INDIAN ARCHITECTURE
(Buddhist and Hindu)

© D. B. TARAPOREVALA SONS & CO. PRIVATE LTD.

Sixth Reprint 1971

PRINTED IN INDIA

Printed by K. L. Bhargava at K. L. Bhargava & Co. Impression House,
G. D. Ambekar Marg, Bombay 31 and published by R. J. Taraporevala for
D. B. Taraporevala Sons & Co. Pvt. Ltd., 210, Dr. Dadabhai Naoroji Road,
Bombay 1.

TO THE MEMORY OF

FARROKH ERACH BHARUCHA

In token of years of happy friendship, cultured advice and shrewd guidance which were at all times invaluable

PREFACE TO THE THIRD REVISED EDITION

IN the course of preparing this volume for a third printing, the opportunity has been taken to revise the letterpress and certain additions have also been made to some of the chapters. A few more illustrations have been introduced, and where better photographs have become available these have replaced the prints originally provided.

Tangier   P. B.

PREFACE TO THE SECOND EDITION

THE first issue of this book being almost immediately exhausted, the steady demand for a reprint has led to its reproduction in the form of a second edition.

In this new publication, apart from a general revision of the original work, several chapters have been added dealing with the architecture of the countries adjacent to India, and specially including those referred to as "Greater India." It is believed that in its expanded form, the volume may prove of greater value in view of this more comprehensive treatment of the subject.

Srinagar, Kashmir   P. B.

PREFACE TO THE FIRST EDITION

IT was the original intention to produce this work on INDIAN ARCHITECTURE in one volume, and the letterpress with the material as a whole was prepared accordingly. In the course of publication, however, it was found expedient to modify this plan, and to bring the work out not only in two separate volumes but in the form of two independent books. The first of these confines itself to the Early, Buddhist and Brahmanical aspect of the subject, and is therefore entitled "INDIAN ARCHITECTURE, BUDDHIST and HINDU" while the second deals with the development of Moslem architecture in India up to modern times and is entitled "INDIAN ARCHITECTURE, THE ISLAMIC PERIOD." It is believed that the issue of the work in this manner will enable it to be more conveniently studied and handled more easily than if it were produced in one rather bulky volume.

A considerable number of authorities and others have been referred to from time to time for verification of certain passages in this work, but it is not possible for all these to be mentioned by name, although my thanks are herewith recorded to one and all. In addition to these inquiries for information, the following, among others, have been instrumental in providing photographs for the illustrations : the Director General of Archaeology in India, and the Superintendents of the various circles of the Archaeological Survey; the Archaeology Departments of the Independent States such as Hyderabad, Baroda, Mysore, Gwalior and Kashmir ; the Superintendents of Museums as for instance Madras, Bombay and Muttra, and the South Indian Railway Co., Ltd. In all cases while acknowledging my indebtedness, it should be emphasized that the photographs supplied are copyright by each of the institutions named.

It is only my duty, however, to express my gratitude for the special help I have received from the following : Mr. Farrokh E. Bharucha for reading the manuscript and giving me the benefit of his valuable advice as to the form of the work and other relative matters ; to my draftsman Babu Nityananda Das Ray for the skilful and intelligent manner in which he has worked from my sketches and drawings to produce many of the illustrations ; to Messrs. Taraporevala for their enthusiastic co-operation in the work of publication at a very difficult time, and the willing acceptance of my occasionally exacting demands ; and, finally, to the Hon'ble Mr. Justice Edgley, I.C.S., not only for some carefully considered deductions relating to the chronology of the rock-architecture which will be found in an Appendix, but also for so readily undertaking the labour of correcting the proofs.

Calcutta   P. B.

CONTENTS

CHAPTER   PAGE

REFERENCE BOOKS. A list of these will be found at the end of each chapter. There is a short General Bibliography at the end of the book.

LIST OF ILLUSTRATIONS

CHAPTER I

INTRODUCTION : THE INDUS CIVILIZATION (c.B.C. 3000-2000) [1]

THE VEDIC CULTURE (c. B. C. 1500-800)

MANY efforts have been made to express in a few words the precise meaning of Architecture and its relation to human experience. Lethaby has approached the subject most nearly in stating that " Architecture is the matrix of civilization"[2]. To such a definition it may be added that viewed historically architecture remains as the principal visible and material record, through the ages, of man's intellectual evolution. Each great cultural movement has made its own particular contribution to the art of building so that the aspirations of the people and even their way of life stand revealed in substantial form for all to see. And in India man's ideals have found expression in numerous noble monuments showing that few countries possess a richer architectural heritage. To the student the value of these productions needs no emphasis, for from such achievements it is possible to reconstruct much of the past and to visualize the social and political conditions of the country as phase succeeded phase, and one period merged into another.

In each of the major historical developments of architecture there is one basic principle underlying its conception, and one which is supremely distinctive. With the Greeks this was refined perfection ; Roman buildings are remarkable for their scientific construction : French Gothic reveals a condition of passionate energy, while Italian Renaissance reflects the scholarship of its time. In the same way the outstanding quality of the architecture of India is its spiritual content. It is evident that the fundamental purpose of the building art was to represent in concrete form the prevailing religious consciousness of the people. It is mind materialized in terms of rock, brick or stone.

This characteristic of Indian architecture is emphasized by the treatment of its wall surfaces. The scheme of sculpture which often covers the whole of the exterior of the building is notable not only for the richness of its decorative effect, but for the deep significance of its subject matter. Here is not only the relation of architecture to life, but transcendent life itself plastically represented. Carved in high or low relief are depicted all the glorious gods of the age-old mythology of the country, engaged in their well known ceremonials, an unending array of imagery steeped in symbolism, thus producing an "Ocean of Story" of absorbing interest.

In view of this character for rich treatment it is strange to find that the earliest known phase of the building art in India, recently excavated, discloses a style of structure which has been described as aesthetically barren as would be the remains "of some present day working town in Lancashire." This development in the dawn-age of the country has been designated the "Indus Civilization," as the records of its culture have been found buried in the soil of the regions bordering on the river Indus. A comparison of these remains with those of other countries of which the chronology is known, as for instance Mesopotamia has indicated that the Indus Civilization was in a fairly matured state as early as 3000 B.C., so that its origin may go back to a still more remote age. Two separate sites have so far been excavated, but there are mounds and other evidences which imply that it extended over a considerable portion of north-west India and even beyond, thus embracing "an area immensely larger than either Egypt or Sumer." Whether it was distributed over the remainder of the sub-continent remains to be seen, but there is an opinion "that this culture spread to, even if settlements were not actually made in, the Ganges valley."[3]

The two sites at present explored are at Mohenjo-daro (*Sindi*, "the Place of the Dead") in Sind, and at Harappa in the Southern Punjab, which disclose the foundations of two cities in numerous well-defined strata, denoting that they flourished over a long period. Although the investigations have revealed a culture in which the buildings of its people had no great artistic value, the finished quality of the materials employed, the high standard of their manipulation, and the stability of the construction as a whole is astonishing. In the first place the builders of these cities had acquired no little experience of town-planning, as proved by the methodical manner in which they were laid out with straight streets at right angles, the main thoroughfares running almost due north and south, east and west. The principal buildings were also fairly regularly orientated having their sides towards the cardinal points ; while each city was divided into wards for protective purposes. All the walls of both houses and public buildings were constructed with a pronounced batter or slope, but it is in the substance and preparation of these edifices that the artificers showed such exceptional knowledge. In both cities the buildings were composed entirely of burnt brick, which in size were on an average rather larger than the common kind used in the present day. They were laid in mud-mortar in what is known as "English bond", that is a course of stretchers alternating with a course of headers, care being taken to break the joint where necessary, the entire process indicating that the Indus builders were thoroughly experienced in the technique of the bricklayers' craft. This method of construction applies mainly to the foundations and walls of the buildings, but as these were very substantial it seems probable that they were two or more stories in height. The upper stories were composed largely of wood, the roofs being flat and built of stout beams covered with planking finished with a top-dressing of beaten earth. No instance of the use of the true arch has been discovered, openings being generally

---

[1] The late Dr. Mackay preferred the term "Harappa Civilization" or "Culture" in place of the older term "Indus Civilization," which recent discoveries have shown to be too comprehensive. In so doing he has followed the usual practice in archaeology of naming a culture after the site where it was first discovered.

[2] *Architecture, p.* 7, Home University Library.

[3] *The Indus Civilization* by Ernest Mackay, London, 1935.

spanned by wooden lintels, but several instances of the corbelled arch formed by oversailing courses of brick have come to light. In view of the persistence with which the Indian builder until the late medieval period clung to the latter method of bridging a space, this fact is significant.

Of the different types of building comprising these cities, dwelling houses both large and small predominate, but there are a certain number of more important edifices, built for various purposes. Among them may be identified large structures probably used as market halls, store-rooms or offices ; another arranged around two spacious court-yards which may have been a palace ; several halls possibly for religious usage, and at Mohenjo-daro a very complete bathing establishment. Yet although all the buildings were constructed of materials and in a manner far in advance of their time, their style is one of such stark utilitarianism that they cannot aspire to be works of architecture ; in effect they represent a very practical form of building construction. There is of course the possibility that on these edifices some kind of mural decoration may have been applied, such as carved wood or colour, but if so this has completely disappeared. The impression therefore conveyed by these remains is that the country was populated by a busy community of traders, efficient and precise in their manners and customs, but devoted to a life of materialism, thus lacking in that aesthetic intuition which demands and naturally creates an artistic environment.

Subsequently a third site was explored, that of Chanhu-daro, eighty miles south-west of the better known Mohenjo-daro, in an effort to find a site that would give more information as to the beginnings of this civilization other than those already investigated. Alternatively there was also the prospect of throwing additional light on the dark period between the disappearance of the Indus culture and the entry into India of the Aryan speaking peoples, presumed to be about 1500 B.C. The results were however not specially informative. The strata at Chanhu-daro seems to go a little further back than the other sites, but it was deserted about 2000 B.C. This part of the country must at the time have had its attractions, but it appears to have had the great disadvantage of persistent floods which eventually forced its population to move. As a whole the inhabitants of these parts seem to have been a migration from the west—the direction of Iran—and when they moved it was probably eastwards, where they would have become assimilated into a yet older population and thus have lost their identity.[1]

Here it may be remarked that in comparison with the rich remains revealed by excavations in other fields of research of relatively the same early age, the discoveries at Mohenjo-daro, Harappa, and Chanhu-daro, in the Indus Valley, have produced a disappointingly small amount of material of an artistic nature. As far as the present evidence testifies the inhabitants of these parts possessed no pronounced aesthetic aspirations, as the severely practical treatment of their buildings bears witness. Nor do they seem to have held any marked religious convictions, as the absence of temples, shrines or tombs, on which they might have expressed themselves architecturally, or artistically by means of painting or sculpture, is significant. In view of the innate sensibility, and outstanding record of artistic achievement

maintained throughout the entire historical period of the Indian people, such a sterile beginning awaits further investigation. One explanation may be that this pre-historical population of the western regions of what is now India, was by no means indigenous, but the result of a racial drift from other and even remote parts, migrants who, having exhausted the resources of their own native land, were driven to seek "fresh woods and pastures new" out of sheer necessity. Such favourable conditions were discovered by them in the virgin soil and primeval forests of the lower Indus river where they eventually settled, and began the work of clearing and cultivating the newly acquired territory. In the course of time they multiplied and spread over much of the expanse watered by the lower reaches of the "Five Rivers," developing into a large and important agricultural and commercial colonization, centering mainly on the two cities of Mohenjo-daro and Harappa. But as a people they appear to have possessed very commonplace ideals, the pattern of their lives disclosing "an almost puritanical utilitarianism," an existence restricted in its spiritual outlook, their minds pre-occupied with the subject of material needs. Accordingly, when the natural productiveness of the land declined, owing apparently to unrestrained exploitation, the civilization itself declined, having served its purpose and run its allotted course leaving no heritage except that of a definitely provocative order, remains of which recent explorations have brought to light. Further research may however tend to enliven this somewhat uninspiring view, which is indeed relieved to a certain extent by the emergence from the deeply buried records of this long lost civilization, of a small series of examples of plastic art each having a very distinctive character. So diverse, however, both in their nature and intention as well as in their material and its manipulation are these relatively small and in every instance portable specimens of art craftsmanship that it seems within the bounds of possibility they were not the product of indigenous hands but importations from other and extraneous schools of culture, objects expressly acquired in the course of trade relations to satisfy the occasional cravings of a few enlightened individuals for some pleasing article to adorn the otherwise severe simplicity of their surroundings.

The "Indus Civilization" declined probably some time early in the second millennium B.C., for the excavations reveal that its cities were then falling into a state of decay. At a later date the deserted appearance of this part of India was remarked on by a Greek writer who relates that here were "the remains of over a thousand towns and villages once full of men." [2] In spite of its virile character and the experienced methods of construction that were achieved at this early age in India this powerful and well founded culture died out without appearing to influence in the slightest degree the nature of the building art that followed. It is possible that some great cataclysm cut across the current of events making an entirely fresh beginning necessary. Some such an interruption is not unknown in the world's history as the advance of civilization is not always a steady progression but may become an intermittent phenomenon. A case in point is that of the Myceanized Greeks of the thirteenth century B.C., and at a much later date the Romanized Gauls, who in both instances relinquished their methods of permanent construction to revert to temporary habitations of wattle and daub.[3] As in Europe so in India. After the

---

[1] Dr. Mackay, Lecture at the Royal Soc., of Arts, March 1937.
[2] Aristobolus, Frag. 29—Strabo XV. C. 693.
[3] *Architecture* by Christian Barman. London 1928, p. 17.

decay of the Indus Civilization when the art of building again comes into view, this no longer consists of well laid out cities of finished masonry, but takes a much more rudimentary form of humble village huts constructed of reeds and leaves and hidden in the depths of the forest. The culture of the people was beginning again.

The exploration of origins reveals the motive power which gives an art its initial impetus. And it is in the primitive culture of a people that these origins are to be found. Primitive art is the matrix of the higher, and is the source from which more advanced forms are derived. The Vedic culture of India provides the material for a study of the first efforts at building construction, when man's efforts were made in response to a need, and before any ideas of architectural effect were conceived. This culture, which produced the elementary type of forest dwelling referred to above, appeared probably towards the end of the second millennium B.C. ; it was the outcome of the great Indo-Aryan migration from the north-west, and which in the course of time laid the foundations of the Vedic Age. That those responsible for this culture were unrelated to the people of the Indus civilization seems fairly clear, as there was a wide difference in the conditions under which each of these populations existed, in their mode of life, and notably in the type of building produced by this method of living. On the one hand the inhabitants of the Indus region, as already shown, were mainly traders and town-dwellers, while on the other hand the Vedic people were of the country, wresting their living from the fields and forests. As far as is known the latter were originally nomads, an offshoot of an immense and obscure migration, who, on settling down in the plains of India, became partly pastoral and partly agricultural, having as their habitations rudimentary structures of reeds and bamboo thatched with leaves. It was not therefore from the fine houses forming the towns of the Indus civilization, but from such temporary erections as these, and the various simple expedients devised to meet the needs of the forest dwellers that Indian architecture had its beginnings. Its foundations were in the soil itself and from these aboriginal conditions it took its development.

From a variety of sources it is possible to visualize the kind of building that the early settlers found suitable for their purpose. Considerable miscellaneous information is contained in the Vedas, those lyrical compositions which have been preserved through three millenniums, while ingenuous vignettes depicting the life of the times are carved in bas-relief on the stupa railings of Barhut and Sanchi. In addition there is the significant character of the subsequent architecture which reproduces in many of its aspects the type of structure from which it originated. Supplied with this material we see the people living in clearings cut out of the primeval forest, just as some of the small cultivators at the present time in India, notably in parts of Bengal, still carve their homesteads out of the bamboo jungle. But these early immigrants had to protect themselves and their property from the ravages of wild animals, and so they surrounded their little collection of huts (*grama*) with a special kind of fence or palisade. This fence took the form of a bamboo railing the upright posts (*thabha*) of which supported three horizontal bars called *suchi* or needles, as they were threaded through holes in the uprights. (Plate I, Figs. 1 and 4.) In the course of time this peculiar type of railing became the emblem of protection and universally used, not only to enclose the village, but as a paling around fields, and eventually to preserve anything of a special or sacred nature. In the palisade encircling the village, entrances also of a particular kind were devised. These were formed by projecting a section of the bamboo fence at right angles and placing a gateway in advance of it after the fashion of a barbican, the actual gate resembling a primitive portcullis (*gamadvara*). (Plate I, Figs. 1 and 2.) Through the *gamadvaras* the cattle passed to and from their pasturage, and in another form it still survives in the *gopuram* (cow-gate) or entrance pylon of the temple enclosures in the south of India. But, more important still, from the design of the bamboo gateways was derived that characteristic Buddhist archway known as the *torana* a structure which was carried with that religion to the Far East, where as the *torii* of Japan and the *piu-lu* of China it is even better known than in India, the land of its origin.

The huts within the village enclosure were of various shapes but it is fairly certain that at first those of a circular plan predominated. Students of constructional origins have remarked on primitive man's natural tendency towards rounded forms, and give as instances pots and baskets. Incidentally, as shown in the bas-reliefs, the earliest Indian seat resembled a round inverted basket. In the case of the building art the foundations of the old city of Rajgriha in Bihar which probably flourished about 800 B.C. indicate that circular buildings were then common, and even at the present day village store-houses in parts of India are often round structures of bamboo. In the Vedic village huts were of the beehive pattern made of a circular wall of bamboos held together with bands of withes and covered either with a domical roof of leaves or thatched with grass. A remarkable illustration of this may be seen in the interior of the rock-cut Sudama cell in the Barabar hill group, where every detail of the timber construction is copied in the living rock. (Plate IX, Fig. 2.) At a later date in the evolution of the Vedic hut the circular plan was elongated into an oval with a barrel roof formed on a frame of bent bamboos also covered with thatch. Soon some of these huts were arranged in threes and fours around a square courtyard and the roofs covered with planks of wood or tiles. In the better class houses unbaked bricks were used for the walls, and the doorways were square-headed openings with double doors. One device to maintain the barrel shape of the roof was to stretch a thong or withe across the end of the arch like the cord of a bow, in a word an embryo tie-rod. (Plate I, Fig. 3.) This contrivance constricted the chord of the arch and produced a shape resembling a horseshoe, a type of archway commonly referred to as the *chaitya* or "sun-window," which became characteristic of the subsequent architecture of the Buddhists. It will be seen therefore, that a very ancient usage underlies many of these village forms, which is significant in view of the ensuing structural developments. Such primitive shapes and expedients as the railing and the gateway, the rounded hut with the heavy eave of the thatch, the barrel-roof with its framework of bent bamboos, all in a greater or lesser degree influenced the style which followed. As to the decorative character of these forest dwellings there is little doubt that this was obtained by means of colour applied on the mud walls. Huts in the remoter villages of India, notably in Orissa, are still almost invariably whitewashed and patterns of archaic designs in red pigment (*haematite*) painted on this white ground. The symbolism in such patterns suggests a very early origin which may go back to Vedic times.

Towards the middle of the first millennium B.C., the social system of the Vedic community so expanded that towns arose at certain important centres, where the traditional structural features of the village were reproduced on a larger scale and in a more substantial form. Owing to a fierce rivalry that had sprung up between the various groups, the towns, which were the capitals of states, were strongly fortified. They were therefore, of necessity surrounded by a rampart and wooden palisades while within this enclosure the buildings were also almost entirely of wood. The Vedic civilization now enters on an era of timber construction. In many countries there is an age when the inhabitants lived in forests so that they became closely identified with their woody environment, as their ancient folklore frequently testifies. According to the natural disposition and trend of these people the period during which they practised wooden construction was long or short but it was inevitably followed in the course of time by the employment of more permanent materials for building purposes. With the early inhabitants of India the timber age appears to have been a long one, due no doubt to the vast extent of the *Mahavana* or "Great Wood" in which they were cradled, picturesque references to which find a place in their epics. So closely connected with their existence were these forests that the early people developed a dexterity in wooden construction of a very high standard. Their pronounced manipulative skill in this material may be accounted for by their prolonged apprenticeship to the woodworkers' craft when they were forced to rely on the trees around them for many of the necessities of life. In the Rig-Veda the carpenter is recorded as holding the place of honour among all artizans as on his handiwork the village community depended for some of its most vital needs. It is not remarkable therefore, in view of this timber tradition that its constructional features were freely and closely imitated in the rock and stone architecture which eventuated and was the form of expression for many centuries afterwards.

Cities largely of wooden construction, therefore, began to appear in various parts of the country, and according to Dhammapala, the great Buddhist commentator they were planned by an architect of the name of Maha-Govinda who is stated to have been responsible for the lay-out of several of the capitals of northern India in the fifth century B.C. This is the first mention of an architect in the annals of the country. In principle these cities were rectangular in plan and divided into four quarters by two main thoroughfares intersecting at right angles, each leading to a city gate. One of these quarters contained the citadel and royal apartments another resolved itself into the residences of the upper classes, a third was for the less pretentious buildings of the middle class, and the fourth was for the accommodation of traders with their workshops open to view as in the modern bazaar. Of the quarters reserved for the citadel and palace a fairly detailed account has been handed down, and the general arrangements of the royal residence have so much in common with the later medieval palaces of India that it seems evident the latter were a continuation of an ancient convention. Although the long interval of two thousand years separates the Vedic palace from that of the Mughals, both were built round an inner courtyard within the citadel and both had a large central window for the *darshan* or salutation of the king. Both had a wing reserved for the royal ladies with pleasure gardens, having fountains and ornamental waters attached. In each there was an official enclosure containing audience and assembly halls, a court of justice, a music gallery, and near at hand an arena for wrestling displays and contests of wild beasts. But whereas the pavilions of the Mughals were of marble, the building art in the Vedic era was at the primitive stage when even the royal residences had not advanced beyond thatched roofs.

In spite, however, of the evidence of the literary records which indicate that much of the building construction at this early date was of a temporary nature, the one example that has survived proves that some efforts were already being made to produce stone masonry of a durable character. The beginnings are seen in the city wall of Rajgriha, the ancient capital of Magadha, now a vast area of ruins in the Patna district of Bihar. Immensely strong and of cyclopean proportions this wall consists of a rough pile of massive undressed stones, each between three and five feet in length, but carefully fitted and bonded together. The core between is composed of smaller blocks less carefully prepared with fragments of stone packed within the interstices ; no mortar appears to have been used. This type of masonry seems to have been carried up to a height of about twelve feet, above which was erected a superstructure of wood and brick, or stone and brick combined. It is noteworthy that the same system of walling is found in the primitive masonry of the Pelasgicum of the Acropolis at Athens, with which it is probably contemporary. The desire for some stable method of construction was evidently being felt, but at this stage the skill and experience were lacking.

REFERENCES

Cambridge History of India, Vol. I, Ancient India, Cambridge, 1922.

Mackay, E., *The Indus Civilization*, London 1935.

Marshall, Sir, J. H., *Mohenjo-daro and the Indus Civilization*, 3 vols. London, 1931.

Piggott, S., *Prehistoric India*, London, 1950.

CHAPTER II

BUILDING DURING THE ROLE OF THE EARLY MAURYAN DYNASTY (c. 400 B.C.)

WOODEN ORIGINS

A STRONG firm government administered over a large territory usually implies an advance in human endeavour, and with the rise of the Mauryan dynasty towards the end of the fifth century B.C. which established for the first time a single paramount power in northern India, marked cultural progress was made. Among other achievements the art of building, stimulated by royal patronage, took a notable step forward, as Megasthenes' account[1] of the Mauryan capital of Pataliputra (near Patna) plainly shows. This Greek ambassador who resided at the court of the emperor Chandragupta about 300 B.C., presents us with a striking picture of the great Indian ruler's stronghold. Occupying a narrow parallelogram about nine miles long and a mile and a half broad, it ranged along the banks of the Ganges like an immense castellated breakwater, surrounded by a stupendous timber palisade, with loopholes for archers and protected externally by a wide and deep moat. At intervals were bastions with towers, over five hundred in number, and it was entered by as many as sixty-four gates. Within the walls was the royal palace, evidently a much more spacious and elaborate edifice than that erected by any previous ruler in the country. The main portion of this imperial residence consisted of a series of hypostyle halls containing pillars of wood each of which "was clasped around with vines embossed in gold and ornamented with designs of birds and foliage in gold and silver, thus excelling in magnificence the famous royal plaisances of Susa and Ecbatana." Apart from the picture of barbaric splendor that such a description conveys, in this city with its unending wooden walls and beetling bastions, and in the centre the palace formed of golden pillared halls, there are indications that India as represented by the Mauryan dynasty was beginning to look even at this early date to the more progressive civilizations beyond its western boundaries for architectural inspiration. For the hypostyle hall had long been a feature of the palaces of the Persians, and Polybius (x. 24) remarks that the columns at the courts of Ecbatana were of cedar and cypress, " all covered with silver plate," a form of structure and decorative treatment not unlike that which Chandragupta appears to have reproduced in his palatial residence at Pataliputra.

Of the fortifications surrounding this great capital city of the Mauryan empire nothing has survived except fragments of the wooden ramparts unearthed at Bulandi Bagh, near Patna, the beams of which by their size prove that the Greek envoy's account of its dimensions was by no means exaggerated. An idea may be gained from the foundations which consisted of timbers laid in parallel lines like railway sleepers each twelve to thirteen feet long, corresponding to the thickness of the stockade at its base. To these horizontal beams upright posts were tenoned, some of them nine feet high, but it is not possible from such scanty remains to estimate its total height. That this technical method of timbering was common to other races, widely separated

and acting independently, is shown by the same principle being utilized by the Romans, as a scene on Trajan's Column depicts, while Caesar's description in his "Commentaries" of the wooden walls of the Celts might apply to those at Pataliputra. "They employ pieces of wood perfectly straight, lay them on the ground in a direction parallel to each other at a distance apart of two feet," etc. An upper portion of the Mauryan stockade preserved in the Indian Museum, Calcutta comprises immense teak-wood posts connected by transverse bars, suggesting that it was an enlarged adaptation of the Vedic village railing previously described.

Megasthenes' too brief account of the civic architecture of his time is amplified by material derived from another and entirely different source, namely the pictures of various historic towns carved in bas-relief on the Buddhist monuments, which although produced a little later are no doubt substantially representative of the building art at this period. On the Sanchi gateways as backgrounds to battles and processions, there may be seen portions of such famous cities as Kapilavastu the place of the Buddha's birth, Kusinagara under the walls of which was waged the "War of the Relics," Uruvilva the scene of the serpent miracle, and Rajgriha, the old Magadhan capital. All these towns appear to be of one established type, strongly fortified and surrounded by high walls having battlements with the merlons corbel-stepped after the manner of those in the Assyrian bas-reliefs. Outside is a moat in which the sculptor with an artist's eye has floated lotus and other aquatic plants, while the whole is enclosed within the usual railing palisade. Specially noticeable are the city gates all of which are designed in much the same style, that of the main entrance to Kusinagara carved on the south torana at Sanchi being so carefully delineated and in such detail that it is possible to reproduce it in perspective, together with its surroundings, as shown in the Frontispiece. The bas-relief shows a tall entrance pylon, with the gateway defended by a square bastion projecting on each side, the whole of a very serviceable nature yet not devoid of architectural effect. Near the gateway is what seems to be a formidable angle-tower, while overhanging the walls are pillared balconies, loggias, railed balustrades and "magic casements" which give an excellent idea of the romantic character of the Buddhist sacred cities. No reference to these pictures in stone at Sanchi would be complete without a remark on the figure subjects to which the architecture forms only an artistic setting. For instance the royal procession issuing from the gates at Kusinagara with the emperor Bimbisara at its head might have been the source of inspiration for Blake's lines in the "Song of Liberty." "The jealous King, his grey-brow'd councillors, thund'rous warriors, curl'd veterans, among helms, and shields, and chariots, horses, elephants, banners, castles, slings, and rocks."

---

[1] *Ancient India as described by Megasthenes and Arrian*, by J. W. M'Crindle, 1877.

Apart from the fortifications and city of Pataliputra there has also survived one concrete record of the wooden construction of the palace, of such a high standard of workmanship that it is a definite proof of the Mauryan artificers' accumulated experience in working in timber. This consists of a number of massive teakwood platforms each thirty feet in length, found buried deep in the silt and apparently introduced as a kind of raft to support the foundations of the facade or propylaeum of the palace. Composed of beams jointed together "with a precision and reasoned care that could not possibly be excelled," they illustrate "the absolute perfection of such work and those who executed them would find little indeed to learn in the field of their own art, could they return to earth to-day."[1]

This high appraisement of the Mauryan artizan's skill as a worker in wood is confirmed by other evidence of a unique character. Owing to the Indian craftsman's traditional genius for imitation every detail of this early form of timber construction has been most faithfully reproduced in the numerous and very complete examples of rock architecture which followed, so that although the wooden originals have perished their exact facsimiles remain preserved in the living rock. In no other country has the carpenters and joiners craft as practised over two thousand years ago been so fully and accurately recorded. With the material thus provided it is quite possible to extract in theory this timber-work from the rock-cut halls of the Buddhists and conjecturally reconstruct it in its original form. The drawing on Plate III illustrates this procedure as it represents a transcription in wood of an excavated example at Kondane of the first century B.C., now buried in the forest of the Western Ghats. This early Buddhist production cut out of the cliff face consisted of a *chaitya* hall or temple and its attached monasteries, so that two characteristic types of structure are depicted, one arched over by means of a barrel-vault roof and the other having a flat roof.

The timber used by the early Indian carpenters and builders was teak, carefully trimmed into the required shape with an adze. Not a large variety of joints were employed, most of them being of a simple but effective order and the workmen knew their application thoroughly ; where these required to be pinned, bamboo pegs were inserted. The foundations were prepared by means of beams laid in the manner already described in the construction of the city walls and to these the uprights, such as the pillars, were tenoned. Most interesting is the construction of the vaulted roof, as it is worked out on somewhat the same principle as the arch braced timber roof of the Gothic builders of Europe evolved many centuries later. In the Indian method the structural membering of the vault was supplemented by a series of curved wooden ribs or groins placed in close order, the whole system anticipating a solution of the problem of arching a space in a most satisfactory and at the same time artistic manner. The flat roofed edifices were planned and executed in an equally workmanlike fashion, with pillars supporting the wooden girders, above which were beams and joists placed and jointed in correct position to carry the requisite weight.

Such was the structural system employed in the framework of these timber buildings, but how this was filled in and finished is purely conjectural. In all probability a filling of plaster (*chunam*) was added and painted white as there are frequent allusions in the ancient Pali texts to great edifices "gleaming white like a cloud", an effect evidently considered the height of achievement. As to the decorative treatment of this wooden architecture, the facades of both the vaulted hall and its attached monastery show that the early carpenter was able to manipulate his material so as to produce the most artistic results, although each effort at embellishment had its practical use. The great arched window admitted light into the vaulted hall through its tracery, while the balcony in front was a minstrels' gallery ; the projecting casements on each side were priests' chambers, and below on the left was a room for the sacristan. Similar decorative but purposeful structures from the frontage of the adjoining building, covered balconies being prominent features as they are in the architecture of the country at the present time. Some of these features are amplified in Plate IV, as for example the system of lighting the smaller rooms by means of bamboo lattices, and in certain instances the entire balcony was a mesh of plaited bamboo strips held together on a framework of wood. This device was the precursor by many centuries of the *pinjra or* "cage-work" so common in the later buildings of Upper India as well as the *meshrebiya* of Egypt and other Islamic countries. These and many other technical and artistic expedients of this early phase of timber construction may be seen literally petrified and thus imperishably preserved in the later rock architecture of the Buddhist period.

----

[1] *Archaeological Survey of India*, 1912-13, p. 76.

REFERENCES

Jackson, V. H., *Notes on Old Rajgriha*, Arch. Survey of India, 1913-14.

M'Crindle, J. W., *Ancient India as described in Classical Literature*, Westminster, 1901.

M'Crindle, J. W., *Ancient India as described by Megasthenes and Arrian*, London, 1877.

Smith, V. A., *The Early History of India from 600 B.C. to the Muhammadan Conquest*, 3rd Edn. Oxford, 1914.

Spooner, D. B., *Excavations at Pataliputra*, Arch. Survey of India, 1912-13, pp. 53ff.

Waddell, L. A., *Report on the Excavations at Pataliputra*, Cal. 1903.

CHAPTER III

ASOKA, AND THE BEGINNINGS OF THE BUDDHIST SCHOOL (cir. B.C. 250)

UP to the middle of the third century B.C. the course pursued by the building art in India has been only indistinctly visible, as it is obscured by the mists of time. So far therefore any account of its progress has been based very largely on evidences of a miscellaneous order such as certain structural remains and various investigations from which the foregoing conjectural impressions have been compiled. Now however, supposition hardens into fact and the picture hitherto ill-defined comes with an almost dramatic suddenness sharply into focus. This effect was brought about by the policy of the third Mauryan ruler of Magadha, the emperor Asoka who ascended the throne in B.C. 274. An early decisive step taken by this monarch was his acceptance of the teachings of the Buddha. Soon it had become apparent to him that the religious beliefs of his subjects were inclined to be indeterminate, and that a radical change in their spiritual outlook was desirable. That the country was ripe for some form of conversion was also obvious. The existing cults consisting mainly of visionary speculations and intangible abstractions were proving unsatisfying, and men's minds were in a receptive mood fully prepared for a doctrine founded on a more substantial basis. In other words there was at this period what may be described as a religious vacuum. And Buddhism redressed this void. Included in its precepts was a material object of veneration, such as the worship of sacred relics, which made a direct appeal to a people perplexed and disillusioned by unconvincing observances. Accordingly in B.C. 255 Asoka inaugurated Buddhism as the state religion of the country. The correctness of the royal reformers' precognition is proved by the whole-hearted manner in which the Buddhist faith was assimilated by his own people and furthermore by the astonishing rapidity with which its tenets were conveyed to and its ritual observed in most of the countries of Asia.

With this change in the religious system of India also came a marked advance in the arts. Buddhism essentially a graphic creed, art became its handmaid, so that wherever it penetrated it was accompanied by forms and symbols expressive of its teaching. In India this early Buddhist art was of a special kind as it was the result of the Mauryan emperor's own personal predilections, and its productions have been referred to as those of the Asokan School. Its elements were due to the ruler's initiative, they were practised only during his reign, and they ceased when it ended ; it was therefore essentially autocratic in its character. But although this first manifestation of Buddhist art was confined within such seemingly narrow limits, and its actual productions were relatively few in number, they were of such exceptional power that they influenced to a notable degree much of the art that followed. The significance of this school lies in the fact that it marks the beginning of an era when India through Buddhist thought was in a position to dictate to the rest of Asia its religion, its symbolism, and its art.

The principal contributions made by this school to the art and architecture of the time were some six in number, consisting of the following : (1) a series of edicts inscribed on the rocks, (2) a number of tumuli or stupas, (3) certain monolithic pillars, (4) several monolithic accessories to shrines, (5) the remains of a vast palace, and (6) a group of rock-cut chambers. Among these productions that more directly affected the course of the art of building were the stupas on account of their structural significance, the monolithic pillars in view of their artistic qualities, the rock-cut chambers because of their technique, and the palace for its architectural associations.

The order in which these manifestations took form, and the manner of their execution may be explained. Possessed of great ideals, as Asoka's policy throughout plainly indicates, one of this ruler's most earnest desires appears to have been to institute a permanent record of the establishment of the Buddhist faith within his now widely-spread dominions. A craving for a symbol of stability occurs in the early evolution of most nations, a need for some "substantial link which holds them to the soil" and is a stage in the development of racial self-consciousness. As a case in point the Pharoahs realised this when in their inscriptions they boasted of having erected "everlasting stone monuments," in honour of the gods. Some such reflection no doubt inspired the Emperor Asoka when as a beginning he carved his famous edicts on the living rocks, proclaiming as they do, in plain terms that his efforts should result in the "long endurance of the Good Law." These inscriptions, although many have survived, were not, however, sufficiently striking to suit his purpose ; what was evidently in his progressive mind was the creation of a memorial of such a permanent nature that it would outlast time itself. With this in view he caused to be raised in many parts of his empire circular tumuli of brick, sacred mounds commemorative of the Buddha. These "stupas", as they have been called, from the Prakrit word *thupa*, were not unknown in India before this date, but their shape, like that of the pyramid, implies durability.

As the stupa from the nature of its structure was subject to disintegration owing to the rigours of the climate, it became necessary for the Mauryan Emperor to seek for some still more lasting method of achieving his purpose. Aware no doubt that other nations were using stone, he began therefore to "think in stone," and in the course of time an impressive monument symbolizing the creed was devised in the form of a pillar, a lofty free-standing monolithic column, erected on a site especially selected on account of its sacred associations. A number of these Asokan pillars were distributed over a wide area and a few bear ordinances inscribed in a manner similar to the edicts on the surfaces of the rocks. The effect of such columns, some of them as much as fifty feet in height, each carrying above its capital a magnificent Buddhist emblem, on the minds of a people hitherto living in a somewhat restricted wooden building tradition was no doubt very great. But these remarkable monuments were by no means the only sculptured stone objects wrought in this manner. With them were other monolithic productions, such as railings, stupa finials in the form of umbrellas, lion thrones, colossal figures, and the pillars of an immense hypostyle hall in the royal palace at Pataliptura, all of which show that the stonework of the

Asokan school was of a highly diversified order. Added to these objects of a mobile character was another and more static development of the stone cutter's art in the form of a group of sanctuaries excavated in the rocks of the Barabar hills near Gaya in Bihar, obviously the work of the same skilled hands. But, whatever form it took one unique quality marks all the stone productions of the Asokan period, one technical characteristic which is never omitted so that even a small fragment may be immediately identified, is the high lustrous polish resembling a fine enamel with which the surfaces, even of the rock-cut chambers, were invariably treated.

Finding expression from wood in another and more lasting material such as dressed-stone is a decisive step in the cultural evolution of a people. But the manner in which this step was taken under Asoka's direction, and the results it produced are both of more than ordinary significance. Appearing as these sculptured forms do, fully matured, at a time when Indian art was still in its infancy, and without any previous preparation, is a phenomenon which needs some explanation. The stones themselves provide the answer. The unerring precision with which they were worked and chiselled show that those who quarried and carved them were no novices at their craft, as would have been Indian artificers, but had generations of experience behind them. The shapes and decorative forms employed are few of them indigenous, but on the other hand are obviously derived from the art repertory of another and more advanced people. Such exotic forms are not difficult to identify as some of them are clearly of Greek, others of Persian and a few perhaps of Egyptian extraction. This development of the art of working in stone, therefore, which Asoka introduced into the country represents an Indian offshoot of that forceful Graeco-Persian culture which flourished with such vigour in Western Asia some centuries before the Christian era.

At this juncture a brief reference to the source of the culture from which Asoka drew his inspiration seems indicated. From c. 500 B.C. and the ensuing 170 years the pulse of Asiatic culture throbbed in what was then the fertile land of Persia, and as a result there developed in the capital cities of that great empire, the nearest to India, a classical art school composed of Pharoic-Hellenic-Iranian elements of a distinctly effective character. This school was probably partially dispersed by Alexander's conquest of Persia together with the downfall of the Achaemenid dynasty in 330 B.C., but the unsettled period which then ensued was rapidly followed by the extension of the Macedonian empire in the east by means of Greek colonies, such as that of Bactria, which brought the full force of Hellenism to the very borders of Mauryan India. What actually happened to the exponents of the original Achaemenid school under such conditions can only be a matter of conjecture but that they and their successors continued to flourish under the intelligent patronage of the Asiatic Greeks, producing works with still more marked Hellenistic features cannot be doubted. It was at this stage of the movement that the Indian emperor Asoka conceived the project of erecting his imperishable and symbolic monuments to the Buddhist faith, and instinctively turned to the descendants of the workmen who had already shown such proficiency in their construction of the stately palaces of the Persian kings.

To attain his object the Mauryan monarch adopted the common practice of royal art patrons, and brought into his service a group of experienced foreign artists of a sufficiently adaptable nature to put into effect his progressive ideas. Historical instances of such a procedure are numerous, but some of those which account for the particular character of the Achaemenid art of Eastern Persia and in the course of time of that of the Asokan school, have a direct bearing on the style which afterwards appeared in Buddhist India. For instance in the production of their magnificent palaces at Persepolis and Susa, the Persian kings made use of talent drawn from the leading art schools of the then known world. Even without the recorded statement of Diodorus that Egyptian artists worked on these buildings, such attributions as the winged globe and the cavetto cornice are proofs of their employment in this enterprise. Side by side with the skilled craftsman from the Nile were stone carvers from Lonia[1] noted for the fineness of their workmanship and minuteness of detail, evidences of which may be recognised in the high quality of the reliefs on the palace walls. Masons' marks from the Greek alphabet on the Hall of a Thousand Columns which forms such an important part of the Persian palace indicate that artificers from Hellas took their share in the construction, while in the realm of the fine arts there is the testimony of Pliny (xxxiv, 68) that the Greek sculptor Telephanes of Phocaea was attached to the courts of both Darius and Xerxes.

In these circumstances it is not difficult to account for the form and character that the giant pillar and the other lithic productions of the Asokan period assumed. From the columned halls reared under the orders of the Achaemenid kings, from their sculptured reliefs and their inscriptions on the rocks as at Behistun, the Indian monarch obtained some of his inspiration, and from the ranks of those who produced them he secured the skilled artificers to aid him in his projects. In short it may be presumed with some degree of certainty that, attracted by the emperor's assured patronage, there was eventually gathered in a quarry workshop near Chunar in Bihar a small group of imported workmen trained in the Graeco-Persian traditions and engaged to collaborate with a number of selected Indian craftsmen to fashion these the first dressed stone objects to be produced on Indian soil.

Of the achievements of this composite school established by Asoka, the free-standing pillars are unquestionably the most notable. Originally there appear to have been about thirty of these monoliths, of which the remains of some ten are in existence. Two of them, with lion capitals, are still standing in situ, and in fairly good condition, one at Kolhua (Bakhra) and the other at Laurya Nandangarh, both in the Champaran district of Bihar. Of the remainder, those of which the capitals have survived are now preserved in the Indian Museum. In selecting an appropriate standpoint for the pillars, several appear to have been erected on sites sanctified by the Buddha, while others marked the course of a Pilgrim's Way to the holy places. The line of pillars in the Champaran and Muzaffarpur districts—at Rampurva, Laurya Araraj, Laurya Nandangarh, and Kolhua were evidently placed at intervals along the ancient royal route from Pataliputra to the sacred land of Buddhism on the borders of Nepal. It is possible that the one at Sanchi belonged to a series which lay on a more western line of approach. In no instance do the pillars appear merely as

---

[1] H. Brunn, Griechische Kunstgeschichte (Munich 1893-97).

isolated monuments, as in the vicinity of each of them are the remains of stupas and other buildings showing that they formed part of the structural accompaniments of an extensive Buddhist settlement. Each pillar consisted of a plain unornamented shaft, circular in section, from thirty to forty feet in height, and arising straight out of the ground without any suggestion of a base, tapering like the trunk of a tall palm tree. At the top of this shaft which is two feet in diameter is a campaniform capital its abacus acting as a support for a large sculptured Buddhist symbol, the whole combination attaining a height of nearly fifty feet. Apart from their Buddhistic significance the Asokan pillars are expressive of a very ancient and widespread belief, and were in the first instance inspired by man worshipping among the groves and great trees of the forest. A suggestion of this tree worship may be seen on the bas-reliefs of the Barhut railing (cir. 150 B.C.) where tall palm trees reminiscent of pillars are conventionally placed at the sides of some of the scenes, while about the same date are the devotional columns with palm leaf capitals at Videsa (Besnagar). With the reverence for trees came a veneration for huge stones and boulders, the sacred and mystical character given them being but a prelude to shaping them into upright forms. Columns were gods in early days and the forerunner of the temple, "and this stone which I have set up for a pillar shall be God's house" (Gen. 28, v. 22.)

The aesthetic properties of the pillars are concentrated in the design and execution of the capitals and superstructure. These portions of the monuments which together average seven feet in height are in one piece of stone, while the shaft of the column consists of another separate piece, the two being joined by a copper bolt accurately fitted into the tenons made for it without the use of cement. The bolt in one of the Rampurva pillars has been preserved, and is a barrel-shaped piece of metal over two feet in length, showing that those who employed this copper dowel were quite aware of the destructive action of iron and other metals in such circumstances. The capitals themselves, which are some three feet in diameter, are campaniform in shape consisting of a series of fluted petals elongated and which, falling together, take the form of a bell. In most instances the capitals are cut to one specified pattern, the exception being that at Nandangarh, which appears slightly stunted in its proportions, while the abacus and other features are somewhat different, so that it is possible this particular example was an early and experimental effort. There may be some symbolic connexion between the campaniform capital and the bell (*ghanta*), as this in a conventional form, was used early in Indian decoration, and it also figures prominently in the temple ritual. But the boldly marked fluting the section of which is unmistakable, has an undoubted foreign origin, exactly similar fluting being not uncommon on Persian and Greek pillars, as may be seen on the bases of those at the palace of Artaxerxes II (B.C. 404-358) at Susa, and on the capitals of the Ionic temples of Apollo at Naukratis and Diana at Ephesus, both of which were built about 560 B.C. Above the Asokan capital is a circular abacus having its broad edge carved with ornamental borders of a special character. On some of these are repetitions of Buddhist emblems, as for example the goose (*hamsa*), but on others, as in the case of the bull capital at Rampurva, there are such well-known conventional motifs as the honeysuckle and palmette, the bead and fillet, and the cable moulding, each one of direct Hellenic extraction. These motifs may not be in exact

accordance with the most approved classical models, but any deviation from the original pattern is no doubt due to their long journey from the Aegean starting point.

It is however in the massive Buddhist composition poised above the abacus that the greatest imagination has been shown, and symbolism utilized to its utmost extent. Most of the superstructures consist of figures of animals, each of which has a mythological meaning. Together they symbolise the four quarters of the universe, the elephant being the guardian of the east, the horse of the south, the bull, as at Rampurva, of the west, and the lion, as in the Nandangarh example, of the north. All four animals are carved in relief on the abacus at Sarnath, by far the finest of the entire group, evidently signifying that, although this pillar was primarily associated with the north by its position and the conventional group of lions above, it was also intended to commemorate by the addition of the great wheel which these beasts support, the proclamation of the Good Law of the Church of the Four Quarters. [1] Such were the Buddhist interpretations, but not a little of this animal symbolism was drawn, in the first instance, from Vedic sources. The Rig Veda gives the place of honour among all wild beasts to the lion, which roamed the jungles of India until comparatively recent times, while a swift or galloping horse represented the sun, and the bull Dyaus or Indra the sky-god, all of which are illustrated on the abacus of the Sarnath capital. From this and other evidences it is clear that much of the primitive Buddhist symbolism as expressed in its art was a continuation of the Vedic mythology, (Plate VII).

As works of art the Asokan pillars hold a high place. They are boldly designed, finely proportioned, and well-balanced conceptions, fulfilling admirably the purpose for which they were intended. This purpose was solely monumental, as they are free-standing pillars, not part of an architectural composition, an object which has been kept in view throughout. The animals, which are the main features in the scheme, are noble conventional representations, spirited yet dignified, ideal examples of their kind. Few works of this nature could be more arresting than the broad sculptural treatment of the bull on the column from Rampurva, a superb creation, simply and truthfully rendered. Even this excellent specimen, however, has its equal in the group of four addorsed lions surmounting the Sarnath capital, who unfortunately lose some of their effect by being deprived of the massive wheel of metal they were meant to support, that "Wheel of Order" which the Rig Veda tells us "rolls around the Heavens" : but the pose of their limbs and the tense muscular anatomy are the work of an accomplished hand. These lions are manifestly a Hellenic attribution, their masks (originally provided with metal eyes) and flowing manes recalling the lion-headed spouts on Greek and also Roman buildings, (Plate VII, Fig. 2.). For the quality of the workmanship in their production there can be nothing but praise, the bold contours of the figures in the round, the subtle modelling of the relief, and the unerring confidence of the chiselling being remarkable.

In sharing the credit for these masterpieces, it is felt that the symbolism and imagination, their spiritual message so to speak, was supplied by the Indian mind while most of the technical skill, together with certain decorative elements, were the work of the imported craftsmen. But the brilliant polish which gives such a finality to the work was

---

[1] V. Smith, *History of Fine Art in India*, p. 60.

the result of Indian thought and labour, as there is evidence of an indigenous aptitude in this aspect of the stone-cutters' art. As a proof, few objects could be more delicately wrought or highly polished than the crystal reliquary [1] from the Piprahwa stupa, which has been assigned to this epoch, and was the handiwork of a *pasana-kottaka* or hereditary stone-cutter. The lustrous finish of the crystal was obtained by the laborious application of an agate burnisher, and somewhat the same process was adopted in the pillars and other sandstone objects. In completing their handiwork with this glazed effect the Asokan artificers were following the procedure of all early stone-workers, as the aim for instance of the 12th dynasty Egyptian masons was a " glassy surface," while the ideal stonework of the Greeks is described in the Homeric poems as "polished shining-glistening." It is doubtful, however, whether the creations of any of these great building nations could compare in this particular respect with the brilliant enamel-like finish obtained by the Mauryan craftsmen. So striking is its appearance that in the fifth century it excited the admiration of that observant Chinese pilgrim Fa-hien, accustomed as he must have been to the famous polished lapidary of his own countrymen, for he writes that it was "shining bright as glass." And even inspite of over two thousand years of the most destructive climatic conditions these monuments retain much of their highly glazed surface at the present day.

The efforts of the Asokan sculptors were not, however, directed entirely to the production of religious monuments, as these craftsmen were also employed in the preparation of some of the most important parts of the Mauryan emperor's palace. This appears to have been a very remarkable conception so much so that it had the legendary reputation of being not the work of man but having been magically raised by Yakshas or supernatural beings. As late as the visit of Fa-hien this traveller was so impressed that he states it was "made by spirits who piled up the stones, reared the walls and gates, and executed the elegant carving and inlaid sculpture work in a way which no human hands of this world could accomplish." Shortly after the pilgrim's visit, having been in existence for over six hundred years it seems to have been almost entirely destroyed by fire, so that the only material records of its design and character have been obtained by excavation, where in the silt of Kumrahar, a site to the south of the present city of Patna, its ashes have remained for fifteen hundred years. From these investigations the palace appears to have been an aggregation of structures enclosed within a high brick wall, the most important of which was an immense pillared hall in three stories on a high stylobate and covering a square of two hundred and fifty feet side. The columns which supported the roof were probably in rows of fifteen with fifteen pillars in each row, set at distances of fifteen feet from each other, centre to centre, making a total of two hundred and twenty-five pillars in all. The ceiling of one of the stories may have been supported by colossal stone caryatid figures as traces of these have been discovered within the bays formed by the pillars. Little more than fragments remain of the stonework used in the palace but the polish on most of them indicates that a good deal of this was used in its construction, and for a variety of purposes. It is fairly certain that all the pillars of the hypostyle hall were of stone as the numerous broken portions testify, while one example has been discovered almost complete, a highly polished cylindrical shaft tapering like a pine trunk some twenty inches in diameter at its base, and when

---

[1] Indian Museum, Calcutta.

entire about twenty feet in height without any signs of a base or capital. On this pillar was inscribed a mason's mark similar in many respects to a symbol used in the rock-carving at Behistun in Persia. The wide intercolumniation of the pillars shows that they must have supported wooden beams and in fact much of the building appears to have consisted of wood, hence its destruction by fire.

From these remains it has been deduced that the arrangements of Asoka's palace at Pataliputra were inspired to some extent by those of the Achaemenids and that the grouping of the buildings within a walled enclosure corresponds in some respects to the complex of palaces at Persepolis, the pillared hall being in close agreement with the Hall of a Hundred Columns built by Xerxes. The mason's mark on the pillar seems to confirm the fact that Persians or Medes were employed in some of the work, and that the idea of the colossal supporting figures, or atlantes, bears some relation to the bas-reliefs representing figures supporting upper stories on their upraised arms in the tomb of Darius at Nakshi-i Rustam and the Throne Room at Persepolis. Although only a few pieces of figures presumed to be atlantean have been recovered at Pataliputra, that the Mauryan craftsmen knew how to produce statues of heroic size is proved by several of these having been found in various parts of the country, including two large and sculpturesque Yakshas or *chauri* (fly-whisk) bearers excavated near Patna. It was probably figures of this kind that supported the wooden roof of Asoka's palace, for one of the upright bars of the Barhut gateway, executed at a slightly later date, displays a small model of a figure-pillar which has every appearance of having been copied from some traditional type. Atlantes and caryatid supports, as for instance the dwarf capital on the Sanchi gateway, and the pillar of the *chankrama* or sacred promenade at Budh Gaya, besides many later examples, all show that pillars of a similar nature were a favourite architectural device with the Indian builder. As to the facade of Asoka's palace some idea of this may be gained from a carved stone in the Mathura Museum, possibly dating from the first century A.D. It depicts the frontage of an important building in two or more stories, each storey formed of a continuous arcade of horse-shoe archways with bays between. Each bay contains a hanging balcony supported on a pillar and the central doorway of the whole is evidently part of a large projecting portico.

Differing widely in intention from the foregoing, but, as the technical treatment of the carving and the enamel-like polish of all the surfaces testifies, evidently belonging to the same school, are the rock-cut sanctuaries in the hills about nineteen miles north of Gaya. In all there are seven of these chambers, four on the Barabar hill and three on the Nagarjuni hill half a mile north-east. In addition there is another example called the Sitamarhi situated some thirteen miles south of Rajgriha and twenty-five miles east of Gaya. The two first-named groups have been quarried with infinite labour out of the large boulder-like masses of quartzose gneiss which form this range, a site evidently selected as an ideal retreat amidst pleasant, although wild surroundings. They contain several inscriptions from which it is seen that they were prepared to the order of the Emperor Asoka for the use of certain Ajivika ascetics, followers of a sect which was not Buddhistic but related to the Jaina religion. These chambers have two special interests as on the one hand they are the earliest examples in India of the rock-cut method, and on the other some of them are exact copies in the rock of existing structures in wood and thatch. On Plate VIII the interiors of some of the cells have been extracted so to speak, from their rock-bed and reconstructed in order to illustrate the kind of building they were supposed to imitate. The two most notable, the Lomas Rishi and the Sudama have been cut adjacent to one another on the Barabar hill, and their interiors are very similar, while the former is exceptional as it is the only one which has an ornamental facade. From the sectional drawing of the Sudama (Figs. 1 & 2) the interior arrangements may be understood. The doorways, notable for their sloping jambs, of both Sudama and Lomas Rishi are in the long side of the chamber, clearly an expedient due to the configuration of the whale-backed hill which prevented the excavation being made axially. Inside is a barrel-vaulted hall 32 ft. 9 ins. by 19 ft. 6 ins. and 12 ft. 3 ins. in height. At the end of the ante-chamber and entered by a central interior doorway is a separate circular cell 19 ft. in diameter with a hemispherical domed roof 12 ft. 3 ins. high at its centre. Exteriorly this cell has an overhanging cave like a thatch and, most singular of all, its walls have irregular perpendicular grooves in imitation of upright battens of wood or bamboo. In a word it is an exact lithic copy of a beehive hut, and almost every part of the surface has been burnished until it resembles glass.

Remarkable though these interiors are, the facade which surrounds the doorway of Lomas Rishi is the *chef-d' oeuvre* of the group, as it is an accurate reproduction of the gable end of a wooden structure chiselled in the rock-face (Plate IX, Fig. 1). The stone-cutter has copied in every detail the handiwork of the carpenter. Two stout uprights inclined slightly inward and some 13 ft. in height form the main support while into the upper ends of these are jointed the two principal rafters, other subsidiary rafters lying parallel. On the rafters is fixed the curved roof composed of three laminated planks, the lower extremities of which are kept in place by short tie-rods, circular in section and obviously turned on a lathe. The doorway, some 7½ feet high, is recessed within a semi-circular archway above which are two lunettes forming a kind of fanlight. In the lower lunette is carved a procession of elephants, while the upper is filled with a diaper pattern of lattice-work both designs evidently being copies of perforated wood. The elephants are exquisitely modelled, and are performing an obeisance before stupas which are introduced into the lunette as solid supports to the openwork. Surmounting the gable is a finial which by its shape is derived from a terra cotta original ; every detail of the facade is sharply chiselled and each part still retains its high polish, the whole except for a few fractures looking as if it had been cut but yesterday.

Of the remaining examples of the group, that now called the *Gopi* or Milk-maid's cave on the Nagarjuna hill is the largest. It is a plain tunnel-like excavation rounded in plan at each end, measuring 44 ft. long by 19 ft. wide and it is 10 ft. high to the apex of its vaulted roof. Over the doorway is an inscription stating that it was excavated to the order of the emperor Dasaratha on his accession to the Mauryan throne. This and two other inscriptions elsewhere are evidence that the school established by Asoka was still in existence at the time of his grandson towards the end of the third century B.C. but after then it appears to have abruptly ceased. Extending over a period of less than fifty years, this movement had no growth and no decline, so that it emerges not so much as a school but as an outstanding episode in the early history of Indian art. One and all of its productions

are of surpassing interest, and some of them are of a significance which has been rarely excelled. It also had far-reaching implications as some of its motifs and forms of expression are to be seen wherever Buddhism found a foothold. For instance the bell-shaped capital of the monolithic pillars was frequently reproduced under varying conditions but always identifiable as of the "Persepolitan" order. It was, however, the excavated chapels that were destined to have the most remarkable effect as the examples in Bihar were the beginnings of that magnificent development of rock-architecture which has no equal in any other country. But even more potential than these material manifestations was the factor of technique, for it put a new power into the hands of the Indian artizans, teaching them how to win stone from the quarry, how to dress and chisel it, and even to apply it to building construction in the form of pillars. But there, strangely enough, it ended. Of the working and setting of stones, of joining them in courses, in a word of the art of stone masonry it conveyed nothing. The country was apparently not yet prepared for such an innovation. Building in wood had been so perfected that the Indian workman saw no reason for a change. Evolution does not always proceed by imperceptible gradations but sometimes advances according to a kind of cultural quantum theory, progress being restrained by the very excellence of previous experience. Some circumstance of a like nature may account for the tardy appearance of stone construction in the building art of India.

Such an expressive architectural feature as the capital appearing in so significant a form as that devised by Asoka, brings into view the various patterns of capital which figure in the building art of this and the subsequent period. A series of examples is illustrated in Plate X having been selected to show certain sources, influences and affinities connected with the Mauryan types.

In the upper compartment of Plate XI an attempt has been made by means of diagrams to explain the origin of a motif appearing in a variety of forms, and with marked persistence in all the earlier developments of Indian architecture. This shape, which owing to its fluted treatment is unmistakable, in most frequently found in the capital, but it also occupies a prominent place as a finial, as well as a decorative element repeated in the quoins of the *sikharas*, or spires, of the later temples. It is a melon-shaped feature ordinarily referred to as the *amalaka*, and popularly supposed to be derived from a common fruit of that name, otherwise known as the *emblic myrobalan*. There is more probability however, that it has reference to the *amalasila* or "pure stone", an object which appears early in Indian art, and is of very remote origin. This again brings it into association with the ring or "cogged" stone, those mystical perforated stones which are found among the remains of many primitive people, while its connection with the *norbu* or "precious jewel" in the Lamaism of Tibet is also clear. That it is a relic of some sacred and very ancient ritual is shown by the fact that it is usually represented enshrined in a specially shaped casket. The difficulty experienced by the sculptor in expressing the presence of the precious symbol in the casket was overcome in two ways, by placing it above the receptacle as in the illustration from Besnagar (Fig. 4), or depicting it within a box reduced to a mere framework as at Bedsa (Fig. 3 and 5). Later, the fluted treatment of this motif may be identified in many architectural features of the *chaitya*, *vihara*, and temple, and it is not unlikely that, blended with the fluted bell-shape, it eventually emerged as the *kalasa* or vase of the Gupta period, as at Udaigiri and Tigawa (Plate X). But there are few elements in early Indian architecture which have more remote, sacred, or mystical origins than the *amalaka*.

Additional light has been thrown on the early form of the stupa hall by the excavations carried out at the ancient site of Bairat in Jaipur State. Here have been discovered the remains of a Buddhist temple, not rock-cut, but constructed of brick and wood, probably the only one of its kind so far unearthed. Of its early date there can be little doubt, as relics of a typical Asokan character were found in its vicinity, so that it is presumed to have been erected about B.C. 250. Circular in plan and formed of panels made of large wedge-shape bricks it is contained within a peripteral range of twenty-six octagonal wooden pillars. Around is a circumambulatory path with a wide entrance on the east leading to the stupa in the interior. That the primitive stupa hall was probably a circular cell has already been referred to, illustrations of which are shown in Plate VIII, and there is actually a rock-cut example of the first century B.C. in the Tulja Lena group at Junnar (Fergusson, History of Indian Architecture, Vol. I p. 158). Plate VI shows a conjectural reconstruction, from the existing remains, illustrating this significant early phase in the evolution of the Buddhist Chaitya hall.[1]

ROCK-CUT CELLS IN BIHAR

BARABAR HILLS	..	(*a*) Karna Kaupar,
		(*b*) Sudama,
		(*c*) Lomas Rishi,
		(*d*) Visvajhopri.
NAGARJUNI GROUP	..	(*a*) Gopika (Milkmaid)
		(*b*) Vahijaka,
		(*c*) Vadalhika.
SITAMARHI	..	(13 miles south of Rajgriha, 25 miles east of Gaya).

---

[1] Daya Ram Sahni *Archaeological Remains and Excavations at Bairat*, Jaipur State 1937.

REFERENCES

Cunningham, A. *The Ancient Geography of India : Buddhist Period.* London, 1871.
Foucher, A. *The Beginnings of Buddhist Art and other Essays.* Paris and London, 1917.
Longhurst, A. H. *The Story of the Stupa.* Colombo, 1936.
Smith, Vincent A. *Asoka, the Buddhist Emperor of India.* Oxford, 1909.

CHAPTER IV

THE BUILDING ART UNDER THE SUNGAS AND ANDHRAS

(cir. B.C. 185 to A.D. 150)

THE co-ordination of Church and State established by the Emperor Asoka was not long maintained after his death in 232 B.C., as the Mauryan empire itself broke up in 185 B.C. and the greater part of the country reverted to Brahmanical rule. The nominal successors of the Mauryans were the Sungas, a power which was supreme mainly in the northern and western regions, and which lasted until c. 70 B.C. The Sungas were supplanted by the Andhras, who had long been paramount in the west and south of India, assuming the title of "Lords of Dakshinapata", or the Deccan, until they also were overthrown about 150 A.D. Under both these Brahmanical dynasties the Buddhists on the whole appear to have been treated with toleration as the numerous monuments produced by them plainly testify. For more than three centuries, before and after the beginning of the Christian era, Buddhist architectural activity seems to have prevailed, and it has been found convenient therefore to classify the works of this period either as Sungan or Andhran according to the particular dynasty under which they were produced. For a space of time after the fall of the Mauryan rule a state of transition supervened while the form of Buddhism found by Asoka went through the process of changing its authority from the throne to the priesthood, the latter having been apparently organised with this in view. The art naturally followed the same course as the religion, there being a static interval between the cessation of the autocratic art of Asoka and the beginning of a new or hierarchic phase. The position of architecture at this stage may be defined.

Of the many places in his dominions that the Mauryan Emperor had consecrated by the erection of stupas, a certain number from various causes had been invested with special sanctity and importance. Although the imposing monolithic pillars raised in the vicinity of several of these shrines their sacred character was appreciably augmented, it was to the stupa, as the symbol of the Buddha, that the pious pilgrims paid their most fervent devotions. At this early date it is fairly clear that these tumuli of brick, endowed as they were with great spiritual significance, were in appearance somewhat uninspiring. They consisted of a masonry hemisphere some 70 feet in diameter and about 35 feet high, solidly constructed of large unburnt bricks each of which averaged the large size of 16 ins. × 10 ins. × 3 ins. In the centre of this domical mound or *anda* (egg) a small space was usually left for a receptacle containing a relic of the Buddha and on the summit as a mark of dignity was raised a wooden parasol (*chhattrayashti*). This honorific umbrella was in some instances, as in the stupas at Sarnath and Sanchi, made of polished stone fashioned by the sculptors of the Asokan School, as fragments of these have been preserved. The brickwork surface of the dome was finished off with a thick layer of plaster, in which at intervals recesses were left for the reception of small lamps to be lit on festival occasions. Over all a certain amount of colour and gilding was applied, and it was also the custom to furnish them with festoons of flowers and drapery together with banners and flags. As the Buddhist ritual consisted of circumambulating the stupa, a processional passage (*pradakshina patha*) was provided by enclosing the monument within a wooden railing (*vedica*) leaving a space for promenading with an entrance at each of the cardinal points. At least one of these stupas, very much in the state described above, still survives, appearing as a rough white-washed mound rather incongruously set amidst an aggregation of later and more finished artistic accessories. Such is that at the shrine of Shwayambhu Nath in Nepal, which has been continuously worshipped for over two thousand years.

At this period, therefore the stupa was in appearance but little removed from the ordinary be-flagged wayside shrine of which many may be seen in various parts of India at the present day. Towards the middle of the second century B.C. a change becomes observable. By this time the Buddhist religion had fully recovered from the removal of Asoka's guiding hand, and the orders of monks had developed into a numerous and powerful monachism having substantial resources, rich benefices, and whose influence accordingly was a great force. In spite of the fact that the movement had been deprived of its direct imperial patronage it still maintained its hold on a large community and many of the Buddhist shrines had become increasingly popular places of pilgrimage. With this resurgence of the creed came a revival of the arts which accompanied it, and what is generally referred to as the Sungan period of Buddhist art began. The initial steps in the movement consisted principally in effecting improvements to the stupa in an endeavour to present this essential symbol of the creed with a more dignified architectural appearance. As a whole the refinements took the form of replacing the impermanent materials of which these monuments had hitherto been composed with others of a more stable nature, in a word stone was employed where previously had been brick and wood. The manner in which this transformation was brought about may be understood by tracing the alterations that were made during the ensuing century to the few rare examples of the period that have been preserved. Chief among these is the shrine at Sanchi in Bhopal State, Central India, the history of which has been disclosed by excavation, and may be followed step by step from the raising of the first brick stupa by Asoka through all its phases until medieval times. Another stupa, at Barhut in Nagod State, Central India, also provides much valuable material, while a railing and its accessories at Budh Gaya in Bihar, throw further light on the progress of Buddhist art at this time. These comprise the principal actual remains, but there were other Buddhist sites where similar structural conversions were taking place, but of which only the barest records have been preserved.

Taking the sequence of events at Sanchi as typical of the movement as a whole, one of the first measures of reconstruction at this sanctuary began as early as 150 B.C., when the existing stupa was enlarged to nearly twice its previous size. In carrying out this important alteration Asoka's brick tumulus was not removed but left intact in the interior of the new construction, for as with religious buildings of more than one creed it was regarded as an act of impiety to demolish an edifice once consecrated. It thus became a deed of merit to encase a stupa within a large "envelope" (*achchhaday*), and a number of these monuments, as for instance that of Jagat Singh at Sarnath,[1] and another at Manikyala in the Punjab, show as many as three and four stupas each enclosed one within the other. In the enlargement of the stupa at Sanchi the new structure was made to cover an area of 120 feet in diameter, and to rise to a total height of 54 feet, the size it is at the present day. (Plate XII, Fig. 1.) Around it was also added a terrace (*medhi*), 16 feet from the ground, thus providing a separate and upper ambulatory passage, access to which was obtained by a double stairway (*sopana*) on the southern side. The whole of the building was then finished off by means of a facing of dry masonry composed of hammer-dressed stones laid in fairly even courses, a technical process of some importance because it appears to be the first instance of true stone masonry being used for constructional purposes in an Indian building. At about the same time the flattened crest of the dome was surmounted by a superstructure of a particular design consisting of a square railing enclosing a pedestal (*harmika*) which supported the shaft *yashti*) if a triple umbrella, every member being made of stone. This form of finial is only seen in the very earliest type of stupas, as almost immediately afterwards another and more universal kind was devised in which the *harmika* was expanded above into a shape resembling an inverted stepped pyramid.

Such a marked increase in the dimensions of the Sanchi stupa led to much of the old work surrounding the Asokan original being swept away, including the wooden palisade which enclosed the processional path. This timber structure was now replaced by a plain stone railing of massive proportions, standing eleven feet high and with an entrance at each of the cardinal points. No feature of Buddhist art or architecture is more characteristic than this railing. It was the emblem of protection dating from the Vedic times and even earlier. It encircled the village sanctuary, it fenced around the sacred Bodh tree, and in miniature it was adapted as a casket to enshrine the holy relics, besides serving many other purposes, religious or secular, structural and decorative. The railing at Sanchi on account of the largeness of its proportions and austerity of its treatment is one of the most impressive productions in the whole range of Buddhist constructional art. Its uprights consist of octagonal posts nine feet high from the ground-level and placed at the close interval of two feet between each. Connecting these posts are three horizontal rails or bars, each two feet wide and separated only by a narrow space of three and a quarter inches. Over all was placed an immense beam, its upper side rounded, forming a coping stone to the whole. For a ponderous structure of this nature there was no real necessity, a much smaller and finer form of barrier would have been equally effective and in accordance with the dimensions of the remainder of the scheme. It seems to represent the result of some backward vision connecting it with an earlier phase of evolution when man delighted in the raising of great stones—the megalithic age—as may be seen in such monumental productions as Stonehenge in England and Zimbabwe in Rhodesia, and in the monoliths of the Khasis, in Assam. All these rear up their stupendous members with the object of causing amazement, awe, and for the purpose of wonder-working. And as distinctive as were the proportions of the Sanchi railing was its method of construction. Although all the various parts are fashioned out of stone, each is a copy, in many respects, of the wooden original it is presumed to have replaced. The shapes and more particularly the joints of the railings are those usually employed by carpenters, as may be seen in the tenons of the uprights (*thaba*), and the scarf jointings of the copings (*ushnisha*), neither of which are methods appropriate for stone bonding. There is also the peculiar form of the triple cross-bars (*suchi*), the lenticular section of which was obviously derived from the bamboo rails of the village stockade. It is evident therefore that these typically early Buddhist structures were produced at a very formative stage, a phase not so much in the evolution of the craft itself, as in that of the craftsman who made them, at a time when his mind was still thinking in wood, although his hands were working in stone. This workman had also not realized the separate properties of these two different building materials, and had yet to learn that things can be done with one that are not always suitable in the other.

Some idea of the size of the Sanchi stupa at this period of its history may be obtained by comparing it and its railing with the dimensions of Stonehenge as it now appears. The diameter of the outer railing at Sanchi is 120 feet, while the outer circle of Stonehenge is 106 feet. In height the former is 11 feet, whereas the outer sarsens of the latter are 13½ feet. The gateways at Sanchi are 34 feet high, while the five trilithons at Stonehenge are 22 feet. In their average proportions therefore the two monuments are not very dissimilar.

Somewhat similar changes as those effected at Sanchi appear to have been carried out in the stupa of Barhut, a site which was possibly a halting-place on the pilgrims' route to the Buddhist holy land. In this instance, however, the brick stupa was not enlarged, as it retained its original dimensions of some 68 feet in diameter, but the railing around it was reconstructed. In size the Barhut stupa was only about half that of Sanchi, its railing being a little over seven feet in height, but in marked contrast to the solid simplicity of the latter, every portion of its stonework is richly carved in bas-relief portraying incidents in the *jatakas*, or scenes connected with the life of the Buddha. What remains of the railing is now preserved in the Indian Museum, Calcutta, where, apart from its Buddhistic significance, its sculptured stones display incidents of contemporary social life of surpassing interest. At another site more intimately associated with the Buddha, namely the great shrine at Budh Gaya, an important railing was also erected, its shape, having however, to conform to the square plan of the building it enclosed, was not circular but disposed around a quadrangle measuring 145 feet by 108 feet. Although in much the same style as the Barhut railing, in size it is slightly smaller, as it is only 6 feet 8 ins. high, and its general dimensions are less massive. From these more slender proportions and its refined treatment, as well as from the character of the bas-reliefs it is presumed to be later than either the Barhut or Sanchi examples, and has been assigned to the early part of the first century B.C. This date has been substantiated by inscriptions on two of the rail pillars, which appear to connect its erection with the Sungan period. There is considerable variation in the quality of the carving, some of it showing the rather crude ingenuousness of the Barhut style, while other parts denote the beginning of a fluency in line and composition

---

[1] *Archaeological Survey of India*, Report 1907-08, Plate XVIII.

particularly noticeable in the border of animals on the coping. This is due perhaps more to the varying skill of the carvers than to any differences in style or date. With the railing at Budh Gaya there was also constructed a *chankrama* or promenade consecreted by the Buddha as he walked on this spot, which was afterwards converted into a pillared passage or corridor and possibly covered by a roof. The pillars had stepped pedestals with vase-shaped bases, and one shaft remains, decorated with a very graceful caryatid figure. This type of figure found much favour with the stone-masons of the early Hindu period specially in the Muttra district, the place of contact of several schools, where fragments have been found of a caryatid motif very attractively rendered. Unfortunately the buildings at Budh Gaya at different times and from various causes have suffered much, and although even now they might solve several constructional and artistic problems, well-meaning, but injudicious restorations have obscured such evidence as remained.

The erection of substantial stone railings to enclose the sacred portions of stupas and shrines was not, however, the only elaboration effected in these structures. Entrances, particularly of religious buildings have been regarded in several of the great historical style as architectural features pre-eminently suitable for ornamental treatment, and the openings in the stupa railing through which admission was obtained to the ambulatory were an invitation to add some kind of imposing gateway to the scheme. This took the form of a *torana* (Skt. from *tor*, a pass) a special kind of entrance archway designed on the same principle as the wood and bamboo portcullis to the Vedic village, (Plate I, Figs. 1 and 2.) From its not infrequent appearance in the bas-reliefs the torana seem to have been accepted as the traditional type of ceremonial portal, so that it was an appropriate addition to the Buddhist sanctuary. The earliest known torana is that which formed the entrance to the eastern side of the Barhut stupa, the only surviving example of four similar gateways, and it bears an inscription stating that it was "built during the reign of the Sungas" (184-72 B.C.). In the composition of this structure as a whole, as well as in some of its elements, there are indications that it was the production of workmen, who had been in contact with Hellenistic and other foreign schools. Kharoshti letters engraved as mason's marks on the stone suggest that some of its character may be ascribed to sculptors from the north-west of India, but on the other hand it is just as likely that it was a heritage of the quarry workshop that Asoka had established at Chunnar, not so far distant. As evidence of the alien attribution there are fluted bell-capitals of the Persepolitan order, with addorsed gryphons above and the frequent use of the Hellenistic honeysuckle motif, specially noticeable in the large spreading acroteria forming its apex. Some of the figured balusters between the architraves of this gateway are small scale copies of the colossal statues of the Asokan period, a reminiscence perhaps of the atlantean supports in the columned hall of the Mauryan palace at Pataliputra. Such are a few of the characteristics of the Barhut torana, but although the oldest example of the style and displaying much that is artistic and instructive, it is entirely eclipsed by a series of similar gateways of a richer and far more impressive design which were shortly afterwards erected at Sanchi. (Plate XV.)

The gateways of Sanchi are five in number, four of them forming the entrances to the main stupa, while there is one isolated in front of another adjacent stupa (No. 3), which was built in the first century B.C., the gateway having been added somewhat later. Although all are of the torana type and have been made to provide an important part of the scheme as a whole, they are really decorative additions not an essential part of the structure nor introduced to meet any special need. This ornamental purpose is realized when it is seen that the framework of each gateway was utilized entirely for the accommodation of the sculpture with which it is so lavishly overlaid. In their intention therefore these toranas recall the doorways of Romanesque and Gothic churches which Ruskin has remarked depict the Bible in stone, the Buddhist example displaying in the same graphic manner much of the philosophy and inspiration of the creed it served. Few portals in any style of architecture can excel the array of rich symbolism and imagery which has been portrayed with such dramatic intensity on the Sanchi toranas, the result entirely of Indian tradition and genius.

In view of this prodigality of embellishment it is not easy to separate the constructional from the ornamental, but relieved of its sculptured overlay, the actual framework of these gateways resolves itself into a comparatively simple structure. Each one consists of two square upright posts 15 feet high, prolonged vertically and connected above by three separate lintels between each of which is a row of ornamental balusters. The total height of this erection is some 34 feet with a width of 20 feet at the broadest part. When it is understood that the thickness of the whole averages only two feet, and that it stands alone without any struts or similar supports, it is a matter for astonishment that any of these gateways should have remained in position for some two thousand years. Added to which they are definitely top-heavy, and the method of jointing, as in the case of the accompanying railings, was technically irrational. Their purely indigenous composition is shown in a variety of ways, notably by the absence of any recognized form of pillar and capital, the first principles of which the Indian workmen had not yet assimilated. Although the Asokan column was before them, and even introduced into the ornamentation, the square upright for a pillar with a square slab above as an abacus was as far as the builders had advanced in the evolution of this almost universal architectural feature. Nevertheless the method of support by means of atlantean figures and also of animals was well understood and artistically applied, as the groups of dwarfs, elephants, and lions introduced for this purpose plainly show.

Although the preparation of the four principal gateways at Sanchi may have extended over a period of nearly fifty years, the style of work throughout is fairly consistent. The first to be erected, towards the latter half of the first century B.C. and therefore during the supremacy of the Andhras, was the one at the southern entrance of the great stupa. This was followed, probably at an interval of a decade between each, by the northern, eastern, and western. Stylistically, however, they resolve themselves into pairs, the southern with the northern, the eastern with the western, the finest workmanship being on the southern example and the less skilful on the northern. Of the isolated torana before stupa No. 3 there is little to distinguish this from the western gateway of the main stupa and it was probably executed either at the same time or a little later. All of them appear to have been the production of a local school of artificers who carried on their trade in Besnagar, a populous town five miles away, the men thus employed being not masons accustomed to handling stone, but workers in the minor and applied arts. As a proof of this the southern gateway bears an inscription to the effect that it was made by the ivory carvers of Videsa (Besnagar). That those engaged in this and similar artistic crafts took their share in contributing their best to these gateways is shown by the variety of materials used in their composition. Mortice holes and slots indicate that there were not a few additions in metal, such as festoons and bells—a large bell and chain was probably suspended from the middle of the lowest beam—and some of the figures of elephants had ivory tusks decorated with gilt metal bands. The general character of these toranas with their skilfully wrought ornamental features but at the same time immature constructional practice, seems to postulate that at this period the applied arts were in advance of the functional, and that the Indian workman was so preoccupied with decorative effect that he overlooked some of the essential principles manifest in all good building construction. In comparison with the unadorned solidity of the railing the elegant intricacy of the gateways is an illustration of contrasts, the one acting as a foil to the other and notwithstanding that at the utmost there is only an interval of a century between the two projects, each seems to imply a different state of consciousness. The real facts responsible for such an apparent incongruity were that the two conceptions although produced as complimentary portions of the same scheme had each a separate aim. The ponderous beams and sense of collective power expressed by the massive proportions of the railing were an effort to impress the beholder as he progressed under its broad shadow with a majestic reminder of his individual insignificance, while the deep mysticism and soul-stirring episodes depicted with such consummate artistry on the toranas were afterwards introduced into the composition in order to stimulate his emotions to the highest degree, when in a receptive state. The efflorescence of symbolism contained in the accessories to the stupa coloured the art of India throughout much of its subsequent course, and the shape of the torana itself became a characteristic architectural feature whenever Buddhism prevailed.

Even before these additions were made to the Sanchi stupa a number of buildings were erected in its vicinity to serve the needs of worshippers, or for the use of those whose duties were connected with the shrine. Two types of structure came early into evidence, one being a temple for the performance of the ritual, and the other a monastery for the residence of the priests. The temple, or chaitya hall arose out of the particular demands of the Buddhist religion. With the appearance of a material cult-object in the form of the stupa (chaitya), some building for the accommodation of facsimiles of this divine symbol, together with shelter for the convenience of those who came to pay their devotions to it, became necessary. Hitherto the religious rites of the people had been conducted in the open air under the shadow of the trees in the sacred groves, so that a structural house of prayer had not been required. No tradition for a temple being in existence, something suitable had to be created *ab initio*. The general shape of the stupa, and the ritual of circumambulation naturally suggested a building a portion of which should be circular in plan with a domical roof. Some such structure had long been the abode of hermits and other holy persons, and their beehive huts with conical roofs and thatch, sanctified by usage, could be readily adapted to contain the stupa. That a rudimentary shelter of this kind was the beginning of the chaitya hall is proved by the character of the rock-cut chambers of the Asokan period in the Barabar hills. The inner cells of both the Lomas Rishi and Sudama examples were seemingly prepared for the reception of stupas, and are lithic copies of circular huts

having thatched roofs with heavy over-hanging eaves, even the scantlings of the walls being faithfully reproduced. (Plate IX). Two other instances of this primitive origin preserved in widely separated parts of the country may be seen, one in a rock-cut chamber at Guntapalle in the Kistna district of the Madras Presidency, and another similarly rock-cut at Kondivte near Bombay. The former, which on stylistic grounds can only be a little later than those in the Barabar hills, is a copy of a circular hut with its conical thatched roof resting on a framework of wood like an inverted basket, and the stupa it accommodates is still in situ (Plate VIII Fig. 7). The example at Kondivte is of an early manner, although it is itself later, and is evidently a survival of an old type which also shows a stupa within a circular cell (Plate VIII Fig. 4). To the inner cells an ante-chamber was attached, those in the Barabar hills being barrel-vaulted, the two compartments communicating by a doorway. Structural examples of this rudimentary arrangement appear to have been built at Taxila about the first century B.C. of which the foundations of the apsidal temple at Sirkap are an illustration (Plate XVI Fig. 2). It was not long, however, before the wall separating the cellar, from the ante-chamber was found superfluous, and when it was removed the basilica-shaped Buddhist chaitya hall came into being. The earliest temple of this shape is No. 40 at Sanchi, dating from Mauryan times or a little later. There are also several buildings of much the same kind depicted on the bas-reliefs, and from the two sources a reconstruction has been attempted in Plate XVI Fig. 4. Exteriorly the temple at Sanchi was rectangular in plan, but one end of the interior was apsidal. The unusually high plinth was reminiscent of an expedient found necessary on the low ground of the plains to raise buildings above flood level, while the side entrances were copied from the rock-cut chapels which had their openings in this position owing to the shallow contour of the rock in which they were quarried, a practice soon to be discarded. A singular feature in the temple was that it contained a row of pillars aligned down the centre of the nave, an arrangement which has also been found in the early temples of the Greeks. The Sanchi temple appears to have been built mainly of wood, the pillars and railings being of this material, and the roof also was of timber covered with tiles. Owing to the impermanent nature of their construction no chaitya-halls of such an early type have survived.

The other building required in connection with the Buddhist shrine was a monastery or *vihara*. As India was the birthplace of monasticism the origin of this structure is possibly older even than that of the stupa, and certainly of the chaitya-hall. *Cramanas* or forest-dwellers practised asceticism from very remote times, living in leafy huts or natural caves and tending the sacred fires, as may be seen in several scenes of the bas-reliefs (Plate XVIII Figs. 1 and 7). It was probably from among these hermits that the emperor Asoka recruited his first order of monks, forming them into an organised society to ensure the church he had founded being properly maintained and its constitution preserved. And just as these wandering ascetics were resolved into groups as the first step towards the establishment of a monastic system, so their huts were grouped around an open space to make the first monasteries, as the subject of the Jetavana scene on the Barhut railing testifies. From some such elementary beginning was evolved the conventional arrangement of a hostel consisting of a series of cells enclosing three sides of a square courtyard, the remaining side being left open for the entrance. Places of residence in the

VEDIC VILLAGE SHOWING GATEWAY AND FENCE ①

BUDDHIST TORAN AND RAIL DERIVED FROM ABOVE ②

CONSTRUCTIONAL DERIVATIONS FROM SANCHI BAS-RELIEFS ③

④ FROM SANCHI ⑤ FROM KARLI

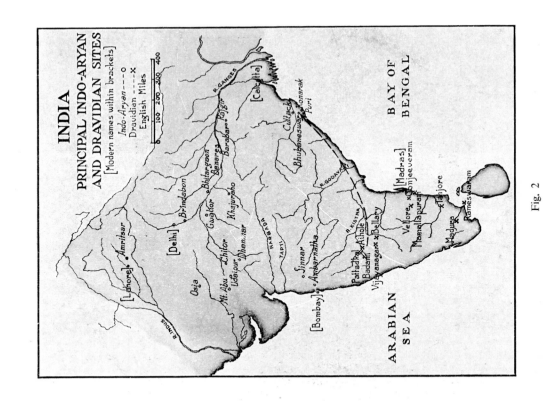

Fig. 2

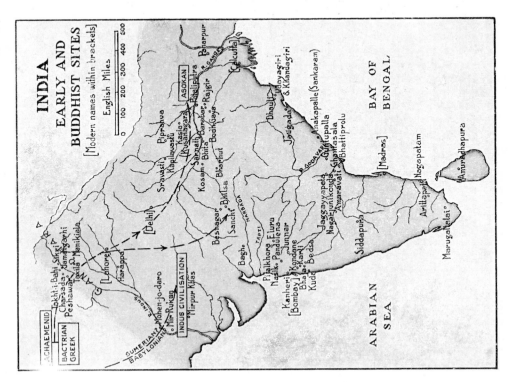

Fig. 1

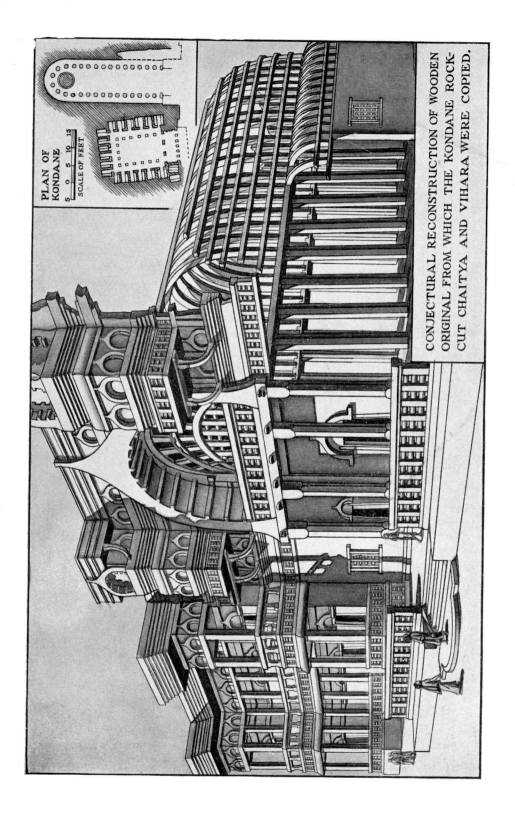

PLAN OF
KONDANE

5   0   5   10   15
SCALE OF FEET

CONJECTURAL RECONSTRUCTION OF WOODEN ORIGINAL FROM WHICH THE KONDANE ROCK-CUT CHAITYA AND VIHARA WERE COPIED.

BHAJA

LOMAS RISHI

UDAI-GIRI, ORISSA

KARLI

KARLI

KONDANE

BHAJA

UDAIGIRI, ORISSA

WOODEN CONSTRUC-TION FROM ROCK-CUT EXAMPLES.

P.B.

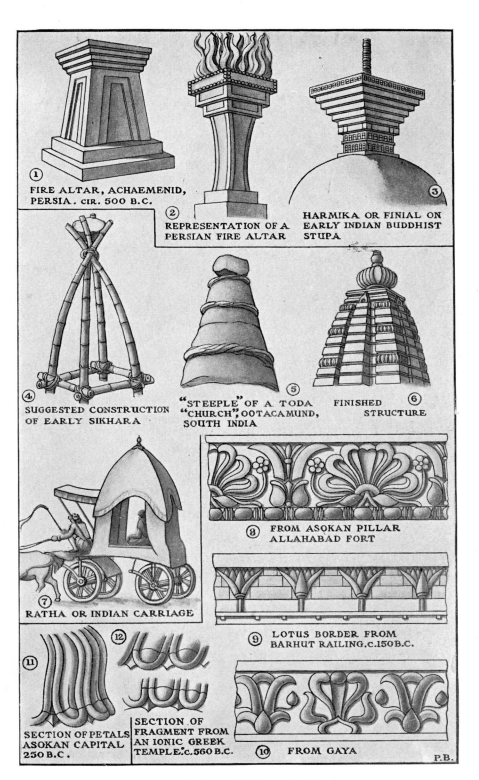

FIRE ALTAR, ACHAEMENID, PERSIA. CIR. 500 B.C.

REPRESENTATION OF A PERSIAN FIRE ALTAR

HARMIKA OR FINIAL ON EARLY INDIAN BUDDHIST STUPA

SUGGESTED CONSTRUCTION OF EARLY SIKHARA

"STEEPLE" OF A TODA "CHURCH", OOTACAMUND, SOUTH INDIA

FINISHED STRUCTURE

RATHA OR INDIAN CARRIAGE

FROM ASOKAN PILLAR ALLAHABAD FORT

LOTUS BORDER FROM BARHUT RAILING. c.150 B.C.

SECTION OF PETALS ASOKAN CAPITAL 250 B.C.

SECTION OF FRAGMENT FROM AN IONIC GREEK TEMPLE. c. 560 B.C.

FROM GAYA

P.B.

Conjectural Origins : Details

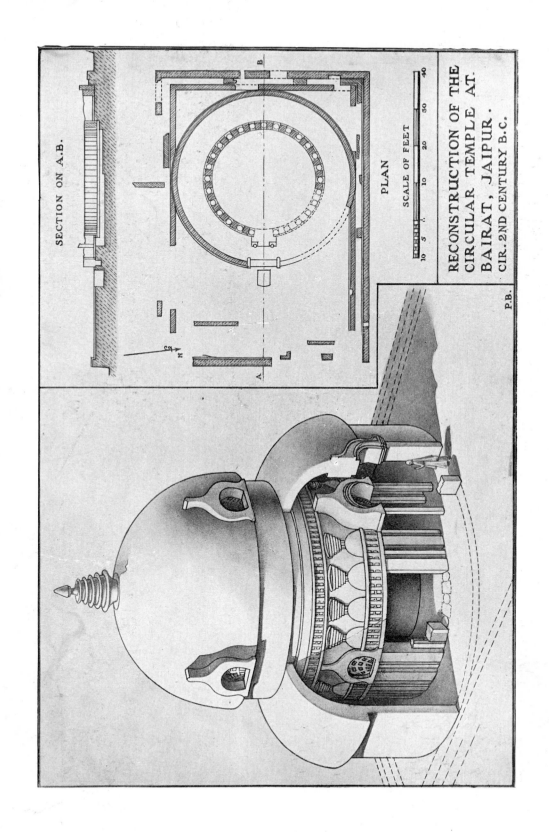

SECTION ON A.B.

B

PLAN

SCALE OF FEET

RECONSTRUCTION OF THE
CIRCULAR TEMPLE AT
BAIRAT, JAIPUR.
CIR. 2ND CENTURY B.C.

P.B.

Fig. 3

Fig. 5

Fig. 1

Fig. 1. Sarnath, Benares. Capital (restored) of monolithic column ; Asokan,
c. B.C. 250.

Fig. 2. Baalbek, Syria. Lion-headed spout ; Roman, 2nd Century A.D.

Fig. 3. Budh Gaya, Bihar. Carved stone border from throne ; Asokan,
c. B.C. 250.

Fig. 2

Fig. 4

Fig. 4. Rampurva, Bihar. Border from monolithic column ; Asokan, c. B.C. 250.

Fig. 5. Sanchi, Bhopal. Capitals from Northern Gateway, c. 25 B.C.

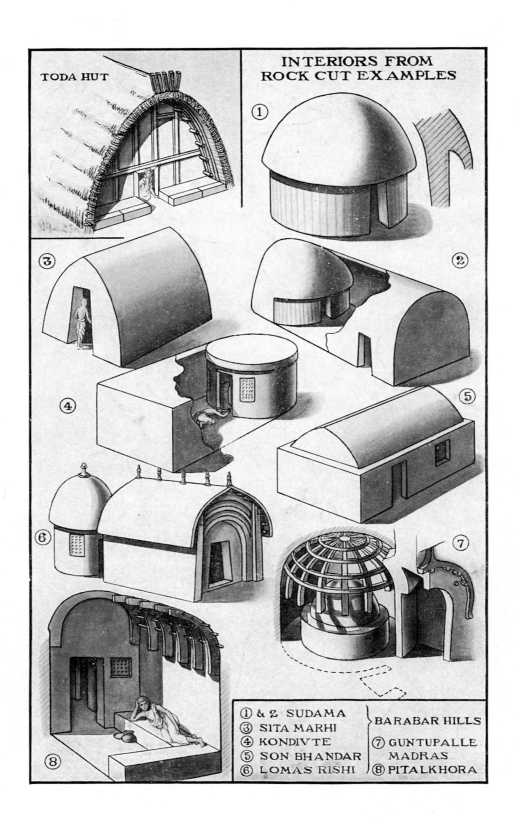

TODA HUT

INTERIORS FROM
ROCK CUT EXAMPLES

① ② SUDAMA
③ SITA MARHI
④ KONDIVTE
⑤ SON BHANDAR
⑥ LOMAS RISHI

BARABAR HILLS

⑦ GUNTUPALLE
MADRAS
⑧ PITALKHORA

east were generally planned on this principle, with the rooms opening on to an interior quadrangle, their backs forming a plain outside wall, the whole being so designed to secure both privacy and protection. The monasteries adopted this method but also added an inside verandah supported on posts and carried round the square in front of the monks' cells to provide a convenient means of communication. As these hostels sometimes appear to have been attached to the chaitya-hall they resemble in certain respects the cloisters similarly annexed to the abbey church of the West, the courtyard corresponding to the cloister-garth, and the pillared verandah to the ambulatory. Built mainly of wood and other perishable materials, all the early Buddhist *sangaramas* have disappeared, but reproductions of them on the bas-reliefs supplement our information as to their design. They were not infrequently of two stories, having barrel roofs with horse-shoe gable-ends, light being admitted through dormer windows. The outer facade containing the entrance was decorated with a certain amount of woodwork including a pillared portico supporting a balcony,—a coign of vantage from which to view processions and other ceremonials taking place on the terrace below. At first these viharas were comparatively modest structures of a purely utilitarian character, but as monachism in India was destined to increase immeasurably during the succeeding millennium, monastic buildings of great size and importance were erected, their style and arrangements reacting not a little on other forms of Indian architecture.

The building activities in the neighbourhood of Sanchi immediately previous to the Christian era were not however entirely confined to the stupa and its accessories, nor even to the Buddhist religion. Besnagar the nearest town was a prosperous and important centre, the capital of the western dominions of the Sungas, with a considerable Hindu population. Here was a Brahmanical shrine of some prominence dedicated to the divinity Vasudeva, and apparently a temple, but only a few fragments of which have survived. In close proximity to this building there were erected several votive pillars one of which is still standing, and the remains of others have been found (Plate X). These pillars, particularly the one in situ, have a threefold significance. In the first place they appear to be the earliest known monuments of stone associated not with Buddhism but with the Hindu religion, secondly they show in their decorative treatment an increased understanding of the principles of design, and thirdly the one still in position bears an inscription which not only fixes the date with certainty but records on incident of some historical importance. The inscription states that it was a Garuda pillar raised in honour of the god Vasudeva by Heliodorus, son of Dion, who was a resident of Taxila and had come to the court of the local prince Bhagabhadra as an envoy from the Indo-Bactrian king Antialkidas. In these few lines a whole chapter of early history is condensed pointing to the relations that existed between this part of India and the Greek kingdoms of the Punjab, as well as to the fact that Heliodorus, a Greek, had adopted an Indian faith, and the inclusion of the name Antialkidas gives 140 B.C., as the approximate date of its erection.

The Heliodorus pillar is a monolithic free-standing column with a bell-capital carrying a figured superstructure, thus reproducing in its general appearance and intentions the Asokan pillars of nearly a century earlier. But in size it is considerably less than the Mauryan example, standing when its finial was complete, not quite thirty feet high and its proportions generally are more slender. The shape and

fluting of the campaniform capital are of Persepolitan extraction, but at the same time bear a marked resemblance to the capitals of the Barhut torana, with which it was contemporary. In the ornamentation of the shaft, the lower part of which is octagonal and the upper sixteen sided, with a band above of thirty-two facets, there may be seen the beginnings of a method of enriching this part of the pillar which was developed with notable effect in the columns of the later styles. Other carvings on this monolith consist of festoon designs, a border with geese in pairs (a common Buddhist pattern), and such Hellenic motifs as the bead-moulding and the honeysuckle. Where these Besnagar pillars manifest a definite departure is in the treatment of the abacus, which now appears as a large square coffer between the capital and its superstructure. Something of the kind may be observed in the massive block which overhangs the capital of the Asokan pillar at Kothua (Bakhra) acting as a base to the figure of the lion above, from which the idea may have been obtained, and it is worthy of note that when this enlarged type of abacus became still more pronounced, as in the early temples of the succeeding style of the Guptas, the lion motif accompanied it. (Plate XXXIV). The remaining pillars at Besnagar, of which only fragments now survive were provided with palm-leaf capitals of singularly graceful design. (Plate X).

One important technical fact emerged during the excavations of the Vishnu shrine at Besnagar, which was that portions of the foundations consisted of bricks cemented together by a well-made grade of lime mortar, the first instance known in India during historical times of the use of cement in bonding masonry. This is direct evidence that the early builders knew of the properties of a cementing material but it found little favour with those who followed, and only on a few occasions was a bonding composition used to any extent until it was introduced by the Muhammadans in the thirteenth century.

The advances made in art and architecture during the three hundred years that passed under the rule of the Sungas and Andhras were considerable. They may be resolved into four phases : (1) stone carving, (2) symbolism, (3) stone construction, and (4) the beginnings of the temple or chaitya hall, and the monastery or vihara. As to the stone carving this, both in design and technique appears to have made appreciable progress, as the plastic treatment of the Barhut railing and the Sanchi toranas is eloquent proof. It may be useful to compare these two examples as a century separates the dates of their execution, but it should be remarked that they may not represent definite stages in development so much as the productions of two different schools. In any case the earlier work, that at Barhut, approaches that of the wood-carvers' technique, and there is an ingenuousness about it that suggests it has only recently emerged from a phase of folk-art. On the other hand the carving on the Sanchi toranas is more sophisticated, there is a feeling of conviction in its manipulation, and it is not by any means experimental although it still displays much naivete both in ideas and workmanship.

But where these two conceptions have broken fresh ground, especially at Sanchi is in the imaginative symbolism with which they are so freely adorned. Most of the emblems employed were of very ancient usage going back into Vedic times, but here they are materialized and brought into the service of Buddhism, the wheel, the tree, the trisula, the lotus, the mounted gryphon, and many other magical motifs appear in these sculptures to be reproduced in a variety of forms in the subsequent art of both Buddhists and Hindus. Specially significant are the dwarf-shaped creatures supporting the cross-bars of the gates at Sanchi, like leprechauns their origin is unknown but that they wielded some mystic power is certain for they found their way into the capital of the pillars of the medieval Indo-Aryan temples. Representational, visionary, with the artlessness of youth and always warm and human, this Buddhist plastic art at Barhut and Sanchi expresses that dawning of consciousness which marks all early artistic effort, but is rarely shown better than in these examples.

Of the constructional advances shown in the stupas and

other records of this age it can be said that the art of masonry building was moving slowly. As already indicated it was retarded by the high standard of previous experience obtained in the field of timber construction, and the change of material from wood to stone was a long-drawn-out process. That progress was being made is manifest in the hammer-dressed encasement of the Sanchi stupa which marks a definite step, but the railings and toranas show how the technique of the old timber method persisted. Of the forms of the building art that were beginning to appear in the temple structure these are represented by the merest fragments, and the development that was taking place in the architecture of such buildings is based on these remains which have made certain conjectural deductions possible.

TABLE SHOWING THE DATES OF THE DEVELOPMENTS AT SANCHI, BARHUT,

BUDH GAYA AND BESNAGAR.

SANCHI (Plate XII, Fig. I.)

(The numbers in brackets are those given in the Archaeological Survey Reports.)

Asokan 274-237 B.C.	.. Great Stupa (No. 1) (Original brick mound.) Lion monolithic pillar (10) near S. Gateway. Stone umbrella as finial	c. 250 B.C.
Sungan c. 185-70 B.C.	.. Temple (40) Plinth	c. 200 B.C.
	Great Stupa (1) Stone covering, larger Umbrella, Harmika, and Finial as a whole. Ground Railing, Stone Pavement covering hill-top .. .. ..⎫ Stupa (2) Ground Railing .. .. ⎬	c. 150 B.C.
	Great Stupa (1) Railing round berm and flanking steps	c. 100 B.C.
	Stupa (3) with Railings	c. 50 B.C.
	Temple (40) Pillars	c. 50 B.C.
Andhran c. 220 B.C.- 150 A.D.	.. Great Stupa (1) Four Gateways (Toranas) ⎫ .. .. (1st South, 2nd North, 3rd East, 4th West.) ⎬ Stupa (3) Gateway .. .. ⎭	c. 25 B.C. c. 25 A.D.

BARHUT

Asokan	.. Original Stupa	c. 250 B.C. (?)
Sungan	.. Gateway and Railing	c. 150 B.C.

BUDH GAYA

Sungan	.. Railing	c. 75 B.C.

BESNAGAR

Sungan	.. Vishnu Temple (destroyed) ; Pillar of Heliodorus	c. 140 B.C.

REFERENCES

Beal, S. *Some Remarks on the Great Tope at Sanchi.* (Journal Royal Asiatic Society, 1870.)
Bhandarkar, D. R. *Excavations at Besnagar.* Archaeological Survey of India. 1913-14, 1914-15.
Burgess, J. *The Great Stupa at Sanchi* (Journal Royal Asiatic Society. January, 1902.)
Cole, H. *Preservation of National Monuments in India.* Great Buddhist Tope at Sanchi, Calcutta 1885.
   „   „- *Third Report of the Curator of Ancient Monuments in India.* Calcutta, 1884.
Codrington, K. de B. *Ancient India from the Earliest Times to the Guptas.* London, 1926.
Cunningham, A. *The Bhilsa Topes.* London, 1854.
Maisey, F. C. *Sanchi and its Remains.* London, 1892.
Marshall, J. H. *Guide to Sanchi.* Calcutta, 1918.
   „   „   *Monuments of Sanchi.* Archaeological Survey of India, 1913-14.
   „   „   Sir John, and Foucher, A. *Monuments of Sanchi.* Calcutta, 1940.
Vogel, J. Ph. *The Garuda Pillar of Besnagar.* Archaeological Survey of India, 1908-9.

CHAPTER V

BUDDHIST ROCK-CUT ARCHITECTURE : THE EARLY OR HINAYANA PHASE

2nd Century B.C. to 2nd Century A.D.

ABOUT the same time that the Buddhist communities at such places as Sanchi, Barhut, Budh Gaya and similar sites made sacred by Ashoka's stupas were elaborating these with structural additions, another and entirely different architectural development was becoming manifest in another part of the country. This took the form of Buddhist monastic establishments consisting of large halls and chambers, having notable architectural pretensions, not however, built of wood or stone in the customary manner but hewn out of the living rock by means of the pick, and finished off by the dexterous application of the chisel. It has been already shown that a beginning had been made in this direction by the rock-cut chambers in the Barabar hills, but after an interval of over half a century this method was revived on a much grander and more ambitious scale. Eventually as a form of architectural expression it assumed remarkable proportions, as there are as many as twelve hundred excavations of this nature, both large and small, in various selected localities. Rock-sculpture and rock-architecture have been practised in many countries in the past, particularly in Egypt and Assyria, by the Greeks in Lycia, and the Romans at Petra, while in Persia under the Achaemenids, and later by the Sasanids as seen at Naksh-i-Rustam, both found considerable favour. But in none of these instances did the art of the rock-cutter show so wide a range or such audacity and imaginative power as in India, where some of the most original examples of architecture produced in this manner may be seen. Specially does this apply to the great prayer-halls of the Buddhists, as within their pillared aisles there is something not only majestic but magical, as if they were the abode of spirits or supernatural beings, the carved and painted images on their walls giving substance to this impression.

The fashioning of architectural forms out of the living rock, or rock-architecture, occupies a very prominent place in the development of creative art in India. Yet in spite of the admittedly high aesthetic character of these productions they have never been allowed that position in the field of art to which they are fully entitled. Ever since these examples of rock-architecture became a subject of study, it has been the custom to refer to them as "caves", implying that they were natural grottoes in the mountain side, the haunt of wild people, and still wilder animals. No word would be more misleading to designate these wonderful records of man's handwork, as many of them are large and well planned temples, skilfully wrought and chiselled out of the solid cliff, and to define which the term rock-architecture is the only one which can adequately describe their workmanship. If, however, the usually accepted definition of architecture as "good construction truthfully expressed" is applied, then on account of their technique alone they cannot be classed as architecture in the strict sense of the work. These rock-hewn forms are expert achievements but they involved no constructional principles, nor do they display any functional properties, their columns signify no adjustment of support to load, the arches carry no weight, nor do they counteract any thrust, in the whole operation no structural intelligibility is required, as no problems of this nature arise. In a word rock-architecture to all intents and purposes is not architecture it is sculpture, but sculpture on a grand and magnificent scale.

It has already been shown that more than one form of early art in India was part of a widely spread cultural development in western Asia transmitted through the influence of Persia when that country was ruled by the Achaemenids towards the fifth century B.C. And it seems probable that the rock-architecture of the Buddhists originated from the same source. For although a period of two hundred years separates the two movements, as this form of expression did not begin to appear in India until the third century B.C., the rock workmanship of each country bears a singular family resemblance. A comparison between the facade of the tomb of Darius at Naksh-i-Rustam near Persepolis, and that of the Lomas Rishi "chapel" in Bihar, although the latter is on a much smaller scale, reveals that the textural properties of the two productions have not a little in common. Rock-architecture appealed to the Indian mind for several reasons. In the first place its stability, as it was as immovable as the mountain of which it formed a part, was undoubtedly an attraction to a people living very largely in impermanent structures of wood and wattle. Secondly, it was acceptable to the Buddhists because from the earliest times natural caves and grottoes were the favourite abode of hermits and anchorites, a custom which even now survives in Nepal and parts of Tibet, where a Lamaistic form of Buddhism still prevails. Such habitations were therefore not only associated with religion but had also the sanction of tradition. But the principal reason was the great increase in the conventual life of the country at this time. From the ancient practice of asceticism, common in the Vedic period, it was but a step to that of monasticism, a system which all the world over has induced its followers to retire into rocky fastnesses, forest recesses, or lonely deserts, there to dedicate their lives to the rare worship of the self-absorbed. Some such convictions, perhaps accentuated by the pressure of religious intolerance, for the ruling powers belonged to the Brahmanical faith, were largely responsible for extensive monastic establishments flourishing within these secluded mountain retreats.

The production of this particular form of architecture was maintained for a very long period, as the first examples date from the third century B.C., and it continued to be practised throughout the whole of the first millennium only falling into, disuse in early mediaeval times. As associated with the Buddhist religion, rock-architecture in India resolves itself into two distinct movements, separated by a fairly long interval. The earliest or Hinayana phase lasted until the second century A.D., a period of some four hundred years, when for the time being it seems to have naturally declined. Then ensued three centuries of inactivity, but it revived again about the fifth century A.D., after which it was carried on for several centuries with great vigour and attained its richest and most varied form, not only in the hands of the Buddhists but also through similar efforts on the part of the Brahmans and Jains. The present outline is concerned only with the first and earliest phase, as developed by the followers of the Hinayana sect, who observed what is known as the "Lesser Vehicle," or primitive aspect of the creed. In its art this primitive Buddhism is distinctive on account of one important convention, for it ordained that in all its productions the bodily form of the Buddha should not be portrayed, in the works of the *Brahmajala Sutta*, "on the dissolution of the body neither gods nor men shall see him."[1] It may be noted that similar restrictions occur in other creeds, as shown by the Hebraic commandment in consequence of which no graven image appeared in the Temple, and the Islamic prohibition regarding representations of the Prophet. In the Hinayana art the spiritual presence of the Master is attested by the introduction in the iconography of certain intimate personal attributes, such as an empty throne, a footstool, cushions, or foot impressions, these symbolized forms being readily recognised and understood by the initiated, but the figure of the Buddha, being sacrosanct, was always omitted. With this convention in mind the classification of Buddhist art and consequently its architecture into its two main divisions is not difficult. It should be observed however that in certain instances attempts were made by the later theistic hierarchy to convert Hinayana monasteries into the Mahayana order by superimposing figures of the Buddha on the earlier work. Such palimpsests may, however, be readily identified, as may be seen on the rock-cut chaitya hall at Kanheri and also at Nasik.

These Hinayana rock-cut monasteries represent a definite regional development, as they are limited to the western side of India, many of them lying within the Bombay State. Taking Nasik as the centre they are all situated within a circle having a radius of less than two hundred miles from that town. Here in a configuration of rugged hills known as the Western Ghats, the terrain is naturally adapted to admit this form of architectural treatment, as much of it consists of horizontal strata of amygdaloid and cognate trap formations of considerable thickness and marked uniformity of texture. The edges of these strata terminate in nearly perpendicular cliffs, which provided an ideal surface for the type of rock-architecture contemplated. This architecture resolves itself into some ten separate groups of conventual establishments, each group being separate and self-contained, and each originally consisting of a prayer-hall and its accompanying monastery. The prayer-hall or Buddhist temple, and usually referred to as the *chaitya hall*, as it accommodated a chaitya or stupa, took the form of a large vaulted hall having an apsidal end and divided longitudinally by two colonnades into a broad nave and two aisles. In the apse stood the stupa, also carved out of the natural rock, consisting of an elaborated representation of the structural tumulus previously described. But the most striking fact in connection with the plan and general design of the Buddhist chaitya hall is its undeniable resemblance to the Graeco-Roman basilica, a type of structure which was being evolved in Europe about the same time. In spite of this similarity and their almost contemporaneous emergence, it is extremely unlikely that the two forms of hall were in any way related. The plan and arrangements of the basilica were such as would occur to anyone devising a commodious place of assembly. On the other hand the gradual process

---

[1] *Dialogues of the Buddha* trans. by Rhys Davids, p. 54.

of formation to the chaitya hall from its very primitive beginning has been already explained, while its more advanced shape as seen in these rock-cut examples, was brought about by the growing requirements of the Buddhist ritual. The side aisles and apsidal end were for the purpose of processions and circumambulation of the stupa, and the nave was provided for the congregational service. (Plates XIX, XX and XXI.)

The other architectural formation in these rock-cut retreats was the monastery proper, an arrangement of apartments for the accommodation of the monks, and known as a *vihara*. A typical vihara consisted of a square central hall entered by a doorway, in front of which was a vestibule, verandah, or portico. Out of the central hall doorways opened into square cells carried still further into the rock, each of which was the abode of one of the brotherhood. The original plan was for one of these viharas to be situated close to the chaitya hall, but as the priestly community increased, more cells were required to be excavated along the cliff side. These provided quarters for the ordinary members of the community, but there were others of a superior rank who felt it more seemly to live in chambers separated from the main group, of which an example is vihara number 4 at Karli. In addition there were those rare individuals on a still higher plane who claimed to be Arhats or Bodhisattvas, each of whom on account of his status lived alone in a single cell by itself, examples of which may also be seen at Karli. Communication between all these various forms of abode was maintained, where necessary by flights of steps, but in some of the larger monastic establishments, the cells are so numerous that the cliff side is honeycombed with them, recalling the nesting burrows of birds such as swifts in a disused quarry.

The style of architecture employed in the rock-cut monasteries was of a very significant and evocative character. It took the form of reproductions, as far as the unusual conditions admitted, of existing structural originals, the general shape of such wooden buildings as well as every detail, even to the joints and fastenings of the carpentry construction, being exactly imitated in the natural rock. And as a proof that, except for the excursions into the rock medium, those who produced this form of architecture were still living in a wood-building age, the rock work itself was supplemented by a substantial amount of wooden construction attached to its surfaces. These additions are shown in both the exteriors and interiors of the rock-cut work, for on the facades of the large halls there are numerous mortice holes for fixing elaborate wooden frontages, while inside in several instances an intricate falsework of wooden groins even now adheres to the rock-cut vaulted roof. There is every evidence, therefore, that the earlier examples of this process were practically half-timbered. Although one cannot fail to be impressed by the technical ability displayed in the production of the rock architecture of the Hinayana period, such a servile imitation of one method in another and entirely different material postulates that those concerned were in an early stage of their architectural experience and in the field of building construction still had much to learn.

The remarkable manipulative skill displayed in fashioning these architectural forms in the rock—for the actual workmanship is incredibly precise—implies that the workmen employed were by no means mere beginners, but on the contrary had served a long apprenticeship to this highly specialised form of quarrying. But strangely enough there are no evidences of experimental undertakings or trial cuttings, no gradual growth, no progressive stages are recorded, the art emerges as does more than one architectural development in India, in a fully matured state. In fact the earliest examples of all these excavated halls, are the most perfectly aligned, planned, and wrought with every line mathematically straight and every angle true. What actually happened when the rock-cut monasteries were first contemplated is, however, tolerably clear, as it can be read in the manner of their formation. The priests who conceived the idea of these retreats called on the master rock-cutters to prepare halls and habitations suitable to their needs. As there was apparently no precedent for such a method of production, the only alternative which presented itself was to repeat in the rock those structures in wood which had already been found serviceable in the past. As from various causes several of the examples have been left unfinished, it is possible to follow each stage of their execution. A selected portion of the naturally steep scarp of the hill side having been roughly cleared until it was perpendicular, a level ledge or platform was thus provided from which the workmen could begin their operations. On this vertical surface the facade of the hall or monastery was marked out, the particular shape that it assumed being a material help in excavating the interior, as in the centre was a large window-opening through which access to the upper part could be obtained. By means of this wide aperture also, the debris from the interior could be removed without difficulty and on this account it was left entirely open until the completion of the work, when it was filled in with a framework of wood. With the spoil excavated from the interior the forecourt in front of the facade was built up.

At an early stage in the proceedings, however it is evident that a small chapel with cells attached was first cut near the site of the main hall in which two or three monks entrusted with the direction of the work could live and conduct their usual ritual. Such chapels may be seen in the monasteries at Bhaja and Nasik, each a perfect specimen in miniature, and undoubtedly the earliest of their group. At Nasik also one chamber (No. 14) appears to have been cut first of all in order to provide accommodation for a priestly "resident architect" or "clerk of works", so that he could always be present to supervise the excavation of the main hall above. Having outlined the frontage, the work of hewing this into shape was begun from the top, as it was the practice to commence with the upper portions so as to have the advantage of the rough rock below for footholds, thus dispensing with scaffolding. In the interior the same procedure was followed, the ceiling or roof being first cut and completely finished, the work being gradually carried downwards. To be sure that a correct alignment was obtained the artificers gauged their direction by means of a rough driftway, and then progressed by cutting deep furrows with a tool resembling a heavy pickaxe, after which the intervening ridges were knocked out, the surfaces being dressed with a broad-edged chisel.

From the markings left on the walls of rock it is possible to realise the sensitive understanding of the master craftsman, and to discern his hand making that "feathering" movement of the chisel, as he feels his way trying to avoid flaws in the strata or twists in the grain that might ruin the effect. There are evidences of that strong delicacy required so as not to crack or splinter the rock, and also to finish its surface pleasingly. This fine finish was obtained by means of a chisel a little over a quarter of an inch in width. Except for the preliminary work with the pick the cutting was done entirely by the aid of hammers and chisels, as there are no signs of such expedients as the drill or wedge. It seems that the same workmen who performed the rough quarrying also chiselled the carving, for had these two operations been the work of separate hands, portions of the rock would have been left boasted in readiness for the finer manipulation of the sculptor. If such a division of labour was the practice, it has certainly left no trace, although several of the halls remain in an unfinished state, from which it is inferred that the man who worked the pick also handled the chisel—he was quarryman and sculptor combined. As to the kind of tool used in the work there are no records except a few discarded chisels which were unearthed when investigating the foundations of the Heliodorus pillar at Besnagar. These are made of iron, the working of which was well known in India at an early date and there is little doubt that the picks and chisels were of the same metal.

Of the two kinds of structure, the chaitya hall and the vihara that were copied in the rock-cut manner, the more important from every point of view was the chaitya hall. There are eight of these belonging to the Hinayana period as follows : Bhaja, Kondane, Pitalkhora, Ajanta (No. 10), Bedsa, Ajanta (No. 9), Nasik and Karli, probably executed in the order named. The two at Ajanta are part of that long series of both Hinayana and Mahayana monasteries all on one site comprising altogether as many as four chaitya halls and over twenty viharas, but this instance of grouping is exceptional and will be explained in due course. All the eight examples were excavated just previous to the Christian era, the first four in the second century, and the remainder in the first century B.C. To these may be added two chaitya halls from a numerous and miscellaneous group at Junnar, one of which is small but complete while the other is unfinished, but they are both of the same type and date as that at Nasik. Finally, executed towards the middle of the second century A.D., is the chaitya hall at Kanheri on the island of Salsette adjacent to Bombay, which marks the end of the Hinayana movement as far as its rock architecture is concerned.

The chronological sequence in which the chaitya halls were executed is based mainly on the principle that the earlier the example the closer it copies wooden construction. Another guide is the slope of the interior pillars, as it is assumed that their inward inclination was derived from wooden posts so slanted in order to counteract the outward thrust of a heavy timber roof, thus the greater the angle of the rake, the nearer the relation to its wooden prototype. Moreover there is the particular shape of the arch forming the main feature of the facade, the curve of which is the subject of change as the style progresses, so that the rule also may be applied that the more rudimentary the curves the earlier the example. This may be proved by reverting for the moment to the previous group in the Barabar hills containing the initial effort in rock architecture, that of the chapel of Lomas Rishi, the facade of which shows a gable-end consisting merely of an arrangement of laminated boards, bent rather than curved to a suitable angle (Plate XXV, Fig. 1). About a century later in the earliest example of the Hinayana series now being described, that at Bhaja, the characteristic horse-shoe arch first appears in the facade, but it is of the stilted variety and its indecisive curves suggest that this distinctive feature was undergoing a process of formation (Fig. 2). The facade of Kondane followed and denotes an advance, as there is a slight inward return to the spring of the arch, and the whole is more vigorous and firm in outline. At Ajanta (No. 9) and at Karli (Fig. 3) the chaitya arch has arrived at its early maturity, being composed of a subtle and refined combination of curves, a shape which it retained for the remainder of the Hinayana period. Afterwards, in the succeeding Mahayana style as in chaitya hall No. 19 at Ajanta (Fig. 4), the arched aperture tends towards exaggeration, it becomes constricted at the base, and more florid in its curvatures until, as in the seventh century facade of Visvakarma at Ellora, it is no longer a horse-shoe arch but almost a complete circle (Fig. 5). Finally, when the chaitya arch motif appears as a decorative feature in the Brahmanical temple, it assumes a variety of forms of which Fig. 6 is an illustration. As an ornamental accessory known as the *kudu*, a kind of miniature acroterium, it is frequently used to break the line of the cornice in the Brahmanical architecture of the south.

A reference to the diagrams on Plate XX, will indicate that the chaitya halls varied considerably in size, and although perhaps at a first glance, notably at Karli, the interior suggests a Norman nave, none of them approach the average dimensions of an ordinary abbey-church in the Gothic style. For purposes of comparison it may be noted that the size of that at Ajanta (No. 10), one of the largest, is appreciably less than that of the somewhat similarly shaped hall in Henry VII's chapel, Westminster Abbey, London. Although the apsidal end of the chaitya hall is a characteristic feature of its composition, one of the series, namely Ajanta (No. 9), is square-ended but even in this instance the interior colonnade carries out the apsidal plan. The pillars forming the colonnades in all the earlier examples appear as copies of plain wooden posts, chamfered into an octagonal section, and without either capitals or bases. It was only towards the end of the style that it became the custom to elaborate each different member of the pillar and its entablature, thus forming it into some semblance of an " order." From the first, however, the exterior and frontal aspect of these chaitya halls was regarded as of great architectural significance, and accordingly considerable ingenuity and artistic skill was expended on the design of the facade. In most instances the actual front was composed of a massive pillared portico or vestibule which in the earlier examples has disappeared. Behind this was the facade which consisted of a great horse-shoe archway above, with a wall or screen below, having one or more doorways giving access to the nave and aisles. But undoubtedly the most conspicuous feature of the front-age was the opening or window occupying the centre of the archway, and through which the light was admitted into the body of the hall. This chaitya or sun-window a form of rose-window and fan-light combined, was clearly an enlargement and elaboration of the dormer window of the Vedic hut, with its projecting cowl to keep off the sun and the rain. In shape it is a stilted semi-circular aperture divided into lunettes by means of curved wooden transoms held in place by braces, also of wood, and radiating like the spokes of a wheel. As an architectural conception, and at the same time as an artistic and effective method of introducing light, this very early form of a traceried window is a remarkable achievement.

Taking the chaitya hall of Bhaja first, as undoubtedly representing the initial effort, this example is singularly instructive (Plate XXII, Fig. 1). The entrance, and facade generally, owing to the action of time, and the climate, have now become a great open archway, bringing the entire interior of the hall into view. Such, however, was no more the designer's intention than would be a Gothic church with its west front removed. Originally the whole of the open space was filled in with a highly finished and appropriate wooden construction, which completely screened the lower portion, and affected to no little extent the appearance of the upper parts of the facade. From the shape and position of the mortice holes, aided by decorative representations in the bas-reliefs, it is possible to reconstruct the scheme of this wooden frontage. The simple but substantial framework on which it was built took the form of a letter H, the two uprights fitting into each side of the rock-cut archway, the cross-piece being a horizontal beam connecting them and holding them into position. The lower half was then filled in by a screen containing one central and two side doorways, while above the cross-beam was projected a hanging balcony supported on four pillars, the whole constituting a spacious and elegant portico. The facade of wood was ornamented in the same manner as the rock-cut oriels still existing on each side, with lattices and brackets in keeping with the remainder of the scheme. There is little doubt that this timber and rock conception was an architectural composition of considerable merit, ingenious in its construction, and not lacking in artistic effect.

In the interior of the hall at Bhaja, woodwork was also freely applied, the closely ranked roof ribs as well as the finial (*harmika*) of the stupa with its umbrella being all originally of this material. But even with these additions it must have had a definitely austere appearance, although its proportions are good. It measures 55 feet long and 26 feet across, the side aisles being 3½ feet wide. The pronounced slope of the pillars which are five inches out of the perpendicular in a total height of 11 feet produces an effect which is not altogether pleasing, but the high stilted vault above, 29 feet from the floor level, is a fine piece of work and to some extent compensates for the unusual slanting formation of the colonnade. As to the stupa this central feature in its present condition is rather a plain conception in two simple parts consisting of a cylindrical base supporting a tall domical body with a " railing " finial. It is more than probable however that the stupa, together with most of the surfaces of the hall itself, were freely decorated with wooden additions, plaster reliefs, and figure subjects in coloured fresco.

The next example, the chaitya hall at Kondane, displayed a facade of much the same type as the preceding, except that the upright beams on either side of the archway instead of being entirely of wood were in this instance partly carved in the rock, thus implying a small but progressive step in the evolution of the style (Plate XXII, Fig. 2). Much of the interior has been destroyed but enough remains to show that its dimensions were slightly larger than those of Bhaja, as it is 66 feet long 26½ feet across and its height is rather more than 28 feet. The more finished line of curvature of the facade archway has been already described. Out of the entire series of Hinayana chaitya halls, those of Bhaja and Kondane, being the oldest, are most informative, as they record in a striking manner the methods and expedients, not only of the rock-carver but also of the wood-worker at this early date.

The two remaining examples of this class, that of Pital-khora and Ajanta (No. 10), although considerably ruined, appear to have been of much the same order as the two previously described. In the case of the former, another advance in the development may be seen by the treatment of the roof-ribs in the side-aisles which instead of being of wood are carved out of the rock, evidently a further attempt to reduce the wooden attachment. Owing to a fault in the strata some of the pillars had to be completed structurally, and the stupa having disappeared the probability is that it was built up in the same way, either of stone or wood. The length of this chaitya hall when complete must have been over 50 feet, and it is 34½ feet wide with a height of 31 feet. The last of the series, Ajanta (No. 10), by its large size shows that the artificers were becoming bolder in their conceptions, as it measures as much as 100 feet in length, is 40 feet wide and 33 feet high ; in this instance also the ribs of the side-aisles are not of wood but cut out of the rock and they radiate from the end pillars singularly like groins from a Gothic boss. As to the stupa this is somewhat elaborated, its circular base being in two tiers, and the dome is rather more than a hemisphere, indicating a step towards that elongation of its elevation which characterised the later forms.

Of the next class of chaitya halls, judging mainly by the design and treatment of the facade, Ajanta (No. 9) and that known as Pandulena at Nasik are the two principal examples, as both have no wooden additions to their frontage, the whole having been carved out of the rock. The Ajanta facade is a singularly well-balanced design recalling in some respects of Gothic rood-screen, with a doorway in the centre and a window on either side, each opening being protected above by an elegant cornice thrown out on brackets like a shallow portico. Over this is what corresponds in the Gothic parallel to the rood-loft, a broad sill or ledge used as a minstrel's gallery, and rising above the whole is the sun-window within a chaitya arch of graceful curves. On the flat surface around the archway are carved as objects of decoration several small lattice windows, conventional renderings of the projecting casements copied so realistically from wooden originals as seen on the previous type at Bhaja and Kondane. As already mentioned the plan of this hall is a rectangle and moreover the ceiling of the side aisles instead of being curved is flat, while its pillars are perpendicular. Originally the vault of the nave was braced with wooden ribs which, however, appear to have been regarded as superfluous and accordingly were removed at an early date. This left a broad surface of the wall above the colonnade similar to a triforium, which was seized upon by the sixth century painters of the famous Ajanta school as an appropriate space for their mural frescoes.

The other example of this small class, the Pandulena at Nasik, with which may also be included the unfinished Manmoda chaitya hall at Junnar, although both differ considerably in their details from the foregoing bear a general resemblance as they are also entirely carved out of the rock and have no porticos or wooden vestibules. A feature of the facade in both instances is a lunette carved with symbolic design, in the Pandulena this is above the doorway, but in the Manmoda it fills the upper space of the archway over the sun-window. In both frontages the decoration on the wall around the main archway contains fresh motifs particularly that on the Pandulena where sculptured in relief there is an arcade containing pilasters of the " Persepolitan " order. The interior of the Nasik example also shows that its designers were beginning to recognise the decorative value of the pillar as instead of these being treated merely as posts, they have introduced on some of them a rudimentary capital in the form

of a square abacus. A singular fact however in this connection is that more attention was paid to the embellishment of the bases of the pillars than to the capitals, as here for the first time the pot-shaped base is met with, a motif presumed to have been derived from the primitive expedient of embedding a wooden post in a pot to protect its lower extremity from the ravages of insects or the effect of damp. Another noticeable feature which distinguishes the pillars of this chaitya hall are their proportions. Instead of the broad and massive piers of most of the rock-cut temples, these are tall and slender, with a diameter of one eighth of their height, a proportion very near to the finest Greek and Roman models of approximately the same date. Immediately within the interior of the Pandulena above the doorway there are grooves and sockets for the attachment of a musicians' gallery, which was fixed inside the hall and not as in other examples in the form of a balcony across the outside of the facade. In the design of the stupa there is expressed by the tall proportions of the cylindrical base a still further desire for height in this central object which became more marked as the style advanced.

The maturity of the early series of chaitya halls is shown in the two very fine examples at Bedsa and Karli, in which the scheme of the facade differs very materially from any of the preceding. In both instances the outstanding feature of the exterior takes the form of a massive propylaeum carved out of the rock face and serving as a kind of vestibule to the arcaded screen in its rear. That at Bedsa which is probably the earlier, is composed of two columns between pilasters, planned on the same principle as the entrance to a *distyle in antis* type of Greek temple. Only a restricted view of this notable conception is possible as the approach to it is marked by masses of rock left in the rough on either side, for some purpose which is not clear. It is the design and execution of the pillars and pilasters of the portico which make the facade such a remarkable production, as by means of an elaborately carved superstructure they act as supports to the main beam of the roof, all however in one solid piece as the entire frontage is carved out of the natural rock. Derived from the Asokan free-standing monoliths the pillars show the extent of their departure from the classical model during the interval of two hundred years. The companiform capital remains only slightly altered, and there is the sculptured group above corresponding to the carved Buddhist symbols on the original. But the vase-shaped base, the octagonal shaft, and various additions to the capital are innovations, several of which suggest a survival from a primitive and indigenous source. The eye is instinctively attracted by the group of figures and animals surmounting the capitals, each of which consists of a male and female figure lightly clad but with heavy ornaments seated astride kneeling animals, on the one side horses and on the other elephants. These groups are exceptionally vivid and spirited examples of rock sculpture, evidently the work of a master craftsman in this medium. Above the figures are the beams, binding joists, and other wooden features of the portico roof all copied most literally in the rock the whole being completed by a parapet of railing design carried across the entire front. Within the portico is the inner facade with its arrangement of archway, sun-window, and entrance doorway all placed according to the conventional disposition of these essential elements. The interior of the chaitya hall is severely plain, the pillars being merely copies of octagonal posts without bases or capitals, although on some of the shafts are carved Buddhist symbols. An appreciable amount of woodwork in the form of vault ribs and other additions was originally attached, but most of it has disappeared within recent years and at one time there were traces of fresco painting with which the pillars and also the stupa were decorated. The hall is small in size, being only 45½ feet long and 21 feet wide.

It was however at Karli that the Hinayana type of chaitya hall reached its culmination, as this example is a most impressive production. The exterior, owing either to a flaw or fall in the rock face is now unsymmetrical, as much of the right side of the facade has become completely obscured, but no doubt as first conceived it was a well balanced composition of somewhat the same style and massive proportions as Bedsa. But at Karli the two large columns, which are the main feature of its form of frontage, were differently disposed, not comprising part of the " construction " so to speak, as they were wholly detached. They were therefore free-standing pillars, one on each side of the facade and slightly in advance of the entrance, which with their lion capitals they appear to guard. The plan of raising two pillars in front of a temple is a very ancient one— before that of the moon god at Ur, 3000 B.C., two wooden columns were raised, and it was probably the same thought that moved the Egyptians to erect a pair of obelisks at the entrances to their temples, while in the porch of Solomon's temple at Jerusalem two pillars of brass were set up as objects of veneration.[1] The pillars at Karli appear to have been the result of the same belief, their great size striking the imagination of the worshipper and filling his soul with reverence and awe. Seen from the ample terrace facing them made up of the debris obtained from the excavation, these colossal columns and their symbolic superstructure formed an imposing introduction to the wonders beyond. Each pillar stood on a wide cylinder of rock and with its companiform capital and group of addorsed lions supporting a large wheel possibly of metal, it was at least fifty feet in height, equalling that of the Asokan column at Sarnath by which the entire conception was certainly inspired. The addition of the base, the sixteen sides to the shaft, the fluted abacus above the capital with its *harmika* forming a square pedestal for the lions, are however all deviations from the original model and indicate a further Indianization of the Persepolitan prototype.

Behind the two lion columns or *sinha-stambhas*, was the vestibule to the hall, the front face of which was formed by a rock-cut screen having a triple entrance below and a pillared clerestory above. On the space between these upper and lower openings, corresponding in some respects to a triforium, numerous mortice holes may be seen for the attachment of a minstrel's gallery of wood which extended right across the front. The wooden addition has completely perished but it was an important feature in the design of the facade and would improve its effect ; access to this hanging gallery was obtained by means of a stairway at the back of the lion column on the left side. Passing through one of the doorways in the screen the vestibule is entered and the whole inner frontage with its sun-window, decorated arcading, and sculptured figure compositions, comes into view (Plate XXIII). The greater part of the inner wall of the vestibule is occupied by the towering horse-shoe archway within which is recessed the sun-window, portions of the wooden tracery in the opening being still in situ, but the lower section with its semi-circular screen of wooden

trellis-work is missing. In the spandrils on each side of the great archway, and also on the narrower ends of this vestibule are carved in the rock tiers of chaitya arcading separated by bands of decorative railings, a very dignified method of ornamenting these subsidiary spaces. Below, some of the panels are filled with figures in relief, but several of them are later Mahayana impositions, and as they were not part of the original scheme they do not harmonise with the rest. Perhaps the most spirited motif in the entire composition is the series of supporting elephants at the ends, each half life-size in high relief and originally provided with tusks of ivory. By such artistic treatment and skilful distribution of all the decorative and symbolic elements, some of them repeated and alternated like a theme in music, the minds of the votaries were attuned and thus prepared for admission into the mysterious and sacred hall of the stupa.

Entrance to the chaitya hall was obtained by means of three doorways, the one in the centre being reserved for the priests, and others of high standing, and was approached by a raised pathway on each side of which the floor was sunk to form shallow cisterns filled with water. The ordinary devotees stepped through these shallow pools on their way to the side doors, a procedure which compulsorily cleansed their feet from the contamination of the outer world. Of these who have been privileged to enter this grand interior there must be few who have not been profoundly moved by the solemn permanency and appropriateness generally of its pillared aisles (Plate XXIV, Fig. 1). Although the largest of its kind, its dimensions are not great as it has only 124 feet long, 46½ feet wide and 45 feet high, so that it would go inside the choir of either Wells or Rouen cathedral, yet within its hoary precincts one ceases to think in terms of space and only in those of time. Many more than a thousand years have passed since the rustle of pilgrims' feet in procession last echoed through its shadowed colonnades, or priests filled the high vault of the nave with their chanted liturgy, but the atmosphere of religious emotion which was then created still lingers. There can be nothing but admiration for those who, urged by their passionate devotion for the Great Teacher, could conjure out of the bare hill-side such a majestically imposing and at the same time supremely artistic place of worship.

The interior of this chaitya hall owes much of its architectural content to the manner in which its three principal elements have each in themselves been treated and then combined to produce a co-ordinated whole. These are the colonnade, the vaulting, and the great sun-window. Taking the colonnade first, the pillars forming it are thirty-seven in number, and are closely set, much more so than any previous example, as the space between each is but little more than the width of the column itself. Those encircling the apse have plain octagonal shafts, as in all the other halls of the series, while the fifteen on each side are highly carved and decorated, repeating in their design, the theme of the larger free-standing lion-columns (*sinha-stambhas*) of the exterior. Each pillar consists of a vase base on a plinth, an octagonal shaft, a campaniform capital with spreading abacus, and each is finished off above by a fine group of sculptured statuary. To the conception of this colonnade the interior owes much of its strength in repose, but it is from the figure composition it supports that the principal vitality of effect is obtained (Plate XXIV, Fig. 2). These carved groups are all somewhat similar, but there is sufficient variation in

---

[1] 1 Kings, Chap. 7.

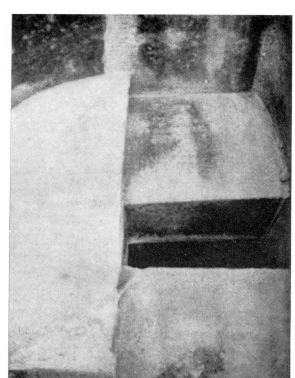

Fig. 2

Fig. 3

Fig. 1

Fig. 1. Lomas Rishi, façade.

Fig. 2. Sudama. Rock-cut imitation of planking in interior.

Fig. 3. Sudama. Rock-cut eave of interior.

Barabar Hills, Bihar : Rock-cut Cells, 3rd cent. B.C.

X

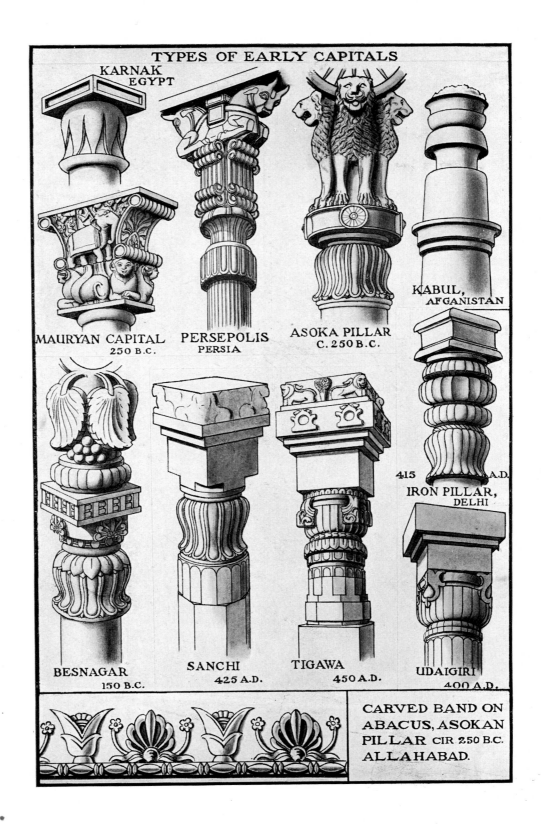

TYPES OF EARLY CAPITALS

KARNAK
EGYPT

MAURYAN CAPITAL
250 B.C.

PERSEPOLIS
PERSIA

ASOKA PILLAR
C. 250 B.C.

KABUL,
AFGANISTAN

BESNAGAR
150 B.C.

SANCHI
425 A.D.

TIGAWA
450 A.D.

415   A.D.
IRON PILLAR,
DELHI

UDAIGIRI
400 A.D.

CARVED BAND ON
ABACUS, ASOKAN
PILLAR CIR 250 B.C.
ALLAHABAD.

① ② ③ ④ ⑤ ⑥

⑦ ⑧ ⑨

⑩ ⑪

EVOLUTION OF DRAVIDIAN CAPITAL

⑦ KARLI 150 B.C.
⑧ LADH KHAN, AIHOLE 5TH CENT. A.D.
⑨ MAMALLAPURAM 7TH CENT.
⑩ KAILASA 9TH CENT.
⑪ KORVANGULA EARLY 10TH CENT.

⑫ PLAN OF DUMBAL TEMPLE OF DODABASAVANNA 12TH CENT.

STELLATE PLAN

10 0 10 20 30
SCALE OF FEET

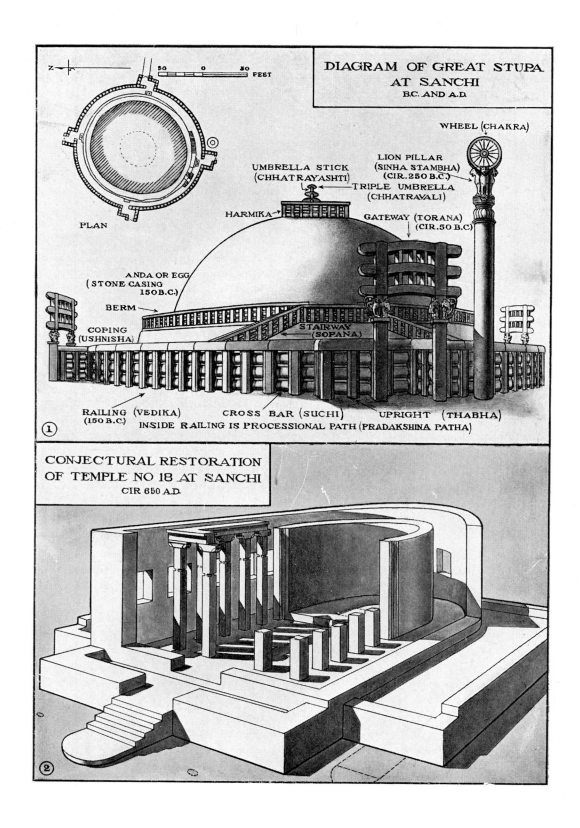

DIAGRAM OF GREAT STUPA
AT SANCHI
B.C. AND A.D.

WHEEL (CHAKRA)

LION PILLAR
(SINHA STAMBHA)
(CIR. 250 B.C.)

UMBRELLA STICK
(CHHATRAYASHTI)

TRIPLE UMBRELLA
(CHHATRAVALI)

HARMIKA

GATEWAY (TORANA)
(CIR. 50 B.C.)

PLAN

ANDA OR EGG
(STONE CASING
150 B.C.)

BERM

COPING
(USHNISHA)

STAIRWAY
(SOPANA)

RAILING (VEDIKA)
(150 B.C.)

CROSS BAR (SUCHI)

UPRIGHT (THABHA)

INSIDE RAILING IS PROCESSIONAL PATH (PRADAKSHINA PATHA)

①

CONJECTURAL RESTORATION
OF TEMPLE NO 18 AT SANCHI
CIR 650 A.D.

②

Fig. 1.   Barabar Hills, Bihar.   Lomas Rishi (c. 250 B.C.)

Fig. 2.   Budh Gaya.   Railing (c. 75 B.C.)

Fig. 3.   Barhut Stupa : Upper part of Gateway (c. 150 B.C.)

Fig. 4.   Budh Gaya : Architectural details on Railing Pillar (c. 1st Cent. A.D.)

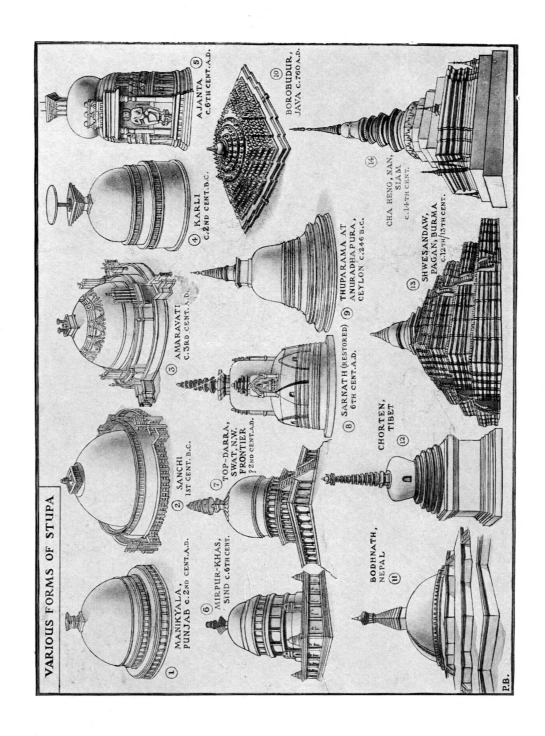

VARIOUS FORMS OF STUPA

1. MANIKYALA, PUNJAB c.2ND CENT.A.D.
2. SANCHI 1ST CENT.B.C.
3. AMARAVATI c.3RD CENT.A.D.
4. KARLI c.2ND CENT.B.C.
5. AJANTA c.6TH CENT.A.D.
6. MIRPUR-KHAS, SIND c.6TH CENT.
7. TOP-DARRA, SWAT, N.W. FRONTIER ?2ND CENT.A.D.
8. SARNATH (RESTORED) 6TH CENT.A.D.
9. THUPARAMA AT ANURADHAPURA, CEYLON c.246 B.C.
10. BOROBUDUR, JAVA c.760 A.D.
11. BODHNATH, NEPAL
12. CHORTEN, TIBET
13. SHWESANDAW, PAGAN, BURMA c.12TH/13TH CENT.
14. CHA HENG, NAN, SIAM c.14TH CENT.

P.B.

Sanchi, Bhopal.   Northern Gateway (partially restored) of Great Stupa ; 1st cent. B.C.

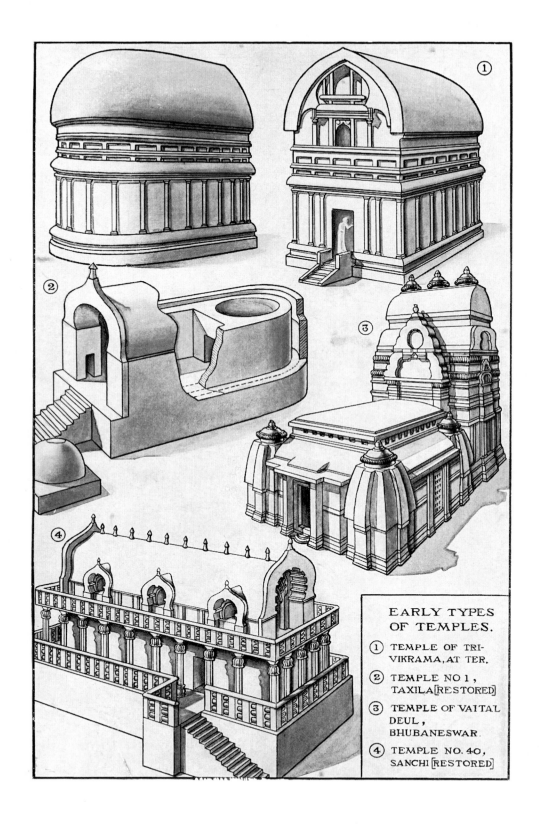

EARLY TYPES
OF TEMPLES.

(1) TEMPLE OF TRI-
VIKRAMA, AT TER.

(2) TEMPLE NO 1,
TAXILA [RESTORED]

(3) TEMPLE OF VAITAL
DEUL,
BHUBANESWAR.

(4) TEMPLE NO. 40,
SANCHI [RESTORED]

their design to prevent monotony, and they merge themselves into a kind of sculptured frieze of great beauty. Each group consists of two kneeling elephants, each animal bearing a male and female rider both wearing resplendent head dresses and loaded with a wealth of jewellery. On the reverse side of these groups, within the side aisles, they are also richly carved, but here horses take the place of the elephants, the former having originally been decked with metal trappings, and the latter provided with silver or ivory tusks. The figures were allegorical and intended to signify the opulence and power of the rulers of the earth on their lordly elephants who kneel in humility before the sacred shrine of the Buddha.

Above the rich zone of chiaroscuro produced by this frieze of figures rises the high arched vault of the roof, the mystery of its shadowed space vaguely defined by the narrow projecting ribs or wind-braces, not carved out of the rock, but fashioned out of separate pieces of wood attached to the surface by means of plugs or socketed into grooves. These braces are wide flat planks with a curved outline, approximating the shape of an inverted ship's hull, the grain of the wood being usually continuous in the curve as in the mediaeval roofs of Europe, while at the apsidal end they converge to a centre as do the ribs of a Gothic vault. Remains of coloured decoration on the wooden accessories imply that at one time much of the interior was painted. Under the semi-dome of the apse is the stupa, a plain yet dignified composition, its cylindrical base in two diminishing tiers, the sole embellishment being two bands of railing in imitation of balustrades, clearly suggested by the custom of an upper and lower processional path around this symbol as at Sanchi. The body, a plain hemisphere, is surmounted by a massive *harmika*, or finial, decorated with a rail pattern in low relief, and high up over the whole spreads a large wooden umbrella carved in the pattern of a lotus.

Such are the arrangements of the colonnade and the vaulting, with the stupa as the focal point of both these essential parts of the scheme. But although the architectural, decorative, and symbolic fundamentals have been so carefully worked out, there is little doubt that the interior of the hall owes much of its appearance to the position and treatment of that most characteristic feature, the sun-window of the facade. On this great aperture depends the whole system of lighting, as the interior is produced on the same principle as a tunnel with one end closed—it could only be illuminated from one direction. But the method by which the open end was manipulated to make the most of the conditions thus imposed shows no little thought and skill. The aim of the designer was to deflect the glaring sunshine outside through this opening to be distributed, modified, and subdued, so that it is projected not so much as light, but as an effulgence, into all parts. It was, therefore, first filtered between the openings of the clerestory in the fronton screen, then broken up by the wooden grille of the sun-window as through a mullioned oriel, finally to fall evenly on the stupa itself like a delicate mantle of light yet edging it with a black shadow. From this central feature it shaded off imperceptibly by modulated half-tones among the surrounding pillars, to be lost in the comparative gloom of the aisles, thus conveying the impression of a fathomless cavern extending indefinitely into the depths of the mountain. There are few lighting effects more solemnly beautiful than the soft luminous atmosphere diffused in this manner through the sun-window at Karli.

With the great effort at Karli, the Hinayana phase of rock architecture seems to have spent itself as although viharas for the accommodation of the still increasing communities of monks continued to be added to these retreats, no more chaitya halls were excavated for some time. At the monastery of Junnar, however, a number of chambers, most of them of a relatively small order, were in the course of production over a considerable period, some perhaps as early as the second century B.C., and others in the first century A.D. In one of the groups on this site known as the Tulja Lena, there is a small chaitya hall, which is different from any other and may be a survival of a very ancient type. It is circular in plan and 20 feet in diameter with a stupa in the centre over which rises a dome about 18 feet high supported on twelve plain octagonal pillars, the whole composition being on the same principle as the monopteron style in Roman architecture, of which the temple of Vesta in the Forum Boarium of Rome is an example. Apparently a reproduction in the rock of a primitive structural shrine, it was a form probably not uncommon at one time and of which there are representations on some of the early reliefs, as for instance on the railing at Barhut.

There are several other small chaitya halls at Junnar, not apsidal, but consisting of rectangular chambers without pillared aisles and with a stupa at their further end ; their exteriors contain neat little vestibules with pillars *in antis* similar to those at Bedsa although on a much smaller scale. Light is admitted into the chamber through the doorway, as the chaitya arch although forming part of the facade is not perforated. In another group on this site, that of the Ganesh Lena (No. 6), there is one chaitya hall, small, yet so perfect in its design and production as to merit special reference. It is of the same dimensions as the hall at Nasik, and the treatment of its pillars is similar to that on some of the viharas there, while the groining also is not wood but rockcut, the style of the whole indicating the first century A.D. as the probable date of its execution. The interior measures only 45 feet in length, but the five pillars on each side of the aisles are carved in the same manner and almost as elaborately as the much larger examples at Karli. Instead however of the elephant and rider motif of the latter, the capitals support animals only, such as pairs of tigers, elephants, and sphinx. The admirable proportions of this hall and the richness of its decoration, although all compressed within a limited space, make it a typical example in miniature of Buddhist rock architecture.

There remains only one other Hinayana chaitya hall, that at Kanheri, which is in a class by itself, as it was the last of this type to have been produced, having been excavated, according to inscriptional evidence, as late as 180 A.D. Up a slight incline, and surrounded by pretty woodland scenery, through which meander and murmur shallow streams, this monastic retreat must have provided a pleasant haven for meditation and seclusion. In its style of architecture the chaitya hall, is, in effect, a decadent copy of that at Karli, but only about two-thirds its size. Its history is plainly observable from the sculpture on the facade. First cut out of the rock in the second century A.D., it was probably never completed, but none the less it was in use by the Hinayana brotherhood for some time. Then, as with others prepared for a similar purpose, on the decline of the creed, it fell into disuse for several centuries. On the revival of the Buddhist religion in its Mahayana form about the fifth century A.D., it was again taken over and occupied by the monks, its exterior, by means of additional sculpture, being made suitable for the theistic ritual then prevailing. Some of the sculptured forms, subsequently introduced, are now the most striking part of the composition, as apart from certain smaller figures on the facade, the result of the same movement, at each end of the vestibule there is a colossal statue of the Buddha over twenty-five feet high. Only the exterior of this chaitya hall is affected by later impositions, the interior remaining as originally designed.

Although a rather bare and obviously unfinished example, Kanheri provides some useful information as to the disposition of the exterior of these chaitya halls, besides explaining the arrangements in front of Karli before the fall of the cliff destroyed its symmetry. In front of the exterior at Kanheri is a well-defined courtyard, contained within a dwarf wall, and entered by a flight of steps ; as this wall is decorated with a rail-pattern in bas-relief, with figures of doorkeepers (*dwarpalas*) on either side, the whole scheme forms an attractive frontal approach. Within the forecourt, on each side, are the *sinha stambhas*, or " lion pillars ", as at Karli, but at Kanheri, apart from several differences in detail, these pillars are not free-standing but attached to the rock, like large and prominent plasters " *in antis* " More-over the middle of the octagonal shaft is interrupted by a " cushion " member, and above the abacus are the remains of supporting figures, or gnome-like atlantes, which appear conspicuously, in a somewhat similar capacity, in the architecture of the mediaeval period. Beyond the *stambhas* is the outer facade, a plain wall-screen with three tall square-headed openings below, and a range of five windows, in the form of a clerestory, above. As the surfaces of this rock screen contain many mortice-holes, it is clear that it was in practice little more than a stable support for a considerable amount of woodwork, including a hanging gallery for musicians. It is noticeable that every portion of the chaitya hall is patterned with holes for attachments, so that much of it was presumably supplemented with timber construction. This is significant, as it goes to prove that as this type of excavated hall progressed, it began to return to its earlier form of being more than half-timbered.

Behind the front-screen is a vestibule in the back-wall of which are three doorways with the chaitya or sun-window above. The sun-window, usually the richest feature of the scheme, in this instance is little more than a bare semi-circular aperture, and is obviously unfinished. Inside, the interior takes the form of the conventional apsidal hall, surrounded by a colonnade, the dimensions being 86 feet in length, 40 feet wide, and with a height of 50 feet. The 34 pillars completely encircling the nave, are closely set, being short massive columns, only a few of which are ornamented, and in much the same manner as those at Karli. The impression conveyed by this chaitya hall is, that, while the architectural technique shows signs of deterioration, the plastic embellishment, particularly of the figures, has maintained its quality. Taken as a whole, however, Kanheri represents a distinct falling away from the high standard of its prototype, plainly signifying that it was a final effort before the early phase of rock-architecture, owing to the decline of the Hinayana doctrine, came to an end.

All these monastic retreats, once the focus of Buddhist spiritual life, eventful and active, have now been deserted for many centuries, and until recently had become the abode of wandering fakirs, people of the jungle, and even wild animals. But the picture they presented in the days of their pride, when they were the home of a large ecclesiastical community, is not difficult to visualize. For although Buddhism has departed from these regions, the ritual, as it was performed two thousand years ago, is still observed in the monasteries of Tibet, from which the ancient ceremonial, as conducted within the rock-cut halls may be reconstructed, and the whole scene brought to life. The day would begin with a burst of trumpets and the strumming of drums from the minstrel's gallery in the chaitya hall facade, the sounds echoing up the mountain side and calling the monks to prayers. Soon the forecourt and vestibule would fill with an assembly of saffron or yellow clad priests, who amidst a cloud of incense, would proceed to walk in procession around the aisles, and, afterwards, to enter the nave where coloured mats had been already placed in front of the bases of the pillars on which they would sit. On the right hand side, near the stupa, would be a raised wooden throne, draped and cushioned for the abbot. Then would follow the service, consisting of readings and chantings from the sacred books, with occasional accompaniments from the trumpets and drums now stationed inside the hall, the entire proceeding being one of great reverence combined with a remarkably artistic effect. For the coloured robes of the priestly congregation, and the richly woven mats and cushions, would be caught up by the fine fresco paintings on the walls above, to the whole of which the architectural treatment of the interior would provide a grandly solemn setting.

REFERENCES

Fergusson J. *Illustrations of the Rock-cut Temples of India.* London 1845.
Fergusson J. and Burgess J. *The Cave Temples of India.* London 1880.
India Society. *The Bagh Caves.* 1927.

CHAPTER VI

ROCK-CUT ARCHITECTURE

(A) THE HINAYANA BUDDHIST VIHARAS OR MONASTERIES

(B) THE ROCK ARCHITECTURE OF ORISSA (2nd Century B.C.)

THE rock-cut viharas, or monastic "houses" of the Hinayana Buddhist order, although not of such architectural importance as the chaitya halls or temples described in the previous chapter, contain many significant features. Among other interesting facts, their planning and treatment generally throw considerable light on the system which prevailed in these retreats, and reveal the manner in which the practical requirements of the community were provided for. In their broad aspect they also demonstrate that the Buddhist monachism of India had much in common with the monastic establishments of Europe, a condition due to the similarity in their aims. For instance the Buddhist monks, as did their Cistercian brethren, planted the houses of their order in wild and desolate places, for apparently the same reasons that they might conduct their observances undisturbed by the distractions of any human environment. In a like manner their habitations had a similar beginning, for just as the cloister with its simple lean-to roof on stone pillars was the first step in the construction of the Benedictine monastery, so the early Buddhist vihara consisted of an open court, corresponding to the cloister-garth, enclosed also by a lean-to roof propped up by wooden posts. Then, in connection with the former were developed the "carralls" or small study-rooms, whereas in the latter these took the form of cells leading out of the central court. In the course of time the full complement of each type of monastery, whether European or Buddhist, was composed of a dormitory, a common room, a refectory or frater, a kitchen with other service amenities, and, in the case of the former a fish pond, and the latter a tank for the water supply. As a proof of the fact that both communities occasionally broke away from the rigid discipline of their order to indulge in a little relaxation, certain sinkings in the shape of small cups in the stone benches in the one instance, and in the rock flooring in the other, indicate that the Benedictines in their spare moments played some such game as Nine Men's Morris, and the Buddhists the national Indian game of *pachisi*. Finally, and in the same way that, after the Dissolution, the monasteries in England lay in ruins, so the rock-cut viharas on the decline of the Buddhist faith were completely deserted and left to crumble into decay; where at one time these numerous halls pulsated with spiritual life, they have now for centuries been the home of the jackal and the bat.

As already indicated the architectural significance of the excavated monasteries of the Hinayana sect lies in the fact that they are facsimiles, in the rock, of structural buildings devised to meet a similar demand, and which undoubtedly existed in considerable numbers. All these rock-cut viharas were by no means alike in their design, they took a variety of forms, but a representative example of the earlier or Hinayana type may be distinguished from that of the later or Mahayana, by several well-defined characteristics. Chief among their typical features was the open simplicity of the central hall, for, with one or two exceptions, this assembly room was a large square compartment, its space uninterrupted by any formation of pillars or colonnade. (Plate XLIX, Fig. I.) Further, the cells opening out from the central hall always contain couches or beds also formed in the rock, and there is often a small recess for use as a locker cut in some convenient position. Owing to the situation of the couch in such small cells, which average only nine feet square, the doorway is not in the centre but to one side of the outer wall. In these rock-cut copies of the structural original it is quite easy to see that the central hall corresponded to the open courtyard, while the facade, vestibule, and cells were all translations, in the rock medium, of the conventional wooden type of viharas, of which owing to their impermanency, no examples have survived.

An illustration of the Hinayana system of monastic retreat may be seen at the famous Buddhist settlement of Ajanta, where, for a long period, a relatively small group of the early type were the only examples. This first series consisted of five excavations in all, two of which, Nos. 9 and 10, are chaitya halls, while there are three viharas, Nos. 8, 12, and 13 (Plate XXV). It will be noted that No. 11 is omitted from the series as it is a Mahayana vihara rather awkwardly interposed at a much later date. Chaitya hall No. 10, with its attached vihara No. 12, were the first to be cut, vihara No. 13 being added shortly afterwards to accommodate the increasing body of monks. Then, most probably because the priestly community had been still further augmented to justify the production of another house of prayer, chaitya hall No. 9 was excavated, together with vihara No. 8 as its accompanying monastery. Of these early viharas, No. 12 provides a simple but typical example of the single-storied variety, although its facade has almost entirely disappeared. Around its square central hall is carved that horse-shoe arcading characteristic of the work of this phase, its upper portion resolving itself into a pleasing frieze. Every feature is planned and cut with remarkable precision, the facility with which the artificers chiselled out the surfaces and finished off the ornamentation being noteworthy.

Another vihara in one story is that attached to the left side of the chaitya hall at Kondane, a representative example, save that it is one of the rare exceptions of the Hinayana type in which the central hall is not plain, but pillared. The exterior, although much of its lower part has broken away, is a very interesting production, as originally it consisted of a pillared portico, the end walls of which still remain. Projecting over this portico is a massive cornice, together with a feature corresponding to an entablature, every detail of which is an exact copy of intricate wooden construction. Within the portico is a screen wall with three square-headed openings, forming the doorway and a window on each side. Inside is a large hall measuring 23 feet by 29 feet, surrounded by a colonnade, and with cells opening out from the three interior sides. The pillars of the colonnade support roof beams with bridging joists and other structural details, all faithful imitations of a timber original. An instructive motif carved on the end wall of the portico is a conventional representation of a chaitya hall facade, from which it is possible to gain no little information as to the final appearance of these frontages. The other Hinayana monastery with pillars in its central hall is that at Pitalkhora, but of this example all that remains are a few of the cells. These cells, however, are not plain square rooms as in all the other viharas, but small vaulted chambers with ribbed roofs and lattice windows, reproductions in miniature of the work of the carpenter (Plate VIII, Fig. 8). The exteriors are as ornate as the interiors, as between the overarch of each doorway is a Persepolitan pilaster surmounted by addorsed animals or gryphons.

The single storied type of Hinayana vihara in its most decorative form may be seen in a series of three examples at Nasik, particularly in the treatment of their exteriors (Plate XXIX). Judging by the style of their design and workmanship, supported by inscriptional evidence, they appear to have been executed in the first century A. D. According to their inscriptions they have also been named, Gautamiputra (No. 3), Nahapana (No. 8), and Sri Yajna (No. 15), Nahapana having been the first to be excavated, followed shortly afterwards by the two others. All have columned porticos and large central halls without pillars, out of which open the usual range of cells containing in most instances stone beds. In their general appearance the porticos of these three viharas are much alike, but the variations in the details are notable, particularly in the design of the pillars. The series of four, with a half pillar at each end, which form the Nahapana facade, are almost exact copies of those in the interior of the Ganesh Lena chaitya hall at Junnar, both of which in their turn having been derived from the portico pillars at Bedsa, every detail, from the lotus-base on the stepped pedestal below to the animal groups on the abacus above, being the same.

In the facade of the Gautamiputra example at Nasik the designer has worked out a somewhat similar scheme, but with elaborations, as in addition to the range of pillars forming the portico, he has placed their bases behind a richly carved dwarf wall, while below he has sculptured a row of giant figures appearing to carry the entire structure, by means of projecting beams, on their shoulders like an immense tabernacle. Under its enormous weight these stalwart atlantes, rising out of the earth, with bulging muscles stagger along, seeming to represent elemental beings from an underworld, forced into the service of the creed. Above the portico is a broad architrave supported on the superstructure of the pillars, each of which consists of either a pair of elephants, bulls, gryphons or other beasts, while there is a a fine border of animals, alternating with a scroll of foliage, the whole rendered with exceptional spirit. The entrance doorway in the inner wall of the portico is a square-headed opening surrounded by an elaborate ornamental composition in which are included figures of an unusual character. In some respects the treatment of this doorway recalls that of the Sanchi toranas, as it has lintels or crossbars with voluted ends, but like most of the rock-carving at Nasik, although it retains the principles of the style, shows a marked originality and independence in certain details.

The remaining example of the three large viharas at Nasik, the Sri Yajna, may have been the last to be executed, but it was produced in much the same form as the others of the group. Then, several centuries afterwards, when the Mahayana priests took over these early monasteries, the interior of this particular vihara appears to have been considerably altered in order to make it suitable for the performance of the later theistic ritual. Such a procedure presented no special difficulties, as the floor was merely sunk so as to provide a square dais towards the middle of the central half, and a cella excavated at the far end with a pillared antechamber for the accommodation of a large image of the Buddha; the style of this alteration indicates that the seventh century was the date of its conversion.

Contemporary with the monasteries' excavated in the Western Ghats, another group of rock-cut halls and cells was being produced on the eastern side of the country, near Cuttack in Orissa. This resolves itself into a collection of chambers, not Buddhistic, but attributed to the opposing belief of the Jains, as in their treatment there are certain features implying a connexion with the latter creed. Nor are there any chaitya halls, for they consist in most instances of a formation of cellular retreats recalling in some respects the viharas of the western Hinayana type. The close grouping on two low hills, not far removed from the famous Brahmanical fanes of Bhubaneshwar, supplies additional proof, if such were required, that this area was of special sanctity, the whole country around having sacred and historical associations. To Orissa, as its share in the precious relics of the Buddha, fell the left canine tooth, and the holy city of Dantapura, the "Town of the Tooth", where this priceless possession was at one time deposited, lay in the vicinity of one of the neighbouring towns, either of Bhubaneshwar or Puri, although all traces of it are now lost. As a token of the antiquity of these parts, near at hand is Dhauli hill, where is inscribed one of the rock edicts of Asoka, guarded by a fine sculpturesque representation of an elephant. The two tree-clad hills in which the rock-cut chambers are situated, are, together, locally known as Khandragiri, but the northern elevation is called Udaigiri. Separated by a defile, between them wound the "Pilgrims Sacred Way", or *Via Sacra*, to Bhubaneshwar, where it is likely there stood, in early days, a stupa—the pilgrims' goal.

According to an inscription carved on the rock of a shallow natural cave on Udaigiri, called the Hathi Gumpha, the mean date of these excavated chambers corresponds to about B. C. 160. This inscription records, among other information, the chief episodes in the reign of king Kharavela, ruler of Kalinga, the ancient Orissa, including his conquests of a great portion of the north and east of India. Kharavela was by religion a Jain, and appears to have been personally interested in the priestly community who had selected these hills as a place of retreat. It is just possible that the small group of Ajivika hermits responsible for the excavated chapels in the Barabar hills, having lost the protection of Asoka on the death of that monarch, migrated to Orissa, not only to be under a Jaina ruler, but in order to continue their system of living in cells cut in the rock.

All the excavations of the Orissan group appear to have been made within the 150 years previous to the Christian Era, after which the production ceased, although on the Khandragiri hill, a short revival took place as late as the medieval period, when a few Jaina cells were added. In its general character this group seems to imply an independent development, having but little in common with any other rock architecture of the country. Yet there are certain fundamental forms, both architectural and decorative, found in all this excavated work, which indicate that whether

Buddhist or Jain, or whatever the locality, it was all part of the same movement, originating from one source, the beginnings of which had been introduced into the country by Asoka a century before.

The principal object of these excavations was obviously to provide a monastic retreat, the chambers and cells being cut out of the coarse sandstone of which the hills are composed. As the country around consists mainly of a laterite formation, the selection of this sandstone outcrop, on account of its more workable character, is understood. There are in all some thirty-five excavations, large and small, but only half of them are of any significance, some sixteen of which are in the Udaigiri hill, while there is only one of any importance on Khandragiri. Apparently laid out on no regular plan, they were evidently cut in convenient places and connected by paths, still traceable through the glades of trees. Two of these retreats consist of single cells only, three or four combine several cells having a portico with the remains of a courtyard in front, while the four largest and most elaborate are composed of galleries of chambers in double stories and overlooking a quadrangle. None of the courtyards is covered in, as are most of those in other parts of India, but the fact that they are open to the sky may be due to the shallow configuration of the rock in which they are cut. Compared with the Asokan examples, or those in the Western Ghats, the workmanship on the Orissan monasteries is clumsy and crude, but such conditions may be partly accounted for by the rough texture of the sandstone. Moreover it seems to have little or no connexion with the remarkably fine phase of structural architecture and plastic art which developed in its vicinity at Bhubaneshwar and elsewhere under Brahmin patronage some centuries later. The local generic name for these Orissan monasteries is "gumpha", meaning a cave, and each is distinguished by a picturesque or appropriate prefix, as for instance the Ganesh (or Elephant) Gumpha, so called on account of two sculptured elephants forming a prominent part of the conception.

The architectural features of the more developed Orissan monasteries consist of their facades of pillared verandahs and the cells leading out of them. In the treatment of the former most of the pillars have simple square shafts with bracket capitals, some of the bracket forms being of a very special character. For instance in one example, that known as the Rani Gumpha, or Queen's Cave, the largest and most important of the entire series, there is a bracket of a very primitive order, not unlike the curved branch of a tree. On the other hand in the Manchipuri Gumpha the portico pillars support intricately carved struts made up of figures riding hippogryphs and other compositions of a similarly fanciful nature (Plate XXXII, Figs. 5 and 6). It may be noted that this form of bracket is the prototype of those which are a prominent feature of the Brahmanical rock-cut temples at Badami in Dharwar, produced at least six centuries later. As already observed a distinctive element in all the early rock-cut viharas is the arcading which decorates the walls, and which in the Orissan examples is of an exclusive kind. Instead of being of the horse-shoe variety, the arches of the arcades are almost invariably semi-circular, and their lower ends, corresponding to the "springer" of a true arch, are expanded to enable them to be supported on pilasters. These pilasters have capitals formed of pairs of recumbent animals, a decadent derivative of the Persepolitan type, and a number of them have vase bases. Another feature in some of the Orissan viharas is a ledge or podium carved like a continuous bench around certain of the compartments. Here is seen an early appearance of the *asana*,

a stone seat with a sloping backrest, which in a more developed and highly decorated form became prominent in the temples of Central and Western India of the early medieval period. The cells comprising the interiors are not square as in most of the other viharas, but oblong in plan, and some are long chambers entered by several doors, in shape more like dormitories than single rooms; in place of the stone bed, differentiating the early type of cell, the floor in each compartment is sloped so as to form a couch, and as in many instances the height of the room is only four feet, they can only have been intended for sleeping.

A few of the single cells of the Orissan group are of a very primitive character, and one known as the Bagh Gumpha, or Tiger Cave, is a fanciful production indicative of a somewhat morbid imagination (Plate XXXII, Fig. 4). Carved out of a shoulder of rock projecting from the hill side, the exterior is shaped like the mask of a tiger, the antechamber simulating the gaping mouth, and the cell door within this, the gullet. On the door-jambs, which slope inwards, are pilasters with winged creatures as capitals, and pots for bases. The interior consists of a room only $3\frac{1}{2}$ feet high, but some six feet deep and nearly eight feet wide. Over the doorway is an inscription in characters anterior to the Christian era, stating that it was the abode of an anchorite named Sabhuti, who, reclining in this narrow cell resembling a tiger's maw, seems to have passed his life literally in the jaws of death.

It has been already remarked that there are no chaitya halls in this monastic retreat, but the example which more nearly corresponds to a temple, is the Rani Gumpha, probably executed about B. C. 150 (Plate XXXI, Fig. 1). This "abbey church" is a double storied production with its cells ranged around three sides of an open courtyard, the fourth side comprising the frontal approach. A broad terrace, projected from the upper story, was originally supported on structural pillars, either of wood or stone, and these formed the verandah of the ground floor. A stairway cut in the rock at the side gave access to this upper terrace, on one face of which there is a spacious throne, with arms and a foot rest, evidently the seat of honour of the abbot or other high dignitary. While the general arrangements of the cells indicate that most of them were for the accommodation of the monks, there are several supplementary chambers and recesses evidently devised for special purposes connected with the ritual, either as robing rooms or for the preparation of offerings. In addition there are rooms for storing the sacred vessels and vestments, with a place for the custodian or sacristan. (Plate XXXI, Fig. 1).

That the open courtyard and its overlooking terraces were specially designed for some spectacular kind of ceremonial seems fairly clear, and a clue to the form that it took is also provided. For around the walls of the upper story there is a long frieze consisting of figures engaged in a series of connected episodes of a distinctly dramatic character (Plate XXXI, Fig. 2). As these same scenes are repeated in part, in one or more of the other viharas on this site, they evidently represent some vivid epic in the heroic age of the people. It may be inferred therefore that this arrangement of courtyard and terraces forming the Rani Gumpha constituted an open air theatre in which the scenes depicted in the sculptured frieze around it were brought to life by being performed on festival occasions as a kind of Passion Play, in the same way that the so-called Devil Dances are celebrated in the monastery (*gumpha*) quadrangles of Tibet. If so, the peculiar formation of the gumpha is at once explained, and its various parts fall into their proper place. Moreover it is not difficult to picture the courtyard occupied by the actors in this drama, while seated on the terraces, like an amphitheatre, with the high priest enthroned in the central position, would be a closely grouped background of spectators, the whole forming a brilliant and moving pageant amidst the dark encircling groves.

The architectural treatment of Rani Gumpha is characteristic of the Orissan style of rock-architecture as a whole, and provides the key to the entire movement. In the design of the pillars supporting the verandahs and the pilasters of the mural arcading two traditions are represented, the former on the one hand shown by their simple bracket capitals that they are of indigenous origin derived from a wooden prototype; on the other hand the pilasters on the walls with their capitals formed of addorsed animals are debased descendants of the Persepolitan order, still identifiable although rough and coarse in their technique. Yet in spite of the appearance of this classical motif, there is much in the decorative nature of the arches to connect it with the early structural art of the country. It is fairly clear that this ornamental arcading was suggested by the wooden barge-boards at the gable-end of the ordinary house, adapted and repeated so as to become mere embellishment. It is possible to see by the manner in which each member of the arcading fulfils its purpose, the arch "riding" firmly on the pilaster capital, the "railing" string-course fitting securely into the expanded "springer", with the central positions of this rail-moulding supported on corbels, all of which are reminiscences of a structural experience of no common order. Of the plastic decoration of a less conventional nature on the Rani Gumpha, there are certain floral forms boldly modelled and singularly Gothic in their execution, but the chief interest centres in the figure scenes, the frieze already referred to being full of spirit and dramatic power. There are also single figures of life-size proportions sculptured in prominent positions, some of them armed with spears acting as guardians or doorkeepers. Of striking appearance are two burly individuals mounted on ponderous animals, the one seated on a bull being strangely Assyrian in its modelling and conception as a whole. Within the cells of this gumpha there are the remains of a system of water-supply, apparently conveyed from a rock-cut cistern above, and distributed by means of channels throughout the entire composition, but whether for ablutions, or connected with the ritual is not clear.

Other monasteries on this site, treated in much the same manner as the preceding, but simpler in their formation, are the Ganesha Gumpha, the Manchapuri Gumpha, and the Ananta Gumpha. The Ganesha, or Elephant cave, is probably one of the earliest examples and displays several interesting features. It is excavated in a ledge, or terrace, of rock, the exterior consisting of a columned verandah, some thirty feet wide and six feet in depth, and approached by steps flanked with figures of elephants. This scheme of sculptured animal guardians to the entrance of a rock-cut hall appears here for the first time, but it was afterwards developed with considerable effect in the Brahmanical temples excavated much later at Ellora and Elephanta, with the elephants, however, replaced by lions. The pillars forming the facade of the Ganesha Gumpha were originally five in number, and are of a type frequently found in this group, the shafts being, in section, square above and below, but octagonal in the centre, with a figure bracket at the top to support the overhanging cornice or eave. At each end of the facade is projected a pilaster *in antis*, not however repeating the conventional design of the pillars, but boldly carved in the shape of a figure—a doorkeeper, or *dwarpala*, armed with a huge spear, and above him, forming the capital to the pilaster is a kneeling humped bull. Executed a little later, the Manchapuri Gumpha or "House of Earth", and the Ananta Gumpha, the latter being on the southern, or Khandragiri hill, are composed of elements and motifs not unlike those in the Ganesha Gumpha just described, and which are common to the group as a whole. These sculptured forms, especially when used in the bracket capitals, as for instance the figures astride hippogryphs, have a very ancient appearance, and seem to have emerged from an early phase of art and building construction, of which all other records have disappeared. As already remarked a similar motif was revived several centuries later in the rock-architecture of Badami, but it is so rare and distinctive as to suggest a lost tradition of some importance. The productions at Khandragiri are coarsely rendered, and not of a high standard of design or workmanship. Moreover they seem to have been an end in themselves, as except in the few details referred to, they led to no further development, their forms died early in the Christian era leaving no heritage. On the other hand this Orissan rock architecture has every appearance of being a final copy, or the last stage, of a cultural movement which at one time had no little significance a method of expression strictly regional, but of a profound and moving order. What is left merely represents it in its decay.

At the ancient city of Junagadh, in Kathiawar, the existence of a considerable group of "caves" indicates that here at one time was settled a thriving religious community manifestly Buddhist and Jain. One of the Asokan inscriptions on a rock at Girnar a mile east of the city is proof of the antiquity of this settlement and also of its Buddhistic origin. The remains of cells suggest that here was at one time a monastery for the accommodation of a large fraternity, while some of the more elaborate excavations, particularly those in the Uparkot, or citadel, by their design seem to signify some special form of ceremonial or ritual. These halls, apparently for communal purposes, are in two stories connected by a winding staircase, with a lower story having broad recesses all round its walls surmounted by a typical frieze of Buddhist chaitya arches. The upper chamber to which is attached a small refectory, also contains a tank and is surrounded by a corridor. But the most striking feature of this compartment are the six columns supporting the roof, which on account of their rich carving, from base to capital, stand out both in their design and technique as the production of one or more experienced craftsmen. No other workmanship quite of this character is known in these parts, and it seems as if here, early in the Christian era probably about 300 A. D., a small group of rock-carvers of exceptional ability flourished for a time and then to have disappeared.

REFERENCES

Bengal District Gazetteer (*Puri.*) Cal. 1908.

Cunningham, A. *Archaeological Survey of India*, Vol. XIII, Cal. 1882.

Fergusson, J. and Burgess, J., *Cave Temples of India*, London, 1880.

Gangoly, M., *Orissa and Her Remains, Ancient and Medieval*, Cal. 1912.

Mitra, Rajendralal, *Antiquities of Orissa*, Calcutta 1875, etc.

CHAPTER VII

THE MAHAYANA OR THEISTIC BUDDHIST MONASTERIES OF GANDHARA (B.C. 250 to A.D. 450)

DURING the centuries immediately before and after the beginning of the Christian era, it has been shown that the Buddhist communities in the middle and southern parts of the peninsula were actively engaged in producing monuments, such as masonry stupas, wooden chaitya halls, and rock-cut monasteries, according to the prevailing Hinayana system of the Buddhist faith. In the region towards the north-west of the country, however, a movement of a very different order was becoming apparent, and one which was destined to react, in a marked manner, on the cultural activities, of the people. The principal characters concerned in this great drama, which had Hither Asia as its setting, were offshoots of four races, or nationalities : (1) Greeks, (2) Parthians, (3) Scythians, and (4) Indians. It was the aspirations of these people, which caused what is now the country of Afghanistan, and the North-West frontier of India, to become the meeting place of streams of culture issuing from both European and Asiatic sources. And as a result there emerged in the early centuries of the first millennium, a form of Indo-Buddhist art, in itself of considerable significance, but still more important on account of its implications, as it affected, to some extent, much of the art of Asia.

Briefly, the developments which ensued enabled Buddhism, by this time the prevailing religion in these parts, to interpret its oriental preceptions by means of an occidental medium, for it brought into the service of the Buddhist faith, the formative and rational art of Greece. In other words, it placed in the hands of the Buddhists, who, hitherto, had been content with a symbolical and non-representational mode of expression, plastic creations of an anthropomorphic character, so that they introduced into their buildings, figures and statuary based upon the Hellenic model. In conjunction with this departure they also borrowed freely from the architecture of the same classical school. The distinctly composite style thus evolved, which displayed a fusion of Hellenistic elements with Buddhist ideals, has sometimes been defined as Graeco-Bactrian, and also Graeco-Buddhist, but the designation now usually adopted is the geographical one of Gandhara, as the region from which it emanated bore that name. The country of Gandhara, before and after the beginning of the present era, corresponded approximately to the modern districts of Peshawar and Rawalpindi together with the eastern portion of Afghanistan.

The manner in which this current of Hellenistic art culture found its way into Central Asia there to take form on the walls of the Buddhist monasteries, was the outcome of the imagination and genius of Alexander the Great, king of Macedonia (356-323 B.C.). For it had its origin in the country of Bactria, one of the Greek colonies founded by this conqueror in the first half of the fourth century B. C. as part of his ambitious scheme for a world dominion in the East. This extreme eastern outpost of the Macedonian Empire occupied a rich tract of land lying between the mountains of the Hindu Kush and the river Oxus, corresponding in a large measure to Northern Afghanistan, and now known as Balkh. The favourable position of such a powerful colony of Greeks enabled it to shed the living light of Hellenic culture over a wide area, and there can be few more romantic episodes than that of this European community making its home in so distant a land, where for nearly two centuries it maintained, as far as environment would permit, a close reproduction of the traditional Greek city-state. That it was a country of some consequence is shown by the fact that, at the height of its power in the third century B. C. Bactria boasted of as many as sixty large towns, and the legendary fame of its magnificent palaces was remarked on by the Chinese pilgrim Hiuen Tsiang as late as the seventh century A. D. For a time the colony kept in constant communication with the parent empire by means of a line of Greek cities across the west of Asia, so that direct stimulation of all forms of Hellenic culture was not lacking. As a proof of this contact the coins issued by the earlier rulers of Bactria are equal in artistic merit to the finest mintages of the Greeks, and from such evidence alone it seems clear that its satraps must have retained in their service artists of the first rank. Moreover the rulers appear to have enriched their palatial abodes, and their subjects their sumptuous villas, with portable statues and reliefs, and thus by surrounding themselves with objects of Greek art endeavoured with considerable success to uphold the aesthetic instincts of their race. Unfortunately, owing to its situation, Bactria lay in the track of the invading hordes which from time to time swept across this portion of the continent, so that in effect all the material evidences of this remarkable colonization have long since been obliterated.

Yet in spite of subsequent effacement, the records of the Greek occupation, and its association with the Buddhists of India can readily be followed. After maintaining itself as a colony for nearly two hundred years, about 250 B. C., Bactria considered it expedient, for political reasons to sever its connection with the Macedonian empire, and accordingly the country assumed independence under a Greek king named Diodotus. From now onward it became self-contained, and more or less isolated as its intercourse with the western world began to be intermittent. Finally in the third century B. C. owing to the intervention of the rising power of the Parthians, who occupied a country corresponding to the modern Khorasan, through-communication in that direction practically ceased. Nevertheless although the territorial conditions were unfavourable, an infiltration of culture from the west, through Hither Asia, seems to have persisted, and the flow of art from the fountain head of Hellas still continued. But by this time it was not the untouched productions of the Attic school which found their way to Bactria, for on their journey they became impregnated with some of the aesthetic ideals of the Parthians, and so there developed towards the second century B. C., what has been referred to as a Graeco-Parthian phase. Material records are somewhat meagre as to the character of the art of the Parthians, but it appears basically to have taken the form of a revival of the ancient Persian style, as this existed under the Achaemenids in the sixth century B. C. The Graeco-Parthian phase therefore, while displaying a Hellenistic foundation, contained reminiscences of those monuments associated with the golden age of Cyrus and Darius, and their royal cities of Pasargadae and Persepolis, of which the motif known as the Persepolitan capital is a symbol.

Such were the conditions which prevailed in the countries beyond the north-west frontier of India about the beginning of the second century B.C. At this juncture, however, the increasing supremacy of the independent, although still Hellenistic kingdom of Bactria, caused its ruler, Euthydemus to contemplate an expansion of his power. Any movement westward would have been abortive owing to the Parthians having strengthened their position in what is now northern Persia, while the invasions, of a nomadic horde from the north made any advance in this direction also impossible. On the other hand the dismemberment of the Mauryan empire in India, which began in the last half of the third century B. C., was an opportunity not to be lost, and accordingly in 190 B. C., the Bactrian king carried Greek rule across the Hindu Kush, down the Kabul valley, and into the plains of Hindustan. By this achievement a considerable tract of northern India was brought under the dominion of the Bactrian Greeks, who were now at the height of their power. An Indo-Greek kingdom was established under Demetrius who was styled "King of India", as he ruled over the country of the Indus.

There is little doubt that had this forward policy of penetration eastward persisted, and concerted action taken, the decaying Mauryan empire of India would have fallen an easy prey to the victorious Asiatic Greeks, with a possibility of the entire country becoming Hellenized. But it is also fairly clear that, owing to long separation from their native land, their stamina had deteriorated and their staying power was sapped, so that the limit of their attainment had been reached. Dissensions among themselves, the division of the newly conquered territory into a number or petty principalities, increasing pressure from the Parthians, and the menace of the ever-advancing nomadic tribes, all combined to make their position insecure. The beginning of the final phase came in 125 B.C. when Bactria itself, the original Greek stronghold, was overwhelmed by the Scythians, a Mongolian horde which was sweeping down from the north. Forced out of their homeland by this disaster, the Bactrian Greeks became confined to their more recently acquired possessions in the Indus valley and the Punjab, which they administered from Sakala, the modern town of Sialkot, but with much diminished power and prestige. Gradually compressed within a territory of ever-narrowing limits, they lingered on until A.D. 60, when the whole country was devastated by the relentless onslaught of the Scythians, who eventually founded the Indo-Scythian empire of the Kushans (A.D. 20-225). With this invasion the last vestiges of Greek rule in India disappeared.

The disintegration of the power of the Indo-Greeks which took place in the first century A. D., would, in ordinary circumstances, have coincided with the inevitable decline of the Hellenistic culture that was an accompaniment of their rule. It was however the reverse that actually occurred. For, at the same time that the dominion of the Greeks was ending, a movement was being created which was the means of reviving and maintaining in a remarkable manner some of the characteristics and structure of their art. This took the form of a development of the Buddhist religion of such intensity and purpose that it can have had few equals. The focus and centre of the movement was the country of Gandhara, and it expressed itself by the establishment of a very large number of monasteries, so that, like the cult of

Lamaism in Tibet, it is evident that an unlimited proportion of the population was employed in the service of the creed. As owing to the course of history, Afghanistan has, during most of the last millennium, been inhabited by a most zealous Islamic people, it is not easy to visualize this country as a stronghold of the Buddhists faith but, that such was the case, is proved by the profusion of its structural remains. For over the entire country the ruins recording the Buddhist occupation are visible, chiefly in the form of monasteries situated on the crest of the hills or on the mountain slopes, in the same manner as the innumerable white pagodas are distributed on the heights following the course of the Irrawady river in Burma. Around Peshawar, Rawalpindi, and in the Swat valley and its neighbourhood, ruins of monasteries may be counted by the dozen, while in the Kabul valley alone there are some fifty examples. These buildings, some of them very extensive, together with many other structural and even rock-cut evidences, testify that this territory was not only the home of a large population of devout followers of the Great Teacher, but also that they expressed their devotion in a material and substantial form.

The architectural style employed in the monasteries, and their plastic and painted embellishment, as will have been gathered, was of a special character. While the intention of the buildings, as well as their surface treatment, was fundamentally Indian, for the religion they served was essentially the result of Indian thought, on the other hand there was much in their structure and mode that was appropriated from the art of the Greeks. In their design there are numerous motifs of purely Hellenic origin, as for instance the Corinthian capital, pediments, entablatures, medallions and mouldings, of a debased classical order, built into stupas, shrines, temples and other religious edifices of an entirely Buddhistic foundation. To these Hellenistic adoptions were also added ornamental elements of Parthian extraction, such as the fire-altar, the addorsed animal capital and other forms identified with the art of that empire.

It was however in the sculpture, with which these Buddhist monuments were so lavishly endowed, that the Gandhara style was most distinctive, and which fully entitled it to the name of Graeco-Buddhist. Much of the particular character that this plastic art assumed, was the result of a notable change which was taking place at the time in the constitution and principles of the creed. The Gandhara Compositions mark the beginning of the movement, when the Hinayana or primitive system of Buddhism was being superseded by the Mahayana or theistic system, a reformation which provided a broader and more progressive interpretation of the teachings of the Buddha. This newer doctrine inclined towards the deification of the Buddha as a personal saviour, and also created other Buddhas besides considerably increasing the mythological nature of the belief as a whole. One of the effects of such an endeavour was greatly to stimulate image worship, and in the production of plastic representations of divine forms on the Buddhist monuments, the Hellenistic methods provided the means. And so there appeared in the art of these parts, statues of the Buddha and other sacred figures, posed, modelled, and draped, after the Greek manner, and according to the Greek ideal. This Hellenistic ascription, however, went even further. So powerful was its influence that it contributed characters from its own Olympian system to the Buddhist pantheon, with the result that such well known pagan deities as Hercules, Pallas Athene, Eros, and Bacchus, thinly disguised but still identifiable, are included in some of the Gandhara compo-

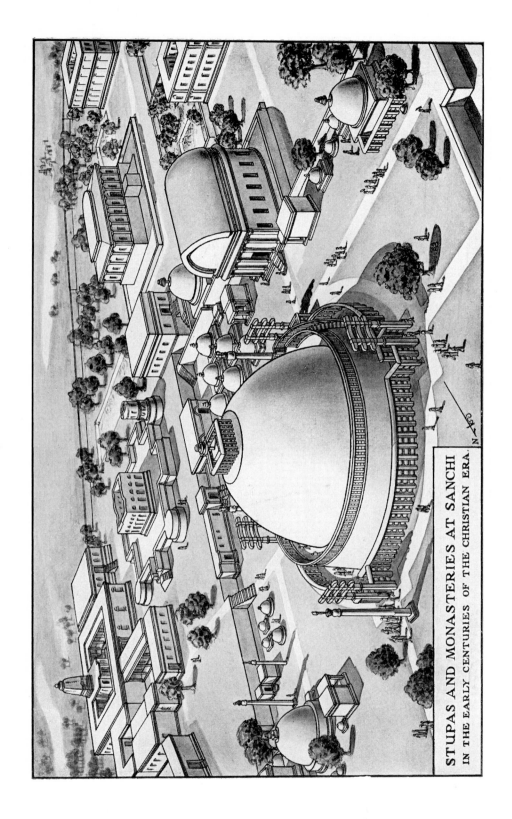

STUPAS AND MONASTERIES AT SANCHI
IN THE EARLY CENTURIES OF THE CHRISTIAN ERA.

HUT AND PILLARS, KASHMIR

PRIMITIVE SHRINES
FROM EARLY BAS-RELIEFS
1 SANCHI
2 MUTTRA
3 AMARAVATI
4 GANDHARA
5 SANCHI
6 GANDHARA
7 GANDHARA

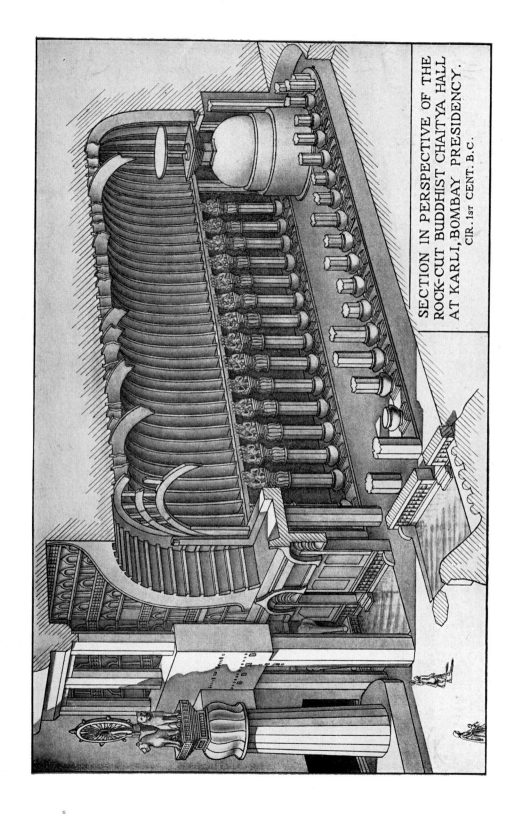

SECTION IN PERSPECTIVE OF THE ROCK-CUT BUDDHIST CHAITYA HALL AT KARLI, BOMBAY PRESIDENCY. CIR. 1st CENT. B.C.

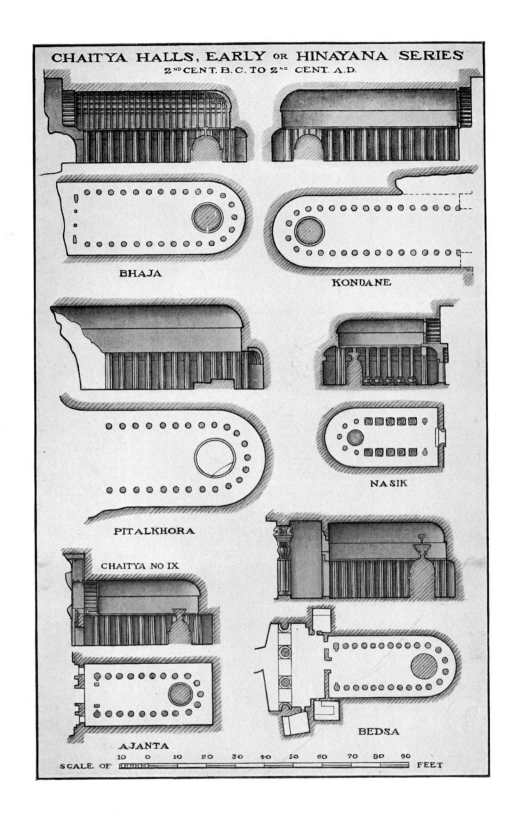

CHAITYA HALLS, EARLY OR HINAYANA SERIES
2ND CENT. B.C. TO 2ND CENT. A.D.

BHAJA

KONDANE

PITALKHORA

NASIK

CHAITYA NO IX

AJANTA

BEDSA

SCALE OF 10 0 10 20 30 40 50 60 70 80 90 FEET

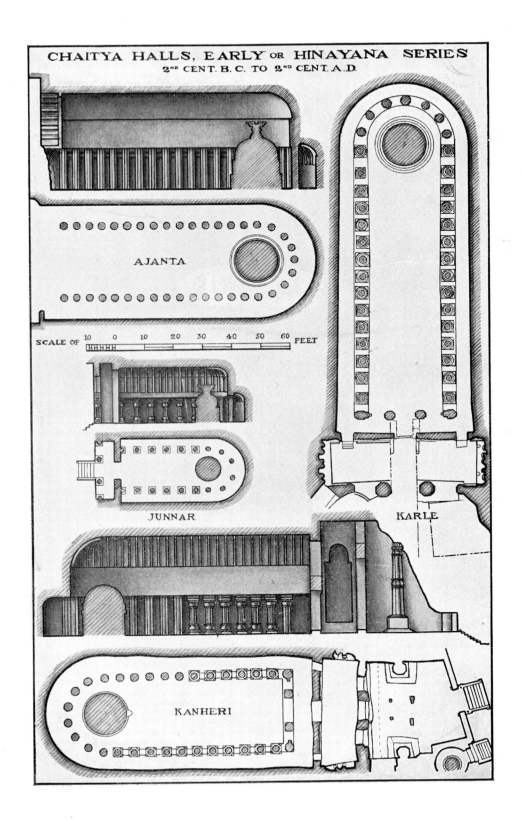

CHAITYA HALLS, EARLY or HINAYANA SERIES
2ND CENT. B. C. TO 2ND CENT. A.D.

AJANTA

SCALE OF 10 0 10 20 30 40 50 60 FEET

JUNNAR

KARLE

KANHERI

Fig. 1. Bhaja.

Fig. 2. Kondane.

Facades of rock-cut Chaitya-halls : 2nd cent. B.C.

Fig. 2

Karli Chaitya-hall, Vestibule, c. 2nd cent. B.C.

Fig. 1

Ajanta, Facade of Chaitya-hall, No. 26, 6th Century A.D.

Fig. 1

Fig. 2
Karli Chaitya-hall ; 2nd cent. B.C.

sitions. But no architectural element common in these monasteries epitomises the style more concisely than that of a Corinthian capital with a small figure of the Buddha enthroned amidst the leaves of the conventional Greek acanthus. The impact of the two cultures, illustrating the mysticism of Buddhism superimposed on the rationalism of the Greeks, is crystallized in this architectural motif.

It will no doubt have been already inferred that, of all the Gandharan monuments, the monastery is the most frequent and also the most typical of the style. This religious establishment consists usually of a somewhat irregular aggregation of buildings, in which, however, there are two main structures, the stupa, and the *sangharama* or quarters for the monks. The planning of some of these monasteries was obviously fortuitous, often consisting of a complicated grouping of structures, an arrangement which may be traced to the fact that they sometimes occupied the site of ancient stupas, which, afterwards enlarged and elaborated, gathered around them many miscellaneous buildings, including chapels, priests, houses, and innumerable votive stupas, so that there is little schematic co-ordination. Such were those of Dharmarajika, at Taxila, and of Jamalgarhi, thirty-six miles north of Peshawar, also the great group of sanctuaries at Charsada in the Peshawar valley, and at Manikyala near Rawalpindi, besides several others in Afghanistan. Some, however, of more moderate size, and unencumbered by any traditional foundation, were designed with an attempt at symmetry, as for instance those at Takht-i-Bahai, north of Hoti Mardan, and Mohra Moradu and Jaulain, at Taxila. But whatever the scheme, the central feature was the stupa, whether it was of the large reliquary type as at Manikyala, or the devotional kind, standing within its own court, as at Takht-i-Bahai. There is evidence that the original shape of the stupa of this region was in the form of the traditional hemispherical mound, as devised by the emperor Asoka, a shape which, at Manikyala, in spite of repeated enlargements, it still retains. But the tendency of the Gandharan builders was to depart from the orthodox yet commonplace tumulus, and to develop it into an architectural composition of more inspiring proportions and character. Their aim was the creation of a structure of more height, which they obtained by elevating the stupa on a tall platform, and by elongating the body of the stupa upwards. The upper surface of the platform, which was approached by a flight of steps, became the processional path, while the stupa itself, being composed of a series of diminishing drums and surmounted by a slender many-tiered umbrella, began to assume the appearance of a pagoda. So lofty were some of these stupas, that the Chinese pilgrims have described them as pagodas, and it is not impossible that in the same way as the Buddhist-Indian *torana* gateway became the *torii* of Japan, so the many-storied stupa of India may have given some of its character to the multiple-pitched roofs of the Chinese temple. In addition to changes in the proportions of the stupa, plastic ornamentation, often brilliantly coloured, in the form of cornices, mouldings, niches, arcades, modillions, and other quasi-architectural elements, were freely applied. Against a background of the bare and featureless mountain side, these richly patterned and painted shrines, although perhaps inclined to be garish, would present an effective and colourful picture.

One of the most representative examples of this type of monastic sanctuary is that at Takht-i-Bahai, which, although ruined, is still understandable. In spite of the varying levels of the rocky spur to which it so picturesquely

clings, it has been designed on an axial plan with all its parts logically arranged. The principal buildings are contained within a rectangle of approximately two hundred feet in length, and consist of (a) the stupa court on the south, (b) the monastery on the north, and (c) an intervening terrace for the reception of votive stupas, small chapels, and similar structural contributions. To the west of the monastery is a conference or assembly hall, the remainder of the site being taken up by various subsidiary edifices, their exact uses at present not having been determined, but they were probably, a refectory, vestment chamber, kitchens and servants quarters. Of these structures, the court (a) with its stupa, was the main feature and was accordingly most artistically treated (Plate XXXIII). The courtyard was an open quadrangle measuring 45 feet by 55 feet, and in the centre, on a platform of 20 feet side and 8 feet high, rose the tall tapering stupa, which with its six-tiered umbrella, reached a total height of 50 feet. An elegant stairway on the north side gave access to the platform for circumambulation, but the ordinary processional path was around the quadrangle at the base. Enclosing the court on three sides was a range of small chapels, each containing a cell or niche, not as in the Hinayana examples for the accommodation of the priests, but, in accordance with the reformed system for the reception of either a statue of the Buddha, or a votive stupa. The roofs of the chapels were so designed that a cupola alternated with a trefoil vault, each an architecturally decorative motif and depicting a separate constructional tradition, for the former was derived from the anchorite's bee-hive hut, and the latter from the conventional shape of the chaitya hall. These particular roofs over the miniature chapels of the monastery are a distinctive feature of the Gandhara style; in their construction no true arches are found, as the method invariably employed was that of corbelling.

By means of a passage and flights of steps on account of the difference in levels, the court of the stupas was connected with the monastery (b) as a church with its abbey. The passage traversed the open space (c) reserved for stupas and other symbols contributed to the shrine as acts of merit, while the front walls of the monastery facing this enclosure, were also made into a range of cells to contain votive offerings of structural form or imagery. The monastery proper or sanghrama for the accommodation of the monks was built on a plan common to all such Buddhist structures, and consisted of ranges of cells around a central courtyard. These rooms were simple and unadorned, but, on the walls between each chamber, and protected by a verandah, it became the custom to place large figure groups, often of stucco and vividly coloured, which caused these usually sombre retreats to become animated picture-galleries of sacred subjects.

Although monasteries were the most representative buildings of the Gandharan style, the excavations at the ancient and historical city of Taxila, near Rawalpindi, have thrown considerable light on various other forms of architecture of this period. One structure at Jandial (Taxila), presumed to date as early as the second century B.C., provides an excellent illustration of the penetration of the Greek building art into such a distant field. It takes the form of a distyle-in-antis type of Hellenic temple, adapted to suit the conditions of some local belief, probably Zoroastrian. Not a large edifice—no Greek temple is remarkable for its size—its entire length over all being only 158 feet, and its width 80 feet, it was surrounded by a peristyle, and its interior included a vestibule, a *pronaos* or porch, a *naos* or sanctuary, and, at the rear, an *opisthodomos*, or back porch. Where it differed from its prototype was that between the back porch and the sanctuary there was a solid mass of masonry with deep foundations, this part evidently being intended to carry a heavy superstructure or tower, probably 40 feet in height. But what is most significant is that the sandstone capitals of the portico were not of the Corinthian but of the Ionic order, and also the shafts were not monolithic, as is usual in Indian architecture, but built up in the Greek manner by means of separate drums fixed with dowels, while the rest of the structure is of plastered limestone and *kanjur*. In the design and execution of the frontal portion of the Jandial temple there is fairly clear proof that only Greek masons in close touch with the Attic school could have produced stone-work of this character (Plate XXXIV).

Sealed up for centuries within the mounds of Taxila, and now exposed by excavation, are many other remains showing how in this region several distinct civilizations met. Among the structures thus revealed there is the base of a stupa at Sirkap, probably erected in the first century B.C., the ornamentation of which shows how elements appertaining to each culture were sometimes introduced into one production. On an architectural foundation of a quasi-Corinthian order, with pilasters and a moulded entablature, there may be seen such an agglomeration of motifs as a Buddhist chaitya arch and torana, a Greek triangular pediment, an Achaemenid niche, and an Iranian fire-altar. Included with these elements is the figure of a double-headed eagle, after which this stupa has been named, a symbol believed to have been of Scythian origin, from which source it afterwards found its way into the imperial arms of Russia and Germany ; but it also travelled southward to appear in the insignia of Vijayanagar in the Deccan, and it even penetrated into Ceylon. On the same site at Taxila, the remains of a palace have been unearthed, apparently of Parthian foundation, but in the disposition of its parts it bears a marked resemblance, although on a smaller scale, to the plans of the Assyrian palaces, as for instance Sargon's great palatial residence at Khorsabad. Most eastern palaces were laid out on the same general principles, with the apartments arranged around open courtyards, one portion for public and official purposes, the other for the private use of the royal family, with a wing and enclosed garden reserved for the ladies. In all such palaces, and at all periods, two large and important halls were invariably provided, one for the public and the other for private audiences. And in many other particulars, the planning of these royal residences in India, from this Parthian example at Sirkap to the magnificent palace fortresses of the Mughals, the builders followed the same general tradition.

The age of the Gandharan buildings may be presumed from the character of the sculptures, the test applied being, the more Hellenistic the sculpture, the earlier the date. Some of the examples indicate by the spontaneity and confidence of their handling that they were not far removed from the first phase of the Alexandrian school of Greek sculpture, which was at its zenith in the second century B.C. Another class appertains more to the style of the statuary recovered from the site of Herculaneum, near Naples, and therefore related to the Graeco-Roman school of the first century B.C. But the bulk of the Gandharan sculpture was executed in

the subsequent period, during the rule of the Indo-Scythians or Kushans (A.D. 20 to A.D. 225), in the first centuries of the Christian era, for it was at this time that Mahayana Buddhism received its greatest encouragement in northern India under the patronage of the Kushan king Kanishka (c. A.D. 123-153). Much of the work produced under this regime was of a somewhat mediocre kind, and can only be described as of a "commercial" character, prepared in large quantities by artizans of not very special artistic ability. It is not difficult to see that the increasing demand brought into being many studio-workshops, supervised by Asiatic Greeks and their descendants, assisted by a subordinate staff of indigenous craftsmen, whom they had trained to copy their style and technique.

The method employed in the construction of the Gandhara buildings was of a rather commonplace order. They are of stone masonry, composed of a schist, which is readily available in these parts, and in the earlier structures the walls were built of ordinary rubble. An advance was made on this slightly primitive system about the first century A.D., when a form of masonry known as diaper-patterned rubble appears. It consisted of using larger irregular blocks of schist with their outer surfaces dressed before being laid in position, and the spaces between filled with stone snecks. Later, and in certain localities, an improvement on this method was effected, the larger blocks being more carefully prepared and dressed, while the stone snecks were replaced by courses of small bricks, fitted into the interstices with some precision and skill. The better type of masonry was that employed in the buildings raised during the reign of Kanishka, whose great "pagoda", of which the remains have been excavated near Peshawar, was of this kind. It is interesting to note that construction, of exactly the same order, is to be found in some of the larger houses of Rajputana and Central India built during the nineteenth century.

The Gandharan style of architecture continued to be practised throughout the supremacy of the Kushans, and although their power declined in the third century A.D., the monasteries were not noticeably affected, as in the year 400, when the Chinese pilgrim Fa Hian passed through the country, they appear to have been in a relatively flourishing condition. The first serious check to Buddhism in Gandhara took place however about fifty years later, when through the iconoclastic zeal of Mihiragula—the "Attila of India", who, with his hordes of barbarian White Huns, is said to have destroyed sixteen hundred stupas and sanctuaries.[1] From this calamity the religion in northern India never fully recovered, although Buddhist monasteries and other buildings continued to be erected, mainly in regions far outside the country of Gandhara, until a much later date.

Until quite recently, the art of Gandhara was considered by the authorities of the time as a form of expression of marked merit, due entirely to its Hellenistic character. This was a period when all styles of art were tested by the Attic standard. Now that a broader view is taken this Graeco-Buddhist movement has been relegated to its proper place, its productions being regarded as indefensibly hybrid. Yet its plastic and painted forms influenced to no little degree the arts of Asia, chiefly on account of their emotional significance and the definite message they conveyed. On the other hand, on the architecture of those countries which accepted Buddhism, however, and particularly on the building

---

[1] M. A. Stein, *Rajatarangini*, Vol. I, p. 89.

art of India, the Gandharan style had little effect, owing to its lack of power. Its monasteries and stupas were the result of a remarkable current of religious fervour and passionate feeling, but such qualities, in themselves, do not necessarily create a great art. There are evidences that although the art of Gandhara was conveyed by means of the Buddhist teaching to many parts of India, its aesthetic character moved the people but little. Latent within them was a much greater art of their own.

Reference may be made here to a phase of art development, based on the type of architecture which evolved during the first millennium, and which concerned a region having as its centre the ancient Mathura (Muttra), a city on the right bank of the Jumna. Subsequent cataclysms have however destroyed almost completely the many buildings, Buddhist and Brahmanical, which at different times proclaimed the flourishing state of both these religions in this part of the country, so that only the barest fragments have survived as a record of their architectural greatness. Of the examples illustrating this movement it is hardly possible to form an opinion, but from the sculptures embellishing these stupas and the temples sufficient remains have come to light to indicate its character and effect. From these relics it has been found that the schools of the Mathura period had great influence on the arts of many parts of India as a whole and it also becomes evident that the buildings, of which numerous specimens of carvings are the only existing record, had a similar influence on the styles of architecture which prevailed for a long period on the Gangetic plain, and even far beyond.

The first development of the Mathura movement is disclosed by a number of stone carvings torn from railings and gateways which decorated Buddhist and Jain shrines built during the domination of the Kushana dynasty. Beginning with the ruler Kadphises in the first century, under the patronage of his successor, the great Kanishka, this early school attained its meridian when stupas, Buddhist temples and monasteris were erected throughout this region in large numbers. From the remains it is clear that similar structures consecrated to the Jain faith were also not uncommon. Under the Kushanas, who ruled over a vast territory extending from north west India into the Gangetic plain, what is known as the Gandhara school, depicting that style of Graeco-Roman art carried eastward by the philhellene Parthians, attained its maturity. Evidence of this debased classical influx are found in the sculptured remains left of the Mathura school, and it is therefore probable that the contemporary architecture was also affected, although of this there is no direct knowledge. But the real basis of the Mathura movement was not so much the result of an attenuated Attic trend, as a derivative from indigenous sources, for instance from the important Buddhist monuments of Barhut and Sanchi. Judged therefore from the scanty remains, the architecture of Mathura would have exhibited characteristics of the Buddhist stupa, its railings and gateways, rather than classical porticos from Graeco-Roman sources. Torana lintels have been unearthed, carved with architectural features obviously reduced reproductions of full scale structural originals, which show that the chaitya arch and other Buddhist elements were the main forms used in the building art of Mathura at this time. On the other hand, later, when Hinduism gained ascendency, on the site of the Buddhist sanctuaries, were erect temples of a grand order, such as that on the Katra dedicated to Vishnu under the name of Kesava Deva, since despoiled by the Mughal Emperor Aurangzeb in the seventh century to give place to the mosque which now occupies the centre of its enclosure. But there is every reason to believe that this temple was built in conformity with Brahmanical ideals, with mandapa, cella and sikhara, according to the accepted plan of the Hindu temple structure. In Mathura, if that ancient and sacred city had not been almost obliterated at a later date, there might have been found, architecturally illustrated, that change from the chaitya hall of the Buddhists to the temple of the Hindus, a chapter in the development of religious building art in India which is regrettably missing.

REFERENCES

Foucher, A. *L'Art greco-bouddhique du Gandhara.* Paris 1923.
Grunwedel, A. *Buddhist Art in India* (Eng. trans.) London 1901.
Marshall, J. H. *Guide to Taxila.* Calcutta, 1918.
Rawlinson, H. G. *Bactria, The History of a Forgotten Empire* (1912).
Smith, V. A. *The Jain Stupa and other Antiquities of Mathura.* Allahabad 1901.
Spooner, D. B. *Excavations at Shah-yi-ki-Dheri*, Arch. Sur. of Ind. An. Rep. 1908-09. Cal. 1912.
    „   „   *Excavations at Shahr-i-Bahlol.* Arch. Sur. of India 1909-10. Cal. 1914.
    „   „   *Excavations at Saheth-Maheth*, Arch. Sur. of India. An. Rep. 1907-08. Cal. 1911.
Vogel, J. Ph. *La Sculpture de Mathura*, Paris 1930.

CHAPTER VIII

BUDDHIST ARCHITECTURE IN SOUTHERN INDIA

(200 B.C. to 4th Century A.D.)

BUDDHISM, and the art that served it, developed in Southern India in much the same manner as in the rest of the country, but there were certain variations in its form of architectural expression, due mainly to the difference in environment. The religion was communicated to the people of the south by Asoka's personal zeal, as several of his rock edicts testify, but the movement seems to have confined itself mainly to a relatively limited area on the eastern seaboard, towards the lower reaches of the Kistna and the Godavari rivers. Here, on several sites are the remains of extensive Buddhist sanctuaries, some rock-cut, others structural, while a few are a combination of the two modes, but nearly all bear evidences of an early foundation. It is doubtful however whether any of the work now visible is of the Mauryan period, and the real activity most probably began after the break-up of the dynasty, and with the rise of the Andhran supremacy in the south about 200 B.C. The power of the latter was centered in this part of their dominions, as the first Andhran capital, Crikakulam (probably the present Sreewacolum), and also the later capital, Dhanyakataka (Dharamikota or Amaravati), were both on the banks of the Kistna, so that the religion flourished where the population, wealth, and patronage, were greatest. Except in this region, and a short distance along the sea coast to the north of it, Buddhism appears to have made no lasting impression in the south of the peninsula as a whole, where Brahmanism has, from time immemorial, been the prevailing belief.

There are two sites where rock-cut architecture is in evidence, one at Guntupalle[1] in the Kistna district, and the other on the Sankaran Hills in the Vizagapatam district. The former has been already referred to, because, it is here that the small circular chamber has been found which explains the kind of shelter that was first erected over the stupa— the beginning of the chaitya hall (Plate VIII, Fig. 7). This chamber is 18 feet in diameter, and the domical roof with its circular ribbed framework is 14 feet 9 inches in height, the whole suggesting a primitive hut, its early origin being proved by the design of the doorway, which, on grounds of style, cannot be very much later than that of the Lomas Rishi in the Barabar Hills. It has been presumed therefore that this rock-cut retreat at Guntupalle may have been begun as early as 200 B.C. The remainder of this *sangarama* consists of two separate groups of chambers forming a large and a small monastery, the ruins of a brick-built chaitya hall, and many stupas of various sizes most of them rock-cut, although there are a few structural. No real attempt at any coordinated plan seems to have been made in arranging the cells of the monasteries, which are crowded together, probably because other chambers were at a later date inserted in the available intervening spaces. The facades show round-arched doorways, and windows with a projecting dormer archway above, and the radiating spokes of a blind chaitya window filling the space between, the whole approximating

the early Hinayana type of vihara decoration, but all rather coarsely executed and displaying little aptitude for this kind of work.

Much the same criticism applies to the other group of Buddhist remains on the Sankaram hills, which, as a whole, may be later in date than the preceding, indeed some portions of the scheme appear to belong to the Gupta period (from c. A.D. 350). As with several of these rock-cut retreats, the plan had to conform to the configuration of the hill-top on which it is situated, so that its arrangement is irregular and scattered.

The principal remains consist of a large number of monolithic stupas, a series of rock-cut chambers, and the foundations of an extensive structural monastic building. The stupas, of various sizes, are mostly carved out of the out-cropping rock, and are nearly all hemispherical in shape standing on cylindrical drums, their proportions being similar to those in the early Hinayana chaitya halls of the Western Ghats, some of which may therefore be anterior to the Christian era. Standing on the summit of the eastern hill, the main establishment at Sankaram comprises a large rock-cut stupa on a square base, with the ruins of a capacious rectangular complex in axial relation to it. The latter was a monastery, with the monks' cells arranged round a large quadrangle, its interior measuring 150 feet by 70 feet, within which were symmetrically disposed three apsidal buildings, evidently chaitya halls. Some of the monolithic stupas here are the largest of their kind, the main one in the front of the monastery, at its circular base being 65 feet in diameter, but its upper part has been demolished. Although there are indications of an early foundation on this site, it seems clear that its most flourishing state was during the Mahayana period, (from c. A.D. 450) as the character of the few surviving pieces of sculpture denotes. There is the quality of coherence in the planning of this part of the scheme, with its well-proportioned monastic buildings confronting the great stupa, but the workmanship itself is on the whole crude and unskilled. The remains at Guntupalle, and also those on the Sankaram Hills, are remarkable more for their antiquarian interest than for their artistic or architectural values.

If, however, the craftsmen in the south of India evinced no special genius in rock-architecture and its appurtenances, on the other hand, as distinct from these, some of the early Buddhist structural monuments, notably the stupas, show not only commendable technical experience in their production, but an artistic perception of a particularly high order. There are the remains of at least eleven such structures, most of them, including the largest, being distributed throughout a circular area of seventy-five miles radius from Ellore, a town situated between the deltas of the Kistna and the Godavari. A list is given at the end of the chapter, but

---

[1] Annual Report, Arch. Dept., Southern Circle, Madras 1916-17.

the most notable were those at Jaggayyapeta, Bhattiprolu, Ghantasala and Amaravati, which, at the beginning, of the Christian era, as examples of the Buddhist style of architecture, could have had few equals. What gave the stupas of the south their imposing appearance and artistic character was that, apart from the grand towering dome, most of them were constructed with an exterior surface of white marble richly carved in bas-relief. Unfortunately time, and the ruthless hand of the spoiler, have dealt hardly with these monuments, and in most instances nothing remains except the foundations with fragmentary portions of the marble casing, but in spite of this almost entire obliteration, it is possible, from the existing records, to gain a very fair idea of their style.

To form their immense mass, as well as to provide an adequate support for the marble and concrete casing of the exterior, the foundations and body of the stupa were constructed of brick, which, in the earlier examples as at Bhattiprolu and Gudivada were built solid. Later, other expedients were adopted to secure strength and at the same time economy of material, the core of that at Jaggayyapeta having masonry floors stretching across the interior at stages in the height, while that at Ghantasala, perhaps the most scientifically constructed of all, consisted of cross-walls forming compartments in the centre, with other walls radiating towards the circumference like the spokes of a wheel. As usual in all this early brickwork the bricks themselves, some of which appear to have been kiln-burnt, were of great size, not infrequently measuring as much as 24 ins. × 18 ins. × 4 ins. From the proportions of this brick core and the remains of the outer covering, some idea of the dimensions and the general appearance of these southern stupas may be obtained. As to shape and height, that at Bhattiprolu, which was probably one of the first to be built, the low hemispherical mound similar to the large stupa at Sanchi was followed, but in subsequent examples the dome was raised by the base being stilted, to comply with the natural demand for something loftier and of more commanding aspect. In the marble casing, the southern builders had a much more chaste material to deal with than the sandstone covering of the northern type, but in none was marble applied all over the surface of the brick core, only the lower portions were so embellished the remainder being of moulded plaster painted white. Even the upper part of the dome at Amaravati, the most sumptuous of all these stupas, was finished off in the same manner. One of the characteristic features of this class of stupa, and one which was a notable endeavour to enrich considerably their architectural appearance, was the addition, in each example, of a pronounced structural offset to the base of the dome at the four cardinal points. This took the form of a rectangular projection, in the interior of which was accommodated the staircase leading to the upper processional path, as may be seen in one of the stupas in Ceylon, that at Ruwanwaeli (c. 160 B.C.). (Plate CL.) Outside and below, this offset was elaborated into a recessed shrine, or altar-piece while above it ended on a level with the upper terrace, to which it formed an extension or platform to provide a base for a row of five slender pillars or stelae. These aryaka, or "worshipful columns", free-standing and completely detached, may have symbolised the five Dhyana Buddhas, a reflection as it were, of certain ethereal embodiments dwelling in the skies. As an ornamental attribution to the domical shape of the stupa, this projection, with its graceful pillars, was an admirable device, and gives an unusually artistic distinction to the southern type.

Although of varying dimensions, the plan and general composition of the stupas of the south were approximately the same, and the description of one will suffice for all. Undoubtedly the finest of these monuments was that at Amaravati, which occupied an elevated site on the south bank of the Kistna river, where was also situated Dhanyakataka, the later capital of the Andhras. In the early years of the Christian era this city was a place of great importance, and towards the east of it was a large area containing the Buddhist sanctuary with the stupa its dominating feature. Of the Andhran capital nothing now remains, and of the towering white monument which was undoubtedly its chief glory, little more than an irregular trench now marks its original position, while such of its marble covering that has survived, has been transferred to museums.

Records of its plan together with fragmentary accounts of its dimensions have been preserved, but of its shape, proportions, and composition as a whole, little evidence of a material nature exists. From such meagre data it would seem almost a hopeless task to attempt to recreate the appearance of this monument, and thus to recapture some of its former physical and spiritual splendour, were it not for one remarkable fact. It was the practice to include in the carved decorations of the stupa, small duplicate copies of itself in bas-relief, showing clearly and in full detail exactly what the main structure was like. Certain portions of the ornamental scheme consisted of a series of panels in the form of a frieze or dado, each panel containing a conventional but quite definite representation of the stupa, the intention being to combine an appropriate design with the merit of endless repetitions of the same immaculate symbol. With these as a guide a fairly accurate conjectural restoration of the building becomes possible. (Plates XXXV and XXXVI).

From inscriptions, as well as from the character of some of the sculptural fragments, it is inferred that the Amaravati stupa in its earliest form may have been built about 200 B.C. Later, a very complete reconstruction of the monument took place, and much of its final effect may be assigned to the half century between A.D. 150 and 200. Certain of the sculptures indicate that it was begun during the Hinayana period of Buddhism, gradually changing during the progress of the work into the Mahayana form of the belief, as the introduction of numerous representations of the Buddha himself plainly prove. In size it was the largest of all stupas, as the base of the dome on the ground was 162 feet across, while outside and concentric with it was a railing enclosing the pradhakshina patha, the entire monument thus measuring 192 feet in diameter. Various calculations have been made as to the height, but to be in reasonable proportion with its width, this would be from 90 to 100 feet. Around the dome, some 20 feet from the ground, there was an upper processional path, with the offsets previously mentioned projecting from it opposite each of the entrances, and each displaying the five prominent aryaka pillars. There was a balustrade about eight feet high around the terraced path, a feature which probably led early writers to assume incorrectly that there were two railings, an inner and an outer one. This balustrade to the terrace appears to have consisted of uprights which, instead of being joined by bars had a rectangular slab morticed between, on the same principle as a railing excavated on the site of the Vishnu shrine at Besnagar (c. 140 B.C.). It was probably on the inner side of these panels that the reproductions of the stupa already mentioned were sculptured in bas-relief, as although at least a score of copies have been preserved, on none of them is this emblem to be seen. It is safe therefore to presume that, as they were not visible in a general view, they must have formed the inner ornamentation of the terrace balustrade.[1]

Elaborate as were the carvings on the stupa itself, this decoration was excelled by the richness of the accessories surrounding its base. These consisted of the ground balustrade, the processional path which it enclosed, and the four entrances. The outer railing was about thirteen feet high and composed of the usual arrangement of uprights, connected by three bars, and surmounted by a massive coping, but the entire scheme was so overlaid with ornamentation that its structural framework is hardly recognizable. Here it may be noted that a discrepancy occurs between the carved copies and the monument itself. For, curiously enough, in all the examples of the former, the sculptor probably with an artist's licence, has depicted four bars, while the actual remains show the traditional number of three only. Within the ground balustrades was the ambulatory, a corridor fifteen feet wide with free-standing pillars placed at intervals, each bearing a small stupa or similar sacred insignia. To enter this passage, in place of the *torana* of the northern type, another kind of portal was devised, in which the railing, where it was interrupted by the opening, was projected so as to form an open portico fronted with pillars, and with two pairs of sedent lions on its coping. As with all buildings of a like nature, the Amaravati stupa did not stand alone, but was surrounded by a courtyard which in the course of time became filled with an aggregation of votive stupas of varying sizes. Towards the western side there are the foundations of a structure which may have been a monastery or even some form of prayer hall, but as with several other remains of a somewhat similar order, it is too fragmentary to be identified.

As already stated this monument to the Buddhist faith has now completely disappeared from the site it occupied, while the surviving marble bas-reliefs have been transferred to the sculpture galleries of Madras and Calcutta, and also to adorn the main staircase of the British Museum, London.[2] But in its day there can have been few structures in southern India more inspiring or impressive. When it is understood that the whole of its marble surfaces were carved in relief with a fineness approaching that of ivory, some idea of the richness and pulsating effect of the conception as a whole may be realized. In the design and treatment particularly of the figure compositions depicting incidents in the life of the Buddha, there is expressed a verve and abandon which is inimitable. Each scene mirrors some touching manifestation of emotion, while the exquisite subtlety of the modelling

is reminiscent of that on an Athenian stele. So vividly poignant are many of the groups they seem to imply that the sculptor was communicating some of his own soul into the people he portrayed as if his chisel and mallet were not mere tools but for the time being formed part of himself. If its architectural appearance was in any degree equal to its plastic embellishment then the Amaravati stupa was indeed a superb achievement.

Yet the question then arises was this great marble production, with all its refinements ever a convincing example of the building art, in a word, was it truly and objectively architectural ? By its very nature the tumular formation on which it is founded unless it departs materially from its original intention, can never attain that elegance of proportion or grace of form which are the essentials of a finished work of art. In its globular mass there could have been little that was rhythmic, or that could arouse real aesthetic satisfaction. It contained no interior hall, so that it served no special functional purpose, it merely formed a grand structural foundation on which to picture in form and colour the story of the Great Teacher. The Amaravati stupa could not stand high therefore as an architectural accomplishment, but there is little doubt that for the sheer beauty of its sculptured enrichment, in which aesthetic excellence, dramatic quality, and religious significance were combined, it was unrivalled.

In spite of its stability of formation and strength of construction, the southern India stupa was not destined to a long life. The fragility of its artistic accessories and the value of the material of which it was composed soon made it the prey of the despoiler. Moreover, Buddhism in these parts began to decline as early as the fourth century A. D., after which date all such monuments fell into a state of neglect. The end followed rapidly, as is shown by the account of Hiuen Tsiang who passed through here in the year 636, for he remarks that "monasteries had been numerous, but were mostly deserted and ruined."

BUDDHIST REMAINS IN SOUTHERN INDIA

ROCK-CUT

(1) Guntupalle. 6 m. west of Kamavarapukota in the Ellore *taluk* of the Kistna district, and 28 m. north of Ellore railway station.

(2) Sankaram. 1 m. east of the *taluk* town of Anakapalla on the N. E. line of Madras and S. Mahratta Railway.

---

[1] Dr. F. H. Gravely, late of the Madras Government Museum, remarks as follows with regard to the reconstruction of the Amaravati Stupa as illustrated on Plate XXXV. "In his book Amaravati Sculptures in the Madras Government Museum Dr. C. Sivaramamurti confirms (pp. 25-26) Jouveau-Dubreuil's observation on the stupas in this area that "the height of the cylindrical base is just that of an average man, the frieze thus being on eye level," which does not agree with your reconstruction in which it is shown as about three times as high as the approaching pilgrims and well above the top of the rail as is shown for artistic reasons (but incorrectly) in the surviving chaitya slab." Apart from the fact that a complete study of the remains of this stupa can only be made by consulting the much more comprehensive collection of material now displayed in the British Museum, such proportions as those referred to above would, if applied, in practice, ruin entirely the graceful elevation of this monument, a solecism which it is hardly possible its designers would be capable of. Further investigation of the mass of material distributed throughout the various museums and libraries seems necessary before the problem can be solved, and a revision of this conjectural restoration attempted. Moreover, it was the custom (which even now prevails) always for the designers of buildings containing rich and delicate workmanship to place this well above the reach of the spectator, for reasons which are obvious to all who chance to see the inquisitiveness of many of those who visit these institutions.

[2] Since removed and re-arranged.

STUPAS

(1) Jaggayyapeta (Kistna Dist.) diam. 31½ feet

(2) Pedda Maddur (Guntur Dist.) „ 44 „

(3) Pedda Ganjam   (No. 1) „ 74 „

     „   „   (No. 2) „ 38 „

     „   „   (No. 3) „ 32 „

(4) Bhattiprolu (Kistna Dist.)   „ Stupa 132 feet
                                    „ Railing 148 feet

(5) Gudivada (Kistna Dist. 22 m.
     N. W. of Musulipatam)   diam. 130 feet.

(6) Ghantasala (Kistna Dist.
     13 m. West of Musulipa-
     tam)   „   c. 122 „

(7) Garikapad (Kistna Dist.) „   81 „

(8) Amaravati (Guntur Dist.) „ Stupa 162 feet
                                  Railing 192 feet

(9) Nagarjunikonda (Guntur
     Dist.)   height   60 feet

REFERENCES

Burgess, J. *Buddhist Stupas of Amaravati and Jaggayyapeta* 1887.
„   „   *Notes on the Amaravati Stupa*, Madras 1892.
Rea, A. *South Indian Buddhist Antiquities*, Madras 1894.

CHAPTER IX

BUILDINGS IN BRICK

THE opening centuries of the Christian era indicate that practically the whole of the architecture being produced in India was the outcome of the Buddhist faith. It will also be seen that the building art thus developed was being evolved, more or less independently, in three different parts of the country in the west, south and north. The particular form that the religion assumed in each region is plainly shown by the character and appearance of its monuments. In the west, as exemplified by the rock-cut halls in the Western Ghats which, upto this time were entirely the result of the Hinayana system, this primitive phase of Buddhism was approaching the end of its course, the arid and almost sterile treatment of the Kanheri chaitya hall (c. A. D. 180) marking its decline. In the south, where the style reached its zenith in the Amaravati stupa (c. A.D. 250), the life of the creed was prolonged by an infusion of the more advance Mahayana thought, but here too it was soon to be overwhelmed by the surrounding Hinduism. Only in the north, in spite of political vicissitudes, did it maintain its hold, its vitality being due very largely to its Mahayana character, as shown by the Gandhara monasteries with their marked Hellenistic attribution. This theistic form of the belief, with its classical iconography, had by now been conveyed across the Punjab to the ancient and sacred city of Mathura (Muttra), which became a stronghold of this later system of Buddhism for several centuries. The Mathura of those days has however almost entirely perished, as it lay directly in the path of the invading Muhammadans, but Mahmud's own account of its architectural mangificence before he destroyed it, that it contained "more than a thousand structures, the greater number in marble" speaks for itself. What records have survived show that here two traditions met, the Hellenistic current from Gandhara passing into the deep pool of indigenous art, as represented by the remains of Barhut and Sanchi. It was the synthesis of these two very different but equally potent movements, as expressed in the monuments of Mathura, that enabled Indian art to maintain its continuity in the more northern regions throughout this period.

From Mathura the Mahayana system of Buddhism was carried further into the Gangetic plain, where both the creed and the building art which served it, experienced a late but exuberant flowering in the famous monasteries, universities, and sancturaries of the Buddhist Holy Land. These numerous and vast aggregations of buildings which grew up on the sites sanctified by the Buddha, are now in most instances mounds of ruins, but investigations have shown that they were almost entirely constructed of brick. The skilled handling of much of this brickwork denotes that it was a method of building which had been in practice for a very long period, of which, there have already been notable examples. Its great antiquity has been proved by the advanced stage building in brick had attained as early as 3000 B. C. in the cities of the Indus civilization. Considerably later, although perhaps not so carefully prepared as the houses of Mohenjo-daro and Harappa, were the stupas of Asoka, but they were compact serviceable structures built with large and strongly made bricks. Following this,

the brick foundations of a Vishnu shrine at Besnagar in Bhopal of the second century B. C., prove by the nature of the materials employed, and the manner of their laying, that the high quality of this method of construction was being maintained. From these various sources it seems fairly clear that an important phase of brick building was partly conterminous with and succeeded the period of wooden construction described in Chapter II. Moreover it has been found that buildings of this character were produced in different parts of the country, but more particularly in the north, culminating in a great development of brick architecture, which prevailed throughout most of the first millennium. It is only logical therefore that in any classification of the art of building in India the position of the brick phase, while following that of wood, should precede that of dressed stone.

As would be expected brick architecture flourished principally in the great alluvial plains of the country where good clay was easily obtainable, but the theory of the availability of material should not be pressed too far. Much depends on the human element, and the preference of a people, under certain conditions, for the particular type of building which would best suit their purpose. As an illustration of this choice of material immense buildings almost entirely composed of brick, were constructed during the early mediaeval period at Mathura and Benares, although the extensive sandstone quarries of Rupbas and Chunar were readily accessible. Brickwork, if properly prepared, and other things being equal, has durable qualities little inferior to those of stone masonry, besides it has the advantage of being composed of small units, the flexibility of which gives greater constructional possibilities. On the other hand the use of such small elements adds to the difficulties of bridging spaces, as in the case of roofs, doorways, and all openings. The Indian builder endeavoured to overcome this disability by resorting to very large bricks, some of the earlier examples being over twenty inches long, several times larger than the modern article. There was a tendency to reduce the size as time went on, so that within limits it may be said that, the larger the brick the earlier its date. But the builders soon found that even by employing exceptionally large bricks spaces could not be readily spanned so that it became the practice to introduce beams of wood over the doorways and windows, many of the earlier brick buildings thus containing a moderate amount of timber. Later, when the properties of stone for such a purpose began to be recognised, instead of wooden supports, lintels of stone were used and a phase then ensued when brick buildings with stone stressings found favour. It does not, however, follow that in every locality the two phases, of brick with wood, and brick with stone, were in the above sequence. In certain parts this order may, for various reasons have been reversed, but as a whole, constructional evolution in the art of building progressed generally on these lines.

Examples of brick architecture in India are of a somewhat miscellaneous order, but they may be resolved into four groups, (1) Buddhist Chaitya Halls, (2) Brahmanical temples,

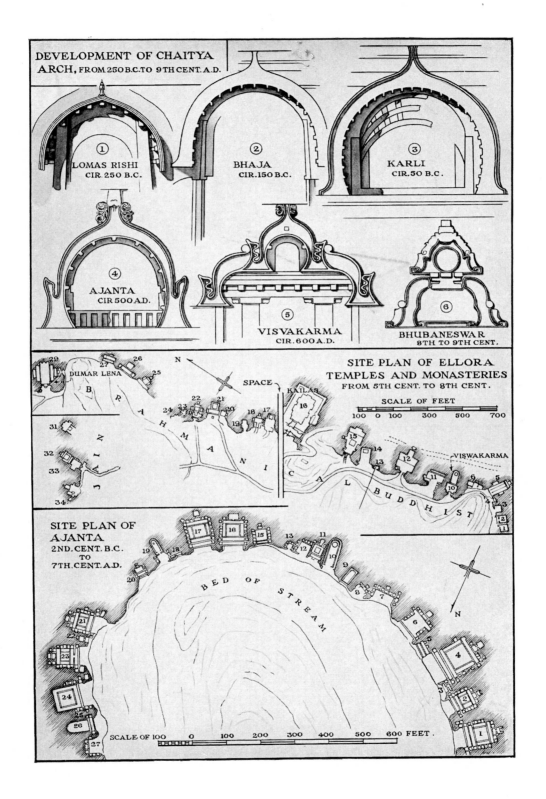

Fig. 1
Junnar (Poona Dist.) Rock-cut facades, Manmoda group, Nos. 1 and 3.   c. 1st cent. B.C.

Fig. 2
Ajanta, general view.
(*By Courtesy of Anton Schroll & Co., Vienna*)

Kondane Chaitya Hall, showing position in rock-face.
(*By Courtesy of Anton Schroll & Co., Vienna*)

Ellora, Kailasa.

Fig. 1. Gautamiputra Vihara (No. 3)

Fig. 2. Vihara No. 10
Nasik : Rock-cut facades. Early 2nd cent. A.D.

① SMALL VIHARA
AT BHAJA (CIR.150 B.C.)
② PLAN
③ ROCK-CUT LATTICE
④ ALTAR IN VARANDAH
⑤ DETAIL OF ARCADING

SCALE

0   25   50
FEET

Fig. 1

Fig. 2
Udaigiri, Orissa. Rani Gumpha. c. B.C. 150.

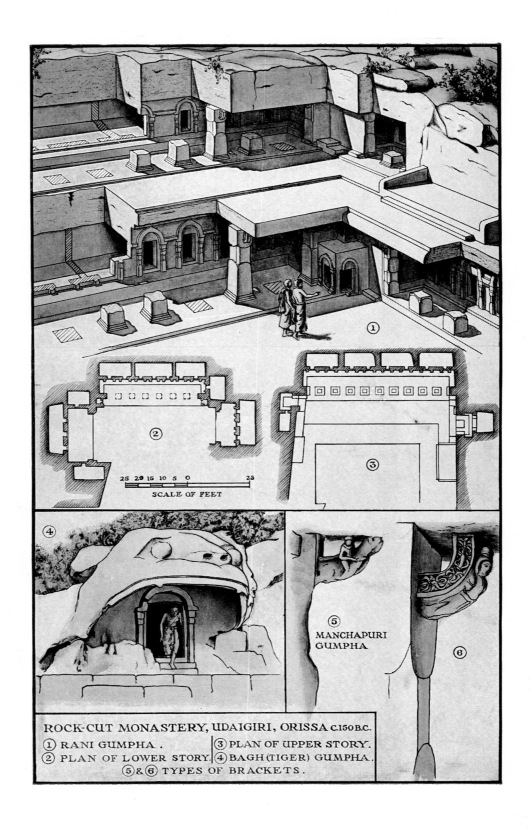

ROCK-CUT MONASTERY, UDAIGIRI, ORISSA C.150 B.C.
①RANI GUMPHA.   ③PLAN OF UPPER STORY.
②PLAN OF LOWER STORY.④BAGH (TIGER) GUMPHA.
       ⑤&⑥TYPES OF BRACKETS.

SCALE OF FEET
25 20 15 10 5 0   25

MANCHAPURI
GUMPHA

(3) the Monasteries and Sanctuaries of the Buddhist Holy Land, and (4) the Stupas of Sindh. The buildings forming the first group are two only in number, and are relatively small structures possessing no outstanding architectural merit. They are important, however, not for what they are intrinsically, but for their significance, as they are Buddhist structural temples in thier original condition, and the only surviving examples of their kind. Situated widely apart, although both are in the southern portion of the peninsula, one at Ter near Sholapur, but within the old State of Hyderabad,[1] and the other at Chezarla in the Kistna district of the Andhra State, they are presumed to have been built as early as the fifth century A. D. Both owe their preservation to having been at a later date appropriated to Brahmanical uses, as a rectangular hall, or *mandapam*, was subsequently added to make them suitable for the Hindu ritual. Buildings of this type were no doubt common about the beginning of the Christian era, when Buddhism had its adherents all over the country, but on the decline of the creed, particularly in the south, they were allowed to fall into decay. Both temples, excluding their mandapas, are of approximately the same dimensions, the exterior length of each being about thirty feet, the Chezarla example in its other proportions being slightly the smaller. In style they are singularly alike, both having apsidal ends, "keel" vaulted roofs, "chaitya" gable fronts, with a wide cornice moulding of the rock-cut order all round the building at the junction of the walls and the roof. A flat ceiling about $7\frac{1}{2}$ feet from the floor conceals the construction of the vault at Chezarla, but at Ter the roof is quite open, showing that the vault was obtained by corbelling out each course of brickwork and covering the whole with a coating of plaster. The bricks in each instance are the same size, being $17'' \times 9'' \times 3''$, the large dimensions serving as additional evidence of their date, as they are less in dimensions than the Mauryan and yet larger than the Gupta. Although little more than a chapel the chaitya at Ter is a well-proportioned structure, the pilasters which form its principal exterior decoration being quite suitable for their purpose, while the sunk panels above the cornice and the treatment of the gable-end have all been carefully considered. (Plate XVI, Fig. 1.) The example at Chezarla is more florid in its ornamentation especially in the upper story, the plainness of the lower portion being relieved by a series of four windows with chaitya arched pediments. These two small buildings explain to a certain extent the external appearance of the structural temple of the Buddhists, hitherto only known through the rock-cut chaitya halls, which have no exteriors except their facades. In both these brick chapels and the rock-cut halls there are constructional features, inherited from the same primitive type, either wood or thatch, so that their inter-relationship is tolerably clear.

The second group of brick buildings comprises a number of Brahmanical shrines, also widely distributed, and extending over several centuries of time. They may be divided into three sub-groups consisting of (*a*) a temple at Bhitagaon in the Cawnpur district, together with several shrines of a later date in its neighbourhood, (*b*) a series of temples at Sirpur and Kharod in the Raipur district of the Madhya Pradesh, and (*c*) two small Hindu shrines at Ter near Sholapur (Bombay State). The earliest and most remarkable of this group is the temple at Bhitagaon, probably

built during the fifth century A.D., and on account of its unique character, standing in a class by itself. (Plate XLI, Fig. 5). On grounds of style the only other brick building to which it bears any resemblance is the Buddhist temple at Budh Gaya, which, in its original form appears to have been erected about the same date, but the size and intentions of the two structures are so different, that they have been referred to separate groups. It is worthy of note that a stylistic similarity also exists between the Bhitagaon temple and a number of Indo-Buddhist shrines constructed of stone on the Djeng plateau in Central Java, dating several centuries later, but manifestly of Indian extraction.[2] The temple at Bhitagaon[3] is a tall tower-like edifice rising in diminishing stages to a height of about 70 feet, and standing in the centre of a fairly high plinth. It is a square of 36 feet diameter in plan, but has double recessed angles, and on the east side there is projected a porch approached by steps, and leading by a passage to an interior chamber or cella 15 feet square. Like the majority of early Brahmanical structures it was not a temple for an assembly of worshippers, but a shrine or repository for an image. The interior is quite plain but displays certain constructional expedients, which for a building of so early a date are of considerable interest, as the porch and cella are both covered over by domical vaults, and the passage connecting the two by a wagon-vault.

The exterior is much ruined but it seems not improbable that the upper part of the tower was finished by means of a short "keel" roof, not unlike that of the Vaital Deul temple at Bhubaneshwar (Plate XVI, Fig. 3), and also of the Telika Mandir at Gwalior (Plate CXVI, Fig. 2) both built several centuries later, but demonstrably survivals of an earlier type. Its proportions appear to have been quite good, but it is in the architectural treatment of its surfaces that the builder has shown his skill in overcoming the disadvantages of flatness and want of shadow, inherent in structures composed of small elements such as brick. Variety has been obtained by introducing at the right intervals prominent string-courses, broken by recessed planes with sunk panels all arranged in excellent relation, not only to one another, but to the scheme as a whole. Effective use has been made of a motif derived from Buddhist sources, consisting of a decorative adaptation of the chaitya-arch converted into a niche for the reception of figure-subjects of terracotta, and applied freely all over the building. The bricks of which this shrine is built are of a large size measuring $17\frac{1}{2} \times 10 \times 3''$, and the general construction shows marked technical ability, so much so that there is little doubt that it represents a phase of the building art which was well-understood and had a long tradition behind it. As almost the sole surviving record of this early phase, which must have been of no little importance during the first centuries of the Christian era, the Bhitagaon temple has a special interest. There are other shrines in its vicinity, much later in date as they are presumed to have been erected in the tenth century, which although varying in style, are designed and constructed on the same simple principles, showing that this method of building persisted in these parts for a long period.

The group of brick temples in the Raipur district,[4] in spite of being some distance away, and also of a later date, as they are assigned to the tenth century, show a certain

[1] Arch. Sur. Rep. 1902-03.

[2] Influences of Indian Art (India Society) p. 66.

[3] Arch. Sur. Rep. 1908-09.

[4] Arch. Sur. Rep. 1909-10.

affinity to the example at Bhitagaon. In this locality there are the remains of several similar structures, but the one which is in the best condition, and retains most of its original appearance, is the temple of Lakshmana at Sirpur. (Plate XXXVII). It is a building having the same tower-like proportions, with a projecting porch leading to a single cell in the interior, and the whole stands on a high plinth. At its base it measures 22 feet side, and when complete was probably at least 60 feet high, although the upper part is much injured. In front there are the remains of a pillared hall (mandapa) which however appears to have been a later addition. The entire building is of brick with the exception of the inner entrance to the sanctuary, which consists of a wide doorway elaborately carved in stone and leading to a cella 9 feet 9 inches side. Where this comparatively small structure excels—and the same qualities may be observed in other shrines of the group—is in the dispositions of its parts, the design and distribution of its decorative elements, and the character of its construction generally, all of which denote artistic and technical knowledge of no mean order. The attractive effects of light and shade obtained by the receding planes of its walls, intersected by the carefully adjusted horizontal lines of the deep string-courses also show considerable architectural experience. Equally pleasing is the relief ornament which is of a conventional type, applied in the best of taste, and in keeping with the composition as a whole. The most noticeable feature is a deeply recessed false window in the centre of each side; this is divided into panels by mullions, and each panel contains a carved pattern intended to represent open-work, evidently derived from a wooden lattice. Nearly all the ornamentation was chiselled out of the brickwork after the walls were built, the necessary parts having been left boasted for this purpose, and the carving carried over the joints as if the whole were in one piece. The average size of the bricks is $17'' \times 9'' \times 3''$, and the surfaces of each have been laboriously rubbed down to a smooth finish, thus enabling the joints to be kept particularly fine. In all its aspects the Lakshmana temple definitely proves that it was the handiwork of craftsmen who had served a long apprenticeship to this method of building.

The two Brahmanical shrines at Ter, dedicated to Uttaresvara and Kalesvara,[1] are small and dilapidated brick buildings, dating a little later, perhaps, than the chaitya hall of the same place and previously described, but they are valuable because they illustrate a stage in the evolution of the builders' art in which records are few and far between. Introduced into their brick construction are wooden beams and door-frames, a method presumed to antedate those in which stone was employed for the same purpose. In the Uttaresvara shrine these wooden supports are beautifully carved, rivalling in this respect the finely moulded bricks of the reminder of the building. Where wooden beams could not be used, as in some of the upper portions, the courses of brick were corbelled forward until they met, as already referred to in the neighbouring chaitya hall. The bricks measure $16'' \times 9'' \times 2\frac{1}{4}''$, so that it is possible these shrines may have been built as early as the sixth or seventh century, the style of their ancient woodwork marking them as rare examples of their kind.

The buildings of brick described so far, although several have unmistakable artistic merit, are not remarkable for their size, and some have only been introduced here in order to represent certain stages in the development of this method.

[1] Arch. Sur. Rep 1902-03.

Where the Indian builders were allowed free scope to work out large schemes of brick architecture, was in the production of the immense monastic establishments which, in the first millennium gradually rose upon a number of sites consecrated to the Buddha in the holy land of Bihar and the adjoining country. Chief among these were certain places of pilgrimage specially sanctified because they were intimately connected with the life of the Buddha himself, such as Kapilavastu, the place of the Nativity, and also of the "Great Renunciation", Budh Gaya, the scene of the "Enlightenment", Sarnath, where in the Deer Park (*Isipatana*) he "set in motion the wheel of the Law", and Kusinagara (Kasia) where he entered Nirvana. To these may be added the University of Nalanda, the Jetavana monastery at Saheth (Sravasti), and an important shrine and hermitage at Paharpur in the Rajshahi district of Bengal, besides many other Buddhist resorts of a similarly hallowed character. On all the religious centres there grew up in the course of time, large aggregations of buildings, such as stupas, shrines, temples, colleges, and monasteries grouped together within a spacious enclosure, and all constructed mainly of brick. Of these vast sanctuaries, teeming with religious life and supporting thousands of monks, so large that they have been likened to university towns, which existed in such profusion in the Gangetic plain from the fifth to the twelfth centuries, nothing remains to mark each site but a shapeless conglomeration of ruins, save the great temple at Budh Gaya, now 'so restored that much of its original appearance is lost. But from a variety of sources such as excavation, literary records, and other data, some idea of their architectural style may be obtained.

The structural complexes comprising these sanctuaries appear to have been laid out on no generic plan, as in most instances they consisted of miscellaneous collections of buildings, added to from time to time according to the need. For instance excavations at Nalanda have disclosed a long sequence of buildings erected and re-erected on the same site after intervals of ruin and desertion, the entire period ranging from approximately the sixth to the twelfth century A. D. Many of the other sites show evidences of the same chequered history. Fundamentally they were immense conventual establishments brought into being by the remarkable expansion of monastic life that arose at this time, inspired originally by the eremitical tendencies of the Buddha himself, and developed by his followers. But what is significant is that their most flourishing period coincided with that great wave of monachism which swept across the whole of the then known world from Arabia through Egypt as far as the extreme west of Europe. The Buddhist monastic movement in its Mahayana phase was therefore an Eastern manifestation of the same ideal, which took the form of a desire on the part of large communities of all nations, irrespective of differences in their belief, to withdraw from the outer world and to seek seclusion in an inner one of their own. Whether in the east or in the west, the allocation, disposition, and general character of these early religious retreats suggest some connection or common inspiration. Enclosed within high walls with watch towers and a single massive guarded entrance to ensure internal discipline, these fortress-like conditions signify that, although their primary object may have been a religious one, they could readily be utillized as refuges wherein the priests and their following could retire on occasion, and bid defiance to an intolerant ruler or resist the antagonism of the supporters of opposing creeds. Such monastic strongholds were not unusual in several countries, a classical instance being that of St. Catherine on Mt. Sinai built by Justinian in 530 A. D. the ramparts and embrasures with which it was provided belying its otherwise peaceful intention. Precautions of a similar kind were also necessary in the Buddhist monasteries of India, as the ruling power was ordinarily Brahmanical, and where moreover, in spite of their considerable following, the Buddhists were a minority community during most of their history. The militant character of these ecclesiastical foundations was reproduced later in the Lamaseries of Tibet, several of which, such as that at Gyantse with its fortified walls and guarded gate-house, were evidently part of the same movement as that which produced the enclosed monastic sanctuaries of Bihar. In a like manner were prepared the temple-cities of the Jains on the western side of India, with their battlemented walls and formidable bastions, while the same apprehension existed to a lesser degree among the Brahmins, as some of the great walled temples in Southern India plainly testify. But an excellent example is the temple of Jagannath at Puri, with its outer and inner walls and guarded gateway. Except that it has no monastic establishment, a system which has no counterpart in Hinduism, Puri resembles in some of its main aspects the Buddhist sanctuaries of the early mediaeval period now being described, as it consists of a spacious sacred enclosure containing shrines and temples, around which has gradually grown up a large town to minister to its needs.

That these Buddhist sanctuaries were of an immense size is shown by the extent of their ruins, as is instanced by the wall surrounding the mound at Kasia, which forms a rhomboid 1,250 feet side and encloses an area of thirty-six acres while the site of Nalanda measures 1,600 feet long and is some 800 feet wide. Within these enclosures were three main essentials—a stupa or group of stupas, a temple and shrine combined, and hostels for the numerous orders of monks. Each sanctuary also included some sacred object special to itself, and generally of a spectacular nature in order to attract pilgrims, the colossal statue of the Dying Buddha at Kasia being a case in point. In every instance this central feature, together with the stupa and other religious monuments, occupied one portion of the enclosed area, where they were generally arranged in juxtaposition, either in axial relation to each other or side by side. Separated from this consecrated portion by a wall was the monastic enclosure, which itself was divided into an inner and outer ward having communicating entrances or a central avenue of approach as at Sarnath and Nalanda, the whole leading up to the main shrine. Out of the immense mound which, for a thousand years has been the only visible record of Nalanda's greatness, several corner towers have been excavated and are a token of the style as a whole. They depict a late flowering of the Buddhist architecture of India, and are composed of a series of well-proportioned stories and tiers divided by prominent cornices of the rock-cut type, decorated with chaitya-arched niches containing figures. (Plate CXXXII). The existing remains show that most of these buildings were of a very substantial kind usually standing on massive plinths

or terraces of solid brick, heavily moulded, and decorated with stucco statutary in high relief. Some idea of their scale may be gathered from the dimensions and character of the large gatehouse to the monastic area at Sarnath, the plinth of which was 61 feet wide with a depth of 28 feet. On each side of the doorway were broad bastions of elegantly moulded brick, while the interior contained several rooms. Little more than the foundations of this building survive, but these are so large and solid that it is clear they carried a high superstructure presumably comparable to the lofty pyramidal *gopurams* of Southern India. (Plates LXXVII and XXXIX).

That great height was a feature of the architecture of these sanctuaries is proved by the frequent remarks of some of the Chinese pilgrims who saw them in their prime. Fa-Hien[1] at the beginning of the fifth century and Hiuen Tsiang[2] in the seventh, were both much impressed by their tall proportions, one referring to " a great vihara some two hundred feet high", and the other to a shrine containing " a copper image more than eighty feet high in a six storied building";[3] moved to ecstasy the latter writes that at Nalanda "the soaring domes reached to the clouds, and the pinnacles of the temples seemed to be lost in the mists of the morning". Through the charmed eyes of these adventurous monks we may envisage the glittering metal roofs, the glazed tiles of brilliant colours, the pillars of the pavilions richly chiselled in the form of dragons, the beams painted red or ornamented with jade, the rafters resplendent with all the colours of the rainbow and the balustrades of carved open work, all of which are set down in the picturesque accounts of their pilgrimages. Now, to adapt the words of Prospero, these vast conceptions are "like the baseless fabric of a vision, the cloud-capp'd towers, the gorgeous palaces, the solemn temples, yea, all which it inherits is dissolved and, like the insubstantial pageant faded, leaving not a rack behind."

From the bare mounds which for centuries have covered up the remains of these shattered structures, it is a relief to turn to the well-preserved shrine of Budh Gaya, the sole living example of the style. Yet, paradoxically, the very preservation of this monument has been its ruin, for so heartlessly and inintelligently has it been restored, that it now gives but a poor idea of its architectural character as originally designed. Fortunately there are a few records, illustrating it before it was altered, so that it is possible theoretically to restore it to something like its previous appearance. This material comprises a "sealing", and a few small ancient replicas, which show it as a building very different from its present reconstruction. Taking the general formation of the building it now consists of a high and broad terrace, or plinth, of 50 feet wide and some 20 feet high, on which rises a lofty pyramidal tower, square in section, and its summit about 180 feet from the ground. At each corner of the terrace is a turret, a copy to a smaller scale of the central tower, so that, as a whole, the composition corresponds to a *panchayatana* or five-shrined temple of the Hindus. Such is the existing appearance of the monument. (Plate XXXVIII, Fig. 1) On the other hand

---

[1] *Fa-Hien. Translated from the Chinese* by H. A. Giles, London 1880.

[2] *La Vie de Hiouen Thsang* by Stanislas Julien.

[3] In Tibet, forming the central features of a Lamasary on the highway from India approaching the important Lamaistic city of Gyantse, there is an example of somewhat these dimensions, showing the manner in which this feat of the combination of sculpture with architecture was effected. The colossal statue of the seated Buddha in this instance not of metal but built up of composite structural materials is enclosed within a pagoda-like building in several stories with apertures at each stage from which a portion of the figure may be viewed, the uppermost bringing the spectator face to face with the immense sacred visage.

while the sealing and the models depict it as a tower not dissimilar in proportions, they represent it as distinctly different in its architectural treatment. For instance there are no smaller corner turrets, which were evidently introduced by the Burmese Buddhists through whose interest it was extensively rebuilt as early as the 14th century. Moreover the front of the building on the eastern side, (as according to legend the Buddha sat under the Bodh tree facing the rising sun) shows a commodious arched recess, apparently trefoil in shape, enshrining a large figure of the Buddha, seated in the preaching attitude. Approach to the image was obtained by means of a tall flight of steps, and the entire conception was enclosed by a railing entered also from the east through a torana gateway. Within the courtyard formed by the railing an Asokan lion pillar may be seen, and on each side stands a colossal statue recalling the two Asokan Yaksha figures from Patna, now in the Indian Museum, Calcutta. Outside the enclosure, on the north, there appears a monastery, while the area on the south is occupied by groves of trees, also another torana gateway, with numerous other details not possible to identify. (Plate XL, Fig. 8).

Just as the existing structure is in effect a misrepresentation of the original, so the accessories of the tower, and its embellishment, are but inferior imitations of the old work. It is true the main lines of the ornamentation appear to have been correctly followed, as each side of the building is divided vertically into five recessed planes, and horizontally into seven zones, both planes and zones diminishing upwards in order to conform to its tapering configuration. Also the zone on each face contains a row of five niches, but where are now empty recesses, the sealing shows in each a statuette of the Buddha, the entire surface presenting a form of architectural enrichment not unlike that employed with such effect at Bhitagaon, where there are repetitions of the chaitya-arch motif enshrining figures. A similar alteration is seen in the finial surmounting the whole structure, for originally there appear to have been prominent turrets at each corner of the apex while in the centre is what may be a stupa with a *harmika*, and a triple umbrella, with flags, festoons and banners.

In spite of its alterations, however, from the general shape of the temple at Budh Gaya it is possible to gain some idea of the type of architecture that flourished in the Gangetic region during the first millennium, especially in the character of its towers, which were one of the features of the style. So frequent were these tall structures, each marking a vihara or monastery, that they are credited with having given the country anciently known as Magadha, its name of Bihar (Vihara). Such fragments of the monasteries that have been excavated, together with the temple at Budh Gaya, show that they represent an architectural development of remarkable power and dignity, but very often of a picturesque and romantic order, in which the qualities of symmetry, regularity of planning, and balanced composition were not consistently observed. The almost complete disappearance of these immense sanctuaries was partly due to the somewhat impermanent nature of their materials and construction, which, under the severe climatic conditions, would need constant repairs. But the main cause of their decay was undoubtedly brought about by the decline of the Buddhist faith, by which the monasteries were gradually deserted, and finally became empty ruins. From the number and extent of the mounds, now all that is left of these one time populous centres of religious life, it is clear that even

the face of the country was very different from what it is at the present day. The multiple fanes of these great sanctuaries reared themselves majestically in scores of different places, and were a centre of attraction not only to the inhabitants but also to devotees from distant lands.

The last group of buildings in brick is to be found not in the region of the Ganges but represented by a number of ancient sites near the lower Indus in Sindh, Buddhism, and the form its monuments assumed, having no doubt been conveyed by means of that great water-way from the country of Gandhara to this western territory. For the Sindh buildings appear to be a rather later development, in brick, of the "Graeco-Buddhist" stone structures of the northern frontier, the change in constructional method being due to the difference in the building material available in an alluvial plain, and that of a mountainous country. Yet in some respects the Sindh brick architecture, notably in its technical and decorative aspects, shows a certain affinity to that of the Gangetic plain previously described, and was no doubt indirectly influenced by the forceful nature of that style. The monuments so far investigated in Sindh are all stupas, and date from about the fifth or sixth centuries A.D. Around these stupas were grouped monasteries, and the usual assembly of buildings associated with sanctuaries of this kind, of which however only the barest traces remain. Indeed the stupas themselves are in every instance in a very ruinous condition, but from two examples out of their number enough has been preserved to enable their general appearance to be conjectured. Like the Gandhara type they were raised on high square terraces, the domical portion mounting up in series of superimposed tiers its walls decorated with an ornamental arcade of quasi-Corinthian pilasters, much in the manner of similar structures in the frontier tract of the Upper Swat. This treatment of the dome may be seen in the remains of the stupa at Thul Mir Rukan, a fine dignified monument, one of the least ruined of the group, where it is apparent that the series of diminishing stages were disposed in agreeable relation to one another, each stage being defined by a cornice and plinth with a prominent roll-moulding as the chief member.

The nature of the terrace on which the Sindh type of stupas was built, has been revealed by excavations on the site of another of its kind, that of Mirpur Khas. (Plate XL, Figs. 9 and 10). Rising 18 feet from the ground this has a side of 50 feet, and the base of the circular structure above measured 37 feet diameter, thus leaving ample space on the upper surface of the platform for a processional path. The domical portion has almost completely disappeared but from the dimensions of its plan, its total height, including the finial, could not have been less than 60 feet. Three sides of the terrace were perfectly regular retaining walls divided up into shallow compartments by pilasters, each compartment being enriched with a conventional niche in the centre, a simple yet very effective form of decoration. But the middle portion of the remaining side, that on the west, was projected so as to give place to a structural addition of an unusual character. Some kind of portico with flights of steps leading to the upper platform of the terrace was the principal exterior feature, thus forming the entrance to the shrine. In conjunction with this was a vestibule leading to three chambers, the whole comprising a small triple sanctum tunnelled out of the solid brickwork of the basement. Each of these cells evidently contained a statue of the Buddha, so that the monument as a whole was a combination of a temple below and a stupa above.

The placing of an image within a dimly lighted chamber to satisfy a craving for something mysterious and mystical, in addition to the great dome rising above in the stark sunlight outside, is here apparent. How this desire grew and was met, is shown by the sombre interiors and darkened sanctums of the later Buddhist and Brahmanical temples of the mediaeval period.

The decoration on all these brick buildings, whether in the dry zone of Sindh or the humid plain of the Ganges, was of the same general character, due largely to the nature of the material of which they were constructed. But there is something more than a difference in material between the architectural manipulation of brick and that of stone. The former has a technical procedure of its own, as the brick builders appear to have been a separate class of workmen carrying out their schemes after their own manner. This may be noticed in the type of moulding employed, and the practice of projecting or setting back the surface planes, as well as other effects readily obtained in brick construction. Various processes were employed to produce the relief ornamentation, some of its being moulded, some chiselled out of the bricks after they were placed in position while in some instances the patterns were carved in the clay when it was in a plastic or "green" state previous to firing. In addition to these methods which were used mainly in producing the repeating designs or "arabesques", much of the figure work was boldly modelled in high relief either in terracotta or stucco. The terracotta panels at Bhitagaon and in the Kachchi Kuti at Maheth, both evidently belonging to the same school of the fifth and sixth centuries, are extraordinarily good examples of this form of decoration, and display a vigour and action which are most praiseworthy. Confronted with the actual finger-prints of the potter, burnt in the clay as seen in some of these panels, in spite of the intervening centuries, one seems in closer touch with the craftsmen of the past than in the case of any other process or at any other period.

As to the actual quality of the materials employed in these structures, the bricks themselves were usually prepared of well-puddled clay with their beds so smoothed that they fitted very accurately. No specific system of bonding is observable, but the method of headers and stretchers was followed, care being taken that no two joints came over one another. Between the joints a mixture of clay was interposed as an adherent, but only a very thin layer, as the bricks were brought into close contact. Lime mortar appears to have been known at this time although but only two instances of it have come to light, one in the foundations of a temple at Besnagar (Bhopal, Madhya Pradesh) of the second century B.C.[1], and the other at Budh Gaya, where it was sparingly employed. The character of the brickwork excavated at Besnagar is very remarkable for so early a date, as the beds of the bricks were grooved to hold the lime mortar, which on being analyzed was found to be of a kind far in advance of the Phoenician and Greek varieties, and approaching more closely to that used by the Romans.

The difficulty of bridging over spaces in brick buildings has been already referred to, as well as the fact that it was the Indian builder's practice to meet this difficulty by inserting lintels of wood or stone. Another method employed to span a void was by means of oversailing the courses of brick until they met, a serviceable but not particularly scientific form of arch found even as early as in the Indus civilization of 3000 B.C., (Plate XL, Fig. 1). The next logical step of a people committed to brick construction would have been, in ordinary circumstances, some method of placing these brick units in juxtaposition, so that they would act as supports to one another, either on the principle of the true arch, or even in the form of the arch itself. This step, however, was never taken, the accepted explanation being that the Indian builder, from the first, mistrusted the stability of such a structural expedient, because, in his own words "the arch never sleeps." That he consistently adhered to this inhibition is proved by the fact that, with one or two relatively unimportant exceptions, the true arch is never found in any indigenous building in India, not appearing in the country until introduced by the invading Muhammadans in the thirteenth century. The few occasions in which the Indian builder experimented the arch, occur in the brick structures just described as for instance the temple of Bhitagaon, the stupa of Mirpur Khas, and the shrine of Budh Gaya. (Plate XL). At Bhitagaon there is a round arch in the porch composed of bricks in the form of radiating voussoirs, but placed edge to edge while the vault of the passage into the sanctum is a variation of the same system. In the three interior shrines at the entrance to the Mirpur Khas stupa, the vault of the central cella was corbelled, but those on each side were arched by means of a series of brick rings, the top and bottom edges of the bricks being curved to the contours of the vault, while the other edges radiate towards a centre.

It was however in the entrance to the shrine at Budh Gaya that a form of brick arching was most boldly employed, two slightly different methods being noticeable. In one of these the bricks of the arch were placed edge to edge, as in the previous instance (Plate XL, Fig. 3) but in another, horizontal courses of brick alternated with others placed upright, as in Plate XL, Fig. 5. This portion of the building has now been completely covered up by subsequent restorations, and moreover it is just possible these particular arches were not in the original structure, but introduced by the Burmese masons during the process of reconstruction by them in the fourteenth century. In support of the Burmese attribution it may be mentioned that there are brick arches of exactly the same type in several early mediaeval buildings in Burma, as may be seen in the Pettuk pagoda at Pagan, dating from the eleventh century. All the instances in India of the use of the arch occur in brick buildings presumed to have been erected about the fifth century A.D., and the arrangement of the bricks in each building is practically the same, that is those constituting the voussoirs were laid flatwise and made to adhere sufficiently to those behind to enable the ring to be completed without support. This method is precisely similar to that used in the Palace of Chrosroes at Ctesiphon, on the Tigris, built about A.D., 250, and in view of the intercourse known to have been maintained between the Sasanian court and India at that time, it may have been then that it was introduced.

At Sarnath, near Benares, there is the Dhamek Stupa built with a substantial core of brick, but faced with a very solid "envelope" (achchaday) of stone masonry, which however is manifestly a later addition, a stupendous piece of work left unfinished but a reconstruction has been attempted on Plate XL, Fig. 7. What makes this ruined and rather shapeless monument of special interest is the unusual scheme

[1] Arch. Sur. Rep. 1913-14, p. 205.

for the decorative treatment of the stone facing, which includes ornamental elements some having significant implications. The remains of these are on the lower story of the structure—it may have been the intention to decorate in a somewhat similar manner the entire surface of the upper domical portion but this is too damaged to determine—and from the character of the stone carving it obviously dates from the early Gupta period, cir. A.D. 350. This lower circular story is divided into compartments by eight projections, in outline curiously resembling the tapering tower or "Sikhara," the principal architectural feature of the Hindu temple style which followed, with an arched niche recessed in the centre of each to contain a statue of the Buddha seated in one of the eight conventional attitudes on a low moulded throne. Over some of the surfaces surrounding this scheme a diaper pattern carved in floral scrolls appears to have been contemplated a very rich and elegant idea. But the most original and striking designs are those forming a wide border carried around its lower circuit, one of which is floral and the other geometrical, each

expressive of its own historical traditions. The floral one a spiral motif, typically Gupta in style is a combination of flowing wave-like curves simulating flower stems supporting at intervals a many-petalled sunflower medallion, an artistic conception of notable beauty and grace. Apart however from its intrinsic elegance it stands forth as the archetype of that distinctive border of spiral curves and foliated medallions which adorns the "screen of arches" forming the facade of the Qutub Mosque at Delhi erected many centuries later under the very different conditions that then prevailed during a Muslim regime. The other pattern, encircling the building contiguous with the foregoing, and in pleasing contrast to its rhythmic fluency, as it is devised on a geometrical system of straight lines, is a rare example of this form of treatment in the field of Indian decorative art. Each of the eight areas between the projecting niches, contains a running "fret" design, all different as each is based on a separate combination of lines, figures and angles, among which interpretations of the "swastika" and the "key" element may be identified. (Plates XXXVIII and XLIII).

REFERENCES

Archaeological Survey of India, Report 1908-09.

Cousens, H., *Buddhist Stupa at Mirpur Khas*. Arch. Sur. of Ind. An. Rep. 1909-10, Cal. 1914.

Cunningham A., *Mahabodhi, or the Great Buddhist Temple at Budhagaya*, London 1892.

Mitra, Rajendralal, *Buddha Gaya*, 1878.

Sahni, D. R. *Guide to the Buddhist Ruins of Sarnath*, 1933.

CHAPTER X

THE GUPTA PERIOD (c. A.D. 350 to 650)

TOWARDS the third century A.D., the scarcity of architectural records throughout the greater part of the country is significant of the general conditions that were prevailing at this time. It is true that in the north-west and in the Gangetic plain the Hellenic influence on the one hand, combined with the growth of the Mahayana system of Buddhism on the other, kept the northern school alive, and much the same applies to the relatively limited movement in the south, with Amaravati as its centre, but the rest of India was going through a period when the creative faculties of the people were in a state of inactivity. The same century saw the passing of an era, the cultural productions of which, initiated by the Emperor Asoka some five hundred years before, may be referred to as those of the "Primitives". Politically, the end of this phase was emphasized by the almost simultaneous collapse of two powerful dynasties, that of the Andhras (c. 225 A.D.) in the south, and of the Kushanas (c. 236 A.D.) in the north. In the sphere of religion there was also a pause, owing to the spiritual fires lit by the Mauryan ruler having evidently burnt themselves out, as testified by the decline of the Hinayana system and the forms of expression that this doctrine had made its own. A somewhat similar condition, it may be noted, arose about the same time in Europe, when the illumination of the Greek genius died out, except for the solitary lamp kindled at Byzantium. And in India, for the time being, the people had reached the limit of their resources so that an interval of stagnation ensued.

A reaction followed, as also took place in the occidental parallel when the Renaissance awoke the European mind to fresh life and activity, but in India the response was earlier. For the fourth century heralded the dawn of an epoch, which eventually developed into what has been generally accepted as a time of India's greatest intellectual awakening. Several forces operating at the same time contributed to produce this high summit of attainment. In the first place, a large portion of the country came under the stabilized rule of the strong and cultured dynasty of the Guptas, whose diplomatic relations when at their zenith, about 400 A.D., extended from the Oxus to Ceylon. The personal patronage and scholarly encouragement of these rulers created an atmosphere favourable to a revival of all forms of human activity, spiritual and material. Secondly, owing to the fact that the Guptas were by religion Brahmanical, and also because the country itself was prepared for it, great stimulation was accorded to Hinduism, the innate faith of the people, so that they were mainly of one mind. And, lastly, the unification of the state under one authority engendered a national spirit to give birth to ideals which transformed every phase of thought and every form of action. Among the effects of this fortuitous synchronisation of circumstances was that produced on the arts of the age, and notably on that of architecture. In the art of building, two progressive movements of fundamental significance are discernible, one relating to its aesthetic character, and the other to structural procedure. The former marks the begetting of a new sensibility, a change from the mere imitative to the infinitely creative, from the servile copying of meaningless forms expressive of an undeveloped mind and unskilled forces, to a reasoned application of the first principles of architectural composition. The latter records the use for the first time of dressed stone masonry, a pronounced step in the technique of building construction, the introduction of which placed a new power in the hands of the workman. It was when the art was in such a formative state that there emerged the earliest known conception of the Hindu "house of god" And with the appearance of this type of building, architecture composed of stone masonry made its beginning.

Previously all shrines connected with the Brahmanical faith appear to have been of a very impermanent order. An ancient commentary, the *Satapatha Brahmana*, incidentally describing one of these before the Christian era, states that it comprised two sheds "formed of posts and beams covered with reeds and mats," thus seeming to imply that a very primitive shelter was all that custom ordained in the ceremonial usage of this belief. That such was the practice is shown by the bas-reliefs of Barhut and Sanchi, of the second and first centuries B.C., the fire altars and *naga* tabernacles of the non-Buddhists being either entirely uncovered or merely protected by temporary erections, from which it may be inferred that the service and ritual were ordinarily performed in the open air. (Plate XVIII). What may be the oldest known actual remains of a Brahmanical stone structure are the foundations of a Vishnu shrine at Besnagar (Bhopal, Madhya Pradesh), adjacent to the Heliodorus pillar, and therefore not likely to be later than the second century B.C. The form this building took is not clear. The reason for the almost complete absence of any stable religious edifice, is due to the particular character of the belief upto this period. Consisting mainly in the propitiation, by means of offerings on an altar, of certain abstract powers representing natural forces and phenomena whose presence was everywhere, under such conditions any kind of earthly abode would have been meaningless. In the course of time, however, there grew up a desire for something more positive than spiritual essences, a need for some material interpretation of the religious ideal. And so by degrees there developed a demand for an embodiment of these impersonal powers, which, early in the Christian era crystallized, and, before the fourth century A.D., the object of worship began to assume a visible form, usually a graven image.

This anthropomorphic conception of a deity naturally called for some habitation, and so a structural shrine came into being. The various stages through which the embryo Hindu temple passed are common to the growth of such edifices, first a leafy bower, then a reed hut, and afterwards a cella of wood and brick. Eventually, in the Gupta period it appears as a sanctum of stone, called the *garbha-griha*, literally "wombhouse", a small chamber, square in plan, its interior walls perfectly plain and without any other opening except the doorway, the darkness inside providing the requisite atmosphere of solemn mystery. Within was placed the effigy of the god. Contrasting with the bare walls of the interior, the outer side of the doorway was often richly carved, and in front of this was usually a shallow porch, in the later Gupta examples enlarged into a pillared portico. Such a beginning was in accordance with that of more than one civilization, the earliest sacred buildings consisting of a flat-roofed chamber with a porch in front, Egyptian and Greek temples both showing evidences of having been derived from similar rudimentary origins. In India, on the same principle, some of the first Brahmanical sanctuaries have either flat roofs, or appear to have been evolved from a flat-roofed prototype, and it was not long before the other essential features, such as the pillared vestibule, were added. These early Hindu sanctuaries are comparatively small structures, in size much inferior to the monumental religious edifices which rose later, so that it seems more appropriate to classify them, not as temples, but as shrines or chapels. They are obviously only a beginning, but they are important, because they were the nucleus of the temple proper, being in themselves merely a prelude to such a structure in its more matured form. A number of small sanctuaries of this order, the earliest in the country to be built of dressed stone, have been found in various places in Central India, and there are fragments of others, further afield, which seem to show that buildings of a similar type were fairly common in the Gupta dominions. Included with these stone-built structures is a series of excavated chambers, having structural porticos attached, but all clearly in the same tradition. (Plate XLI, Fig. 1).

The supremacy of the Guptas lasted only for 160 years, but the particular style of art associated with this dynasty was produced over a considerably longer period, the vitality of the movement giving it sufficient momentum to make its influence felt even in mediaeval times. These Gupta buildings date from the fourth to the sixth centuries, the earlier examples, besides being in accordance with the generical formula of a flat roof and pillared portico, possessed other distinctive features. Among the specific characteristics are (a) the shape of the pillars and capitals, (b) the treatment of the inter-columnation, (c) the system of continuing the architrave as a string-course round the entire building, and (d) the design of the doorway. The principal examples of this type now remaining are as follows : a temple at Tigawa in the Jubbulpore district ; the Narasina and the other shrines at Eran (N.E. of Bhilsa) ; Temple No. 17 at Sanchi ; a temple at Bhamara in Nagod State ; a temple at Nachna in Ajaigarh State ; and a group of rock-cut sanctuaries at Udaigiri near Bhopal. Of these the most typical is the Vishnu temple of Kankali Devi at Tigawa,[1] which, in spite of later additions to its frontage, still retains much of its original appearance. (Plate XLII, Fig. 1).

As with all the buildings of the group, the dimensions of the Tigawa temple are unassuming, the sanctum being a square structure of 12½ feet side enclosing a cella of eight feet diameter, while the porch projects in front to the extent of seven feet. A feature of the portico pillars in several of these temples is the intercolumnation, the middle interval being wider than those on either side. The facade owes its character almost entirely to the design of its pillars, which, besides forming the main elements of its frontage are also fully representative of what may be termed the early Gupta "order". Each consists of (a) a massive abacus surmounted by a device of lions, (b) a capital resembling a broad conventional vase, (c) a short shaft of many sides, and (d) a plain square pedestal. A glance will show that in spite of the greatly diminished height this form of pillar is a direct

descendent of the Vishnu column at Besnagar of five centuries earlier, and the lion motif itself is a link with the still older monoliths of Asoka. The other outstanding decorative feature of the Tigawa temple is the doorway to the cella, which also displays in its treatment certain historical connexions. Its expanded overdoor is a survival of the timber age when a wooden beam was placed over the opening and extended beyond the tops of the side posts, to provide additional strength and stability. But it is the shape and subject of the panel at the upper angle of the doorway, that have the most significance. Here is seen an adaptation of the Yakshini motif which festoons the projecting architrave to the Buddhist torana, but transmuted in the Gupta temple to suit the Brahmanical text. Instead of the subject being a dryad embracing a tree as in the earlier composition it becomes an allegory of the holy waters of the Jumna and the Ganges, with a river goddess standing on a tortoise on one side symbolising the Jumna, and on the other side a similar figure standing on a crocodile, or makara, representing the Ganges. This device is a prominent one in the doorway design of many Hindu temples, but only in those of the early Gupta style is it placed in the upper angle. In all buildings of the subsequent period it is carved on the base of the doorpost.

It is instructive to compare the Brahmanical temple at Tigawa with the Buddhist temple (No. 17) at Sanchi,[2] both of which were probably erected in the first half of the fifth century, and are situated not 150 miles apart. (Plate XLII). Their proportions are practically the same, and they both conform to the general characteristics of the Gupta style. Where they differ externally is in the design of the pillars which, in the Sanchi example as would be expected, are in the Buddhist tradition descended from Asoka's bell and lion monoliths. But the difference between these two buildings is something more than one of form, significant though this may be. Each is a statement of a separate experience. On the one hand the Sanchi temple, although clearly a departure from any previous architectural conception, is a precipitation of several ancient traditions displaying the classical art inspired by Buddhist thought in its final mood. There is much to admire in the manner of its composition, in the application of the principles of good building, and the adjustment and interdependence of its parts to form a coordinated whole. But in spite of its original appearance, it is not the beginning of something new, it is in itself an end, the last expiring effort of the "primitives", revivified for the moment by an infusion of the new spirit around it. Nowhere is this shown more plainly than in the bell capital, an arid attempt at a refinement of the full-blooded campaniform capital of the Asokan monoliths. On the other hand the Tigawa example displays no marked architectural perceptions, there are crudities in its composition, but its forms ripple with a refreshing vitality, and pulsate with the nervous energy of exuberant youth. These Gupta shrines are something more than a symbol, they reflect that "sudden glory" which comes with a fresh inspiration, the capital, or "order", providing the keynote. No longer does this present the whitening bones of a dead tradition as in the Sanchi bell example, but a living, growing organism. For the Gupta capital is the purna kalasa, the "bowl of plenty", typifying a renewed faith, the water nourishing the plant trailing from its brim, an allegory which has produced the "vase and flower" motif, one of the most graceful forms in the whole range of Indian architecture.

[1] Cunningham's Reports, Vol. X, p. 41.
[2] Guide to Sanchi, Marshall, pp. 19 & 105.

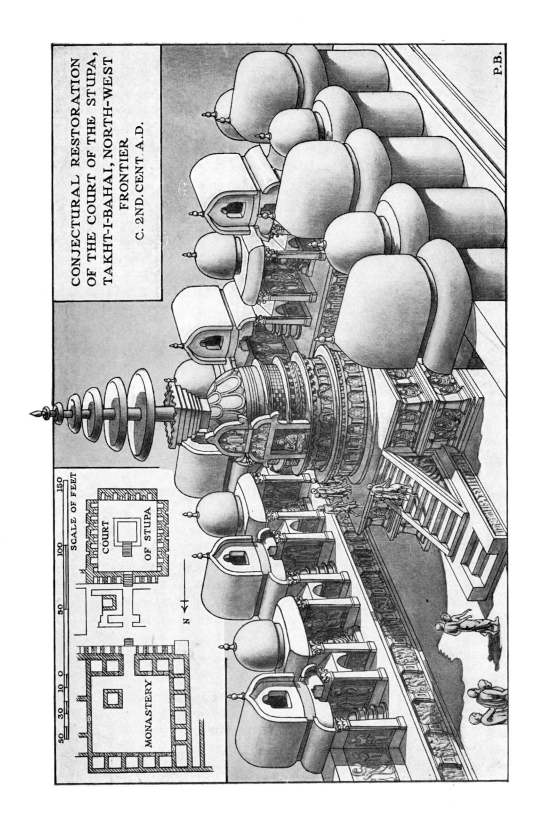

CONJECTURAL RESTORATION
OF THE COURT OF THE STUPA,
TAKHT-I-BAHAI, NORTH-WEST
FRONTIER
C. 2ND. CENT. A.D.

P.B.

SCALE OF FEET

COURT
OF STUPA

MONASTERY

N

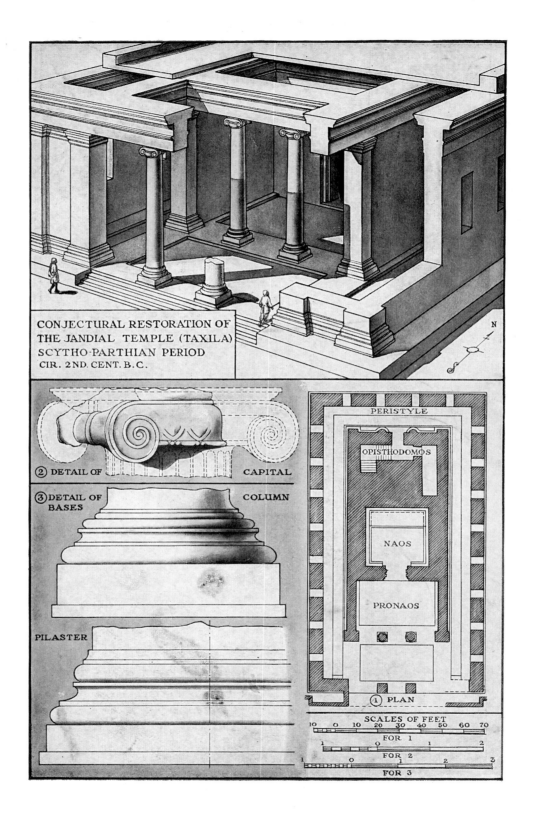

CONJECTURAL RESTORATION OF
THE JANDIAL TEMPLE (TAXILA)
SCYTHO-PARTHIAN PERIOD
CIR. 2ND. CENT. B.C.

N

② DETAIL OF   CAPITAL

③ DETAIL OF   COLUMN
    BASES

PILASTER

PERISTYLE

OPISTHODOMOS

NAOS

PRONAOS

① PLAN

SCALES OF FEET
10   0   10   20   30   40   50   60   70
FOR 1
1   0   1   2
FOR 2
1   0   1   2   3
FOR 3

Fig. 1. Bhaja : Small Vihara. c. 150 B.C.

Figs. 2-3. Capitals from Gandhara.

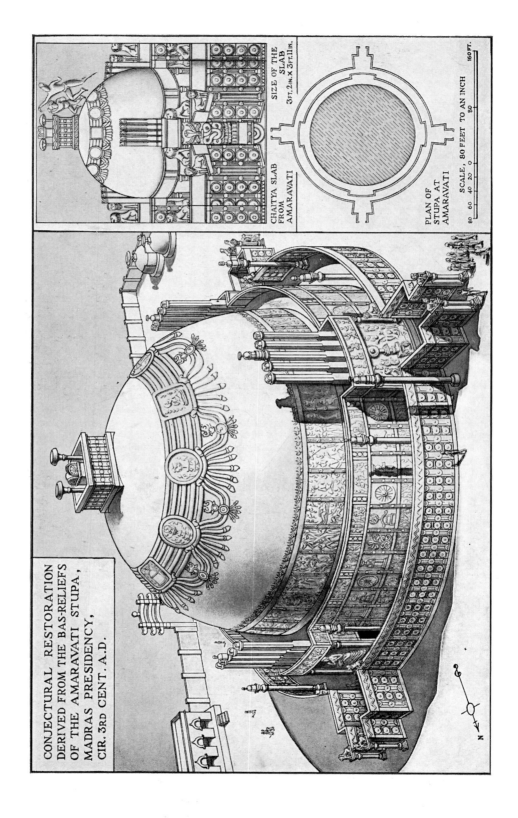

SIZE OF THE SLAB
3FT. 2 IN. x 3 FT. 11 IN.

CHAITYA SLAB FROM AMARAVATI

PLAN OF STUPA AT AMARAVATI

SCALE, 80 FEET TO AN INCH

80 60 40 20 0 80 160 FT.

CONJECTURAL RESTORATION DERIVED FROM THE BAS-RELIEFS OF THE AMARAVATI STUPA, MADRAS PRESIDENCY, CIR. 3RD CENT. A.D.

N

Fig. 2

Amaravati Stupa : Marble bas-relief ; c. 3rd cent. A.D.

Fig. 1

Nasik, Pandulena Chaitya-hall ; c. 1st cent. B.C.

Fig. 2

Fig. 1

Sirpur, Madhya Pradesh : Temple of Lakshmana: c. A.D. 800

Fig. 1.   Budh Gaya

Fig. 2.   Sarnath, Benares : patterns on Dhamek Stupa ; c. 6th cent. A.D.

CONJECTURAL RESTORATION OF THE STUPA, SHRINE, AND MONASTERY AT SARNATH, BENARES. ABOUT 7TH CENT. A.D.

In any account of the art of the Gupta period, a strict adherence to chronological order would have placed the excavated chambers at Udaigiri[1] first, as one of them bears an inscription stating that it was produced in the reign of Chandragupta II, who ruled from A.D. 382 to 401, thus making these as early as the end of the fourth century. But as they are partly rock-cut and partly stone built they are not so typical as the structural examples described above. There are in all nine of these cells in a sandstone hill two miles from Besnagar, and five from Sanchi in the vicinity therefore of an art centre of notable historical reputation. Beginning with what is usually referred to as a "false cave" (No. 1), their numbering most probably follows the sequence in which they were excavated. With the exception of the last of the series known as the "Amrita cave" (No. 9), the rock-cut interiors of the shrines are of little consequence, as they are plain rectangular cells, similar to the structural examples. Their architectural value lies in the treatment of the rock facades, and particularly in the design of the pillared porticos that were built in front of them. As far as the combination of these two technical methods permitted, the general style of each is in the early Gupta tradition. The only one of the series with its frontage fully intact is the "False Cave", so called because it has been adapted out of a natural ledge of rock, which has been made to form both the roof of the cella and its portico. It is a primitive effort, but at the same time it carries out the conventions of the style, with its flat roof, massive string-course, and row of four pillars with the wider intercolumniation in the middle. There is character in the shaping of the pillars, with their capitals of the "vase and foliage" pattern, for, although heavily proportioned, they are in keeping with the rugged strength of the whole. The importance of this "False Cave" lies in the fact that it is probably the earliest Brahmanical sanctum that has survived. (Plate XLI, Fig. 1).

The remaining shrines at Udaigiri are an elaboration of the principles applied in the "False Cave", together with a refinement of the treatment generally, as the work of producing them progressed. Added to these examples, in most instances their rock-cut facades, especially the doorways, are richly carved, and in conjunction with them are certain separate sculptured figure-compositions of a high order. The spirited design and experience of form that the rock-carvings display, when compared with the rudimentary technique of the masonry, are an indication of the uneven evolution of the arts at this particular period. While the carved reliefs show every evidence of maturity, the building art, to judge by these porticoed cells, seems still in its infancy, as they are little more than a step removed from the rustic shelter on the hill-side, with its lean-to roof in front of a natural hollow. Yet, in spite of this lingering archaism, a considerable amount of fine workmanship was expended on their production. Several of the doorways are of the kind already referred to as typical of the Gupta style, with the expanded overdoor and intricately moulded jambs all carved on the prepared surface of the rock. On each side were sculptured in high relief figures of *dwarpalas* to guard the entrance, as well as other mythical beings. In the design of the pillars of the structural portion there are signs of careful thought and patient handling, the pillars being all of the Gupta "order", having square pedestals and octagonal shafts surmounted by a vase-shaped capital.

As the work of producing these shrines proceeded, so they became larger and more ornate, the cells were made more spacious, and the simple porches began to assume the appearance of pillared halls. A stage in this process is seen in the "Bina cave", No. 3, where, in addition to the four pillars forming the front of the portico, there are two smaller pillars on either side. No. 9, known as the "Amrita cave" denotes a further step, as it is the largest, and probably the latest, of the entire series. It has a cella nearly twice the size of the others, which measures 22 feet by 19 feet 4 inches, and four massive pillars some eight feet high have been left in the centre, all hewn out of the rock. The doorway is also richly carved in the rock, and outside was a long structural portico with three openings, to which a pillared hall was afterwards added, the whole forming a composition 27 feet square. Both the plastic and architectural treatment of the Amrita example show that it is the repository of several art traditions. In the first place, in the design of the rock-cut capitals of the inner chamber, the carvers have reproduced something from the Gautamiputra colonnade at Nasik of the first century B.C., as shown by the small fawn-like animals which enrich its fluted bell. Secondly, for the doorway they seem to have received some inspiration from the Sanchi toranas, as parts of it are a memory transcript, incised in the rock, of this type of gateway. And thirdly, the pillars of the portico are of the Gupta pattern with vase-shaped capital. Although this sanctuary contains contributions from these three different sources, yet throughout it displays a quality and temper inherited from the Buddhist art of the Sunga period, thus showing that the Besnagar craftsmen still retained their skill under the Guptas, although four centuries had passed. The fine rock-cut figure compositions, which form part of the shrines are further evidence of the persistent vitality of this artistic school.

Slightly later than any of the foregoing are two buildings in the early Gupta style, which have much in common. These are a Siva temple at Bhamara[2] near Nagod, and the Parvati temple at Nachna[3] near Ajaigarh, both probably erected before 500 A.D. Each is built on the principle of the flat roof, with pillared portico, and although differing in some parts of their arrangements, (for instance the Nachna example has an upper story), their proportions are very similar, and their plans are much alike. The Parvati temple is the simpler scheme, and consists of a square building of 15 feet side, containing a cella 8½ feet in diameter, the whole standing on a square platform 35 feet wide. This platform in both buildings is extended on the front side to an additional 12 feet where it is approached by a short flight of steps. Both temples are much ruined but each had a processional path around the outside of the sanctum, that at Nachna being an enclosed passage, while at Bhamara it was an open promenade. In each case the doorways to the shrine are of the typical Gupta design with their overhanging lintels, figure panels in the upper corner, and ornate treatment generally. But the carved decoration was by no means confined only to the entrances, the Parvati temple contains at the sides some panels with vigorous figure compositions, while there are few buildings for their size that could have displayed such choice embellishment as that on the stones lying around the Bhamara sanctum. For spirited floral scrolls and crisp modelling, the chiselled patterns on its lintels have their equal only in the brushforms of the Ajanta

[1] Cunningham's *Reports*, Vol. X, p. 41.
[2] *Memoirs*, Arch. Sur. Ind., No. 16.
[3] Cunningham's *Reports*, Vol. XXI, pp. 95-97.

frescoes, each medium expressing that quality of exultation and movement which only appear under the most tranquil and favourable conditions.

The early Gupta style reached its culmination in a superb little structure at Deogarh in the Jhansi district, a Siva temple probably dating from early in the sixth century. In this example is seen an effort to throw off the rudimentary and rather ineffective convention of the flat roof, and to obtain some appearance of height. Accordingly the upper part of the sanctum was carried upward in the form of a pyramidal tower, but unfortunately the summit is too ruined for its detailed shape to be made out, although its height when entire could not have been less than 40 feet. This tower-like shrine which at its base is 18 feet side, is further elevated by being placed in the centre of a square terrace five feet high, with a flight of steps in the middle of each side. In the ingenuous disposition of the pilasters, panels, and coping, on the sides of the substructure there is a suggestion of the railing around a Buddhist stupa. But the most notable feature of the Deogarh temple is the arrangement of its portico. Instead of only one of these, as is usual in front of the entrance to the sanctum, there are four of them, one projecting from each side of the central structure, each with a flat roof supported on a row of four pillars, with the customary wider intercolumniation in the middle. All the porticos have fallen but the general appearance of the building is shown in the diagram of a conjectural restoration in Plate XLI, Figure 6. In each part of the temple there is the same exuberance of carving as in the previous examples in this style, the pillars being elaborately chamfered, and the capitals of the vase and foliage type lavishly decorated with pendent scrolls.

But the most ornate of all these features is the doorway, which although designed in the mode of the period, is so charged with decorative additions that the principle of the projecting lintel, so characteristic of the style, is almost obscured. The underlying motif takes the form of a pavilion archway with pilasters on each side supporting an architrave of dormered gables, the whole being skilfully adapted to frame the doorway. This ornamental archway bears some relation to a style of semi-secular architecture found in the backgrounds of the mural paintings which about the same time were being produced at Ajanta. The structures, which probably suggested the introduction of these architectural elements into the sculpture and painting of the Gupta period, were apparently pavilions of a portable kind having wooden pillars, turned on a lathe, and lacquered and coloured, to be set up like tents for the accommodation of the imperial court as it moved about the country. The regal nature of this equipage, with its graceful lines caught the eye of the artist who was prompt in applying it in his more lasting decorative schemes. In the Deogarh temple the ornate character of the doorway is repeated in the sculptured treatment of the three remaining sides of the building. But on these portions the central feature of each takes the form of a sunk panel or false window, five feet high and four feet wide, framed in an architectural setting of pilasters and architrave, and containing a profoundly moving religious figure composition carved in high relief (Plate XLI, Figs, 2 and 3). Here it is possible to see one of the purposes of the projecting porticos, as they protect these icons, and aid in consecrating them as a kind of altar-piece. When com-

plete, this building was unquestionably one of rare merit in the correct ordering of its parts, all alike serving the purpose of practical utility, yet imbued with supreme artistic feeling. Few monuments can show such a high level of workmanship, combined with a ripeness and rich refinement in its sculptural effect as the Gupta temple at Deogarh.

In addition to the temples there are other productions of this period of an architectural character. These are several free-standing pillars chief among which are the Budhagupta monolith at Eran,[1] and the famous Iron Pillar at Delhi.[2] The former, which bears a date corresponding to A.D. 484-5, is a graceful composition with a faceted shaft surmounted by a lion abacus, but the whole effect is marred by the mean fluting and attenuated proportions of its bell capital. The object of the column is to support aloft a statuette of the god Vishnu, a well-executed work dignified by an expansive radiated halo. As it is 43 feet high it equals in this respect the pillars set up by Asoka, but it has not the massive simple grandeur of those classical models.

The other example, the Iron Pillar at Delhi, is an entirely different conception, and, in several respects is unique (Plate X). Prepared to the order of king Kumaragupta[1] about A.D. 415, it was originally erected on a site near Mathura, being removed to its present position in the Kutub Mosque at Delhi in mediaeval times. Its 'total height, including the capital, is 23 feet 8 inches and it is composed of pure malleable iron, the entire weight exceeding six tons. The high technical skill required to forge such an object which, until recently, would have taxed the resources even of the largest foundries is a remarkable tribute to the genius and manipulative dexterity of the Indian iron-worker. When first set up it bore on its summit an image of a *garuda*, the "vehicle" or attribute, of Vishnu, which has now disappeared, but even without this feature the design of its superstructure, although outwardly little more than a pleasing combination of conventional mouldings, has interesting implications. This superstructure may be resolved into three separate parts, the uppermost being the square abacus, identified as a refined adaptation of that which usually surmounts the Gupta "order", a shape later to become universal whenever an ornamental throne or pedestal was required. Below is a melon-shaped member, in which it is possible to recognise a phase in the evolution of the "cushion" or "vase" motif, to be used with such effect at a slightly later date. And, lastly, there is the campaniform capital, marking one of the last appearances of the Persepolitan attribution, here however still retaining the vigorous outline and rounded fluting of the original model. Although, in some of its details there is a subtle grace, the Iron Pillar as a whole is not a work of art of exceptional merit, but as a landmark denoting the dividing line between the age of primitivism and the beginning of the early mediaeval era, it is important.

At this time when the building art was largely in a state of indetermination, seeking direction, it is only natural that certain structures were produced which it is not easy to classify. One of these at least is of sufficient interest to deserve reference. This example, probably dating from the fifth century, consists of the remains of a pillared portico in the Mukandwara Pass of Kotah State, and is composed of immense blocks, suggesting such a giant handling of stone that only its precise cutting and fine carving save it from being

---

[1] Cunningham's *Reports*, Vol. X, p, 81.
[2] Journ. Roy. As. Soc. 1907, pp. 1-18,

characterised as cyclopean. While there is something not unattractive in the ingenuous chamfering which breaks up the mass of the pillar shafts—a decorative treatment remotely related to the Buddhist railing pillar—the fabric in its entirety has a definitely archaic flavour, recalling that massive strength and dexterous simplicity of the "sturdy Dorians" in Greek architecture. It shows little knowledge of construction, the only problem solved being that of placing one stone on another, the first step in the art of masonry building. Yet this method was typical of the Gupta style, when it was the practice to employ blocks of stone much larger than the relatively small size of the building justified. But economy of material, without loss of strength and stability, is a matter of experience, which was yet to be gained. The stones in the Gupta shrines are, as a rule, well cut with the surfaces finely dressed, but there was no mortar, all the masonry being of the dry order. An experiment in jointing stonework, however, was made in the construction of the Deogarh temple, as here the blocks were held together with iron dowels.

REFERENCES

Banerji, R. D.   *Arch. Sur. of Ind.*,   Memoir No. 16.

Cunningham, A.   *Archaeological Survey of India*, Report Vol. X.

Havell, E. B.   *Zenith of Indian Art, Ostasiatische Zeitschrift.*, Ap.-June, 1914.

Smith, V. A. *Indian Sculpture of the Gupta Period A. D. 300-650.   Ostasiatische Zeitschrift*, Ap.-June, Vol III, 1915.

CHAPTER XI

CHALUKYAN ARCHITECTURE : ITS BEGINNINGS AT AIHOLE AND BADAMI

(c. 450 A.D. to c. 650 A.D.)

ALMOST at the same time that the Gupta shrines were being built in Central and Northern India, another and apparently independent movement, but having much the same implications, was making itself felt in a part of the Deccan. This was inspired and put into effect through the initiative and energy of the rising race of the Early Chalukyans, a power which began to assert itself in Southern India about the fifth century A.D. It was clearly the result of an enthusiasm which was religious in origin and in intensity of purpose. The first efforts of the Chalukyans are represented by a considerable group of stone-built shrines and temples at Aihole,[1] now a somewhat decayed village in the Bijapur district of Dharwar. The majority of these structures are Brahmanical, although a few are Jain, and all appear to have been erected in the period between A.D. 450 and 650. With the structural edifices at Aihole may be included a series of rock-cut pillared halls at the neighbouring town of Badami, executed in the latter half of the sixth century. So early, and so informative are they, especially at Aihole, that one is tempted to presume that here, on this relatively obscure site, the Hindu structural temple, not only took an introductory form, but, as far as this part of India is concerned, had its beginning. For in several of the examples it is possible to see the first emergence of the temple structure, if not its actual birth.

The temples at Aihole consist of some seventy buildings, about thirty of which are contained inside a walled and bastioned enclosure, while the remainder, owing to want of space, are disposed within its vicinity. It is, in fact, a town of temples. Unlike the contemporary Gupta structures, which are distributed over a wide area, the Early Chalukyan group is confined to this one locality, so that it was a comparatively restricted movement, but one of great vigour and promise. At Aihole, for the space of two centuries, the art of temple building must have been conducted with fervour and energy, when it finally ceased, the centre of religious activity being transferred, in the middle of the seventh century, to the town of Pattadakal, some fifteen miles distant, where a later phase of the style ensued (Chapter XIV). As with the Gupta temples those at Aihole have flat or slightly sloping roofs, but the latter in some instances are surmounted by a small upper story or tower (sikhara), which appears to have been subsequently added. The chief difference between the two types lies in the treatment of the structure in front of the sanctuary, which, in the Dharwar group, even in the earliest examples, assumed the character of a pillared assembly hall, or mandapa. The addition of this feature to the Aihole structures implies a step forward in the development of the completed temple design. None the less, judging from the varied forms of these Dharwar buildings, it is clear that no definite decision had yet been reached as to the type of structure most suitable for Brahmanical worship. As will be seen, it seems as if both priests and builders were seeking for a formula which would fulfil the requirements of the creed.

Mainly on account of its primitive appearance the temple known as Ladh Khan is considered to be the oldest building of the Aihole group, and has accordingly been assigned to the middle of the fifth century. There are others of much the same style, such as that named Kont-gudi, as well as two shrines in its immediate vicinity, but Ladh Khan is the larger and more significant. Partially obscured and defaced by modern accumulations, the general appearance of this structure as it now stands, is unimpressive. In shape it is a comparatively low, flat-roofed building, its plan being a square of fifty feet side, and over all rises a small supplementary story of later date. Three of its sides are completely enclosed by walls, two of which are relieved by perforated stone grilles, but from its fourth side, forming its eastern front, there is projected an open-pillared porch. The interior consists of a hall, which resembles a pillared pavilion, as it contains two square groups of columns, one within the other, thus providing a double aisle all round. A large stone effigy of a bull (nandi) almost fills the central bay, while at the far end is the cella, not, as is usual, a chamber leading off the main hall, but built within it, and against the back wall. With the exception of the Siva symbol of the nandi, which has been put into the building afterwards, for as the dedicatory block shows, it was erected as a Vishnu temple, it is clear that, as far as the body of the structure is concerned, this arrangement is original, no part of it is an afterthought, none of it was subsequently added. Yet it is also just as clear that, for the purpose for which it was constructed, it was not by any means a suitable building for the ends it had to serve, as it fulfils few of the conditions necessary for the performance of the Brahmanical ritual. The reason for such inappropriateness is that, although it was intended for a temple, it was an adaptation of another structure devised for an entirely different object. This was an edifice planned for secular and civic use, the santhagara, the village mote, moot, or meeting hall.

No examples of the santhagara have survived, but it appears as a very early institution in Indian village life[2]. From descriptions in the ancient texts, it was a structure specially built in order to enable the elders of the community to meet and settle matters relating to their social and economic intercourse. It was probably the only public building in the village, and took the form of a flat-roofed open edifice without walls, so planned that the deliberations within might be visible to, and shared by, the public outside. Persons taking part in the proceedings were seated in a specified order, with the president occupying "the chair" in the middle. It is not difficult to trace these conditions in the temple of Ladh Khan. The pillars of the open exterior are still visible, but are now converted into pilasters, as the

---

[1] Arch. Sur. Rep. 1907-8, p. 189.

[2] Cambridge History of India, Vol. I, p. 176.

spaces between have been filled in with masonry to provide seclusion for worship. Such an alteration shut out the light, so that the perforated windows became necessary. The seating arrangements, being no longer required in the main hall of the temple, were omitted, but were retained in the portico, as a concession to the public, like those in a church porch. It seems not improbable that this rather distinctive type of stone bench, or podium, the relics of which enclose the portico, was continued right round the mote-hall for the use of the members of the assembly while its sloping back, acting at the same time as a seat-rest, formed a dwarf wall to keep out animal intruders. But the most difficult problem was to decide on a suitable place in the scheme for the "holy of holies", which was solved by the simple expedient of inserting it as an additional interior chamber against the end wall. (Plate XLIV).

Apart from the extemporaneous nature of its composition, the Ladh Khan temple contains several notable features. Although the plain square shaft and bracket capital is a characteristic of its style, an elaboration of this occurs in the pilasters placed at each of the exterior angles of the building. The shafts of these taper slightly at their upper ends, above which is a "cushion" capital with an expanded floral abacus supporting the bracket. This is probably the first appearance of a particular form of capital of great importance, because it afterwards became almost universal in the architecture of Southern India, representing, as it does, the "order" of the Dravidian style. Another element in the temple, and one already alluded to, is the stone seat of the portico, with its sloping back-rest. Here is seen the beginning of the *asana*, which developed into an ornamental feature used with considerable effect in the entrance halls of many mediaeval temples. The construction of the roof is peculiar, and is the original of a system which continued to be practised for a long period, for even as late as the thirteenth century it is found in the Chalukyan-Hoysala temples of Mysore (Chapter XXIX). It consists of large flat slabs, near the joints of which grooves were chiselled, with a corresponding ridge at the edges. Covering the entire length of the joints, long narrow stones were placed fitting into the grooves, on the principle of ordinary roofing-tiles, but to a much larger scale. In the shape of these stone ribs there is, however, a suggestion of a timber origin, while the heavy overhanging eaves of the roof which, in some instances also show ribs underneath, have been derived from thatch. That the temple of Ladh Khan was the near product of a primitive movement is shown by the nature of its masonry, which is composed of great archaic looking blocks dressed to level beds and placed one upon the other without any cement or similar binding composition. The walls are of disproportionate strength, yet not uncouth, although denoting a wasteful use of material, significant of inexperienced workmanship. The character of the portico is typical of the style. The prodigious shafts and ponderous brackets of the pillars, and its low beetling cornice are expressive of exultant strength, while the carving on its exterior has an elemental, almost savage beauty, reminiscent of that on the buildings of the Anglo-saxons, which has the appearance of having been produced by the means of an axe. As in all the workmanship at Aihole, it is stark, strong, and enduring, the utterance of a robust and vigorous people having great potentialities but, at present, of undeveloped powers (Plate XLV).

In direct contrast with the architectural formation of the foregoing, but at the same time illustrating another experimental stage in the development of the temple structure, is the Durga temple at Aihole (Plates XLVI, Fig. 2, and XLVII Fig. 4, also XLIV and XLV). This example is a Brahmanical version of the Buddhist chaitya hall, adapted to suit the service of the former creed. It has already been established that Buddhist buildings of a similar type were not uncommon in many parts of India in the early centuries of the Christian era, while there is an actual example at Ter, not far distant from Dharwar (Chapter IX). The Durga temple, which most closely follows this model, was probably erected during the sixth century, and is an apsidal-ended structure measuring externally 60 feet by 36 feet, but in addition there is a large portico on its eastern front 24 feet in depth, so that its entire length is 84 feet. Raised on a particularly high and heavily moulded plinth or stereobate, the topmost tier of its flat roof is 30 feet from the ground; over the apse a short pyramidal tower, or *sikhara*, has been subsequently added. among other notable features in the design of the Durga temple is its peripteral exterior, or pteroma, a passage formed by the colonnade of a verandah which is carried right round the building, and joins up with similar pillars comprising the portico. This portico is approached by two flights of steps, one on each side of the front, and inside it is a vestibule, also pillared, within which is the entrance doorway. The interior consists of a hall 44 feet long, and divided by two rows of four pillars into a nave and two aisles, with an apsidal shaped cella, recalling the naos of the Greeks, at its far end; the aisles are continued round this cella as a processional passage. Light is obtained both for the central hall and for this passage by means of stone grilles, those at the sides being square and those in the apse circular in shape, and each is filled with an elegant carved and perforated pattern. The roof of the nave is raised higher than that of the side aisles, so that in almost every particular, not only in the treatment of its parts, but in the nature of the building as a whole, it is a literal re-statement of the Buddhist chaitya hall.

Another temple of the same kind is that of Huchchimalligudi, a smaller and simplified form of the preceding, for it has no apsidal end, and is without a peristylar verandah. As with the other examples at Aihole, to it has also been added a *sikhara* of later date. Unlike the richly carved Durga temple, it has a relatively simple exterior, the plainness of its walls being relieved by one pattern only, a singularly elegant motif of a floral vase, repeated in panels along the *asana* or sloping surface of the portico. The interior is a rectangular hall divided into nave and aisles by two rows of pillars, three on each side, with a processional passage carried around the square sanctum. Its plan is quite ordinary except that it contains one additional feature. This is a vestibule, or *antarala*. Hitherto in no temple has there been found any sign of an intermediate chamber in front of the cella, but in Huchchimalligudi something of the kind is beginning to appear, rather a primitive affair, but showing that some form of "pronaos" was becoming necessary. It consisted in this instance of introducing a masonry screen, with a doorway in the centre, between the two innermost pillars of the nave, thus providing an intermediate compartment between the main hall and the cella. It has every appearance of an afterthought, and is obviously an early attempt, and perhaps the first of its kind.

A temple having the appearance of being one of the last to be built at Aihole, and which is proved by an inscription recording its erection in A. D. 634, is the Jain temple of Meguti. In more than one particular it indicates that the building art by this time had made some progress. There is an improvement in the quality of the masonry, as smaller blocks of stone have been used, and other advances in technique are noticeable. More delicacy is shown in the treatment of the ornamentation, as seen in the design of the bracket capitals of the exterior pilasters in comparison with the coarse scrolls of the earlier buildings. Various refinements of a like nature denote increased experience in craftsmanship, but on the other hand there are few signs of any marked advance in the planning and general arrangements. This temple still retains the square pillared hall enclosing a central shrine which, together with other features, are evidences that the builders continued to be preoccupied with the mote-hall tradition, beyond which they had made little progress, so that no suitable temple scheme had yet been evolved. Portions of the building have been left unfinished, and the incomplete state of the carving serves to prove that it was the practice to chisel the plastic decoration on the structure after it was built, instead of preparing it beforehand in the quarry. This method may have been borrowed from the rock-cut technique, and much of the sculpture on the Aihole buildings, as well as the shaping of the masonry itself, savours of the natural rock treatment. As there are two minor examples of excavated temples, one Brahmanical and the other Jain,[1] in the immediate vicinity, such influence is not unlikely. That there was a guild of craftsman, highly skilled in rock-architecture, is manifested by a remarkable series of excavated temples at Badami, situated only fifteen miles away, and now to be described.

Badami, a corrupted form of the ancient "Vitapi", was a stronghold of the founders of the Chalukyan kingdom early in the sixth century. Picturesquely nestling at the foot of steep cliffs and by the side of a small lake, it contains several buildings of an early date, but what is most interesting is a series of four pillared halls excavated in the scarp of a hill overlooking the south-east side of the town. Three of these are Brahmanical, and one is Jain; in that numbered 3 of the former there is an inscription to the effect that it was prepared in A. D. 578 in the time of Mangalisa, the son of Pulakesi I, who selected the site for his capital. Such a precise and authentic date not only provides a valuable landmark in the history of rock-architecture as a whole but also denotes that this particular series of pillared galleries was among the earliest of its kind, for the only other rock-cut shrines upto the present belonging to the Brahmanical faith were the Gupta examples at Udaigiri in Bhopal State (Chapter X), and the somewhat elementary productions at Aihole. The group at Badami proves, by the high standard of the workmanship, that considerable progress had been made in this form of architectural expression in such a short interval. These four temples are connected by a causeway inclined up the face of the cliff, and each appears originally to have had an open court in front; in addition to the forecourt, that of the largest is enclosed by a structural retaining wall, the approach being by means of a flight of steps and through a doorway composed of excellent ashlar masonry, the whole carried out with a simple dignity recalling a good classical model. In their general appearance and interior arrangements these excavated temples are all of the same type, as each includes three features, a pillared verandah, a columned hall, and a small square cella cut deep into the rock. There is no outstanding architectural effect attempted in the exterior, the facade showing merely the range of pillars forming the verandah, save that a running border of grotesque figures in the form of rollicking urchins (*gana*), probably

gnomes or earth-spirits, is carved in relief on the stylobate of each (Plate XLVII, Fig. 2). In contrast to this unassuming, yet serviceable frontage, is the treatment of the interior, on the enrichment of which the rock-carver has concentrated his utmost skill, so that the spectator, passing from the bright sunlight outside into its darkened pillared halls, finds himself bewildered by the wealth of symbolism and mystical imagery which surrounds him on all sides, and appears to extend indefinitely into the interior gloom.

Of such excellent quality is the sculpture and decoration generally, that, as in the case of the Gupta temples, their forms emphasise the progress that had been made in the plastic art of the time, in comparison with that of architecture. Moreover the wealth of carving conceals to some extent the shortcomings of the plan. For there is an uncertainty and indecision in the design of these sanctuaries as a whole, which can only be explained by the fact that the arrangements of the Brahmanical temple were still unevolved, the correct shape and disposition of its parts having not yet been assured. This is shown by the inapt proportions of the pillared halls, which end at their further extremity so abruptly that the compartment has the appearance of being truncated, or that its further progress had been stopped for want of explicit directions as to its form, a condition particularly noticeable in No. 3. Such uncertainty, in its turn, may have affected the columniation, which is not always symmetrical and, denotes some hesitation in the grouping of the pillars. For instance there is a wider interval between the two middle rows, suggesting, yet hardly confirming, a central aisle, and in No. 3 the idea of a double colonnade was possibly derived from a similar disposition of the pillars seen in the temple of Ladh Khan at Aihole. On the other hand the proportions of the interior may indicate a concession to the exigencies of the rock-cut mode, there being some correlation between the wide frontage and the shallow depth, the former giving the maximum light, and the latter the maximum space which this would efficiently illuminate. In these excavated temples the pillar is the most important element in the composition, and on their design depends much of the architectural effect. Most of the shafts of the columns are square in section, although those forming the inner colonnade of No. 3 are many-sided. Of the capitals to the pillars two kinds predominate, one in which the bracket is the chief feature, and another which is cushion-shaped. Combinations of the two forms are also seen. Above, are massive entablatures, while cross-beams supported by gryphons, having a curious resemblance to Gothic gargoyles, divide the ceilings into sunk panels like coffers each containing a carved pattern replete with symbolical devices. (Plate XLVIII, Fig. 1).

It seems probable that the Brahmanical halls at Badami were all excavated within a relatively short space of time, but the one belonging to the Jains was added nearly a century later. Of the three former, the largest and most important example bearing the dated inscription, and dedicated to Vishnu, was first begun being followed by No. 2, the smallest, also, Vaishnavite, which is only half its size; the last to be produced was No. 1, in this instance a Sivaite shrine which, in its dimensions, is intermediate to the other two. Although in comparison with other rock-cut examples, those at Badami are not large, yet the proportions of No. 3 are not inconsiderable. The exterior width of its verandah, or what corresponds to a facade, is nearly 70 feet, and is composed of a colonnade of six pillars in addition to a pilaster at each end.

---

[1] *Cave Temples of India* by Fergusson and Burgess, pp. 404 and 491.

Its extreme depth into the rock, including the cella, is 65 feet, but the assembly hall with its 14 columns only takes up half of this, thus making the shape, of the chamber twice as wide as it is deep, not a commendable ratio in view of its position in the plan. The average height of the whole is 15 feet. Every portion is richly carved, either with figures in such high relief as to be almost in the round, or with ornamental patterns so delicately chiselled as to resemble line engravings. Most striking of all is the treatment of the portico pillars on which considerable imaginative effort has been expended. Over the moulded cushion-capitals massive brackets have been superimposed, each sculptured into a figure-composition of great boldness. In addition to these, on the outer side and supporting the under-frame of the eave or cornice, struts have been projected, carved into images of hippogryphs and other fabulous monsters similar to those which seven centuries earlier, were cut out of the rock to enrich the *gumpha* of Manchapuri at Udaigiri in Orissa. (Chapter VI). This under-frame of the cornice was apparently suggested by the wooden battens which support a thatched roof.

Apart from being smaller, the two other Brahmanical temples of the series differ from the preceding in the arrangement of the pillars within the columned hall. In each instance the columns are eight in number and so placed as to be equidistant from each other, except in the spacing of those in the central aisle, where the intercolumniation is slightly wider. Although this alignment of the pillars is an improvement on that of No. 3, it still suggests some uncertainty as to their correct disposition. The facade of each of the smaller temples consists of a colonnade of four pillars forming the verandah on the inside of which are two pillars at the entrance to the central hall. The exterior of No. 1 is 42 feet wide, while that of No. 2 is 33 feet, and in comparing them relatively with No. 3, they both penetrate further into the rock, the entire depth of No. 1 being over 50 feet from its front steps to the back wall of the cella. It is from the more considered nature of their plans, and also from the restrained character of the sculpture, that the slightly latter date has been attributed, the latter showing itself particularly in certain refinements in the mouldings, as for instance those around the entrance to the pillared hall of No. 2, which are astonishingly modern in treatment.

Turning to the Jain example, at Badami, which may have been executed in the middle of the following century, it is apparent that it was inspired by the Brahmanical group, and is practically a copy of these adapted to suit the Jain ritual. Its dimensions are less than the others as the facade with its four pillars and bracket capitals is only 31 feet wide, and the depth of the whole is but 16 feet. Although an interesting production, it merely testifies to a temporary revival in the seventh century, of the rock-cutter's art in this locality, after which it appears to have entirely ceased.

REFERENCES

Cousens, H., *Ancient Temples of Aihole, Arch. Sur. of Ind., An. Rep.* 1907-8 Cal. 1911.

„　　„　*Chalukyan Architecture, Arch. Sur. of India,* 1926.

CHAPTER XII

THE ROCK-CUT ARCHITECTURE OF THE MAHAYANA BUDDHISTS

(cir. A. D. 450 to 642)

STIMULATED also by the cultural conditions and atmosphere of toleration created during the Gupta regime, the Buddhists at the same time revived their architectural activity, particularly in its rock-cut aspect, in which they had already shown a marked proclivity. No doubt its exponents persisted in this form of production as it was a method with which they had long been familiar and also probably, because it presented no serious constructional difficulties. This Mahayana rock-cut architecture is restricted to certain specified localities in Western India, chiefly in the hilly country of the Ghats, such as Ajanta, Ellora, Aurangabad, and a few scattered retreats of lesser importance in the same region. At Ajanta, as described in Chapter V, a Hinayana order of priests had towards the beginning of the Christian era, excavated a group of large halls and monastic abodes, after which a quiescent period of four centuries intervened, when this Buddhist hierarchic settlement again sprang into life. On the other Buddhist site, that at Ellora as distinct from Ajanta, no earlier excavations had been made, it was previously unoccupied, so that here an entirely new undertaking was initiated by the Buddhists, and eventually developed, under the Jains and Brahmans into the most important and comprehensive range of rock-cut monuments in India. The Mahayana Buddhist movements, both at Ajanta and Ellora, appear to have begun simultaneously about the middle of the fifth century, but the other group, that near Aurangabad, which was probably an off-shoot from Ellora, may be dated slightly later. After the seventh century, as far as the Buddhists were concerned, this form of expression ceased, in fact this date marks the termination of Buddhists architectural effort in India, with the exception of the brick-built monasteries of the north, as produced in Bihar and the Gangetic plain. (Chapter IX). Although the rock-cut monasteries of the Buddhists at Ellora are of great interest, the real glories of the site are the subsequent works of the other religious communities, the Hindus and the Jains, as will be shown later (Chapter XV).

In its broad sense, and in the formation of its productions, this later phase of Buddhist rock-cut architecture displays no marked departure from that of the earlier period, as the Mahayana priestly community still adhered to the two types of religious institutions established by convention, namely, the chaitya hall, or temple, and the vihara, or monastery. It was, therefore, not so much in the content, as in the stylistic treatment of these that a dissimilarity is observable, such changes as were made being largely conditioned by the changes in the nature of the creed. The most noticeable transformation, and one which gives a key to the whole movement, may be seen in the presentation of its iconography, as the deification of the Buddha permitted the introduction of his image into the art, an opportunity for statuary sometimes of colossal proportions, of which the Mahayana sculptors took full advantage. In its architectural arrangements, the most characteristic of these two types, of excavated halls, that containing the chaitya, was but little affected by the changes in the Buddhist doctrine, as it continued to maintain its traditional formation, of which the essential elements were the nave, aisles, apse, stupa, and vaulted roof. The same however cannot be said of the other class of rock-cut hall, the vihara, which underwent considerable alteration. In this monastic type of hostel an innovation which affected both the plan and intention and one which at once distinguishes the Mahayana vihara from the Hinayana, is the change produced in the disposition of the innermost range of cells. The appropriation of these cells originally serving as dormitories for the monks, and their conversion into sanctuaries for the reception of images of the Buddha, is significant of the alteration in the belief as a whole. It meant, firstly, that the vihara was now fulfilling the functions of both abbey and church, secondly, that relic worship was being supplanted by image worship, and thirdly, that the dominating cult of Hinduism was not only influencing the Buddhist doctrine, but also vitally affecting its art and architectural practice.

The most notable of these monastic retreats, that of Ajanta, provides an excellent illustration of the evolution of Buddhist rock architecture, as here it can be followed throughout its entire course. In addition to its architectural qualities, the situation of this group is romantic and inspiring as it consists of a range of excavated galleries extending in a sickle-shaped curve along the face of the cliff for over a third of a mile, and overhanging the waters of a pretty stream, cascading through the ravine below. Here are aligned twenty-eight monastic halls of various sizes and they have been numbered in sequence, beginning with No. 1 at the western extremity, and finishing with No. 28 at the eastern end. Four of these are chaitya halls or temples, and the remainder consist of viharas or monasteries. (Plate XXV). As previously explained, taken as a whole they represent two independent movements, separated by a hiatus of over four centuries. The first group, comprising Nos. 8, 9, 10, 12 and 13, as they belong to the much earlier Hinayana system, has been already described (Chapters V and VI). The others, twenty-three in number, illustrate the later of Mahayana movement, and form the series now under reference. Begun towards the middle of the fifth century they were in course of production for a period of two hundred years, the excavation of one hall after another, at irregular intervals, being carried on during the whole of this time. Then, as shown by the unfinished condition of the last example, the work came to an end in A. D. 642, a date which marks the death of the Chalukyan king Pulakesin II and the conquest of the country by the Pallava king Narasimhavarman I.

The Mahayana rock-cut halls at Ajanta resolve themselves into five groups, according to the following circumstances, and order of execution. When about 450 A.D., this monastic retreat was revived and began its second phase, for a time the two now ancient Hinayana chaitya halls (Nos. 9 and 10), sufficed for the actual service but the monastic dwellings being inadequate, more cells became necessary to provide for the additional priests. The earliest group

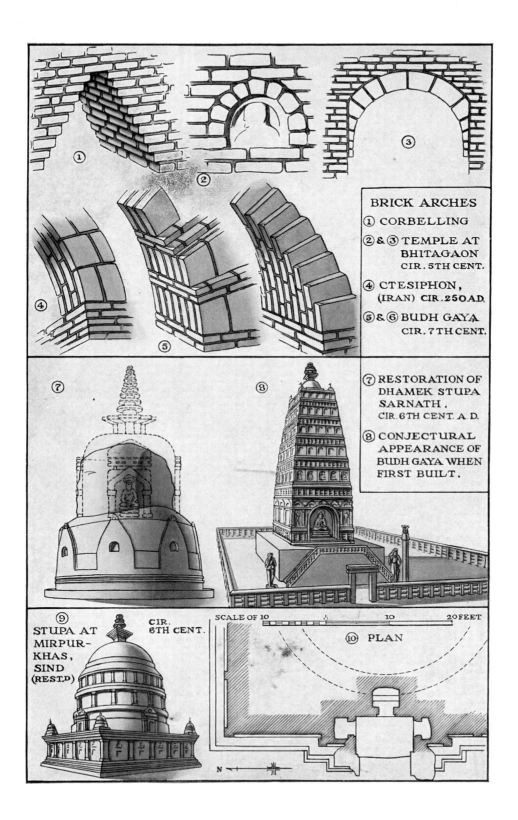

BRICK ARCHES

① CORBELLING

② & ③ TEMPLE AT
   BHITAGAON
     CIR. 5TH CENT.

④ CTESIPHON,
   (IRAN) CIR. 250 A.D.

⑤ & ⑥ BUDH GAYA
     CIR. 7TH CENT.

⑦ RESTORATION OF
   DHAMEK STUPA
   SARNATH.
     CIR. 6TH CENT. A.D.

⑧ CONJECTURAL
   APPEARANCE OF
   BUDH GAYA WHEN
   FIRST BUILT.

⑨ STUPA AT
MIRPUR-
KHAS,
SIND
(REST.D)

CIR.
6TH CENT.

SCALE OF 10   10   20 FEET

⑩ PLAN

N

FORMS OF
EARLY TEMPLES

① UDAIGIRI
BHOPAL. C. 400 A.D.

② GUPTA TEMPLE
SANCHI. C. 415 A.D
[BUDDHIST]

③ LADH KHAN
AIHOLE. C. 450 A.D.

④ DURGA TEMPLE
AIHOLE. C. 500 A.D.

⑤ BHITARGAON.
NEAR CAWNPUR
C. 400 A.D. [BRICK]

⑥ DEOGARH NEAR
JHANSI C. 500 A.D.

Fig. 1
Jubbulpore Dist. : Temple at Tigawa ; c. 5th cent. A.D.

Fig. 2
Sanchi, Gupta Temple (No. 17) : c. 5th cent. A.D.

Fig. 1
Sarnath, near Benares ; detail of Dhamek Stupa ; c. 6th cent. A.D.

Fig. 2   Fig. 3
Jhansi Dist. : Details of Temple at Deogarh; c. 6th cent. A.D.

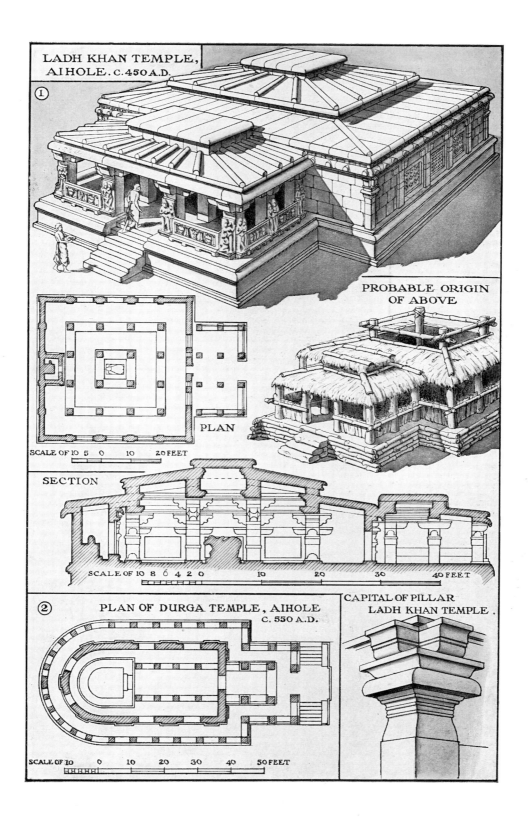

LADH KHAN TEMPLE,
AIHOLE. C. 450 A.D.

①

PROBABLE ORIGIN
OF ABOVE

PLAN

SCALE OF 10 5 0 10 20 FEET

SECTION

SCALE OF 10 8 6 4 2 0 10 20 30 40 FEET

② PLAN OF DURGA TEMPLE, AIHOLE
C. 550 A.D.

SCALE OF 10 0 10 20 30 40 50 FEET

CAPITAL OF PILLAR
LADH KHAN TEMPLE.

Fig. 1.   View from South-west.

Fig. 2.   Detail of Porch.
Aihole, Dharwar : Ladh Khan Temple ; c. A.D. 450.

Fig. 1.   View from South-west.

Fig. 2.   Passage (pteroma) round exterior
Aihole, Dharwar: Durga Temple, A.D. 500.

Fig. 1
Aihole, Dharwar: Durga Temple, portico; c. A.D. 500.

Fig. 2
Badami, Bijapur Dist.   Rock-cut Temple No. 2; 6th cent. A.D.

therefore of the series, viharas Nos. 11, 7 and 6, in that order, were added. These sufficed for a time, but, after some fifty years, still further accommodation for the priests was demanded, and also another and more appropriate hall of worship became desirable. This brought the second group into existence, consisting of Nos. 15 to 20, probably the finest of the whole series; it included also the small, but elaborated chaitya hall No. 19. (Plate XLVIII). A little later, a third and separate group was begun on the extreme west of the line, being partially detached from the others owing to an intervening water course. Of this group, viharas numbered 21 to 25 were first cut, followed by chaitya hall No. 26, all probably dating from the end of the sixth century. As time went on, and the popularity of the order increased, even more monastic hostels were needed, and so early in the seventh century the fourth group was added on the eastern extremity, thus accounting for viharas numbered 1 to 5. Finally, the last group was undertaken, consisting of two more viharas at the western end and opposite extremity of the line. These are numbered 27 and 28, and it is obvious from their partly completed state that the workmen were disturbed in the course of their operations, dropped their tools, and never returned. This took place towards the middle of the seventh century, when the site was abandoned for ever in consequence of the historical event referred to above.

The approximate detailed dates therefore of the entire movement at Ajanta are as follows :—

HINAYANA SERIES (2nd century B. C. to 2nd century A.D.):

Vihara No. 8, chaitya hall No. 9, chaitya hall No. 10, Viharas Nos. 12 and 13.

INTERVAL (2nd century A.D., to cir. 450 A.D.).

MAHAYANA SERIES (A.D. 450 to A.D. 642):

Viharas Nos. 11, 7 and 6 (A.D. 450-500).

Viharas Nos. 15, 16, 17, 18, 20 and chaitya hall No. 19 (cir. A.D. 550).

Viharas Nos. 21 to 25, and chaitya hall No. 26 (A.D. 550 to 600).

Viharas Nos. 1 to 5 (A.D. 600-25).

Viharas No. 27 and 26 (A.D. 625-42).

Such is the conjectural sequence outlining the execution of this monastic retreat, which in its high time must have presented a scene of exceptional spiritual and artistic activity. Now silence broods over the whole valley, the rock face is animated only by the brilliant sunshine, and within the pillared halls are mere whispers and shadows. At its most flourishing period, Ajanta must have accommodated as many as two hundred monks, and supplementing the monastic establishment, throughout much of its history, there would have been a considerable community of artisans and craftsmen engaged in the work of quarrying out, sculpturing, and decorating with mural paintings its numerous and extensive galleries. Of the manner in which the works were executed or the personnel of those employed, whether some of them were artist-monks, or all were lay exponents of their various crafts, can only be a matter of conjecture. But, whatever the system, in this remote valley there existed for some two centuries a school of art of marked power, religious intensity and originality. So much so that it seems not improbable Ajanta was the the fountain head of a movement that influence Buddhist art in no little degree wherever that creed flourished, extending even as far as China and Japan.

The earliest sub-group in the Mahayana style at Ajanta, consisting of three viharas numbered 11, 7 and 6, forming the initial productions of the later movement, are examples of a transition stage, when the threads of the previous effort were again being taken up. Although differing materially from the original Hinayana type, they still clearly owe something to wooden forms, especially in the arrangement of the pillars in the main hall which seems to be an adaptation of materials used in a structural prototype. In No. 11, the first to be cut, the design of the four pillars suggests a square shed, or similar shelter, occupying the centre of the courtyard of the structural building (Plate XLIX, Fig. 2), while No. 7, next in order of production shows how two such erections placed side by side, became necessary in a structure of larger dimensions (Fig. 3). The lower story of No. 6 which may have been cut shortly afterwards, combines the system of the four central pillars of the previous examples, with the plan of another series of pillars all round the main hall, the latter corresponding to those supporting a verandah, a complex and almost confused arrangement which was not repeated (Fig. 4). The sequence of experiments indicated in this group led to the final conception seen in the upper story of No. 6 which contains a colonnade on all four sides, a satisfactory and logical system of columniation adopted in all the subsequent vihara halls (Fig. 5). It is, however, to some of the details in the lower story of this vihara to which attention is specially directed, as it has several unusual features. This particular example appears originally to have had a verandah on its exterior which has crumbled away, so that its facade now presents a doorway, with a rectangular window on either side. At some early date the doorway has been recut and slightly enlarged, but much of the old work still remains. The doorway has the overhanging lintel characteristic of the early Gupta style (c. 450 A.D.) with a recess at its outer extremities, most probably intended as a receptacle for a figure, in wood, of the river-god. Below the recess is a nook-shaft with vase-capital, base, and a pedestal in the shape of a caryatid and an elephant, the whole forming a singularly artistic composition. In the interior of this vihara, the grouping of sixteen pillars, contained within a hall approximately 54 ft. square produces a congested appearance, modified to some extent by the simplicity of their design. These pillars are unlike any others at Ajanta, as little more than a simple moulding suffices for the capital, while the shafts are chamfered, and they have no bases.

After a period of experiment, as shown in the diversified arrangement of the first group of the Mahayana viharas, the plan of the monastic hall became more or less standardized, although the detailed treatment of the succeeding groups shows considerable variety and fertility of invention. Of the remaining examples, the finest are Nos. 1, 4, 16, 17, 21 and 23, the high water mark of the whole series being attained in No. 16, dating from early in the sixth century, while the supreme efflorescence of the style may be studied in the carved and painted embellishment of No. 1, which was probably produced a century later (c. A.D. 625). Both Nos. 1 and 16 are of approximately the same size and designed on much the same lines, each having an exterior verandah 65 ft. long, a main hall 65 ft. square containing a surrounding aisle formed by a colonnade of twenty pillars, such being the average dimensions of the Ajanta viharas. Around the hall and verandah of No. 16, is recessed a series of sixteen square cells, and on the innermost side, cut deep into the rock, is a spacious sacrarium containing a seated figure of the Buddha.

Although the Mahayana viharas at Ajanta show many pleasing features, and are wonderful examples of the rock-cut mode, they are easily surpassed in design and execution by the chaitya halls. There are two of these Buddhist temples in the series, of which No. 19 is the earlier and finer. This chaitya hall is not large, the entire height of the exterior being 38 ft. with a width of 32 feet, while its interior measures 46 ft. by 24 ft., so that in its proportions it is not dissimilar from Trinity Chapel in Canterbury Cathedral, with the exception of the lesser height which is only 24 feet. It corresponds also in size to the already existing chaitya hall No. 10, the smaller and later of the Hinayana series, and, as with the other Mahayana example (chaitya hall No. 26), it follows the earlier type in having flat ceilings to its side aisles. Chaitya hall No. 19 appears to have originally possessed a singularly well-proportioned entrance court with side-chapels, a scheme which serves as an attractive prelude to the facade. This facade has only one doorway, instead of the usual three, but in front of it is projected a pillared portico of such elegant design as to give its character to the whole. The roof of the portico forms a massive entablature, the upper surface of which was probably used as a minstrels' gallery, and at the back rises the chaitya window, the entire height of the facade being 38 ft., with a width of 32 ft.

The interior is divided into nave and aisles by a colonnade of fifteen pillars, in addition to two at the entrance, all closely set, and eleven feet high. These pillars have richly patterned shafts, with cushion capitals and ponderous brackets above. Supported by the brackets is a broad triforium or frieze, five feet wide, divided into panels, and continued right round the nave. Over all rises the vaulted roof, with the ribs no longer additions in wood, but carved out of the rock itself. Every portion of the scheme is elaborately sculptured, particularly the bracket capitals and the triforium frieze above. Images of the Buddha, empanelled, canopied, or niched, are the leading feature, but, in contrast to these static figures, are groups of aerial beings, some mounted on winged animals, others in full flight, the whole forming an animated conception of great charm. But the interior is merely the setting or background for the stupa which it enshrines. This sacred emblem stands on a slightly elevated platform within the centre of the apse. At each side of the step leading to the platform erect and alongside the corresponding pillar, was originally sculptured a life sized statue of the stupa guardian. Although they have now almost entirely crumbled away, the effect when complete of these two attendant figures, silent and impassive as the living rock out of which they were carved, must have been impressive indeed. The stupa is a composite monolith some 22 ft. high, its apex therefore nearly touching the vault of the apse above. In spite of the double dome forming the body, and other complexities, the traditional shape of the tumulus may still be traced, but the stupa as a whole, has been so elongated and elaborated that it bears really little resemblance to the low semi-spheroidal brick mound from which it was anciently derived. The face of the domical portion has now been converted into a pillared niche and canopy, its shallow recess occupied by a large image of the Buddha in high relief. Above the dome rises a tall finial in tiers, consisting of a *harmika*, three diminishing parasols, and a vase, the last being almost lost in the sombre gloom of the roof. The soaring height and general intention of this stupa recall the tapering spires of reliquaries found in some Continental cathedrals. (Plates XLIX and L).

The other chaitya hall of the series is No. 26, and was excavated at least fifty years later than the preceding. Although an exceedingly fine and rich production, it is clear that the style had arrived at its adequate fulfilment, the turning point had been reached, and no further progress in this particular form of architecture could be expected. Such an inference is established by the fact that there is not that correlation, or equilibrium of its parts which is so satisfying in the earlier example. It is approximately one third larger in its dimensions, as it measures 68 ft. long, 36 ft. wide, and 31 ft. high, while, besides the two at the entrance, it contains 26 columns, each 12 ft. in height. The architectural treatment of this hall is in much the same style as No. 19 but the ornamentation has been increased, as may be noticed in the additional member introduced into the capital of the pillar, the recessing of the panels, with the elaboration generally of the triforium and in the insertion of decorative features wherever a space offered. The stupa is an imposing conception, overlaid with a wealth of carving, but as a whole it lacks the graceful proportions and rhythmic effect of the earlier type. Externally this chaitya hall has been much damaged, as a broad pillared portico which extended across its entire front has disappeared, thus detracting considerably from the appearance of the facade. Inside the portico it is entered by three doorways, and above is the chaitya window against a background of richly carved figure compositions. There is almost an excess of sculpture in this example, most of it of a slightly monotonous order, which, together with the method of its execution are further proofs that the decline of the style was imminent. (Plate L. Fig. 1).

In these later examples of chaitya hall and in fact in the Mahayana rock-architecture as a whole, not only the wooden construction itself is discarded, but much of its imitative character has been eliminated. It is true a timber framework with its curved transoms is retained in the opening of the chaitya window, and the ribs of the vaulted roof have every appearance of woodwork, but, except for these, the wooden attribution has lost its previous emphasis. The workmen employed in such productions were now realizing the differences in the material they were handling, and were becoming increasingly aware of the fact that each medium demanded a different technique. Instead, therefore, of copies in the rock of slender wooden beams and carpenters' joinery as in the Hinayana examples, advantage was taken of the solid rock to effect an appearance of mass, weight, and volume, carving being freely distributed to enrich and lighten the whole. The later halls thus present a definite style of architecture, more flexible, sophisticated, and plastically ornate, than any which had hitherto prevailed. Much of this was brought about by the cultural sublimation which had developed in the consciousness of the people themselves, whose experience had now become more matured, they were no longer mere imitators but had acquired a reasoned aesthetic sense. The Ajanta Mahayana rock-cut monasteries display evidences of a growing appreciation of architectural values, and mark a distinct advance in the art evolution of the country.

Although contemporary, and, in a direct line only some sixty miles distant, it is possible to detect in the Buddhist rock-architecture at Ellora, a slight difference in character from the corresponding series at Ajanta. Both monastic establishments being more or less self-contained, each may have had its own particular system, or doctrine, which reflected in the style. Moreover there is a difference in the terrain of the two places, a circumstance which no doubt affected their architectural treatment. For instead of the almost vertical cliff as at Ajanta, the halls of Ellora are excavated out of a ridge of low hills, pushed up from the vast plateau of the Deccan. At Ellora the Buddhists were the first of the three great religious communities to occupy this site, so that their monasteries are in the most favourable position, being at the southern end of a scarp of the plateau, where it throws out a horn to the west. Here they practised their religion for some two centuries, from A.D. 450 to 650 during which period the group of twelve rock-cut halls belonging to the Buddhist creed were produced. This series may be resolved into two sub-groups, Nos. 1 to 5 known as the "Dhedwada group", and a group slightly later in date consisting of Nos. 6 to 12. Each sub-group comprises a prayer-hall and its attached monasteries. In the case of the earlier examples, the monks appear to have conducted their principal worship in the large pillared hall known as the Mahanwada (No. 5), an unusual type, as it consists of a combination of prayer-hall and monastery. In the later group the religious ceremonies were probably more according to convention, and performed in the chaitya hall No. 10. Save for the great hall of the Mahanwada, which is of a special character the monasteries of the earlier group differ very little from those at Ajanta. They are single-storied excavations, entered through a verandah, with a large central hall having a shrine-chamber or cella beyond. Of this type No. 2 is the most noteworthy, as it has a square hall of 48 feet side, with a colonnade of twelve massive pillars forming an aisle all round. Where it is exceptional is that in place of the usual series of cells leading out of this hall, a side gallery has been added, formed by a supplementary row of four pillars, a plan which has produced, on each side of the hall, a kind of iconostasis, with its back wall divided into compartments containing groups of statuary in bold relief. Such a departure in the interior arrangements of the monastery, is further evidence of the conversion of the hostel with its residential cells into a house of prayer, brought about by the changes effected in the creed.

An architectural feature which emerges about this time, is a type of pillar and capital thoroughly distinctive of the rock-cut technique. Of massive proportions, the lower half, which corresponds to the shaft is a plain square prism, while the upper portion is round in section, vertically fluted, and elaborated into a capital consisting of the compressed "cushion" forms. This became the dominating type of capital and pillar and together with the other type already referred to as the "vase and foliage", constituted the two "orders" in all subsequent rock-cut architecture. So different in every aspect are these two capitals—the "cushion" and the "vase",—that it is clear they are the outcome of two entirely different but parallel traditions.

Of the other halls in this early group, the Mahanwada, or No. 5, is by far the largest and most remarkable, and, owing to its uncommon design, is in a class by itself. It measures 117 feet deep by 58½ feet wide, exclusive of two fair sized side recesses, and is divided into a nave and two aisles by twenty four "cushion" pillars in two rows. In addition it has twenty three cells opening out of its sides. At the far end is a transverse vestibule, beyond which is a square cella containing a seated figure of the Buddha with his attendants. Down the centre of the nave, two low, narrow and parallel platforms have been left in the rock, extending the whole length of the hall, an unusual feature, of which there is only one other instance, namely the "Maharaja" or "Durbar Hall" at Kanheri ; from this

circumstance it may be inferred that, although many miles apart, both were designed for the same form of ceremonial usage. What the usage was is revealed by the Lamaistic services in the monasteries (gumphas) of Sikhim and Tibet, obviously a survival of those which prevailed in Buddhist India centuries before. There the priests (lamas) sit in two lines facing one another on raised platforms, the abbot on a higher seat at the head and on the right, with the altar and holy image beyond, all of which conforms to the Mahanwada plan. It was evidently in order to suit a similar type of ritual that the Mahanwada prayer-hall at Ellora, and the "Durbar Hall" at Kanheri were designed in such a manner.

The second, and presumably slightly later sub-group of Buddhist excavations at Ellora, consisting of Nos. 6 to 12, is notable for the extent and size of the monasteries, and the character of its chaitya hall. Two of the monasteries are by far the largest of their kind, as they are the only examples in three stories, and rise to a height of nearly 50 feet, with ample courtyards in front. Of these, No. 12, known as Tin Thal, or "Three Stories" is the most striking, and also the most commodious, as it has sufficient cells to lodge at least forty priests, while its assembly halls would provide, at the same time, room for congregations of many times that number. This capacious hostel and abbey combined is entered through a rock-cut gateway, which opens on to a quadrangle 108 feet wide, and 60 feet deep at its centre opposite the entrance, on the far side of which the facade rises in three equal tiers, each story being indicated externally by a verandah on eight square piers. The plain appearance of the exterior, with its bare entrance yard, is unusual, the whole being practically devoid of any vestige of ornament, recalling that of a severely utilitarian tenement house. As a contrast to this austere character of the facade, on entering the monastery it will be found that the interior of each hall is enriched with considerable sculpture, and interest in the production as a whole revives when it is found that each story is differently treated and each is of no little aesthetic and architectural merit. Beginning with the ground floor, access is obtained through a pillared verandah, 112 feet across and 43 feet deep, divided transversely into three aisles by means of three rows of columns of eight each, making 24 pillars in all. Extending into the rock at right angles to the verandah, is another pillared hall 35 feet across and 44 feet deep having three aisles of three pillars each. At the far end of this vestibule-hall is the shrine-chamber, a cella 23 feet across and 15 feet deep, containing a seated image of the Buddha, with other images in relief on the walls. Doorways in the sides of these halls lead to small square cells some twelve in number. In one of the cells on the right side, facing the facade, is a staircase for ascending to the floor above, or first story.

This first story of the Tin Thal comprises one large compartment 112 feet across, 72 feet deep, and 11½ feet high, divided into five transverse aisles by five rows of pillars of eight each, thus producing a hall of forty pillars. On the far side are two supplementary pillars fronting a vestibule 38 feet wide by 17 feet deep, beyond which is the cella, a square chamber approximately 20 feet wide enshrining a seated figure of the Buddha. The walls all round the hall and vestibule are recessed for the reception of Buddhist images in high relief. Staircases on either side of this great hall lead to the second or top story, where another form of interior will be found. Here is a verandah of eight pillars as already noticed in the description of the facade, behind which is a hall, cruciform in plan, as it consists of a nave driven axially into the rock, flanked by a wing or transept on each side cut at right angles. The nave is a rectangular hall 78 feet deep and 36 feet wide divided longitudinally by two rows of pillars of five each. Each wing is also divided transversely, by two rows of pillars of three each the width of the whole being 118 feet, exclusive of the cells, 18 in number which open out of it on all sides. At the far end of the central hall is the cella, a square chamber of 20 feet wide containing the usual seated Buddha image with standing attendant figures round the walls.

The other three-storied vihara of this group No. 11, misnamed the Do Thal, or "Two Stories" (as until recently one story was hidden under an accumulation of earth), is not so large or so spacious in its interior arrangements as the foregoing, but it is planned on somewhat similar lines. Where it differs is in the shallow nature of its halls, some of which are verandahs only, and there are no cells for the monks. Another vihara of the same group No. 6, has more interest because of its transverse plan, which is not dissimilar to the uppermost story of the Tin Thal, but without its system of pillars. The shape of this particular monastery indicates that it may have been a preliminary effort at a cruciform system, an arrangement which was adopted and elaborated later by the Hindus in the halls of the Dumar Lena and of Elphanta. In some of these viharas notably in the Tin Thal there will be found the most precise and mathematically accurate craftsmanship throughout the entire range of rock-architecture. Lines are straighter, angles more correct, and surfaces more true than in any other examples, indicating that at Ellora in the seventh century, rock-architecture, in its technical aspect, had reached its culmination.

There now remains of this sub-group, the most notable production of the whole Buddhist series at Ellora, namely chaitya hall No. 10, commonly known as the Visvakarma, or "Lord of the Arts", as it has the reputation of being specially frequented by artisans particularly those of the carpenter caste. As a more orthodox type of Buddhist prayer-house, and the only one of its kind on the site, it resembles in many respects the two almost contemporary Mahayana chaitya halls at Ajanta previously described, although it is appreciably larger, as inside it measures 85 feet by 44 feet, with a height of 34 feet. It is not quite so richly carved as the Ajanta examples, as the twenty-eight pillars of the "vase and foliage" order, which divide it into nave and aisles, are, for the most part, comparatively plain, but otherwise its interior is planned and decorated on much the same general principles. The central feature of the hall, the stupa, manifests in its particular treatment a still further stage of development, showing that, although retaining the shape of a reliquary, it becomes little more than a substantial foundation for the support of a large projecting shrine or niche, containing a seated figure of the Buddha. As a whole, the interior of the Visvakarma chaitya hall marks a logical step in the evolution of the Buddhist house of prayer, its appearance changing gradually but surely in response to the changing character of the creed.

Although such a conversion may have had only a moderate effect on the inside of this temple, it shows itself with marked emphasis in the treatment of the exterior. This exterior is prefaced by a fairly large formal courtyard surrounded by a pillared arcade, that on the two sides providing

the verandahs to apartments in their rear. At the far end rises the facade of the temple itself, and it is here that the most expressive innovation is discernible. Hitherto the great sun-window had been an important constituent attribute of the Buddhist chaitya hall exterior from time immemorial, the horse-shoe arch over the entrance meaning something more than an architectural motif, it was an emblem of deep traditional significance. In the facade of the Visvakarma, it is true, some recollection of this experience still lingers, but the result is reduced and transformed until it becomes meaningless. As a whole the scheme of the frontage is resolved into two parts by a broad entablature carried horizontally across the centre, the upper surface of which acted as a minstrels' gallery similar to many of the previous examples. Nor are the arrangements of the lower portion of the facade at all exceptional, as it consists mainly of a range of pillars comprising the portico, not unlike those of the latest chaitya hall (No. 26) at Ajanta. But it is in the space above the entablature, where the sun-window should be placed that the most noticeable alteration has been effected. Here, the chaitya arch has been compressed until it forms a relatively small circular opening, below which is a transverse foliation, converting the whole into a kind of trefoil. Across the lower part of the triple formation thus produced an architrave has been carried on two pillars, a treatment so obviously a copy of wooden construction, that it suggests a reversion to the timber method. On this facade however there are two features of more than usual expressiveness. These are the two canopies over the niches at the extreme sides of the composition, each of different design. In them we seem to detect the two forms of shrine, which, derived from Vedic originals persisted eventually to become, as will be shown later, the basis of the two styles of Hindu temple architecture, the Indo-Aryan, and the Dravidian. The one on the right, as proved by the ribbed melon shape of the *amala sila* or sacred stone, is the Indo-Aryan, while on the left is the canopy which afterwards became the characteristic feature of the Dravidian style. In the design of this facade may be observed an attempt at originality, which failed because it lacked inspiration. The Buddhist rock-cut architecture closes on this note, the sun-window of its chaitya halls was, in the earlier examples a noble symbol, in the somewhat meaningless form it assumes in the Visvakarma, the last of its kind, it becomes a portent. (Plate XLII, Fig. 2).

The Buddhist rock-cut monasteries of Aurangabad,[1] consist of three groups of excavations situated in a precipitous scarp of a hill about a mile north of that city. One of these groups contains a chaitya hall and four viharas, and another has four viharas, while a third has three "caves" of no particular significance. The viharas show by their style that they belong to the sixth and seventh centuries, being probably the latest of their kind, and are valuable as they are evidence of the manner in which Buddhist art, in this medium, was merging into that of the Hindus. On the other hand the style of the chaitya hall (No. 4) at Aurangabad is conflicting, as it displays certain characteristics that imply a very early date, possibly contemporary with the Hinayana group at Ajanta, and therefore not later than the third century A.D. If however it is an example of the Hinayana type, attached to it should be a vihara in the same early style, but none of the existing viharas on the site fulfils such conditions. This chaitya hall, which is much ruined, is a small example, as it measures 40 feet long by 32 feet wide, and the features which recall the previous movement are the

---

[1] See "Indian Art and Letters" India Society, Vol. XI, No. 1.

simple design of the stupa, and the treatment of the apse triforium. With regard to the stupa, this resembles the relatively low and plain examples of the Hinayana type, such as at Karli and others of the same period. The mural pattern on the triforium is singularly characteristic of the early phase, as it consists of an arcading of narrow arched panels of a kind which is one of the distinguishing features of the preceding style. Moreover there are other circumstances, such as the rib-vaulting of the roof, and the plainness of the interior as a whole, all suggestive of the earlier movement. It is not impossible therefore that this chaitya hall was an ancient production, with which was its accompanying and contemporary vihara, the latter, however, having been re-cut and elaborated into one of the later examples, on the revival of the creed at a subsequent date.

Of the viharas at Aurangabad, those numbered 3 and 7, are the finest and also the best preserved, and more important still, each illustrates a different form of plan. No. 3 is of the more general kind, in which the cella leads out of the pillared hall, being cut deep into the rock. On the other hand the cella of No. 7 occupies the centre of the main compartment, while a passage for ambulation is carried around it, an arrangement which is not common, and is probably a survival of some early tradition. When, shortly afterwards, the Hindus began their series of rock-cut temples at Ellora, a few of these were planned on much the same system, as for instance that known as the Rameswara. Another distinctive feature of the Aurangabad viharas is their plastic treatment, which takes two forms, one consisting of designs executed in moderate relief and chiefly on the pillars and their superstructures, the other of bold figure sculpture carved almost in the round. The pillars have capitals composed of a combination of the bracket with the vase and foliage motif, while in vihara No. 1 supplementary struts have been introduced, each a figure-subject of graceful design resembling those at Badami in temple No. 3. In addition to the rich character of the capitals, the entire shaft of the pillar is elaborately carved into designs of foliage and figures, particularly noticeable in No. 3.

But it is in the larger figure carving that these viharas at Aurangabad excel, as some of the sculpture is of an unusual kind. There are several compositions containing representations of deities, some of them goddesses of massive proportions and voluptuous in form, for to comply with the requirements of the rock technique, this boldness of relief is in accordance with their architectural setting. It is, however, in the innermost shrine of vihara No. 3, that the most striking productions are found, for here are two groups of figures, almost life-size, and of surpassing interest. Each group consists of a number of votaries, kneeling in devout adoration before a colossal statue of the Buddha on his throne. There are both males and females, some offering garlands, others with clasped hands, and all displaying a touching eagerness in their attitude and expression. In the garments, head-dress and ornaments, and also in their physical appearance, they present a living picture of the people of the period. But they imply much more than a scene of everyday life of the seventh century. These groups of statuary show that when the sculptors were able to break away from their endless reproductions of the conventional and stylised images of the deities, they could depict the human form in its most life-like manner, realistically posed and naturally modelled. It is evident that genuine artistic expression was unduly restrained by the exacting conditions of the existing belief.

REFERENCE

Burgess, J., *Ellora Cave Temples* (Arch. Sur. of Ind. Vol. V), London, 1883.

CHAPTER XIII

THE EVOLUTION OF THE TEMPLE

IN the latter half of the seventh century, as the surviving examples show, the temple structure, in its mediaeval aspect, was beginning to assume a prescribed form. And, just as in describing a Gothic church, one accepts such terms as nave, aisles, chancel, spire etc., so in the Indian temple it will be realized that this building also comprises a number of essential parts, the names of which will figure repeatedly in any account of its structure. The glossary at the end of this work will explain and amplify the various architectural terms which are in general use. It should be noted however that the same words are not always employed in all parts of the country, but where there is a departure from those in common use, as for instance in connection with the important Orissan style, this will be explained in due course.

The principal architectural features of the temple are as follows. Throughout the greater part of the country, the sanctuary as a whole is known as the *vimana*, of which the upper and pyramidal or tapering portion is called the *sikhara*, meaning tower or spire. Inside the vimana is a small and generally dark chamber or cella for the reception of the divine symbol. This cella is the *garbha griha*, or "womb-house", and was entered by a doorway on its inner, and usually, eastern side. In front of the doorway was a pillared hall, or *mandapa*, actually a pavilion for the assembly of those paying their devotions to the divine symbol in the cella. Some of the earlier temples indicate that the mandapa, was a detached building, isolated from the sanctuary by a definite open space, as in the "Shore" temple at Mamallapuram, and originally in the Kailasanatha at Conjeeveram, both near Madras, and built about 700 A. D. A little later it became the custom to unite the two buildings, thus forming an intermediate chamber, or vestibule, and called the *antarala*. Leading up to the main hall, or mandapa, is a porch or *ardha-mandapa*, while there may be a transept on each side of this central hall, known as the *maha-mandapa*. The most complete illustrations of the fully formed and co-ordinated temple structure, are the tenth century examples at Khajuraho, Central India, especially that known as the Kandariya Mahadeo (Chapter XXII). In this class of temple, each portion named above, has its separate pyramidal roof, rising in regular gradation, from the lowest over the porch (*ardha-mandapa*), to the lofty spire over the sanctum. In some parts of the country it became the practice to enclose the temple building within a rectangular courtyard by means of a continuous range of cells, facing inwards, the whole forming a substantial containing wall, and thus ensuring seclusion. One of the first temples to combine all these attributions, and to present a co-ordinated plan was that of the Vaikuntanath Perumal at Conjeeveram (cir. A. D. 740). Most of these early temples have a processional passage or *pradakshina patha* consisting of an enclosed corridor carried around the outside of the cella. (Plate LIV).

It will be seen that, although differing in other respects, there is much the same conventional system and disposition of parts in the Indian temple as in the Christian church, with the nave corresponding to the mandapa, the chancel to the sanctuary, the tower or spire to the sikhara, the cloisters to the rectangular range of cells, and the churchyard, or close, to the temple enclosure. In its plan there is also some resemblance to the temple of the Greeks, with its columned naos before the interior cella, and its pronaos or porch acting the same as the ardha-mandapa of the Indian type. It is not without significance that, as already described, a temple showing Hellenic influence was actually erected, with local modifications, at Jandial in Taxila in the second century B. C. (Plate XXVII). It may be noted, also, that the basic intentions of the Greek and Indian temples were not dissimilar as neither was designed for congregational worship, each being a sacred monument, and an object of devotion in itself. The Indian temple was, in the language of the people, a "dwelling place of the gods", for, in addition to the symbol of the deity within the cella, numerous niches, recesses, alcoves, and altars, were provided as part of the architectural scheme, within which were enshrined sacred images of the immortals, so that the whole structure resolved itself into a place of assembly of the *Devas*, or "Shining Ones".

With the establishment of the temple type about the eighth century A. D., the people proceeded to embark on an era of temple building, which can have few equals, so much so that before long in all parts of the country superb creations fashioned in stone and, in some instances, hewn out of the living rock, could be counted by the score, if not by the hundred. It was an epoch which implied great religious concentration and intensity of purpose, corresponding in some respects to that wave of passionate building which swept over much of Europe in the Middle Ages, and of which it has been said that it was as if the whole population had to a man, been apprenticed to the stone mason. And, to continue the occidental parallel, as Ralph Glaber in his famous history speaks of the "white robe of churches which covered Europe in the eleventh century", so in India every hamlet had its cluster of shrines, and in every town the tall spires of temples rose singly and in groups, as proved by the remains observable all over the country to the present day. With these structural religious edifices were also rock-cut monuments, showing that this method, previously the monopoly of the Buddhists, was in the eighth and ninth centuries, continued by the Hindus and Jains, notably at such famous sites as Ellora and Elephanta. Although the rock-cut form of production displays many instructive features, as will be shown in due course (Chapter XV), it is in the examples of the structural form of expression that the temple architecture of the country may be most intelligibly estimated.

In this matter of appraisement, however, one factor should receive special consideration. This is the spectator's mental point of view. It should be realized that in all works of art, and particularly in the temple architecture of the country, in the mind of the Indian people, the religious, philosophical, and metaphysical qualities of the production take first place, the artistic character being regarded as secondary. The intellect of the age, absorbed largely in divine contemplation, is reflected in the temple ideal, where the spiritual dominates the material. "O ye works of the Lord, praise ye the Lord," signifies this ideal, and the innate aesthetic sense of the people caused each creation to be an inspired work of art. It is from this standpoint that the architecture of India should be viewed, and from this direction approached.

A detailed analysis of the temple structure will show that much of its architectonic character was obtained by the surfaces being treated as if they were an organism of repeating cells. This particularly applies to the tower or sikhara which is often built up of repetitions of the same architectural motif, converted into an element of decoration. In a word the sikhara is composed of an orderly grouping of miniature multiples of itself, and the same applies very largerly to the other parts of the structure. In employing this artistic expedient the designers were proceeding in a perfectly logical and safe manner, for although such a plan may lead to monotony owing to mechanical reiteration, it can never be incongruous, or result in a display of bad taste. But these structural elements repeated so artistically, yet so emphatically, in the temple design are something more than mere architectural motifs ; they have a much deeper meaning. It will be found that each unit or constituent part making up the whole building is a reduced model of what is obviously a shrine, and furthermore that two different types of shrine have been utilized, one kind being employed entirely in one form of temple design, and the other in another. Thus it comes about that the bulk of the temple architecture of India resolves itself into two distinct and separate styles in which the pillars, capitals, mouldings, and architectural details generally differ in each, so that as in the case of Greek and Roman architecture, these buildings may be classified into "orders". In India there are two such orders, which emerge about the eighth century, and have been designated by Fergusson the one as Dravidian and the other Indo-Aryan, the former being found in the south of India, a country anciently known as Dravida, while the latter is confined to the north. In its geographical aspect, however, a dividing line between the two regions occupied by the two modes cannot be definitely drawn, as temples in the Dravidian style extend towards the north as far as Ellora (Aurangabad), while there are Indo-Aryan examples as far south as Dharwar on the upper Kistna ; in fact in the town of Pattadakal in this region, during the eighth century, both kinds of buildings were erected side by side. It should be also noted that the entire area in which Dravidian temples may be found comprises only one fifth of the country as a whole, the Indo-Aryan being distributed over the remainder, and therefore buildings of the latter type are more numerous and more diversified. Much may be said in favour of a regional and ethnological method of classification, but on the other hand the difference in the two styles seems to be more fundamental, and to be derived from some other sources deep down in the early culture of the people.

In support of the presumed very ancient derivation of these two architectural orders it is possible to trace back the particular shrine which, for instance, gives its specific character to the Dravidian style, to the rude shelter over the Naga altars, or those protecting the sacred fires of the non-Buddhists, as depicted on the Sanchi bas-reliefs executed before the Christian era. Its structural features recall even a more primitive expedient for keeping off the rain and enabling the smoke to escape, consisting of a large earthenware bowl inverted with its rim supported on blocks (Plate LIV, Fig. 1), thus providing a crude kind of chimney, still found in domestic buildings to the present day. There seems some probability that in Vedic times the sacrificial altar of each deity was roofed over by a particular form of shelter always associated with that deity, enabling the humblest worshipper readily to recognize each by its shape. So may be explained the occasional appearance in later temples of a range of shrines, square, round, or apsidal in form, as is well illustrated in the Jain temple of Tiruparutikunram near Conjeeveram, while the five "raths" at Mamallapuram may be full-scale monolithic models exemplifying the same tradition. In the course of centuries two only out of these several types of primitive shrines survived and became perpetuated in the two types of temple, their initial meaning having become obscured. In some such mysterious and subtle manner derived from an almost pre-historic experience, the two styles of Indian temple architecture, the Dravidian and the Indo-Aryan, may have had their source, and therefore their geographical distribution may have been more or less fortuitous.

Such an important architectural feature as the *sikhara* or tower, which figures in all the types of temple design in the country, has evoked several theories as to its origin, especially in the form it assumes in the Northern or Indo-Aryan-style. An attempt has been made to prove that this "spire" evolved from the peaked or domed huts of Eastern and Central India, which prevailed in those parts before the beginning of the Christian era. "It is quite evident that such huts, whether of bamboo or wood, were the prototype of the Nagara temple with *sikhara*.[1]" On the other hand it has been endeavoured to show that the *sikhara* of the Northern Indian type of temple developed out of the Buddhist stupa, gradually becoming elongated from the semi-globular mound, through the various credal changes that took place during the early centuries of the first millennium until it finally took the form of a spire or tower.[2] This progress has been carefully traced by means of a number of graded authentic examples illustrating that as Buddhism merged into Hinduism so the symbol of the chaitya eventually merged into the sikhara from the ceremonial umbrella through the stupa to the tower. Another theory, based on the fact that the temple is not infrequently referred to as a *ratha*, or car, and so the sikhara may have been derived from the tall covering of the processional car (*ratha*) which containing an image of the deity was carried about on ceremonial occasions. (Plate V, Fig. 7).

There is little appreciable difference in architectural appearance between the temples of the Jains and those of the Hindus, except that the former preferred enclosed compartments instead of open columned halls, thus ensuring more seclusion for their ceremonial. Nor did the two major divisions of Hinduism, Sivaite and Vishnuvite, affect to any extent the temple structure. The device on the finial of the sikhara distinguishes the temples of each system, the three pronged trident signifying a Siva temple, inside the cella of which will be a *linga* or phallic emblem, and outside on the east, in front of the main entrance, an effigy, of the

---

[1] Dr. Ramaprasad Chanda in *Rupam*, No. 17, Calcutta Jan. 1924.
[2] Longhurst in "*The Story of the Stupa*", Colombo, 1936.

sacred bull (*nandi*). On the other hand above the spire of the Vishnu temple will be a disc, or wheel, and inside the sanctuary a statue of the deity. Other determinating symbols are the dedication stone, which may be seen carved above the doorway of the sanctum on the centre of the lintel, corresponding to the keystone of an arch. Moreover, around the exterior walls of the sanctuary three principal images are often carved, one in the centre of each side, the figure at the back and west generally having some connection with the particular deity enshrined within. The various compartments comprising the general arrangements of the temple are usually co-ordinated axially, being all built on one alignment running east and west, with the entrance to the east. The edifice normally faces east so that the early morning rays of the sun may penetrate into the holy of holies, thus filling it with the fresh glory of the coming day. Such conditions also symbolise the entry of the god into his own temple of the world. This system of orientation, however, is not so strictly adhered to in the temples of the Jains, which sometimes face the north.

As the temple building began to take form, it becomes evident that it obtained some of its architectural character from the older productions of the Buddhists. Such borrowings are readily indentified in the decorative treatment, as for instance the introduction of the chaitya arch (*kudu*), now reduced to a mere ornamental motif, and other similar elements, but the Brahmanical temple builders also brought not only ornamental forms but some portions of the Buddhist architecture itself into their Hindu conceptions. Of the two types of Buddhist monument, the chaitya hall supplied little inspiration, it was too distinctive in its formation and purpose to be readily adapted to other needs, although its unmistakable vaulted roof occasionally survives in the Hindu temple, as for instance in the Teli ka Mandir (eleventh century) at Gwalior, and the singularly interesting Vaital Deul (c. 900 A.D.), at Bhubaneswar both examples of the northern style. In the south, Hindu shrines having the " chaitya " roof with its apsidal end are not so rare, so much so that this form has been given the name of the " elephant back," or *Gajaprishthakriti*, and is illustrated in the Chola temples of Somangalam, Manimangalam (eleventh century), Tennesi, and Magaralu, besides others at Chezarla and Tiruparuttikundram already mentioned. These Dravidian examples were probably based on the rock-cut model of the Sahadeva ratha at Mamallapuram. On the other hand from the other Buddhist type, the vihara or monastery, the Hindu craftsmen seem to have appropriated certain architectural forms of which they made considerable use in their temple design; particularly in the buildings of the Dravidian style. Attributions from Buddhist sources show themselves most plainly in the pyramidal character of the earlier sikhara, doubtlessly suggested by the diminishing stories of the monastery, which was composed of ranges of cells or chapels, one above another around a square court. In the temple these cells were conventionalized and converted into ornamental turrets arranged in tiers, while from the central court may have been derived the pillared hall or mandapa. (Plate CLI).

Although emphasis has been laid on these distinctions in style, underlying the temple architecture of the country as a whole were certain fundamental principles which guided and controlled the art of building in all its phases. There is noticeable throughout the entire movement a standardization of procedure, artistic and structural, implying that the master masons were working not only with one general understanding, but also by means of some comprehensive and well-established technical code. This shows itself unmistakably in the uniformity of the style even where the buildings are situated widely apart, or in the most remote localities. For instance there is much the same character in a temple of Gujarat on the extreme west, as in another at Bhubaneswar on the eastern seaboard, or again in the valleys of the Himalayan foot-hills. Even more remarkable, however, is that a similar stylistic content reveals itself in the distant Indo-Buddhist monuments of Java and Cambodia, postulating that the Indonesian builders were motivated by the same system of aesthetic ideals. In all these structures there may be divergence in the less material forms, but in their broad aspect they express the same thought although in a different idiom.

This co-ordination of architectural practice was brought about mainly by means of two indigenous institutions, both of which played a considerable part in the aesthetic development of the country ; these were the *seni*, or guilds, and the *silpas*, or canons of art. Guilds in India were a very ancient organization, known to have been in existence as early as the seventh century B.C., and therefore the oldest of their kind. At first the craft guilds were maintained by a system of apprentices, whose name, *antevasika*, literally " the boarder," denotes that these young learners were not only professionally but domestically connected with their master's establishment. Later, heredity became the custom, as each craft was specialized, and, like a family property was handed down from father to son. The character of the building art not infrequently necessitated the local guild of masons being moved about the country, and on some occasions the magnitude of their task forced them to settle down near the site of their labours for a generation or more, the great structure on which they were engaged being the sole object of their existence. In this way any large architectural undertaking became an art centre from which a local school and style were derived. For example, in the group of temples at Khajuraho (950-1050), and at Konarak (c. 1250), it is possible to trace the development of individual experience, distilled through long years of " trial and error," during the gradual process of producing such monumental works of art.

What the guilds did for the practice, the other institution, the *silpas* professed to do for the theory. In their more comprehensive form, the silpas were a vast and erudite compilation of canons for guidance in all spheres of human activity, one important section of which, however, concerns itself with aesthetics. At an early date some such regulations appear to have existed in a literary form, as mention is made of them in the *Brahmajala Sutta* of the Digha Nekaya, or " Dialogues of the Buddha," of probably the fifth century B.C. Later, these ancient aphorisms were codified into the silpas, extracts from which have been preserved textually and may date from the sixth century A.D. There are books, mostly in Sanscrit, professing to be transcripts of portions of this immense work, copies of which were widely distributed, as they have been found in the lamasaries of Tibet, and also in Nepal. In the section on Aesthetics the three forms of artistic expression are dealt with, namely Sculpture, Painting and Architecture. That portion relating to the building art, the *Vastusastra*, or " Rules of Architecture (*vastu*)" contains detailed directions for the proper construction of every kind of building, religious and secular, and includes an imposing array of technical rules of proportion and recondite prescriptions, with a fund of astronomical

Fig. 2

Ajanta: Facade of Chaitya-hall No. 19; c. 6th cent. A.D.

Fig. 1

Badami: Rock-cut Temple No. 1, portico; 6th cent. A.D.

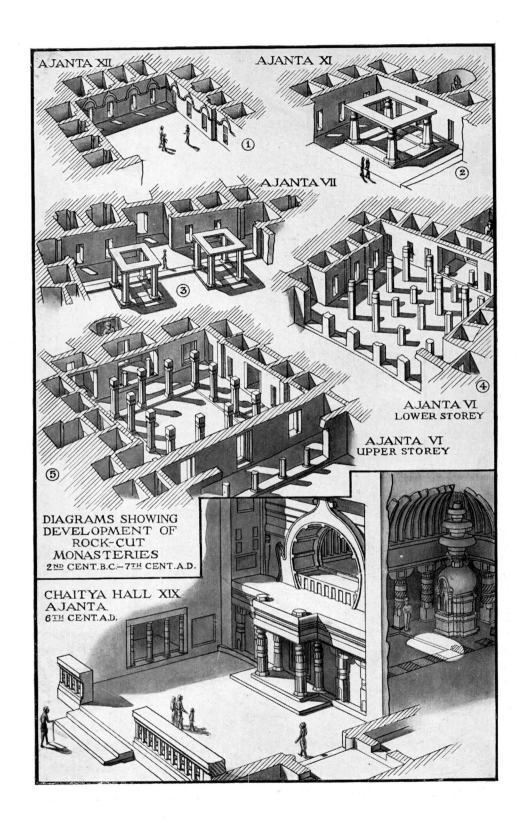

AJANTA XII

AJANTA XI

AJANTA VII

AJANTA VI
LOWER STOREY

AJANTA VI
UPPER STOREY

DIAGRAMS SHOWING
DEVELOPMENT OF
ROCK-CUT
MONASTERIES
2ND CENT.B.C.—7TH CENT.A.D.

CHAITYA HALL XIX
AJANTA
6TH CENT.A.D.

Fig. 2

Ellora: Facade of Visvakarma Chaitya-hall; c. 7th cent. A.D.

Fig. 1

Ajanta: Chaitya-hall No. 26; c. 6th cent. A.D.

DIAGRAMS SHOWING EARLY CONSTRUCTIONAL PRACTICE

① TEMPLE OF PARASURAMESVARA BHUBANESWAR, ORISSA, (8TH CENT)

② SMALL RUINED TEMPLE AT BADAMI, CIR.600 A.D.

Fig. 1
Ruined Temple above Badami; c. 600 A.D.

Fig. 2
Pattadakal: Temples of Kasinath and Mallikarjuna; c. 740 A.D.

Fig. 1
Pattadakal: Temple of Papanath; c. 680 A.D.

Fig. 2
Pattadakal: Temple of Virupaksha; c. 740 A.D.

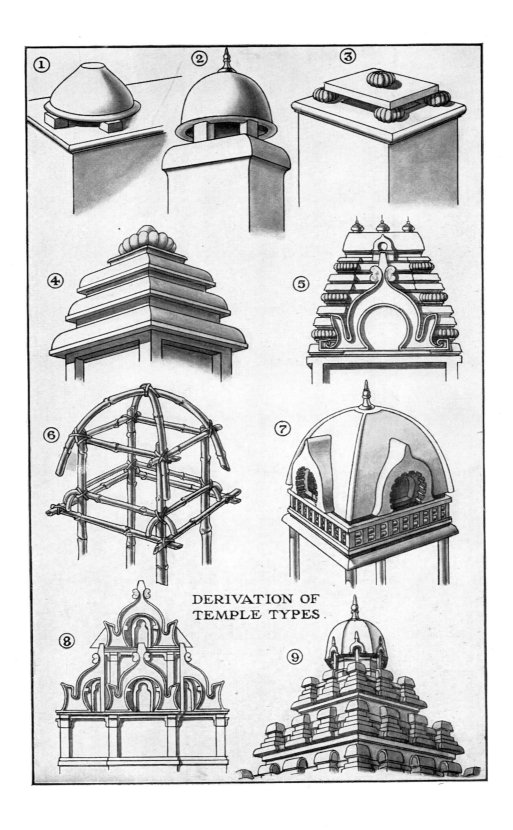

DERIVATION OF
TEMPLE TYPES

LV

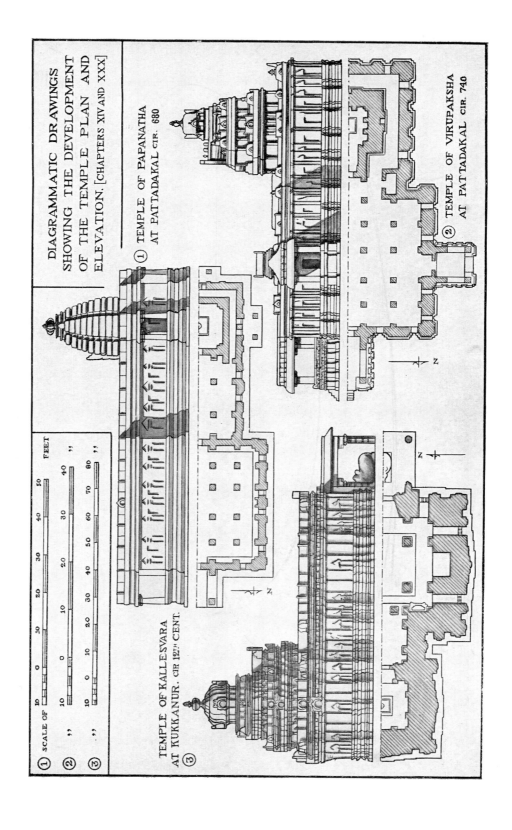

DIAGRAMMATIC DRAWINGS
SHOWING THE DEVELOPMENT
OF THE TEMPLE PLAN AND
ELEVATION. [CHAPTERS XIV AND XXX]

① TEMPLE OF PAPANATHA CIR. 680
AT PATTADAKAL

② TEMPLE OF VIRUPAKSHA CIR. 740
AT PATTADAKAL

TEMPLE OF KALLESVARA
AT KUKKANUR. CIR 12TH CENT.
③

① SCALE OF ___ FEET
② ,,
③ ,,

calculations and religious precepts. Bearing unmistakable evidences of having been dictated by a dominating hierarchy, they recall the ordinances of the Holy Tribunal which stood sentinel over the art of Spain in the mediaeval period, with the result that the artists of both countries were fettered to a prescribed formula. And as in Europe all knowledge and culture were in the hands of the Church, so in India the outlook of men's minds was controlled by priestly influence as their aesthetic productions plainly testify. It was the practice therefore for the silpas to be committed to memory by the Indian artisans, and recited by the master-mason to his staff while at work, thus constituting a technical *lingua franca*, or workshop language. Such a system is in accordance with that by which most instruction is conveyed in the east—the reiteration of passages from books, or the repetition of patterns in drawing, until the lesson becomes second nature. The silpas were designed to place in the hands of the workmen an authoritative text-book on the grammar of his art, which if faithfully followed would make failure impossible. They were also intended to be a means of preserving the inner character of the crafts, and communicating this character wherever these crafts were practised, even in the most remote localities or over the seas.

Corresponding in some respects to the treatise of Vitruvius, the Vastusastra displays the obscurity of that famous Roman architect in his explanation of the "perfect numbers" of the Greeks, many times intensified. There seems little doubt that, although compiled with the best of intentions, the laws of the silpas cast their shadow over the arts, so that they never fully recovered their earlier elasticity and natural charm. In this connection, it may be remarked that at some time towards the middle of the first millennium, there appears to have been a spirit abroad, which aimed at priestly control over all cultural activities, the iron hand of religion being used to restrain complete freedom of expression. That it also affected literature is proved by the *Ahamkara*, or "Rules of Poetics," and there are indications that similar regulations were framed for the guidance of several of the arts. It has been found that any such discipline, operated by a fixed set of rules, is apt to emerge only during periods of intellectual stagnation, and any system devised to compel expression to conform to certain preordained conditions, is bound to impair spontaneity of utterance. The silpas fall into this category, with the result that they stifled initiative and struck at the very root of inspiration. Only the genius of the Indian workman could rise superior to such circumstances—he maintained a living art, not because of the silpas, but in spite of them.

The magic and mystery which many historical buildings inspire, are, in India, attributed to the supernatural powers of certain mythical beings, or others of legendary fame. Some of the finest temples in Central India, are reputed to have been raised by an imaginary prince named Jakanacharya, to expiate the sin of killing a Brahmin, and accordingly he was forced to spend twenty years of his life in this work. On the other hand, a common explanation in most parts of India for any unusual group of structures is, that they were produced in a single night by the Pandavas, those famous sons of Pandu, the heroes of the Mahabharata. In north Gujarat the great temples are ascribed to the piety of the celebrated ruler Siddharaja, King of Gujarat (cir. A.D. 1125), and in Khandesh to the dynasty of the Gavali rajas. Many temples in the Dekkan are said to have been raised through the religious zeal of Hemadpant, a minister of king Ramachandra with the result that some of them of the thirteenth century are rather vaguely styled Hemadpanti. Towering above all these relatively lesser personalities, however, the great force which is universally recognized as divinely responsible for all mechanical and structural enterprises, is the god Visvakarma, "Lord of the Arts," the embodiment of creative power. He is the patron saint of the Indian artificer and all those who work by their hands, one day in their calendar being set apart for his worship, when the tools and instruments of the craft are treated as objects of veneration. Throughout the Epics Visvakarma figures not only as the great architect of the universe, the master of the science of mechanics, but also as the welder of Agneyastra, or fiery weapon, "the executor of a thousand handicrafts, the carpenter of the gods, the fashioner of all ornaments, who formed the celestial chariots of the deities, on whose craft men subsist, and whom, as a great and immortal god, they continually worship." Visvakarma's antiquity is referred to in the Rig Veda (X. 72). "In the earliest ages of the gods, even as a smith, the Lord of Prayer, together forged this universe. With such a personification of omnipotence as their presiding deity, it is not surprising that skilled master craftsmen are sometimes credited with magical powers.

Very few indeed of the names of these master masons have survived, for Indian art as a whole, and particularly its architecture, is anonymous, a fact which applies to the Hindus as well as to the Islamic productions. The name and character of the Indian genius who conceived and supervised the execution of that marvelous masterpiece, the rock-cut temple of Kailasa, is unknown, and that of the Moslem architect who much later planned that unique monument the Taj Mahal is also matter for speculation. Much of this was due to the system by which architecture was treated not so much as an art, but as a craft, the building was not the creation of one man, but the combined and often equal efforts of several, each an expert in his profession and each making his own particular contribution to the whole. Here and there a name has been preserved in the same manner as those of some of the leading master masons of the Gothic cathedrals have been handed down, but not as the names of the great architects of Greece and the Renaissance were known, each of whom was the sole author of the monument with the design and construction of which he was entrusted.

The constructional methods of the Hindus, not unlike those of the Greeks, were of a simple but effective order, showing little inventiveness, or any serious attempt to solve structural problems. No effort was made to apply in their building productions the principles of the equilibrum of forces in action by means of the arch, vault, or other mechanical devices, which, instituted by the Romans, were by this time, being put into universal practice by the architects of the western world. Instead, the Indian craftsman, clinging to his own traditional technique and unmoved by the progress being made elsewhere, achieved his purpose solely by the judicious observance of the laws of gravity, strength being obtained by mass supporting mass, and stability by the solid resistance of weights acting only vertically, all pressure being transmitted directly downwards. In these circumstances mortar was unnecessary because it would have been of no use for distributing the pressure between the courses of the structure : it was therefore very rarely employed, with the result that all Hindu masonry is described as of the "dry" order. The Indian builder knew architecture as a fine or liberal art, but not as a mechanical art. He seems to have resembled the master mason of the Middle Ages in Europe, rather than the architect of the Greeks.

As a rule the Indian masons prepared their building material not on the site of the structure, but in the quarry itself, often some considerable distance away. Here the rough mass of stone, after being won from the living rock, was made into suitable sizes and shapes by cleavage. A groove was sunk along the line of the required division, and holes jumped along this a few inches part. Into the holes thus formed wooden wedges were driven, which, on being wet, swelled, and the blocks split off in this manner. The facing of these blocks was obtained by hammer-dressing, surfaces also being levelled by chiselling parallel lines with a large iron tool, afterwards with a finer one. The presence of numerous fragments of carving in some of the quarries, as for example on the Silasankar hill in Dharwar, from which outcrop the stones used in the Gadag, Lakkundi, and Dambal temples were extracted, points to the sculpture also being executed in the stone-yard. From here the blocks, ready dressed to level beds and carved to pattern, were assembled on the temple site, a staff of workmen being on the spot to lay the stones in their proper courses, and put the finishing touches to the joints in the sculpture. Such a process would necessitate detailed and accurate measurements being made available, while an early record shows that models to scale were also sometimes prepared. In the Upanishads it is related that an architect of the name of Suradevi exhibited to his patron a model of a temple which he had built at Pataliputra.[1] While the foregoing was the general practice of the builders, the alternative process was not unusual, as there are temples which indicate that the masonry was left boasted on the building, so that the carver could chisel it into pattern on the structure itself. An instance of this, among others, is the eleventh century temple of Rajarani at Bhubaneswar, where some of the carving is marked out and left unfinished, thus showing that the Orissan artisan preferred the other method, which is the one almost invariably followed in the West.

Whether it was through much of his life being passed in the quarry workshop under the shadow of the hill-side, his long apprenticeship to the rock-cut mode, or his own innate aesthetic sensibility, the Indian mason shows in his architectural compositions an appreciation of the grandeur of mass and the rich value of shadows to a marked degree. A notable quality in much of the building art of India is that its linear aspect is subservient to its volume, the aim being mass rather than line. It seems as if the imagination of the workman had received special stimulation from his experience in the field of rock architecture when, confronted by the fact that his conception lay imprisoned in the womb of the mountain, he summoned up all his genius to bring about its release. Such an experience added considerably to his powers. Few things could be finer than the great roll cornice used with such effect in many of his earlier works, as for instance in the eighth century Virupaksha temple at Pattadakal, a feature obviously inspired by a rock-cut prototype. Then the distribution of the shadows, and the chiaroscuro generally in his temple architecture, indicate also that for a considerable period he was " thinking in shadows," when pre-occupied with the rock-cut method. This condition communicated itself to the treatment of his interiors, where, not satisfied with an atmosphere of religious gloom, some of his halls were filled with an intense darkness. Only on the occasion of a procession through the aisles were these chambers illuminated, when the delicate tracery of the fretted ceiling, hitherto unseen, was revealed, and the images of the gods were brought to life as their shadows moved to and fro, lit by the fitful torchlight. Outside were the projecting eaves (chajjas), their wide surfaces protecting the facade from the fierce sunlight, and also sheltering it from the heavy monsoon rain. Every portion, every effect, was the product of long years of application. Wherever it was to his advantage the Indian builder made the climate his handmaid, when this was impossible he used his artistic ingenuity in providing against it.

---

[1] *Kathakosa*, translated by C. H. Tawny, p. 150.

REFERENCES

Acharaya, P. K., *Architecture of Manasara*, Oxford, N. D.
    „   „   *Indian Architecture according to Manasara-Silpasastra*, Oxford, 1921.
    „   „   *Dictionary of Hindu Architecture*, Oxford, N. D.
Bose, P. N., *Principles of Indian Silpasastra*, Lahore, 1926.
Gravely, F. H., *Outline of Indian Temple Architecture*, Madras, 1936.
Gravely, F. H., and Ramchandran, T. N., *Three Main styles of Temple Architecture*, Madras, 1934.
Ram Raz, *Essay on the Architecture of the Hindus*, London, 1854.

CHAPTER XIV

THE EARLY CHALUKYAN PHASE AT AIHOLE, BADAMI, AND PATTADAKAL (A.D. 600 to 750)[1]

IN a previous chapter reference has been made to the fact that at the ancient township of Aihole in Dharwar there are indications that this capital of the early Chalukyan dynasty was one of the cradles of Indian temple architecture. Such a probability is shown by several examples, all of a distinctly incipient character, and all erected apparently during the fifth and sixth centuries A.D. Most of them are temples of the flat roofed order, and similar therefore to those of the Gupta style of the more northerly latitude, thus displaying a characteristic which implies an early stage in the process of evolution of this structure. In the Chalukyan temples other stages of development may also be traced. For instance in the most primitive of all, the shrine is in the body of the building, with nothing on the exterior to mark its position from outside. Afterwards a tower was added over the shrine, not only to give this central feature dignity, but also as a means of distinguishing the temple from other buildings. Later, the shrine, or cella, was contained in a structure projected from the western end of the temple and surmounted by a tower. This last development caused the sanctuary to form a kind of annexe attached to the body of the temple, the shrine and tower combined comprising that portion of the structure known as the vimana.

All these stages may be studied in the various temples at Aihole, while the beginning of that significant feature, the sikhara, is also observable. It is not improbable that an early phase of the tower consisted of a series of mouldings or courses of masonry of a very simple order, diminishing as they ascend, thus taking the shape of a stepped pyramid, truncated above and crowned by a ribbed stone, as shown in several smaller shrines on the site. (Plate LVI, Fig. 4). But one of the earliest, judging by its primitive appearance, to assume the sikhara form is that over the Durga temple. This, when complete, instead of being curved in outline, as in the later examples, is almost straight-sided, like an elongated pyramid, but inclined inward at the apex to support the fluted finial (amala sila), a large ribbed stone now thrown down and lying at its foot. There is something singularly interesting in the formation of this temple, particularly in the superposition of its distinctly Hindu tower on an apsidal structure obviously derived from a Buddhist chaitya hall. (Plate XXXVIII). Another at Aihole, the Huchimalligudi, has also been provided with a sikhara, although in this instance it is not raised on an apse, but over a square end. On the front or eastern face of the sikhara, there is a portion projected and shaped like a chaitya-arch, with a circular panel sunk in the centre. This panel contains a carved figure-composition of the god Siva dancing the tandava, a representation of a vigorous performance attributed to the deity when in revelry. Afterwards, the projected portion was gradually extended into a kind of gable, and became the roof of the vestibule in the temple interior. It will be noted that most of the sikharas at Aihole are in the northern or Indo-Aryan style, and may have been improvisations by the local craftsmen, but the primitive simplicity of their design is manifest. (Plate XLVI, Fig. 1).

In addition to the series of Indo-Aryan spires at Aihole, there are several examples of the contrasting or Dravidian style of temple, as for instance, that numbered 53, and the Jaina temple, No. 39, as well as the Meguti temple bearing a date equivalent to A.D. 634, and referred to in Chapter XI. But the remains of these are so incomplete they only suffice to indicate they belong to the southern mode, that most distinctive feature, the tower, being in each case in a state of ruin. For a very early example of the Dravidian style in this region, it is necessary to turn to the town of Badami, situated some fifteen miles from Aihole, and the seat of the Chalukyan dynasty at a slightly later date. Here, among a cluster of temples and shrines three miles west of the town, is the temple of Mahakutesvara, which from inscriptional evidence appears to have been built before A.D. 600. It is a small and almost insignificant edifice, but it is instructive because the tower is complete, and shows this feature with an octagonal domical finial, and surrounded by tiers of miniature shrines, all illustrative of an early phase in the evolution of the Dravidian sikhara. But a larger and slightly more developed structure of much the same type, although undoubtedly of a somewhat later date, is a temple on a spur of the rugged hills which overlook the town of Badami itself, and known as the Malegitti-Sivalaya. In the tower of this temple also, the domical finial is octagonal, and supported by a series of small shrines as in the previous example. The Malegitti temple, however, implies something more than a mere confirmation of a stage of evolution; it is a structure of considerable appearance, besides containing much informative material. It is not large, being only 56 feet in length, but is a massive solid production evidently built to withstand the elements in its exposed position. Consisting of three compartments—cella, assembly hall, and porch, the two former square in plan—its heavy monolithic pillars, ponderous bracket capitals, broad string-courses, and overhanging roll cornice, are all suggestive of the rock-cut tradition. Yet imposed on these starkly elemental structural features is a certain amount of sculpture, in panels, borders, and niches, which, although not exactly refined, possesses a spirit and action implying youth and movement. There is an air of restrained power in this structure and a sense of stability which makes it appear as part of the rock on which it is built. (Plate XLII, Fig. 1).

On another spur, a short distance from the foregoing, is a smaller temple, of much the same type, and which, in view of its crude construction, may be of an earlier date. But the finial of its sikhara is square, not octagonal, a fact which on the other hand may point to a further stage of development. This temple, which is nameless, is much ruined, its interior is exposed so that it is no longer a living structure but a mere shell. Yet from these remains, like an anatomical specimen, it is possible to study more readily its composition and constructional system. In Plate LI, Fig. 2, the details of the temple are laid bare, showing its central cella contained within a processional passage, and in front the pillared hall covered with a sloping roof. The

---

[1] *Chalukyan Architecture* by H. Cousens : Arch. Survey of India, Vol. XLII.

masonry is almost savagely simple in its character, while
the extravagant use of the material gives it a megalithic
appearance.   Although perhaps not so primitive as it seems,
those who produced this building were not expert-masons
or finished manipulators of stone.

These two temples not only overlook the town of Badami,
but they also face towards the series of rock-cut halls described in Chapter XI, and dating from the latter part of the
sixth century.   In comparing the Malegitti temple and its
nameless neighbour, with the rock-cut examples it is difficult
to realize that the former were executed probably a century
later than the latter.   The inferiority of the structural productions as a whole, but particularly of the design and workmanship of the pillars is most noticeable.   There is something
very primeval in the square plain shafts and heavy bracket
capitals of the porches in these buildings specially when
contrasted with the refinement of the fluted pillars and
elaborately moulded struts of the rock-cut halls.   The
clumsiness of the later work when compared with the skilled
execution of the earlier, implies a retrogression in conception
as well as in technique.   But the explanation is that two
such opposing forms of production are evidence of the great
change that was taking place at this juncture in the building
art, a change which went to the very root of architectural
practice.   Hitherto architectural form had been determined
by the rock-cut method, permanence being assured by the
stability of the cliff side.   This system was now about to be
superseded by the use of stone masonry.   Such a change
was however not destined to be a revolutionary one, the
process being very gradual, as the rock-cut method was to
persist for several succeeding centuries.   But rock-architecture had by this time been developed until it had achieved
a high standard of achievement, while on the other hand
the art of building with blocks of stone was relatively in its
infancy.   One can almost imagine the surprise of the rock-
cutters on seeing this new method, which they no doubt
felt was a transitory expedient compared with the lasting
qualities of their own performances.   For although looked
upon in the present age as a common procedure, the art of
placing one stone on another so as to form a strong and
shapely structure had to have its beginning.   And moreover
when finally perfected, masonry buildings were more pliant,
more ductile, and in certain respects even more lasting than
the sometimes crumbling rock.   But apart from its technical
qualities, masonry construction brought a new architectural
content into the temple scheme, for its very nature implied
the important conception of an exterior elevation, an aspect
and dimension hitherto little known to the rock architect,
who dealt almost exclusively with interiors.   From the
difference in the principles of the two methods, the one an
art of building up, the other of cutting down, it seems fairly
certain that each was in the hands of a separate guild of
workmen, operating independently according to their own
particular technique.   Not that they omitted to learn from
one another, the course of both arts shows that there was a
mutual understanding in the matter of architectural style,
but in practice they did not combine, they progressed on
parallel lines.

The next stage in the development of the building art in
these parts may be studied in the temples of Pattadakal, the
third of the Chalukyan capital seats.   Pattadakal is distant
ten miles from Badami, and, on the assumption that the
transfer of the capital took place after the capture of the
town in A.D. 642, it seems fairly certain the earlier temples
on this site were executed during the last half of the seventh

century.   But the Chalukyan dynasty reached the height of its
power under the kings Vijayaditya (696-733) and Vikramaditya II (733-46), so that the actual meridian of the style at
Pattadakal was attained in the first half of the eighth century.
At Pattadakal, temples of no mean order, and in both styles
of architecture are found side by side, a phenomenon which
would be almost equivalent in mediaeval Europe to Gothic
and Renaissance churches being built in juxtaposition and at
the same time.   Moreover certain of these temples which are
in one style, contain architectural details belonging to the
other contrasting style, implying that the buildings represented
a stage of evolution before the conventions of both had been
definitely established.   There are ten temples of consequence
at Pattadakal, four of which are in the Indo-Aryan or northern
style, and six in the Dravidian or southern, as follows :—

INDO-ARYAN	DRAVIDIAN
Papanath Temple (c. 680).	Sangameswar (c. 725).
Jambulinga.	Virupaksha (c. 740).
Karsedesvar, (Karsiddhesvara).	Mallikarjuna (c. 740).
Kasinath, (Kasivisvanatha).	Galagnath (c. 740).
	Sunmeswar.
	Jain temple.

Two of the temples, the Papanath and the Virupaksha, are
larger and more important than the others ; the former is
certainly the older, and it is not improbable that it was built
as the chief temple soon after the capital was founded,
possibly before the end of the seventh century.   Apparently
dedicated in the first instance to Vishnu and Surya, it seems
to have been converted afterwards to the worship of Siva.
The other large temple, that of Virupaksha, is shown by its
inscriptions to have been built during the reign of Vikramaditya II, so that its mean date would be about A.D. 740.
It is dedicated to Siva and may therefore have been built
to take the place of the previous example when the Chalukyan
dynasty appears to have changed over from Vaishnavism to
Saivism.   It is of some significance that of these two temples,
Papanath in the Indo-Aryan style is dedicated to Vishnu, and
Virupaksha in the Dravidian style was built for the worship
of Siva.

The temple of Papanath, both in its plan and in elevation, bears every indication of a conception in course of
formation. (Plate LIII, Fig. 1).   In general appearance
it is a long low composition some ninety feet in length, with
a tower at its eastern end too small and stunted to be in
good proportion with the remainder of the building.   Much
of the inconsistency of its exterior design is brought about
by the illogical arrangement of the plan, which illustrates
perceptibly the uncertainty that existed at the time as to the
correct disposition of the main elements of the structure and
their relation to one another.   In this instance the vestibule,
or *antarala*, is at fault, as the compartment is too large ;
it takes the shape of a square court, containing four pillars
widely set, so that instead of forming a connecting antechamber, it becomes a supplementary assembly hall.   (Plate LV,
Fig. 1).   It is this disproportion in the plan that has produced
a corresponding disproportion in the elevation.   Turning
to the more detailed treatment of the different parts of the
Papanath temple, the interior presents that massive solid
character, both in the bulk of its walls and particularly in
the shape of its pillars, which suggests not only the rock-cut
influence, but also something elemental.   The latter quality
is shown in certain of the larger details such as brackets and
struts half hidden in the upper gloom, in the form of supernatural creatures, recalling some phase of prehistoric evolu-

tion of which all that now remains are like the nightmares of a child, vague, awe-inspiring memories.

The exterior treatment of this building is of much the same nature, but more readily explained. Over the outer walls is a heavy cornice above which is a parapet of ornamental shrines, while below is a substantial basement formed of bold string-courses carried round the structure, like powerful bands binding the whole composition together. It is however in the broad space between these upper and lower members, in a word, the " filling," of the outside wall surface that the most instructive architectonic sculpture has been applied. This consists of a repetition of a feature derived from a particular type of shrine, originally in three dimensions, but now translated for decorative purposes into a bas-relief. Each niche is composed of two pillars, a cornice, and a traceried canopy, the last being essentially of Indo-Aryan extraction. Although all these details, especially the mural shrine motif, are pleasing features in themselves, their disposition on the building shows no special knowledge of architectural design ; the fact that the decorative shrines are regimentated over thirty times round the building, is evidence of a poverty of ideas and an ignorance of spacing and correct distribution which can only be attributed to inexperience. How these inconsistencies were corrected will be explained in the next example. (Plate LIII, Fig. 1).

It was probably less than fifty years after the foregoing, that the temple of Virupaksha was produced, but the progress made in such a relatively short period in architectural composition is noteworthy. (Plate LIII, Fig. 2). So much so that it has been implied the increasing power of the Chalukyan rulers enabled them to call in outside experts to aid the local artisans in their building efforts. If this is correct it was help of a nature which could only have been obtained from those in the employ of the contemporary Pallava rulers on the eastern seaboard, where a movement not unlike that now being described was also taking place. That there were close contacts between the Chalukyans and the Pallavas is a matter of historical knowledge, and that these influenced the architectural productions of the two peoples has also been a subject of considerable research. Confirmation of these influences is presumed to be derived from two sources (a) the evidence of inscriptions, and (b) points of style. With regard to the former there is an inscription on the Papanatha temple which reads that one Chattara-Revada-Ovajja of the Sarvasiddhi-Acharyas, and presumably the architect of the temple, was a builder from the south, possibly, though not necessarily in the Tamil country, and that he was also versed in the technical practices hitherto only known to a certain guild of Kanarese stone-masons. Two inscriptions on the Virupaksha temple also relate to a craftsman from the southern country who built this temple for the queen of Vikramaditya, and whose qualifications are defined in the most fulsome terms. But in no sense can these make it quite clear as some authorities have interpreted, that the Chalukyan king Vikramaditya II, when he conquered the Pallava capital of Conjeeveram in 740, was so struck by the architectural masterpiece of the Kailasnatha temple, that he brought back with him a Tamil architect who was responsible for the Pallava elements in the two temples built by his queens at Pattadakal. As a matter of fact there is in these temples no contribution " from the Dravidian style that was not already in regular use in the Chalukyan country, the only new feature being its combination of elements from both the local styles which previously seem to have influenced one another remarkably little."[1] What happened was that architecture, as this art developed in the south of India, evolved, appropriated, devised and invented certain forms which eventually resolved themselves into buildings now known as in the Dravidian style. During this early primitive period intercourse between the various peoples of the south led to imitations and borrowings, the system of universal technical canons and of craftsmen's guilds were the means by which this intercourse was maintained in the sphere of the building art, and in this manner the style of architecture in the regions of the south came into being.

It becomes tolerably clear therefore that the much improved design and execution of the Virupaksha temple were mainly due to the purposeful application of the Chalukyan builders to the task in hand, who, during the ensuing intervals, made it an occasion to acquire much practical proficiency. This is seen in the better proportions and adjustment of the plan, with its resultant effect on the external formation of the building. Although by no means a finished exposition of the essential parts of the temple system, the size and position of the vestibule, including the junction of the shrine-chamber with the pillared hall, are logical and well-conceived, and mark a distinct advance. Such an arrangement represents however only a stage in the temple development. For the final achievement in this direction it is necessary to compare it with the Chalukyan temples of the early mediaeval period, as for instance the productions at Kukkanur and Lukkundi of the twelfth and thirteenth centuries (Chapter XXX), where the entire composition is shown fully matured (Plate LV, Fig. 3).

None the less there is a bold beauty in the appearance of the Virupaksha temple as a whole, which is best seen in the exterior. It is a comprehensive scheme, as it consists not only of the central structure, but of a detached *nandi* pavilion in front and is contained within a walled enclosure entered by an appropriate gateway. Larger in size than the previous example as it measures one hundred and twenty feet from the front of the porch to the back of the shrine, owing to its balanced composition it is much more pleasing to the eye. This satisfactory effect has been obtained by treating the building as a unity, so that there is a definite coherence and rhythmic grouping of its parts. On the other hand, there is still that heavy solidity characteristic of all such early works, but here it is relieved by an increase in the amount and quality of the sculptured ornamentation. This plastic decoration resolves itself into several classes of workmanship and it seems not improbable that it was the handiwork of as many separate groups of craftsmen. There is the purely architectural detail, such as mouldings, pilasters, cornices and brackets, evidently prepared by the mason's own artificers ; the floral scrollwork together with the richly patterned perforated windows, the production of men specially trained in ornamental carving; the bold animal supports chiselled by artisans accustomed to large schemes ; the intricate bas-reliefs of figure-subjects requiring technical skill combined with a knowledge of mythology; and finally the full sized statuary in the panels and niches obviously designed and moulded by the master-sculptors of the time. The character of this ornamentation, and the manner in which it is applied bespeak more than ordinary knowledge. Although lavishly

[1] Bulletin of the Madras Government Museum, by F. H. Gravely and T. N. Ramachandran, Vol. III, Pt. 1, Madras 1934.

disposed, it is so skilfully co-ordinated with the rest of the structure that no part can be said to show where the building art ends and the plastic art begins. The sculpture flows into the architecture in a continuous yet disciplined stream. So harmonious is the entire conception it conveys the impression that the deepest emotions of its creators were concentrated on its production. The amount of thought expended, not only on the whole, but on each detail is incredible ; every one of its grey weatherworn stones, in spite of the passage of centuries, is yet warm with life and feeling. The Virupaksha temple is one of those rare buildings of the past in which the spirit still lingers of the men who conceived it and wrought it with their hands. (Plate LIII).

It is mainly in the application of this architectural embellishment to the structural background of the temple that progress is most marked. Specially is it noticeable in the treatment of the exterior walls, and more particularly in the area known as the " filling," already referred to in the previous example. This expanse of wall surface between the basement and the cornice, in view of its prominent position in the structure as a whole, invites very considered treatment. Here it has been divided up by means of pilasters, sometimes singly and at other places in pairs, into well-proportioned spaces, the intervening panels being enriched by the introduction of niches alternating with perforated windows. A comparison of the scheme of the wall surface with that of the Papanath example is an index of the gain in the art of architectural mural decoration, which has taken place since that temple was built. But there is something more than a mere improvement in the nature of this filling, there is a difference in the type of unit forming the basis of the composition. This unit, or fundamental element, is the ornamental shrine or niche. Where, in the Papanath temple, these were of the Indo-Aryan kind, in the Virupaksha they are of Dravidian character. The style of each temple is, therefore, not only defined by the shape of the tower, or even by the general formation of the structure, but also by the " order " expressed in the shrine-like niches on its walls. In a word the temple is a development and elaboration of the aboriginal shrine. The northern order of niche, as in the Papanath example, is distinguished by the character of its canopy, which is made up of multiples of a small decorative chaitya arch, grouped so as to form a triangular pattern. (Plate LIV, Fig. 8). On the other hand the Dravidian niche has as its underlying principle a canopy adapted from a single chaitya-arch motif, as illustrated on the Virupaksha temple.

One other point relating to these " orders " emerges in the early temples, which, although small in itself has considerable significance. A close examination of the pilasters on the exterior reveals an unusual convention in their design. This is a narrowing or constricting of the upper end of the shaft where it joins on to the capital. It is possible that such an inward curvature, seen below the neck moulding and forming a kind of shoulder, originated from the campaniform contours of Asoka's bell capital, and is first observable to a very slight degree in the pillars on the verandah of the rock-cut vihara No. 2 at Karli. (Plate XI, Fig. 7). Afterwards this " neck and shoulder " shape became more pronounced on the pillars of the southern style and

wherever seen may be accepted as the sign manual of the Dravidian order. One exception at least may be noted, singularly enough in one of the buildings now being described. The pilasters on the exterior of the Papanath temple are of this particular type, thus recording a symbol of the Dravidian order on an Indo-Aryan structure. But such an apparent solecism only serves to prove that at this early stage a few of the architectural proprieties of each style were still undetermined. There is one other architectural feature on the Virupaksha temple worthy of note. This is a structure rising above the parapet at the back of each of its porches, and which has been indentified as an embryo *gopuram*, that monumental gatehead which dominates all the approaches to the Dravidian temple, and one of the most striking productions in the architecture of the south. Here its final formation is observable, afterwards to develop into the horns and scroll motif on the topmost roof of these towering entrance pylons. (Chapter XX).

It has been shown that the centre of the architectural movement associated with the Early Chalukyans was confined to the triad of ancient capitals, the seats of this dynasty in Dharwar. But a minor development of a somewhat similar character took place, which, although in the same region, yet is an appreciable distance away from the fountain head. At Alampur, a village on the west bank of the Tungabhadra river in the Raichur district of Mysore State, is a group of temples almost identical with some of those described above.[1] These temples are six in number, and are situated inside a fortified enclosure in the same manner as at Aihole. They are however more in the style of the Papanath at Pattadakal, as they have Indo-Aryan sikharas, and may accordingly be assigned to the same date as that example, namely the latter half of the seventh century. Of no great size, as the largest only occupies a rectangle 75 feet by 50 feet, they are structurally very complete, as the walls and spires are in a finished state, and there is a finial in the form of a fluted *amala sila*, in position on most of them. Although appearing to be a modified reproduction of the Papanath type, in plan and in their interior arrangements they show a certain individuality, illustrating what seems to be a local manifestation of the style. In the shape and position of the pillared hall and the shrine chamber, the Alampur structures are not unlike the rock-cut temple of the Ravana-ka-Khai in the Ellora group (Chapter XV), also of the seventh century. That is to say the interior consists of an oblong hall with the shrine at one end, a colonnade of pillars forming a nave and aisles in front, and a processional passage the whole way round. The pillars are not so massive in their proportions as those in the rock-cut example, being tolerably slender and graceful, but they are decorated in the same manner, with the Indo-Aryan vase and foliage capital in evidence, a motif, as already shown, associated with the productions of the Gupta regime. This small group at Alampur, besides throwing further light on the gradual formation of the temple design, also reveals some kind of thought-transmission in the field of architectural expression. In a straight line a hundred miles away to find a small replica of the main movement, but with no accountable association, is an experience, although remarkable, yet not altogether unknown in Indian art history.

[1] Annual Report, Archaeological Dept., Hyderabad, 1926-7, Calcutta 1929.

REFERENCE

Cousens, H., *Ancient Temples of Aihole*, Arch. Sur. of India An. Rep. 1907-8, Cal. 1911.

CHAPTER XV

ROCK-ARCHITECTURE : THE FINAL PHASE

(A.D. 600 to 900)

BY the seventh century, as shown in the previous chapter, the art of building by means of dressed stone masonry had already considerably advanced in certain parts of the country. Yet in spite of the progress made in the sphere of constructional architecture, the rock-cut form of expression had in the course of many years become so inherent a tradition that it continued to be practised until almost mediaeval times. So much so that during the period from the seventh to the tenth centuries the most notable development of rock-architecture took place. An explanation of this method persisting and surviving in India after the rest of the known world had become proficient in the more rational mode of building production, may be traced to a condition of comparative isolation which appears to have prevailed at the time. Intercourse with other civilizations had tended to be rare and intermittent, so that new experiences were not readily acquired. But another and perhaps more important factor that encouraged this ancient procedure, and gave it so long an existence in India, was contained in the instincts of the people themselves. For it is fairly clear that the rock temples were eminently suitable to their religious susceptibilities, the dim-lit columned halls crowded with immense shapes indestructible and hewn out of the earth itself, when compared with their own puny selves, filled them with fear and fascination combined. The solemn mystery of these great colonnaded caverns, yet orderly and symmetrical in their formation, would appeal to minds imaginative and intensely receptive, an innate mental condition to which the impassioned nature of their art plainly testifies.

This final manifestation of rock-architecture in India was confined to three localities : (1) Ellora, where excavated halls under the Buddhists had been already in course of production for two hundred years (Chapter XII) ; (2) the islands of Elephanta and Salsette near Bombay ; and (3) a development under the Pallava dynasty, the rulers of a kingdom approximating geographically to the modern State of Madras. As the works of the last named form the opening phase of the Dravidian style as a whole, they are referred to in the next chapter. The rock-cut groups now to be described are the Brahmanical and Jain series at Ellora, and the Brahmanical examples at Elephanta and Salsette, all excavated between the seventh and the ninth centuries.

It was early in the seventh century, when the activities of the Mahayana Buddhists on this site were drawing to a close, that the Hindu hierarchy began in their turn to prepare a series of columned halls in much the same architectural style as the Buddhist, but adapted to suit their own ritualistic needs. The Brahmanical group at Ellora extends along the west face of the hill for about half a mile, and consists of sixteen excavations numbered 13 to 29 (Plate XXV). The principal examples are : (No. 14) Ravana-ka-Khai or Abode of Ravana, the demon king of Lanka (Ceylon) ; (No. 15) Das Avatar, or the Ten Incarnations of Vishnu ; (No. 16) the Kailasa or Siva's Paradise ; (No. 21) Rameswara, or "Lord of Rama" ; (No. 29) Dumar Lena, sometimes called Sita's Nani, or Bath of Sita. These resolve themselves as follows, into four different types, most of them apparently taking their various shapes in order to conform to the changing requirements of the creed : (*a*) the most primitive, and evidently owing much to the Buddhist vihara, being merely a pillared portico with a cella beyond, as for example the Das Avatar (No. 15). (*b*) Similar to the preceding but with the cella isolated by means of a passage round it, as in the Ravana-ka-Khai, (No. 14) and Rameswara (No. 21). (*c*) Another style in which the shrine is isolated but standing in the centre of a cruciform hall, the whole having more than one entrance, as in the Dumar Lena (No. 29), (The temple at Elephanta, and also the Jogeswara in Salsette are of this type). (*d*) The culmination of the rock-cut method taking the form not of an excavated series of galleries as in each of the previous examples, but one in which a structural temple is copied in all its detail, as in the monolithic temple of Kailasa (No. 16).

The largest and finest of the first type (*a*), and also the most important as it is the only Brahmanical example in two stories, is the Das Avatar (No. 15). This temple is approached through a rock-cut entrance which opens on to a large irregular-shaped courtyard having a detached shrine in its centre. There is a doorway on the left of this courtyard leading to a square compartment surrounded by cells comprising the quarters of the sacristan and store-rooms for the reception of the ritualistic vestments and utensils. The detached shrine is a large and important feature of the exterior, probably intended for a *nandi* image (the bull of Siva), and is in the form of a square four-pillared pavilion surrounded by a verandah with a flight of steps at front and rear. Beyond this rises the facade of the temple, the two stories being defined by two rows, one above the other, of square pillars, recalling a similar arrangement in the frontage of the Tin Thal monastery in the Buddhist group. A short flight of steps gives admission to the ground floor which consists of a compartment 97 feet wide by 50 feet deep, and containing 14 square pillars. A staircase on the left communicates with the upper story, a fine rectangular hall 105 feet by 95 feet having the large number of 44 pillars to support its flat roof. These pillars are arranged in six rows of nine each, with two additional ones at the far end of the central aisle to form a shalow vestibule leading to a square cella enshrining a lingam. The whole of this portion of the conception is remarkable for the plainness, of its treatment, the pillars, save the two in front of the vestibule which are elaborately carved, being simple square prisms with flat abacus capitals. The architecture was however only the framework, or setting, for the handiwork of the sculptor, whose skill is displayed in large sunk panels spaced out between pilasters at regular intervals around the walls. In each of these deep square recesses is illustrated, in exceedingly bold relief, some striking episode from Hindu mythology, those on one side being mostly Vaishnava, while on the other they are entirely Saivite. The effect of such gigantic figures partly hidden by the darkness and shadowy obscurity of the pillared aisles is supremely dramatic.

The second type of excavated hall, the kind distinguished by a processional path around the shrine, is represented by two fine examples, the Ravana-ka-Khai (No. 14) and the Rameswara (No. 21), but except that both have this corridor for ambulation, they have little else in common. The Ravana-ka-Khai is very simple in plan, the whole of it occupying a regular rectangle 52 feet wide by 87 feet deep, two-thirds of the space in front being taken up by the pillared hall, the remainder by the shrine. Around the pillared hall is a row of columns with a double row in front forming a sort of verandah, the capitals of the columns being all of the vase and foliage order. The side aisles are continued so as to give access to the passage round the shrine. This shrine is produced by leaving a rectangular mass of rock in the centre of the far end of the hall, and cutting a cubical chamber within it. On each side of the entrance to the cella are carved a number of figures including two *dwarapalas*, and within is a broken image of Bhavani or Durga the deity to whom the temple was dedicated. Within the walls of the pillared hall are recesses between pilasters in which are boldly carved figure-compositions, on the south side Saivite subjects, and on the north Vaishnavite.

The other example of the processional passage type, the Rameswara (No. 21), is also a relatively simple scheme, but notable on account of the wealth of carving with which all its parts are overlaid. In front is a courtyard in the centre of which is a shrine consisting of a lofty pedestal elaborately sculptured and supporting a figure of the reclining bull of Siva. Just beyond is the facade of the temple, a range of four short and prodigiously bulky columns arising above a highly decorated dwarf wall. This wall is interrupted between the two central pillars to form a doorway to the entrance hall or portico, a comparatively shallow compartment 25 feet deep, but 69 feet wide, these proportions being brought about by the fact that the portico is carried across the entire front, with a further extension of a chamber at each end. Of the pillars inside the entrance hall, which are all of the " cushion " variety, the two on the inner side form three openings, that in the centre facing the cells, while those on each side lead to the processional passage round it. This type of shrine and cella is similar in principle to the previous example, but in the present instance the latter contains a *lingam*. The entrance portico with its massive fluted pillars, the profusion of carved imagery on its walls, and the giant *dwarpalas* (guardians) of its cella standing forth darkly powerful from the inner sanctuary, all combine to give the hall of the Rameswara considerable mystery of effect, but the chief character of the temple is not in its interior. This will be found outside in the architectural treatment of the facade, especially in the shape and design of its pillars. These four columnar groups form the principal feature of the frontage, with a half column completing the scheme at each end. Their short shafts are almost entirely concealed by the dwarf wall which rises in front of them, so that the principal portion presenting itself to view is not the pillar but the capital. The capital is based on that of the vase and foliage order, but over this now familiar conception groups of figures in the shape of brackets have been superimposed, thus giving the motif not only a richer but an entirely different complexion. With their stunted proportions and miscellany of motifs the effect as a whole is one of fantastic extravagance, yet, on the other hand, some of the ornamentation, and particularly the rhythmic forms and exquisite modelling of

the female figures show a feeling for grace of poise and voluptuous beauty which is instinctive.

The third type of excavated temple in which the shrine is not only isolated but contained within a group of halls arranged on a cruciform plan, is illustrated at Ellora by only one example, that of the Dumar Lena (No. 29). Two other rock-cut temples of this class are known, although on entirely different sites, one at Elephanta and the other the Jogeswara in Salsette, but the Dumar Lena is clearly the original by which these were inspired. Where this type differs fundamentally from all others and departs from the rock-cut tradition is in the number and position of its entrances, both the Ellora example and that at Elephanta having three separate portals, one at the front, and one in each wing. Such an innovation was dependent to some extent on the configuration of the hill in which the temple was excavated, and the manner in which some of the difficulties thus presented were met is seen in the varying forms of the plan. All the temples of this class are not only large in area but also in the scale of their parts, and although no doubt they were primarily devised to admit of the passage of important ceremonial processions, the result is an interior architectural scheme of a most impressive order. Much of the effect is due to the system of lighting, which, admitted through the portals from three opposite directions infiltrates into every part of the interior, casting an unending intricacy of shadows thus increasing the contrast and illusion. That it was a type of excavated hall copied from some form of building which has disappeared is not unlikely as the interior arrangements consisting of one pillared aisle passing through a row of columns into another having a different axial direction, seem to suggest a structural derivation.

The Dumar Lena is one of the largest and most imposing temples on the Ellora site, the conditions of its plan being made possible by the shape of the hill in which it is cut. In the interior disposition of its halls, the focal point not only in its ritualistic but also in its architectural aspect, is a massive central shrine, surrounded by gigantic figures guarding the steps on each of its sides which give access to the four doorways of the cella. Leading up to this shrine and partly encircling it is the main hall, a fine rectangular gallery 150 feet long and 50 feet wide, divided into a nave and aisles by a colonnade of five pillars on each side, including the two forming the principal entrance. Flanking the main hall, and opening out of it through a row of four pillars on each side, are the transepts, columned courts communicating with the two lateral entrances, the entire width across the temple between the side portals measuring the same as its depth, 150 feet. This transverse system of halls is not dissimilar in principle to that of a Gothic cathedral, for there are the main or west entrance, the north and south doorways, with pillared aisles from all three converging on to the " high place " confronting the sanctum in the east. (Plate LVI).

The exterior of the Dumar Lena can scarcely be called a facade, as it consists of the three detached entrances, but all of which are of conspicuous design. Each is a wide pillared opening approached by a flight of steps with a statue mounted on a pedestal on either side of a lion, sedent, the head turned inward and one paw raised. With its background of pillars receding into the diminishing light of the interior there is a simple dignity in this conception of an entrance which, in Indian architecture has few equals. All the pillars within the temple are of the " cushion " order,

Fig. 1. Entrance.

Fig. 2. Main Hall
Ellora, Rock-cut Temple: Dumar Lena; 7th cent. A.D.

Fig. 2. The Plinth. The Kailasa. Ellora: 8th cent. A.D.

Fig. 1. Capital from Elephanta

Lingaraja Temple, Bhubhaneswar.

Fig. 1. Trimurti Mandapa

Fig. 2. Varaha Mandapa
Mamallapuram, Madras: Rock-cut Facades; c. A.D. 650.

SHRINES IN GABLE ENDS
OF THE RATHAS AT
MAMALLAPURAM, MADRAS.
7TH CENTURY A.D.

BHIMA RATHA

SAHADEVA RATHA

GANESHA RATHA

Fig. 1.
Badami, Bijapur Dist.:   Temple of Malegitti Sivalaya from N. E.; c. A.D. 700.

Fig. 2.
Mamallapuram: General View of the Rathas (Seven Pagodas); c. A.D. 650.

Fig. 1
Mahishasur Mandapa; c. 650 A.D.

Fig. 2
Shore Temple.

Fig. 3
Shore Temple, Mamallapuram, Madras ; c. A.D. 700.

TEMPLE OF KAILASANATHA
AT CONJEVERAM (KANCHIPURAM).
C. 700 AD.

SHOWING
ORIGINAL ARRANGEMENT
OF THE BUILDING.

CONJECTURAL RESTORATION
OF THE
SHORE TEMPLE AT
MAMALLAPURAM
(SEVEN PAGODAS).
C. 700 AD.

PERCY BROWN.

and are of stupendous proportions being fifteen feet high and five feet wide at the base ; as some of the standing figures are also fifteen feet in height the effect as a whole recalls some of the similarly large-scale productions of the ancient Egyptians. Through the perspective of these ponderous piers, the sculptured shapes of the gods move elusive yet persistent " imaged in dimly-seen titanic forms, looming out of the unknown depths of space and eternity."

As the two other temples of this class are situated elsewhere, a degression from the Ellora site becomes necessary at this stage in order to include them in their proper place. That on the island of Elephanta, near Bombay, and dating from the middle of the eighth century, resembles the Dumar Lena in the general distribution of its parts, but to a rather smaller scale, as its measurements overall are 130 feet by 129 feet. Certain changes in the plan may be traced partially due to the particular shape of the terrain in which the temple is situated, and although there are three entrances, the cruciform arrangement is not so clearly marked, while the shrine is placed in a side aisle instead of opposite the main front. In the proportions, style, and disposition of its pillars, there is a notable similarity to the Ellora example, as they are of the "cushion" order and aligned so as to produce the nave and aisles, with additional rows of pillars on either side to form the wings. The main shrine also, with its huge sculptured guardians, has been treated in the same way as that in the Dumar Lena, and the entrances appear to have been originally of the lion type. The remains of a frontage of this nature, with the sedent lions still in position guarding the flight of steps, may be seen in a supplementary prayer-hall on the east wing of the main temple, a kind of chapter-house, which, although ruined, still retains enough of the original work to show that it was a broad, simple and refined composition, thus providing an elegant and appropriate annexe. There are features in this side sanctuary such as the low level of the floor of the courtyard suggesting a kind of shallow reservoir, which may have an association with *Naga* (snake) worship and water spirits. In several types of early temple, water seems to have played an important part in the ritual, and so influenced not a little their architectural arrangements. Where however the Elephanta temple is superior to all others of its kind is in the character and quality of its sculptures, particularly those on the back or southern wall. Here are three large square recesses, divided off by pilasters each of which bears a gigantic figure of a *dwarpala*. The panel to the left or east contains a spirited representation of Ardhanari, a manifestation of Siva typifying the male and female energies, while the corresponding panel on the right enshrines figures of Siva and Parvati. Both these groups are masterly examples of the plastic art, and pulsate with spiritual fervour, but the most striking of all, that in the central recess depicting the three-faced head of Siva Mahesamurthi is the creation of a genius. Few works of sculpture excel the magnificent treatment of this colossal triple bust in which the whole essence of the creed is concentrated in forms of marvellous refinement and subtlety, curved, and full and alive ; in the white heat of his passion the sculptor seems to have melted the very substance of the rock and infused into it something of his own soul.

The cruciform type ends somewhat tamely in the temple of Jogeswari on the island of Salsette near Bombay, the last of its kind as it dates from about 800 A.D. Although

in some respects larger and more grandiose than the two preceding examples, there is a want of logic in its plan, with little of that assurance in the arrangements that makes these so satisfying. Comprising a rather rambling sequence of entrances, porticos, courts, and galleries, its principal central feature is a square hall of 95 feet side with an aisle all round formed by an inner colonnade of twenty pillars. Within this, in the middle, is the shrine with its four doorways leading to a cella containing a linga. The pillars are similar to those at Elphanta, but except for the carving on some of its doorways, its walls are devoid of sculpture. The main approach is from the east by means of a flight of steps which give access to a portico having a range of four pillars on each side. In the gallery behind these pillars the walls have been carved with figure subjects. Beyond the portico is an open court with an isolated mass of rock left on either side which it was evidently intended to sculpture. Three doorways in the far side of the court lead to another larger portico, with the same arrangement of pillars on each side, out of which three more doors give access to the main hall described above. This range of courts, porticos and main hall is in one alignment and the measurement of the whole amounts to two hundred and fifty feet in a straight line, a longer distance cut in the rock than any other of the excavated temples.

The final type of Brahmanical rock-cut architecture consists of one example only, the Kailasa (Siva's Paradise) at Ellora, which stands in a class by itself, as it is unique. Instead of the underground halls which had hitherto been the practice, its creators threw aside all previous conventions and boldly undertook to reproduce in the virgin rock to a very large scale and in full detail a structural temple of the period. Truly has it been said "the Indian artist had an extraordinarily developed plastic sense. No other people has ever dreamed of sculpting such great temples out of the solid rock as he has. Indeed, Indian architecture proceeds, not as ours, according to the principles of construction ; it is rather conceived as an object cut out of a solid material as an ivory figure might be."[1] When it is realized that the ground plan of the Kailasa approximates in area that of the Parthenon at Athens, and that its height is one and half times that of the same Greek masterpiece, some idea of the magnitude of the undertaking may be conceived. In its plan and general arrangements the Kailasa bears a certain resemblance to the Virupaksha temple at Pattadakal (Chapter XIV), even then a recent building, and one which was no doubt at the time considered the last word in temple design. But although the early Chalukyan example may have provided some inspiration the Kailasa is more than twice its size, and is clearly an illustration of the normal development of the Dravidian temple-type, adapted to conform to the particular technique involved. It is only logical that each individual temple at this formative period of the art, should be a copy of its predecessor, but improved and enriched by the accumulation of previous experience. Once the idea of the Kailasa was conceived, its production became a matter of time, patience, and skilled labour, all of which appear to have been readily forthcoming. That it was an expression of exalted religious emotion is obvious but even this condition could not have made such a consummation possible, had it not also had the patronage of a ruler with unlimited resources and who was at the same time moved by the loftiest ideals. This monarch has been identified as Krishna I (757-783) of the Rashtrakuta dynasty of Malkhed. Having subjugated the Western Chalukyans and occupied their territory, the dynasty was at the fulness

---

[1] Roger Fry, "*The Arts of Painting and Sculpture*", p.87.

of its power towards the latter half of the eighth century, during which time the Kailasa was executed. (Plates XXVIII, Fig. 2 and LVII).

The first stage of the work, although laborious, was simple. It consisted in excavating out of the hillside three huge trenches at right angles, cut down vertically to the level of the base of the hill, thus forming a rectangle 300 feet by 175 feet. This operation outlined the shape of the courtyard and at the same time left standing in the middle a large isolated mass or "island" of rock, over 200 feet long, 100 feet wide and 100 feet high at its apex. Beginning at the top, the process of rough-hewing the irregular mass into shape was next undertaken, but those employed on this "pointing" were immediately followed by the sculptors, for each portion of the carved detail appears to have been completely finished as the work progressed downwards, thus avoiding any need for scaffolding. Such a method would naturally lead to deviations from the structural type, as the Kailasa is more closely allied to sculpture on a grand scale than to architecture, the effect being obtained by the process of cutting down, as distinct from building up. This accounts to some extent for the abnormally high plinth, which it was easy to leave in the living rock, and also for the "bridges" connecting certain portions of the scheme, none of which occur in any masonry buildings. Authorities[1] have shown that this method of production by excavation involves much less expenditure of labour than by building, but on the other hand the general effect is marred by the rock production always appearing in a pit, a disadvantage from which the Kailasa obviously suffers. (Plate XXVIII, Fig. 2).

The scheme of the Kailasa as a whole resolves itself into four parts, namely the body of the temple itself, the entrance gateway, an intermediate nandi shrine, and the cloisters surrounding the courtyard. On each side of the courtyard supplementary chambers have been excavated, the one cut into the north wall being a very large pillared hall called the Lankeswara, but these may have been added at a slightly later date, and in any case have little connection with the design as a whole. As regards orientation the axial alignment of the temple is from west to east, but contrary to the usual arrangement of the structural examples, due to its position on the hill-side, the entrance is not on the east, but to the west. The main body of the temple occupies a parallelogram approximately 150 feet by 100 feet with sections of its sides projecting at intervals, like transepts, to support corresponding projecting features above. Much of the imposing character of this portion of the composition is obtained by the lofty and substantial plinth, which is twenty-five feet high, and at first sight has the appearance of a ground story. Above and below, the sub-structure is heavily moulded, while the central space of the sides is occupied by a grand frieze of boldly carved elephants and lions. Standing high on this plinth is the temple proper, approached by flights of steps leading to a pillared porch on its western side, and it is here that its designers rose to the greatest heights. There is no pronounced departure from the conventional combination of the mandapa and the vimana, but the manner in which various architectural elements, all definite and sharply outlined, such as cornices, pilasters, niches, and porticos, have been assembled in an orderly and artistic manner to form a unified whole, is masterly. Then over all rises the stately tower in three tiers, with its prominently projecting gable-front, and surmounted

by a shapely cupola, reaching up to a total height of ninety-five feet. But this is not all. Around the wide space of the platform at the base of the vimana five subsidiary shrines have been fashioned out of the rock, each an elegant reproduction to a reduced scale of the main theme, to which they serve as a refrain. The interior consists of a pillared hall, from which a vestibule leads to the cella. This hall is a well-proportioned compartment measuring seventy feet by sixty-two feet, having sixteen square piers in groups of four in each quarter, an arrangement which produces a cruciform central aisle with an effect of great dignity.

The remaining portions of the temple-scheme, although essential to the composition as a whole, are substantially in the nature of accessories. There is the Nandi shrine in front, a pavilion twenty feet square and standing on a solid yet highly decorated base the entire height being fifty feet, in order to bring it level with the rest of the temple to which it is connected by a bridge. On the opposite side this shrine is joined in the same manner with the sole entrance a fine double-storied gatehouse with ample accommodation for the temple guardians, the whole combination forming a suitable introduction to the main design. Encircling the courtyard are cloisters composed of a colonnade of pillars the regularity of which is broken at intervals by the entrances to side chambers ; as a rich background to the central mass nothing could be more appropriate. Finally there are the two-free-standing pillars, or *dhwajasthambhas*, fifty-one feet high, one on each side of the *nandi* shrine, in themselves finished works of art, gracefully proportioned yet strongly stable, their place in the architectural scheme being somewhat analogous to the obelisk in the Egyptian temple. Each bore the trisul, or ensign of Siva, to whom the Kailasa was dedicated, but in addition to this and other symbolism carved on their surfaces, the shape of these pillars has its significance. This is seen in the contours of the capital. During the early stages of the evolution of the Dravidian style, as has been already noticed in the very primitive pilasters of the Ladh Khan temple at Aihole dating from the fifth century, a type of capital was being formulated the distinguishing features of which were a "cushion" member above a constricted neck. A development of this combination produced the Dravidian "order", of which these monolithic columns of the Kailasa are an interpretation, the constricted neck having been transformed into that sloping shape below the cushion cap, a contraction of the outline which is unmistakable. Throughout the entire architectural scheme, pilasters and pillars of the Dravidian order are in evidence, although occasional examples of the "vase and foliage" type of capital have been introduced, showing that in this instance the influence of the northern style still persisted.

The temple of Kailasa at Ellora is not only the most stupendous single work of art executed in India, but as an example of rock-architecture it is unrivalled. Standing within its precincts and surrounded by its grey and hoary pavilions, one seems to be looking through into another world, not a world of time and space, but one of intense spiritual devotion expressed by such an amazing artistic creation hewn out of the earth itself. Gradually one becomes conscious of the remarkable imagination which conceived it, the unstinted labour which enabled it to be materialized (a work of a hundred years), and, finally, the sculpture with which it is adorned ; this plastic decoration is its crowning glory something more than a record of artistic form, it is

---

[1] Ferguson, *History of Indian Architecture*, 1910, Vol. I, p. 348.

a great spiritual achievement, every portion being a rich statement glowing with meaning. The Kailasa is an illustration of one of those rare occasions when men's minds, hearts, and hands work in unison towards the consummation of a supreme ideal. It was under such conditions of religious and cultural stability that this grand monolithic representation of Siva's Paradise was produced.

Of these excavated temples on the Ellora site, there now remains only the final group, the productions of the Jains, probably begun about 800 A.D., and carried on continuously for the following century. This group the smallest of the entire series is set a little apart from the others, occupying the northern horn of the ridge, and consists of five examples, Nos. 30 to 34, but only three are of any importance. One of these, known as the Chota Kailasa (No. 30) standing a little detached from the others, as indicated by its name, is a small copy of the great Brahmanical monolithic temple, the Kailasa, previously described. Only about a quarter the size of the original, the hall being thirty-six feet wide compared with the Kailasa's fifty-five feet, it is a replica of it in most respects, but in the process of reduction, the tower has assumed rather stunted proportions, and is also unfinished. Much superior to this monolithic example are the two temples of the excavated variety, known as the Indra Sabha (No. 32) and the Jaganath Sabha (No. 33), standing close together. Both are in two stories, the larger and finer being the Indra Sabha, apparently the first of the group to be cut, and therefore dating from about 800 A.D. This temple is approached through a rock-cut doorway which opens on to a square courtyard of fifty feet side, much of the central portion of which is occupied by a monolithic shrine in the form of a miniature Dravidian temple. A handsome prelude to the temple proper, mounted on a high flight of steps and with all the details of the original model faithfully rendered, nevertheless this shrine is rather disproportionately large for its surroundings and as in addition there is a large free-standing pillar (dhwajasthambha) over thirty feet high on one side, and an imposing effigy of an elephant on the other, the courtyard as a whole is inclined to be congested. Moreover as three sides of the quadrangle are elaborately carved to produce a two storied facade, such an excess of richness in so confined a space is overpowering. Yet there is much in the treatment of the sides of this frontage that has merit. What may be termed an entablature is one of its main features, consisting of a broad horizontal surface dividing the lower from the upper story, while a similar broad surface surmounts the upper story. Both entablatures are elaborately carved, the upper one by means of a series of shrines with images of the Tirthankars, or Jaina saints in the niches, the lower with a design which includes projecting elephant forms alternating with rampant lions against a background of pilasters and decorative vases. Although all these motifs are exceptionally well-designed and executed, and portions even well-composed, as a whole the facade does not appear to have been treated as a unity, it is an arrangement of very artistic elements but carried out without any clear pre-conceived plan.

The condition of the interior proves conclusively that it was the practice in rock-architecture to carry the completion of the work from above downwards, for while the upper story is entirely finished, parts of the ground floor are only blocked out. It was evidently the intention in the planning of the lower story to supplement the central hall by means of a range of cells, but these have been begun and left in the rough. This central hall, which is approached through a deep pillared verandah, is a square of approximately forty feet side, while beyond is a vestibule, also pillared, leading to the cella containing an image of the saint Mahavira seated on a lion throne. All the pillars have plain square shafts, with simple flat brackets as capitals but in some instances the bases are richly moulded. It is not improbable that these plain shafts would have been carved into ornamental pillars had some untoward circumstances not intervened and prevented their completion. The upper story, which is reached by a staircase on the right of the lower verandah, consists of a cental hall with two additional sanctuaries thrown forward on each wing, the balconies of all three overlooking the open courtyard described above. The main hall in the centre has an elaborate pillared portico while the hall itself, a square of fifty feet side is surrounded by a colonnade of twelve pillars, with an altar in the middle on which originally stood a quadruple image (chaumukha) ; the ceiling immediately over this altar is coved and made to represent an immense lotus flower, with mortice holes at the corners and centre for pendent lamps. At the far end is a richly patterned doorway leading to a cella containing a figure of Mahavira. The two side sanctuaries are in most respects smaller copies of the large hall, with balcony and central chamber all pillared, and a cella with an image at the far end. No other temple at Ellora is so complete in its arrangements or so finished in its workmanship as this upper story of the Indra Sabha, all the large sunk panels between pilasters on every wall being filled with figure subjects, while the pillars, admirably spaced, and on occasion joined by dwarf walls, are moulded, fluted, and faceted, as in no other instance. Yet in spite of its advanced character there is a survival of certain wooden traditions, a curious reversion to the more primitive rock-cut type. Here and there are naive copies of timber expedients, literally translated, as for instance a wooden batten to hold the asana or seat-back of the balcony in its place, is exactly reproduced in the rock technique. There are indications also that a considerable amount of woodwork was introduced to supplement the rock-work, as there are grooves for shutters to the verandahs, and a special arrangement of holes and sockets for the insertion of a wooden trap-door to enable the entrance to the upper floor to be impenetrably sealed. From such evidences it may be inferred that outside these groups of rock-cut religious retreats, the other buildings of the country were of wooden construction, and that the people as a whole were still living in the timber age.

The other notable example of the Jain group, the Jaganath Sabha (No. 33) is in general principles and in the treatment of its major parts, of the same character as the Indra Sabha, but without its regularity of plan. The ground floor is a complex of three sanctuaries unsymmetrically arranged and opening out of a courtyard, much of which has crumbled away. Each sanctuary is self-contained and comparatively small, the hall of the largest being only 26 feet side, consisting of the usual complement of portico, square pillared compartment, and cella beyond. The upper floor is a larger hall much on the lines of that of the previous example except that it is rather smaller as it measures 57 feet by 40 feet, with a colonnade of twelve pillars around the four sides. There is a cella at the far end, and the walls are recessed for groups of figures. Leading out of this main hall by means of an adjoining chamber in one corner, and at an angle to it, is a supplementary sanctuary, similar in proportions and character to those on the ground floor, exact in its workmanship and very complete in all its parts. It is in the richly carved details and perfected finish, particularly of the pillars, all of which are elaborations of the cushion variety, that the Jain examples excel, and also in the precision and accuracy of the cutting generally. Throughout, the workmanship is of a high order, yet the planning, as in this instance, is inclined to be haphazard and improvisatory. Moreover, as in many of the productions of the Jains, in spite of the beauty of the embellishment, or perhaps in some obscure way on account of it, there is a cold and impersonal feeling in these rock-cut halls, which is not found in those of the Buddhist or Hindus, a circumstance of some irony in view of the pronounced humanitarian character of the creed that inspired them.

With the excavated temples of the Jains at Ellora, which were probably completed towards the early part of the tenth century, the rock-architecture of India, to all intents and purposes, terminated. But before this occurred the close of the movement had been already foreshadowed. That outstanding monolithic example, the Kailasa, although representing its culmination, implied, all unconsciously the beginning of the end. When instead of the pillared halls penetrating into the interior of the hill-side their place was taken by direct copies of structural edifices, such replicas, however splendid, ceased to possess that indefinable quality which gave rock-architecture its real incentive. No longer was it an art of long sombre galleries and dim-lit cells peopled with colossal beings in a darkly splendid world, thrilling the devotee with a strange fearfulness into a state of religious awe. Brought out into the brilliant sunlight, much of the atmosphere of haunting mystery departed, and although the beauty of art and workmanship was greater than ever, as the Kailasa plainly testifies, its ancient motives and traditions were lost. Such may have been the metaphysical reason for the cessation of this architectural mode. But there was also the material explanation. By this time structural building had been developing, and there is little doubt that rock-architecture declined and eventually died out on account of the masonry system of production becoming perfected and its greater possibilities known. But for over a thousand years, corresponding approximately to the first millennium, it was a method of expression which flourished in several parts of India to produce some of the most remarkable monuments wrought by the hand of man. Whatever their architectural properties, that many of these excavated temples are outstanding works of art, significant of a people who had the vision and capacity for ideas to conceive them and the skill and audacity to create them out of the unyielding rock, cannot be denied.

REFERENCE

Burgess, J., *Rock Temples of Elephanta*, Bombay, 1871.
Burgess, J., *Rock Temples of Elura*, Bombay, 1877.

CHAPTER XVI

THE DRAVIDIAN STYLE, ITS GENESIS UNDER THE PALLAVAS (c. 600 A.D. to 900)

IT has already been shown that the building art as it was developing in Southern India was assuming a separate form. Also that this form, in view of the fact that it was being practised almost entirely in the Tamil country, anciently known as Dravidadesha, has been referred to as the Dravidian style. This southern type of architecture, it has been found convenient to resolve into five periods, corresponding to the five principal kingdoms which ruled in the south of India during the course of its evolution. These are as follows :

> (1) Pallava (A.D. 600-900) ; (2) Chola (900-1150) ; (3) Pandya (1100-1350) ; (4) Vijayanagar (1350-1565) ; (5) Madura (from 1600).

Of all the great powers that together made the history of southern India, none had a more marked effect on the architecture of this region than the earliest of all, that of the Pallavas, whose productions provided the foundations of the Dravidian style. Originally the political successors of the Andhras, under whose rule the Buddhist architecture of Southern India attained its finest form, the Pallavas came into prominence in the seventh century, and continued paramount in the south until the beginning of the tenth century. The centre of their kingdom lay on the lower reaches of the Palar river, and the chief examples of Pallava architecture are to be found in the country around the town of Conjeeveram (Kanchipuram) the ancient capital. There are however a few instances of the work of this dynasty located as far south as Tanjore and Pudukkottai.

The Pallava dynasty maintained its varying forms of architecture for some three centuries, from A.D. 600 to 900, and its productions resolve themselves into two phases, the first of these occupying the seventh century, and the second the eighth and ninth centuries. In the former the examples were entirely rock-cut, in the latter they were entirely structural. There were four principal rulers during the period of their power, and the works of each phase have been divided into two groups, comprising four groups in all, each of which is named after the king who was ruling at the time.

1st Phase	Mahendra Group, A.D. 610 to 640, pillared halls (mandapas) only	wholly rock-cut.
	Mamalla Group, A.D. 640 to 690, mandapas, and rathas (monolithic temples).	
2nd Phase	Rajasimha Group, A.D. 690 to c. 800, temples.	wholly structural.
	Nandivarman Group, c. A.D. 800 to c. 900, temples.	

It will be seen from the above that the rock architecture of the first phase takes two forms, referred to as *mandapas*, and *rathas*. In this connection, a mandapa is an excavation, while a ratha is a monolith. The former is an open pavilion, and, as excavated in the rock, takes the shape of a simple columned hall with one or more cellas in the back wall. A ratha is in reality a car or chariot, provided by the temple authorities for the conveyance of the image of the deity during processions. But here, by common usage, it refers to a series of monolithic shrines, which are exact copies in granite of certain structural prototypes.

Beginning with the rock-architecture produced during the reign or Mahendravarman (A.D. 610-640), constituting the earlier of the two groups of the first phase, this represents the mode that found favour with the Pallavas in the first half of the seventh century. The examples of the Mahendra group consist of one type only, namely pillared halls or mandapas. In this connection, it is perhaps only natural to infer that because the surviving relics of an ancient civilization are those formed out of the lasting rock, people were acquainted solely with that method. It will be shown however that a true picture of the time would represent these rock-cut halls supplemented by a very considerable miscellany of other buildings structurally formed. Although the latter have perished, owing to their impermanent character, the style and certain distinguishing features of their architecture are preserved by copies cut in the rock. But it is obvious from the examples of the early group, which are fourteen in number, and enumerated below,[1] that the architecture, whether structural or otherwise, of the Pallavas at this particular stage was of a definitely primitive type. Each rock-cut mandapa consists of a pillared hall serving as a kind of portico to one or more cellas deeply recessed in the interior wall. The exterior presents a facade formed of a row of pillars, each pillar averaging seven feet in height with a diameter of two feet, the shafts being square in section except for the middle third which is chamfered into an octagon. An immense and heavy bracket provides the capital, the composition as a whole suggesting as its origin a very elemental structure in which a ponderous wooden beam and bracket were the main features. So plain and simple is the Mahendra type that in the earliest examples, as at Mandagapattu and Trichinopoly, there is not even a cornice above the pillars, but later a roll-moulding was added as at Pallavaram. Afterwards, at Mogalrajapuram, this roll-cornice was ornamented at intervals with a motif known as a *kudu* (acroteria), which is readily identified as the Buddhist chaitya-arch much reduced and converted into an object of decoration.

Towards the end of Mahendra's reign some efforts were made to break away from this singularly plain treatment of the mandapa, as may be seen in the rock-cut temple of Anantasayana at Undavalli, and in the series of shrines at

---

[1] (1) Dalavanur, 10 m. S. E. of Ginjee, in S. Arcot dist., (2) Trichinopoly "Rock Temple," (3) Mandagapattu, 6. m. S. W. of Dalavanur, (4) Pallavaram, Chingleput dist., (5) Mahendravadi, 3 m. S. E. of Sholinghur, N. Arcot dist., (6) Vallam, 2 m. E. of Chingleput, (7) Malacheri, 3 m. N. W. of Gingee, (8) Singavaram, 1 m. S. of Malacheri, (9) Tirukkalukkunram, 9 m. S. E. of Chinglepur, (10) Kilamavilangai, S. Arcot dist., (11) Bezwada, Kistna dist., (12) Mogalrajapuram, 3 m. E. of Bezwada, (13) Undavalli, Guntut dist., (14) Bhairavakonda, Nellore dist.

Bhairavakonda. The former is a definite departure, as although in some senses a mandapa, for it consists of several of these pillared halls one above another, it is fairly clear that it was an attempt to reproduce in the rock technique a pyramidal composition, evidently based on the conventional form of a Buddhist vihara or monastery, as it is in four stories and rises to a height of some fifty feet. Yet except for its size and more complex design, its architectural rendering shows but little advance on the single storied examples already referred to. It is, however, in the series of eight excavated examples at Bhairavakonda, probably the latest of this reign, that a marked step forward is observable, for here is the beginning of the distinctive Pallava type. It is true that here also the mandapas are of the same simple plan as are all the foregoing, but it is in the design of the facade, and specially in the elaboration of the pillars, that a new spirit seems to have entered architectural effort of the time. It is the stage at which the characteristic pillar, or " order," of the Pallava into the style makes its appearance.

Up to this point the pillar in the Mahendra group of mandapas has been a rudimentary type of beam and bracket, serviceable in principle, but the idea of minds evidently in possession of very limited experience. At Bairavakonda, this crude production is still visible, but superimposed on its simple shape is an entirely different and much more sophisticated design of capital and shaft, a formation which has already been referred to as representing the Dravidian mode. And moreover, with the fusion of the two forms of pillar, there was also added another element, that of a lion, a figure of one of these animals being combined with the lower portion of the shaft, and another introduced into the capital. This heraldic beast, which from now onward occupies a prominent position in the architectural productions of the Pallavas, was appropriated by the ruling dynasty, and made to serve as a symbol of their Simhavishnu, or " lion " (simha) ancestry. The Bhairavakonda pillars therefore depict the Pallava order in the making, the blending of the stark realism of the beginner, with the more reasoned results of endeavour. How this order of pillar design, as yet unformed, was refined and adapted until it developed into a type of column of exceptional character and elegance, is shown in the productions of the succeeding reign.

The second group of the first phase of Pallava architecture, mainly executed during the reign of Narasimhavarman I (A.D. 640-68), while still adhering to the rock-cut method, in addition to a series of mandapas, is also represented by a number of rathas or monoliths. Practically all the examples of this group are found on one site, marking the position of the deserted seaport town of Mamallapuram, and named after its royal founder, one of whose titles was Mahamalla. This archaeological record of the one-time might of the Pallavas lies towards the mouth of the Palar river, thirty-two miles south of Madras, and indicates that here was the harbour for Conjeeveram, the capital seat of the dynasty, situated some forty miles up the river. Here the configuration of the coastline was singularly suitable for its purpose, as rising out of the sand near the seashore was a large rocky hill of granite gneiss, aligned from north to south, measuring half a mile long and a quarter of a mile wide with a height of over a hundred feet. Detached from this main prominence, and towards the south, was another and much smaller rocky outcrop, consisting originally of a whale-backed mound of granite about two hundred and fifty feet long and fifty feet high. It was out of these two formations that the rock architecture of the Mamalla group was excavated and sculp-

tured. As already implied, however, in conjunction with the rock productions, there was a large amount of structural architecture some of it of considerable importance, but all of which has perished. There are still visible foundations of a citadel which may be traced on the heights of the large hill and within this were palaces and similar royal residences, apparently built on raised masonry basements, while the buildings themselves consisted of a wooden framework filled in by brick and plaster walls. As was not an uncommon practice, therefore the secular buildings were structural while the halls for religious purposes were quarried out of the natural rock.

One other feature is observable at Mamallapuram, now almost obliterated, but which when in full use gave the town, and particularly its religious architecture, some of its character. This was a well-designed and extensive water system, drawn from the Palar river, and distributed by means of canals and tanks to all parts of the port. There are indistinct but none the less definite traces of this installation, so that in its palmy days such a constant supply of running water must have made it a very pleasing seaside resort. But this was not provided solely for public use, it was also maintained for ritualistic purposes, as proved by the design of some of the temples in which cisterns and conduits appear to have formed an essential part of the scheme. The significance of what appears to be a popular belief in water worship, combined with the Naga or serpent cult, is embodied in a remarkable scene sculptured on the eastern face of the main hill, and now misnamed Arjuna's Penance. This rock-cut drama is an allegorical representation of the holy river Ganges issuing from its source in the distant Himalayas, the water, fed from a receptacle above, cascading down a natural cleft in the rock in the centre of a magnificent picture carved in relief.

Yet even with such vivid relics still in situ, it is difficult to reconcile this deserted area consisting of a bare rocky hill, and desolate sand dunes, with what was once a populous maritime centre. The drifting sands have covered up and obliterated most of its landmarks, while the warring elements of wind and tide have altered the contours of the coastline, so that its ancient appearance can only be imagined. But in its art connections alone this port had more than ordinary significance. For there is little doubt that from Mamallapuram, in the middle of the first millennium, many deep-laden argosies set forth, first with merchandise and then with emigrants, eventually to carry the light of Indian culture over the Indian Ocean into the various less enlightened countries of Hither Asia. Amidst the opalescent colouring of Java's volcanic ranges, and on the lush green plains of old Cambodia, in the course of time there grew up important schools of art and architecture derived from an Indian source. That the origin of these developments is to be found in the Brahmanical productions of the Pallavas, and, before them in the stupas and monasteries erected by the Buddhists under the rule of the Andhras, is fairly clear. It is possible to identify in the Khmer sculptures at Angkor Thom and Angkor Vat, and in the endless bas-reliefs on the stupa-temple of Borobudur, the influence of the marble carved panels of Amaravati, while the architecture that this plastic art embellishes owes some of its character to the rock-cut monoliths of Mamallapuram. In addition therefore to providing the foundations of the Dravidian style of architecture in southern India, the vigorous creations of the Pallava craftsmen exercised considerable effect over a much wider field, and it was from this now deserted port that their art was probably conveyed to more distant lands.

Of the rock-cut examples of Pallava architecture at Mamallapuram, the mandapas may be referred to first : these excavated halls are ten in number[1], and are to be found on various suitable sites on the main hill. In most instances they are of the same general character and proportions as those of the previous group, but much more highly developed, a proof of the rapid progress that took place during the short period that intervened. None of them is large, their approximate dimensions being as follows :—width of facade 25 feet ; height from 15 to 20 feet ; depth overall including cella 25 feet ; pillars 9 feet high and 1 to 2 feet wide diameter ; cellas, rectangular and from 5 to 10 feet side. It will be seen from these measurements that the mandapas are relatively shallow halls or porticos, and are remarkable therefore not for their size but for the exceptional character of their design and execution. This character is shown in two ways, first in their architectural treatment, and secondly in the disposal and quality of the sculpture combined with the architectural forms. As regards the former, except for the pillars which are the main features of the composition as a whole, the actual architectural treatment is of the simplest kind. On the facade there is a roll cornice decorated with chaitya arch motifs (kudu), and above this a parapet, or attic member, formed of miniature shrines, a long one alternating with a short one. The remainder of the scheme both inside and out consists principally of pilasters of mouldings acting as a framework of the figure sculpture, the display of which appears to have been one of the prominent objects of the mandapa idea. For it is fairly clear that the rock-cutter was primarily and fundamentally a sculptor, and these pillared halls were regarded very largely as a means of presenting to the visiting devotees pictures of mythological and other subjects produced in this plastic manner. Not that the treatment of the architectural features was in any way inferior to the relief work, some of the architraves, cornices and strings-courses being as finely wrought as the figures. As an instance the precision with which the basements were designed and executed is admirably shown in the Varaha mandapa, where the stylobate has been sunk so as to form a long narrow receptacle for water. (Plate LIX, Fig. 2). Apart from the manner in which this important part of the facade has been conceived and carried out so as to compel ablutions before entering the temple, it is an excellent illustration of the artistic handling of a purely material adjunct.

As in all rock architecture of a similar type, the pillars, especially those of the facade, are the principal elements in the composition, and those of the Mamalla group are no exception. The beginning of the Pallava order of the column has already been referred to in the works of the previous reign, but the Mamallapuram mandapas show this feature in its rich maturity. In some of the examples the crude block bracket is still much in evidence, primitive traditions usually die hard, but on the other hand some of the pillars as for instance those on the exterior of the Mahishasura mandapa are singularly graceful conceptions, when the purpose and peculiar technique are taken into consideration. A further development, with the addition of the heraldic lion forming the lower half of the shaft, is seen in the facade pillars of the Varaha mandapa, one of the most finished examples in the entire group. But the culmination of this lion form of pillar is represented by the two interior columns of the former mandapa, so different from any of the others, yet refining

and combining all their attributions, implying the accomplishment of a craftsman of more than ordinary powers. The lion as a pillar base is not an uncommon motif in the architecture of several civilizations. It is found in late Roman work, and also in Lombardic Romanesque buildings of Europe dating from the eleventh century, but in these occidental examples the shaft is usually supported on the animal's back. In the Pallava type the pillar is made to rest on the sedent animal's head, and, in the case of the lion in the Mahishasura interior, it is not the horned grotesque of the mandapas, but a more natural leonine figure yet sufficiently conventionalised to suit its architectonic purpose. The remaining members forming this particular class of pillar are equally well designed, the fluted and banded shaft (stambham), the refined necking (tadi), the elegant curves of the " melon " capital (kumbha), and its lotus form (idaie) above, with its wide abacus (palagai), are all so united as to produce an " order " of marked propriety and stability. (Plate LXII, Fig. 1).

Passing now to the other type of rock architecture of Mamalla's reign, namely the series of monolithic temples called rathas, and widely known as the " Seven Pagodas", these exemplify an entirely novel form of expression. Although in much the same architectural style as the mandapas, they enunciate a completely different idea. Each is obviously a replica, quarried out of the whale-backed rock previously mentioned, of a separate type of religious structure evidently common at the time, and built largely of wood, as is shown by the beam-heads, rafters and purlins faithfully represented in the granite reproduction. Each example, with all these features is so well preserved as to be perfectly comprehensible, but the question at once arises, what was the object and intention of recording so faithfully and with such infinite toil each architectural type, as if it were a full sized model, or to be regarded as a standard pattern for the guidance of the temple builders ? Solitary, unmeaning, and clearly never used, as none of their interiors is finished, sphinx-like for centuries these monoliths have stood sentinel over mere emptiness, the most enigmatical architectural phenomenon in all India, truly a " riddle of the sands". Each a lithic cryptogram as yet undeciphered, there is little doubt that the key when found will disclose much of the story of early temple architecture in Southern India.

As with all the rock productions of the Pallavas, the rathas are of no great size, the largest measuring only 42 feet long, the widest 35 feet, and the tallest is but 40 feet high. They number eight in all,[2] and, with one exception, are derived from the two types of structure hitherto attributed to the Buddhists, the vihara or monastery, and the chaitya hall or temple. The exception is that known as Draupadi's ratha, the smallest of the series, as well as being the simplest and most finished. This example is merely a cell or pansala, and the shape of the roof indicates plainly that it was a copy of a thatched structure, most probably a form of portable shrine belonging to a village community, as shown by its sub-structure. For its base is supported by figures of animals, a lion alternating with an elephant, their attitudes suggesting that they are bearers of a heavy burden. Such an idea is occasionally represented in Indian architecture of the temples and shrines borne along by supernatural creatures, or supported on poles by grotesque human beings, thus implying

---

[1] (1) Dharmaraja, (2) Kotikal, (3) Mahishasura, (4) Krishna, (5) Pancha Pandava, (6) Varaha, (7) Ramanuja, (8) Five celled Saivite, (9) & 10) unfinished.

[2] North-west : Valaiyankuttai and Pidari. South : Draupadi, Arjuna, Bhima, Dharmaraja and Sahadeva. North : Ganesh.

that these religious constructions were sometimes not fixtures, but could be carried in procession or moved about from place to place. The portable shrine represented by Draupadi's ratha may have some connection with certain models of tabernacles depicted on the gable ends of the remaining rathas, to be referred to hereafter. (Plate LX).

Of the vihara or monastery type of ratha at Mamallapuram, all of which are square in plan and pyramidal in elevation, there are five examples, varying in size and in their details, but all treated in the same architectural manner. In shape and appearance these vihara rathas seem to have been evolved out of a building composed of cells arranged around a square courtyard, the inner court being afterwards covered in with a flat roof on pillars. In the course of time, as the community of monks occupying the monastery increased another story was added, and, finally, still another, the whole structure eventually being finished off with a kind of domical roof. In the rock-cut interpretation of this composition, the cells have lost their original character and intention, and become modified into ornamental turrets, while other substantial alterations have been effected in order to make it suitable for its new purpose. The transformation from a Buddhist hostel to a Hindu shrine is best illustrated in the largest of these vihara rathas, that known as the Dharmaraja, enough of which has been completed to show the full architectural style of the exterior, as well as the manner in which it was proposed to treat the inner compartments. As regards the elevation, this is in two parts, a square portion with pillared verandahs below, and the pyramidal shape or sikhara (tower) formed of the converted cells, above. With its strongly moulded stylobate, its lion pillared porticos casting their deep shadows, the scintillating appearance of its turreted roof, this type of design is not only an effective production in itself, but it is a storehouse of pleasing forms and motifs, besides being replete with potentialities. That such promises were amply fulfilled is shown by the architectural monuments developed from this rock-cut model which evolved later.

Even more significant than the foregoing are the remaining three examples of rathas known as Bhima, Sahadeva and Ganesh, which appear to be based on various types of chaitya hall, or Buddhist temple. They are all oblong in plan, and rise up into two or more stories, while each has a keel or barrel roof, with a chaitya gable end. The Sahadeva type is apsidal, and structural replicas of this form were erected at a subsequent date, of which the later Pallava temple of Vadamallisvara is an example. A still more informative instance of the chaitya hall type is Bhima's ratha, which is a copy of a building in two stories, the upper story displaying a perfect representation of a keel roof with a gable at each end. A similar effect was produced later in two structures of the Indo-Aryan order, the tenth century temple of Vaital Deul at Bhubaneswar, Orissa (Chapter XXI), and in the eleventh century Teli-ka-Mandir in Gwalior Fort (Chapter XXVI). The remaining ratha of the group, that of Ganesh, is in some respects a combination of the two previous examples, but it is different inasmuch as the entrance is through a pillared portico on its long side. Not only were these three rathas the prototypes of temples, but they were also the pattern out of which was evolved an important later development, for it was on their oblong plan, diminishing stories, and specifically, the keel roof with its pinnacles and gable ends, that the *gopuram* was based. It is possible to see here the beginnings of those great towering pylons forming the entrance gateways to the temples of the south, and which give their chief character to the Dravidian style. (Plate LVII, Fig. 2.)

These monolithic shrines were of Saivite attribution, and in their proximity are images, also carved in the rock, of a lion, an elephant, and a bull, symbolising respecitvely Durga, Indra, and Siva. Yet the fact that these Siva shrines are in a style of architecture traditionally associated with the Buddhists, seems to imply that they were a type of structure not the monopoly of any one religion, but had a common origin. There is evidence in support of this in certain emblematical subjects carved within the gable ends of the three chaitya hall examples, each of which is full of allegory. (Plate LX). And in more than one of them there is a central symbol not unlike a stupa. Each gable illustrates a conventional or diagrammatic rendering of a prayer-hall, the curved barge-boards taking the place of the vaulted roof, the decorated brackets on either side simulating the ribs of the vault, while, most significant of all, the central object is a tabernacle or sacred relic. Each of these representations of tabernacles or reliquaries takes a different form, just as the ratha on which it is depicted also is of a certain design, so that both ratha and reliquary may be identified as belonging to one another. It is possible therefore that each ratha is a shrine consecrated to one of the manifestations of Siva, its shape being conditioned by the tradition which has ordained that it should take such a form for that particular manifestation.

A remarkable feature of the Pallava rock-architecture is the fine quality of the figure sculpture which adorns both mandapas and rathas. But in its plastic form it was only part of a movement, which, extending over the whole of southern India, found expression in a school of sculpture of a grand classical order. Most of this is in the rock-cut technique, of which that on the Kailasa at Ellora, and at Elephanta, are rather later examples, but some of the finest and earliest productions were the work of the Pallavas. These figure subjects at Mamallapuram are endowed with that same passionate spirit which pulsates in the Christian art of Europe of the corresponding date, but with even a finer feeling for form and more experienced craftsmanship. There is a notable sense of restraint and refined simplicity specially in the bas-reliefs of single figures, yet even more pronounced in several of the larger sculptured dramas, as for instance in the Vishnu panel of the Mahishasura mandapa, which has some of the breadth and rationality shown in the sculpture of the Greeks towards the end of their first period. In view therefore of the superb quality of the Pallava plastic art it is not surprising that the schools of scultpure which developed out of this movement in Java and Cambodia displayed also the same high artistic character.

From the unfinished state of nearly all the rock architecture at Mamallapuram, much of it lacking that final effort which would have made these shrines really serviceable, it would seem as if some unexpected political cataclysm had intervened, causing the rock-cutter to throw down his mallet and chisel and hasten away, never to return. History records no such upheaval, so that an explanation must be looked for elsewhere. What these incomplete shrines reveal is that the patronage of Narasimha Mamalla having ended with his death in A.D. 674, under his successor Rajasimha a new architectural movement began. For with the rule of this king, the rock method ceased, no further labour was put either into the excavated mandapas or the monolithic rathas, in a word as a form of expression it became obsolete.

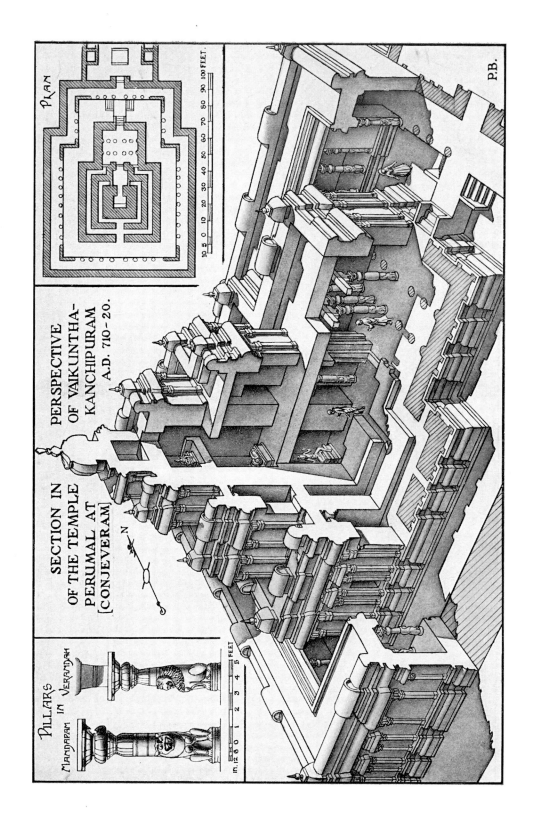

PLAN

PILLARS IN VERANDAH

MANDAPAM

SECTION IN
OF THE TEMPLE
PERUMAL AT
[CONJEVERAM]

PERSPECTIVE
OF VAIKUNTHA-
KANCHIPURAM
A.D. 710–20.

P.B.

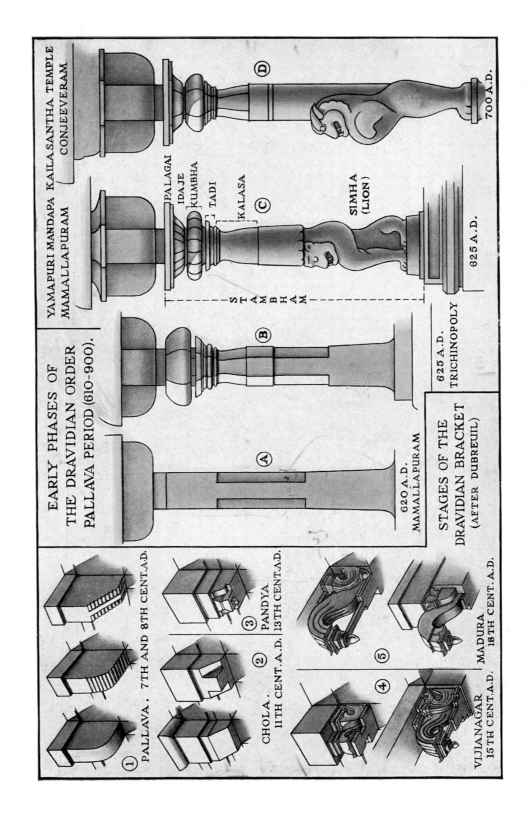

EARLY PHASES OF THE DRAVIDIAN ORDER PALLAVA PERIOD (610-900).

YAMAPURI MANDAPA MAMALLAPURAM

KAILASANTHA TEMPLE CONJEEVERAM

PALAGAI
IDAJE
KUMBHA
TADI
KALASA

SIMHA (LION)

S T A M B H A M

Ⓐ 620 A.D. MAMALLAPURAM

Ⓑ 625 A.D. TRICHINOPOLY

Ⓒ 625 A.D.

Ⓓ 700 A.D.

STAGES OF THE DRAVIDIAN BRACKET (AFTER DUBREUIL)

① PALLAVA. 7TH AND 8TH CENT. A.D.

② CHOLA. 11TH CENT. A.D.

③ PANDYA. 13TH CENT. A.D.

④ VIJIANAGAR 15TH CENT. A.D.

⑤ MADURA. 18TH CENT. A.D.

Fig. 1
Srinivasanalur, Trichinopoly Dist.: Temple of Koranganatha; c. A.D. 940.

Fig. 2
Darasuram, Tanjore Dist.: Alankara Mandapa in Aiyravatesvara Temple; c. A.D. 1350.

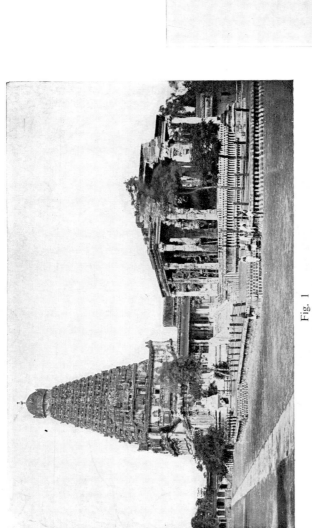

Fig. 2

Tanjore: Great Brihadeswara Temple; c. A.D. 1000

Fig. 1

Fig. 3

Fig. 2

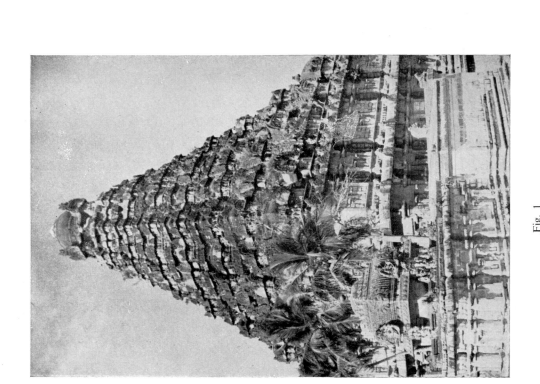

Fig. 1

Gangaikondacholapuram Temple; c. A.D. 1025.   Near Kumbakonam.

Fig. 2

Tiruvarur Temple, Tanjore Dist. : Detail of Gopuram; c. A.D. 1600.

Fig. 1

Gangaikondacholapuram Temple; c. A.D. 1025.

Vijayanagar (Hampi), Vittalaswami Temple: 16th century.

Fig. 2
Srirangam Temple near Trichinopoly: "Horse Court": c. A.D. 1590.

Fig. 1
Taddpatri : Pillar in Gopuram of the Rama Temple ; 16th century.

Instead of the permanent yet inflexible carving of the granite, the art of structural building was taken up, as it was being realized that this process gave greater powers to the workman, it provided him with more freedom, so that he could place his structure where he pleased, and make it what shape he liked. The only limit to his performance was the extent of his knowledge of the principles of the mason's craft, and the size and strength of his materials. With the reign of Rajasimha therefore the second phase of Pallava architecture opens, in which all the buildings are entirely structural. The production of the first temples of this phase, and called the Rajasimha Group, began towards the end of the seventh century and occupied the whole of the eighth century, during which period several notable buildings were erected.

Of the Rajasimha mode there are some six examples, comprising the " Shore," Isvara, and Makunda temples at Mamallapuram ; a temple at Panamalai in the South Arcot district ; and the temples of Kailasanatha and of Vaikuntha Perumal at Conjeevaram. Three of these are of major importance as each illustrates a stage not only in the style as a whole, but in the development of the temple formation, in much the same manner as that already shown in the contemporary art of the Chalukyans on the other side of the Peninsula (Chapter XIV). These three examples are the " Shore " temple, and the two temples at Conjeevaram. The first Pallava building to be constructed of dressed stone was the " Shore " temple, so named in modern times as it stands on the extreme foreshore of the ancient port. (Plate LXII, Figs. 2 and 3). Although the earliest known production in this technique of the Pallavas, as it dates from the last years of the seventh century, the materials of which it is composed and the manner in which they have been applied indicate a certain amount of latent experience in the art of building construction. As a proof of its excellent workmanship for over a thousand years the " Shore " temple has endured on this exposed spur of rock, buffeted for half the year by the monsoon rollers, at other times.

" The grey sea creeps half-visible, half-hushed,
    And grasps with its innumerable hands
        Its silent walls."

Yet even with the ceaseless activity of the sea on the one side, and the insidious menace of the drifting sands on the other, its twin towers are still erect and its shrines remain intact, immutable it stands, a silent record of a great but almost forgotten people.

Owing to its unusual position, and also to the intention of its creators, the plan of the Shore temple is not according to custom. The underlying idea was that the cella should face eastwards overlooking the sea, so that the shrine might be illuminated by the first rays of the rising sun, as well as being plainly observable to those approaching the harbour in ships. For it was a landmark by day and a beacon by night, as out amongst the breakers still rises a stone pillar on which a lamp would be placed to shine across the waters and guide the mariner to his anchorage. Such an arrangement, however, with the cella actually on the ocean's brim, left no room for a forecourt or assembly hall, and not even for an entrance gateway, all of which had to be placed at the rear of the shrine. In this instance therefore the central building is surrounded by a massive enclosure wall, entry being obtained through the western side of the courtyard which was left entirely open. But quite early in its production this simple scheme was complicated by two additional

shrines being attached, rather unsymmetrically, to its western end, one of which provides the smaller spire, as well as what at first sight appears to be the main entrance. It is these two supplementary shrines which have converted the Shore temple into a double towered monument, unconventional in its grouping, and a little difficult to comprehend.

While it is quite clear that the central buildings comprising the Shore temple are a development of the monolithic rathas of the previous phase, specifically from that of the Dharmaraja ratha, the difference in treatment between the two types of the temple is considerable. The change in technique from the rock-cut to the structural partly accounts for this, and the interval separating the execution of the two productions, although not great, would also have some effect. And there was, of course, a new ruler on the throne, whose personal predilections may have had some influence. But even these factors, significant though they may be, can hardly account for the difference not only in temper and in trend, but in the forms as well, which appear in this first structural example of the Pallava period. In principle the monolithic Dharmaraja ratha and the Shore temple are the same, there is the square lower story, and the pyramidal tower in diminishing tiers above in both conceptions, but there is another and original ideal motivating the design of the Shore temple, particularly noticeable in the shape of the tower. This is shown in the obvious desire of the builders to rid themselves of the vihara incubus, and to devise a building more architecturally rational, in a word to shake off the shackles of its prototype and give effect to their own rising genius.

And so we see in the composition of the Shore temple, more rhythm and more buoyancy than in the monolithic rathas, a lightness and a soaring quality that was however not entirely due to the more tractable technique. But there is also another important component in the structural example, which although relatively a matter of detail, was destined to give not a little of its character to the later Pallava art. This is the appearance in the architectural scheme of a very pronounced type of pilaster, a rampant lion in prominent relief, and which finds a place wherever such a structural form with an ornamental support is required. In the Shore temple this heraldic lion, erect and holding up a Dravidian capital, projects from every angle, and is also introduced at intervals around the lower part of the entire building. As the style progressed this leogriff motif became more frequent and more characteristic so that it may be generally regarded as the identifying symbol of the Pallava style. As in the case of numerous motifs in Indian art, the origin of this rampant lion pilaster is a mystery, it suddenly appears in the temple design without any marked prefigurement, save for one small representation of it on the unfinished ratha of Valaiyankuttai of the previous reign in the shape of an insignificant bracket. It is strange that from such a rudimentary detail much of the character of the Narasimha architecture should have developed.

There was however considerably more in the formation of the Shore temple than the central buildings described above, as these were surrounded by an outer rectangular enclosure containing many interesting features. (Plate LXIII, Fig. 2). In the first place it seems evident that portions of the ground plan of the enclosure consisted of a system of shallow cisterns, which could be flooded on occasion, so that it resolves itself into a type of water temple. Some of the conduits and receptacles may still be traced, and it is clear that they constituted an essential part of the lay-out. The water to feed this system was brought by a canal and conveyed by sluices throughout the building, any overflow being carried down a rocky cascade in the rear of the shrine and into the sea. The surrounding wall was an imposing structure, its parapet and coping crowned by figures of kneeling bulls, while at close intervals all round the exterior projected boldly carved lion pilasters ; on the western side admission was obtained through a richly orna-mented doorway. This doorway was the main entrance and led into a corridor one side of which was formed by the inner face of the enclosure wall, the other by a large rectangular building, probably an outer mandapa, but only the foundations remain. Halfway along each of the long sides of the corridor, there was a pillared arcade containing an altar, possibly provided for Naga worship, as all the courts and passages around could be filled with water. A feature of this corridor was a series of carved panels on the side walls, each containing a figure-subject illustrating some striking mythological episode—a picture gallery in stone.

Not long after the erection of the Shore temple at Mamallapuram, another Siva temple the Kailasanatha was begun at Conjeeveram, the capital seat of the Pallavas, situated forty-five miles south-west of Madras. Conjee-veram, in the early centuries of the Christian era, was a place of considerable importance, probably the leading city of the Carnatic if not of Southern India. As the home of Dharma-pala, the great commentator, a contemporary of the famous Buddhaghosa of the fifth century, it appears to have been a centre of intellectual life, while its fine series of temples are proof of its religious activity extending over a long period. For here may be studied the Dravidian style of temple architecture from its genesis under the Pallavas beginning in the 6th century to its culmination at Vijayanagar as late as the 15th and 16th centuries, a period of a thousand years of development. The temple of Ekambaranatha illustrates in one or other of its compartments every feature of this evolution, while a study of the Kailasanatha should form the basis of any investigation of the Dravidian building art. Dealing first therefore with the latter example, the main shrine of this structure was built during the reign of Rajasimha, so that its approximate date is A.D. 700, although the actual completion of the temple as a whole was under-taken by his son Mahendravarman III, but, with the exception of a few additions to the east end of the enclosure, it is all as originally conceived. The scheme resolves itself into three separate parts, consisting of a sanctuary with its pyramidal tower, a pillared hall or mandapa, the whole contained within a rectangular courtyard enclosed by a high and substantial wall composed of cells. At a much later date, probably in the fourteenth century, the two isolated buildings, the sanctuary and the mandapa, were joined together by a spacious intermediate hall or *antarala*, to accord with the ceremonial of the time. This mediaeval addition has robbed the main structure of some of its architectural appearance, and it is better to visualize it without such an intervening compartment as shown in Plate LXIII, Fig. 1. It will be seen from the drawing that the main building is the tall sanctuary at the eastern end of the enclosure, and that in principle it conforms to the monolithic prototype of the Dharmaraja ratha. But there are certain elaborations, particularly in the supplementary shrines attached to and projecting from its three free sides, which aid considerably its effective presentation.

Every aspect of this temple is replete with informative features, as it illustrates in all its parts the trends of the style. The cells comprising the interior of the enclosing wall, the design of the wall with its parapet of cupolas, the sturdy, primitive shape of the mandapa pillars, the constant repetition of the rampant lion pilaster, these, and the composition of the building as a whole, make the grey pile of the Kailasanatha a most fascinating study. Yet undoubtedly its most interesting portion is the pyramidal tower or sikhara for it is in the distinctive treatment of this feature that the development of the Dravidian style may be best observed. From the somewhat compressed forms of the monolithic rathas to the more loosely-knit elements of the Shore temple, we now arrive at a further effort to present the sikhara in a suitable architectural form, well-proportioned, substantial, yet at the same time rhythmic in its mass and elegant in its outlines. Such was evidently the aim of its designers, and within certain limits some of these desired conditions have been fulfilled. There is still however occasion for more refinement in the shape of this tower, for although it marks another stage of evolution, it obviously falls short of that perfected maturity which was subsequently achieved.

Apart from the main structure of this temple there are certain arrangements in connexion with the entrance to the courtyard which are noteworthy. This part appears to have been produced under the direction of Mahendravarman III, and evidently marks a deviation from the original plan. In place of what should have been the main gateway, a large subsidiary chapel has been introduced, complete with cella, vestibule and stairway approach, the actual doorways into the courtyard being relegated to openings on either side. Although a place of worship, the Mahendravarmanesvara shrine is built in such a manner, as, with its accompaniments, to suggest the beginnings of the gopuram, or entrance pylon. That the masons were by this time realizing the importance of selection in the matter of their building materials is shown by the fact that in the Kailasanatha, while the foundations of the temple are of granite, the upper portions are of sand-stone, thus providing a hard and firm sub-structure to carry its weight and a more plastic substance for the sculpture. Unfortunately at a somewhat distant date repairs to the latter became necessary, when these were effected rather ruthlessly by means of concrete.

About a decade later, the temple of Vaikuntha Perumal, also at Conjeeveram, was built, and here the Pallava style of architecture is seen in its most mature form. This temple is slightly larger and more spacious in its proportions than the previous example, and instead of the principal parts such as the cloisters, portico, and sanctuary, being separate buildings, they are amalgamated into one architectural whole, as may be seen in Plate LXIV. Square in plan, having a side of nearly 90 feet, the eastern or front portion is carried forward 28 feet to provide for an entrance portico. The exterior of this formation presents what might have been a high and somewhat uncompromising outer wall, but its surfaces have been so enriched with semi-structural and ornamental motifs that it blends admirably with the sikhara towering above the whole composition but actually rising from the shrine within. Inside the outer wall are the cloisters, consisting of a colonnade of lion pillars, with a passage for processions continued right round the building between this and the central structure. The central edifice is in two parts, the sanctuary and its portico, but these are so combined as to form this portion into one building. The portico, or what corresponds to the mandapa, is interiorly a square compartment 21½ feet side, having a transverse aisle of eight pillars, and it leads by means of a vestibule to the cella, a rectangular chamber over which rises the pyramidal vimana tower. This vimana is square in plan, externally having a side of 47 feet, and its tower rises to a height of 60 feet from the ground. It is in four stories, each with a passage round its exterior, a cella in the centre, and a corridor encircling two of these for circumambulation. Although there is not in the Vaikanta temple the living freshness and ingenuousness of the Kailasanatha, yet it has many commendable features, for it displays an economy in the disposal of its parts together with a skilful marshalling of the main elements so as to produce a unity of conception, which has resulted in a building having considerable architectural merit.

The last phase of the second group of buildings executed during the Pallava regime marks the end of the productions of this dynasty. It represents the works prepared during the rule of Nandivarman and his successors, and depicts the mode in practice in these parts during the ninth century. No buildings of any note were erected at this time, but there are a few small temples which show the direction of the movement. The principal examples are six in number as follows :—two temples at Conjeeveram, the Muktesvara and Matangesvara ; the Vadamallisvara temple at Orgadam near Chingleput ; the temple of Virattanesvara at Tiruttani near Arkonam ; and the Parasuramesvara temple at Gudimallam near Renigunta railway junction. The fact that all the temples are of small size, and are mere reproductions of the previous manifestations are proofs that

the might of this one-time powerful dynasty was declining, its end began with its defeat by the Western Chalukyans in the middle of the eighth century. Among the examples of this late development, the older are the two temples at Conjeeveram, and are simply copies to a smaller scale of the style which prevailed in the previous reign, except that the building ·is entered through a two pillared portico which forms the facade. The four remaining temples of the group, which appear to have been executed somewhat later, indicate that at this date another prototype found favour, as they are all based on the apsidal example represented by the Sahadevaratha at Mamallapuram. All these buildings, by their lack of virility connote the diminishing power of the dynasty, and towards the end of the tenth century, production practically ceased. But even if the art appears to have died, it passed by no means into oblivion. Such a movement, although perhaps it has left no large works of genius, was at the same time remarkable for the spirit and vigour of its performance. These qualities had a far-reaching effect. For to the Pallavas is the credit of having kept burning brightly the torch, which, kindled by the Buddhists in the early centuries of the Christian era as seen at Amaravati, was bequeathed to these Simhavishnu "lion" kings. Later, its flame glowed with renewed brilliance in the hands of the Cholas and subsequent rulers in Southern India, as their architectural undertakings eloquently testify. But perhaps its most potent influence was that which it transmitted beyond the seas, to the countries of Indonesia, where its effulgence, reflected in the vast monuments of those civilizations, shone with even greater splendour than in the land of its origin.

REFERENCES

Jouveau-Dubreuil, G., *Archaeolgie du Sud de L'Inde*, Paris, 1914.

„   „   *Dravidian Architecture*, Madras, 1917.

„   „   *The Pallavas*, Pondicheri, 1907.

Longhurst, A.H., *Pallava Architecture* (Memoir of the Archaeological Survey of India, No. 17) Simla, 1924.

Rea, A., *Pallava Architecture* (Archaeological Survey of India), Madras, 1909.

CHAPTER XVII

THE DRAVIDIAN STYLE

THE TEMPLES OF THE CHOLAS (A.D. 900 to 1150)

THE unsettled state of the Tamil country, brought about by the conflicts between the various dynasties such as the Pallavas, Cholas, Pandyas, Chalukyas, and Rastrakutas, all striving for supremacy, precluded any great cultural advance or any notable enterprises being undertaken during the last centuries of the first millennium. Out of this struggle for power the Cholas finally emerged triumphant, and proceeded in the course of time to become paramount in Southern India. Their dynastic history began about 900 A.D., and their rule attained its meridian a century later, declining towards the middle of the twelfth century, when it succumbed to the rising power of the Pandyas. During the first century of this 250 years of their supremacy, the Cholas found themselves principally engaged in territorial aggrandisement, as they extended their dominion as far as the Ganges in the north, and included Ceylon in the south, while a portion of Burma also came within their influence.

Preoccupied as the dynasty was in this manner, the buildings attributed to the Cholas during the tenth century are not many, nor are they large, and they imply a local rather than an imperial development. A certain number of examples are to be found in and around the State of Pudukkottai, and are all small temples built entirely of stone. Among them mention may be made of the Sundareswara temple at Tirukattalai ; the Vijayalaya temple in Nartamalai, with a circular sanctuary of an unusual order ; and the triple temple the Muvarkoil in Kodumbelur, of which however only two of its sanctuaries are preserved. The first two of the group were executed in the ninth century, so that they are probably the earliest of their style, while the triple temple may be ascribed to the tenth century. Other temples in Pudukkottai territory are as follows : Mucukundesvara in Kolattur taluk ; Kadambar in Kadambarmalai, Nartamalai; and Balasubrahmanaya in Kannanur, Tirumayam taluk.[1] Similar structures, may be found as far south as S. Arcot, such as in Tiruppur, Visalur, Panangudi, and Kaliyapatti, in Kolathur taluk, and in Enadi, Tirumayam taluk. The importance of all these buildings, however small many of them are, may be realized when working out the development of the Dravidian style at this formative stage. Most of them are constructed of well dressed granite blocks accurately coursed and bonded. Dating from the 9th and 10th centuries, that they are in the early Chola style is fairly evident, but at the same time Pallava features are observable, while their relation to the monolithic rathas at Mamallapuram may be noted. As a connecting link in the progress of the building art in Southern India each example is worthy of study. All these small structures are very complete in their formation and display a freshness and spirit in marked contrast to the last productions of the declining style of the Pallavas. So much so that they appear to herald either a new movement, or to denote some stimulation received from another and more virile source. The latter assumption is the more likely

as all the temples of the group show by the treatment a close affinity to those of the more distant Chalukyans than to any revival of the style of their predecessors the Pallavas. Such influence although a little remote is not improbable as at this time the Chalukyans were again extending their power, and under their later rulers the building art, as will be shown hereafter, was much encouraged. This relation of the Chola temples at Pudukkottai of the ninth and tenth centuries to the productions of the early Chalukyans may be observed specially in the shape of the domical finial of the sikhara, which has a double flexured contour similar to that in the temples of Badami and Pattadakal. (Chapter XIV).

For the purposes of study however reference may be made to a larger and more distinctive example of the early architecture of the Cholas, the temple of Koranganatha at Srinivasanalur in the Trichinopoly district. (Plate LXVI). This was built probably during the reign of one of the first of the dynasty, Parantaka I (907-949), and therefore dates before the middle of the tenth century. Its peculiar name is due to a local legend which records that on completion it was defiled by a monkey (korangu), and thus was never consecrated. Consisting of a pillared hall, or mandapa, with its attached sanctuary or vimana, its total length is 50 feet, the former occupying a rectangle 25 feet by 20 feet, and the latter a square of 25 feet side. The height of the sikhara or tower is 50 feet, while the cornice of the mandapa measures 16 feet from the ground. A small hall having four pillars comprises the interior, with a vestibule and passage beyond leading to the cella, a square chamber of 12 feet side.

These dimensions serve to show that the Koranganatha is a building of modest proportions. Compared with the temples of the previous period, although conceived on the same general principle, there is a marked change in the method of architectural treatment. In the composition of the exterior it displays a noticeable simplification in all its parts, which are also more reasoned in their forms and in their distribution ; an elimination of much of that detail which frets the surfaces of the later Pallava example is likewise observable. Moreover, it is proof that the builders had acquired an appreciation of the value of plain spaces, together with due sense of the character and correct location of the architectural features required for the purposes of embellishment. That dominating element of the previous style, the lion motif, both sedent and rampant, has disappeared, the pillars and pilasters which this leogriff invariably adorned, being converted into purely abstract conventions of mouldings and other similar forms. The Chola conception of the Dravidian order of capital at this stage is admirably illustrated by the pillars of its interior. (Plate XI, Fig. 11). Two changes from the Pallava type of order are discernible, one relating to the capital itself, the other to the abacus above. In the capital a neck moulding (padmabhandam) has been introduced where it joins on to the shaft, thus appropriating

---

[1] Chola Temples in Pudukkottai, by Venkataranga Raju, Journal of the Indian Art Society, Calcutta, 1937, p. **78** et seq.

to itself a segment of the upper part of the shaft, and adding another member to the lower part of the capital in the form of a vessel or pot (kalasa). As to the abacus, the palagai or "plank", is much expanded, so that combined with the flower-shape (idaie) underneath, it becomes the most striking element in the order. There is good proportion and suitability expressed in this example of the Chola pillar and capital.

In addition to the strictly architectural treatment of its exterior, there is a considerable amount of sculpture on the wall surfaces of the vimana, consisting chiefly of full-length figures installed within recesses, each about half life-size and in very bold relief, so that in a manner they recall the images of saints occupying niches in Gothic cathedrals. On the centre of the southern wall of the Koranganatha there is a particularly well rendered scene representing the goddess Kali as Dakshina, with Saraswati on her left and Lakshmi on her right, while below is Asura, the enemy of the gods, and around are various gana-devatas, or lesser deities. Compared with the plastic art of the previous period, in the Chola sculpture there is the beginning of that voluptuous treatment of the human figure in which the image is in such high relief that it resembles statuary in the round rather than relief work. Such however is the usual course in the development of the sculptors' art, a progress from the conventional to the representational, as may be observed in the change from the first to the second period of Greek sculpture.

Another ornamental feature of some interest appears in the Chola buildings, and is illustrated in the Koranganatha example. As already indicated the devices of heraldic lions and other supernatural beasts were eliminated in the temples of this period, but a different animalized motif now emerges. It takes the form of a string-course, frequently repeated, containing a row of gryphons heads, the use of which as a decorative element in the temple scheme was continued throughout the subsequent periods of the Dravidian style. Some signs of this striking motif are discernible in the early Chalukyan temples but it is not observable in the Pallava examples. These gargoyle-like heads squirming under the weight of the superimposed masonry, as if their bodies were immured within the joints of the structure are, rakshasas or earth-spirits, so imprisoned that they may guard the temple, but at the same time they are helpless to cause it harm. Here we seem to see something that corresponded to the "bestiaries" of the West, those representations of fabulous creatures so popular in Europe about this date and which are believed to have had their origin in the East. Although usually in pictorial manuscripts, these "unicorns, yales, leopards, and fire-breathing panthers" were not infrequently carved on Gothic churches in much the same manner as those on the Chola temple. Taken as a whole the temple at Srinivasanalur, although decidedly unpretentious, appears as an unaffected illustration of a transition stage in the evolution of the Dravidian style. It denotes that the Cholas at this period were passing through a process of formation in their architectural culture, treasuring their traditions but at the same time exercising their discretion with regard to what was handed down to them, thus restricting their aspirations to accord with their undeveloped ideals.

In the course of time, however, maturity was attained, as the two magnificent temples of Tanjore and Gangaikonda-cholapuram, erected less than a century afterwards, abundantly testify. In comparison with the temple of Koranganatha, they are as cathedrals to a parish church. Both built within the first quarter of the eleventh century, they prove that, during the intervening period, the Chola dynasty had been made aware of its vast power, and had had its character revealed to itself. The first ruler to become conscious of this sense of their own might was Rajaraja the Great (985-1018), which he proceeded to inaugurate by a superb architectural monument. It must have been a profoundly spiritual impulse which moved this ruler to commemorate the material achievements of his line in the great Siva (Brihadesvara) temple at Tanjore erected about the year 1000. (Plate LXVII). Apparently the largest, highest and most ambitious production of its kind hitherto undertaken by Indian builders, it is a landmark in the evolution of the building art in southern India. In size alone, regardless of its superb architectural treatment, its proportions are considerable, as the main structure is 180 feet long, above which rises a massive pyramidal tower 190 feet high, and from these dimensions some idea of the magnitude of the work and the courage and skill required to complete it may be realized. Except for the Great Lingaraja temple at Bhubaneswar in Orissa (Chapter XXI), which even then was a recent production, with a sikhara of 160 feet in height, few buildings had been raised of a greater height than 60 feet. As a measure of its size the vimana is equal in height to the central tower of Worcester cathedral, but the temple as a whole is only two-thirds the area of this Gothic example.

The Tanjore temple is composed of several structures combined axially, such as a Nandi pavilion, a pillared portico, and a large assembly hall, all aligned in the centre of a spacious walled enclosure. But the main feature of the entire scheme is the grand tower of the vimana at the western end which dominates everything in its vicinity. Much of the dignity and power of this fine pyramidal pile lies in the simplicity of its parts, which are three in number, consisting of the square vertical base, the tall tapering body, and, over all, the graceful domical finial. The first of these, the vertical base, covers a square of 82 feet side, and rises perpendicularly to a height of 50 feet. From this the pyramidal body mounts up in thirteen diminishing zones, until the width of its apex equals one-third of its base. On the square platform thus formed stands the cupola, the inward curve of its neck producing a pleasing break in the otherwise rigid outlines of the composition while the bulbous dome poised like a light but substantial globe is a fitting finish to its soaring character.

The architectural manipulation of the surfaces of this fine tower is in keeping with its mass. Specially noticeable is the scheme of decoration applied to the walls of the lowest and upright portion which is divided into two stories by a massive overhanging cornice recalling those of the rock-cut example. Except for this powerful horizontal member the underlying idea is vertical in intention, the two ranges of pilasters above and below being reminiscent of the super-columniation in the Roman facades. Combined with these pilasters are remarkably ingenious motifs and devices showing great fertility of invention, as for instance a conventional foliation, or "tree of knowledge" which enriches so effectively the deeper recesses, and other similar elements. Then, occupying the middle of each compartment is a figure-subject, each statue the central object of its own setting, providing a crowning achievement to the whole. Yet in spite of the supremely imaginative quality of its embellishment the critical eye may discern that, although each feature is an excellent effort in itself, taken as a whole the components do not always co-ordinate, in short, this portion of the facade consists of an assembly of admirable artistic elements, but not in every instance architecturally adequate.

Turning to the tapering section of the vimana, the effect of this pyramidal mass is enhanced by the rich manner of its treatment. Its surfaces are patterned by the horizontal lines of the diminishing tiers intersecting the vertical disposition of the ornamental shrines, thus producing an architectural texture of great beauty. Finally there is the contrast of the rounded cupola at the summit, its winged niches on all four sides relieving the severity of the outline just where this is required. In erecting this vimana on the principle of a pyramid its builders were on safe ground, for such a form not only conveys the impression of solid strength and stability, but is in reality the most permanent structural shape yet devised and men unconsciously tend to produce handiwork that will last. But there is much more than a desire for durability in this example of Chola architecture, for with its qualities of powerfully adjusted volume there is at the same time a sense of graceful balance so that when seen either close to or from afar its upward sweep is such that it appears to hang in the air. Unquestionably the finest single creation of the Dravidian craftsmen, the Tanjore vimana is also a touchstone of Indian architecture as a whole.

The other great building produced during the Chola ascendency, the temple of Gangaikondacholapuram is a monument evidently erected in a spirit of emulation, to excel, in richness and grandeur its predecessor. (Plate LXVIII). It is attributed to Rajendra I (1018-33), and is all that remains of an extensive capital city, which this ruler built as a record of his power and his pride. Situated about seventeen miles from the town of Kumbakonam, this fine structure now stands in solitary state, except for the mud huts of a village straggling around it, as centuries ago the tide of life receded from these parts leaving it like a great stranded shell. Nature with artistic hand has endeavoured to veil its abraded surfaces, not always for its structural good, with festoons of foliage, so that it appears as a lovely grey-green pile slumbering amidst the tangled verdure of a wide neglected garden. Built by a king for the purposes of his own religious ceremonial it has now become the occasional resort of the local idlers, and even its existence is known only to a few.

The date that this grand temple was erected was about 1025, less than a generation after that at Tanjore, and although it is in much the same style, the increased elaboration of its architectural appearance is not without meaning. For the Chola dynasty at this time had attained its most affluent state, and it is therefore fully expressive of its triumphant domination. Larger even in plan than its predecessor it is however less in height as the vimana measures only 150 feet from the ground. The temple building itself occupies the middle of an immense walled enclosure designed partly for defensive purposes as there is a substantial bastion at the south-east angle and another smaller one on the west. With its long axis from east to west the entire plan of the temple building forms a rectangle some 340 feet long and 110 feet wide, having its main entrance on the east. This main doorway gives access to the assembly hall, a relatively low building 175 feet by 95 feet and containing over 150 pillars, all rather slender and of comparatively ordinary design. In this many columned hall there is the beginning of those famous " thousand pillared mandapas " which were to constitute an important feature in all the large temples complexes of a later date. The arrangement of the pillars

in the Gangaikondacholapuram interior is peculiar as they are in colonnades and stand on a solid platform four feet high which however is divided down the centre by a passage or aisle on the ground level, while a similar passage on the same level is carried all round the hall. Between this pillared hall and the sanctuary is a vestibule or transept, running at right angles to the axis of the building, and leading to the north and south doorways, both deeply recessed side-entrances approached from outside by flights of steps. Two rows of massive square piers, eight in all, cross this vestibule, beyond which, hidden in darkness, lies the " holy of holies " in the womb of the vimana itself. (Plate LXVII).

Taken as a whole this assembly hall, comprising the entire frontal portion of the temple, both as regards its exterior as well as its interior is a large but uninspiring production, almost barn-like in its plainness. The pillars of the interior are an attempt to give it character, but without much success, while a still greater effort to provide it with some external appearance was made in connexion with the main entrance on the east. There are indications that a grand portal was here contemplated, certain of its elements such as the giant figures in high relief on either side, the pylons in front of these, the wide stairways, the immense basement mouldings, and the colossal image of the bull (*nandi*) leading up to this entrance are almost Assyrian in their dimensions. But for some reason the builders failed either to co-ordinate these fine components, or left the entire scheme incomplete, in either case this eastern front seems to represent an outstanding architectural ideal unfulfilled.

But whatever criticisms may be applied to this portion of the temple, without doubt the tall pyramidal vimana which towers over the western end is a superb achievement. On plan it is a square of 100 feet side, and as in the Tanjore example, is resolved into the three typical features of the Chola Dravidian sikhara, consisting of the upright ground story, the tapering body, and a domical finial. Like its predecessor also its vertical base is in two stages each defined by a heavy cornice casting horizontally a broad cordon of shadow, while the pyramidal body is in tiers, although here there are only eight of these diminishing zones, thus accounting for its lesser height. Where the contours of the tower differ from the previous example is that in place of the strong straight lines and planes of the Tanjore vimana, curves have been introduced, the outline formed by the quoins or external angles of the pyramidal form being made slightly concave, while the surfaces between have been embowed so as to become slightly convex. Such curves give the mass an increased richness, but detract from its power. There is a voluptuousness in the later structure, the beauty of ripe femininity, in contrast to the masculine strength of the earlier type. But in comparing these two architectural productions they present much more than a difference in kind. Stately and formal as an epic may epitomise the Tanjore vimana, while the later example has all the sensuous passion of an eastern lyric, but it seems to go even deeper than that. Each is the final and absolute vision of its creator made manifest through the medium of structural form, the one symbolizing conscious might the other sub-conscious grace, but both dictated by that "divinity which has seized the soul".

No account of these two monuments would be complete without a reference to the statuary with which the square foundational portion is embellished. Most of this takes the form of single figure subjects each occupying its appointed niche in the scheme as a whole. For instance the dancing figure of the god Nataraja is located in a panelled recess on the south-west corner, Siva within the flaming lingam is on the west face, Ganesh the elephant god is on the south, and Chandi Kesa Angrahamurti on the north and so forth, each expressing a spiritual as well as a material embodiment of the deity represented. On the spaces around are depicted attendant beings such as flying *Apsaras* (nymphs), sprawling *Gana-devtas* (lesser divinities), and contorted *Yakshas* (supernatural creatures), with a border of writhing *Rakshasas* (goblins) at the foot of each story. A feature of the lowest portion of the vimana is the character and volume of the base mouldings on which this great pile takes its stand. In few other styles has the importance of a stylobate been so fully understood, with the result that its courses are in complete accord with their function, their proportions are massive without being unduly heavy. Especially does this apply to the ponderous torus and its supporting member, the scale of which, although immense, implies strength combined with equilibrium. The sense of stability expressed by such means in the bases of the Dravidian buildings during this period and also afterwards has rarely been excelled.

Under the Chola rulers as these two imposing monuments testify, the architecture of the south attained its culmination, and with this effort the dynasty seems to have remained content. The movement neither declined nor died after its supreme achievement, but none the less it had manifestly spent its force, for no specially remarkable buildings appear to have been erected after this date. The two temples here described are however sufficient in themselves to establish the architectural reputation of the Chola power.

REFERENCE

Jouveau-Dubreuil, G., *Archaeologic du Sud de L'Inde*, Paris, 1914.

CHAPTER XVIII

THE DRAVIDIAN STYLE

UNDER THE PANDYAS (cir. 1100 to 1350)

THE impulse and achievement which culminated in the grand temples of Tanjore and Gangaikondacholapuram early in the eleventh century were not maintained, for less than a century later the Chola power diminished, after which the building art in the Tamil country ceased for a time to hold the high position it had previously attained. The Cholas were succeeded by the Pandyas, who, although they encouraged to a certain degree the visual arts, do not appear to have been a notable building dynasty. During the period of over two centuries that the Pandyas dominated the south of India, the Dravidian style continued to develop, but few outstanding architectural contributions were made to this southern movement, and no pronounced attempts to continue the magnificent tradition which they had inherited from their predecessors have been recorded. Moreover, as far as the temple structure was concerned, new tendencies were in the course of formation, which although they affected but little the architectural style, influenced to a considerable extent that type of edifice it had become the custom to erect. Up to this point it had been the practice of the builders to apply their finest craftsmanship to the body of the temple itself, and specifically to its most sacred part, the vimana, which they made the most resplendent feature of the temples of the Cholas. With the advent of the Pandyas this usage ceased, and instead of the sanctuary continuing to be the central architectural production, the builders' skill was diverted in order to give prominence to some of the supplementary or outlying portions of the temple scheme.

One of the reasons for this change of objective was that of sentiment. Distributed throughout the country on sites of great religious antiquity were a number of buildings of no particular artistic character, but on the other hand of marked sanctity, because enshrined within them were images of deep and lasting veneration. Custom at the same time ordained that, although these edifices were aesthetically insignificant, it was considered undesirable either to pull them down and erect others in their place, or even to change their appearance by structural alterations or improvements. These shrines therefore remained practically untouched, retaining their humble and somewhat primitive state, and also preserving at the same time that atmosphere of pristine holiness with which they were originally endowed. Religious emotion with regard to such edifices had however to find some form of expression, and it did so by exalting their environment, surrounding them by high walls to emphasize their sanctity, and making the entrances to the enclosures thus formed into gateways of imposing size and rich appearance. One of the results of this procedure was to give the temple confines the appearance of a fortress or citadel, as the outer scheme consists of a series of concentric walls enclosing open countryards or *prakarams*, and approached through high watch-towers. The walls were purely utilitarian structures of no aesthetic value, being not infrequently provided with an inner platform, and battlemented, obviously as a means of defence in case of emergency. In contrast to the relative plainness of the walls, the tall gateways were made into productions of considerable architectural character, as they formed immense piles in themselves as well as providing a basis for a wealth of plastic embellishment. In the course of time these pylon-like entrances were introduced so frequently into the temple scheme, that they have become the most striking feature in the architecture of the south.

The gopuram, as this type of temple portal is called, derived its name in the first instance from the " cow-gate " of the Vedic village, afterwards becoming the city gate, and subsequently the monumental entrance to the temple. Elementary prototypes of this characteristic architectural feature have been already referred to, as for instance in the shrine at the entrance to the Kailasanatha temple at Conjeeveram (Chapter XVI), and also in the early Chalukyan temple of Virupaksha at Pattadakal (Chapter XIV), both examples illustrating the gopuram in a very rudimentary stage. As with a number of conspicuous elements in Indian architecture of various kinds there is no definite process of evolution, the object, although not exactly self-originated, suddenly emerges in a relatively mature state. So it was with the gopuram, the earliest developed examples of which appear as the gateways to the southern type of temple during the period of the Pandyas in the twelfth and thirteenth centuries.

A typical example of a gopuram depicts a building oblong in plan rising up into a tapering tower often over one hundred and fifty feet in height, and entered by a rectangular doorway in the centre of its long side. Its similarity to the more familiar Egyptian propylon, which is much the same in mass and proportion, and also the entrance to a temple, is obvious, but any such impression is mainly due to both structures, having pronounced sloping or battered sides. Almost invariably the two lowest stories of the gopuram are vertical, and are built of solid stone masonry thus providing a stable foundation for the superstructure which is usually composed of the lighter materials of brick and plaster. This superstructure is pyramidal in shape as it is composed of a series of zones or tiers diminishing as they ascend. The average angle of slope from the vertical is 25°, and the width at its truncated apex is approximately one-half of its base. On the flat summit is mounted a particular kind of elongated roof with gable-ends, and no portion of the design is more significant than this barrel-valued uppermost story. At this stage it will have become apparent that the outstanding features of Dravidian temple architecture are its two types of tower, the vimana and the gopuram. These two towers represent the final manifestation of two ancient forms and traditions, as exemplified by the top story of each. The vimana being square in plan and structure has as its finial a rounded cupola. On the other hand the plan of the gopuram is oblong, and accordingly its crowning feature is in the form of the oblong vaulted roof, unmistakably a survival of the keel roof of the Buddhist chaitya hall. It is not difficult therefore to see in these two characteristic formations of the Dravidian style the last phase of the two archi-

Vellore Temple in Fort.   Kalyan Mandapa; c. 16th century.

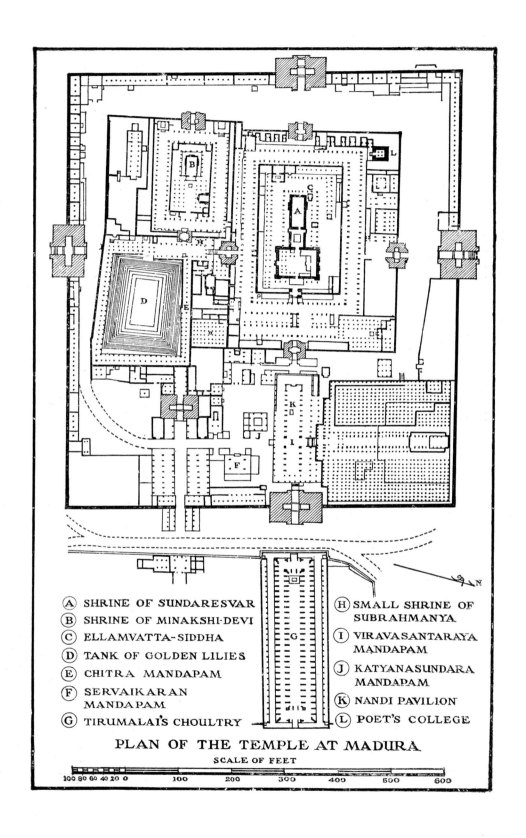

A SHRINE OF SUNDARESVAR
B SHRINE OF MINAKSHI-DEVI
C ELLAMVATTA-SIDDHA
D TANK OF GOLDEN LILIES
E CHITRA MANDAPAM
F SERVAIKARAN MANDAPAM
G TIRUMALAI'S CHOULTRY

H SMALL SHRINE OF SUBRAHMANYA
I VIRAVASANTARAYA MANDAPAM
J KATYANASUNDARA MANDAPAM
K NANDI PAVILION
L POET'S COLLEGE

PLAN OF THE TEMPLE AT MADURA

SCALE OF FEET

100 80 60 40 20 0   100   200   300   400   500   600

Fig. 1. Temple of Tiravulur.

Fig. 2. Great Temple at Madura.

GREAT VAISHNAVA TEMPLE
AT SRIRANGAM, NEAR
TRICHINOPOLY
13TH TO 18TH CENT. A.D.

Fig. 1. Madura Temple, Swami Singothanam: Entrance to Main Shrine.

Fig. 2. Tanjore. Subramania Temple; c. A.D. 1750.

Madura Temple, Southern Gopuram.

Fig. 2
Madura, Tirumalai's Choultry. Portrait and "Yali" pillars;
c. A.D. 1623-45.

Fig. 1
Trichinopoly. Interior of Jambukeswar Temple; c. A.D. 1600.

Fig. 1
Travancore.   Suchendram Temple.   16th century.

Fig. 2
Corridor in the Temple of Rameswaram; c. 17th century.

tectural types of the Buddhists, the monastery and the temple, the vimana deriving from the vihara, and the gopuram from the chaitya hall.

When once established the general principles of the design of the gopuram were fairly consistently maintained, and no radical changes in its architectural structure are recorded. But owing to variations in its appearance and surface treatment it is possible to resolve these gateways into two classes. As regards their main shape there is one type in which the sloping sides are relatively straight, firm and rigid in their contours, and appertaining in their mass more to the strictly pyramidal figure. In keeping with its geometrical form, the decoration of this variety is of a conventional order, usually architectural in its character and consisting of pillars and pilasters applied in such a manner as to produce the different stages of its conformation. In the other class of gopuram the sloping sides are not straight but curved and concave, so that the entire building has a soaring upward sweep which, although not entirely substantial, is very impressive. In addition the surface treatment is of a more florid nature, figure-subjects predominate, while every portion is plastered thick with images in a bewildering manner. Here are represented " all the mystic and many weaponed deities of the Siva pantheon, infinitely multiplied and repeated and reduced and carried in rising ranks, and receding tiers, up to the horns of the topmost roof." The roof in this more ornate class of gopuram is indeed a fantastic production with its cornuted gables and its ridge line breaking out into a row of tall pinnacles it forms an appropriate climax to the fretted and pullulating mass below. (Plate LXXVII).

Most of the Pandya gopurams, being the earliest of their kind, are however of the simpler and more conventional variety, and their decoration is mainly of the architectural type. From this architectural treatment of the gopurams, and also from other sources, it is possible to observe in the design of the pillar and capital a further stage in the development of the Dravidian order. Two changes in these distinctive features may be recorded, which differentiate them from the order of the previous period. One occurs in that characteristic member the *idaie*, or flower-shape, a motif which corresponds in some respects to the echinus in the Doric capital of the Greeks. In the hands of the Pandya sculptors this flower element was given a scolloped edge, thus presenting it with a foliated and more exquisite appearance. The other alteration is in the form of the *bodigai* or corbel of the bracket overhanging the capital, which has been converted from a purely conventional and abstract member into a moulded pendent or " drop." (Plate LXV, Fig. 3). In addition to the above the *palagai*, or " plank," which serves as an abacus to the order, and throughout the style has been remarkable for its outstanding width, is in the Pandya type of capital of exceptional proportions and projection, some of these stone " planks," although only two inches thick, are as much as 4½ feet in diameter. It is by such details peculiar to the order that the identification of the buildings of this period may be confirmed.

In referring to the Dravidian temple at this stage of its evolution Dubreuil,[1] has not inappropriately likened the procedure by which the temple precincts were expanded, to the phenomenon of the growth of a tree trunk, the cross section of which shows a number of concentric rings each

an annual contribution to its thickness. On the same principle the earlier courts of the Pandya temple are those towards the centre, while each concentric wall with its gopurams records successively a later addition. The older gopurams therefore are usually the smaller ones nearer to the innermost shrine, and one of the first examples of its kind appears to have been that in the second enclosure wall of the temple of Jambukesvara near Trichinopoly, probably built in the twelfth century. There are several features in this gopuram which are clearly a " carry-over " from the preceding style of the Cholas, so that it is really an illustration of the transition between the two modes. These earlier features are details in the order as seen in the design of the pilasters, for while the *idaie* or flower-shape of the capital remains plain and unscolloped as in the Chola type, the *bodigai*, or corbel of the bracket is elaborated after the Pandyan pattern. Although relatively small matters such details are a clue to the style and date of this presumably first example of a fully developed gopuram.

Later and more typical examples of the gopuram as it matured under the Pandyas are as follows :—another entrance subsequently added to the temple of Jambukesvara and known as the Sundara Pandya gopuram, built about 1250 ; a gateway on the eastern side of the temple of Chidambaram, of the same date ; one on the eastern side of the inner enclosure of the temple at Tiruvannamalai (Tirumalai) cir. 1300 (Plate LXXIV) ; and a gopuram of the great temple at Kumbakonam, cir. 1350. Of this series the eastern gateway at Chidambaram is perhaps the most characteristic of the period, and as it bears an inscription of the Pandya ruler Sundara who reigned in the middle of the thirteenth century its date is authenticated. In plan this gopuram occupies a rectangle 90 feet by 60 feet, while the two stories comprising its vertical substructure are together 35 feet high, the total height of its seven stories including the roof being 135 feet. There is still much of the old traditional beauty of the Chola style in the design of its structure, the lower stories in stone masonry being but little different from those of the Tanjore vimana of 150 years before, except that there are elaborations in the details, which distinguish the existing mode. Above, the surface treatment is of the architectural kind, consisting of rows of pillared niches and pavilions, each with a foliated canopy, thus presenting a pattern of arcading alternating with a zone of ornamentation, an effective appearance without being too lavish. All these gopurams of the Pandya period are of much the same character as the foregoing, and although a type of structure which relies for much of its effect on the rich nature of its surface decoration, the restraint exercised in the earlier examples is commendable.

So far the Pandya period has been represented solely by monumental gateways, but there is one example of a complete temple which may have been erected during this regime. If, as presumed, it was produced under the Pandyas, on grounds of style it must date towards the end of their rule, therefore during the first half of the fourteenth century. This is the temple of Aiyravatesvara at Darasuram in the Tanjore district. (Plate LXVI, Fig. 2). The main structure of its composition, in a word the temple proper, is in plan very similar to the two great temples already described of the previous period, as it consists of a long rectangular building of no great height rising up into a pyramidal tower or vimana at its western end. On the other hand around

---

[1] *Archaeolgie du Sud L'Inde*, by Jouveau-Dubreuil, Paris, 1914.

this central feature and forming part of the architectural scheme, as they are all within the same enclosure, are several other edifices, the whole comprising a small but compact group of buildings of notable expressiveness. A system consisting of a group of religious structures, in addition to the one central temple, was an arrangement which now began to develop, but may be resolved more logically to the subsequent period, as it is particularly characteristic of the Vijayanagar manner. The architectural treatment of the Darasuram example however is obviously in the late Pandya mode, as is clearly shown in the design of the pillars, the capital and bases of which bear the unmistakable scolloped edge of this period, while the bracket above the capital has a cyma recta curve, all distinguishing features of the Dravidian style at this juncture.

One architectural motif freely used in parts of this temple recalls a much earlier phase of the southern style. It is the reappearance, as a support to the walls, of the leogriff pilaster, that rampant animal form so characteristic of the Pallava period. Emerging first in the rock-cut mandapas of Mamallapuram, it disappeared for several centuries to be revived in its original shape on the Amman shrine of this temple of the Pandyas. Such an instance of architectural atavism is not by any means rare in the building art of India, yet it is a little strange to meet again these almost forgotten leonine creatures, but they fall into their place in the later building and in perfect accord with their environment in spite of the long interval of disuse. A somewhat similar animal form going back almost to the same early phase is seen in another kind of pillar at the Darasuram temple on a building known as the Kalyan mandapa. This is a sedent gryphon attached to the shaft of the column, but its body is attenuated vertically, thus appearing by its pose to prefigure those very striking horse and dragon groups which rear themselves in such spirited attitudes to form the columns of the succeeding period.

In the gradual progress of the style the temple of Darasuram is an example of some significance. Compared with the gopurams which are typical of the Pandya period there is a definite change not only in architectural treatment but in the broader aspect of ideals. The temple denotes that a movement was being made away from the relatively robust and disciplined productions of the Pallavas and Cholas, towards a richer and more elegant effect. It implies an effort to animate the style with a new tempo, not with the idea of giving it greater powers, but with the object of arresting attention by increasing its emotional appeal. This building therefore is of no little consequence as it illustrates the middle period of architectural development in the south, marking the stage of transition between the affluent maturity of the Cholas, and the exquisite though extravagant productions of Vijayanagar.

REFERENCE

Jouveau-Dubreuil, G. *Archaeologie due Sud de L'Inde* ; Paris, 1914.

CHAPTER XIX

THE DRAVIDIAN STYLE

UNDER THE VIJAYANAGAR DYNASTY (cir. A.D. 1350 to 1565)

BEGINNING in the middle of the fourteenth century, a change came over the spirit as well as the substance of architecture in Southern India, when, after the somewhat temperate productions of the Pandyas, the country gradually became enriched with buildings in a style showing that the people had been aroused to a life of greater fulness, and one which moved them to express with marked freedom and fluency their aesthetic aspirations. The power which gave impetus and direction to such a movement was the forceful dynasty which established the Vijayanagar empire and dominated the Dravida country for over two centuries, from 1350 to 1565. This Hindu empire came into being in response to a vital need, that of preventing the all-conquering Mahommedans, who had already overrun the rest of India, from crossing the dividing line of the Kistna river, and thus completing the subjugation of the country by bringing the final portion, that of the extreme south, under their rule. Something of the sacred importance of their trust, that of preserving intact the last remaining independent Hindu territory, may have stimulated and sustained them, and enabled them to build up a dominion of exceptional stability and strength. The capital of this great empire, extending from the Kistna to Cape Comorin, was the palatial city of Vijayanagar, for a time one of the foremost cities in Asia, which, occupying a strong strategic position on the banks of the Tungabadri river, stood like a bulwark against the ever-present menace from the north. That it was a period when princely encouragement was given to the arts is proved by the architectural remains in this now deserted city, which, although grievously ruined still contains much that is wonderfully rich and beautiful. Its religious buildings, and those in other parts of Vijayanagar territory, show that no longer was it the practice to produce large unified compositions as in the Chola period, but on the other hand to devise groups of structures of moderate proportions, distinguished however by the exquisite character of the architecture and their sumptuous plastic embellishment. Indian architecture, at all times remarkable for the profuseness of its applied decoration, at this stage of its development reached " the extreme limit of florid magnificence ". It is a record in stone of a range of ideals, sensations, emotions, prodigalities, abnormalities, of forms and formlessness, and even eccentricities, that only a superimaginative mind could conceive, and only an inspired artist could reproduce. The sole parallel, but a relatively remote one, is the Baroque movement in Europe, as it is expressive in a degree of the same political and social conditions. And just as the Baroque was the final issue of the Renaissance, so the almost contemporary movement in Southern India represents the supremely passionate flowering of the Dravidian style.

Some of the changes in the character of the religious architecture at this time are due to changes that were taking place in the structure of the creed. The elaboration of the ceremonial observances, brought about partly by the more pronounced anthropomorphic attributions of the deity, produced a corresponding elaboration in the temple system by increasing the number of buildings within the temple enclosure, and also to a certain extent altering their intention. In addition to the main temple in the middle, there are separate shrines, pillared halls, pavilions and other annexes, each having its special purpose and each occupying its appointed position in the scheme. One of these is the Amman shrine, a subsidiary temple usually situated to the north west of the main building and slightly behind it ; in it is enshrined an image of the consort of the deity to whom the temple is dedicated, he himself occupying the cella of the central structure. Another and even more important building, generally placed towards the left and front of the east entrance, is the Kalyan mandapa, not infrequently the most ornate structure of the entire group. This is an open pillared pavilion, with a raised platform for a throne in the centre for the reception of the deity and his consort on the annual celebration of their marriage ceremony.

Much of the intricacy and rich beauty of the Vijayanagar type of temple was produced by the number and prominence of its pillars and piers, and the manner in which they were sculptured into the most complicated compositions, strange and manifold, so that each becomes a figurative drama in stone. Pavilions containing groups of columns form the principal part of the architectural scheme, and it is by the artistically ingenious character of many of these supports that the buildings of this style may be identified. A very striking type of pillar design and also the most frequent is that in which the shaft becomes merely a central core for the attachment of an involved group of statuary, often of heroic size and chiselled entirely in the round, having as its most conspicuous element a furiously rearing horse, rampant hippogryph or upraised animal of a supernatural kind. Another type, sometimes combined and also alternating with the foregoing, shows encircling the central column a cluster of miniature pillars, slender, mystical, and dreamy, like Gothic nook-shafts. Of the less complicated form of column there is one which is often found in conjunction with others, where the shaft is composed of a series of small-scale shrines copied from original full size structures and arranged in zones one above the other on the same principle of the repeating " cells " on the sikhara and gopuram. Lastly there is a fairly common type which appears throughout the later phases of the Dravidian style consisting of a cubical motif alternating with wide bands and chamfered, so that portions of the shaft are eight or sixteen sided. Almost all these different kinds of pillars have ornamental brackets forming part of their capitals, as found in every stage of the Dravidian order, and usually below the bracket is a pendant or *bodegai*, the changes in the design of which throughout the style have already been traced. (Plate LXV). In response to the demand for more richness of detail during the Vijayanagar regime this pendant was elaborated into a volute terminating in an inverted lotus bud, its different shapes thus providing a minor but reliable index to the period.

There are a number of buildings in the Vijayanagar style of architecture distributed throughout the Dravida country, but the finest and most characteristic group is in the deserted city of Vijayanagar itself. It is not improbable that the peculiar terrain on which this capital is situated may have had some indirect reaction on the style. Strategic reasons account for its location, but it is not easy to understand why such a tossed and tumbled jungle of sun-blasted stones, with only limited open spaces intervening, should have been selected. In, and amongst, and even on these gigantic and often grotesquely shaped boulders, the monuments are erected, strewn over a turbulent landscape having the appearance of a planet long since dead. So closely associated are the buildings with the rocks from which they were constructed, that it is difficult at times to tell where nature ends and art begins. Some of these naturally fantastic shapes may have stirred the imagination and directed it towards the invention of strange creatures such as chimera and other fabulous forms with which the style abounds. One advantage of such a site was the ease with which the building material could be obtained. This may account for the immense and multiple piers of the temples being monolithic, each formed out of one large block of granite, levered the short distance from the quarry to its place in the pillared hall, and there carved into shape on the spot. In addition to the local granite a dark green chlorite stone, more amenable to the chisel, was readily available, so that the two kinds of masonry are seen side by side. Whether it was the result of these two differently textured stones, or perhaps more likely the presence of two separate schools of plastic art, the difference between the character of the granite sculpture and that of the chlorite is very marked. The former is graphically conceived but crudely and almost childishly fashioned, while the latter is sharply cut and skilfully modelled giving the appearance of being produced by workmen having long experience and age-old traditions.

The principal temples in the city of Vijayanagar are the Vitthala and the Hazara Rama, but there are several others of no little interest. The Vitthala, although not the grand temple of the city which is traditionally ascribed to the Pampapati temple, is by far the most exquisitely ornate building on the site. Begun by Raja Krishna Deva in 1513, it was continued by his successor Achyuta Raja (1529-42) but owing to its elaborate character was never entirely finished. It stands within a rectangular courtyard 500 feet long by 310 feet wide, which is surrounded by cloisters formed of a triple row of pillars, entrance being obtained through three gopurams, those on the east and south being the more important. At least six separate structures, mostly in the form of pillared halls are within this stone-flagged enclosure, the largest, that of the main temple occupying the centre, while the others are disposed around in their prescribed position. The central building is dedicated to Vishnu in the form of Vitthala or Vithoba (*Panduranga*), one of the embodiments of the god Krishna, and is a long low structure of one story averaging 25 feet in height, and in length 230 feet, aligned from east to west. Its lack of height is partly due to its being incomplete, for any superstructure that it ever possessed, being of brick and plaster, has fallen into decay. Although appearing externally as one long building, it consists of three distinct compartments, namely an *ardha-mandapa* or open pillared portico in front, a *mandapa* or closed assembly hall in the middle, and the *garbha griha* or sanctuary in the rear. The part which first attracts attention on account of its supremely rich appearance is the maha-mandapa, or portico, a columned pavilion, not square in plan as it has deeply recessed sides, but measuring 100 feet across its extreme length and width. Standing on a moulded

plinth five feet in height with flights of steps, elephant guarded, on its three free sides, the whole composition is heavily shadowed by means of an immensely wide double-flexured eave, above the parapet of which rises an irregular outline of brickwork turrets, the remains of the original superstructure.

The chief feature of this columned hall, however, is its range of pillars, fifty-six in number, each twelve feet in height, forty of them regularly spaced as a kind of colonnade or aisle around its outer edge, while the remaining sixteen form an oblong court in the centre. (Plate LXX). Each pier comprises an entire sculptured group in itself, being fashioned out of one large block of granite, and each is a variant of much the same type of design. Clusters of delicately shaped columns form the central portion of these broad supports, some of which are four and five feet across, while interposed between them is the afore-mentioned rearing animal motif, half natural half mythical but wholly rhythmic, the said architectural character of the one acting as a foil to the free and animated sculpturesque treatment of the other. This scheme surrounds the central core of each pier, joining together above to form a single massive capital and below to unite in one moulded pedestal or base, while the colonnade as a whole is so closely spaced as to produce an effect of bewildering intricacy. Then over the piers are bracket supports of prodigious size combined with profusely carved entablatures and above all a flat ceiling ornamented with sunk lotus flowers. When it is understood that every stone is chiselled over with the most elaborate patterns, some merely finely engraved, others modelled in high relief, while not a few are so undercut as to be almost detached, the tropical exuberance of its composition will be realized.

The remainder of this central temple building, the part which is attacked to the preceding and formed by the ardha-mandapa and the sanctuary combined, resolves itself into a unified rectangular structure 135 feet long and 67 feet wide, its exterior walls embellished with that conventional arrangement of pilaster, niche, and alcove combination, which, in one form or another, appears as surface decoration in almost every phase of the Dravidian style. This mandapa or assembly room, which is entered from the east front through the ardha-mandapa described above, has in addition two-side-entrances, each having steps and a pillared porch of some size. Its interior is a square hall of 55 feet side surrounded by an aisle of 12 pillars with four others in the centre, one at each corner of a square dais. At the far end of the assembly hall is the doorway to the cella, behind which is a corridor or vestibule leading to the chamber of the god, enclosed within the solid masonry of the vimana. This vimana, or last of the three compartments of the central building, is externally 75 feet long and 72 feet wide, and is a little unusual in its plan. Apparently a processional passage, not included in the original scheme, became necessary, and was evidently improvised while the temple was still under construction. The floor of this ambulatory for structural reasons had to be on the same lever as the courtyard, so one descends into it by two flights of seven steps, as into a crypt, one flight on each side of the vestibule leading to the cella. Such an expedient implies some unexpected change in the ceremonial at this date.

The remaining buildings within the Vitthala temple enclosure are all in the same ornate style as the main structure, but one of these, the Kalyana or "marriage" mandapa is even more superbly wrought. Placed according to convention slightly to the side and front of the principal entrance to the temple, it consists of an open pavilion resembling in some respects the ardha-mandapa, as it is designed in much the same manner, but is little more than half its size. Standing as they do within a few paces of one another, these two pillared halls present an architectural combination of astonishing richness. The Kalyana has the same kind of high plinth, with deeply recessed sides and flights of steps in the centre of three of them, its plan measuring 62 feet either way at the widest part. Again there is the voluptuous double flexured cornice with a turned up outer edge reminiscent of the pagodas of China, and below is a grouping of piers, each with its girdle of detached shafts of most graceful and elegant proportions. There are as many as forty-eight in all, of these piers, of which twelve are placed around the square throne in the centre of the pavilion, the remainder forming a double arcade around its sides. Aligned with the main axis of the temple, and facing the east or principal entrance to the ardha-mandapa is another monument of no little beauty and significance. This is the ratha or chariot of the god, a reproduction in masonry, with realistically revolving stone wheels and to a fairly ample scale, of a temple car, with every feature imitated in granite, even to the elephant forms which guard the steps. As with all the structures of the period its upper part, in the form of a sikhara, was of brick and cement, but this has been dismantled. The position of such an artistic piece of symbolism in the foreground is well thought out, as it leads up to the fine effect of the main building beyond.

In view of the irregularity of the ground on which the capital seat of the Vijayanagar kings was built, there could be little attempt at symmetry in its town-planning, and the disposition of the different quarters of the city is therefore not readily determined. One portion however has been identified as the citadel, and within this walled area the imperial buildings were grouped. Among these is a comparatively small but highly ornamental temple known as the Hazara Rama, in which the royal family and members of the court worshipped, and may therefore be referred to as the Chapel Royal. Its private character is emphasized by the twenty-four feet high wall with which the courtyard is surrounded. According to inscriptions it was begun by Krishna Deva Raya in 1513, and in spite of being of very moderate dimensions, is perhaps the most completely finished example of its kind, as not only is the superstructure intact, but included within the enclosure is an Amman shrine, a Kalyana mandapa, and all the other subsidiary structures found in the larger type. It is entered on the east through a finely proportioned but flat-roofed porch, which leads to an assembly hall having as its main feature a group of four massive black-stone pillars, one at each corner of a central square. These four columns are of unusual design as their shafts are built up of contrasting geometrical shapes, a cube alternating with a fluted cylinder all copiously carved, while each capital is a very substantial four-branched foliated volute, each volute terminating in the characteristic knop.

There are two other entrances to the assembly hall of this temple, one on each side and each provided with a porch ; these however communicate with the courtyard, but at the far end of the hall is the doorway to the sanctuary in the cella of which was originally enshrined an image of Vishnu in the embodiment of Ramachandra. Passing down the steps of one of the side entrances and crossing the small and high walled enclosure the temple scheme is revealed. The main building which is towards the centre

of the courtyard is remarkable for its vimana, with its lower story of stone and its pyramidal sikhara of brick rising above. This sikhara, although considerably worn, consists of a regular grouping of replicas of itself in three tiers surmounted by a cupola, the whole rather under fifty feet in height. Slightly to the side and rear of the vimana is the Amman shrine, in style a smaller reproduction of the main structure, with the exception of the crowning member of its sikhara, where, in place of a cupola, a keel roof has been adopted, derived from the Buddhist chaitya hall. In both buildings these brick and plaster superstructures were originally finished off with paint in bright colours a treatment which must have contrasted somewhat strongly with the sober natural tone of the stone masonry of the lower story. Yet this stonework itself has a singularly colourful appearance as each wall is elaborately carved in that architectural pattern of niche and pilaster, which by this time had become characteristic of the Dravidian style. There are not many buildings, however, of the period in which this very appropriate scheme of mural relief decoration has been more skilfully designed and disposed than on the temple of Hazara Rama.

Within the walls of the citadel at Vijayanagar there are the remains of certain buildings, obviously of a secular order, in which only the lower portions have escaped the destruction wrought by the conquerors of the city after the fateful battle of Talikota in 1565. Yet so beautiful are these coursed and moulded terraces that if their superstructures now overthrown and broken were in any way their equal, they fully justify the eulogies of those who, visiting the city in its prime, described it in such glowing terms. Two of these substantial masonry basements stand out above all others, the larger, known as the King's Audience Hall, and another rather smaller called the "Throne Platform", or by some the "House of Victory", as it is recorded that it was erected in commemoration of Deva Raja's return from his conquest of Orissa in 1513. Both terraces seem to have been surmounted by pillared pavilions above which rose pyramidal roofs, the whole structure, according to the contemporary accounts, being several stories in height. It is also not unlikely that these royal pavilions when in use were the Dravidian equivalent to the two large halls which invariably found a place in the design of the imperial palaces in India and Persia, later to be known as the Diwani-Am and the Diwani-Khas, or halls of Public and Private Audience respectively. The platform of the King's Audience Hall, which may have been the Diwani-Am, still retains the sockets of its pillars, and there appear to have been ten rows of these, each row containing ten pillars, so that it was a "Hall of a Hundred Pillars". Fragments of these lie around from which it seems that they had cylindrical shafts, bracket capitals, and square bases. Three spacious stages, one above the other, diminishing as they rise, make up the solid foundation of this terrace, up which mount fine flights of steps, with the retaining walls decorated by means of mouldings and string-courses, broad, bold and precise, to conform with the monumental character of the building of which they formed such a substantial part.

The basement of the other building, the Throne Platform, presumably intended for private audiences, as in the previous example, is in three diminishing stages, each square in plan, the side of the lowest being 132 feet and the uppermost 78 feet, access to the latter being obtained by stairways with the usual elephant decorated side-walls. There is even less evidence as to the type of pavilion which surmounted this broad expanse of masonry, but if it was as distinctive in style as the upper of the three stages, the one on which it took its stand, it must indeed have been a work of surpassing elegance. This highest stage of the platform is in marked contrast to the two below, as these are merely plain masonry plinths, their part in the scheme being to raise the entire composition to a considerable height, the value of such a procedure in giving additional dignity to the whole being well understood by the builders. It is interesting to note however that for the edification of those lowly ones who were not admitted into the special audiences, the vertical retaining walls of both these lower platforms were converted into picture galleries by means of bands of figures and animals carved in bas-relief and of a most entertaining description. As a foil to this broad effect the uppermost stage was subjected to an entirely different treatment to prepare the eye for the noble superstructure it supported. Its horizontality is emphasised by a series of boldly moulded courses, sharply projected, and fashioned out of lengths of stone like huge beams, carved and placed in position with a skill and precision showing long practice. As an effort at decoration of a purely architectural order this platform is a singularly effective production, in its handling not unlike some of the later workmanship of the Gothic style in Europe.

No remains of this city recall more vividly the story of the forgotten empire of Vijayanagar than these massive terraces, still impressive examples of architecture in spite of their mutilated superstructures. For here the ruler of this rich region sat in state on his golden throne to view the pomp and pageantry symbolising the greatness and wealth of his possessions, an Indian replica of the "Field of the Cloth of Gold", a spectacle which at that very time was taking place in the West. Even in their dismantled condition these elevated and orderly piles of masonry with their finely moulded revetments retain some of the glamour and romance of that brilliant period when Vijayanagar, the "City of Victory" was one of the most famous capitals of the East.

It has been already mentioned that buildings in the Vijayanagar style also arose in other parts of the southern empire, as for instance at Vellore, Kumbakonam, Conjeeveram, Tadpatri, Virinjipuram, and Srirangam. Among them the temple in the fort at Vellore is prominent, its Kalyana mandapa even excelling in the luxuriant character of its carving the buildings of the capital, being considered the richest and most beautiful structure of its kind. Nothing could exceed the spirit or vigour of the hippogryphs and dragons of its pillars, or the fineness and prodigality of the ornament. In the centre pillars of the pavilion there is a reversion to the sedent lion motif, as seen at least six centuries earlier in the rock-cut Yampuri mandapa at Mamallapuram, but with every part of this archaistic element elaborated to accord with its more florid environment. The gopuram to this temple is characteristic of the style during the sixteenth century, as shown by the execution and disposal of its various traditional forms such as the foliation of the predestal (*padmam*), the pavilion-canopied niches, the voluted chaitya "antefixes' (*kudu*), and the flamboyant pilasters (*kumbapancharam*) in the alcoves. (Plate LXXII).

There is much the same unrestrained exuberance in the architectural treatment of the large Kalyana mandapa of the Marghasakesvara temple at Virinjipuram, in the North

Arcot district, the verve and abandon of the rearing chimeras and the exquisite refinement of the detached pillars around the corner piers, appearing to be the spontaneous expression of a people of great spirit. At Conjeeveram there are two temples with pavilions in the Vijayanagar style, that in the Varadarajaswami, a "hundred pillared mandapa" being composed of a maze of closely set pillars each consisting of a bizarre grouping of imaginative statuary with stone-cutting of a high order, while the other, the Ekambaranatha contains a "thousand pillared mandapa" decorated with the same fantastic form of sculpture. To gopurams at Tadpatri belonging to the temple of Rameswara are patterned in a close filigree of convoluted carving, and finally, there is the famous so-called "Horse Court", or Seshagiri mandapam at Srirangam near Trichinopoly, with its colonnade of furiously fighting steeds each rearing up to a height of nearly nine feet, the whole executed in a technique so emphatic as to be not like stone but hardened steel. (Plate LXXI, Fig. 2).

The repetition of the "horse" motif in the pillars of this period which seems to attain the finality of extravagance in the Horse Court at Srirangam, is remarkable. A rampant animal was a notable decorative element in the architecture of the Pallavas, the earliest phase of the Dravidian style, a feature which became a permanent gift to the building art of the South. During the Vijayanagar regime this motif, in a much more developed form, appears so frequently that it dominates every conception, until it becomes an obsession. Such conspicuous creations, when they persist in this manner, usually imply some vivid experience ever-present in the sub-consciousness of the people, a mass psychosis which they are unable to suppress. Several mysterious subjects of a like nature figure in Indian decorative schemes, one of the most constant depicting a dwarf-like creature, downtrodden and compelled to support buildings, or carry enormous weights, a conventional representation reminiscent of some conquest in the twilight of their history of an aboriginal race and since condemned to everlasting slavery. There are others equally graphic which either tradition or instinct ordains should be reproduced in the country's art. The rampant horseman in the later Dravidian buildings is an illustration of this mental phenomenon, and also reveals the spirit of the times, as the Vijayanagar era corresponded in some respects to that age of chivalry and romance which prevailed in mediaeval Europe. Save that they were on a lesser scale, the conditions in the Tamil country were not very different from those which produced the Crusades, except that in India the movement was mainly defensive, while in Europe it was more aggressive. Both people were faced with much the same peril, that of an impending Islamic subversion, to oppose which called for the highest valour and personal heroism. That the armed forces of the Vijayanagar empire were of the finest calibre, inspired and led by rulers of great audacity and daring, is proved by the long period of two centuries during which they kept their hereditary foes at bay, whereas almost every other part of the country succumbed at once. Something of this temper, a feeling of exultant invincibility translated into the power of good over evil, seems embodied in the art of this period and to account for these colonnades of splendid cavaliers nonchalantly astride gigantic rearing chargers and engaged in furious combat with fabulous creatures, an episode singularly analogous to that of St. George and the Dragon in the West.

REFERENCES

Longhurst, A. H., *Hampi Ruins*. Madras, 1917.
Sewell, R., *A Forgotten Empire* (*Vijayanagar*). London, 1900.

CHAPTER XX

THE DRAVIDIAN STYLE

MADURA : THE FINAL PHASE (from cir. A.D. 1600)

AFTER the fall of the Vijayanagar Empire in 1565 brought about by the confederacy of Muhammadan principalities in the Dekkan, the Hindu element in the Tamil country, owing to the pressure of Islamic aggression, was forced further south eventually to establish itself with the city of Madura as its capital seat. Here, and in certain other towns in the extremity of the peninsula, under a dynasty known as the Nayaks, the Dravidian style assumed its final form, which has lasted almost until modern times. Hindu architecture, as produced during this period, flourished principally under the rule of the greatest member of this line, Tirumalai Nayak, who reigned from 1623 to 1659, and through whose patronage many of the finest works were created. In the field of religious architecture, the Madura style, as it has been found convenient to call it, appears to have been a revival and continuation of the building procedure of the Pandyas (1100-1350), which, it may be recalled, consisted in improving and extending the existing shrines, so that these attained much greater magnificence. This method of temple development had been a common practice from early mediaeval times, as the historical records of many southern Indian temples testify, but under the Nayak regime, beginning in the seventeenth century it received notable encouragement, with the result that a number of ancient foundations became expanded into structural complexes of vast size and impressive appearance. In some instances such conditions were arrived at by gradual stages, additions to the temple-scheme being made at different periods, the final effect being obtained after a long course of years ; on the other hand, in certain examples the greater part of their existing formation was produced by a single effort made at one particular time. In either case the result was much the same as both methods present what at first sight appears to be a rather confused grouping of buildings devoid of any pre-conceived plan. From some of the less complicated of these compositions, however, in spite of recent aggregations, it is possible to establish some kind of system underlying their layout.

It is fairly clear that the expansion of the southern Indian temples was occasioned by a corresponding expansion of the temple ritual, the forms and ceremonies of the creed having become considerably elaborated, a condition which naturally reacted on the arrangements of the building in which they were celebrated. Some of this increase in the structural formation was due to the wider powers accredited to the deity of the temple, who it is possible to envisage in two capacities, a spiritual and a temporal. In his spiritual capacity the deity remained enshrined within the darkened mystery of his cella, where passively he received the homage of the devout. To provide for such a condition there is therefore an inner portion of the temple, strictly reserved and secluded as the sacred habitation of the god. On the other hand on certain prescribed occasions this divinity personifies a less abstract embodiment and emerges from his retreat in his temporal capacity, assuming a physical form not unlike that of an earthly sovereign of the olden time. When in

this state therefore he is led forth in procession to take part in festivals and ceremonials of a semi-mundane but imperial character, and accordingly for this specific purpose the outlying precincts of the temple are largely utilized. It will be seen that, in such circumstances, and to conform to these two contrasting appearances, the temple resolves itself into two main formations, an inner, covered, and most sacred part, and an outer, open, more public and less sanctified part. The former, comprising the central portion, may consist of two flat-roofed courts, one enclosed within the other, which in most of the temples cover a fairly large rectangular space. Within the inner of these two courts is the sanctum, the cupolas of which, often richly gilt, may be seen thrusting itself through the flat roofs, thus denoting the focal centre of the entire scheme. In contrast to the guarded seclusion of this inner portion, the outer part of the temple area is formed of a concentric series of open courtyards called *prakarams*, enclosed within high walls, but open to the sky as they are too large to be roofed ; these *prakarams* provide ample space for buildings connected with the more secular aspect of the ceremonial.

The process of enlargement of the temple plan proceeded on the following lines. Beginning from the centre, the cella and its portico, both together comprising the sanctum of the temple, were the first and foundational structures, and these sometimes took the form of a temple in miniature, that is to say they consisted of a small chamber and its forecourt, the usual origins of a shrine. The preliminary step in expansion was to enclose this shrine within a spacious flat-roofed structure the innermost court referred to above. No doubt the object of such an addition was to protect the original sanctuary, and at the same time to emphasize its sacred character. Within this court there grew up pillared aisles and other interior arrangements of a like nature, the entrance to the whole being through a small gopuram or gateway in front and on the east. In the course of time the covered court itself became contained within another structure of the same type, and the same process of dividing up its encircling corridors by means of pillars and pavilions was adopted. To this court there were ordinarily two entrances, east and west, or front and back, each being marked by a gopuram larger than the last. This generally completed that portion of the temple which was wholly covered and sacrosanct.

The next step towards enlarging the temple formation was that of enclosing the entire composition within a rectangle by means of a high boundary wall, an intervening space being left all round to provide a wide open courtyard, or *prakaram*. This enclosure was entered by gopurams, one on the east and the other on the west, the former being usually the larger as it was the principal doorway. Within the space thus enclosed various structures were erected, chiefly pillared halls or subsidiary shrines, and also certain buildings of a semi-religious character such as granaries, and store-rooms for the safe-keeping of the ceremonial supplies. After a time another larger rectangular area was added, concentric with the last, and also contained within a still higher enclosing wall, leaving another appreciable space between the inner and outer perimeters. As many as four entrances were often made in this wall, one in the middle of each of its four sides and each consisting of a gopuram greater in size than any of those previously erected. At this stage therefore some architectural effect becomes visible, being obtained by the series of gopurams aligned along the axis of the temple, with two others to balance at its sides. Within this outermost enclosure two large and important structures are generally found, one being a hypostyle hall of a thousand pillars, and the other a square tank of water for ablutions, lined with steps and surrounded by an arcade. (Plate LXXV).

Some such plan was no doubt the intention and ideal, and something of the kind forms the basis of most of the great Dravidian temples of later date, but it was a procedure which, in a systematic manner, was rarely put into practice. In some cases the scheme has been disproportionately enlarged, as for instance in the temple of Srirangam where there are as many as seven concentric rectangular enclosures each with its entrance gopurams, the whole equal in area to that of a fair sized town. These *prakarams* were often contributed as acts of piety by the ruling family, and as the boundary walls were generally crenellated, the royal donors could not have been unaware of their defensive properties as a place of retreat in time of trouble.

The likeness of some of the larger temples of this period to those of the ancient Egyptians will no doubt be noticed, but any such analogy is more apparent than real, although a comparison brings into relief certain interesting facts. A seeming similarity is produced by two causes, namely the presence of the entrance pylons, and the form of the layout. As already observed the principle of the batter, or inward slope, as for instance in the gateways, must always owe something through the association of ideas, to the monuments of the Nile valley. The Dravidian gopuram and the Egyptian propylon are however two very different structural conceptions, in the former the doorway is an opening through the centre of a single edifice, the latter is a double composition with the doorway produced by an opening between the two sloping towers. As regards the layout, both types of temple, the Pharoic and the Dravidian, begin with these high and imposing entrances and, what is equally significant, their arrangements within have in a measure an uncommon resemblance. From such massive entrances the courts comprising the interior progress by diminishing stages, each compartment leading to a lesser, until the whole scheme terminates in one relatively small and inconspicuous cell in the centre. A system of structural composition of this nature is however generally regarded as contrary to the accepted rules of good building, in other words it is a negation of the fundamental principles of rational architectural procedure, as it starts with the large and impressive and finishes with the small and insignificant. Yet it is possible that in both the Egyptian and Indian instances the underlying concept was primarily not architectural but spiritual, they were planned with the object of engendering religious emotion in the mind of the devotee. He was first confronted by the majestic entrance towers which filled him with awe, and then led on by a process of progressive abasement from one hall to another, each smaller and dimmer than the last, until, he finds himself, reduced to infinitesimal nothingness as in a dream before the mystery of the darkened shrine, into the holy of holies and in the presence of the god himself.

Undoubtedly this was the intention of the Egyptian design, because each of the great temples of the Pharoahs was a unity definitely established from the first, being begun and ended with the one object in view. Not so the Dravidian temple, which, although it eventually attained much the same form and aimed at the same ideal, achieved these by a different and even inverted process. There was no conscious plan in its arrangement, no decisive preliminary conception, it gradually evolved from a small nucleus in the form of a shrine, until in the course of time it spread out into the indeterminate and, in some respects, unsystematic complex it now presents. It was fashioned not by thought or imagination but by means of a gradual aggregation of parts, many of them added without any particular attempt at a co-ordinated whole. Developed according to need very much in the manner of a mediaeval town, the temple plan resolves itself into a moderately harmonious agglomeration but lacking that quality of inseparability between form and content, the observance of which is the basis of all great works of architecture. While one cannot fail to be impressed by the profoundly religious atmosphere, emotional and often intellectual in which many of the southern Indian temples are steeped, making them as in the temple of Madura, a vast composite symbol of essential Hinduism, as an architectural entity they do not hold a high place.

But even if the late Dravidian temple as a whole fails to produce a unified architectural effect, there are certain of its elements, which, regarded either individually or collectively are of considerable artistic merit. Two of them are preeminent, consisting of exteriorly, the gopurams, and, interiorly, the pillars, either singly or in colonnades or groups. During the Madura period the gopuram reached its maturity, and some of these great pylons are not only thoroughly characteristic of the southern style, but are most imposing examples of the building art. As by far the most impressive features of the temple scheme, not only do they make a direct contribution to the whole, but they are of marked importance in shaping its parts. A certain number are what may be termed of the first class, that is 150 feet high and over, and some of them, rising up to as many as sixteen stories, and, literally, "sky-scrapers", attain the height of nearly 200 feet. In the centre of the long side is the doorway, a square-headed opening about 25 feet high, forming a kind of corridor through the structure, with rooms on either side for the accommodation of guardians and doorkeepers. Out of one of these rooms leads a staircase by means of which the summit may be reached, with a wide landing at each story. In its external treatment the height of the gopuram is emphasised by lines leading vertically, upward tendencies being obtained by the sides not being flat but having perpendicular sections projected. Then across this verticality are carried the lines of the diminishing storeys in horizontal tiers, so that the entire mass becomes a rich pattern of the vertical and the horizontal. In the later examples the surfaces were also embellished with groups of plastic imagery from which an idea of the inexhaustible resources of Hindu mythology may be gained, as some of them are computed to display as many as a thousand figures, the majority considerably over life-size. (Plate LXXVII).

Turning to the interior of the later Dravidian temple the pillars are the principal feature, and although these, as a rule, have not the florid elegance of the previous style, from which they were directly derived, they still retain some of their vigorous character. These pillars are never very high, averaging only about 12 feet, but in no other style

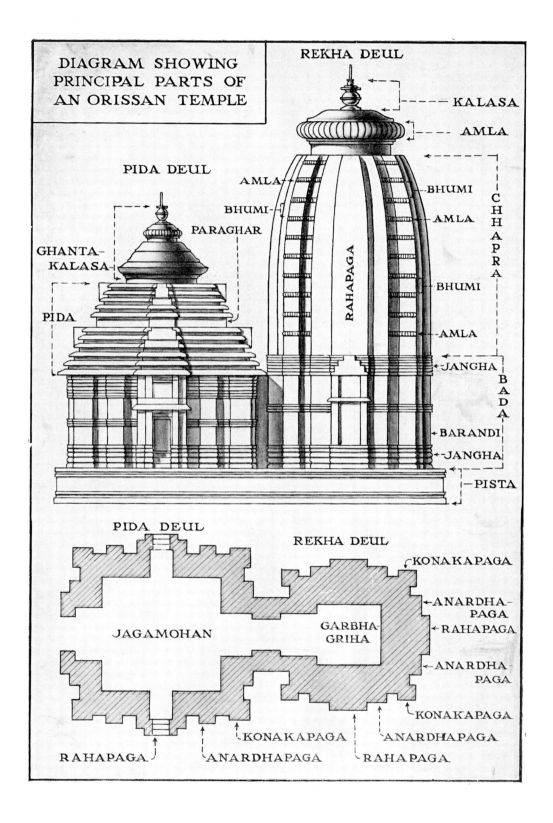

DIAGRAM SHOWING PRINCIPAL PARTS OF AN ORISSAN TEMPLE

REKHA DEUL

KALASA

AMLA

PIDA DEUL

AMLA

BHUMI

BHUMI

AMLA

PARAGHAR

GHANTA-KALASA

RAHAPAGA

BHUMI

PIDA

AMLA

CHHAPRA

JANGHA

BADA

BARANDI

JANGHA

PISTA

PIDA DEUL

REKHA DEUL

KONAKAPAGA

ANARDHA-PAGA

RAHAPAGA

JAGAMOHAN

GARBHA-GRIHA

ANARDHA-PAGA

KONAKAPAGA

KONAKAPAGA

ANARDHAPAGA

RAHAPAGA

ANARDHAPAGA

RAHAPAGA

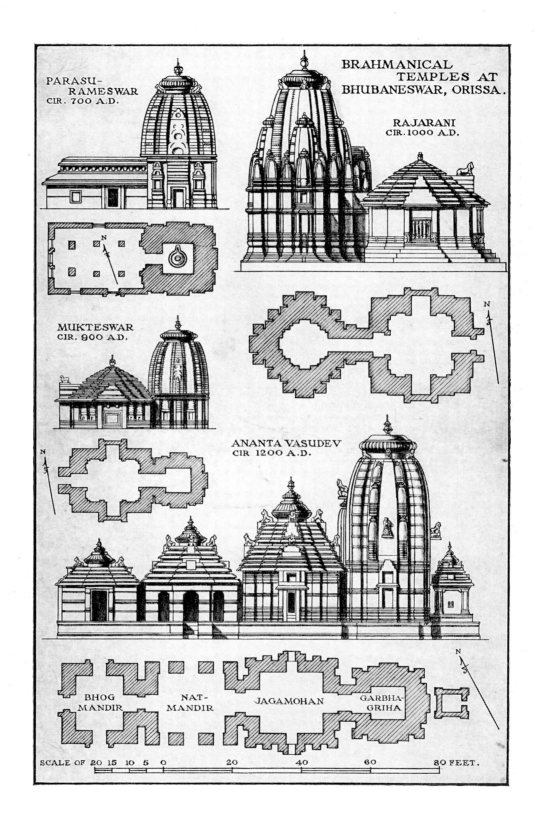

PARASU-
RAMESWAR
CIR. 700 A.D.

BRAHMANICAL
TEMPLES AT
BHUBANESWAR, ORISSA.

RAJARANI
CIR. 1000 A.D.

MUKTESWAR
CIR. 900 A.D.

ANANTA VASUDEV
CIR 1200 A.D.

BHOG
MANDIR

NAT-
MANDIR

JAGAMOHAN

GARBHA-
GRIHA

SCALE OF 20 15 10 5 0   20   40   60   80 FEET.

Fig. 1

Fig. 2   Fig. 3
Bhubaneswar: Parasrameswar Temple (before restoration); c. 8th century A.D.

Fig. 1.   Mukhteswar Temple from S.E.; c. A.D. 900.

Fig. 2.   Wheels on the Temple of the Sun, Konarak.

Fig. 2
Raja Rani; c. A.D. 1000.

Bhubaneswar Temples.

Fig. 1
Vaital Deul; c. A.D. 850.

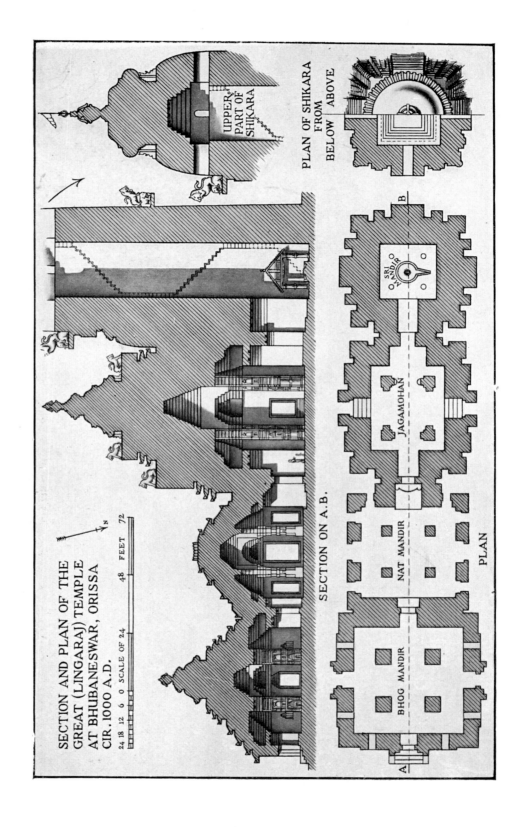

SECTION AND PLAN OF THE
GREAT (LINGARAJ) TEMPLE
AT BHUBANESWAR, ORISSA
CIR. 1000 A.D.

24 18 12 6 0 SCALE OF 24   48   FEET   72

N

UPPER
PART OF
SHIKARA

PLAN OF SHIKARA
FROM
BELOW ABOVE

SRI
MANDIR

JAGAMOHAN

NAT MANDIR

BHOG MANDIR

A   B

SECTION ON A.B.

PLAN

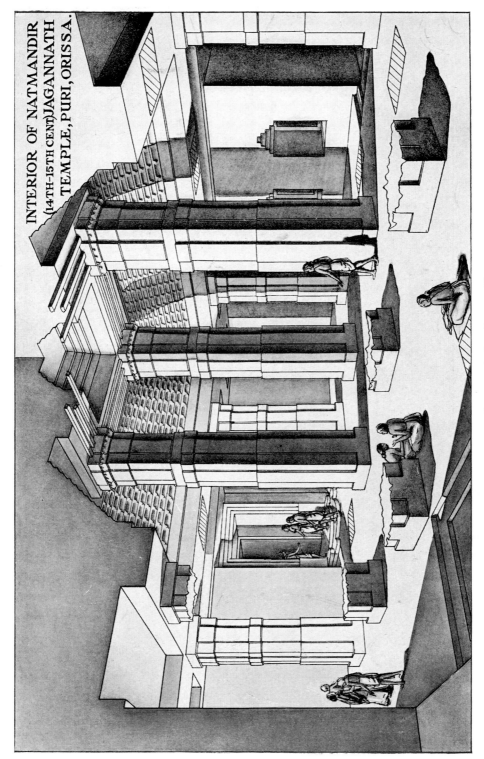

INTERIOR OF NATMANDIR
(14TH–15TH CENT.)JAGANNATH
TEMPLE, PURI, ORISSA.

Puri: the Natmandir. Note the iron beams ceiling.

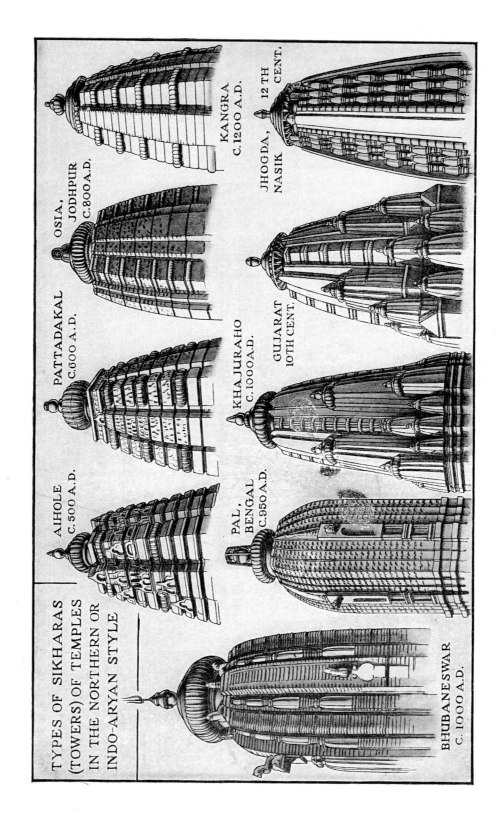

are they found in such profusion. As an example there are at least a thousand pillars in the temple of Madura, in addition to an equal number in the hypostyle hall, making a total in this one temple alone of two thousand pillars in all. They are mainly of four kinds, consisting of a square moulded and patterned example, the simplest of all ; the rampant dragon ; the figure, usually of a deity ; and the portrait, often of the donor or one of his family. All of these support ponderous and complicated superstructures in which crouching dragons and foliated brackets predominate. Although the first kind is relatively a simple composition in some instances it is enlarged into an immense square pier, with the radiating brackets above spreading out like the branches of a tree, as may be seen in the central court of the Jambukeswara temple near Trichinopoly. (Plate LXXVII). Most common of all is the second kind, that of the rearing dragon type already noted in the Vijayanagar temples, a motif still retaining its spirited curves, but restrained and stylised in the hands of the artists under the Nayak regime. This hippogriff formed the favourite design in the hypostyle halls of a thousand pillars, and individually there is much in its lines and shapes which is commendable, but when reiterated so insistently it becomes wearisome. The best example may be seen in the thousand pillared hall at Madura, where not only are the dragons exceptionally well-rendered but their superstructures are cleverly composed. This specially applies to the gryphon bracket-system above the capital and its combination with the beam it supports, the whole being balanced and finished off in a masterly manner by the dropping knop.

Of the two kinds of pillar in which the one represents a deity and the other the donor of the temple there is not very much difference, as both have figures often over life-size attached to their shafts, but they are more elaborate and complicated than any others. Unlike the classical atlantean type of support most of these Dravidian figures have little structural significance, as although they are often complete statues in the round, they are held only by attachments to the pillar shaft. There are instances however where they are so designed as to form some slight additional support to the pillar as may be seen in one of the corridors of the Minakshi shrine at Madura. The most remarkable group of deities combined with the structure are those ornamenting the court of the Swami Singothanam, or entrance to the main shrine of Sundareswara, (Siva) at Madura, a bewildering synthesis of contorted figures and multifarious architecture. (Plate LXX). Less common in the portrait-pillar, although images of donors and other personages are found sculptured on the monuments of southern India from the earliest times.[1] At Srirangam, at Srivilliputtur (Ramnad), in the Brihad-Isvara at Tanjore, and in the Pudu-Mandapa at Madura, are examples of this form of pillar, in most instances the portrait image being attached to the front of the pillar-shaft. (Plate LXXVIII, Fig. 2).

The number of temples of the Madura class is nearly thirty, but the following are the more important : Madura, Srirangam, and Jambukesvara, both near Trichinopoly ; Tiruvarur, Rameswaram, Chidambaram, Tinnevelley, Tiruvanamalai and Srivilliputtur. Of these the temple at Madura, having the merit of being largely built at one time, is most typical of the architectural style as this prevailed in the seventeenth century. It is a double temple, as it has two separate sanctuaries, one dedicated to Siva and the other to his consort the goddess Minakshi. These two shrines, which are really temples within a temple, occupy the largest space inside the main enclosure. The outer wall of this surrounds an area which is nearly a square as it measures approximately 850 feet by 725 feet, with four large gateways one towards the centre of each of its four sides. Admission is usually through the gopuram on the east which communicates with a fine pillared avenue over two hundred feet long and nearly one hundred feet wide. This leads directly to a smaller gopuram, forming the eastern entrance to the second *prakaram*, a rectangular enclosure measuring 420 feet by 310, also having four gateways one in the middle of each side, but all smaller than the preceding. Most of this second enclosure is covered in with a flat roof, but it is partly open on the northern side. Within, there is again another covered court, its sides 250 feet by 156 feet, and with only one entrance, a doorway on the east. Only so far are the uninitiated allowed to proceed, but it is outside this entrance, in what may be termed the nave and transepts of the temple, that the most elaborate part of the scheme and the most intricate grouping of pillars are to be found. Inside this last enclosure the sacred shrine itself is situated, a structure consisting of three compartments, an assembly hall, a vestibule, and the cella, the last being surmounted by a small sikhara which penetrates through the flat roof covering the whole of this portion of the temple, and may be seen from the outside rising like a golden crown in its midst. All the courts, corridors, and halls making up these enclosures have colonnades of pillars, often strange and unreal in their design, arranged in long lines or groups forming diverse vistas in all directions. (Plates LXXIV and LXXIII).

The other sanctuary of the Madura temple, that of the consort, or associate deity, Minakshi, the "fish eyed", so called as this form of eye is traditionally regarded as of surpassing beauty, is an enclosure attached to the south side of the foregoing, somewhat to the rear, and is a half-size reproduction having one compartment within another, of the adjacent Siva sanctuary. Its exterior measurements are 225 feet by 150, and it is entered by two gopurams, that on the east being comparatively small, but the western one is larger. Rising above the flat roof between the two is the cupola of the shrine, as in the Siva temple. Lying towards the front of the Minakshi sanctuary, in the angle made by that and the Siva enclosure, and forming an important feature of the temple as a whole is a rectangular sheet of water surrounded by steps and with a pillared portico on its four sides. This is the "Pool of the Golden Lilies," an artificial reservoir measuring 165 feet by 120 feet, its pictureseque appearance being considerably enhanced by the great mass of the southern gopuram, over 150 feet high, as its background and reflected on its surface. (Plate LXXVII). Not far from the north-east corner of the tank in the outer enclosure is a fair sized gopuram placed across the line of approach to the Minakshi sanctuary, marking a processional passage to that shrine from the outside, and thus indicating an independent entrance. Large and small there are eleven gopurams to the Madura temple, the four outer ones being of the first class as they are all over 150 feet high. There is one other important and spacious structure in the temple scheme and that is the court of a thousand pillars, added about the year 1560 by Arianayakam Mudali, minister of the founder of the Nayak dynasty. This hypostyle hall occupies an appreciable portion of the north-east angle of the outer *prakaram*, covering a space of 240 feet by 250 feet. Its

---

[1] *Portrait Sculpture in South India*, by T. G. Aravamuttam, London, 1931.

front, which faces south, lies alongside the wide pillared approach of the main entrance, and the doorway is also on the same side. Symmetrical in its arrangements the interior consists of central aisle with a double row of columns on either side, leading up to a small shrine at its northern and dedicated to Sabhapati ; behind the colonnades forming the aisle are row upon row of pillars making up the total of 985 in all. As with the other halls forming this temple the hypostyle hall has no architectural exterior, it is merely a low flat-roofed structure, remarkable only for its interior with its unending range of grotesquely carved piers.

Outside the main enclosure, but in axial alignment with the eastern gopuram from which it is separated by an inter-vening busy thoroughfare of traders' shops, is the large supplementary hall of the Vasanta or Pudu Mandapam, commonly known as Tirumalai's Chaultri. This is in the shape of the parallelogram measuring 330 feet by 105 feet and is recorded to have taken seven years to build, from 1626 to 1633, being a contribution to the temple scheme by Tiru-malai Nayak. Its use is as a reception hall or temporary place of residence for the presiding deity during a certain festival season of the year. Divided longitudinally into a nave and two aisles by four rows of pillars, all elaborately carved, the long columned perspective of its interior, although lacking in feeling, is rich and impressive. Towards the centre of the hall the regularity of its line of pillars is inter-rupted by a group of these columns being accorded different treatment from the others. On their shafts are sculptured, in the round, ten life-size statues each of which portrays a king of the Nayaka house of Madura, the last of the line being that of Tirumalai (1623-52) the builder of this fine mandapam. (Plate LXXVIII, Fig. 2).

By far the largest of these Southern Indian temples is that of Srirangam near Trichinopoly, which differs from the Madura temple in two particulars, as it is a single temple having only one sanctuary, and its construction, instead of consisting of mainly one effort, extended over a long period of time. An unusual feature in the plan is that it is laid out from north to south instead of the almost invariable orientation from east to west. It is dedicated to Vishnu, and although many of the buildings date from the seventeenth century, being due to the munificence of the Nayak princes, who made their second capital at the city of Trichinopoly, it contains evidences that other portions are of an earlier period. There are inscriptions which connect it with the Pandyas in the thirteenth century and with Vijayanagar in the fourteenth century, while the celebrated "Horse Court", previously described (Chapter XIX), shows that the rulers of the latter empire maintained their interest in the building in a practical manner until well into the sixteenth century. As at present its dimensions are indeed remarkable as the outermost wall is a rectangle of 2880 feet by 2475 feet, enclosing an area of over a quarter of a square mile, and including large, small, and also unfinished, 21 gopurams, 13 of which may be seen following the axial line of the temple from one point of view. Within this area are six other prakarams, making in all seven concentric enclosures, with the shrine in the centre, much on the principle of a nest of caskets, one inside the other, with the treasured contents in the innermost. The three outer courts, the latest to be added, are not of any special architectural significance, as they extend through, and into the surrounding town and are almost lost in the maze of the bazaar. The gateways of some of them may however be distinguished rising above the house tops, forming a long series of pylons each higher than the

last, the line finally ending in the two unfinished gopurams of the seventh enclosure. Of these two incomplete gateways that on the south side or main approach sufficient has been constructed to show that had it been finished according to the usual proportions it would have attained the stupendous height of nearly 300 feet, equal to that of Giotto's campanile at Florence, and rather less than the dome of St. Pauls, London. (Plate LXXV).

The architectural portion of the temple therefore may be said to begin at the fourth court, the outer wall of which measures 1235 feet by 849 feet, with a gopuram in the middle of three of its sides, on the north, south, and east, that on the east being the finest and largest in the entire scheme. Near this eastern gopuram, and within the fourth enclosure in its north-eastern angle, is the hall of a thousand pillars, a flat-roofed structure occupying a rectangle 500 feet by 160 feet. Arranged in rows within are over 900 carved granite monoliths, all leading up to a shrine at the far end. Con-sidering the amount of labour expended in this hypostyle hall it is a somewhat unimpressive production. Except for the "Horse Court", the remaining buildings within this prakaram, which consist of a few pillared pavilions, are of no particular importance. The next or third enclosure measures 767 feet by 503 feet, with a gopuram on its north and south sides, the latter being the principal entrance, as it opens on to a fine pillared hall known as the Garuda Mandapam. Towards the middle of this mandapa is a shrine with a cupola which rises like a minor dome above the surrounding flat roofs. At the side of the pillared hall is a covered tank, the surya-pushkarani, and at the opposite or northern end of this prakaram is another tank, horse-shoe in shape, called the Chandra-pushkarani, the two comprising the "Pool of the Sun" and the "Pool of the Moon" respec-tively. The second enclosure is also entered by gateways on its north and south sides, and measures 426 feet by 295 feet. It is a covered court occupied mainly by pillared pavilions, with a long processional pillared passage on its western side. Within this is the first or innermost enclosure, having its entrance on the south side, and its sides being 240 feet by 181 feet, while the object it contains is the sanctuary and its cella. The sanctuary is a square compartment, and the room around the cella is also rectangular, but the actual chamber within is circular, the shape of the whole resembling a small chaitya hall as may be seen by its golden domical roof projected above the flat roof outside.

A very comprehensive idea of the formation of this grand temple-complex may be obtained by ascending the eastern gopuram, as from its elevation the entire plan is laid at one's feet. Here it is possible to trace out all the different mandapams, which combined, present a wide expanse of uninspiring flat roofs, with here and there a golden cupola asserting itself to indicate the position of some specially sacred shrine. Towards the centre of the scheme the inner-most sanctuary may be recognized by its apsidal vault of gold, while nearer the main southern entrance is another larger cupola, marking the Garuda shrine within the third enclosure. Attached to this Garuda mandapa on its eastern side lies the Surya-pushkarani, the Pool of the Sun, and within the same enclosure, but at its northern end and identified by its curved shape is the Chandra-pushkarani or Pool of the Moon. On the opposite side of the temple from the spectator, in the distance, may be discerned two fair sized gopurams one behind the other, the western counterpart of those on the side from which the spectator is taking his stand. Some distance in front of these, within the third *prakaram* on its western side, five cylindrical structures are visible, which, together with other large erections in their vicinity are buildings used as granaries, as much of this portion of the temple is reserved for storing and suchlike purposes. Except for the fact that from this high standpoint the general disposition of the temple is made intelligible, there is little of interest in its succession of flat roofs, but following the axial line to the north and south, the view of the long series of gopurams already mentioned is impressive, the distant ones losing themselves among the roofs of the surrounding houses and palm trees. Of these thirteen gateways at least six are notable for their size, while the two unfinished examples at the far end, one of which on the south has a considerable portion of its lower storeys erected, were intended to be of colossal proportions.

The temple of this type which has the finest architectural interior is that of Jambukeswara, situated within a mile of the previous example of Srirangam, and laid out on much the same pattern, but considerably smaller in size. It consists of four concentric enclosures, the two outer being open *prakarams* while the two inner are covered courts. The principal entrance is by a gopuram on the east, leading to a pillared avenue passing through a large hypostyle hall with one hundred and twelve pillars on either side. To the right beyond this intricacy of columns is a spacious pool, surrounded by a tall double-storied arcade. Continuing along the main approach, and passing through a gopuram with a pillared portico projecting on each side of its doorway, the second enclosure is entered. Opposite lies the doorway which leads to the covered portion of the scheme, and it is from this entrance that the finest portion of the architectural effect may be observed. The doorway opens on to one arm of a cross formed by avenues of columns, the intersection of the arms widening out into a capacious square court or central hall. Within this are four immense square piers, one at each corner of a square, leaving an open space or "crossing" in the centre for the four symbols of the creed, the *lingam, nandi* (bull), *dwajastambha* (flag-staff) and *balipatam* (sacred jewel). Massive as are the solid shafts of these piers, ornamented with a triple pilaster on each face, their capitals and superstructures are even more stupendous, as they spread out like inverted pyramids into a phenomenal width. Around this central group of piers at some distance from them are the ranges of pillars forming the outer edge of the central court, a kind of pillared facade with receding avenues of pillars in their rear. This large and dignified composition of nave, aisles, and transepts, is the prelude to the innermost court containing the shrine, the doorways being on its further side beyond which admission is limited to Hindus only. No Dravidian temple interior of this period gives a better idea of the style at its best than the large central court of Jambukeswar. (Plate LXXVIII, Fig. 1).

Although all these Southern Indian temples have evolved on much the same lines and disclose plans and general arrangements in which there is a certain similarity, several possess some special feature to distinguish them from all others of their class. A notable example is the temple of Rameswaram of which the chief glory consists in its pillared corridors, which not only completely surround it, but form avenues leading up to it, so that combined they are calculated to aggregate three thousand feet in length. The breadth of these fine columned passages varies from seventeen feet to twenty-one feet, and their height from floor to roof is about twenty-five feet. Richly decorated pillars of good proportions and closely set continue along the entire length,

each pillar being twelve feet in height and rising from a moulded stylobate five feet high. In almost every direction therefore there is an unending perspective of columned halls, those on the north and south sides being particularly effective as they are over seven hundred feet in length. The general scheme of the Rameswaram temple consists of a double shrine enclosed within three concentric perimeter walls, the outer of these measuring eight hundred and eighty feet by six hundred and seventy-two. Like the temple at Madura most of it in its present state was planned and constructed within one period although on a very ancient and sacred site, as remains of the original shrine are still in evidence. These comprise a few small structures near the western exterior which differ in their orientation from the remainder of the temple, and from their style may be as early as the twelfth century. Externally, as the temple is enclosed all round within a plain wall twenty feet high, there is no architectural effect save that of a very fine gopuram on the eastern side. This gopuram which forms the principal entrance to the second enclosure, is recorded to have been begun about 1640, and then left unfinished, to be completed within modern times. It is in eleven stories and about one hundred and fifty feet high, with good proportions and the contours of its angles straight and strong, the scheme of decoration being of the architectural order without much figure work. Two other much larger gopurams have been begun on the north and south sides of the outermost wall, but only their lower stories have been finished. (Plate LXXIX).

The Siva temple at Chidambaram consists of a large group of buildings, the construction of which has extended over several hundred years, each century making its contribution until it has attained its present form. As with most of these shrines it originally rose on an ancient site, some of the inner parts being of legendary antiquity, but there are definite records of its existence before the tenth century, and some inscriptions of the eleventh. The east gopuram was erected in the thirteenth century, the Parvati temple added in the fourteenth or fifteenth century, the north gopuram in the sixteenth century, and the hall of a thousand columns in the seventeenth century. With such a history it is surprising, there should be any symmetry in its plan, yet the scheme is not without a certain regularity, and the orientation, right-angles and parallels, have been maintained throughout. There are evidences of four encircling enclosures, some unfinished with high massive walls of stone, the courtyards being paved with granite, and the whole covering thirty-two acres in extent. Its outermost wall forms a parallelogram measuring one thousand and forty feet by seven hundred and eighty feet, but the fifteenth century Parvati temple encroaches on its north-west angle affecting the uniformity of the plan, although adding to its area. The enclosure wall of the outer *prakaram*, of which only the south-west portion is finished, is entered by four gopurams, one in each side, that on the east being the Sundara Pandya erected about 1250 (Chapter XVIII), and that on the north being built by Krishna Deva towards 1520. The usual entrance was by the Sundara gateway as it leads directly to the main temple contained within a square court of three hundred and twenty-five feet side with entrances on its east and west sides. Within this enclosure is the shrine, dedicated to Natesa, where no doubt the earliest structures will be found, but admission is restricted. It is recorded however that the inner shrine is in the form of a temple car mounted on wheels and drawn by horses, by no means an unusual temple design, as may be seen at Konarak, and the Alankara mandapa at Darasuram, to mention only two examples. One of the chief features of the Chidambaram sanctuary is its portico which is composed of fifty-six pillars of intricate pattern.[1]

All the main structure comprising the temple of Natesa lies to the south-centre of the entire walled-in space, leaving a relatively large area on its northern side. Here are two important annexes to the temple scheme, consisting of a large tank or Sivaganga, and a thousand pillared mandapam or Rajasabha. The former is a sheet of water 275 feet by 175 feet bounded by flights of steps and pillared arcades, with the fine north gopuram in its rear, which reflected in the water forms an effective scene. Alongside is the hypostyle hall, a rectangular building 338 feet long and 197 feet wide and containing a thousand monolithic columns each ornamented with carving, but owing to most of these being dull and rather mechanical repetitions the appearance as a whole is somewhat monotonous.

Two temples both planned on much the same general system, and which depict relatively compact but comprehensive examples of the later Dravidian style are at Tiruvarur in the Tanjore district, and at Tiruvannamalai. Both have records associating them originally with the earlier period of the southern mode, the former bearing inscriptions referring to the Chola period (850-1100), and the latter displaying in the east gopuram of its third circuit stylistic evidences that this gateway was built about 1300. Such temple therefore appears to have developed in the traditional manner, from what was at first a village shrine, through successive stages until it attained the ample proportions it now presents. The Tiruvarur temple contains a double shrine dedicated to Siva and his consort in the form of Valmikesvara, the two sanctuaries being placed side by side within a cloistered court measuring 191 feet by 156 feet, the only entrance being by a gopuram in the middle of the eastern side. This inner shrine, the nucleus of the whole, is recorded to date from the early fifteenth century, and probably existed in the same form for more than a century, when a second enclosed court was added increasing the whole to a square of 470 feet each way. With this were built two gopurams, on the east and west. Finally about 1700, the outermost circuit was constructed, measuring 957 feet by 726 feet having two large gopurams on the east and west, and three more of lesser size at other points. At the same time a thousand pillared hall was begun on the eastern side of the outer enclosure, but never finished. One of the finest features of the Tiruvarur temple is the eastern gateway, which although constructed as late as the early eighteenth century is as good an example of Dravidian art as can be seen anywhere. The three lower stories are particularly well produced, the lowest with its broad pilasters alternating with sunk recesses containing rearing hippogryphs being boldly conceived, while the two above have magnificent roll-mouldings and plinths carrying pillared niches in which are enshrined black basalt images remarkable for their architectonic treatment. (Plate LXIX, Fig. 2).

Of the remaining temples of this group most of these are repetitions, with certain variations, of the foregoing. That at Tinnevelly is a double temple dedicated to Siva and his consort Parvati and therefore divided into two almost equal proportions, the whole occupying a rectangle 580 feet by 756 feet. Each deity is accommodated in a sanctuary towards the centre of the area, each containing a cella and portico and entered by a gopuram on the east. There are four other gopurams as entrances to the outer enclosure, and another for communication between the two separate enclosures. Tanks and pillared pavilions occupy most of the outer circuit, while extending along the whole of the southern side is hypostyle hall of a thousand pillars, measuring 520 feet by 63 feet, the pillars being arranged in rows of ten with a hundred in each row. Another temple in the Tinnevelly district is that at Srivilliputtur, notable for a gopuram which is two hundred feet high. An example of the later type, being built mainly of brick and plaster, it is in thirteen stories exclusive of the superstructure forming its roof. This superstructure is an excessively tall composition resembling a hall with a chaitya roof, elaborately ornamented with a great *suraj mukh*, or "sun-face" above its gable-end, and a row of immense vase pinnacles along its ridge. It belongs to the class of gopuram with the contours of its angles slightly concave, a structural expedient giving a curved outline to its mass, which, while adding to the sweeping effect of height and grace, deducts from it virility and strength.

Proofs of the Dravidian master-builders losing little of their traditional skill even within comparatively recent times may be seen in the temple of Subramaniar, a relatively small building, introduced into the courtyard of the great Siva temple at Tanjore in the eighteenth century. (Plate LXXVI, Fig. 2). For some time the perfection of the design and workmanship of this architectural gem led authorities to believe that it belonged to the early mediaeval era, that it was in fact more or less contemporary with the majestic structure to which it is an appendage. It bears no inscriptions, but the date has been determined by its style, particularly that of its architectural embellishments. The position of this supplementary temple, which is dedicated to Subramaniar, the south Indian name of Kartikeya, the god of war, is at the north-east angle of the enclosure, where it occupies a space of 120 feet by 35 feet, with a sikhara about 55 feet high, approximately the proportions of a typical parish church in England. A glance will reveal that the Subramaniar temple in all its details is very much more ornate in style than the larger eleventh century building at its side, but the elaboration of its parts does not make it meretricious as its ornamental features are so skilfully distributed. Compared with the Siva temple it is at once obvious that its plastic ornamentation belongs to a widely different and later date. In the course of the six centuries which separate the two structures, the style has advanced considerably, it has accumulated much, some perhaps not for its betterment, although as a whole it is a most satisfying composition. There is an animation in its sculptured relief with its pulsating light and shadow, every shaft is fluted, many mouldings ribbed, capitals and bases are scalloped, all its details have been wrought in a school where the desire for enrichment was insatiable. There could be no finer tribute to the genius of the Indian artisan than that he could squander ornament so recklessly yet produce a building which, although exuberant, is still in good taste. It is well that the Dravidian style which persisted for over a millennium in varying phases, should end on this note, a small but admirable example of a mode that had become decadent, but a very brilliant decadence in no wise discreditable to its creators.

---

[1] Furgusson, J., *History of Indian and Eastern Architecture*, Vol. I, p. 374.

REFERENCE
Jouveau-Dubreuil, G., *Archaeologie du Sud de L'Inde*, Paris, 1914.

CHAPTER XXI

THE NORTHERN OR INDO-ARYAN STYLE

ORISSA (A.D. 800 to 1250)

AT this stage a regression becomes necessary, back to the early mediaeval period, in order to take up the beginning of the other great style of Indian architecture which it has been found convenient to designate the Northern or Indo-Aryan. Unlike the Dravidian style just described, this Indo-Aryan development was not confined to a relatively restricted area such as the southern extremity of the peninsula, but was practised in one form or another over at least three quarters of the northern portion of the sub-continent. And also unlike the southern mode, on account of the examples being more widely distributed, it is not possible to treat its various phases dynastically, but they will be dealt with geographically, so that each will be described according to the region in which it flourished.

These regional developments are some six in number, the majority of which correspond in some degree to the main territories into which the country as a whole is divided. One of the earliest movements, and one of the most definite in its evolution, was that on the eastern seaboard, in the State of Orissa, or, according to its ancient name, Kalinga. Rather later in its origin, and, as it is confined to one locality and one period, so that it consists of a group rather than a movement, are the examples at Khajuraho in Central India, all of which were built in a hundred years, from A.D. 950 to 1050. Further west and spread over the country of Rajputana and the adjacent portions of Central India, are the remains of many temples, representing what may be termed a post-Gupta period as it was in this direction that the Gupta empire extended. South of this region, an important epoch of temple building took place in Gujarat and Kathiawar, the former being specially rich in architectural remains as the artistic traditions of its people are noteworthy. Still further south, in the Deccan, a phase of the building are prevailed in which the most southerly examples of the Indo-Aryan style are found. Finally, as they are rather of a distinctive character a few temples in the Fort at Gwalior and a local development at Brindaban near Muttra are referred to as small separate groups. Although each regional manifestation has its own particular qualities, there is throughout the entire range of this type of architecture, a certain undercurrent of thought resulting in a standardization of forms, principles, and procedure, which indicate that fundamentally all these examples belong to the same wide movement.

For reasons already stated the temples of Orissa provide the most logical beginning for a study of the Indo-Aryan style. The main group is concentrated in the town of Bhubaneswar where there are over thirty examples. But a few miles from this temple-town are two of the largest and most important buildings in this locality, the temple of Jagannath at Puri, and the remains of the Temple of the Sun at Konarak. Apart however from the central development, a considerable distance along the coast towards the south, as far away as Ganjam within the Madras State, there is a small group in this style at Mukhalingam, which

has no little significance. In the other direction from Bhubaneswar, towards the north, an offshoot of the movement is to be found in a series of ruined shrines in the State of Mayurbhanj between Orissa and Bengal, while still further north on the southern borders of Bengal and Bihar there are a few structures of somewhat the same general character. It will be seen therefore that along a wide belt of country extending for some four hundred miles in a north-easterly direction, parallel to the coastline of the Bay of Bengal, this type of temple is fairly common. The earliest of these may date from the eighth century A.D., and the largest and latest of all, that of Konarak was erected in the middle of the thirteenth century, so that for nearly five hundred years during the early mediaeval period this part of the country was the scene of sustained architectural activity. So much so, that it recalls a similar and almost contemporary phase of cathedral building in Europe, when the builders, the rulers, the priests and the people were overpowered by their faith which found expression in the production of religious monuments. And in the same manner in Orissa so many fine examples persisting over such a period of time, make it possible to trace the gradual evolution of this particular movement without difficulty, an opportunity from various causes not presented in anything like the same continuity elsewhere.

There is reason to believe that this style of temple architecture approached the eastern region from its southern extremity, spreading northward to form the main development in Orissa. Although the small series at Mukhalingam may not comprise the earliest examples, that the beginning was made in this locality is not unlikely. It has already been shown that a type of temple in a primitive Indo-Aryan style had begun to appear as far south as in the territory of the Chalukyans as early as the sixth century A.D., implying that it may have originated in that quarter. (Plate XLVI, Fig. 1). That there can have been any direct connection between the early Chalukyan structures on the south-west, and the temples of Ganjam on the east is somewhat improbable, but the fact remains that certain architectural affinities are observable which suggest a linking up of the temple design in these two divergent places. If such a correlation is admitted, it may be traced to the political contact which no doubt existed between the Ganga kings of western India on the one hand, and the Ganga dynasty of Kalinganara, now the modern Mukhalingam, on the other. It was from their capital in Ganjam that the country of Kalinga, at present called Orissa, was administered by the Eastern Gangas from about A.D. 600. By some such means the cultural activities of the Early Chalukyans may have been conveyed to this region on the east, where, beginning from the eighth century certain architectural forms appear, which bear a resemblance to those produced slightly earlier at Aihole and Pattadakal. (Chapters XI and XIV).

The small group of temples at Mukhalingam consists of three examples, namely Mukhalingeswara, Bhimesvara and Somesvara, whose foundations probably date from the time of the old capital, when its rulers were in touch with the movements in the south and west of the peninsula. These buildings are now very much restored, but the renovations do not appear to have deviated materially from the general shape of the original structure. From their appearance, and specially from the character of their carving, in their present form they may date from the ninth or tenth centuries. The most striking example of the group is the temple of Mukha-lingeswara, which in plan, is an incipient type of a *panchayatana*, or temple of five shrines, as apart from the central sanctuary, there are four minor shrines one at each corner. In spite of its presumed Chalukyan origin, in some of the carvings with which the facade is decorated, the presence of a certain kind of scrollwork pattern, and the unmistakable "vase and foliage" order of the pilasters, implies some influence of the Gupta style, which prevailed more in the north and north-west of India towards the seventh century A.D. But at the beginning of its course any movement is the ready recipient of such forms as are conveyed to it from all sources to become incorporated in its productions.

Turning now to the main group of temples in the Orissan style in the neighbourhood of Bhubaneswar, several facts become apparent which indicate that nevertheless in many of its aspects this architectural movement was very largely of an independent nature. Not only are the plans and general treatment of these religious structures of a special character, but the building art has a separate and distinct nomenclature of its own. The generic name for a temple is *deul*, but as the building in the first instance consisted very often of a sanctuary only, the same word was employed for this tower-like structure also. In front of the *deul* is a square building or assembly hall corresponding to the *mandapa* in other parts, but here known as the *jagamohan*. These two edifices combined constitute the essentials of the Orissan temple type. As the style progressed and also as the temple ritual was developed, other buildings were found necessary, and were added to the front of the assembly hall, thus presenting in the larger examples a series of structures all in one axial alignment. The two buildings usually supplemented were first the *Nat-Mandir* or Dancing Hall, and secondly in front of this the *Bhog Mandir* or Hall of Offerings. Standing on a basement or a plinth (*pista*), these halls were invariably of one story only, and the elevation of each consisted of two parts, a cubical portion (*bada*) below, and a pyramidal roof (*pida*) above. In the same way the lower and upright portion of the *deul* or tower is called the *bada*, but above that it is resolved into three parts, comprising the tall middle portion or *chhapra*, the flat fluted disc at the summit known as the *amla*, and its finial or *kalasa*. This glossary might be extended indefinitely, as the Orissan mason has a technical name for every section, member, and moulding, but except to the actual workmen, many of these serve no useful purpose and a full list would only confuse. Some of the more important terms are shown in the diagram on Plate LXXX.

Compared with the other regional development in the Indo-Aryan style, the Orissan temples as a whole are of the astylar order, pillars being notable by their absence. In some of the earlier examples the pillar finds a place, suggested no doubt by other modes, but as a rule it was not favoured. In a few of the larger halls however some such support became a structural necessity to sustain the heavy weight of the pyramidal roof, and accordingly a group of four solid piers, one at each corner of a four-square system of roof beams was introduced. One of the most remarkable

characteristics of the Orissan temple is the plan and featureless treatment of the interior contrasted with the profusely ornamented walls of the exterior, the surfaces of which are charged with a superfluity of plastic patterns and forms. The difference between the rich carving on the outside, and the simple unadorned planes of the interior can only be accounted for by the existence of some esoteric tradition which the builders either instinctively followed, or were compelled strictly to observe.

For the purposes of study the temples of Orissa may be resolved into three groups, according to their date and style. These are as follows : (1) Early, cir. A.D. 750 to 900 ; (2) Middle, cir. A.D. 900 to 1100 ; (3) Later, cir. A.D. 1100 to 1250. Out of the very large number of temples belonging to these groups, there are some twenty of consequence which are classified below.

EARLY PERIOD cir. A.D. 750 to 900—

Parasrameswar	at Bhubaneswar.
Vaital Deul	,,	,,
Uttaresvara	,,	,,
Isvareswara	,,	,,
Sutru Ganesvara	,,	,,
Bharatesvara	,,	,,
Lakshmanesvara	,,	,,

MIDDLE PERIOD cir. A.D. 900 to 1100—

Mukteswara, cir.	975	at Bhubaneswar.
Lingaraja	,,	1000	,,	,,
Brahmeswar	,,	1075	,,	,,
Ramesvara	,,	1075	,,	,,
Jagannath	,,	1100	,, Puri.

LATER PERIOD cir. 1100 to 1250—

Ananda Vasudev	at Bhubaneswar.
Siddhesvara	,,	,,
Kedaresvara	,,	,,
Jamesvara	,,	,,
Meghesvara	,,	,,
Sari Deul	,,	,,
Somesvara	,,	,,
Rajarani	,,	,,
Temple of the Sun at Konarak, cir. A.D. 1250.

It will be seen that of the Early Period there are seven examples, all of them at Bhubaneswar. Three of these, Sutru Ganesvara, Bharatesvara, and Lakshmanesvara are ruined shrines of small size situated near the much later temple of Rameswara. The remaining four are all fully formed temples, namely Vaital Deul and Iswaresvara, both of which are in the town and within the same enclosure ; Uttaresvara, in north of the Vindu-Sarovara tank, and Parasrameswar, on the outskirts of the town. The buildings of this group vary considerably in size and shape, but all display that spirit of ingenuousness which betokens the early effort. Their primitive character is obvious in the architectural treatment, and there are also discernible forms and elements derived from a number of sources, showing wide contacts and various influences. But it is in the plastic decoration of their exteriors that this unsophisticated nature is most in evidence, and it is illustrated in both the subject-matter and its method of representation. For in these carved patterns there are artists' memories or previous experiences, mysterious insertions and fragmentary statements, introduced sometimes irrationally and without full knowledge of their meaning, while some of the motifs are frankly of Buddhist extraction. Two of the early examples at Bhubaneswar, the temples of Parasrameswar and Vaital Deul are of surpassing interest and throw no little light on the origins of the style.

Judging mainly from its appearance, the oldest building of the entire series is the temple of Parasrameswar, a small structure, but with every stone of an informative nature. (Plate LXXXII). It consists of a sanctuary with its pillared hall, in other words a deul and its *jagamohan*, the entire length of the two being only 48 feet, while the sikhara of the former is but 44 feet high. In size therefore it may almost be regarded as a "museum piece", but in effect this little building is much more than that, for with the other example, the Vaital Deul, these two temples constitute a "lithic primer" on the beginnings of the Orissan mode. The shape of the tower of the Parasrameswar is definitely rudimentary, as it is thick-set and "heavy-shouldered", with an immensely wide fluted *amala-sila* or coping stone. A low rectangular structure comprises the hall of the temple, and this is provided with a double roof and plain massive eaves, while there is a doorway in each of its three free sides and four perforated stone windows. In the interior of the *jagamohan* are two rows of pillars, three in each row, producing a miniature nave and aisles ; these pillars were originally monoliths having plain square shafts, no bases, but with voluted bracket capitals. They supported a massive architrave raising the ceiling of the nave higher than the aisles, thus forming an embryo clerestory. The interior is perfectly plain, whereas the walls of the exterior are intricately and profusely carved. (Plate LXXXII, Fig. 1).

One inexplicable feature in connection with this temple is the character of the juncture between the pillared hall and the sanctuary, which seems to imply that the two structures were built at different times. The sanctuary may have been added a generation or so later, to take the place of an earlier edifice which had probably fallen into decay. On the other hand there are indications that the *jagamohan* itself may have been the subsequent addition, although on grounds of style this does not appear likely. In any case the joining of the two structures is a haphazard piece of work, as the end of the pillared hall covers up some of the carving on the face of the sanctuary. Moreover, the sculpture is not of the same character in the two buildings, some of that on the *jagamohan* being so naive as to be classed as a folk-art. But one portion stands out as being a production of exceptional merit, namely the two stone grilles, one on each side of the west doorway. (Plate LXXXII, Figs. 2 and 3). These represent figures of young dancers and musicians with trumpet and with shawm, lute and cymbal, so grouped as to form perforated stone windows. In some respects these panels might be reproductions in stone of one of Della Robbia's glazed terracotta reliefs, excelling even the work of that famous Florentine in their vigour and rhythm, and evidently the creation of one who has left this brilliant work of art as the sole record of his inimitable genius.

The method of construction used in this building serves to confirm its early origin, as the masonry consists of stones of large size kept in position by means of their weight and balance, aided by a system of interlocking flanges, so that no mortar or cementing material is needed. (Plate LI, Fig. 1). An interesting comparison may be instituted between this temple, and the somewhat earlier temples of the Chalukyans at Aihole. It will be seen that the tower of the Parasrameswar example, although inclined to be heavy and crude, is an improvement on the Indo-Aryan type of sikhara subsequently added to the Aihole buildings. Moreover the incipient form of clerestory introduced into the Orissan temple is also an advance on the double roof of the Durga and Huchchimaligudi temples of the Chalukyan group, from which however it may have been derived. It is the peculiar treatment of such features, which suggests that some communication of impressions may have been maintained between these two centres, thus enabling the Orissan mason to benefit by the experiences of his fellow craftsman in the Deccan. On the other hand, there are certain portions of the architectural ornamentation in the Parasrameswar temple, such as pilasters with vase and foliage capitals, a motif usually associated with the Gupta mode, indicating, as already mentioned, that there were also influences from the more northerly source. Taking all these factors into consideration it may be inferred that the approximate date of the Parasrameswar temple is towards the end of the eighth century, a date which also marks the introduction of the Indo-Aryan style of architecture into this region.

The other temple illustrating the early phase, the Vaital Deul, was evidently erected rather later than Parasrameswar, although it may be contemporary with the sanctuary of that example, which it has been shown may have been a subsequent addition. But the Vaital Deul is a very different conception, and derives from another an entirely different tradition. (Plate LXXXIV, Fig. 1). For it is obvious that the tower of its sanctuary is not only allied more to the southern style as exemplified by the Dravidian gopurams, but like those structures, its original ancestor was the chaitya-hall of the Buddhists. In spite, however, of its elongated vaulted roof in two stories, with its ridge finials and chaitya-arch gable ends, all expressive of the Buddhist type, there is every evidence in the distinctive quality of its architectural treatment that fundamentally it is of Indo-Aryan extraction. In its own manner the *jagamohan*, or hall in front of this sanctuary is also of uncommon design. This is a rectangular structure, but embedded in each angle is a small supplementary shrine, a replica in miniature of an Indo-Aryan vimana, so that it is, in effect, an example of a *panchayatana* or five-shrined type of temple, but in a nascent stage of its evolution.

The Vaital Deul is a comparatively small building, its plan measures only 18 feet by 25 feet, and its height to the ridge of its keel roof is barely 35 feet, but within this limited compass there is much that is informative, and much that is strangely beautiful. Its chief effect is contained in the tower, the proportions of which are most satisfying, but in addition to the well-balanced arrangement of its parts, the handling of its surfaces, and the manner in which the architectural decoration is disposed, all denote a highly trained aesthetic sensibility. This specially applies to the flat projections, like shallow buttresses, placed around the *bada* or base of the structure. There are four of these on the narrower side of the tower and five on the wider, each of which contains in its centre a recess enshrining an image sculptured in bold relief and each about two feet in height. These projections, richly patterned, alternate with flat uncarved recesses, the contrast thus afforded producing an admirable appearance. Then in the front of the tower, thrown out above the roof of the *jagamohan* is an elegant foliated gable, a development of the Buddhist chaitya-arch, with the Hindu

Tandava motif or Dancing Siva within a circular panel in place of the sun-window, that characteristic feature of the Buddhist temple facades.

The second group of buildings comprising the "Middle Period" of the Orissan style, and dating from cir. 900 to 1100 A.D. consists of a series of temples which represent the movement at its early maturity or prime. What is believed to be the first example of the phase is the small temple of Muktesvara situated with a number of others on the outskirts of the town of Bhubaneswar, and probably built about A.D. 975. (Plate LXXXIII, Fig. 1). It is a miniature gem of architecture as it is not only a highly finished structure, ornamented with fascinating carved patterns, but in addition it is approached by an arched gateway, or torana, of the most elegant design and execution (Plate XCII). There are certain details in the design of this temple, which enable its date to be fixed with tolerable accuracy as for instance the shape of the vase base of the pilasters, the character of the bracket supports to the figures, and the modelling of the figures themselves, all of which imply a slight immaturity as if they were still in course of development. That its elements are a considerable advance on those of Parasrameswar and Vaital Deul of the previous group is quite clear, but that it is also not so finished in its forms as the remaining examples of the series, is likewise apparent. The Mukteswara temple is 45 feet long, 25 feet at its widest part, and its tower is hardly 35 feet high, but although of such limited dimensions it is all so exceptionally well proportioned, and its parts so skilfully adjusted that it readily attracts the eye. In its surface decoration there is such beauty of form that all its surfaces resolve themselves into one harmonious effect, but a large figure-design repeated on each side of the tower stands out on account of its vigorous grace. The torana archway in front of the entrance is one of the most original conceptions throughout the entire style, and evidently the production of an artist having superior vision and skill, with a mind above his fellows. This detached portal consists of two pillars supporting around arch within a semi-circular shaped pediment, the whole very substantially proportioned, but all its parts lightened and diversified by exquisite carving. The Mukteswara temple is one of the few temples of the Orissan group which has sculptured decoration in its interior.

But the most representative examples of the "Middle Period" are two temples of monumental proportions, the Lingaraja (cir. A.D. 1000) at Bhubaneswar, and the Jagannath (cir A.D. 1100), at Puri, the former being not only the finest living example of the Orissan group, but it ranks as one of the foremost architectural productions of the country. (Plate LVIII, Fig. 4). The Lingaraja, or Great Temple of Bhubaneswar, occupies the centre of a large quadrangular enclosure measuring 520 feet by 465 feet, contained within a high and solid wall, on the inner face of which is a platform, so that on occasions it could be patrolled and defended. Within the enclosure many subsidiary "chapels" and shrines have been grouped around the main temple, contributions by ardent devotees as acts of merit. The presence of this great central building in the midst of numerous smaller replicas cannot fail to recall the practice of the Buddhists in congregating their votive chaityas around the large central stupa. Such an arrangement however not only applies to the system within the Lingaraja enclosure, but also in its wider aspect to the large concentration of temples within and around the town of Bhubaneswar itself, plainly indicating that this neighbourhood was a place of great veneration, a

holy land of profoundly religious significance. It is not unlikely therefore that the locality was the site of a deserted sanctuary belonging to previous movements, either the sacred town of Tosali of the Buddhists, or the Ekrama Tirtha of the Jains. The ancient usage of these two creeds of grouping their shrines in this manner was therefore maintained by the Hindus.

As it stands at present the Lingaraja consists of the four structures which comprise the fully developed Orissan temple-type, namely the *Deul*, or *Sri Mandir*, as it is called in this particular instance, and corresponding to the Vimana in other parts ; the Pillared Hall or *Jagamohan*, in other words the mandapam ; the Dancing Hall, or *Nat Mandir*, and the Hall of Offerings, or *Bhog Mandir*. (Plate LXXXV). These buildings are all disposed on the same axis, which extends from east to west, but they do not all date from the same period ; the temple as originally designed was composed of only the two structures, the Sri Mandir, and the *jagamohan*, the two other halls being added probably a century or more later. These supplementary buildings, however, became responsible for certain structural alterations to the original scheme. Before they were added the only entrance to the temple was that on the east or front of the jagamohan, which formed the main doorway. When the Nat Mandir was built in front of this, another doorway became necessary. This was effected in a rather crude manner by cutting a rectangular opening below the southern window and thus converting it into a portal, a disfigurement it is true, although not such a serious one, as it all fits into the carved surface of the wall.

Undoubtedly the most impressive feature of this temple is the great tower of the Sri Mandir, as it dominates not only the entire composition, but the whole town of Bhubaneswar with its height and volume. At its base it measures 56 feet side, although owing to its projecting faces or *pagas*, it is not square in plan, as the sides are indented by regular chases. In its elevational aspect for approximately one-third of its height the sides are vertical, the lower portion of which constitutes the *bada* or ground-story, distinguished from the rest of the tower by a separate form of surface treatment. At the height of about 50 feet the contours of the structure, up to this point vertical, begin to incline inwards, speeding up into a pronounced parabolic curve to produce the "shoulder" at 125 feet from the ground. Above the curves of the shoulder rises the neck or *beki*, over which is the ponderous fluted disc or *amila-sila*, supported by sedent gryphons, the whole being crowned by a vase-shaped finial (*kalasa*) bearing the *trisula* or trident of Siva. All the middle section of the tower is richly textured by means of horizontal mouldings, which, carried in lines across the recessed chases of the sides produce a suitable background for the attachment of certain selected motifs. These motifs consist of a vertical line of miniature *deuls*, small-scale replicas of the tower itself, which fill in the angles of the recesses, and, on each side taking the shape of a prominent projection is a representation of a lion crushing down an elephant, a frequent symbol in the architecture of Orissa. Within the tower is the cella 19 feet square, but instead of a ceiled chamber it is continued upwards somewhat in the manner of a well, or chimney, forming a hollow space throughout the entire height.

The jagamohan which was built at the same time as the tower, the two forming the original temple scheme, is in plan not the customary square, but an oblong measuring

CONJECTURAL RESTORATION OF THE TEMPLE OF THE SUN KONARAK, ORISSA. C. 1250 A.D.

Fig. 1

Fig. 2. Temple of the Sun at Konarak; c. A.D. 1250.

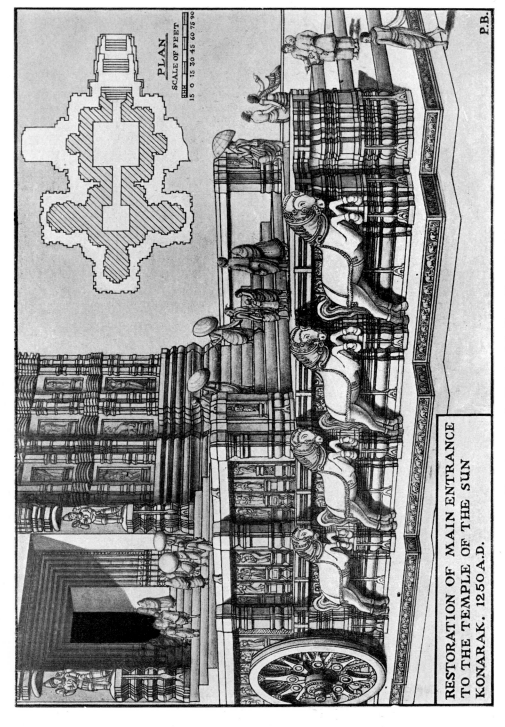

RESTORATION OF MAIN ENTRANCE
TO THE TEMPLE OF THE SUN
KONARAK. 1250 A.D.

PLAN
SCALE OF FEET
15 0 15 30 45 60 75 90

P.B.

The entrance to the Temple of the Sun.   Konarak, Orissa.

Fig. 2

Fig. 1

Khajuraho: Temple of Kandariya Mahadeo; c. A.D. 1000.

Fig. 1. Torana from Mukhteswar Temple, Bhubaneswar; c. 900 A.D.

Fig. 2. Khajuraho: Ceiling Construction of Kandariya Mahadeo Temple; c. 1050 A.D.

XCIII

Fig. 2
Kandariya Mahadeo Temple, construction of ceiling.

Khajuraho Temples; c. A.D. 1000.

Fig. 1
Visvanath Temple, capital of pillar

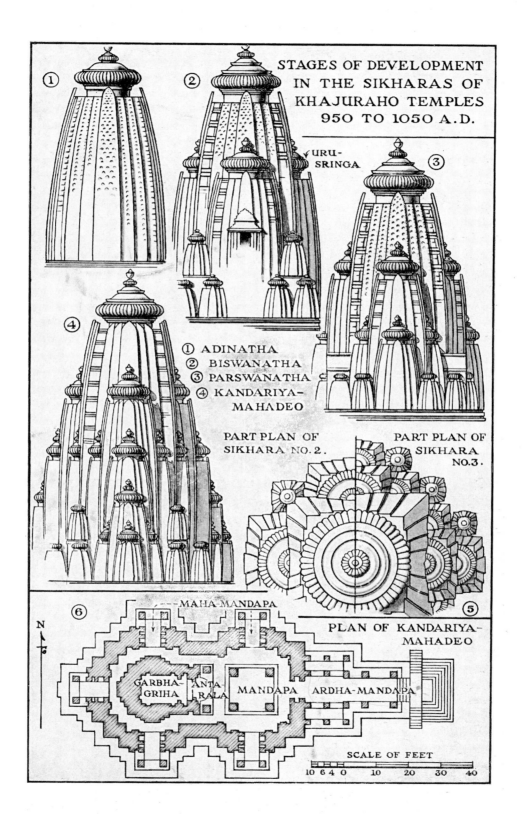

STAGES OF DEVELOPMENT
IN THE SIKHARAS OF
KHAJURAHO TEMPLES
950 TO 1050 A.D.

URU-
SRINGA

① ADINATHA
② BISWANATHA
③ PARSWANATHA
④ KANDARIYA-
MAHADEO

PART PLAN OF
SIKHARA NO. 2.

PART PLAN OF
SIKHARA
NO. 3.

PLAN OF KANDARIYA-
MAHADEO

MAHA-MANDAPA

N

GARBHA-
GRIHA   ANTA-
RALA   MANDAPA   ARDHA-MANDAPA

SCALE OF FEET

10 6 4 0   10   20   30   40

Fig. 1.   Khajuraho: "Ghantai" Temple; c. A.D. 1050.

Fig. 2.   Kiradu, Mewar: Temple of Shiva; 11th century.

72 feet long and 56 feet side. Its lower story or *bada* is 34 feet high and like the tower is composed of a series of recessed chases. Above this square portion rises the substantial roof in the shape of a pyramid, the lower part square and stepped, the upper part round and fluted, the whole attaining the height of 100 feet from the ground. The additional halls of the nat and bhoga mandirs, although belonging to a somewhat later date, are in much the same style as the jagamohan, and compose not inharmoniously with the architectural scheme as a whole except that they unduly prolong its line. As already mentioned the interiors of these halls are plain single cells, the walls being entirely devoid of ornament, and the ceilings, composed of oversailing courses of masonry, are treated in an equally simple manner. Each hall however has a group of four massive piers in the centre to support the solid mass of the roof, and these have sculptured patterns on their shafts. (Plates XCII and XCIII). It is difficult to believe that the workmen who showed such restraint in the production of these austere interiors could be the same as those who were so profligate with their decoration on the outer walls of the same buildings. Not only did the artists produce on the exterior wall surfaces figure compositions of an intricate nature and absorbing in subject, but in every part the multiplicity of detail, the fertility of invention, the fantasy and caprice of the patterns, are astonishing. And this plastic decoration is not unsystematic, the orderly manner in which it is applied, and the discipline employed in its distribution recall the foliated panelling, canopied niches, and spiralled nook-shafts of some of the Gothic cathedrals of Europe.

Out of the infinity of forms which appear on the Orissan temples at this time one architectural feature emerges of unusual character. It is best described as a mullioned window, although so designed as to admit but little light and even less air. Openings for such purposes are not common in Indian temple architecture, the brilliant sunshine is reflected into the interior without any need for windows, the object being to restrain this searching light, not to encourage it, and to preserve that half shadow half darkness which gives these halls their religious solemnity. The Gothic cathedral, with more voids than substance, illustrates the other extreme, where light, and more light, was the architect's constant aim in a climate of low visibility. An Orissan temple window is devised on the simple principle of a rectangular opening filled with a row of uprights at close intervals, but the manner in which this scheme is decoratively handled converts it into a notable work of art. As a framework to the opening the carver indulged in a variety of mouldings, pilasters, and cornices, according to his fancy, but it was in the design of the uprights that he introduced the most delicate forms. In the temples of lesser importance these mullions took the shape of graceful balusters, like small tapering pillars with moulded capitals and bases perfectly proportioned and skilfully fashioned. But in the larger temples, as for instance in the Lingaraja, each upright in addition to its upper and lower decoration, carried on its shaft a female figure, voluptuously modelled and languorously posed, the whole conception presenting an effect of exuberance evidently expressive of the luxuriousness prevailing in the existing social environment.

Yet however rich and splendid this plastic art on the walls of the Lingaraja appears, unquestionably the crowning achievement of this temple is the grand mass of the tower, which as a work of architecture is not unworthy of any age or people. It may not possess the shapely poise of a thir-

teenth century Gothic spire, or the refined tapering profile of a mosque minar, nor has it the firm repose of some of the mediaeval companili of Southern Europe, but as with all such productions it represents a supreme effort to attain height combined with a finished architectural appearance, and by means of its dignified proportions, balanced stability, and breadth of treatment this ideal has been accomplished.

The other notable example of the middle period is the famous temple of Jagannath at Puri, an appreciably larger building than the Lingaraja, and the principal parts of it erected about a century later. There are records that it was originally built as a pillar of victory by Chora Ganga, the conqueror of Kalinga in 1030 A.D., but that it was not consecrated until A.D. 1118. The probability is that on this site the ruler raised a commemorative column on the occasion of his conquest, but about A.D. 1100 its place was taken by the present structure. Built on the same principle as the Great Temple, at Bhubaneswar, and consisting of four edifices in one alignment, it first comprised the deul or sanctuary, and its assembly hall or jagamohan, in which condition it appears to have remained until the fourteenth or fifteenth centuries, when the nat and bhog mandirs were added. As now completed the extreme length of these four buildings in a line is 310 feet, with a width of 80 feet, while the tower is nearly 200 feet in height. Moreover as it stands on an eminence, it presents a singularly commanding appearance, its soaring deul providing an imposing landmark across the low-lying country for many miles around. This elevated position suggests that the Jagannath temple occupies the site of some still more ancient monument, not improbably the shrine of the Buddha's tooth at Dantapura, before that precious relic was transported to Ceylon.

But except for its impressive proportions, the architectural effect of this temple is disappointing, as in its treatment it is merely an arid replica of its predecessor at Bhubaneswar. Much of its inferiority is however due to certain extensive renovations which became necessary a century or more ago, when the original stone masonry decayed, owing probably to centuries of action by the sea air. Unfortunately these restorations appear to have been effected by means of solid applications of cement, which have made its close appearance heavy and lifeless, a mere hulk of what it was when first conceived. Yet in spite of its cement overlay, the tower still retains its imposing mass from which it is possible to see that Orissan architecture continued to be a moving and living art. This is shown by the improved shape noticeable in its contours generally, and specifically by the overhang of the shoulder, which in this instance has been reduced to a more graceful line, giving its profile additional refinement and balance. As already mentioned two of the halls of the temple were added at a later date, and the ornamentation which so profusely adorns these structures is stiff and stylized, clearly implying a period when the style had begun to decline. One of the halls, the nat mandir, a large building of some 80 feet side, has its ceiling supported by as many as 16 pillars in 4 rows of 4 each, the only real example of a hypostyle hall in Orissa.

There are other features in the Jagannath temple at Puri, some of considerable significance and implying affinities of a widely separate kind. One of these concerns the character of its inner enclosure, for like the Lingaraja it stands within a spacious courtyard surrounded by a high wall, forming a rectangle 440 feet by 350 feet. Around the main building in the centre, distributed over the remaining area are some 30 or 40 edifices of various shapes and sizes, each a shrine or chapel, the whole representing the same system as that at Bhubaneswar, but in this instance as all the structures are grouped on higher ground, they approach still nearer to the Buddhist stupa tradition. Another feature is connected with the outer enclosure, as there are three of these encircling walls, known poetically as the "Three Garlands", a reference to the custom, universal in India, of adorning divinities and high personages with wreaths of flowers. The outer wall 20 feet high, was added at a later date concentric with an inner one and containing a space 665 feet by 640 feet, having a gateway in the centre of each side. These gateways, although substantial structures with pyramidal roofs, bear no resemblance to the gopuram type of the southern style, but the principle of such architectural entrances, and the additional enclosed area, is analogous to the arrangement of pylons and *prakarams*, which about this time were becoming a characteristic of the Dravidian temple, seems more than a coincidence.

The third period or "Later" style of Orissan architecture which flourished about 1200 A.D., includes a number of temples, none of which is large, but all are remarkable for their rich and finished appearance. From the monumental compositions of the previous period to these moderately sized but profusely decorated examples of the builders' art implies a definite change in values, a condition already observed in connection with the evolution of the Dravidian style when the immense pagodas of the Cholas were succeeded by the smaller, more intimate, and exquisitely ornamented halls of the Vijayanagar period. There are at least a dozen temples at Bhubaneswar representing this later phase of the Orissan style, the majority of which consist of the two basic parts only of the temple type, the deul and its jagamohan. On the other hand the most striking of all, the Ananta Vasudeva, resolves itself into a reduced copy of the much larger and previous type, as it comprises the full complement of four buildings all in one line, although in this instance, too, the nat and bhog mandirs both appear to have been a subsequent addition. The largest example of the "Later Period", it has a length of 125 feet with a breadth of 40 feet, and its tower is 68 feet high, while the whole structure being built on a substantial plinth, a rare feature in most of the temples of this group, it presents a reasonably impressive effect. (Plate LXXXI).

Had it been finished in the manner in which it was begun, nothing would have exceeded the grace and elegance of another temple of this period, the Rajarani, probably one of the last of its class to be built. As it is, the *deul*, which is practically complete, displays a refinement in its curves and contours denoting not only an advance in the art of composition, but an appreciation on the part of the craftsmen of a more subtle feeling for form. Much of the improved effect has been obtained by a change in the distribution of the decorative elements comprising the tower, so that a more fluent volume and mass is the result. No one who has seen the Rajarani temple, and also those of the Khajuraho group shortly to be described (Chapter XXII), can fail to notice the similarity in the shape of this particular Orissan deul, and the sikharas of the Central Indian type, which strike a new note in this aspect of temple design. The tower of the Bhubaneswar example is remarkable for the beauty of its formation, but the attached jagamohan, mainly because it has been left in an unfinished condition, consists of much that is interesting. Apart from its promise of artistic qualities

equal to that of the deul, one can see from the designs on its walls, some merely inscribed, others blocked out, but all incomplete, the manner in which the architectural decoration was effected. As in all these productions in the preparation of which the work has been interrupted, the toolmarks are so fresh and clear that the human element seems still to linger, implying that the craftsman is shortly returning to his task. But from this example, and also another of the group, the Siddhesvara, it is clear that the practice of the Orissan builders was to block out the structure in the mass, leaving its surfaces "boasted" awaiting final treatment with the sculptor's chisel. The small temple of Siddhesvara is notable in this particular, for it appears as a relatively plain building, yet it is quite obvious that it was the intention to elaborate all its parts with carved decoration, but for some reason, probably financial, this never matured.

There is one other factor in the design of the Rajarani temple, which is a further indication that this example is a departure from all the others of the group. It will be seen that the plan of the sanctuary, although in its general configuration is in the shape of a square, has both its exterior and interior surfaces so elaborately recessed that it becomes almost circular in appearance. Moreover the plan is not aligned so that its sides are in the same plane as the rest of the building, but the whole structure is placed diagonal to it. Such an arrangement is an exception in the plans of the Orissan temples, where the sides of all the buildings are in the same alignment. But, as will be shown later, this setting of the plan of the sanctuary diagonally to the plan of the hall in front of it was not infrequently adopted in the temples of other parts of the country, and one which was speedily developed as it produced an added variety and contrast of effect in the elevational appearance of the structure as a whole. The Rajarani temple was an early example of the diagonal treatment in its plan, and may have pointed the way to the employment of the same principle in the other regional styles.

There now remains the grandest achievement of this Eastern School of architecture, the Temple of the Sun at Konarak, standing entirely by itself, some twenty miles in a north-easterly direction along the sea-coast from Puri. Built in the reign of King Narasinha-deva (1238-64), it has become a deserted ruin, a great mass of masonry, rising like a pyramidal mound above the sand-dunes, and forming from the sea a prominent landmark known as the Black Pagoda. Although so much of it has fallen, enough remains to make a conjectural reconstruction possible, and to show it in its finished state. Abul Fazl, who was the Emperor Akbar's official historian, and who appears to have seen the temple before it became a complete ruin, eulogizes it, about 1585 in the Ain-i-Akbari as follows : "Even those whose judgement is critical and who are difficult to please stand amazed at the sight." Yet it is doubtful whether it ever actually attained the appearance as depicted in Plate LXXXVIII for there are fairly clear proofs that it was never quite completed as before the ponderous stones that formed the upper portion of the tower could be put into position, the foundations began to give way. Some of the large sculptured blocks intended for the summit lie at the foot, not only unbroken, but unbruised, whereas had they fallen from such a height they could not fail to show signs of serious damage or fracture. The conception of this temple was that of a genius, but its colossal grandeur outstripped the means of execution, for its materialization was beyond the capacity of its builders, its scale was too great for their powers, and in the constructional part they failed. It was, however, a magnificent failure, for without unduly straining the imagination, it is possible to see even in its ruin, that it was one of the finest architectural efforts the Indian master-mason ever made.

The temple of Konarak is dedicated to Surya, the Sun-god, to whom some of the largest and most remarkable temples have been consecrated, as for instance Martand (9th century) in Kashmir (Chapter XXXI), and Modhera (1026 A.D.) in Gujarat (Chapter XXIV). In its design the Orissan temple is in a class by itself for several reasons. Firstly, it represents the crystallised and accumulated experience of several hundred years of this type of temple building, so that no longer is it a fortuitous range of separate structures, as in the Lingaraja and Jagannath examples, but a reasoned and systematic co-ordination of its parts into an architectural unity. Where another hall is needed, as the nat mandir, this, although detached, in order to conform to the demands of the ritual, is nevertheless made to accord with the scheme as a whole. The Temple of the Sun at Konarak therefore illustrates in every aspect the fulfilment and finality of the style. Further, in its conception the building is unique on account of its supremely imaginative character. The traditional representation of the Sun-god visualizes this deity standing in Time's winged chariot urging on his team of seven horses, with which he blazes his way through the heavens. These he unyokes at sunset so that

When he has loosed his coursers from their station
Straightway Night over all spreads her garment

(*Rigveda*, 1, 115, 4).

This spirited allegory moved the designers to translate it into temple form, to realize it as a great spectacle in stone, the building to be fashioned like a *ratha* or wheeled car being whirled along by the seven horses of the sun. The base of the structure therefore is an immense terrace with 12 giant wheels, (Plate LXXXIX), each nearly ten feet high fixed on either side, to simulate the vehicle of the god, and in front is a wide flight of steps, its sides supported by seven richly caparisoned steeds, rearing and straining in their harness as they strive to drag its great bulk along. On the high platform thus formed the temple building was raised in two conjoined parts, consisting of a large hall or jagamohan, 100 feet side and 100 feet high, and a still larger deul or tower rising to the great height of some 225 feet from the ground. At the base of this deul three subsidiary shrines were attached, with outer staircases leading up to spacious recesses each containing a life-sized but minutely carved chlorite statue of the deity. To complete the scheme, facing the main flight of steps the nat mandir was erected, a detached structure, square in plan and with a pyramidal roof, the whole on a high plinth, while placed around were a number of artistic and structural accessories such as a free-standing pillar, a refectory, several supplementary shrines, and separate groups of statuary, all enclosed within a courtyard 865 feet by 540 feet, having entrance gateways in three of its sides. Finally, to add to the richness of its appearance, as well as to the mysterious nature of its ceremonial the builders have filled out the pattern of this great structural composition by means of sculptured forms and intricate designs applied without stint to its immense surfaces, some of outstanding beauty, but others of such a shamelessly erotic character that they have no parallel in any known building.

Such are the bare outlines of the principal components of this stupendous undertaking, which the superb craftsmanship of the artisans at that period almost succeeded in completing. But, as if the powers of good resented the perpetuation of the evil it portrays, it now lies a colossal ruin, all that remains moderately intact being the jagamohan or assembly hall, as a record of the character of the whole. (Plate LXXXIX, Fig. 1). In its damaged condition this temple recalls the torso of some famous classical statue, shorn of its limbs, battered and broken, half buried in the sand, but still identifiable as a noble work of art. The portion that is preserved, the assembly hall, although considerably injured, is a notable architectural production. At first sight presenting an appearance of infinite elaboration, reduced to its lowest terms it resolves itself into a comparatively simple formation as it consists of two main elements, a *bada* or cubical portion, and its pyramidal superstructure or roof (*pida*). The surfaces of the *bada* are in recessed chases, so that its plan is not a plain square, and on the same principle the shape of the roof, although it has the form of a pyramid, its outlines are interrupted by angles, projections, and curves, presenting a scheme of varied complexity. The proportions of this edifice are correspondingly simple, as the main cornice marks the centre of the structure, the width of the *bada*, or cubical part, is twice its own height, and the entire width of the building is equal to its altitude. Other dimensions are similarly uninvolved. There are three doorways, one in the middle of each of its free sides, each approached by a flight of steps, but the eastern or principal entrance is a noble conception. Leading up to the main portal is a wide stairway, flanked by the rearing and straining horses, three on one side and four on the other, the whole composition an inspiration, splendidly realized.

Much of the imposing appearance of this great structure has been obtained by the treatment of the pyramidal roof. The square portion consists of three tiers diminishing as they ascend, the wide spaces between each stage opening out into platforms for the accommodation of a number of boldly sculptured groups of statuary of heroic size, all performing on musical instruments, an innovation which gives it a vivid human vitality. Each of these tiers is stepped, the two lower with six, and the uppermost with five string courses producing a pattern of horizontality of the utmost architectural value. Above this the apex of the pyramid is gathered up into a massive circular finial, fluted, curved, and moulded, a subtle contrast to the square portion below. The principle on which the roof was designed and executed is similar to that in all the buildings of this region, but in this instance it is elaborated, enlarged, and improved with admirable results. The interior of the hall is now inaccessible, as it has been permanently sealed up in order to preserve it from further subsidence, but it consisted of one large single cell, sixty feet side, the ceiling supported by four huge solid piers, and the whole of its walls, in marked contrast to the rich plastic treatment of its exterior surfaces, severely plain. At the far end of the hall a vestibule led to the sacred cella, a square chamber of twenty-five feet side enclosed within the solid mass of masonry forming the *deul* or tower. This great tower has disappeared, except for its foundations, so that although its general dimensions may be conjectured with a certain degree of exactitude, no record of its style is known. It is however tolerably clear that it followed the usual shape and proportions of the Orissan type of tower, and in view of the progressive character of the rest of the building, it was probably an advance on the

Lingaraja form, appertaining more in its volume to that of the Jagannath example at Puri, but with its curves of the refined and fluid order of the Rajarani temple at Bhubaneswar.

Of the buildings within the enclosure forming the remainder of the architectural scheme, the most important is the nat mandir, a richly designed hall confronting the main entrance to the temple, but separated from it by an interval of thirty feet. This space had as its centre a graceful pillar, or *khirti-stambha*, bearing aloft a small image of Arjuna, but this free-standing column was transferred some considerable time ago to adorn the eastern entrance of the Jagannath temple at Puri, where it still remains. The character and location of these supplementary structures were all in accordance with the composition as a whole, the nat mandir, being a lesser building in the same style as the great structure it faces, thus acting as a refrain to the main theme. Another detached edifice was a small although complete shrine towards the south west portion of the enclosure, dedicated to Ramchandra, treated in the same ornate manner, but on the south east a large building for service purposes, probably a refectory, was plainly designed in keeping with its utilitarian object. Of the gateways to the enclosure, as well as the retaining wall, nothing is left, but there are several colossal groups of sculpture, intended to occupy salient positions on the line of approach, which are still preserved, although not now on their original sites. Some of these groups are superb works of art, not realistic, but idealistic and architectonically treated, so that they all form part of the scheme. Such are two monumental statues of war-horses, their impetuosity restrained by armed attendants, which for spirit and power recall the Chinese productions of the Han period, but combined with the indigenous Indian rock-sculpture tradition. That the entire conception was worked out so that every element, large and small, was not only perfect in itself, but in proportion and intention in complete agreement with every other element is abundantly clear. Each part proclaims its correct architectural application, and the whole is assembled in such a masterly manner that the result is an ordained and convincing uniformity.

In studying the statuary on this building one is struck at once by the expert manner in which each figure, or group of figures, has been so modelled that not only are they architecturally conceived, but they also merge themselves into the building so as to form part of the structure itself. One cannot help comparing this treatment with some of the famous compositions of modern times, where the architect having designed his building, decides that here in one position or there in another a figure or group of statuary may be imposed on his architectural background as a form of enrichment or to emphasize a point of interest. And so the statuary is produced, separately, beautiful no doubt in itself, but detached or isolated, in no sense a part of the composition as a whole ; in other words it is an "exhibition" piece of stone, marble, or bronze. Several hundred years ago, the Orissan master-mason intuitively devised his sculpture so that it is embodied in his building scheme and so forms an integral part of his architectural ideal.

As already observed the sculpture with which this architecture is adorned is of an equally high order. Few buildings can boast of such an unrestrained abundance of plastic decoration as this vast structure, every portion of the exterior being moulded and chiselled either in the form of abstract geometrical ornament, conventional foliage, mythical animals. fabulous beings half-human with half-serpent coils, figures satanic and figures divine, of every conceivable motif and subject known to the Indian mind, and in a technique which ranges from patterns cut with the minute precision of a cameo to powerfully modelled groups of colossal size. As far as the mural decoration is concerned the system on which it was applied has as its basis a framework of vertical and horizontal courses, recalling in some respects the warp and weft of a woven textile, the relief ornament presenting an intricate tapestry of form, amazingly beautiful. Yet much of this relief work depicts subjects which, according to the ordinarily accepted standard in such matters are grossly obscene. These indicate the emergence of a particular phase of Hinduism, known as Tantrism, the *maithuna* ritual of which is represented in the carving on this temple. Such a conception is not however limited to the temple of Konarak; it finds expression at intervals not only in the art of the country but also in its literature, both prose and poetry.[1] Nor is it confined to one region, for in its plastic form it appears on the temples of Khajuraho in Central India, at Madura, and in certain of the eleventh century temples of the Dekkan, as for instance at Balsane in Khandesh, and in the Asvera at Sinnar in the Nasik District.

But nowhere are its observances more blatantly exploited than on the walls of the temple of the Sun at Konarak, the figure sculptures of which are very largely representations of sexual perversion. In Orissa at this period the *maithuna* movement appears to have obtained a firm hold on a considerable section of the community, while it is worthy of remark that the carvings reproduce an ethnological type, very distinctive in apearance, which is now never seen. It is not improbable that this temple was erected on such a remote site in order that the practices so wantonly illustrated might be ceremoniously conducted by its addicts in an underworld of their own. The ultimate result was the same as that which has overtaken other races who have abandoned themselves to such unnatural pursuits. Konarak is deserted, the hierarchy and its following have died out, and even in the distant towns where this debased thought also appears to have prevailed, the people show symptoms of its deplorable effects. Whether this form of worship was so deep and widespread that its consequences caused much of the original Orissan stock to disappear and its place to be taken by others, is outside the present subject, but it is significant that the raising of such stupendous monuments as were then produced seems beyond the capacity of the present populace.

It has been noted that these plastic obscenities are confined entirely to the exterior of the temple, so that it is presumed the elemental observances they represent were performed outside, which may account for the plain interior of the great hall, appearing, by contrast, relatively pure and holy. Such, however, is only one of the mysteries attached to this vast solitary pile, which for centuries has been slowly subsiding into the dust. But its disfigured beauty cannot be concealed, nor its sinister character suppressed, the drifting sands around ceaselessly whisper it, although as ceaselessly they endeavour to hide it. Yet once every year the stillness is shattered, the temple again comes to life to recall scenes of its ancient glory, when, stirred by some strange instinct like that of migratory birds, pilgrims in their thousands converge from long distances to worship the

---

[1] Vasanta Vilasa : the doctrine of Parakiya Rasa ; the poetry of Chandi Das, of Vidyapati and of Jayadeva.

sun-god within its precincts. For one whole day its broken walls pulsate with religious emotion, and its crumbling courts echo with fervent prayers from people of all classes. Then "night over all spreads her garment", and by the following dawn the place is deserted, the devotees have filtered away in groups across the sands towards the horizon, and the great ruin sinks again into solitary silence, steeped in its own dark thoughts.

Owing largely to the dismantled condition of much of this building some idea of its construction, as well as that of other examples of the style may be readily obtained. Most of the masonry is composed of blocks of laterite, but certain portions such as the doorways, and also some of the larger and more important images, as for instance those of the god Surya himself, are minutely carved in chlorite. The courses of laterite are not bonded with mortar, as the masonry is of the dry order, but they are held together mainly by a system of counterpoise, the weight of one stone acting against the pressure of another, much of the stability being a matter of balance or equilibrium. In the case of the deul or tower, to counteract any lateral thrust the entire structure was weighted at the summit by means of the massive melon-shaped disc or *amla*. To raise these great blocks into position, they appear to have been ramped up inclined planes of earth as is the usual practice in the East, and it is believed that to provide a centering for the roof of the jagamohan at Konarak the whole of the interior was filled with a core of earth or sand, which was afterwards removed through the doorways. The ceiling of this hall, which followed the pyramidal shape of the exterior, was a remarkable effort of construction, as it was corbelled out by means of oversailing courses of masonry, each course projecting beyond the one below, thus enabling the sides to converge gradually towards the crown. This system was not however sufficient in itself, and stone lintels were introduced carried on four solid piers. But even this arrangement was not considered adequate support for such an immense superstructure, and, accordingly, a very ingenious plan was devised to supplement it. Each laterite lintel was reinforced by a number of wrought iron beams, while many others, like girders, were disposed about the ceiling, the whole forming an iron grid, or framework, of great strength. Some of the metal beams are as much as thirty-five feet in length and over seven inches thick, one fragment measuring eleven inches in section. These beams were not cast but obviously forged, and the larger ones were evidently produced by welding together a number of "blooms" of wrought iron by means of a hammer. In no other part of India was such a process employed, but it appears to have been the usual method in Orissa, as most of the larger temples were constructed on the same principle, the jagamohan of the Lingaraja at Bhubaneswar, being clearly of this type. The method may be readily studied in the interior of the Gundichabari Garden temple at Puri, which unlike many of the others, is accessible to the general public.

As previously mentioned the Orissan style had a northerly development which penetrated into a region comprising the western portion of the State of Mayurbhanj, the Burdwan district of Bengal, and the Manbhum district of Bihar, where a few scattered examples have been located. These are all relatively small structures, few of which have porticos, as they usually consist of a simple deul or tower containing the cella, so that they appertain more to shrines than temples. In Mayurbhanj these are found only at one place, in the small village of Khiching near the western frontier of the State, at one time the capital of a principality which flourished during the eleventh and twelfth centuries, when they appear to have been erected. Most of the shrines are in a very ruined condition, but they seem to have formed a group, with one in the centre larger than the others, the base of this being as much as thirty-five feet side. The architectural style of the Khiching examples is very similar to that of the Orissan group, but the wealth of carving and figure sculpture with which they are decorated is slightly different in its handling, suggesting the existence of a separate and local school of plastic art. Still more to the north the shrines in the Burdwan and Manbhum districts show more individuality in their design, the increased distance from the centre of the movement causing them to be less under the influence of the parent style. There are several examples of the phase at Barakar in Burdwan, and another at Telpuki in Manbhum presumed to date from the end of the Pal dynasty of Bengal in the 11th century. These buildings however are more closely allied with the regional style as it developed in Bengal, and will be described in connection with the architecture of that part (Chapter XXXI).

Possibly on account of the mistrust of the arch, or lack of expedients for spanning a wide space, the road-bridge does not appear to have figured in the structural activities of the Indian builder prior to the Muhammadan period. Rivers were usually crossed by ferries, and in the dry season were traversed by temporary causeways. There are however a few bridges of an ancient type, notably two of Hindu workmanship in Orissa, one known as the Tentulemul bridge at Jajpur in the Cuttack district, and another, the Atharanala bridge two miles north-east of Puri. The latter spanning the Madhopur stream is reputed to date from the eleventh century, and although not in its present condition of such early construction, it is almost certainly of pre-Muhammadan origin. Although built entirely on the corbel system of oversailing courses of masonry, this elevated causeway maintains the character of a bridge as it is not entirely horizontal in its elevation. For towards the centre of its 280 ft. length it is raised up on two larger piers where the spans also are wider. These spans are nineteen in number, eight feet wide and corbelled out of piers seven feet in width, the whole supporting a roadway thirty-eight feet across. That when first built the bridge was treated as a work of art is proved by the remains of sculptured lions and elephants in its composition, that well-known motif of the Orissan style, which figures repeatedly in all the architecture of this region. The other example at Jajpur is of much the same character, but smaller in its proportions, and probably dating from the same period.

REFERENCES

Arnott, M. H., *Report with Photographs of the Principal Temples at Bhubaneswar*, London, 1903.

Bose, N. K., *Canons of Orissan Architecture*, Calcutta, 1932.

Gangoly, M., *Orissa and Her Remains : Ancient and Mediaeval*, Calcutta, 1912.

Mitra, Rajendralal, *Antiquities of Orissa*, Calcutta, 1875, etc.

Mukhalingam, *Epigraphia Indica*, Vol. IV, No. 24 (1896-97).

CHAPTER XXII

THE NORTHERN OR INDO-ARYAN STYLE (*continued*)

THE KHAJURAHO GROUP, CENTRAL INDIA (A.D. 950 to 1050)

ONE of the most refined and finished manifestations of Indian architecture in the Indo-Aryan style is to be found in a group of temples at Khajuraho in Central India. Moreover these buildings not only represent the mode in such an elegant form, but the majority of them, in spite of the fact that they have weathered the climate for a thousand years, and withstood neglect for nearly as long, are still well-preserved and in good condition. Having now been deserted for several centuries, no regular ritual is held within their halls, so that the spectacle of such noble monuments standing isolated and meaningless amidst fields and jungle is a moving one. Situated a hundred miles south-east of the town of Jhansi, these temples are over thirty in number, most of them occupying a site measuring approximately a square mile in extent, and when first built appear to have been disposed rather unsymmetrically around the borders of an ornamental sheet of water. Unlike those of Orissa, the Khajuraho temples do not illustrate a development over a long period of time, for, as shown by inscriptional evidence, they were all erected within the relatively narrow interval of a hundred years, from about A.D. 950 to 1050. They imply therefore a brilliant episode in the history of Indian temple architecture rather than the progressive course of a concerted movement, representing one of those rare occasions when religious emotion and unstinted patronage coincided with a flowering of artistic genius to find expression in a group of buildings of the highest aesthetic standard and the utmost significance.

These temples were built during the supremacy of the Chandela rajas, a dynasty noted for its structural productions, although their buildings partook very largely of undertakings of a utilitarian character, such as reservoirs and similar public works. No doubt this royal house extended its patronage to the temples of Khajuraho, but their grouping appears to have been due not so much to dynastic encouragement, as to a combined sacerdotal impulse of a marked tolerant and comprehensive nature, as they represent different beliefs, several of them being Saivite, others Vaishnavite, and some Jaina. The congregating of a number of temples on one site is not uncommon in India, but an assembly on such a scale as those at Khajuraho implies some special object. It seems not improbable that a powerful hierarchy which then existed conceived the idea of founding a central seat of religious life and learning, not monastic, as this finds little favour in the systems of either the Brahmans or the Jains, but in an organization of religious orders, not unlike that planned by the Oratorians in Italy in the sixteenth century. In any case, whatever the ideal it stimulated the building art to a remarkable degree as these buildings amply testify. But as at Konarak in Orissa, it is proved by the carvings on several of these temples, that the same sinister ritual which degraded that monumental conception also prevailed at Khajuraho, and it is possible that the religious community concerned suffered the same fate. Such may be one of the explanations for the almost complete absence of life within the precincts of these beautiful buildings, and their disuse over such a long period of time.

The Khajuraho temples have a definitely individual architectural character, different from that in any other part of the country. In the first place instead of being contained within the customary enclosure wall, each stands on a high and solid masonry terrace, the intention being no doubt to detach itself in this manner from its temporal environment. On the broad platform thus produced, each temple has been erected, not as a number of conjoined buildings, but as one unified structure, all its parts so incorporated as to form a compact architectural synthesis. None of them is of any great size, the largest is only slightly over a hundred feet in length, so that they are by no means imposing edifices, but they rely for their appearance on their elegant proportions, graceful contours, and rich surface treatment. The method by which such admirable results were attained becomes evident on analysis, as those who built them were obviously experienced in the practical requirements of the structure, and accordingly began with the plan. (Plate XCIV, Fig. 6). On the ground this took the general shape of a Latin cross with its long axis from east to west, the sole entrance being on the east, at the foot of the cross. This shape was divided into three main compartments, namely the cella or *garbhagriha*, an assembly hall or *mandapa*, and an entrance portico or *ardha-mandapa*. Supplementing these are the *antarala* or vestibule to the cella, and, in the more developed examples, the transepts or *maha-mandapa*, together with a processional passage around the cella.

With the plan so simply and logically projected, the formation of the elevation presented no difficulties, and the designers showed great intelligence and aesthetic knowledge by the manner in which they carried out their handiwork. The mass, or volume comprising the Khajuraho temple-type moves in an upward direction, its trend is towards height, in much the same way as an aspiring quality is a characteristic of the Gothic church. Raised up on its lofty terrace, the building resolves itself into three main parts, consisting of an emphatically high basement story, above which are the walls and openings of the interior compartments, while over all is a grouping of roofs culminating in the tall and graceful sikhara. To accentuate the soaring impulse there are a number of pronounced vertical projections, which not only lead the eye upwards, but produce a variety of vertically inclined and well-disposed passages of light and shade. The architectural treatment of these three main elements forming the elevational aspect of the structure shows consummate skill. A rich and diverse series of mouldings lightens the substantial proportions of the plinth, the spreading base of which seems to grip firmly the pavement of the terrace, like the roots of a symmetrical and well-grown tree. The intermediate portion of the building above this, comprising the central feature of the scheme and enclosing the halls of the interior is handled in an equally artistic manner. Where the remaining surfaces of the structure are solids, here the builder has introduced his voids, consisting of a horizontal range of window openings, thus, bringing in light and air, and at same time throwing a vivid band of intense shadow athwart the whole composition. There are few more attractive conceptions in the field of Indian architecture than these lovely balconied openings, and few, either structurally or aesthetically, more appropriate to their purpose.

There is however another outstanding feature on this central zone of the temple exterior, a decorative motif and one which fills in the wall spaces between the openings mentioned above. This takes the form of two, and sometimes three, parallel friezes, conjoined and following the alternate projections and recesses of the walls and carried round the entire building. Peopled with groups of statuary moulded in high relief, and in dimensions rather less than half life-size, these friezes present a moving pageant and never-ending procession of lifelike forms, shapely in appearance, exquisite in workmanship and of inexhaustible interest. On one temple alone, that of the Kandariya Mahadeo, the figures thus depicted are six hundred and fifty in number, and each building accommodates a similar community in proportion to its size. (Plate XCI). Some of the figures are apparently ideal human beings, while others are divine personages, but all are in elegant attitudes and some are posed with a Hellenic grace recalling the rhythmic forms on a classic vase. Unlike the sombre saints who look down from Gothic niches, those on the walls of the Khajuraho temples are of a warm and gladsome nature, living in a happy golden age, when time was one long sequence of pleasurable experiences. With such an animated throng ever present on these structures it is not remarkable that the architecture pulsates with a human vitality not ordinarily found in the building art.

Each on the main compartments of the temples was distinguished by a separate roof, the smallest and lowest being the portico, next in height came the central hall, the two sweeping up in line of mass to the tall shape of the tower or sikhara, surmounting the whole. Unlike the Orissan type which is pyramidal, the Khajuraho roofs are domical in contour, but their surface texture in horizontal strata is much the same. The external appearance of these temples owes not a little of its grace to the grouping of these roofs and their centripetal movement towards the spire, suggestive of the rising peaks of a mountain range converging on to the highest pinnacle. This effect, however, has not been obtained without an occasional overcrowding of its parts, as for instance where the roof of the mandapa impinges on the sikhara, but this defect is of minor consequence where all is so well-ordered and coherent.

The touchstone of the Indo-Aryan type of temple is the design of the spire, and the examples of this dominating feature at Khajuraho are the most refined and elegant of their kind. The graceful shape of these sikhara has been effected in two ways, on the one hand by the subtle lineament of the main curves, and on the other by the rhythmic disposal of the subsidiary members attached to them. It is only necessary to compare the Khajuraho form of sikhara with the Orissan type to realize the beauty of the former with its flowing profile. In the first place the contours at Khajuraho are more taut and tenuous, the tempo of the lines is accelerated as they mount up in a more decided incline. But the principal refinement is obtained by the design and distribution of the miniature turrets or urusringas, which it was the practice to superimpose on the sides to break up the mass. The

manner in which the craftsmen at Khajuraho played, and even juggled with these elements in the formation of the sikhara is proof of a long apprenticeship to this kind of work. The principle is illustrated in Plate XCIV. In the simpler examples the builders began by attaching a fairly large flattened half-spire against the lower portion of each side of the central structure, the quoins of which were continued down until stopped by another miniature turret or urusringa at the junction of the tower with the substructure. With this as a basis, in the larger examples the scheme was elaborated by means of each of these attachments being duplicated and even triplicated about the lower part of the structure, as are turrets around a Gothic steeple. It will be readily seen that such a system resulted in more melodic outlines to the volume, the fluency thus achieved adding fresh beauty to its strength.

Turning now to the interiors of the Khajuraho temples it will be at once realized that these were designed strictly according to the requirements of the ritual, combined with the necessity for a certain economy of space. There is only one entrance, that on the east, and this is approached by a singularly tall flight of steps rising steeply owing to the excessive height of the plinth, but increasing its dignity. The doorway, like some of the other openings in the interior, has its lintel festooned with a cusped archway or foliated form of strut, so finely fashioned as to appear more like ivory carving, or even a hanging drapery than chiselled stone. Through this doorway one enters a passage or porch, which expands into a rectangular portico or ardha-mandapa, the whole with open sides, the ceiling carried on pillars, and sloping seat-backs or asana as dwarf walls. Opening out of this portico is the main hall or mandapa, a moderately large square compartment with four pillars in the centre supporting the beams of the roof. (Plates XCII and XCIII). On each side of this hall extending laterally, are the transepts or maha-mandapa connecting with the balcony windows of the exterior. The furthermost side of the main hall communicates with the vestibule or antarala, a shallow passage with a large moonstone step (chandrasila) leading up to the ornate doorway of the cella, an opening which repeats in its festooned lintel the design of the main entrance.

Contrasting with the excessively plain treatment of the Orissan interiors, the halls of the Khajuraho temples are richly decorated with sculpture. As the principal compartment is the mandapa this exhibits several notable features, functional and ornamental. The average size of the mandapas at Khajuraho is only 25 feet square, no great space to cover with a roof, but the weight of the domical mass of masonry above, and the relatively elementary structural system employed, made it difficult to achieve in a single span. The method adopted of oversailing courses could only be self-supporting within certain limits, so that a process of under-pinning became necessary. This took the simplest and most natural form of four pillars, one at each corner, with four beams in the shape of a square framework under the ceiling ; on the same principle by which he would prop up his wooden hut, so the Indian mason supported the main roof of his temple. Yet this plan is structurally sound, and he proceeded to make it artistically beautiful, for the manner in which sculpture was applied over its surfaces is superb. Those portions specially selected for treatment were the capitals of the pillars, the architrave, and the ceiling itself. The capitals are structurally of the bracket order, but so overlaid with ornament and figure-sculpture that this is obscured. Above and below are the contorted forms of grotesque dwarfs, curious atlantean creatures without which no capital in the fully developed Indo-Aryan style is complete, and they are accompanied by rampant gryphons at the angles. But in the spaces between these strange and unearthly beings, as a foil to their forbidding appearance, are inserted female figures of enchanting grace and loveliness, either in the act of dancing or posed in some flexuous attitude, each a finished statuette in itself carved out of a separate slab of stone and morticed into sockets prepared for its reception. If this is an effort to express the triumph of beauty over ugliness, or to contrast the bestial with the spiritual, then the artist has fully succeeded in his object. (Plate XCIII, Fig. 1).

The substantial architraves above these capitals are also highly decorated with figure compositions of an animated nature, but it is in the design and execution of the ceilings which they support that the sculptor has exercised the greatest ingenuity and artistic skill. Here it is that we come into contact with a portion of the temple structure, which in many of the regional developments, has been regarded as a subject for the most intricate plastic embellishment. In every part of the country it seems to have been imperative that the ceiling of each compartment in the temple should be elaborately patterned, and, as will be shown later, in certain circumstances to overlay its curved surfaces with scenes of imagery and allegory of timeless origin and profound meaning. And more often than not the interior of the temple is so lacking in light that these upper portions of the halls, although so exquisitely sculptured are in deep shade or even in complete darkness. None the less it was the practice to include these richly carved ceilings in the temple interior, many of which by their character and technique seem to indicate that the preparation of these and the fixing of them in position were in the hands of a separate guild of craftsmen who specialised in this particular kind of work.

In this ceiling treatment of the Khajuraho temples the shallow dome over the central compartment or *mandapa* was that on which the finest work was produced, although even the porches and outlying chambers were often equally elaborated. The design selected was usually a geometrical one, an arrangement of intersecting circles, which on plan form a combination of cusps or quatrefoils, but in section are a series of semi-spherical recesses, or shell-shapes, with a long richly-carved pendant dropping from the centre of each. In a typical example of one of these ceilings the entire surface is a swirling pattern of circles and semi-circles recalling stones thrown into a pool. It is a method not unlike stalactite vaulting, but composed almost entirely of spherical instead of octagonal elements, and there are also observable some of the principles employed in Gothic fanvaulting, although worked out to a much smaller scale. Each stone of these ceilings was carved separately, according to a stencilled pattern, and the whole composition fitted together temporarily on the ground. Then, when all the parts were complete, and the jointing perfected, its components were hoisted up on to the roof and dropped into position one by one so that they interlocked, each course supporting that above it. The complex nature of the designs, the patience and skill required to carve, fit, and finally assemble each piece in its correct position, while in the end the entire work is invisible on account of the darkness of the compartment it covers, is an illustration of one of those insoluble problems occasionally found in the building art of the country.

¹ *Archaeological Survey of India, Cunningham*, Vol. II, 1871.

The main group of temples at Khajuraho, consisting of at least a dozen buildings, is that to the north-west of the site, where they are arranged in two lines, with both Vaishnavite and Saivite shrines standing side by side. In some instances the dedication is a matter of doubt, while the designation of a few may have been subsequently changed. Each of these two lines of structures consists of one large temple, with others slightly smaller alongside, and, for the purposes of study, each has been given a serial number.¹ The largest of the entire series is the Siva temple of Kandariya Mahadeo (No. 3) the first of the most westerly line, and its dimensions are 109 feet in length, 60 feet in width externally, with a height of 116½ feet above the ground or 88 feet above its own floor. (Plate XCI). Its plan is that of a double-armed cross, as not only is it provided with transepts to the mandapa, but it has another pair with windows to give light to the processional passage, while there is also a similar aperture for illuminating this corridor in the rear. The compartments of the interior are six in number consisting of the portico, main hall, transepts, vestibule, sanctum, and ambulatory. These arrangements affect very considerably the shape and architectural appearance of the exterior, which is an effective combination of lines and masses, bold projections being balanced by receding bays, the whole being held together by a well-devised system of horizontal passages of carving. Standing on a broad terrace with ample space all round, the base is formed of a plinth thirteen feet high sloped rapidly upwards by means of a succession of prominent stringcourses. This sloping substructure is surmounted by a kind of dado supporting the massive inclined seat-backs or *asana*, above which appear the window openings divided up by pillars, with the wide eave, or *chajja*, overhanging the whole. Over each of these eaves rises an elaborate gable formation blending itself in the array of turrets leading up to the roof. Apart from the masterly composition of these major parts there is over the whole of this building a vibrant sensibility produced by the rich and colourful texture of its gallery of sculptured forms.

There are two other temples at Khajuraho planned on the same principle as the Kandariya, with double transepts, but they are both one-sixth less in size. These are the Siva temple of Visvanath (No. 7), and the Vishnu temple of Chaturbhuj (No. 10), the former measuring on the ground 87 feet by 46 feet, and the latter 85 feet by 44 feet. Both appear to have had small supplementary shrines at each corner of their platforms, so that they are examples of the *panchayatana*, or five-shrined type of temple. On the Vishvanath temple there is an inscription which records that it was built about 1000 A.D. Two other temples of a fair size are the Vishnu temple of Devi Jagadambi (No. 5) measuring 77 feet by 50 feet, and that of Chhatr-ko-patr (No. 6) dedicated to Surya, the Sun-God, measuring 87 feet by 58 feet, both of which have only one pair of transepts, and are on plan and in elevation very elegantly proportioned. The Devi Jagadambi is a good example of the simpler type of temple-design, as it has only four compartments, the ardha-mandapa or portico consisting of only one chamber, instead of two, and there is no processional passage round the cella.

The Jain temples grouped together on the south-east of the site are some six in number, in varying states of preservation, and as a whole their architectural character differs but little from the Brahmanical examples. Their only

Delhi: Temple pillars of the 8th and 9th centuries re-erected in the cloisters of the Qutb Mosque.

Fig. 1

Fig. 2
Osia, Marwar: Temple of Surya; c. 10th century.

Fig. 1.   Kiradu, Mewar: Vaisnav Temple; 11th century.

Fig. 2.   Osia, Marwar: Temple "No. 2"; c. 9th century.

Fig. 1

Fig. 2
Kiradu, Mallani Dist., Mewar: Someswara Temple; 11th century.

Fig. 2

Fig. 1

Udaipur, Gwalior: Udayaswara Temple; 11th century.

Fig. 2
Torana at Rewah: Central India; c. 11th century.

Fig. 1
Udaipur, Udayaswara Temple: Vedi pillar in interior; 11th century.

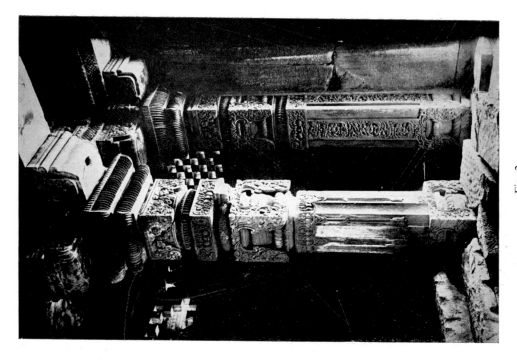

Fig. 2
Gyraspur, Gwalior: Mala De Temple; Pillars in Main Hall;
10th century A.D.

Fig. 1
Gyraspur, Gwalior: "Ath Khumba" (Eight Pillars);
9th century A.D.

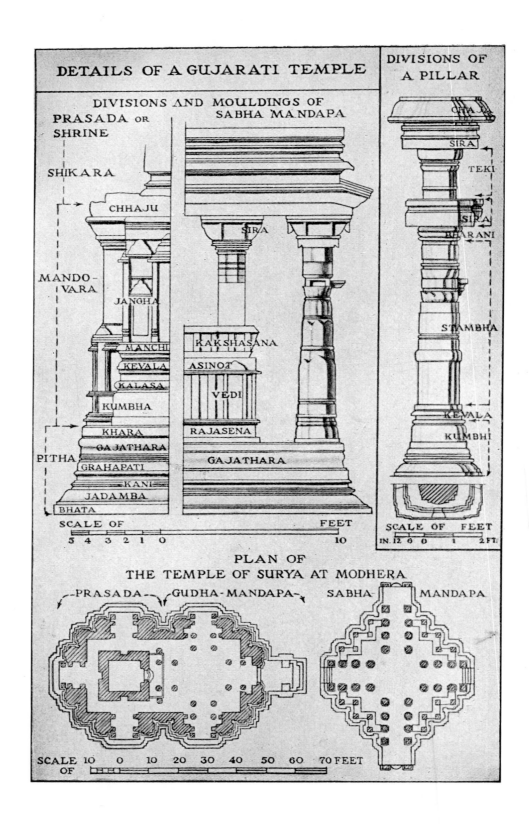

DETAILS OF A GUJARATI TEMPLE

DIVISIONS OF A PILLAR

DIVISIONS AND MOULDINGS OF SABHA MANDAPA

PRASADA OR SHRINE

SHIKARA

CHHAJU

MANDO-VARA

JANGHA

MANCHI

KEVALA

KALASA

KUMBHA

KHARA

GAJATHARA

PITHA

GRAHAPATI

KANI

JADAMBA

BHATA

SIRA

KAKSHASANA

ASINOT

VEDI

RAJASENA

GAJATHARA

CHAJ.

SIRA

TEKI

SIRA

BHARANI

STAMBHA

KEVALA

KUMBHI

SCALE OF   FEET
5 4 3 2 1 0   10

SCALE OF FEET
IN. 12 6 0   1   2 FT.

PLAN OF
THE TEMPLE OF SURYA AT MODHERA

PRASADA — GUDHA-MANDAPA

SABHA — MANDAPA

SCALE 10   0   10   20   30   40   50   60   70 FEET
OF

divergence from this type is in the almost complete elimination of any voids in their elevation, or anything resembling the window openings which are such pronounced features in the temples of the other groups. The result is that the absence of these striking elements causes the external appearance of the Jain temples to be somewhat monotonous, a condition which the sculptor has tried his best to relieve by elaborating the parallel friezes of statuary. These rows of figures, having now no architectural interruptions, dominate the entire scheme being continuous right round the structure, with portions projected like buttresses at intervals in an attempt at variety. These projections are carved into the shape of pillared niches enshrining images of special sanctity, with the occasional introduction of a kind of miniature balcony having sloping balustrades (*asana*) behind which is a group of small figures, a conceit more fanciful than architectural. The most complete example of the Jain group is the temple of Jinanath (No. 25), an oblong building measuring externally 60 feet long and 30 feet in breadth, with a projected portion at each end, that on the east forming the entrance porch. One oblong hall also forms the interior, within which are two compartments, comprising a pillared portico in front, and an enclosed cella beyond, leaving a wide processional passage all round the entire hall. Except that it is laid out in this manner to suit the requirements of the Jain ritual, the architectural treatment of this temple follows much the same principles as the Hindu examples.

There is one ruined shrine at Khajuraho, standing a little apart from the Jain group, but evidently belonging to that creed, which has attracted considerable attention on account of what may be described as the Attic beauty of its constituent parts. (Plate XCV). A building in this condition, like the trunk of a mutilated figure, sometimes acquires undue merit for the sole reason that it is a fragment, the remains of something entirely great, but there is little doubt that the Ghantai temple when complete was a gem of its kind, evidently the handiwork of a group of the most accomplished craftsmen of the time. It consists now of merely a cluster of some twelve pillars, each over 14 feet high, standing on a moulded plinth 45 feet by 25 feet, and supporting a flat roof, the whole originally having been enclosed by walls. What is left bears some slight resemblance to the portico and cella in the Jinanath temple on the same site, but the brackets on the pillar shafts, the flat roof, and its detached position seem to suggest that it may have served some specific purpose in the Jain ceremonial. In its dismantled condition one can only admire the elegance of its pillars and the richness of the carved doorway. Some of the pillars are most gracefully proportioned, tall slender shafts, octagonal below and circular above, clasped around at intervals with girdles of delicate carving, and surmounted by an appropriate bracket capital.

South of this Jain group, near the Kurar Nala, are two Brahmanical temples, one of which called the Kunwar Math (No. 30), and dedicated to Siva, is as fine as any of the Brahmanical examples on this site. It is 66 feet long by 33 feet broad externally and is composed of the usual five compartments, the whole being designed and decorated in the traditional Khajuraho style. Remains of other temples, evidently of the same period, have been located still further afield, as for instance at Jatkari 1½ miles south of Khajuraho, while even as far away as in Rewa State, there is the Vishvanatha temple at Maribag, a small example but clearly of the same type. It is however in the principal group of these buildings as seen at Khajuraho itself that interest mainly centres, for in its deserted courts the spirit of the time still seems to linger, not only in its architecture but in the multitude of silent yet moving forms on its temple walls, depicting a race of people who appear to belong to another world—a world of sensuous mystery, where sober reality is unknown.

REFERENCES

Cunningham, A., *Archaeological Survey of India*, Vol. II, 1864-65.
Griffin, Sir Lepel, *Famous Monuments of Central India*, 1886.

CHAPTER XXIII

THE NORTHERN OR INDO-ARYAN STYLE—(continued)

RAJPUTANA AND CENTRAL INDIA (8th to 11th Centuries)

A DEVELOPMENT of great beauty in the art of temple building expressed itself in parts of Rajputana, Central India, and the adjacent country in the last centuries of the first millennium. Such a virile movement as that inspired by the Gupta dynasty in the fourth, fifth and sixth centuries was naturally succeeded, even after the decay of that intellectual regime, by a later flowering of a singularly rich and lovely nature. Unfortunately much of this fine form of architecture lay in that part of the country which suffered most from the earlier invasions of the Muhammadans, so that examples are comparatively rare and fragmentary. This succeeding phase of the Gupta style flourished from about the eighth to the eleventh centuries, shortly after which the demolition of many of the temples in northern India by the followers of the conquerors not only removed the existing examples, but brought to an end any further building of this kind.

Some idea of the amount and quality of the temple architecture produced in these parts may be obtained from an examination of the remains built into those two famous Islamic monuments, the Qutb Mosque at Delhi, and the Arhai din ki Jhompra at Ajmer, the earliest architectural efforts of the Afghan invaders. From inscriptional evidence it is known that twenty-six temples were dismantled to provide materials for the Delhi mosque, the number of pillars in which amounts to 240. Each single mosque pillar however is made up of two pillars of the temple type, one being placed above the other, thus giving a total of 480 in all, or an average of rather more than eighteen pillars from each temple. But the Ajmer mosque is a much larger structural compilation containing some 235 pillars, and in this instance instead of two, three of the temple examples are superimposed, so that nearly a thousand pillars were used, representing the spoils of at least 50 temples. These calculations may be served to explain the scarcity of indigenous architectural remains within the vicinity of the cities of Delhi or Ajmer. Most of the temples thus demolished appear to have been of moderate proportions, and notably peristylar, their numerous pillars and capitals, with the carved ceiling they supported, being their principal architectural feature. In the mosque at Delhi these temples appear to have been mainly those of the eighth and ninth centuries, the beauty of some of the capitals being remarkable, indicating that they were excellent examples of the post-Gupta style. On the other hand the components of the Ajmer mosque seem to have been derived from structures of a rather later date, probably of the tenth and eleventh centuries, as the vase and foliage capital signifying the Gupta order is rare, and the shafts of the pillars are not fluted but octagonal in section. Although torn from the buildings they were designed to embellish, these beautiful examples of Hindu workmanship are probably seen to better advantage in their present position than in the obscurity of the temple mandapa. (Plate XCVI).

To what extent the post-Gupta art and architecture derived its exquisite quality from the cultural conditions that prevailed in this region during the latter half of the first millennium, can only be conjectured. Such a galaxy of intellectuals as that which comprised the "Nine Gems" at the Court of Ujjain, including the celebrated dramatic poet Kalidasa, and, later, Bhavabhuti, the Indian equivalents respectively of Shakespeare and Goethe, implies an epoch having real unity, corresponding in a measure to some of the great creative developments of the West. That this scholarly movement influenced all forms of expression is shown by the architecture of this period, and it is clear that it was a time when men's minds were working in accordance with high aesthetic ideals. In its cultural aspect therefore it suggests the age of Pericles, rather than that of the Elizabethans, with the addition of a profoundly religious trend. One of the chief characteristics of the great literary masterpieces of this period, and one which is insistent throughout, is an abundant sympathy with and love of Nature in her most florescent mood ; and in this warm, colourful environment live and luxuriate chaste and graceful female forms. Such an emotional atmosphere could not fail to react on the visual arts, and specially on the plastic embellishment of the temples. Can we not see therefore in these buildings, in the elegant scrolls of foliage clustering round column and capital, mouldings and cornice, some of that fondness for blossoming trees, trailing verdure, lotus lilies, and "pale red trumpet flowers", which so frequently comprise the setting of these poetical dramas ? And have not some of the love-idylls inspired those voluptuous feminine figures adorning pediment, bracket, and strut, embodiments of Sakuntala, daughter of the celestial nymph of whom Kalidasa sings?

> Her lip is ruddy as an opening bud,
> Her graceful arms resemble tender shoots ;
> Attractive as the bloom upon the tree,
> The glow of youth is spread on all her limbs.

There is much of this sentiment and passion in the art of the post-Gupta period, particularly in its sculpture, while some of the lilt and melodic cadence of the poetry is observable in the rhythm of its architectural forms.

There are several groups of buildings which exemplify this movement, most of them unfortunately fragmentary owing to subsequent vicissitudes. One of these displaying structural records of great beauty is in the Saugor district of Central India. Here at Eran are architectural remains extending over a period of some six centuries, from the fifth to the eleventh, beginning with the monolithic pillar of Buddhagupta of the fifth century and including a series of shrines dedicated to Varaha, Narasimha, and Vishnu, all of the later Gupta era. Ten miles away is Pathari where the seventh century is represented by a monolithic column, and here also is the temple of Kotheswara which may be of the ninth century. At Gyraspur, further south, in the ruins known as the *Ath-Kambha* (eight pillars), and the *Char-Kambha* (four pillars) are portions of the columned halls of two temples of the ninth and tenth centuries, while the building called the Bagramath, and the temple of Mala De are of the early tenth century. (Plate CII). Finally, at Udayaspur, there is the temple of Udayaswara dating from the middle of the eleventh century, and showing by its style an affinity to the Chandela group at Khajuraho. (Chapter XXII). In the design of each of these structures, whether ruined or entire, there is some feature, or group of features, entirely expressive of the period each represents, such as the typical Gupta order of the capital at Eran, the carved pillars in the Mala De temple with their foliated motifs characteristic of the post-Gupta style in its richest and ripest mood, the faceted shafts of the *Ath-Kambha* with patterns as fine as old Chinese ivory carving, and the logical planning of the red sandstone temple of Udayaswara. All the records of this series however are distributed over a relatively wide area, for a more compact group of structures illustrating the movement, the temples at Osia in Rajputana may be selected.

The village of Osia,[1] thirty-two miles north-west of Jodhpur, is an example, not uncommon in India, of a considerable city whose substance has departed, and only the spirit remains. This spirit, battered and broken, still exists in the form of some sixteen Brahmanical and Jain temples, the majority now in a neglected condition, but a proof that for four hundred years religion was a very real thing in the life of its people. These relics of its past greatness occupy two sites, one consisting of a group of eleven temples of an early phase on the outskirts of the modern village, while the remainder, rather later, are on a hill to the east of it. The temples forming the earlier group appear to have been built in the eighth and ninth centuries, and although comparatively small structures, their size is compensated for by the elegance of their architecture and its applied art. What is also striking in these temples is the variety in their design, no two are alike, one and all show an individuality of conception and an originality of composition, which is unusual in a country where there is a tendency to repeat a standard pattern and where unalterable convention is strictly observed.

Three early temples of the series at Osia, probably built in the eighth century, and dedicated to Harihara, are small but particularly pleasing in their design and rich in their embellishment. Two are of the *panchayatana* class, so that with their four additional shrines they form very attractive compositions. They are raised up on plinths, as in the Khajuraho group, but on the other hand their sikharas resemble the early Orissan type, except that they are more refined in their contours. In Nos. 2 and 3 of this Harihara trio, the mandapa is an open pillared hall, with the lower part of the pillars supporting the characteristic sloping seat-back or *asana* and every part is tastefully carved. (Plate XCVIII, Fig. 2). This plastic decoration is well shown in the entrance to the sanctum of temple No. 2 and also in the pillars of one of the shrines attached to No. 1. There is a naivete and freshness in this carving, although it is profusely applied, and there are the same ingenuous qualities in the architecture, which is also skilful in its execution.

A temple of equal elegance, although more restrained in its treatment, and probably a little later in date, is that dedicated to the sun-god Surya, and in some respects the most graceful of the entire group. (Plate XCVII). Much of its effect has been obtained by the original design of its frontage, to which two tall fluted pillars have been added, giving this aspect almost a classical appearance. This temple is also of the *panchayatana* type, its four subsidiary

shrines being connected by a cloister (*sal*), which not only provide shelter for visiting devotees, but also served the purposes of an enclosure wall. In its proportions and style this building displays no little dignity, while both in the shape of its sikhara, and in the manner of its pillar ornamentation, it is admirable. As an example of the "order" of this period the pillars of the portico may be referred to, the "vase and foliage" motif forming the capital and the base, together with the band breaking the slender lines of the shaft, are the work of an experienced hand. In its architecture and in its art this temple is an illustration of the supreme, almost loving care bestowed by the craftsmen on their handiwork, each example in the course of its production being evidently regarded as a *chef-d' œuvre*.

The most complete example of the Osia group is a Jain temple dedicated to Mahavira, as it consists of a sanctum, a closed hall, and an open porch, immediately in front of which is an ornate torana or gateway. It appears to have been first built at the end of the eighth century, and then repaired and added to in the tenth century, so that it is a record of development over two periods. This is shown by the changes in style of the building throughout, but particularly in the character of the pillars, in which it is possible to compare those of the mandapa belonging to the original structure with the later examples in the second porch ; this latter apartment or *nal* mandapa is so called because it was erected subsequently over the *nal*, or staircase, leading into the interior of the building. To add to the history of this temple, the torana or entrance archway appears to be even a still later addition, probably made in the eleventh century. In this one building alone, therefore, it is possible to follow the course of the style over a period of several centuries. One of its outstanding features are the pillars of the porch, as they represent the post-Gupta order in its ripest state. That this form of pillar found favour for some considerable time is shown by almost exactly the same design figuring in the temple of Mala De at Gyraspur, which can hardly be earlier than the tenth century. It also appears in the triple-shrined Vaishnava temple near Amvan in Kota State, and in the temple of Kalika Mata at Chitorgadh, all evidently of equal date. (Plate CII).

From each temple at Osia the progress of the style may be studied, for instance in that known as the Pipla Devi, a stage in the development of the pillar is illustrated. This temple is provided with a large *sabhamandapa*, or assembly hall, in which there are as many as thirty pillars, apparently dating from the end of the tenth century. Although there is much to admire in their treatment, these pillars seem to indicate that a point had been reached when the art had passed its fine freshness, and was becoming stylized and stiff. The flutings of the shaft in the earlier model have been replaced by recessed angles, which are carried through the entire length of the pillar and even into the capital. Instead of each member of the order being distinct, they merge into one another, the effect becoming confused. A similar treatment of the pillar is noticeable in another temple in this area, the Jageswara at Saladi in Godvad, Jodhpur State, which is known to have been built towards the end of the tenth century, and therefore confirms the date of the approaching decline.

To carry the movement to its final phase there is a temple to the east of the village called Sachiya Mata, the foundations of which may date from the eighth century, but most of it,

---

[1] Archaeological Survey of India Report, 1908-09.

as now standing, was executed towards the middle of the twelfth century. In plan it has an octagonal space, or nave, in the centre of the assembly hall, with a pillar at each angle supporting a shallow dome, an arrangement of the interior which began from the eleventh century. The spire of this temple is complex in design with supplementary turrets or *urusringas* attached to its sides, which, with other similar features proclaim its later date.

The significance of the pillar and its capital in the temples at Osia has been already emphasised, but in some of the examples, that distinctive motif, the "vase and foliage", attained its supreme form. Although not universal, this type of capital may be regarded as the "order" of the Indo-Aryan style, and in the hands of some of the sculptors it has been made into a singularly graceful feature. One of the most elaborate examples of the vase-and-foliage convention may be seen in the porch pillars of the Mahavera temple of the eighth century. Not only is this element introduced into the capital of the pillar, but, with a slight modification, it also serves as the base. This enrichment however did not satisfy the Indian artist, it was merely one incident in his design, for over and above this he piled on other ornamental devices almost smothering the pillar with the wealth of his inventiveness. There is a feeling that he was endeavouring to express the outpourings of nature in her most bounteous mood, that tumultuous fertility of tropical growth, but on occasion his exuberance becomes strained so that the palate cloys and the eye tires from such a display of sheer sensuousness.

No account of the temples of the Osia group would be complete without a reference to the doorways, particularly those which form the entrances to the shrine chamber. In most of the temple architecture, these are the features on which the decorator concentrated all his knowledge and skill, thus corresponding in their wealth of story to the doorways of a Gothic cathedral in the West. The fact that the shrine entrance led immediately into the divine presence seems to have given wings to the artist's imagination, so that here we find portrayed, by symbol and image, whole volumes of folk lore and mythology for those who can see but cannot read. On the lintel are represented the nine planets or *navagraha*, while below are ornamental niches each enshrining some well-known incident. Simulating a key-stone is the dedicatory block, often depicting a figure or emblem associated with the divinity within the cella, while in panels down the jambs are figure-subjects of lively interest. Decorative mouldings outline the doorway, among which is a motif of double spirals continuing right round the opening delineating the intertwined coils of the snake Sesha, the king of the Nagas or serpent race, a device signifying an endless destiny or eternity. The river goddesses of the Ganges and the Jumna figure at the base of the jamb, to which position they were relegated after the Gupta era ; one of the conventions of that period was to include these deities at the upper angle of the doorway, the sixth century marking the date of this change.

With this post-Gupta development in Rajputana may also be classed one example of the Indo-Aryan style in this region, which on account of its technique is rare, as it is rock-cut. This is a Brahmanical temple at Damnar, a site fifty miles south-west of Jhalra Patan and evidently contemporary with an extensive series of Buddhist excavations in its proximity, which may date from the eighth or ninth centuries. Standing a little apart from the Buddhist group, this temple has several noteworthy features. It is approached by a passage cut in the rock some 282 feet in length, at the end of which a rectangular pit has been excavated leaving a mass of rock in the centre out of which the temple has been formed. Its plan is not however a simple one, as in addition to the central shrine it is surrounded by as many as seven entirely separate but smaller shrines all symmetrically grouped so as to form the whole into one unified but somewhat complex composition. Differing from the *panchayatana* or five shrined temples, which in one form or another are not uncommon, there are several examples of this combination of eight shrines, such as the temple of Kotheswara (cir. ninth century) at Pathari, and the Udayaswara (eleventh century) at Udayapur, but the rock-cut temple at Damnar is apparently the archetype of all these. Apart from its plan, this temple is of the usual design consisting of a sanctum, a pillared hall and a small two-pillared portico, the extreme external length of the whole being 50 feet, and its widest part is 35 feet. It is quite finished, even to its interior, the mandapa consisting of a hall 21 feet square, with four central pillars and eight side pilasters supporting a flat recessed roof. Except for its rock technique, and the fact that it is eight-shrined, there is however nothing of special architectural merit in this rather unusual adaptation of the northern style.

As an example of a rock-cut temple in the Indo-Aryan style, that at Damnar is not alone, for there is one other group of excavated shrines in this mode, not however in Rajputana, but in a more remote locality. At Masrur in the Kangra district of the Punjab Himalayas, quarried out of a rectangular mass of sandstone is a complex of monoliths, in style similar to the temple at Damnar, and also of the same date, the eighth century A.D.[1] Although so far apart, these two solitary examples of the Northern mode by this method are sufficiently alike to be classed together. The Masrur conception was obtained by excavating two parallel cuttings leaving an intervening mound of rock measuring 160 feet by 105 feet. Out of this mass one principal temple was carved surrounded by eight smaller ones, the sikhara of the former being of the simple type as in Plate XCVIII, Fig. 2, while the capitals of the pillars are of the vase and foliage order, elaborate in design and finish, fully characteristic of their period.

The post-Gupta development, as expressed in the west and central region, was undeniably a rich aftermath of the intellectual regime of the imperial Guptas, the earlier manifestation signifying that first creative impulse which heralds the birth of a new era, the later, under the steadying influence of time, producing the exquisite second flowering, as exemplified by the remains at Osia, Eran and elsewhere. But in reality these groups of buildings only represent one aspect of a much wider cultural movement which extended into most parts of the country. For there is ample evidence that during the latter half of the first millennium the arts generally were approaching a very high level, and in several instances had actually attained their golden prime. The great school of rock architecture which was nearing its glorious end, and the building art in its structural form which was beginning its grand achievements, indicate that the spirit of progressiveness was a very living force at this time.

[1] Archaeological Survey of India Report, 1912-13.

REFERENCE
    Bhandarkar, D. R., *The Temples of Osia*, Arch. Sur. of India, An. Rep. 1908-9, Cal. 1912.

CHAPTER XXIV

THE NORTHERN OR INDO-ARYAN STYLE—(*continued*)

GUJARAT AND THE WEST (A.D. 941 to 1311)

ONE of the richest and most prolific developments of the Indo-Aryan style of architecture was that which prevailed in Western India during the early centuries of the second millennium. The majority of the buildings were erected in the interim of over two and a half centuries between Mahmud of Ghazni's expedition to Somnath in Kathiawar in A.D. 1025-26, and the conquest of this part of the country by the Sultans of Delhi in 1298. It is true that the Afghan ruler's raid, with iconoclasm as its prime object, for the time being threw the whole of this territory into disorder, but after his return to Ghazni, the inhabitants appear to have quickly recovered from the effects of the blow, and to have repaired the temples that he had desecrated and despoiled. Then ensued a period of comparative peace in the western region together with a condition of marked material prosperity, one indication of which was the number and character of the buildings produced at this time. The settled state of the country was largely due to the stable rule of the Solanki dynasty, a Saivite line whose power extended over a large area centering around Gujarat, and including Kathiawar, Kach, (Cutch) and much of what is now Rajputana, with the capital at Anahilavada-Pattana, corresponding to the comparatively modern town of Patan, north-west of Ahmedabad. The wealth that came to this part of India was acquired mainly through its geographical position, as Gujarat was to India what Venice was to Europe, the focus of commerce of both the east and the west. And the reaction to this state of general affluence was the creation in substance and sensibility of a form of religious architecture in accordance with the favourable circumstances that then prevailed.

Unfortunately many of the finest buildings are in ruins, while in some instances they have been almost entirely obliterated. Apart from the disintegrating influences of time and climate, spoliation by the Muslim conquerors when the country definitely came under their rule at the end of the thirteenth century, accounted for the complete dismemberment of several of the largest and richest temples to provide materials for their mosques. Much later, at the beginning of the nineteenth century, a devastating earthquake, with its epicentre in Kathiawar, wrought indescribable havoc over Western India, reducing to their present damaged state those buildings which age and the invaders had spared. Its one time splendours of sculptured stone have therefore in too many instances been reduced to crumbling piles of broken and shapeless masonry, but from these remains, and other buildings still preserved, it is clear that the Gujarati craftsmen had inherited an artistic capacity, rich and deep, and their productions are ripe examples of this innate architectural genius. In the preparation of these monuments they received the support and patronage of the people to the fullest extent, for not satisfied with mere stone, the growing opulence of the inhabitants was poured out into the erection of temples built entirely of white marble, having every surface moulded into religious forms mingled with luxuriant fancies. Even these magnificent tokens of the material resources and passionate devotion were insufficient to express adequately the spiritual consciousness of the time, so that it became the custom to encrust with gems and precious stones, not only the images, but also their canopies and shrines. None the less under this apparent excess of superficial richness there is revealed a feeling for architectural form and fitness, which indicates that in the main these Solanki temples were notable for their aesthetic excellence and structural efficiency.

Although many of these building undertakings were directly inspired by the Solanki rulers themselves, some of the finer efforts appear to have been due to the patronage of their ministers and governors, who, more often than not, were prominent members of the Jain faith, and who used their great wealth unstintingly, and with marked broadmindedness in erecting temples, both Jain and Hindu. Two of these exalted personages, the brothers Vastupala and Tejapala, who attained to power in the first half of thirteenth century, may, in certain respect, be referred to as the "Indian Medicis", for as politicians, bankers, and merchant princes, they used their influence and accumulated resources in much the same manner as those celebrated Florentines, the Medicis, patronising and encouraging the arts of Gujarat, as Cosimo the Elder and Lorenzo the Magnificent did for Italian art in the fifteenth century. Yet there seems little doubt that like many mediaeval masterpieces, the Solanki temples were not the produce of one mind, or even a group of minds, but were the spontaneous expression of the entire community, every individual, from the highest to the lowest being moved to take a personal interest in their construction, so that even those monuments which are dismembered and broken still continue to breathe the spirit of that brilliant age.

Moreover, each member of the community had also a material share in the production, as is proved by inscriptional records, for these state that there prevailed a system corresponding to the offering of "first fruits" to the deity of the ancients, or the "tithes" of Christendom, in which each person subscribed according to his capacity. As a beginning substantial grants of money or revenue from land were provided by the ruler or his ministers, after which we learn that the head men ordered "a great assembly on market day and came to an agreement to set apart for the god certain taxes", payment to be made in the form of commodities. Thus "in the market-place the shopkeepers were to give a spoonful of every kind of grain that was sold, while of cotton each shop was to give as much as a man could hold in his hand and the reapers of betel-plants were required to make a contribution when they reap, and so forth, the ministers of the king being ordered to recognize these imposts".[1] Every member of the populace therefore being thus identified with these artistic productions, such a

---

[1] *Archaeological Survey of Western India, Kathiawar and Kachh,* : London, 1874, pp. 236-38.

measure could not fail to implant in one and all the seeds of aesthetic feeling a condition which is reflected in all the handiwork of this time, from the wooden house-fronts of the bazaars to works of the merest utility.

The master-builders with their staff of masons formed an essential part of the pattern comprising this social economy, as they are in a lesser degree and in the more remote localities, to the present day. Relics of the builders' guilds (*sena*) still survive, and descendants of the craftsmen are not infrequently found carrying on their trade in much the same manner as did their forebears in mediaeval times. As an instance, one such, engaged on an intricate architectural undertaking when questioned as to how he could do it without models, plans, or working drawings, significantly touched his forehead, implying that all these material aids were stored in his mind. He then proceeded to chant the ancient rules of the craft, a miscellany of religious formulas and astronomical propositions, unintelligible to most, but thoroughly understood by his workmen, as they followed the directions given in this manner, without a fault. Moreover the care and correctness with which the iconography on the temples was executed is proof that the master-masons had a sound working knowledge of the folk-lore and mythology of the country, most of this information being conveyed to them by means of the *shilpas*, or rules of the craft. None of these workmen appears to have been an artist-priest, although instances are known of one being either by heredity or application empowered to perform the ritual of his creed on holy days, with all its complicated ceremonial. In the ranks of a certain group of artisans within recent years, was a cleric, one of the temple staff whose duty it was to paint the images at the festivals and perform art-work of a like nature, and who was accepted by his fellow craftsmen in the dual capacity of both painter and priest. As shown in the case of mediaeval Europe,[1] the building of temples in India was not done by priests trained in the art, as sometimes supposed, but entirely by the hand of lay artisans, professional masons by heredity, known as *silavats* or *salats*. When the Muhammedan governors after the fourteenth century changed the orientation of the building art from temples to mosques, these masons had no very deep religious or other irreconcilable convictions to overcome, but carried out the orders of their Moslem over-loads without any real break in the continuity of the architectural tradition.

The general structural scheme of the temples of this western group consists of the same system of compartments as in most Indian temples, namely in the first instance, of a shrine with its cella, and a pillared hall or *mandapa*. In the treatment of these two combined formations, while in every example retaining the same specific architectural character, the master-masons showed by the manner in which they handled these conventional parts, considerable versatility and power of invention. The *salat* plotted out his work in confirmity with the established rules, varying this where necessary according to his instinctive artistic ability, employing his own architectural idiom, which however was always correct in grammar, and consequently in good taste. The plans of these temples resolve themselves broadly into two kinds, those in which the two compartments are joined so as to unite the entire building within a parallelogram, and those in which each compartment forms a rectangle, in the latter case the two are attached diagonally. The former system is found usually, although by no means invariably,

in the earlier temples of this period, and of which that of Modhera (eleventh century) if its detached hypostyle hall, or *sabha-mandapa*, is excluded, is a typical example, while the temple of Somnath (twelfth century) illustrates the diagonal arrangement. In all instances both the parallel and the diagonal plans have their sides interrupted at intervals by projected or recessed chases forming angles, which, carried up into the elevation are productive of strong vertical effects of light and shade. Furthermore these angles are also of two kinds, as in one class of building they are straight-sided, and in the other rounded or foliated. Finally, some of the larger examples of these Solanki temples appear to have been in two, and perhaps three stories, but most of this type are too ruined for the arrangements to be quite understood, although the principle on which these storied mandapas were produced may be seen in a temple of another class, namely the Sas Bahu (eleventh century) in Gwalior Fort. (Chapter XXVI).

As regards the elevational aspect of the Solanki type of temple, it will be seen that the architectural scheme is divided horizontally into three main sections, consisting of the basement or *pitha*, the *mandovara* or wall-face up to the entablature or cornice, and the superstructure comprising the roof, in the case of the shrine portion (*vimana*) the spire or *sikhara*. Something of this kind of three-fold arrangement conditions the elevation of the majority of temples in the Indo-Aryan style, but it assumes a fairly fixed convention in those on the western side of the country. Furthermore, the same divisional system may be traced in most of the other architectural productions, such as in the archways, towers, columns or any upright composition. For instance, each of these has a moulded base or basement corresponding to the *pitha*, above which is a vertical portion containing niches and figures, resembling in this respect the *mandovara* or wall-face of the temple. The third or uppermost division of the structure, which may be referred to as the attic portion whether tower or pillar, is designed according to need, for instance in the temple it is a series of ascending stories, and in the pillar, the capital and its entablature or other accompaniments. (Plate CIII).

In the temple design the *pitha* or basement, the upper surface of which forms the floor of the building, is composed of a series of mouldings and string-courses, the more important carved with repeating motifs arranged in an order fixed by convention, the lowest being the *garaspatti* or horned heads (*rakshas*), over this is the *gajapitha*, or elephant fronts, then comes the *asvathara* or horses, and finally at the top is the *narathara*, or human beings. Supported by this basement is the second or middle division, the *mandovara*, the most significant portion of the entire elevational scheme, as it comprises a vertical wall-face reserved exclusively for figure sculpture, so that except for its medial position it corresponds to, and has all the attributes of a wide frieze. On this wall are enshrined in niches and tabernacles bas-relief images of the deities and saints associated with the dedicature of the temple, a sculptured pantheon carried usually right round the building. Then, completing the composition of the temple as a whole, there is the third of these formations, comprising the superstructure, in which the roof of the assembly hall or mandapa is built up in the manner of a low pyramid, composed of horizontal courses, diminishing as they rise, and terminating in the usual vase-shaped finial. It is however in the treatment of the *sikhara* which surmounts

---

[1] *The Monastic Craftsman* by Swartwout, Cambridge, 1932.

the shrine that these western temples are most distinctive, as this spire is no longer one simple member, but a group of members, its lower portion being surrounded by a system of turrets or *urusringas*, these features being symmetrically arranged, each a replica in miniature of the large central structure, and each in such high relief as to be semi-detached or almost "in the round". (Plate CIV, Fig. 1).

The interiors of these temples display several notable characteristics. In this western development the architectural style is definitely peristylar, as groups of elegantly carved pillars form an essential part of its content. These columns are arranged geometrically leaving an octagonal area, or nave, in the centre of the main hall, while outside this they are so spaced so as to constitute the aisles. The shafts of the pillars rarely taper, but are divided horizontally into decorative zones or drums, the upper being less in diameter than the lower, so that they diminish by stages, to finish in a bracket-capital or *sira*. Surrounding the nave the pillars are provided with an extension or attic of dwarf-pillars also bearing bracket capitals, the interval between the upper and lower *siras* being filled by inclined struts or braces each carrying an image, usually a female figure, carved in high relief. These attic pillars, with the architrave above, while raising the height of the nave, also support the central dome, which consists of a shallow bowl-shaped ceiling formed by a succession of overlapping courses, the joints being so concealed by intricate carving that the whole appears as if moulded in one piece. That significant feature of the temple interior, the shrine doorway, is designed so that its decorative scheme composes with that of the pillars, as it consists of horizontal bands of figures and foliage, the textural effect of this portal being that of a richly sculptured stratification.

There appears to be some esoteric reason for the scheme of relief decoration in the interiors of Hindu temples in the Indo-Aryan style, differing in extent from that of the exterior. While there are no limits to the exuberance of the sculpture on the outer walls, some restraint is observable in the amount and its distribution in the interiors. These indications of some form of what may be termed plastic prohibition, vary in different groups of buildings, for instance in the Orissan temples, as already shown, many have almost entirely plain interiors, the bare walls of their assembly halls being in striking contrast to the excessively rich decoration outside. On the other hand at Khajuraho in Central India, more freedom is discernible, a considerable amount of carving being found in the interiors of the temples of this group. Still further to the west, in Gujarat and its proximity, the style shows that only the innermost passages and chambers are devoid of ornament, the remainder of the interior being profusely sculptured. From these circumstances it may be inferred that the original intention was to keep all the temple interiors relatively featureless, either in order not to divert the mind from the divine image, or by reason of some cause of a profoundly spiritual nature. But the irresistible chisel of the Indian carver could not always be repressed by precept, and his art was therefore inclined to intrude into all but the most sacred chambers and their immediate surroundings. The gradual reduction of his sculptured handiwork, combined with a decreasing effect of light as one penetrates further into the recesses of the sanctuary, are particularly noticeable in the fully developed temples of the western school. Beginning with the open sunlit portico or *subha-mandapa*, with its richy wrought pillars, one enters the enclosed and covered aisles of the assembly hall or *gudha-mandapa*, more sombre and less ornate than the preceding. This leads to the vestibule, the panelled and figured framework of the shrine doorway being often the only relief from its plane surfaces ; openings on each side of this indicate the entrances to the dimly illumined featureless corridor of the ambulatory, progression finally ending before the mysterious deeply-shadowed sanctum of four bare walls. Yet heedless of the total darkness of some of the subsidiary chambers, the sculptor's hand could not be stayed, the ceilings of these being sometimes delicately filigreed and scalloped as they would be if illuminated by the bright light of day. Such intricate patterns are only revealed by the aid of a torch, the explanation of this paradox being that they are not intended to be seen by ordinary mortals, but are for the eye of God alone. In the words of Longfellow

> In the elder days of Art
> Builders wrought with greatest care
> Each minute and unseen part,
> For the Gods see everywhere.

Of the type of temple that developed during the domination of the Solanki dynasty, there are examples illustrating the mode that prevailed in each century from the late tenth, to the middle of the thirteenth. A list of the principal buildings is as follows :

10th century .. Temples at Sunak, Kanoda, Delmal, and Kasara, in Gujarat.

11th century .. The Navalakha temples at Ghumli and Sejakpur in Kathiawar : Surya temples at Modhera in Gujarat : Vimala Temple at Mount Abu, Rajputana, and the group at Karadu in Mewar.

12th century .. The Rudra Mala (fragments only) at Siddhapur, Gujarat : Somnath (several times restored) Kathiawar.

13th century .. Tejpala at Mount Abu, Rajputana.

Among the earliest buildings of this period were the four temples at Sunak, Kanoda, Delmal and Kasara all situated within a radius of some fifteen miles from Patan, the old Solanki capital in Gujarat. Presumably dating from about the end of the tenth century, they are all small edifices of comparatively simple parts, consisting of a vimana or shrine with an open pillared portico in front, but although modest in plan and proportions they display in their sculptured detail all the characteristic copiousness of the style. The open mandapa is contained within a dwarf wall, above which, leaning outwardly, is the sloping *asana*, or traditional "seat-back", while the pillars of the interior are square in section with reminiscences of the vase and foliage motif among the decorations of the shaft. Although very complete in themselves there are indications in this small group that the style was in course of development. The best preserved examples is the Nilakantha temple at Sunak, as its *sikhara* is entire, even to the *amalasila* finial, and the building itself is a gem of its kind.

Passing on to the productions of the following century, the eleventh, many large and beautiful temples were erected, some in Kathiawar, others in Rajputana, and several in Gujarat, from the character of which it seems that now was the time when the art of temple building in these regions had found its supreme expression. In none of these temples was this more perfectly achieved than in the temple of Surya at Modhera in Gujarat. (Plates CV, CVI and CVII). Modhera itself at the present time is little more than a collection of huts some eighteen miles south of Patan, but this temple and other remains testify that, when its founders set up a tabernacle to the Sun God, it was a site of no little sanctity. Misfortune, or perhaps neglect, has attended most of the great temples dedicated to this deity, as the ruins of Konarak in Orissa, and Martand in Kashmir, among others, are eloquent proofs, and Modhera is no exception. This Sun Temple has lost its tower so that there is no soaring grandeur, while the roofs of its pillared halls are damaged, and its surroundings generally are decayed, yet even with these disabilities, derelict, and away from the sounding world, it is still a monument of incomparable beauty. According to an inscription, found within its broken walls, its exact date has been revealed as 1026-27, probably signifying the year it was consecrated, when Bhima I of the Solanki dynasty ruled in Gujarat.[1]

In spite of its ruined condition little imagination is required to picture this building as it was when consecrated in the eleventh century. What gave it such a finished appearance was not so much the design of the temple building itself, fine though this structure was, but the appearance of the whole scheme with its architectural setting, including its accessories, which show that as in all good building, the needs and the conveniences of the undertaking were counted as essential as its aesthetic treatment. Accordingly those entrusted with its production confronted the temple with a large sacred pool or kunda, for ablutions, comprising a sheet of water contained within a rectangular arrangement of platforms and terraces interspaced with shrines of various sizes and shapes all so admirably laid out that this part of the composition itself is a notable work of art. On the western side of this ornamental tank, a wide flight of steps ascends through an exquisitely carved and fluted archway, or torana, to the main entrance of the temple. This building was elevated on a broad terrace (kharasila) constructed of solid brick faced with stone which formed an imposing courtyard around it. The temple itself is resolved into two separate structures connected by a narrow passage, consisting on the one hand of an open pillared hall or sabha-mandapa, and on the other of an enclosed rectangular building containing two compartments, the assembly hall or gudha-mandapa, and the shrine or garbha-griha, the axial length of the whole being 145 feet.

Although the two structures comprising the temple building differ from each other in character, as the one is in the form of an open hypostyle hall and the other is enclosed within walls, by the skilful adjustment of their mouldings, string-courses and horizontal elements generally, the composition is so well harmonised as to produce the necessary effect of wholeness. On plan the frontal structure, or sabha-mandapa, is based on a square of nearly fifty feet wide, placed diagonally with the axial line, its sides being interrupted at regular intervals by recessed chases. There are pillared entrances with cusped archways at each of the four corners, and a smaller pillar set within each recessed angle, the whole system forming an adequate support to the wide projecting Cave or chajja, and the triple cornice above. A dwarf wall, richly empanelled with figure subjects,

and surmounted by the leaning "seat-back." encloses the lower part of this arcade, while the upper portion being open presents vistas of its fine interior columnation. What remains of the roof shows that this was in the form of a low stepped pyramid, its horizontal lines being broken by innumerable miniature finials, while above each of the entrances was a group of sculpture. Restoration of this becomes possible owing to the fortunate circumstance that a few pieces of the cornice and lower parts of the roof and tower have survived in situ, so that the type or "order" of building to which the temple belonged is obvious from this clue. The interior of the hall is composed of two aisles of pillars arranged along the diagonals of its square plan, thus producing a cruciform effect. By omitting the central pillars at the junction of these cross aisles, the octagonal space of the nave opens out in the middle of the hall, and above this rises the domed ceiling, elevated higher than the aisles by means of an attic story. As to dimensions the pillars are 13 feet high, the rim of the dome is 17 feet, with its centre 23 feet from the floor level.

The essential parts of the Modhera temple are, however, contained in the enclosed structure at the rear of the preceding, as this includes the shrine. Externally this building is on plan an oblong formation with an extreme length of 80 feet, and a width of 50 feet, having its long sides, not diagonal as in the case of the hypostyle hall, but parallel to the axis of the scheme as a whole. In its design recessed angles are also a distinctive feature of the exterior, while the sole entrance is through a pillared portico on the east, where it connects with the western or rear doorway of the sabha-mandapa. At intervals in the sides are window openings, five in number, each a well-proportioned aperture, and, with its side pillars, relieving the wall surface in an interesting manner. The elevation is composed of the three main divisions already referred to with the basement or pitha consisting of the conventional range of carved mouldings, above which is the spacious mandovara, or panelled wall-face, richly embellished with figure sculpture, each image enshrined in a niche, the principal divinities in the larger and central ones, female figures such as dancers and musicians at the sides, with saints and ascetics in the smaller and less prominent. The superstructure of this building has completely disappeared, but it comprised the traditional arrangement of a low pyra-midal roof over the front portion, and a tall turreted sikhara over the shrine. In both these formations the recessed chases, still visible in the body of the structure, were continued upward, those carried up into the spire providing that element of verticality to its outward appearance which, in its present truncated condition, is lacking. (Plate CVII).

The interior of this enclosed portion is divided equally into two compartments, each consisting of a square of twenty-five feet side, the front or eastern being the gudha-mandapa, or assembly hall, containing eight columns around a central octagonal nave, above which is a highly ornamental ceiling. Except however for a niche in every bay enthroning an image of the sun-god the walls of this hall are plain. Leading out of this compartment, through a shallow four-pillared vestibule, is the shrine-chamber—a square cell with a processional passage around it. Carved decoration is here sparsely distributed, most of it being concentrated on the entrance to the cella. This doorway has its jambs and lintel divided up by mouldings into sections each crowded

---

[1] See an illustrated article in the Magazine " Marg ", Vol. V, Number 1 (Bombay) on the " Sun Temple at Modhera " by Silloo Bharucha.

Fig. 1

Fig. 2
Sejakpur, Kathiawar: Navalakha Temple; 11th century.

Fig. 1

Fig. 2
Modhera, Baroda: Surya Temple, 11th century.

Baroda, Modhera: Surya Temple; 11th century.

Fig. 1.   Modhera, Baroda: Sun Temple, entrance; 11th century.

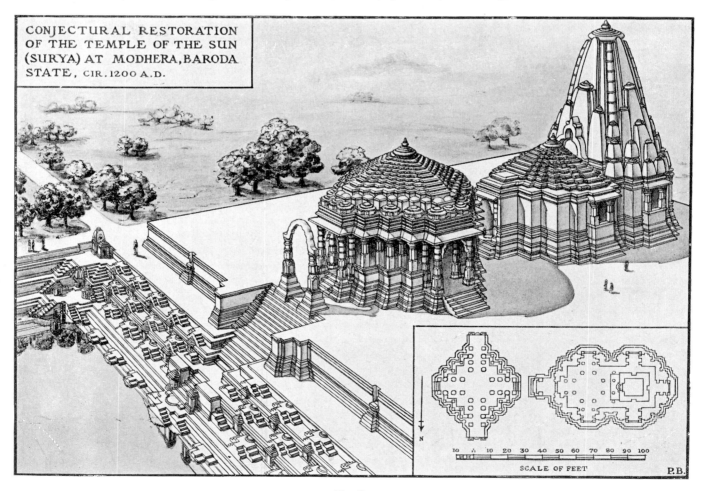

CONJECTURAL RESTORATION
OF THE TEMPLE OF THE SUN
(SURYA) AT MODHERA, BARODA
STATE, CIR. 1200 A.D.

SCALE OF FEET

P.B.

Fig. 2

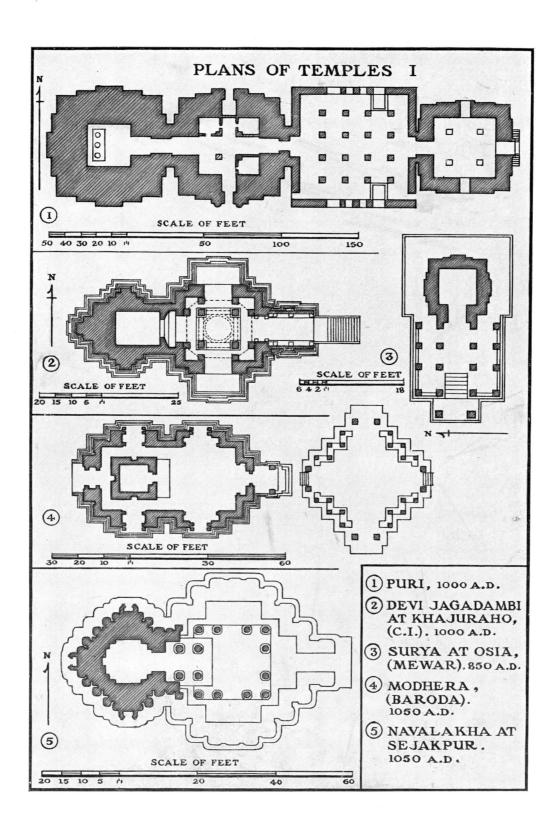

PLANS OF TEMPLES I

① PURI, 1000 A.D.

② DEVI JAGADAMBI AT KHAJURAHO, (C.I.). 1000 A.D.

③ SURYA AT OSIA, (MEWAR). 850 A.D.

④ MODHERA, (BARODA). 1050 A.D.

⑤ NAVALAKHA AT SEJAKPUR. 1050 A.D.

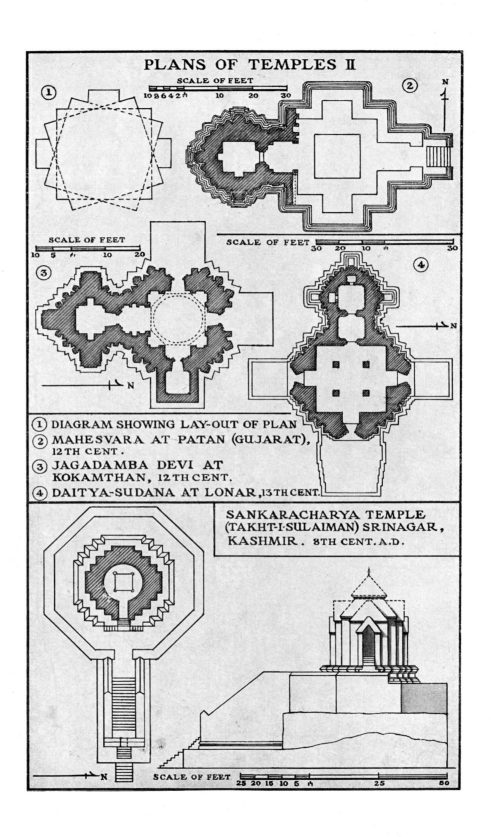

PLANS OF TEMPLES II

① DIAGRAM SHOWING LAY-OUT OF PLAN
② MAHESVARA AT PATAN (GUJARAT), 12TH CENT.
③ JAGADAMBA DEVI AT KOKAMTHAN, 12TH CENT.
④ DAITYA-SUDANA AT LONAR, 13TH CENT.

SANKARACHARYA TEMPLE (TAKHT-I-SULAIMAN) SRINAGAR, KASHMIR. 8TH CENT. A.D.

Fig. 2. Mount Abu, Rajputana: Temple of Vimala Saha: A.D. 1013.

Fig. 1. Ceiling in Dilwara Temple, Mount Abu.

Fig. 1
Ambarnath, Thana Dist. near Bombay: Mahadeva Temple from S. W.; 11th century.

Fig. 2
Jhogda, Nasik Dist.: Temple of Mankesvar; 12th century.

with figures, a somewhat stiff and formal treatment and a forerunner of that rigid and over-strained method of dealing with the door-frame which marks the later style.

In viewing the Modhera temple the aesthetic sense at once responds to the elegance of its treatment and its proportions as a whole, the entire composition being lit with the living flame of inspiration. But apart from its material beauty, its designer has succeeded in communicating to it an atmosphere of spiritual grace. The temple faces the east so that the rising sun at the equinoxes filters in a golden cadence through its opening, from doorway to corridor, past columned vestibules finally to fall on the image in its innermost chamber. In its passage the rays of the heavenly body to which the shrine is consecrated, quiver and shimmer on pillar and archway, giving life and movement to their graven forms, the whole structure appearing radiant and clothed in glory. To see this noble monument with its clustered columns not only rising like an exhalation, but mirrored in the still waters below, is to feel that its creator was more than a great artist, but a weaver of dreams.

About the same time that the Modhera temple was being built in Gujarat, at Mount Abu in Rajputana another temple was being erected, which, although in much the same style, differs from it in several material particulars. This is the temple of Vimala, constructed entirely of white marble and designed to conform to the usage of the Jain religion, being one of the oldest and most complete examples belonging to that creed. It forms one of a group of shrines on this romantic site, as it was the custom of the Jains to build their fanes on the summits of the mountains, high places being regarded as sacred and worshipped as deities, so that in their temples it is true their "foundations are upon the holy hills." (Plate CXXI). As the majority of the temples of this period are deserted ruins, it is refreshing to turn to the Vimala which is well-preserved and still maintains its living character. There is not infrequently an air of reserve and aloofness in the external appearance of Jain temples, as it was the practice to surround them with a high enclosure wall of cells, but within the courtyard thus formed, the architectural mode is broadly in accordance with the general style then current. These ranges of cells around the courtyard are related to the *pansalas* of the Buddhist monasteries, but here they have become transmuted into small chambers lit only from the doorway and enshrining a seated figure of the Jina or saint to whom the temple is dedicated, in this instance that of Rishabhanath or Adinath, the first Tirthankar. Within this range of enclosing cells the courtyard measures 145 feet by 95 feet, where, screened by a double arcade of pillars, stands the temple building, a structure cruciform in plan, its length being 98 feet and its widest part 42 feet.

As is not uncommon in Jain temples the exterior of the Vimala has no special architectural character, all the effect being reserved for the interior. Entrance is obtained through a domed porch on the east, facing which is a six-pillared pavilion with a *samosan*, or conventional representation of the holy mountain of the Jains in the centre, surrounded by ten statues of the founder Vimala and his family each seated on an elephant, this earthly portrait gallery being set apart from the sacred halls of the gods. Passing into the cloistered courtyard it will be seen that the temple resolves itself into an orderly grouping of pillars forming an open portico and vestibule, beyond which is an enclosed portion containing the shrine. The central feature of this columned hall is the usual octagonal space, or nave,

produced by an arcade of eight pillars supporting the dome. At the far end of this on a slightly higher level is the vestibule, extending across the width of the building like a transept having two rows of pillars, and out of this opens the doorway to the shrine. Some idea of the proportions of the columned hall may be gained from its measurements, the octagonal nave being 25 feet in diameter, the architrave alone being 12 feet from the floor, while the apex of the dome is less than 30 feet high. As with most of the temples of this class, the rim of the dome is supported on an attic system of dwarf pillars with convoluted braces between, and all the capitals are of the four-branched bracket order.

When it is realized that practically every surface of the interior, including the pillars, is elaborated with sculptured forms, the rich effect may be imagined, but it was in his treatment of the vaulted ceiling of the nave that the marble carver found his supreme expression. This dome is built up of eleven concentric rings, five of which, interposed at regular intervals, depict patterns of figures and animals, a plastic record of some ancient half-obliterated memory. The lowest contains the fore-fronts of elephants, their trunks intertwined, as many as one hundred and fifty of these in close rank. A few mouldings above is another border representing images in niches, also repeated many times, and again over that a similar course of dancing figures. This is followed higher up in the concavity by a series of horsemen, finishing in the topmost story with more figures engaged in an endless dance. Between these various figured courses are ornamental repeats, gradually becoming more pronounced until towards the apex they culminate in a grouping of pendents not unlike festoons of foliage suspended from the high trees of a forest. But this is not all. Boldly superimposed athwart the lower of these circular rings is a series of sixteen brackets consisting of female figures representing Vidyadevis or goddesses of knowledge, each contained within an aureole, their high semi-detached projection giving them the appearance of supplementary braces supporting the vault. (Plate CX).

In its strictly architectural aspect however the whole of this interior is open to criticism, and specifically this remarkable dome, as it is clearly too heavy in appearance for its relatively slender supporting columns, while the convoluted struts serve only an ornamental purpose, being introduced merely to enrich the effect. Any analysis from this point of view could only emphasize the fact that several of the ordinarily accepted principles of the building art have been disregarded in its composition, the structural properties being obscured by the exuberance of the decoration. Moreover, throughout the entire scheme of plastic treatment, the main theme has been the multiplicity of detail, the reiteration of a motif innumerable times, a ceaseless repetition of deities in human form, the underlying idea being that the more frequently these are reproduced, the more emphatic becomes the message they convey. As their pantheon proves the Indian mind is prone to think in vast exaggerated numbers. The consequence is that when this is presented plastically the eye tires, the faculties become satiated and some of the warmth of life is lacking ; there is not only monotony but a frigidity in its atmosphere, a condition increased by the very perfection of the material of which it is built. For marble of this refined quality should not be fussed and fretted into ornamentation, its natural texture is its chief charm, and to carve it thus is to put it to waste and so misunderstand its intrinsic delicacy and significance. Nonetheless the Vimala temple is a notable achievement, its fame resting not so much on its architecture which has few conspicuous virtues, but on the infinite caprice and inventiveness of its sculptured decoration which seems to be a reflection of the intense religious fervour then existing among the Jain community.

Of the temples in Kathiawar contemporary with the above, and therefore also dating from the eleventh century, that of Navalakha at Ghumli, and a group of the same name at Sejakpur are prominent examples, both grievously dilapidated, but clearly fine conceptions when in their prime. In the case of the former, the plan is on the diagonal principle with the two compartments of the pillared hall and shrine chamber conjoined to form one building, the whole being remarkable for the depth of its projections and recesses, thus producing vivid passages of light and shade. In addition the mandapa is in two stories, and, as it stands on a high and wide platform contained within an enclosing wall or screen, the effect when complete must have been impressive. Of the buildings at Sejakpur one of these still displays enough of its sikhara to show that the feature was composed of a close grouping of semi-detached turrets or *urusringas* at its base, and therefore in this respectfully typical of the style. (Plate CIV). Its pillared hall is a graceful arrangement of large columns forming a nave in the centre, with the succession of smaller pillars around comprising an aisle. The plan of the vimana illustrated the foliated system of projections, and these, carried up into the body of the structure add much to the richness and vitality. Both these Kathiawar examples are of moderate size, that at Ghumli being eighty feet long and that at Sejakpur seventy feet.

As an instance of the wide distribution of this style in the eleventh century, there is an exceptionally rich but severely damaged group of temples at Kiradu in the district of Mallani in Marwar, each temple having many of the characteristics of the Solanki mode. Yet with these may be detected certain Gupta influences, particularly in the pattern of the small turrets of the sikhara, and in the more liberal use of the vase and foliage motif, due no doubt to the proximity of the Gupta territory and the still living records of that style. There are five temples at Kiradu, of which one dedicated to Vishnu is probably the earliest, but the largest and least injured is that of Someswara still retaining much of its tower, and the shell of a magnificent pillared hall, the square shafts of its columns ending in the vase and foliage element, above which is a circular section and a four branched bracket capital. In this temple the basement or *pitha* includes a complete series of the traditional mouldings of the style, consisting of the rows of horned heads, elephants, horses, and men, in that order. Several of the mandapas in the other examples are mere skeletons of their original shape, but from these anatomical remains, the construction and arrangements may be more readily studied. There appear no other temples in these parts so richly wrought, or showing more distinctly a compounding of exuberant art and intensity of devotion than this deserted group at Kiradu. (Plates XCV, XCVIII and XCIX).

That the twelfth century saw a continuation of this architectural activity, as the country remained comparatively peaceful, and its commercial prosperity was maintained, is shown by several important buildings. Among these, two great projects were consummated, consisting of the completion and consecration of the temple of Rudra Mala at Siddhapur, and the further restoration of the temple of Somanatha after its spoliation by Mahmud of Ghazni in A.D. 1025. On account of their ruinous condition, however, both these famous monuments are of little help in tracing the progress of the style, as of the former only a few pillars and an architrave remain in situ after being dismantled at the end of the thirteenth century, in order to provide materials for an adjacent mosque, while the temple of Somanatha, having been restored more than once, and then converted into a mosque, has not much of its original fabric preserved. Undoubtedly the Rudra Mala was, towards the middle of the twelfth century, after it was consecrated by Jayasimha Siddharaja the hero-king of Gujarat (1094-1142), one of the largest and most sumptuously decorated religious monuments in India. Of its wondrous beauty the Gujarati ballad-singer still fulsomely declaims, as the following extract shows :

To the Great Rudra eleven shrines were erected,
Covered with gold like the mountains of Meru,
Columns sixteen hundred were raised to adorn them,
Carved screens and pierced lattices veiled them from without,
Inlaid with gems were the doors of the shrine-chambers,
With rubies and diamonds they glistened like lamp-flames,
And the "Shining Ones" also were festooned with pearls.

It is still possible to trace the plan of this fine structure on the banks of the Saraswati river, its foundations indicating an imposing conception, as with its adjacent shrines all forming part of the composition as a whole, it covered a space 300 feet by 230 feet, the central building itself being 150 feet long and over 100 feet wide. From the portions that remain it seems that the mandapa was three stories in height, and by the same fragments the rich character of the design may be appraised.[1] Not much smaller than the Rudra Mala was the temple of Somanatha, after its reconstruction by Kumarapala in the latter half of the twelfth century, as the main building measures 130 feet long by 75 feet wide. It is now a crumbling and disfigured shell, deserted and desolate, a weather-beaten pile from which most of the glory has departed.[2] Yet these two relics contain sufficient evidence of the great scale, bold planning, and elaborate nature of the Solanki style at this stage of its course.

During the last years of the thirteenth century the Muhammedan rulers at Delhi invaded Gujarat and put an end to the Solanki dynasty. But before the collapse of this indigenous line, one outstanding monument was added to the list of those which arose during their ascendency, and with it the style draws to a close. This building is the Jain temple of Tejpala at Mount Abu, dating from about 1230 A.D., and in proportions, quality of idea, and material, resembling the Vimala temple, already described, and erected on the adjacent site exactly two hundred years previously. So much alike are these two Jain temples, the Vimala and the Tejpala, that it is commonly supposed the one was copied from the other, but it is more probable that the Tejpala illustrates the natural evolution of the style, the few differences proving the really small extent the architectural mode changed

---

[1] Archaeological Survey of India, Vol. XXXII, *Antiquities of Northern Gujarat*, London, 1903.

[2] Archacological Survey of India, Vol. XLV, *Somanatha*.

during the course of the two centuries that separates the raising of the two buildings. Such differences are mainly matters of detail, among which is the treatment of the eight different types of pillars to be found in the later example. The shafts are in most instances circular in section and are evenly diapered with mouldings and conventional or geometrical patterns resembling reticulations. In many of these pillar designs the carver appears to have lost some of his first fine spirit, yet something of the old vigour is discernible in the convoluted struts holding them together, the curves of which are strong and graceful. As a whole however the Tejpala temple has not the freshness of the earlier example, nor does it show such creative energy, for the original ardour of the craftsmen was slowing down. There remains a sense of perfection in its workmanship, but it is mechanical perfection, with an over-refinement and concentration on detail implying the beginning of the decline. The high time of the Solanki style was passing.

A building art of such a virile character as that which flourished under the Solanki rule, did not however confine itself solely to the production of temples, and there are many other structures of a semi-religious or civic character executed at different places during this period. Among these are such erections as *kirti-stambhas* or temple archways, monumental towers, city gateways, tanks and sluices, and *wavs* or public wells. The *kirti-stambha* is a form of torana, usually an accompaniment to the temple design, standing at its outer entrance, but there were some for the ceremonial of swinging the god (*hindola*), from others the scales were suspended for weighing the ruler against gold for charity, and for various similar observances. Two of the finest examples are at Vadnagar in Gujarat, both one time connected with a temple, but of which building not a vestige now remains. That which must have stood at the main entrance of the edifice at Rewah is the most complete and is a typical specimen of its kind. Of a total height of forty feet it consists of two massive and elaborated columns supporting a wide cornice, above which rises a voluted pediment containing figures. The pillars are designed with an upper story or attic, between which is thrown an ornamental cusped arch, making the effect of an archway more apparent. All the parts forming the *kirti-stambha* are devised on the same principles as those employed in the temple design, with the spreading base, figured shaft, bracket capitals, and tabernacled superstructure being of much the same order, but, if anything, even more ornate. There is a sense of stability in their expanding pedestals, and grace in their proportions, but as examples of "riches spawned of riches," their heaped-up sculptured effect is overwhelming. (Plate CI, Fig. 2).

Of the monumental towers there is one exceptionally well-designed example in a style related to that of the Solanki period, and dating from the twelfth century. This *Jaya-Stambha* at Chitor in Rajputana (the earlier of two such structures, as there is another in the same locality of the fifteenth century), was probably a "Pillar of Fame" set up before a Jain temple, which has now disappeared. (Plate XCVI). A temple stands besides the tower but it is a fourteenth century production, evidently built on the site of the original edifice. The tower rises to some eighty feet in height, and is in eight stories, the active principles of this fine conception plainly showing that the craftsmen were by no means slaves to the temple-type, but could, when required, create equally beautiful buildings of another kind and for another purpose. Its foundation is a simple platform from which mount the spreading mouldings of the

basement to support the most prominent feature, corresponding the *mandovara* or wall-space in the temple design, a projecting story consisting of tabernacles and niches containing figures. Above this the stories recede or expand in measured alternation to finish in an open pillared pavilion with a pyramidal roof which forms the summit. Each story is enriched with mouldings, balconied-windows, turrets and other architectural motifs, the whole presenting an appearance of animated variety yet all in perfect unison, a subtle blending of the qualities of beauty and strength.

Examples of the civic architecture of this period may be seen in certain city gates, such as the Rampola at Ghumli in Kathiawar, and a complete series of four, each in the ancient towns of Jhinjuwada and Dabhoi in Gujarat. The walls and fortifications which adjoin these gates, although much ruined, indicate that the whole conception of these fortified towns with their bastions, battlements (*kanjuras*), corner towers, covered ways, and terrepleins was carried out in a thoroughly practical but at the same time in an exceedingly artistic manner. It was on the gateways however that the craftsman's art was mainly concentrated, some of which are remarkably elaborate and even romantic productions. These gates were all double structures, consisting of an inner and an outer curtain, the former being at right angles to the line of entrance of the outer, leaving a small open court between. In most instances the inner gateway only has been preserved, in appearance an intricate and richly sculptured edifice, but the system on which these portals were constructed was comparatively simple. It is clear, they were derived from a wooden prototype, as timber is still actively employed in these parts to the present day. The archway itself, although all of stone, is composed of hammer-beams, struts, and curved braces, in much the same style and on the same principle as the wooden roofs were built in Gothic churches in the west. To attach this archway to the side-walls, six substantial pilasters were built on each side of the gateway, in groups of threes, with a wider space between each group in order to allow the leaves of the door to open back on to the walls. Each of these pilasters supported one of the bracketed archways, a sextuple arrangement of one archway behind the other, thus affording an attractive surface for sculpture, of which the designer took full advantage. It is the nature of the plastic ornamentation which gives these gateways much of their character, as the stone-carver has not only elaborately moulded each constructional member but in the spaces between the beams, struts, and braces he has introduced figures of musicians, dancers, cavaliers and other fanciful creations all treated in a very spirited manner.

It is instructive to compare these gateways with those produced by the subsequent rulers, the Moslems, as each type is thoroughly representative of the widely different ideals of each community. Contrasting with the fundamentally militant, but, at the same time, architecturally satisfying fortress gates of the Muhammedan period, these rare examples of the previous age have no such aggressive qualities, as they are evidently designed quite as much for their aesthetic as for their protective properties. Where the Islamic gateways are definitely practical and architectural, those of the Hindus are just as definitely imaginative and decorative, a relatively peaceful and inviting approach to the city they so characteristically adorn.

At both the towns of Jhinjuwada and Dabhoi the gateways appear to have been built originally in the twelfth century, but some alterations or renovations may have taken place in the thirteenth century, while under the Moslem governors parts of these were reconstructed, and their shapes changed. Yet in spite of vicissitudes several of them still retain much of their indigenous appearance signifying a time when the lintel was the accepted method of bridging a space, and the arch was unused because it was unknown. The finest examples are the four at Dabhoi, one being in the centre of each of the four walls of the city, three of them being, of the type above described, while the Hira or Diamond gate, the main entrance to the town, is a far more ambitious production and therefore in a class by itself. (Plate CXIII). This gateway is thirty-seven feet through, with a clear roadway twelve feet wide between its walls, and a large structure having several rooms for guards and custodians in the wings. On each side of the actual gateway, and within the thickness of the walls, a temple is inserted, the one towards the north being a fairly spacious compartment in the form of a Greek cross, and known as the Kalika Mata, as it was dedicated to the goddess Kali. On the exterior face of this composition the masonry is severely plain, as this was the outer wall but on the inner face, within the city, there can have been few buildings more ornamentally conceived. No regulated plan seems to have been followed, nor symmetry contemplated, as bays alternate with projections, balconies on voluted struts hang from available places, while windows and canopied niches are introduced wherever fancy dictated. In the plastic decoration which runs riot over every one of the architectural features, all the motifs stored in the imagination of the Indian artist have been released to add their share to the tumult of the effect. As a picture of the spirit of the time, fundamentally religious, yet unrestrained by any particular conventions, the Hira Gate at Dabhoi stands almost by itself.

Water forms such an essential part of the religious and economic life of the Indian people that tanks, conduits, sluices, and wells are common in all parts, but none of these have been more artistically treated than in Gujarat. Even such utilitarian objects as the water gates of the reservoirs became in the hands of these craftsmen pleasing works of art, as shown by one of the sluices of the Khan Sarovar Tank at Anihilapattana, with its elegant vase-and-foliage pillars

of the eleventh century. It was however in a special type of public well developed in western India that the *Salaat*, or stone mason, expressed himself most favourably, for some of these *wavs* have marked architectural character. The *wav*, or *baoli*, consists of a cylindrical draw-well, one side of which is open down to the water level, as it is approached by flights of steps descending an inclined passage. Each flight of steps leads to a stage or story, so that the passage becomes a series of narrow galleries, one above the other. By this arrangement the public obtained access to the water without having to make use of the draw-well. Such a structural plan provided an excellent opportunity for the introduction of pillars and pilasters, and groups of these accordingly find a place in each bay. Moreover, the entrance to the passage, and its "skylights" above, together with the mouth of the draw-well itself, invited ornamental treatment, and this took the form of pavilions and kiosks of the pillared variety, the whole combination converting the *wav* both above and below ground into that true test of an artistic consciousness, an object of utility realized architecturally. A few instances of *wavs* of the Hindu period survive, which show that this system of well-construction matured at a comparatively early date, that of the Rani Wav at Anihilapattana, built about 1050 A.D., being one of the largest and most sumptuous of its kind. Little of it now remains except indications of its shape and size but among its ruins one pillar still stands, which is a proof not only of the elegance of its design, but is also an excellent example of the Gujarati order of this period. Less elaborate but better preserved *wavs* of the early kind are the Vethiya *wav* near Mukhana in Kathiawar dating from the eleventh century, and another at Vayad in the old Baroda State built in the thirteenth century. That at Vayad is a characteristic design in four stories or galleries, all well proportioned but somewhat parsimoniously treated as regards detail. The Hindu type of *wav* was however but a prelude to the kind of structure that developed in later mediaeval times under Moslem rule, when besides functioning as a well, or *baoli*, it became enlarged and elaborated into a range of underground compartments and columned courts, a cool and refreshing retreat for the wayfarer from the heat and glare of the bazaars overhead.

REFERENCES

Burgess, J., *Archaeological Survey of Western India*, Vol. II, Kathiawad and Kach, 1876.

     ,,   ,,   ,,   ,,   Vol. IX, London, 1903.

Burgess, J. and Cousens H., *Architectural Antiquities of Northern Gujarat*, Arch. Sur. of W. Ind., Vol. IX, London, 1903.

Burgess, J., *Archaeological Survey of Western India, Belgaum and Kaladgi*, 1874.

Burgess, J. and Cousens, H., *The Antiquities of Dabhoi in Gujarat*, Edinburgh, 1888.

Cousens, H., *The Architectural Antiquities of Western India*, India Society, London, 1926.

CHAPTER XXV

THE NORTHERN OR INDO-ARYAN STYLE

THE TEMPLES OF THE DECCAN (11th to 13th centuries)

A VARIATION of the Indo-Aryan style was produced during the early mediaeval period in a tract of country forming a portion of the Deccan. This tract comprises an extensive area of the middle-west of the peninsula, being contained between the river Tapti on the north, and the upper branch of the Kistna on the south. It is a part of India having notable architectural traditions as it includes within its limits the finest examples of the rock-cut mode, such as Ajanta and Ellora, which in themselves are sufficient to provide a grand source for architectural inspiration. This rock method of expression, to all intents and purposes, was drawing to a close towards the end of the tenth century, so that with the beginning of the structural movement, now to be described a new era of architectural development dawns.

Situated as this region is between two other architectural movements of great power, its productions could not fail to be affected by the characteristics of their style. For on the one hand it extended towards the north in the direction of Gujarat, where a very distinctive type of structure had been evolved under the patronage of the Solanki dynasty, while on the other, towards the south, it was within reach of the influence of the later Chalukyan mode, a manifestation of temple architecture of even greater significance. But although the Deccani temples show evidences of the proximity of these two divergent developments, none the less they also display certain notable features of an independent and original order entitling them to separate treatment.[1]

One of the most prominent of the self-originated characteristics in the Deccani type of temple is observable in the design of the sikhara, which is decidedly different from that of any other region. Instead of the turrets or *urusringas* being grouped around the lower part of this structure, as in most examples, the Deccan sikhara has a pronounced vertical band carried up each of its angles, taking the form of a " spine " or quoin. This feature extends from the lower cornice right up to the finial, and displays functional qualities of a high order, as it follows the main contours of the spire thus holding the entire shape within its firm outline. (Plates LXXXVII and CXI). Then the spaces between these quoins are filled in with rows of small reproductions of the sikhara itself, each supported on a pedestal like an altar, the contrast of this strongly marked repeating pattern with the more delicate diaper on the quoins producing an effect of some emphasis. The same principle was employed in the formation of the other portion of the temple scheme, as the pyramidal roof of the mandapa is composed of diminishing rows of miniature multiples of itself, so that this singularly artistic system is the keynote of the composition as a whole.

A certain originality is also noticeable in the plans of these temples, as in the larger examples they are laid out on a diagonal arrangement, and there is also a marked elaboration in the shape of the walls. A feature of the temple plans in several regions are the projections and recesses of the wall surfaces, which as they mount upwards, catch the light or retain the shade, adding an unusual vitality to the character of the elevational effect. This method was carried to its extreme limit in the Deccani temples so that few structures are more varied or have greater vivacity of appearance than the fluted examples of this large group. In more than one instance this treatment has been carried almost to excess, as in the case of the temple of Jagadambadevi at Kokamthan, where the exterior is so ruggedly patterned as to resemble a form of eroded rock. Fully aware of the effect of this vertical tendency in his scheme and to counteract any undue upward trend the designer threw across the entire composition a close series of horizontal passages, chiefly in the form of mouldings, the two systems combined comprising the architectural make-up of his conception. Many of these mouldings are of a special variety, having a kind of knife-edged section, and named *kani*. The *kani* moulding runs throughout many of the examples like a theme, observable not only on the wall surfaces, but it is particularly noticeable in the design of the pillars, sometimes giving the building a sharp linear effect distinctive of the productions of this region.

The pillars, also of the Deccani style, are of an original order, as apart from the frequent use of the *kani* moulding, they have other decisive features. No struts or detached brackets are used in the capitals, but above the uppermost moulding is a support in the shape of a scroll or volute, almost Ionic in its graceful curves. The vase and foliage motif is conspicuous by its absence, an inadequate attempt to reproduce it however being occasionally discernible. Although the greater part of the pillar shaft is richly moulded, the lower third is usually a severely plain square prism, a contrast almost too pronounced to be pleasing. Yet this was not always the practice, as in some of the larger temples the lower part of the pillar was so profusely sculptured with figures as to form a kind of shrine. To produce the fine mouldings on the pillars, these were turned on a large and somewhat crude type of lathe, a technical process freely employed by the Chalukyan craftsmen, from whom it was no doubt derived, and which enabled the sharp knife-edged section (*kani*) to be readily obtained. A pillared treatment was introduced into the jambs of the shrine doorways in the form of an attached pillar, or nook-shaft, evidently suggested by the pilasters on some of the rock-cut shrines of the previous period. That the rock-cut tradition of this region still lingered is shown in a striking manner by the design of one of these structural temples of the eleventh century. As an example of the living influence of the powerful rock-cut phase, at Balsane there is a temple (No. 5) the plan of which, with its portico, pillared hall, series of cells on either side the cella with its vestibule, is in the arrangement of these compartments, almost an exact counterpart

[1] Mediæval Temples of the Dakkan by H. Cousens, Arch. Sur. of Ind., Vol. XLVIII, Calcutta, 1931.

of a Mahayana Buddhist monastery excavated out of the rock in the seventh century A.D.

Even the largest of these Deccani temples is of very moderate size, that at Sinnar one of the most spacious, being barely eighty feet in its entire length; but these limited dimensions were occasioned, to some extent, by the manner of their construction. The proportions of the building were determined by a unit, this unit being the height of the monolithic shaft of the pillar in the interior, which, in its turn, depended on the greatest length of stone it was economically possibe to extract from the quarry. As all parts of the temple were proportioned strictly according to rule, each member being in fixed ratio to all the others, the pillar shaft served as a standard for the purpose of measurement, and the entire composition was therefore executed to that scale. In view also of the relatively large extent of the territory concerned, the temples of this type are not numerous. Of all kinds there are less than fifty, only ten of which are of real significance. From this selection it is however possible to illustrate each phase of its development, extending over a period of three centuries.

11th century	..	Temple of Ambarnatha, Thana District. Triple-shrined temple at Balsane, and temple of Maheswara, both in Khandesh.
12th century	..	Gondeswara Temple at Sinnar, and the Mahadeva Temple at Jhogda, both Nasik District. Temple of Lakshmi-Narayan at Pedgaon, Ahmednagar District.
13th century	..	Temple of Naganatha at Aundh, Andhra Pradesh.
13th century	..	"Hemadpanti" type. Temple of Daitya-Sundana at Lonar ; Vishnu Temple at Satgaon ; Temple at Mahkar, all in the Deccan.

Probably the finest of the whole group, and also one of the earliest of its kind is the temple of Ambarnatha in the Thana District of the Bombay State. (Plate CXI, Fig. 1). Although not situated strictly within the confines of the Deccan, it is quite clearly of the same style as the temples which developed there. Moreover, it provides a fixed date from which this group as a whole may be considered, as it bears an inscription equivalent to A.D. 1060. In a delightful situation by the side of a long deep pool, this temple, when complete, was a model of rich perfection, typical of the style when the architect had been given a free hand and unlimited time. For there are few buildings of the Indo-Aryan order, which display more refined architectural perception combined at the same time with intricate decoration lavishly but tastefully applied. To the western eye, disciplined to the principle of ornamental passages being balanced by plain spaces, such a tumult of sculptured forms distributed over every surface of the structure, the piling of ornament upon ornament, apparently defying all the accepted conventions of the building art, is bewildering. But a study of this temple reveals the fact that, although the plastic embellishment may lack restraint, and implies occasional formlessness, the architectural and functional treatment of the structure as a whole, is reasoned and logical.

In the first place, the designer's principal aim was clearly variety of effect, and he therefore began by aligning the two essential parts of the temple diagonally astride the axial line, joining them at their inner angles. This produced an attractive plan measuring 90 feet long by 75 feet in width. Then he broke up the sides of this conception by a close series of vertical projections and recesses, in some respects corresponding to buttresses, but without their structural purpose. For the intention of these upright passages was mainly decorative, the object being by this system to elaborate the chiaroscuro, to multiply the shadows and lights and thus attain animation and movement. The remaining architectural treatment of the building, comprising the horizontal mouldings of the *kani* or knife-edged type, the quoins of the sikhara, and the multiplication to a smaller scale of the architectural features to make up the pattern of the structure, were all applied according to the system already described.

This temple is entered by three doorways, one on each of the free angles of the assembly hall, and the interior consists of a single compartment, with attached pillars at each of its eight angles and a group of four forming the square nave in the centre. There is a considerable amount of excellent carving in the ceiling panels and shallow domes of this interior, but it was on the pillars of the main hall that the sculptor was most prodigal with his art, as, from base to capital, these are intricately carved with both conventional designs and figure subjects. The most highly finished are the four detached columns in the nave, each of which on account of its wealth of imagery, of gods in niches and figures in friezes, ceases to be a structural element and becomes a complete tabernacle or altar in itself. (Plate CXIV). Corresponding to these central pillars are those attached to the angles of the hall, each being treated in much the same decorative manner, but in a slightly simpler scheme, the whole effect, although superlatively ornate, being very carefully thought out. Throughout the design and execution of those pillars there is much that recalls the style of those in Gujarat, such as the marble columns in the Vimala temple at Abu, yet there is a certain individuality of treatment that indicates that Deccani productions were a separate effort, but obviously influenced by the power of the widely spread Solanki movement.

Another site containing buildings in this style, and in this instance within the Deccan, as it is in Khandesh, is that of Balsane, where there is a group of nine temples, the erection of which may have extended over a period of one hundred and fifty years. Of these a triple-shrined structure (No. 1) is of much the same design as that at Ambarnatha and no doubt of approximately the same date, but it is smaller in size as it is only sixty-five feet long by fifty feet wide. Although of such moderate proportions it is a building of considerable beauty, while among its many ornate features, the shrine entrance is a most striking production. At the base of this doorway are the usual groups of divinities, and rising above these on each side is the decorative "nookshaft" which characterises the shrines of this class. These shafts support a prominent cornice over which is a range of miniature tabernacles and other similar ornamental motifs all carefully distributed and elegantly designed. Interposed within this scheme are patterned mouldings of figures and foliage which, together with illustrations of symbol and myth, depict all that the artist's fancy could recall and ingenuity conceive. Of the other examples at Balsane, temples Nos. 2 and 3, by their style, may have been built fifty years later, at the beginning of the twelfth century, while No. 4 is notable because in the plan of its shrine exterior, the star-shaped principle appears, allying it with the Chalukyan temples of Mysore. To complete this instructive group is temple No. 5 already referred to as being, in its lay out, almost an exact copy of a type of rock-cut vihara at Ajanta and Ellora, both these monumental developments of rock-architecture being barely fifty miles distant.

Representing the style at its next stage, during the first half of the twelfth century, is one of the most complete and best preserved buildings of the Deccan series, the Gonde-swara temple at Sinnar, in the Nasik district. (Plate CXV, Fig. 1). An example of the *panchayatana* class, as the temple is surrounded by four small supplementary shrines, the whole conception stands on a moulded and stepped platform measuring 125 feet by 95 feet. With a Nandi pavilion facing the eastern main entrance, the group of structures forming the entire composition is symmetrically disposed on this elevated space in a very competent manner. The main building occupying the centre of the platform is elegantly proportioned, its two parts, the sabha-mandapa with the vimana behind rising above it, although obviously separate compartments, are blended into an architectural unity by the same cornice being carried round the whole structure, thus binding them together. Yet the difference in the two portions of the conception is emphasized by the treatment of their roofs, both being composed of miniature models of themselves, those in the sabha-mandapa being short flat shapes characteristic of that structure, while on the vimana they are the taller forms of the sikhara. The extreme dimensions of this building measure 78 feet in length and 67 feet in breadth, and the inside of the pillared hall is only 21 feet square, but the three outstanding columned porticos by which it is entered add not a little to its size, grace, and dignified appearance. Although the general proportions of this temple are as good as any of its class, on the other hand there is a falling off in the quality of the sculpture adorning its walls which seems to indicate that a decline in the style was beginning at this date.

In addition to the Gondeswara temple, Sinnar contains the remains of another temple, which, because it is of a different tradition and date, is of unusual interest. This is the temple of Aesvara, a building in the Chalukyan style, the most northerly example of the mode usually associated with the country of Mysore. Yet, probably owing to its isolated situation, it has assimilated certain features of the Indo-Aryan development of the Deccan, such as the atlantean figures, or *kichaka* bracket above the capitals, a motif unknown to the Chalukyan builders. Moreover, it appears

to have been built as early as the eleventh century, and is therefore anterior to the Gondeswara temple, indicating that it was in existence while that temple was being constructed, but clearly without in any way influencing its northern architectural character. The inference is that, although buildings in the Chalukyan manner were produced over a wide area, they had no marked effect on the indigenous regional manifestation, both types evolving independently.

The course of the style is carried a step further by several temples built probably after the middle of the twelfth century, of which one of a group of five near the village of Pedgaon in the Ahmednagar District is a typical example. This is the temple of Lakshmi-Narayan, a small structure measuring only 54 feet by 35 feet but so finely proportioned and profusely sculptured as to present a perfect but miniature model of its class. A noticeable departure in the architectural character of this building is in the treatment of the pillars, which include in their design the " vase and foliage " element, a motif not found in the previous examples of these parts, but evidently imported from Gujarat. Another original expedient is in the walls of the pillared hall, as these are composed of square panels containing perforated patterns thus admitting more light and air into this compartment than in the older temples. This system appears to have been derived from the Chalukyan style as it prevailed towards the south, where highly decorated and intricately perforated screen walls are characteristic.

During the latter half of the thirteenth century, and also extending into the early fourteenth century a considerable number of temples were built, which are referred to all over the Deccan as in the Hemadpanti style, their production being ascribed to a great patron of temple architecture of the name of Hemadpant.[1] This semi-legendary personage has been identified as most probably a famous prime minister of Ramchandradeva, the last of the Devagiri rajas, who ascended the throne in A.D. 1272. A high and influential official, Hemadpant had a passion for temple building, and appears to have been responsible for the erection of many religious edifices within this region. The temples designated as Hemadpanti are distinguished by their heavy proportions and bald and uninteresting architectural treatment, and, what is particularly noticeable, the scarcity of figure sculpture on their exteriors. Common though the temples of this type are in the Deccan, they are uninspiring conceptions, apparently illustrating the building art of these parts when the real spirit had gone out of it, under the ominous shadow of the impending Islamic domination.

---

[1] Proceedings of the Royal Asiatic Society of Bengal, Calcutta, 1873.

REFERENCES.

Cousens, H., *Mediaeval Temples of the Dakkan*, Arch. Sur. of Ind., Vol. XLVIII, Cal. 1931.
Taylor, Meadows, *The Architecture of Dharwar amd Mysore*, London, 1866.

CHAPTER XXVI

THE NORTHERN OR INDO-ARYAN STYLE—(concluded)

THE TEMPLES AT GWALIOR (11th century) AND BRINDABAN (16th century)

THE sacred buildings within the Fort at Gwalior, as a whole, differ little in their architectural style from those of the surrounding country, although as they form a small series by themselves, they invite separate description. On the other hand the other group included in this chapter, that at Brindaban near Muttra, a hundred miles to the north and built several centuries later, consists of several temples of a specially localized order. Of the earlier series, those at Gwalior, there are some eleven structures of a religious character within the perimeter of this rock-bound fortress, five of which take the form of temples. Out of the five, three only are of importance, while their architectural composition is such as to give them considerable significance. According to an inscription the largest of the three, known as the greater Sas-Bahu was finished in A.D. 1093, and the other two cannot be far removed from this in date, so that all may be regarded as representative of the style in these parts towards the end of the eleventh century, or shortly after.

If any one of this small series is earlier than the others it is that designated the Teli-ka-Mandir, or Oilman's temple, a name for which there is no convincing explanation, a tall commanding structure eighty feet in height, and of a distinctly unusual appearance. (Plate CXVI, Fig. 2). In its conception this building is rather more of a shrine than a temple, as it consists of a sanctuary only, comprising a tower together with a substantial porch and doorway leading to an interior cella ; there is attached to it no assembly hall or mandapa, and none of those pillared pavilions which ordinarily formed part of the fully developed temple structure. Moreover it is also exceptional in that no parts of its plan are square, its shape externally being an oblong, 60 feet by 46 feet, and so is the inner chamber, which is 30 feet by 15 feet, as well as the passage connecting this with the doorway. Naturally the formation of the ground plan conditions the elevation, which apart from its configuration, is also from base to summit treated in a decidedly different manner from any other sanctuaries in the Indo-Aryan style. The most marked departure from the orthodox design of the temple tower is in the composition of the summit or roof. Owing to the oblong formation being continued throughout its height, the upper part of the building is also oblong in shape, and it is clear therefore that it could not be finished off by means of the usual pyramidal construction. But it was evidently never the intention of the designers to complete in it this fashion, for they proceeded to give it a superstructure similar to the vaulted roof of a Buddhist chaitya hall. To emphasize this Buddhist character there is a form of sun-window at either end, a keeled ridge with finials, and pillared arcades derived from the rock-cut colonnade system along each of its longitudinal sides. The porch continues the idea, as it is carried up almost to the height of the roof and appears also to have terminated in a chaitya arch gable.

The Teli-ka-Mandir represents a rare type of Brahmanical sanctuary, for probably the only other example in the Indo-Aryan style with a sikhara of this order, a relic of their distant Buddhist heritage, is the Vaital Deul at Bhubaneswar, a Siva temple of the Orissan group and erected a century earlier. Both these temples, although separated by half the width of the entire sub-continent, are notable illustrations of the manner in which certain thought-forms, evolved during a much earlier movement and based on different ideals, emerged after a long interval to be incorporated in their structural composition.

More orthodox in style than the preceding, are the two remaining temples of the series in Gwalior Fort, both designated Sas-Bahu, literally the " mother-in-law and daughter-in-law," the origin of which nomenclature is also obscure. Both are in much the same architectural mode, the smaller of the two, although an elegant little building, in comparison with the large example, of which it is a reduced and simplified copy, is relatively unimportant. For, apart from considerations of style and structure the large Sas-Bahu temple is a most informative production, its composition and treatment generally adding not a little to our knowledge of architectural development at this period. (Plate CXVII). Dedicated to Vishnu in the last years of the eleventh century, although still a grand pile, this temple is but a portion of the original conception, as only the main hall or mandapa remains, the vimana with its sikhara which was probably 150 feet in height having disappeared. On plan the building is in the form of a cross, the entire length being 100 feet, the width across the transepts 63 feet, while the height of the great hall was originally about 80 feet.

As only the great hall is now the part in existence, it is from this structure alone that the architectural style of the Sas-Bahu can be judged, but it is quite sufficient for the purpose. Externally this maha-mandapa or assembly hall is in three stories, which take the form of open galleries or loggias surrounding the building on all sides. Each story is defined by a massive architrave, with the spaces between occupied by pillars and piers, the effect of the facades being that of large open arcades. The roof is partly demolished, but was an arrangement of diminishing tiers of ornamental masonry rising up into a low pyramidal or domical formation. Undoubtedly much of the vivid and vigorous appearance of the exterior elevation of this structure was obtained by the skilful conception of its plan, one of the underlying objects of which was to enable the facades to be projected into a bold combination of contrasting planes. These planes, interrupted by columns alternating at regulated intervals with openings, have been so devised as to produce a successive correlation of solids and voids, of passages of light merging into graduated shadows, which make the exterior of this building, from all points of view, a composition of more than ordinary elegance.

The interior arrangements of this hall are as artistically ingenious as the exterior. It has been remarked that the building is in three stories, but this does not apply to the

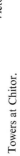

Fig. 2
Victory Tower of Kumbha Rana ; c. A.D. 1450.

Fig. 1
Tower of Fame ; c. 1100.

Towers at Chitor.

Fig. 2

Fig. 1

Dabhoi, Baroda: City Gateways; 12th century A.D.

Fig. 2

Brindaban, Muttra: Temple of Jagal Kishore; 16th century.

Fig. 1

Ambarnath: Mahadev Temple, Pillar in Hall; 11th century.

Fig. 1
Sinnar, Nasik Dist.: Gondeswara Temple; 12th century.

Fig. 2
Brindaban, Muttra: Govind Dev Temple; A.D. 1590.

Fig. 2

Gwalior: Teli-ka-Mandir; 11th century A.D.

Fig. 1

Brindaban, Muttra: Govind Dev Temple, Interior: A.D. 1500.

Gwalior: Larger Sas Bahu Temple; 11th century A.D.

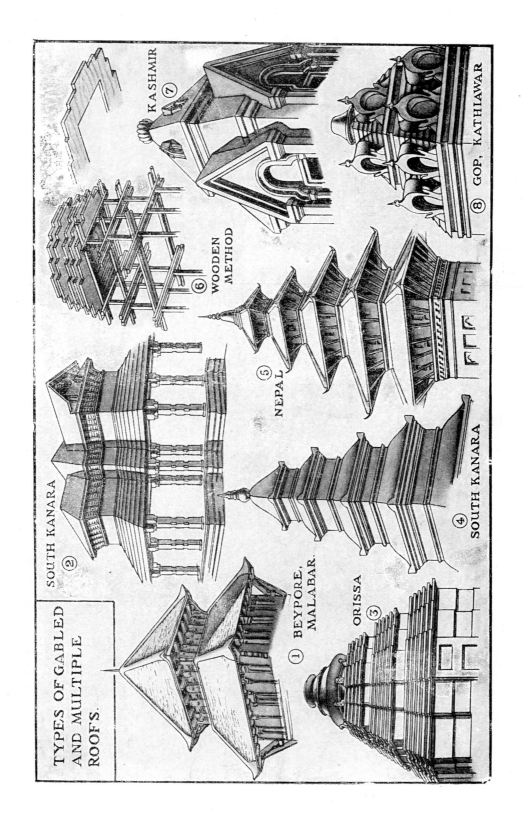

TYPES OF GABLED AND MULTIPLE ROOFS.

① BEYPORE, MALABAR.

② SOUTH KANARA

③ ORISSA

④ SOUTH KANARA

⑤ NEPAL

⑥ WOODEN METHOD

⑦ KASHMIR

⑧ GOP, KATHIAWAR

Fig. 1.   Chandranatha Jain Temple; Mudabidri, South Kanara.

Fig. 2.   Travancore: Thuruvalla Temple;
Temples with Gabled Roofs.

interior which is one large central chamber, contained within the ranges of open galleries forming the outside facades. In other words it consists of one tall compartment only, around which project the loggias, one above the other, which comprise the triple stories of its external elevation. The central hall, however, which corresponds in some respects to the " crossing " of a Gothic church as it is where the nave and transepts meet, was over thirty feet in diameter, a wide space to be bridged by the only method then employed by the Indian masons, and, moreover, above this it was necessary to support the solid stone courses of the roof. The problem was solved by introducing into the interior four massive piers, and on these large but shapely supports the superincumbent masonry was imposed. But such an expedient naturally destroys any effect of open spaces, and makes the interior somewhat congested.

From the design of this temple it is possible to understand the constructional principles adopted by the builders in other large temples of this class, as for instance the Rudra Mala at Siddhapur, that fragment of a one-time immense structure in Gujarat. It reveals to us how these temples in several stories were produced without arches or other scientific methods, but solely by means of the pillar and the beam, a system which had limitations as the interiors of these buildings plainly demonstrate. For they could have no large halls uninterrupted by pillars, no spacious covered courts in their internal arrangements ; their plans were restricted by the length of the stone lintel that could safely carry the required loads, and that this was occasionally miscalculated is shown by the cracked beams in a number of temples, including the Sas-Bahu now described. But there is something more to be learned from this example at Gwalior, not connected with temple construction, but with that of some of the mosques which began to be built a little later. It was on the principle of the Sas-Bahu interior that those pillared naves forming the central feature of the Islamic prayer halls at Ahmedabad and Champaner were evolved, but with more grace, more space, and more refinement than that ever produced in the assembly halls of the temples. Yet it was from these temple mandapas that the mosque builders developed those noble central spaces surrounded by pillars and carried up in stages to the vaulted roof, a conception of rare beauty and one which gives its prevailing character to the *masjids* of Gujarat.

Passing now to the series of Brahmanical buildings at Brindaban of a much later date, this town, although small in itself, figures very large in the minds of many on account of its association with Krishna, as it was the scene of some of this popular god's most notable exploits. Here is a group of five temples, all built of red sandstone, and in a style of architecture different from any others of their kind ; these temples are (1) Gobind Devi, (2) Radha Ballabh, (3) Gopi Nath, (4) Jugal Kishore, and (5) Madan Mohan. The mode adopted in their design is a purely local development, confined solely to Brindaban, and was the outcome of an exceptional concurrence of circumstances. In the first place these temples are relatively late in date, as they were all produced towards the end of the sixteenth century or the beginning of the seventeenth, a period corresponding approximately to that covered by the reign of the Mughal Emperor Akbar (1556-1605). By this time the Islamic style of architecture introduced and fostered by the Muhammedan rulers, had obtained a firm hold, although hitherto confined entirely to the buildings belonging to that creed. Owing however to the " Great Mogul's " notable toleration, the

temples at Brindaban were allowed to be erected in the heart of his dominions, being in most instances built to the order of certain Hindu princes who had allied themselves to the Mughal power. The reason for the selection of this site is explained by the fact that just previously there had been a widespread revival of the Krishna cult, brought about by the preachings of the famous Vaishnava reformer, Chatanya (1486-1534).

The largest and most important of the temples at Brindaban is that of Gobind Devi, built in 1590, now a truncated composition, as its sanctuary was completely destroyed during the reign of Aurengzabe. (Plate CXV, Fig. 2). What remains therefore is the assembly hall or *maha-mandapa* which takes the shape of a spacious cruciform structure, with the eastern arm converted into an extemporary sanctuary in place of the one which originally extended out of this and has disappeared. The present building differs but little in the proportions of its plan from a Greek cross, as its arms from east to west measure 177 feet and it is 105 feet in breadth ; when the sanctuary existed the whole composition may have been as much as 175 feet in length. Externally the principles on which this temple has been designed are not dissimilar from those of other large temples in the Indo-Aryan style, as for example the Sas-Bahu at Gwalior described above, its elevation being formed of several stories containing open arcades. But the manner in which this traditional arrangement has been treated, shows that during the intervening period the builders had acquired an entirely new orientation in the field of temple architecture. The Gobind Devi temple signifies, as comprehensively as any building could do, the change that had taken place in the constitution of this part of the country, owing to the conditions brought about by the Islamic domination, a change, in the case of the building art, from the aesthetically natural to the ordered conventional, from architecture produced largely by rule of thumb, to that resulting from the application of certain well-defined structural principles. One noticeable fact in this temple is the almost entire absence of figure-carving, a circumstance not improbably due to the Islamic usage prohibiting any display of imagery, and communicated to the guilds of artisans by the Emperor Akbar, although that monarch himself was no bigot in this respect. The consequence of these various influences is that while the Gobind Devi temple is an architectural composition of no little formal beauty, consisting as it does of a combination of balconies and loggias, of bracketed archways and moulded buttresses, wide eaves and ornamental parapets, all carefully disposed so as to be in perfect accord with one another, there is at the same time an almost complete absence of that quality of humanism, together with a deficiency in that supreme spiritual content which one has learned to expect incorporated in the design of all Hindu temples of the more orthodox type. In this building more than in any other we see the effect of the imposition of Islamic ideals on those of the Hindus, perpetuated in stone. Even more pronounced is the outcome of this impact on the structural treatment of the interior, which except for the fact that the entire conception appears to be an anomaly, is a very fine architectural effort of great mandapa, instead of being the low curved ceiling usual in the temple design, consists of a high vaulted dome formed of intersecting pointed arches, in its structural procedure not unlike what is known as the four-part pointed vaulting of the Gothic style. This system of roofing in the temple is an illustration of the influence of the contemporary construction of the Mughals being copied and adapted from that used in several of the mosques of this period, as for instance in the aisles of the Jami Masjid (c. 1580) at Fatehpur Sikri, the state capital of the Emperor Akbar. (Plate CXVI, Fig. 1).

Of the remaining temples, that of Jugal Kishore is the most prominent, as its shrine, octagonal in plan, is intact and attached by one of its sides to a rectangular assembly hall. (Plate CXIV, Fig. 2). Although externally the sanctuary is an octagon of 35 feet in diameter, the cella in its interior is a square of only 17 feet side. The interior of the assembly hall is also a square of dimensions differing but little from those of the cella, leaving therefore a great thickness of wall around both compartments. In the case of the assembly hall within this mass of masonry small chambers have been introduced, as well as recesses for images. Around the main eastern entrance there is a considerable amount of carving which has a noticeable Islamic flavour. But the most distinctive portions of several of these Brindaban temples are the sikharas which in style and shape are unique, as they bear little or no resemblance to any other kind of Indian temple spire. They rise from an octagonal plan and taper into a tall conical tower (that of Madan Mohan being as much as sixty-five feet in height) with a broad band of mouldings outlining each angle. At intervals throughout their height are similar bands of mouldings placed transversely, so that the surface effect is that of a series of diminishing rectangular panels. Overhanging the whole at the apex is a ponderous finial, or *amasila*, a flat circular disc, its outer edge ornamented with a border of massive knob-like petals or flutes. The attempt by means of this unusual treatment to achieve something original has been successful, but as a work of art this form of sikhara has not much to commend it.

REFERENCE

Cunningham, A., *Archaeological Survey of India*, Vol. II, 1864-65.

CHAPTER XXVII

TEMPLES WITH GABLED OR MULTIPLE ROOFS

AS in the case of most civilizations, the arts of India have evolved by means of a sequence of movements, one superseding the other, so that a cross-section of the whole would present a series of strata not unlike that of a geological formation. In the course of development most of these art strata have become obliterated by subsequent " deposits," but on the other hand in several instances these movements have been so persistent that portions are still visible, like an outcrop, as proof of their one-time prevalence. Such is a certain type of roof structure of a very distinctive character, which reveals itself in a variety of forms, and in widely different parts of the sub-continent. This roof is of the gabled or multiple order and appears to be a survival of a wooden type, which was apparently not uncommon in India towards the beginning of the Christian era. There are various references by Chinese pilgrims to towers and shrines several stories high which these adventurous travellers saw while in Buddhist India, and of which they brought back small copies for reproduction to the original scale in their own country. It is not unlikely therefore that, as with the distinctive Indian *torana* gateway, which became the *piu-lu* of China, so from these multiple roofed structures of Buddhist India was derived the many storied pagoda of the Far East.

That a form of roof constructed on the laminated or " clinker-built " system of overlapping planks and possibly in tiers, was employed in early Indian building seems fairly clear ; for something of the kind, reproduced in stone, appears in the roofs and sikharas of the temples in the Indo-Aryan style, specially noticeable in those of Orissa. Rathas, or temple cars, in parts of the country are still fashioned of timber in this manner, each horizontal section taking the form of a wooden frame, with blocks fitted between to keep each layer apart, as is still simulated in stone in the temple roof. (Plate CXVIII, Fig. 6). In the architecture of certain parts of the Himalayas, as for instance in the countries of Nepal and Kashmir, reminiscences of the gabled and multiple type of structure still prevail, reproduced in wood, metal, tiles and stone. But it is significant that a somewhat similar manifestation of this Himalayan style of building also occurs in two distant and relatively remote localities in the south and west of the Indian peninsula. One of these developments is found in Kathiawar and repeats certain characteristics of the Kashmir type, while the other, which is as far south as in Malabar, appertains more to the Nepal style.

The temples which appear to have an affinity to those of Kashmir, were produced in Kathiawar by an immigrant tribe known as Mers,[1] during the last half of the first millennium, and therefore contemporary with the Kashmir examples. Both the Mer and Kashmir temples are square in plan, with a central sanctuary, but the principal parallelism is in the formation of the roofs. In each type these are pyramidal in shape, and rise up into two tiers, the upper overhanging the lower, rather in the manner of the stories of a Chinese pagoda. Added to this in the Mer design, although the temples are Brahmanical, there are Buddhist chaitya arches in the form of dormer-windows projecting from the sloping portion, but these, in the Kashmir structure, are in the shape of pediments and trefoil arches. It is not therefore so much a resemblance in the actual elements making up these two types of temple formation that is remarkable, but it is in the principles underlying their construction that there is observable a distinct similarity of motive. (Plate CXVIII, Fig. 7 and 8). In view of their wide geographical separation, any direct contact between the two countries is improbable ; what is more likely is that some mutual pattern of thought-mould evolved, which accounts for this approximation of forms, rather than any interchange of technical experience.

The temples in Kathiawar of this type are at Gop, Kadvar, and Bilesvara, while something of the same character may be seen in a temple at Visavada, and in the temple of Surya at Sutrapada. All are relatively small in size, measuring on an average forty feet across, while the period of their production appears to have been from the sixth to the eighth or ninth centuries. The temple at Gop is certainly the oldest, as it is presumed to be not later than the sixth century, and no doubt introduced the style into these parts. (Plate CXVIII, Fig. 8). It is considerably ruined, but it is not difficult to reconstruct its arrangements from the later but better preserved example at Bilesvara. On plan these structures consisted of a square central shrine, enclosed within a square covered court, the larger size of the latter producing a spacious aisle all round. This aisle was flat-roofed, and out of its centre rose a pyramidal structure covering the shrine and its cella. The chief claim of this type of temple to any architectural merit lies in the treatment of this pyramidal superstructure, which, particularly in the example at Gop, is a well shaped and convincing piece of work. In this instance the central feature rises well above the roof of the aisles, standing up high enough to be called a tower, and its pyramidal portion is in two tiers of square section surmounted by a substantial finial, or *amalasila*, which is circular in plan. On each side of the lower tier are two " chaitya-dormers," while the upper tier has only one, and it is the position, proportions, and general design of these ornamental arched projections that give this building much of its character. In the recess, or niche of each of these chaitya motifs, a figure or miniature altar is enshrined, in one on the western side a statuette of Ganesh is still identifiable, but the conception as a whole has a distinctly Buddhistic derivation. As this type of temple progressed it began to lose its apparently exotic nature, and to conform more to the indigenous Indo-Aryan style, although there is still much of the " vihara " influence in that at Bilesvara, perhaps of the eighth century. Later, the shrines at Visvada, and the Surya temple at Sutrapada, show how it was becoming merged into the conventional form of Brahmancial temple design. Finally, before the end of the first millennium, it has disappeared and seemingly has contributed nothing to the style of building which followed.

---

[1] Archaeological Survey of India, Vol. XLV, Imperial Series, *Somanatha* by H. Cousens.

The other group of temples, recalling the style that appertains to the country of Nepal is still more distant from the Himalayas, as it is situated in the coastal region of Malabar. Of these examples decidedly the most remarkable is located in the small seaport of Beypore, south of Calicut. Here is an ancient Siva temple, the Mahadeva Kovil, which in both design and construction appears to be a deliberate copy of a double roofed Nepalese temple of the late mediaeval period. (Plate CXVIII, Fig. 5).[1] As both types are over thirteen hundred miles apart, the one in a seaside town and the other in a remote valley in the Himalayas, the resemblance is difficult to explain. One theory is that a presumed anthropological connection existed between the Nayars of Malabar and the Newars of Nepal, while another accounts for the pagoda-like attribution by a contact with China by sea as proved by the Chinese type of fishing nets used on this coast.[2]

Less like copies of the Newar shrines of Nepal, but still resembling the architecture of the Himalayas, is a series of temples in South Kanara, a tract of country on the western side of Mysore State. There are as many as sixteen examples of this style, all Jain temples and situated at Mudabidri, about twenty miles north-east of Mangalore, the earliest dating from the twelfth century, and the others at intervals during the following four centuries. Although built of stone masonry, these buildings are clearly copies of wooden construction, as may be seen in the shape and design of their verandahs which have pillars resembling chamfered logs of wood, sloping roofs imitating planks, and gables formed on the penthouse principle, with wide projecting eaves. And in the style of their architecture as displayed in the pyramidal roof of overhanging stories, supported by brackets and struts, they recall the types common in the mountains of the north, as well as to a lesser degree the stone temples of Kashmir. In the case of these Mudabidri temples some of the similarity to the Himalayan style may be accounted for by the builders in each region endeavouring in their construction to solve problems presented by the extreme changes of climate, in mitigating the effect of the fierce tropical sun alternating with heavy monsoon rains. Yet it is difficult to believe that the analogy between the two styles of building and methods of construction is due to both people reasoning alike.

One of the finest of the Mudabidri group is the temple of Chandranatha, which may have been built early in the fifteenth century. It is contained within a high walled enclosure having an entrance on the east, which opens immediately on to a fine free-standing pillar (mana-stambha) in front of the main doorway. The temple building consists of three halls, corresponding to mandapas, all combined and connected with the vimana containing the cella, in which is the divinity, or Tirthankar. It was the custom of two and sometimes three of these compartments to form the front portion of this class of temple, and, each of these to be designated by a name, in the Chandranatha example they are known as the Tirthankara, Gaddije, and Bhiradevi or Chitra mandapas. (Plate CXIX, Fig. 1).

If the exteriors of these temples suggest a wooden origin, the interiors are obviously lithic, as the numerous pillars of the mandapas plainly testify. The Mudabidri type of pillar is a thickset solid production, in all some twelve feet in height, with the lower third consisting of a plain square prism, in marked contrast to the remainder of the shaft, which is circular in section and profusely moulded. As to the capital this is a composition of brackets and pendent lotus buds around a square abacus, the whole a most ornate conception. In their design these pillars are closely allied to what may be referred to as the Chalukyan order, as this prevailed at the time in the country of Mysore. They were produced also by the same technical process, the heavy rounded mouldings being obtained by turning the monolithic shaft in a large lathe. The pillars in the Bhiradevi mandapa of the Chandranatha temple are exceptionally elaborate, the shafts being moulded and chiselled into all kinds of fine patterns. Certain parts of these are undercut into detached lotus petals and miniature balustrades all executed with incredible precision, patience, and skill.

In the neighbourhood of Mudabidri is a series of monuments which in style, character, and intention are even more unusual than the temples. They are tombs of the priests, and are a form of sepulchre practically unique in India, for Buddhist, Jain or Hindu rarely included any kind of mausoleum in their usage. In this instance however it appears to have been a local custom to erect a cenotaph in memory of the temple incumbent, although they bear no inscriptions or other means of identification. The style of these monuments is that of a pagoda-like pyramid rising up into several diminishing stories, each story defined by a projecting cornice, the whole being crowned by a finial. (Plate CXVIII, Fig. 4). There are several of these cenotaphs all grouped together, some of the larger are in as many as eight stories and mounting up to nearly thirty feet in height, but although of original design they possess little that is artistically distinctive.

Another group of temples in the Kanara country, rather more to the north, is in the town of Bhatkal and although constructed of stone, their exteriors are most astonishingly wooden in appearance.[3] They are all built on the double penthouse principle, with expansive stone roofs in imitation of laminated or overlapping planks. No sikhara or tower of any kind rises above these roofs to distinguish them as religious buildings, but in front there is usually an elegant stambha or free-standing pillar forming part of the temple design. Even more expressive of a timber derivation than the roofs, is the system of stone screens which close in the sides of the structure, and are in horizontal slats, like Venetian blinds, or Indian jil-mils. That the construction of these temples is a frank copy of the domestic architecture of the locality, imitated in the laterite for permanence, is shown by the thatched houses of the people being of the same character with battens of palm stems for the screens. In this instance too, the style has been forced on the people by the conditions of the climate the driving rain on the one hand, and the hot humid atmosphere on the other, necessitating protection from the former and ventilation for the latter. (Plate CXIX).

Although the outward form of these temples at Bhatkal is of a purely practical nature, the innate desire of the Indian

¹ The Story of the Stupa, by A. Longhurst, Colombo, 1936.
² An Outline of Indian Temple Architecture, by F. H. Gravely, Madras, 1936.
³ Chalukyan Architecture, by Henry Cousens, Archaeological Survey of India, Vol. XLII, p. 134, Calcutta, 1926.

for ornamentation was not to be denied, for there is no inconsiderable amount of sculpture on those parts of the walls which permit of plastic decoration, and the standing column in front is invariably a graceful conception, as for instance that in the Ketapai Narayana temple of this group. But the interiors provided a better opportunity for embellishment, as they are all designed on the usual system of two conjoined compartments, a pillared hall in front and an enclosed sanctuary in the rear. There were accordingly considerable surfaces available for decorative carving, as may be seen on the walls and coffered ceiling. It was however on the pillars that the sculptors chiefly expended their skill and ingenuity, and these are as artistically treated with mouldings and figures in relief as are many other buildings of a much more pretentious character. As these temples plainly prove even in such remote localities it was part of the sociological system to maintain within the community a group of craftsmen of experience and ability.

REFERENCES.

Brown, Percy, *Picturesque Nepal*, London, 1912.
Longhurst, A. H., *The Story of the Stupa*, Colombo, 1936.

CHAPTER XXVIII

THE TEMPLE-CITIES OF THE JAINS

ALTHOUGH there is no style of architecture in India that can be referred to as Jain, the temples belonging to this religion show by their arrangements that they are neither Buddhist nor Brahmanical, but so designed as to conform to the ritual of the Jains. Mahavira, the last Jain leader, is generally regarded as the founder of the creed, but it is claimed that the same doctrine was propounded during countless ages by a succession of earlier teachers. There are twenty-four of these saints, known as Jinas or Tirthankars, literally " conquerors " or " leaders," and it is from the word " Jina " that the comparatively modern name of Jain is derived. These Jinas, or Tirthankars as they are more commonly called, having become deified, usually occupy similar high places in the Jain temple as the Hindu divinities do in theirs, and shrines are dedicated to them. And just as Jainism has not inaptly been defined as a theological mean between Buddhism and Brahmanism, progressing more or less parallel with these two creeds, so the architecture associated with each belief has also moved on parallel lines. Where the followers of Buddhism and Brahmanism have resorted to the rock-cut form of expression, the Jains have likewise excavated their places of worship, and where these have produced the structural type of temple, so the Jains have built theirs. Whether quarried out of the rock or built of masonry, the general character of the Jain architecture has been very similar in style to that of the Buddhists and Hindus of the same period and the same region.

In one respect however the Jains made a departure, when at some remote age, having appropriated certain " mountains of immortality " as sacred sites, they proceeded to erect on their summits a considerable aggregation of religious buildings, so that these formed what may be termed temple-cities. To use their own words they " ornamented these holy hills with a crown of eternal Arhat chaityas (tabernacles of saints) shining with the splendour of jewels." In spite of the known antiquity of these mountain sanctuaries few of the temples comprising them are earlier than the fifteenth century, and most are much later. Various causes have been responsible for the older buildings having been obliterated, one being the practice of the Jains themselves of pulling down their temples when decayed and erecting new ones in their places, many of the walls bearing evidences of this, as they reveal stones of previous structures having been built into them. Again, the creed during its long history has not been free from internal dissensions, an iconoclastic schism in the fifteenth century possibly being one of the factors responsible for few buildings having survived before this date. On the other hand the peculiarly militant appearance of some of these structural complexes as a whole implies that outside forces may at one time have subjected them to desecration and pillage, from a repetition of which they are now materially guarded. For, as they exist at present, these religious sites are surrounded by embattled walls, with their interiors divided up into tuks or wards, like the inner courts of fortified cities, the crenellated parapets being loop-holed and embrasured, each tuk having massive circular bastions at its angles, entry being obtained through strong gateways. It is a little incongruous to see projecting above this grim screen of defensive masonry a forest of graceful fanes belonging to so peaceful and humane a cult as that of the Jains. (Plate CXXI, Fig. 2).

These temple-cities, or tirthas (places of pilgrimage), are laid out on no specific plan, the buildings being arranged on such level spaces as the contours of the hill naturally provide. In one or two instances they consist of several hundreds of edifices, but contain no human habitation, as except for an occasional watchman, they are at night-time entirely deserted, the gods in their shrines being left to the protection of their own sanctity. Each tirtha represents centuries of devotion which found expression in temple building, and they form the central object of pilgrimages and festivals at frequent intervals. Although many of the temples may seem complicated in appearance, each is designed, as a rule, on the principles common to the religious architecture of the late mediæval period, the elaborations being due to such factors as the addition of numerous supplementary shrines, to the application of double stories, and to the practice of imposing pillared cloisters around all the larger examples. In the style of the individual buildings one variation found only in Jain temples is noticeable, and that is the frequent erection of a class of temple known as chaumukh, or " four-faced." This form of structure owes its shape to the particular character of the image it enshrines, as instead of a single figure facing one way, and therefore requiring only one entrance to the cella, the chaumukh is a quadruple image, or a group of four images, either of one Tirthankar, or of four different Tirthankars placed back to back so as to face the four cardinal points. Such a plan necessitated a shrine chamber with four doorways, a structural alteration which affected very considerably the design of the sanctuary, converting this into a cruciform compartment with an opening on each side. This again influenced the shape of the vimana as a whole, a circumstance of which the Jain builders took full advantage in their treatment of the exteriors of this temple type.

Two of the most important of these temple-cities are on mountains in Kathiawar, one being on the heights of Satrunjaya and the other on those of Girnar. The largest of all is that of Satrunjaya, south of the town of Palitana, and occupying the twin summits of the mountains, two thousand feet above sea level. Crowning these two ridges each some three hundred and fifty yards long, the line of buildings, several hundreds in number, follows approximately the shape of a letter S, one group running along the curve of the northern ridge and another the southern with a connecting group on the saddle forming the loop between. Out of this large number of shrines of various shapes and sizes, a characteristic example is the Chaumukh temple of Adinath standing within the Karalaravasi Tuk at the apex of the northern ridge. Built in A.D. 1618, on the site of a much earlier structure, it shows how the builders put into effect the plan of the " four-faced " shrine. The cell chamber, which is twenty-three feet square, is provided with the four requisite entrances, that on the east side being connected in the usual manner by a doorway with the assembly hall in front. The three other openings have porches leading into the surrounding courtyard, while above each porch rises an elegant second story with balconied windows, a feature having a definitely secular appearance, the whole buttressed against the lower part of the spire. In addition to this amplification of the vimana there is a range of exterior cells incorporated into its western walls and screened by a pillared verandah, a form of supplementary cloisters considerably enriching this portion of the structure. Although tending to produce the effect of one architectural element imposed on another, there is nevertheless a rich animation about this design which is commendable.

Dominating the opposite and southern ridge of Satrunjaya is another temple, not only typical of the style but celebrated for the antiquity of its foundation, as it occupies the most sacred site on the mountain, the *sanctum-sanctorum* of the *tirtha*. This is the Sri Adisvara which stands within the Vimalavasi Tuk, the present structure dating from A.D. 1530, but it fills the place of a much older temple erected in A.D. 960, and there was probably another still earlier. Although simpler in plan than the previous example, as it enshrines only one cella, its architectural elevation, which is notably ornate, has distinctly good features. This specially applies to the eastern frontage with its pillared portico and upper story, the semi-circular arches of each being cusped and braced with the characteristic convoluted strut. Over the mandapa extends a low pitched roof, moulded in lines resembling tiles, with figures of dragons along the ridges breaking the skyline like crockets on a Gothic gable. As a whole this building is however not unified, it is a combination of parts each good in itself, but the process of assembling has not been perfectly accomplished.

The other famous temple-city of Kathiawar, that on the hill of Girnar near the historic town of Junagadh (Uparkot), is situated on the top of a great cliff some six hundred feet below the actual summit, but still nearly three thousand feet above sea level. Although not so numerous a collection of shrines as those on Satrunjaya, from which it is distant barely a hundred miles, a few of its buildings are of an earlier date. As an instance of this, the largest of the Girnar group, the temple of Neminatha, bearing an inscription indicating that it was restored in the 13th century, is probably not very different in its general appearance from what it was when first built about a century before. More recent renovations may perhaps have robbed it of some of its original character, but it is still a building of marked size and distinction. It is possible to obtain a comprehensive view of this temple from a point of the hill above it, the entire scheme depicting a very carefully designed plan. Standing within a quadrangular courtyard measuring 190 feet by 130, it is surrounded by a range of pillared cloisters containing over seventy cells. The temple building is placed towards the western end of this enclosure leaving a wide sweep of pavement in front to add dignity to its proportions, the structure itself having a plan of 120 feet long and 60 feet wide. The mandapa is a handsome hall 43 feet square with an open space in the centre constituting the nave, around which is a colonnade of twenty-two pillars forming the aisles. It is however in the exterior elevation of the vimana that the early character of the temple may be detected, as this is composed of a grouping of turrets around the central tower on a system common in the temple architecture of western India of about the twelfth century.

The manner in which the temple builders of these parts endeavoured to adapt their plans to the Jain observances is shown in another early building at Girnar, the temple of Vastupala Tejpala, so named because it was founded by those two famous ministers under the rulers of Gujarat, who, by their munificent patronage, gave such encouragement to the building art in the west of India during the first half of the thirteenth century. This temple is remarkable as it is a triple structure composed of three separate shrines, each leading out of one of the sides of a square central hall, the fourth side providing the entrance. As usual the shrine on the east is the principal sanctuary, as here in the cella is a statue of Mallinatha, the 19th Tirthankar, but the two lateral shrines contain Jain emblems of marked spiritual significance. Each of these side-chambers is in the form of a pillared hall, the centre, or nave of which is almost filled with a monument of solid masonry, called a *Samosan*, that on the north having a square base and called *Sumeru*, the fabled mountain of Meru, while that on the south is circular in plan and named *Sameta Sikhara*, referring to the sacred mount of Parasanath in Bihar. The lateral arrangement of this temple necessitated a broad frontage having three entrances, above which rise three shallow domes covering the central hall and its two side shrines. In working out this composition, the builders failed to produce any appearance of height, so that the general effect of the elevation is low and flattened although it contains passages which are well-proportioned and have no little architectural merit.

There are several other sacred sites of the Jains, which appertain more or less to the temple-city plan but none of those is equal in architectural character to the two already described. At Sonagarh near Datia in Central India something of the kind has been conceived, as groups of temples in considerable numbers have been built on terraces on the hill side, most of them however of moderately recent date and in a style of architecture of a rather commonplace type, although the appearance of the whole is picturesque. The same may be said of two other sites, that at Kundalpur in the Damoh district of the Central Provinces, where there is a cluster of some fifty temples, and at Mukhtagiri near Gawalgarh in Berar. Parasanath, a hill in Bihar, has profoundly sacred associations although its temples have little but their sanctity to commend them. This short list does not profess to include all those high places where religious fervour found expression in the raising of temples and shrines ; there are other lofty and romantic sites where such buildings may be found, but most of these are important only from their religious aspect, as they consist of venerable but simple monuments, where the devout may perform the rite of *panchanya*, and thus " worship the mountains as the feet of Jina."

Taken as a whole the architectural character of the buildings comprising these "holy cities" of the Jains is not of a particularly high order. Yet consisting of such a large number, and their production extending over a very considerable space of time, they cannot fail to be instructive. But the information they convey is not inspiring, their cold systematic compositions making little appeal. There is a falling away of power in these structures, some of it undoubtedly due to the relatively late period in which many of them were erected, when the first vigour of the style had passed. Compare any of the temples of the twelfth and thirteenth centuries pulsating with a fresh vitality, with those of the later style, and it will at once become apparent that the art was growing nerveless and mannered, the dynamic movement of the one being in strong contrast with the static condition of the other. That something happened to divide the two phases is obvious, and that circumstance was the full force of the Islamic aggression which was experienced at this juncture. For some time the mind of the people was stunned by these subversive influences, and the buildings reflect not only the effect of the religious impact but also the socio-political conditions that then ensued. From this state the country partially recovered, but it was never the same. The old arts continued to be practised, but the spirit of them passed very largely and almost imperceptibly into the more vigorous conceptions of the new power.

In addition to the temple-cities just described, there are other sacred sites, mostly on the western side of the country, on which the Jains have built temples of great size and considerable architectural importance, chief among these, and fully representative of the style, is the Chaumukh temple of Adinatha at Ranpur near Sadari, in Marwar, situated within the Godvad province of Jodhpur State. An inscription on a pillar states that one Depaka was the architect, producing the building to the order of a " devout worshipper of the Arhats," named Dharanaka in A.D. 1439. Some idea of the proportions and complexity of this temple may be gained when it is realized that it covers a space of over forty thousand square feet, an area corresponding approximately to that of Wadham College, Oxford, and that it consists of twenty-nine halls containing as many as four hundred and twenty pillars, the designs of no two of which, are alike. Such a large and extensive conception can hardly claim to be a unified whole, and as a matter of fact it resolves itself into a comprehensive structural scheme consisting of an orderly aggregation of shrines, symmetrically disposed around a larger one in the centre, the entire complex erected on a lofty plinth, and contained within a high and solid boundary wall. This wall surrounding a square of two hundred feet side, is in reality the main feature of the exterior, as it forms the chief elevational aspect, recalling at the same time those battlemented fortifications of the temple-cities, but in this instance treated more architecturally and also more pacifically. Not only does the wall with its massive substructure safeguard the sanctity of the shrines within, but it also emphasises by its almost unbroken circuit that desire for seclusion which seems essential to the devotional ceremonies of the Jains. In place however of the militant crenellations of the temple-city parapets, at Ranpur these take the form of light and graceful turrets, one above each of the sixty-six cells, or *bhamlis*, attached to its inner face. Behind this outwork of pointed fanes rises an array of tall spires and rounded cupolas to produce a charmingly picturesque effect. Of the sikharas there are five, the largest and most prominent surmounting the central sanctuary, with each of the others over a corner shrine, while the cupolas are twenty in number, each forming the roof of a pillared hall. (Plate CXXIII).

From the middle of three sides of the enclosing rectangle project the temple entrances, each a double storied portal of great elegance, that on the west being the largest, thus denoting the principal approach. Each of these entrances leads through a series of columned courts into the main halls of the temple proper. At first sight the interior appears to be a complicated labyrinth of courts and pillared halls, but its regular and balanced composition soon becomes evident. Reduced to simple terms it resolves itself into a temple within a temple, in other words a central sanctuary surrounded by a range of chapels and subsidiary shrines.

The main temple, occupying the middle of the composition, is contained within a rectangular courtyard measuring 95 feet by 100 feet, which space it partially fills as it consists of a large hall standing on a plinth and graced with a hundred pillars. In the centre at the " crossing " or nave of this hall is the adytum, 25 feet square and with four entrances, its interior consisting of a cruciform chamber enshrining the *Chaumukh*, a quadruple image in white marble of Adinath, the first Tirthankar. The rectangular courtyard surrounding this main temple is open to the sky, but the four outer sides are enclosed by the range of supplementary courts referred to above. There are three of these open spaces along each side with a special sanctuary and cella known as the *Khunt-ra-mandar* at each angle, besides four other shrines one on each side of the north and south entrance halls. Such is a bare outline of the arrangements of this temple on its ground floor, but as it is in two stories, practically the whole of it is duplicated above, while portions of it, as for instance the compartments on each side of the main sanctuary, rise up to a third story. These upper stories repeat, in many respects, the disposition of those below, even to the shrine chamber, with its four openings, access to which is obtained from the terraced roofs. (Plate CXXIII).

The principal impression conveyed by this temple is the variety and multiplicity of its parts, yet all are well proportioned and uniformly disposed within the scheme. Then there is the contrast of the pointed spires with the ovoid domes, and the fretted roofs, each of a different character and height, but each signifying the position of some chapel, hall, or tabernacle within. Across these architectural elements move the broad and clear-cut shadows of the wide eaves contrasting with the passages of light on the pillars of the superstructure, such are some of the attractive features of the exterior. In the interior are the unending vistas of the columns interrupted at intervals by open courts, each vaulted compartment ceiled with carving of a most intricate character, and the whole illuminated by either direct or reflected light which is thrown from pavement to pillar, and from pillar to screen to penetrate into all parts. The general effect of this temple may not be that of great architecture, but as a work of inspired art, and at the same time complying with the exacting conditions of the creed, it is a notable achievement.

Another important shrine of the Jains displaying certain architectonic pretensions, and having much the same derivation and object as the temple-cities of western India, lies more to the south of the peninsula, within the confines of Mysore State. Here, some forty miles north of Mysore city is the sacred site of Sarvana Belgola, an imposing natural formation, which in the course of time, aided by the hand of man, has become one of the holiest places of pilgrimage in Southern India. Attributed by some to a date as early as 309 B.C., a community of fugitive Jains settled here, whose leader, Bhadrabahu, became a martyred saint by starving himself to death. By this action the sanctity of the locality was assured, and towards the twelfth century, there had accumulated on its heights a group of monuments, some of them of more than ordinary significance. In its widest aspect this sanctuary comprises two adjacent granite hills, Chandragiri and Indrabetta, each about four hundred feet high, with the depression between excavated to form a large rectangular tank, called Belgola. Although numerous buildings are to be found on this site, those only having any claims to be called serious architecture are the temples,

Fig. 1. Jain Temples at Girnar, Kathiawar.

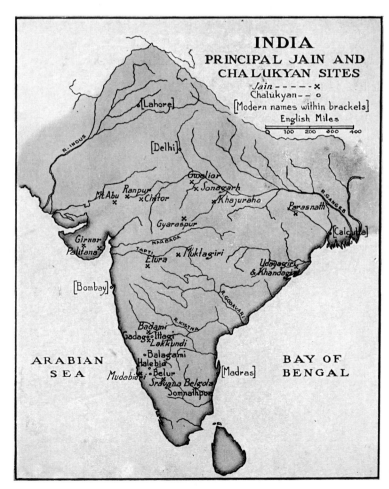

Fig. 2

Fig. 1.   Mount Abu; View of Temples from S.E.

Fig. 2.   Palitana, Kathiawar.

Kathiawar: Satrunjaya Hill; Jain Temples

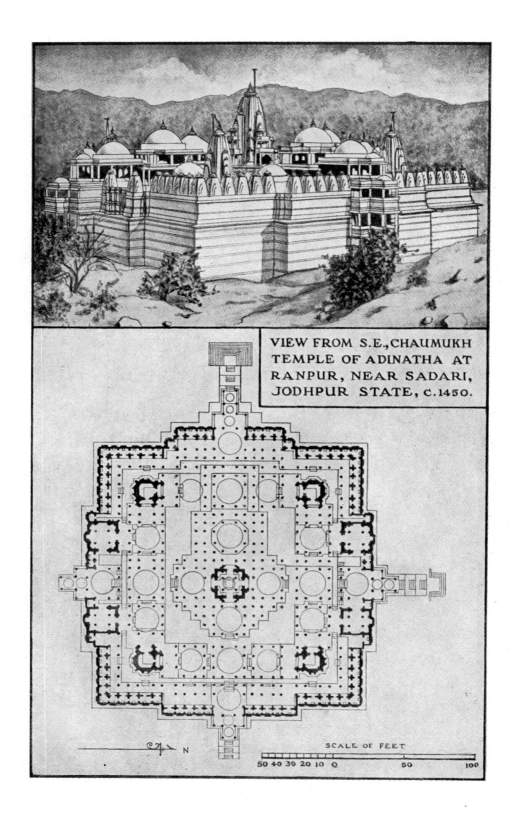

VIEW FROM S.E., CHAUMUKH
TEMPLE OF ADINATHA AT
RANPUR, NEAR SADARI,
JODHPUR STATE, c. 1450.

SCALE OF FEET

50 40 30 20 10 0   50   100

N

Fig. 1.   Halabid, Mysore: Entrance to Hoysalesvara Temple· 12th century A.D.

Fig. 2.   Belur, Mysore: Channakesava Temple interior; 12th century A.D.

Somnathpur, Mysore: Kesava Temple; A.D. 1268.

Somnathpur, Mysore: Kesava Temple, South-west wall; A.D. 1268.

Fig. 2
Belur, Mysore: Channakesava Temple, the Sukhanasi doorway; 12th century A.D.

Fig. 1
Halabid, Mysore: Hoysalesvara Temple South wall: c. A.D. 1150.

known as *bastis* (lit. *basadi*), grouped on the shoulder of the Chandragiri hill. These are fifteen in number, most of them dating from the twelfth century and all are in the Dravidian style of this period, as described elsewhere. The largest and finest of the group is the *basti* of Chamundaraya, which may have been founded as early as A.D. 980, but the present building was probably erected about 1135 A.D. Its dimensions are not inconsiderable, as it measures 70 feet in length, including the portico on its eastern front, and it is 36 feet wide. Except that it has few openings of any kind in its sides in order to conform to the Jain observances, it is of the usual type of the south, with a pyramidal sikhara surmounted by a domical finial at its western end. Owing mainly to the lack of voids in the exterior elevation, the inclusion of which gives such contrast and vitality of effect to the Brahmanical temple of the same period, this Jain temple is inclined to be ineffective and lifeless. The remaining *bastis* on Chandragiri Hill are of much the same character and therefore call for little comment.

Connecting the Chandragiri Hill with that of Indrabetta is the Pilgrims Way, which, passing alongside the holy tank of Belgola, ascends the bare hillside by innumerable steps cut in the granite slope to the walled enclosure encircling the summit of Indrabetta. As a contrast to the *bastis* of Chandragiri, this enclosure contains another class of Jain structure, commonly referred to as a *betta*, although this term, on occasion, may also refer to the sacred hill as a whole. The structural *betta* is not a temple in the ordinary sense of this word, but is an open court surrounded by an arcade or cloisters in the centre of which is a statue of one of the Jain divinities. There is nothing of special architectural merit in the design of these bettas, but they are notable as some of them enshrine standing images of exceptional appearance and also of colossal size. Several such statues, each a monolithic production carved out of the living rock, are to be found in the bettas of the Kanara country, as for instance one at Karkala, over forty feet in height and bearing the date A.D. 1432, and another at Yenur, about thirty-five feet high produced much later, having been erected in 1604. But the earliest and most stupendous of all these great figures is the example on the Indrabetta hill depicting Gommata, son of the first of the twenty-four Tirthankars, which is a most astonishing production. This gigantic image stands over fifty-six feet

high, (scarcely ten feet less than the height of the Great Sphinx in Egypt), and was carved in situ, during the reign of the Ganga king Rachamalla II, to the order of his minister Chamunda Raya about A.D. 983. The story of its creation is quite clear. Originally the granite outcrop forming the hill was crowned by a conspicuously lofty rock or tor, and it occurred to the imaginative mind of the Jains to fashion this solid block of gneiss into a statue of their saint. Entirely nude, as he is of the Digambara or " sky-clad " sect, and representing the ideal ascetic who stood in abstract meditation while the ant-hills arose at his feet and the creeping plants wound themselves around his limbs, this Indian colossus, in spite of defects in its proportions is profoundly revealing. Through the surge and stress of over a thousand years this solemn and impassive figure has defied the elements, and the high finish of its workmanship still remains. Surely Blake in his " Four Zoas " had visions of such a monumental image when he wrote ;

" . . . . Reared his mighty stature ; on Earth stood his feet,
His naked limbs glitt'ring upon the dark blue sky
Where the Eagles cry and Vultures laugh."

There is one other architectural feature, common to the temples of this southern type, which is prominent on account of its high aesthetic properties. This is the *mana-stambha*, or free-standing pillar, an example of which usually confronts the main entrance to the basti, a good instance being that in front of the Parswanathaswami at Sravana Belgola. Planted on a wide-spreading base of several moulded steps, the shaft, square at its lower section, changes to a circular shape having shallow flutes crossed by lateral bands at regular intervals. At the top of the shaft is the capital, usually a fluted vase-motif of Dravidian derivation, and this supports an elaborated superstructure, the design of which gives its character to the whole. This graceful conception of a finial may be likened to a kind of tabernacle based on a wide square abacus, below which is a circular member resembling a full-blown flower. The corners of the abacus are supported by figures or rampant gryphons, while small pillars and finials decorate every projection. As some of these free-standing *manastambhas* are over fifty feet in height they form an artistic and impressive introduction to the temple entrance.

REFERENCES.

Burgess, J., *Satrunjaya*, London, 1870.
   ,,   *Antiquities of Northern Gujarat* (Arch. Sur. of West Ind., Vol. IX, London).
Cousens, H., *Somanatha and Medieval Temples in Kathiawar* (Arch. Sur. of Ind., Vol. XLV), Cal., 1931.

CHAPTER XXIX

THE LATER CHALUKYAN OR HOYSALA STYLE

(A.D. 1050 to 1300)

THE mediaeval temples which have been dealt with so far have been resolved into two main styles of architecture, the southern or Dravidian, and the northern or Indo-Aryan. Early in the second millennium, however, in a large area of the Deccan, a type of temple architecture was developed sufficiently distinctive in character to be regarded as a separate style. This third, or as it is sometimes termed, intermediate style, has been designated by the dynastic name of Chalukyan, which, although not entirely a satisfactory nomenclature, is open to less objection than others. It was a mode of building evolved and practised very largely under the Chalukyan kings or through their influence, as theirs was the paramount power in these parts for the long period from the sixth to the twelfth centuries. The Chalukyans were then overthrown by the Hoysalas, an enterprising and virile race, and it was under the rule of this later dynasty, and mainly within their dominions that the maturity of the style took place. For two hundred and fifty years therefore, from the eleventh to the thirteenth century, a very large number of temples were erected, which in view of the relatively limited period and the restricted size of this region imply a condition of almost unprecedented architectural activity ; so much so that the art of building in this mode developed into a definitely significant movement.

In its broad aspect the course of this movement may be said to have been founded on the instinctive artistic sense of the Chalukyans, and to have culminated through the intellectual patronage of the Hoysalas. Undoubtedly the cradle of the style may be located in that triad of historical towns in Dharwar, at Aihole, Badami, and Pattadakal, where, as already shown (Chapters XI and XIV), throughout the middle centuries of the first millennium some purposeful buildings, but of an unformed character were produced. In the course of time out of this very living beginning the large and important movement of the later Chalukyans was developed. This development was helped very considerably by the fact that the ground where this manifestation took place was well prepared. The artisans of Mysore, the country where the majority of the temples in this style are to be found, possessed an eminent aesthetic sensibility evidently the outcome of a long artistic tradition, which the strong and stable Chalukya-Hoysala rule stimulated and organized with remarkable results. Yet between the type of building that began in Dharwar and the more fully matured temples of the later Chalukyans there are certain fundamental differences. One of the most noticeable of these was brought about by a radical change in the nature of the building material used by the Mysore craftsmen. Whereas the masons of the " three towns " of Dharwar employed large and unwieldly blocks of sandstone, thus producing an appearance of massive stability emphasized by bold plastic treatment, the Chalukya-Hoysala builders resorted to a stone of much finer grain—a greenish or bluish-black chloritic schist. The latter is a close-textured stone, very tractable under the chisel, and specially suited to the preparation of the minute carving which became a pronounced characteristic of the later style. With this change of material, and partly no doubt as the result of it, the masonry of the Mysore temples is more highly finished, the blocks are smaller and better dressed while the construction generally shows considerable technical enlightenment, improvements which are distinctly observable as the style progressed.

There has been a tendency to refer to the Chalukyan style as intermediate between the Indo-Aryan and the Dravidian. Such a position is not exactly in accordance with the facts. For any real evidences of the influence of the northern development are almost negligible, and confined to the occasional introduction of a few motifs, such as a copy of the Indo-Aryan sikhara in some of its architectural ornamentation. On the other hand the effect of the southern style is distinctly marked, mainly because the territory in which the Chalukyan movement flourished was surrounded by that of the Dravidians. Naturally the result of this was that the nearer the Chalukyan buildings were to the southern manifestation, the closer they resemble the Dravidian type, and, conversely, where they are in more remote parts, the more independent is their treatment. In spite of this almost imperceptible gradation of one style into the other it is possible to divide the Chalukyan temples into two regional developments, firstly, those in the more typical style as this evolved within the state of Mysore, and, secondly, those located outside this country, and showing the influence of the Dravidian overlapping and interpenetration.

Of the buildings in the typical style produced by the later Chalukyans, some idea of the importance of the movement may be estimated from the fact that out of over a hundred temples enumerated in Mysore territory more than eighty are in the Chalukya-Hoysala mode. To understand the distinctive character of these temples, their architectural composition may be described under four headings : (1) the configuration of the building, and the shape of the plan ; (2) the treatment of the wall surfaces, (3) the formation of the tower, or sikhara, and (4) the design of the pillars, or the " order."

With regard to the first of these characteristics, that relating to the disposition and general arrangements of the temple, the scheme as a rule is similar to that found in most parts of the country, as it comprises a central structure within an enclosure, the surrounding walls of which contain ranges of cells fronted by a pillared verandah or cloister. The central structure, or main building, in its simplest form resolves itself into the customary three compartments, namely, the cella, or *garbha-griha* attached to a vestibule known as the *sukhanasi*, which connects with a pillared hall or *navaranga*; in front of the last is very often an open pillared pavilion or *mukha-mandapa*. It is however in its actual conformation that the Hoysala temple is distinct from all others. In the first place many of these structures, instead of consisting of a single cella with its pillared hall, are multiples of this system, in numerous instances they are double temples having most of their essential parts in duplicate, and quite frequently they are triple, quadruple, and, in some instances, quintuple in their plan and general arrangements. Further, it was a common practice for main portions of the scheme such as the sanctuary, to have the plan of the outer walls, not laid out by means of right lines and angles but in a series of points, resulting in the conventional figure of a star. There are many temples, especially on the western side of India, which have their plans elaborated into the shape of a star by means of a series of recesses and off-sets, but the indentations and projections thus formed are produced by right angles, or curves on right lines. In contrast to this, in the Chalukyan style, the stellate or *asthabhadra* plan, is worked out on an entirely different principle, being obtained by means of an intricate geometrical device. This consists of a combination of equal squares, each with a common centre, but whose diagonals vary by several degrees, the amount of difference in degrees being in accordance with the number of points required to form the star. (Plate CIX, Fig. 1). Although a special characteristic of the Hoysala temple, the stellate plan is by no means confined to this style alone, as instances of a similar kind are to be found in other parts of the Deccan, such as in the temples of Patna, Kokamthan, and Lonar, in Kandesh, in a temple at Karusa in Andhra Pradesh and in several others in Rajputana and elsewhere.

The typical Hoysala temple-structure stands on a high platform, not rectangular in shape, as its sides project or recede being carried parallel to the lines and angles of the building it supports. This platform is much wider and more spacious than appears necessary, thus leaving a broad flat surface or terrace all round the temple, but it was so ordained for a definite purpose. For in none of these temples is there an interior *pradakshina patha*, and this space provides a suitable substitute for processions or circumambulation.

Turning to the second characteristic of these temples, that relating to the architectural treatment of the wall surfaces, it will be seen that the general effect of these is one of horizontality. Such an appearance is fortuitously emphasized in some of the larger examples, as these for various reasons lack their towers and superstructure so that what remains is a long low building in which mouldings, lines, members, and spaces horizontally applied, predominate. As with most styles there is some difference in the surface design of the walls of the vimana compared with that of the pillared hall, the former resolving itself into three horizontal divisions, the latter into two, but both compartments are connected above by a wide continuous cornice. In both also there is a high and almost vertical basement, in some instances nine or ten feet in height, not formed of mouldings, but made up into a number of bands containing animated continuous designs, and running right round the building. These carved borders are usually ranked in the same conventional sequence, the lowest, on the ground, consisting of a procession of elephants, signifying strength and stability, then a border of horsemen denoting speed, with a band of spiral foliage and *kirthimukh*, or sun-face (a grotesque mask) above ; next in order and most interesting of all as it is on a level with the eye, therefore best observed, is a frieze less than a foot wide depicting a succession of scenes from the great epic poems, a picture-gallery in stone executed with marked dramatic effect and wealth of detail. Then above

this is a border of *yalis*, scaly hippopotamic monsters, presumed to symbolize the sacred river Ganges, spouting spirals of foliage, while crowning all is a running pattern of *hangsahs* (*hamsa*) a kind of goose or legendary bird, which, so the poets say, " swims in the waters of the mind of the great." (Plate CXXVII, Fig. 1). In the elevational aspect of the pillared hall the basement is terminated above by an *asana*, or sloping seat-back, and this feature, including also the whole of the structure below, is referred to as the *jagati*. Rising from the *jagati* are the exterior pillars of the hypostyle hall, their moulded shafts spaced at regular intervals around the building with the intercolumnation filled by perforated stone screens. It is not improbable that the first intention in many of these temples was to leave this pillared hall as an open pavilion, but in order to secure privacy, the spaces between the outer pillars were at an early date closed by stone grilles. (Plate CXXVIII, Fig. 1).

The three horizontal divisions of the vimana wall are even more ornate than the two comprising the pillared hall. As already described the basement of the vimana is a continuation of that around the rest of the building, but above this, and corresponding to the pillar-and-screen treatment of the hypostyle hall, is a wide upright space defined above by a prominent string-course, and which contains one of the most typical features of the style. In the neighbouring temples of the Dravidian mode this middle area, or " filling " of the exterior was enriched by means of pilasters and niches, an abstract conception of notable architectural fitness. The Hoysala craftsman did not exclude this entirely from his scheme but he relegated it, or something like it, to the uppermost of his three divisions, where, compressed between an upper and a lower cornice, it has little architectural significance, and is a mere concession to the traditional conventions of the temple elevation. His object in bringing about this change is quite clear, as by so doing he left a broad space in the most prominent part of his building for an exposition of his skill as a figure sculptor. Here, in this wide wall surface he placed within ornate niches and under foliated canopies the images of his gods, so elaborately chiselled that they can scarcely be regarded as part of the architecture, because each appears displayed as a distinct and independent example of plastic art. (Plate CXXVI). The richness of the effect of this statuary is much enhanced by the stellate plan of the structure as a whole, which producing vertical planes like facets in the body of the building, not only presents more play of surface but also provides a greater variety of light and shade.

The third characteristic of the Hoysala temple is the design and treatment of the tower or *sikhara*, which, on account of its prominence, may be regarded as the key-note of the style. Although it is separated from its substructure, consisting of the walls of the vimana, by a wide projecting cornice or eave, the stellate system is carried through this to produce a fluted effect on the tower above. As in other regional developments the upward tendency is however modified and balanced by a scheme of horizontal lines and mouldings, which resolve the whole tower into an orderly succession of tiers, diminishing as they rise to terminate at the apex in a low parasol-shaped finial. The motifs that make up the horizontal and vertical pattern of the sikhara consist of a complex grouping of miniature shrines and niches, each tier being separated either by a sunk moulding or a fretted string-course. In mass this type of tower has no effective height, and its contours, being a section of a parabola. are not strong in outline. There is a certain plastic beauty in its rich sculptured texture, but architecturally it is formless, and lacks structural strength.

The fourth, and last, of the characteristics which distinguishes this style, relates to the particular shape of the pillar and its capital, in a word the "order". This order was in many respects a development of that of the Dravidian style, with its capital of expanding mouldings, and "foursquare" brackets above. But the pillars themselves took on a special form, owing to a mechanical process by which they began to be produced in this particular region, which very largely conditioned their appearance. As in most Indian temples the pillar shaft is monolithic, and it became the almost invariable practice of the stone masons to fashion and decorate these elongated blocks by turning them on a large lathe. The stone was first roughly shaped to the required proportions, and then mounted in an upright position on a wheel, by means of which the block was rotated against a chisel, set as a turning tool. A baluster-like appearance was the result, the shaft and capital being converted by this process into a series of rounded horizontal mouldings, resembling rings, with the base or pedestal left square. In the preparation of these mouldings and their contours, whether sharp convex rims or deep sunk grooves, the workman showed considerable ingenuity and seems to have been allowed a fair amount of freedom in his designs; there is however one particular form almost always present, a conventional motif to accord with some ancient tradition, and that is a prominent bell-shaped member towards the lower half of the shaft. The manufacture of these lathe-turned pillars was in operation over a wide area in the Deccan, but they are a special feature of the Hoysala temples in Mysore, and must have provided employment for a large number of people, as they are found in great profusion. Incidentally, they provide early evidence of a system of mechanical handling and mass production in the field of building construction. As an enrichment to this type of pillar in the Hoysala temple there was attached a sloping bracket-stone imposed on the turned capital to which it was fixed by sockets. These strut-like brackets were carved out of one slab into images enshrined within leafy aureoles, and are known as *madanakai* figures : so elaborately are they sculptured as to rival in execution and high finish those in the niches on the vimana walls.

The general impression conveyed by these temples is, that, while the basis of their style is Dravidian, in the hands of the Hoysala craftsman it became a very different thing. Unconsciously the workmen altered and adapted the southern mode to suit their own ideals, which were not those of a builder, but those of an art craftsman, such as the sandal-wood carver, the ivory worker, the metal caster, and also the goldsmith. What they produced was in reality not architecture, but applied art. For instance in the fine chiselling of the figures on the exterior walls of the *vimana*, each a separate image in its special setting, one seems to see an enlarged lithic reproduction of the sandal-wood shrines which, even now, are the favourite handiwork of the Mysore artisan. Then, in the *madanakai* brackets, projecting from the upper part of the pillar, there is the touch of the ivory worker, his figures being carved in stone to a large scale to suit the size of the building, but still bearing the fine technique of his ivory original. Further, in some of the strap patterns fixed with " drops " in imitation of studs and rivets, which,

like bronze bands support the under side of the eaves, these recall the cast and hammered effects of the metal worker, a noted craftsman in these parts to the present day. Finally, in the wealth of simulated jewellery with which many of the figures are loaded, with their beaded headdresses, their pendents and tasselled girdles, each part exactly imitated in the stone by means of a riffler and a fine drill, is there not some of the delicate handling of the goldsmith, when he encrusts his silver filigree with precious stones ? Such fine relief on account of its resemblance to the chasings of silver-smiths corresponds to the *plateresco* of the mediaeval Spanish school. Whoever these craftsmen originally were, each type of artificer prepared his plastic contribution as if it were a *chef d'oeuvre*, and this was attached to the temple structure in the manner of an icon placed on a wall. So much so that some of these applied statuettes are inscribed with the sculptor's name, together with a title extolling his genius, recording that he was " an artist of the gods, a delighter of the hearts of the good, and as a bee at the lotus feet of Sarasvati " (divine patroness of the Arts and Sciences).

The effect of this profuse but coherent aggregation of plastic and applied art may be imagined. And just as the Italian buildings of the Renaissance[1] have been styled, perhaps not too happily, as " architects' architecture,"[2] so, with much more reason, the temples of the Chalukyans may be criticised as " artists' architecture " or, even more specifically " sculptors' architecture." For these Mysore temples owe their character more to the chisel of the sculptor than to the stonework of the mason. Gone is the structural basis, the functional framework evolved through the experiences of previous workers in the field, with its bold organic mouldings and supporting pilasters providing stability and strength, and in its place is an arrangement of manifold planes, projections, and courses of masonry, each intricately carved and beautiful in itself, even beautiful in its aggregation, but not, as a whole, amounting to a work of significant architecture in the full sense of the word. No doubt the builders of these temples revelled in their display of plastic exuberance, but, on the other hand, there may have been some object in this unrestrained application of sculptured forms. The master craftsman, possibly reasoned that only the intellectual few would appreciate his efforts to achieve graceful linear contours and balanced formation combined with a logical structural foundation. On the other hand, the masses, although by no means deficient in the aesthetic sense, would more readily understand, and probably more eagerly expect, in their religious buildings, lively representations of their gods, goddesses and divine tutelars, to whom they instinctively appeal for all things concerning their daily life, as well as the hereafter. Then running throughout the entire composition of the temple, were the long bands of the narrative art, illustrating with the utmost detail and in a singularly dramatic fashion, extracts from the nation's mythology and folk-lore, with which even the humblest would be familiar. Under these conditions it is not surprising that the temple-builder became a story-teller in stone, so that his productions appertain more to an illuminated missal transmuted into sculpture, than to a full-scale architectural composition.

The larger and more important buildings in this style are incomplete, as they lack their superstructure of roof

---

[1] W. R. Lethaby, *Architecture* 1912, pp. 232-33.

[2] *The Architecture of Humanism*, by Geoffrey Scott, 1924, pp. 58-9.

and tower which were never finished, or, if so, they have decayed and fallen, only the lower and more fundamental portions remaining. In such circumstances, although wonderful works of art, they do not represent the temple in its full expressiveness, for this, one must look to some of the smaller buildings of which there are numerous examples. Among these are the Lakshmidevi (quadruple, A.D. 1113) at Dodda Gaddavali,[1] the Kesava (triple, c. 1170) at Nagamangala, the Buchesvara (triple, 1173) at Koramangala, the Isvara (double, c. 1220) at Arsikere, the Harihara temple at Harihar (double, 1224), the Kesava (triple, c. 1234) at Harnhalli, the Lakshmi-Narasimha (triple, 1249) at Nuggihalli, and the Kesava (triple, 1268) at Somnathpur.

Most typical and complete is the Kesava temple at Somnathpur[2] situated about twenty miles from Seringapatam, a triple shrine, or *trikutachala*, and illustrating the style in its late maturity. (Plate CXXV). The temple itself occupies the middle of a rectangular courtyard surrounded by sixty-four cells each with pillars in front, the whole enclosure measuring 215 feet by 177 feet, and forming an appropriate cloistered setting. Owing to its combination of three shrines, the temple plan is in the shape of a cross, its greatest length being 87 feet and its width 83 feet, with its sole entrance on the east. These very moderate dimensions enable one, on entering the courtyard through its eastern gateway, to see this building in its entirety at a single glance, and it is indeed a very perfect and finished production, a small, but typical example of the style. So well-balanced and finely proportioned are its parts that no element obtrudes or is out of place, and although the three stellate towers are only thirty feet high, they are fully in accord with the rest of the building. The temple structure stands on a high platform, the outlines of which run parallel to the plan of the building, following the points of its stellate shape, but leaving a space some seven feet wide all round, as an ambulatory. Its plan is fairly simple as it consists of a main pillared hall in the centre, at the western end of which are the three shrines, one in axial alignment with the hall, the others projecting laterally, like transepts, thus producing its cruciform effect. The exterior walls, parapet, and towers are disposed and embellished according to the conventional system already described. A single pillared hall measuring 41 feet long by 30 feet wide comprises the interior, but this is actually a composite of the two compartments of the *mukha-mandapa*, or front hall, and the *navaranga*, or middle hall, the former containing twelve pillars and the latter four, all elaborately lathe-turned in the manner of the style. From each of the three interior walls of the middle hall a doorway leads to a square vestibule or *sukhanasi*, beyond which, in each instance, is the cella. (Plates CXXVI and CXXV).

For a larger and earlier example, as well as one of more historical importance, we must turn to a group of temples at Belur in the Hassan District of Mysore, the construction of which dates from about 1117 A.D. (Plate CXXIV, Fig. 1). These temples are all within one enclosure, and few sights could be more richly picturesque than this assemblage of early twelfth century buildings distributed rather unsymmetrically over its flagged pavements, with the temple of Kesava, evidently the main intention of the scheme, placed towards the centre. Unfortunately this, the principal building of the group, has lost its superstructure, so that it is architecturally unimpressive, but a close inspection reveals a conception of unusual artistic merit. The arrangements of its various compartments produce the customary cruciform plan, the temple with its platform, measuring 178 feet long by 156 feet wide, and its formation consists of a pillared hall having deeply recessed angles, a stellate vimana, with a small square vestibule connecting the two. There are three entrances, one on each of the free sides of the hypostyle hall, each approached by a flight of steps flanked by a pagoda-like shrine, the last a useful note of architectural emphasis. A large and very elegant exterior shrine is also attached to each of the three projecting sides of the vimana, an appropriate addition to this part of the structure. Although the temple at Belur was built a century and a half before the example previously described, as it was one of the first of its kind, while that at Somnathpur was one of the last, it is significant of the conservatism of the Indian artisan that the differences in the treatment of the two temples are slight. There is a little more freedom in the arrangement of the ornamental courses forming the basement, and a less disciplined disposal of the plastic forms on the exterior surfaces, indicating, to a slight degree, that at Belur the style had not completely crystallized. Yet there is one elaboration in this temple not found elsewhere and that is the sculptured figure-subjects on the perforated screens between the exterior pillars of the hypostyle hall. In number there are twenty of these screens, ten of which are treated geometrically, as is common in most of these temples, but the rest are carved to illustrate stories from the Puranas, presenting friezes crowded with beings engaged in the most animated pursuits.

From this temple the best idea of an interior in the style may be gained, although, as in most examples, even here the pillars are so closely set, that no spatial view is possible, and every feature is so overlaid with carving, that the effect is one of congestion, there is no attempt at restraint, breadth, or repose. (Plate CXXIV, Fig. 2). The main colonnades form two cross aisles intersecting in the middle of the hall, where they produce a central bay or nave. These cruciform aisles leave spaces in the angles of the hall in which smaller pillars are placed, and each group of four supports beams enclosing a sunk coffered ceiling. It is on the main pillars and the recessed ceilings that the sculptor has specially directed his artistic ingenuity, and these are most imaginatively and copiously patterned. As the greatest interior dimensions of this *navaranga* are 92 feet by 78 feet, and the total number of pillars amounts to forty-six, all of which, save the four in the central bay, are each of different design, the variety of form and complex character of the whole is astonishing. It seems as if the system employed in the design and construction of these pillars was that of entrusting each example to one head artist and his assistants, who combined as a team to produce their finest work. Set to compete against one another in such a manner, each pillar became, therefore, an individual masterpiece, the fertility of invention and the minuteness of the execution in every instance being phenomenal. One column in the middle hall is so unique in character that it has been distinguished by the name of the Narasinha pillar, for to show his cleverness the sculptor has not only carved its capital, shaft, and base, into a repeating pattern of niches in each of which is enshrined an image, but has ingeniously contrived that the whole pillar could be rotated at will. Yet underneath all

[1] *Mysore Archaeological Series*, No. III, Bangalore, 1919.
[2] *Mysore Archaeological Series*, No. I, Bangalore, 1917.

these interlaced mouldings and intricately finished forms it is possible to see, in spite of this plastic overlay, that the basis of the design is in conformity with the Chalukyan order, that there is throughout a certain conventional combination of elements which is unmistakable. That each detail of the building was the work of specialists in their craft, a not uncommon procedure in other forms of Indian art, is indicated by the fact that on a number of the images, particularly those on the brackets, there is inscribed the name of the sculptor, like a signature, thus showing that each individual artist had contributed to the scheme a selected specimen of his handiwork.

There yet remains the highest achievement of the Chalukyan-Hoysala school of architecture, the temple of Hoysalesvara at Halabid. (Plate CXXIV, Fig. 1). Owing to the truncated condition of this building, for it lacks the whole of its superstructure, its architectural appearance is disappointing, but were its roof and tower in position, rising up to group themselves in balanced mass against the sky, the effect would be distinctly imposing. In spite however of such a fundamental disability, this temple, chiefly on account of the emphatic prodigality of its sculptural embellishment, is, without exaggeration, one of the most remarkable monuments ever produced by the hand of man. The Hoysalesvara was the principal temple within the walls of the ancient city of Darasamudra, which for three centuries flourished as the royal capital of the Hoysala empire. Now, even the name of this city is forgotten, and it has declined into a small hamlet in the Hassan District, called Halabid, some fifty miles north-west of Mysore. Of the temporal power of this one-time great capital-city, of its places and citadels, fortifications and civic buildings, there remain now only grass-grown mounds. Yet of the spiritual life of its people this fine temple is still a standing monument, when all that was material has faded into oblivion. That Darasamudra was the centre of marked religious activity is plainly shown by the remains of numerous Brahmanical and Jain temples grouped within its walls. One of these, the Kedesvara, a building of moderate dimensions, yet beautifully proportioned and exquisitely carved, may have been the " Chapel Royal," as it was in close proximity to the palace and connected with it by a road. But this superb though minor example is entirely eclipsed by the remains of the grand temple of the imperial capital, the Hoysalesvara, designed and erected, as an inscription states, by one Kedaroja, the master builder of Narasimhal (1141-82), the Hoysala king, under the supervision of Ketamalla, chief officer of the public works, and it is as well, in view of the remarkable nature of this building, that their names should be remembered. Its date was therefore after the middle of the twelfth century, a time when the empire was in its first vigour, and from it one may gain the most complete impression of the style.

The Hoysalesvara is a double temple in every sense of the word, as it is two complete temples of exactly the same dimensions built side by side, connected only by their adjacent transepts. The length of each is 112 feet and about 100 feet in width, so that they are not large structures, each approximating in area the chancel of a moderately sized English Cathedral, but, taken together, the two buildings, with their *nandi* pavilions in front cover a fairly large space, as they occupy the greater part of a square measuring over 200 feet side. The entire conception stands on a large platform having angles corresponding to those of the buildings it supports. Each temple is cruciform in plan so that the whole composition on the ground assumes the shape of a double cross joined at its inner arms. The arrangements of each temple resolve themselves into the two usual compartments consisting of a pillared hall and its attached sanctuary ; in addition there is in front, in both instances, a *nandi mandapa*, or open pillared pavilion, the one facing the eastern doorway of the southern temple being a building of considearble size, a temple in itself, but the northern pavilion is much smaller, the inequality of these two supplementary structures being the only unsymmetrical portions of its configuration.

But although in extent it is moderately large, the design of the building is such that it presents little spatial effect as its exterior is broken up by repeated projections and angular surfaces, while the narrow halls of the interior are filled with many pillars closely spaced. The average height of the exterior elevation is 25 feet, but even if the towers and roofs above this were in position, it is doubtful whether it would ever have assumed the appearance of a reasonably co-ordinated composition, as its total conception in two distinct portions could only have produced a balanced grouping of parts, but no effect of a corporate unity. Externally, a certain amount of contrast is obtained by the change of form between the treatment of the sanctuary on the one hand, and the assembly hall on the other, the junction being harmonised in a very skilful manner by the interposition of a massive and profusely decorated buttress. The sanctuary, being stellate on plan, its walls are formed of acute angular projections, while the surfaces of the pillared hall are mainly at right angles. The entire elevation however is blended into a semblance of completeness by the scheme of continuous mouldings, borders, friezes, cornices, and bands of statuary which are carried around the whole building. In general appearance therefore, the elevation resolves itself into a multiplicity of planes, of alternations of shapes, of intervals separated by sharp lights and vivid shadows, of occasional passages of half-tones, but there is little attempt at formal volume or developed mass.

Such is the first impression conveyed by the general appearance of this building, followed by the feeling that, although it is clearly executed in terms of architecture, it is also equally clear that it is architecture of a very special kind. A closer inspection confirms this view. As one proceeds along the broad platform which encircles the conjoint structure, so planned in order to provide space for ceremonial processions, the walls of the temple begin to suggest the analogy of a voluminous illuminated scroll, which is unrolled as one progresses. On it is portrayed, one after another, the whole company of Indra's heaven, each of these immortals enshrined within a structural niche, and canopied by aureola of heavily hanging foliage. Then, as the scroll unfolds, its wide margins become visible, framing the pictures of the divine beings in the centre with rich ornamental borders, comprising repeating patterns of natural forms and conventional animals, scenes of figures illustrating popular myth and legend, one continual complicacy of symbol and imagery, elaborately carved and with infinite detail. (Plate CXXVII, Fig. 1).

This bewildering display of plastic art is principally contained within three parallel spaces carried round the manifold planes forming the outer walls of the temple. The central space is the main object of this most comprehensive sculpture gallery, for each facet is occupied by a minutely wrought representation of a deity, splendidly apparelled, each figure in height half the size of life, and all modelled in exceedingly high relief, the entire frieze constituting a graphic record of the Hindu Pantheon, unusually complete, with all the accessories, attributes and symbols of each celestial being. Below this remarkable exposition of statuary is a wide vertical space comprising the basement or plinth, its total breadth divided into numerous borders, each formed into a running band of carving of the most entrancing variety. There are elephants and cavaliers, sequences of dramatic narrative scenes, strange and mystical motifs, such as the *hamsa* (goose), the *yali* (hippogryph) and all those fantastic creatures whose origin goes back to the most remote ages. The third and upper space corresponding to a frieze, is treated in a more formal manner, as it is mainly architectural in its character, consisting of niches and canopies, mouldings and pilasters, and all shaded by a heavy projecting cornice or eave. This cornice which overhangs the entire wall surface indicates the beginning of the architectural superstructure, now not in existence, but there is little doubt the roof and spire were sculptured in the same lavish fashion.

The above is but a bald outline of the system by which this unending wealth of relief work was distributed over the exterior of this temple, but it is the incredible intricacy with which each detail of this extensive conception was treated that is so overwhelming, filling the spectator with astonishment. In the marvellous minuteness of its technique alone, there is no thought of time, space, or limitations of any kind, and, as to the emotional conditions which inspired this great work, no other known movement can approach it in the intensity of its purpose. Not that the quality of the art thus represented is of the high order of some of the schools of Indian sculpture ; much of the figure modelling is taut and stylized, lacking in breadth and suggestion, but as a sustained *tour de force*, and also as a grand repository of religious thought expressed in plastic form, the walls of this temple are unequalled.

Four entrances interrupt the continuity of this sculptured elevation, two to each temple, and each is approached by a flight of steps with small detached shrines on either side. Two of these doorways are complete, one on the south, and the other on the south-east, both much alike in their design, and both remarkable productions on account of their imaginative treatment and precise workmanship. No special attention has been paid to the shape of the doorway itself, which is a plain rectangular opening, but it is the surroundings which are of such an exceptional character. Much of its design is indicative of the ingenuousness of the craftsman in seizing on realities and converting them into ideals. With this as his aim, he has sculptured on either side of the entrance a statue, in heroic proportions, of a *dvarpala* or door-keeper, a permanent effigy in place of the mobile human attendant, and these two enlarged figures he has elaborated into extravagantly fanciful creations. Each is posed in what is known as the *tribhanga* or three-flexured attitude, head, body and legs at slightly different angles, and each is costumed in a sumptuous array of jewels and tassels of gold, holding large and immensely rich symbols of office, the whole contained within an arched and foliated aureole. The lintel above the doorway is a broad panel twelve feet long and three feet high, even more ornately carved, and illustrating selected episodes from the peoples' mythology and story. Its design resolves itself into an arcaded central space formed by a *lata torana*, or archway, and supported by *yali*, those water-unicorns shaped like huge pachydermatous quadrupeds, spouting convoluted foliage on either side. The principal figure in the centre is Tandavesvara, wildly dancing, supported by other divinities, and a band of musicians accompanying their lord with drum and cymbal. Although there is something very vital in certain portions of these entrance compositions, they show little attempt at anything structural, as conceptions they are formless, appealing mainly on account of their superlatively rich and sensuous appearance. (Plate CXXIV, Fig. 1).

Passing into the temple, the scheme of the interior is congested and complex, owing to the size and near proximity of the pillars, and the accumulation of other elements, but it resolves itself into transverse aisles, with a four-square group of pillars in the space formed by the intersection, thus comprising the nave. What is remarkable however is the manner in which every feature of these columned corridors is loaded with ornament, each shaft moulded and fluted, and each capital supporting a heavily figured *madanakai* bracket, so closely set that they almost touch each other beneath the weighty beams. Such a " systematisation of confusion " rules out any appearance of breadth or space, there are few vistas or open passages as the whole is a labyrinth of fretted columns, sinuous projections, and perforated screens.

The temple at Halabid is the supreme climax of Indian architecture in its most prodigal plastic manifestation. Even if its qualities of composition are not high, at least, as a monument to the phenomenal concentration, superb technical skill, ingenuity, imagination, and profound religious consciousness of those concerned in its creation, it has no peer.

REFERENCE

Mysore, Archaeological Series, Nos. 1, 2 and 3. The Hoysala Temples of Mysore.

CHAPTER XXX

THE LATER CHALUKYAN STYLE

(cir. A.D. 1050 to 1300)

THE buildings in the remaining phase of the later Chalukyan style, as referred to in the previous chapter are located in a region towards the northern border of Mysore State, astride the upper reaches of the Tunga-bhadra river. This area is chiefly occupied by the Kanarese districts and that of Bellary, although it may be noted that examples of the same type of temple architecture are to be found in parts of the Nizam's dominions, and also in northern Mysore. Bounded as this region is, on the one hand by the country in which the Early Chalukyans originated and developed their style at the three towns of Aihole, Pattadakal, and Badami, and on the other by the territory containing the Chalukyan-Hoysala temples of Mysore, this phase of architecture not only affects characteristics from both these movements, but what is more important, it also supplies in some measure a connecting link between the two. It is possible, therefore, by a study of the buildings of this phase, to trace the evolution of the Chalukyan style as a whole from its beginning in the ancient Chalukyan triad of capitals, through the phase now being considered, step by step as it developed, until it arrived at the fully matured examples of the Hoysala school in Mysore, already described (Chapter XXIX). The period during which this style prevailed extended over some two and a half centuries, from about A.D. 1050 to 1300, or even later, after which the advent of the Muhammadans into these parts brought it to an end.

The characteristics of this type of temple may be understood by an analysis of the various parts of these buildings which make up the whole, as for instance their plans, the treatment of the exterior walls, the shape of the towers or sikharas, the pillars or " order," and, lastly, the design and execution of the doorways. With regard to the plan, unlike the Hoysala temples of Mysore, none of them, with one exception,[1] is stellate, as they are all laid out on the principle of right lines and right angles, the whole consistently rectangled. Nor, also with one exception,[2] is the interior ambulatory passage encircling the cella found in these temples and sometimes light is introduced into the inner compartments by means of windows of perforated stone screens. It is also not uncommon for the principal entrances to be not at the front, but at the sides of the structure, as the eastern end is frequently faced by a supplementary cella, shrine, or pillared portico.

As to the surface treatment of the exterior walls, in this particular aspect of the Chalukyan style, this is exceptionally well rendered. Owing to the nature of the temple composition, the outside walls in most regional developments provided a large area for decoration, of which the architectural sculptors took full advantage. This spacious wall surface was due to the fact that windows, or, in fact, voids of any kind, were rarely required. When one compares the brilliant climatic effects of the Orient with those of the west, where many windows are a necessity, as shown for instance in the Gothic buildings of Europe, the lack of such openings in the architecture of India will be understood. Sufficient light for the temple-structure was obtained mainly by reflection through the doorways, and, moreover, the impressiveness of the interior was emphasized by low illumination. In place therefore of any structural features interrupting the exterior surfaces of the building, the designers were faced with the problem of giving an effective appearance to the walls by some form of plastic decoration, preferably having an architectural basis. As already shown in some styles the difficulty was avoided by filling in the wall space with figure sculpture, not infrequently distributed over the surfaces with the minimum amount of order or, restraint. Such an expedient however did not commend itself to the builders of the temples now under reference, as they rose to the occasion in a masterly manner, finishing off their structural scheme with decorative elements of great charm, and applied with taste and experience. For few buildings in India display a more appropriate system of architectural embellishment than the temples in this phase of the Chalukyan mode.

The method of making effective the wall content of the temples was based on that initiated by the earlier Chalukyan builders, as at Pattadakal, in which the principle employed was that very sound one of spacing out the surface by means of pilasters. But the later craftsmen took this simple idea and developed it into a much more elaborate and finished conception. The pilasters are present, their slender shafts dividing the wall into well-proportioned areas, and giving to the whole a functional framework of great architectural value. Moreover, the builders added to the forcefulness of this by alternating much larger structural forms in the shape of half-pillars resembling buttresses, and at the same time a replica, in their design and detail, of the pillars of the open hall in front, a repetition of marked architectural compatibility. Then at appropriate intervals an ornamental niche or shrine was projected, with a wide eave to gather shadow, and above, a canopy, copying the decorated form of the sikhara itself, again a most artistic refrain. Finally, to enrich the whole scheme in a suitable manner a graceful motif, not unlike a standard reliquary, was interposed between the other elements, and supporting a trophy of foliated curves, while the same voluted trophy on a large scale finds a place wherever required. Such is a bare outline of the mural treatment of these temples, a disposition of architectural decoration which must be seen to be appreciated. While no doubt its conception was the result of experience, the ease and fluency with which it was designed and distributed, and its aesthetic fitness to the space it occupied, implies the possession of a natural gift for plastic expression inherited by its creators. (Plate CXXX.)

---

[1] Temple of Dodda Basappa at Dambal.
[2] Saraswati Temple at Gadag.

Fig. 1.   Belur, Mysore: Entrance to Main Temple; 12th century A.D.

Fig. 2.   Gadag, Dharwar: Somesvara Temple from South; 12th century.

Fig. 2

Dambal, Dharwar: Temple of Dodda Basappa; 12th century.

Fig. 1

Gadag, Dharwar: Pillars within Saraswati Temple; c. 12th century.

Fig. 1

Fig. 2
Ittagi, Dharwar: Temple of Mahadev; 12th century A.D.

Fig. 1
Lakkundi, Dharwar: Kasivisvara Temple from S.W.; 12th century.

Fig. 2
Kashmir: Temple of the Sun, Martand; 8th century A.D.

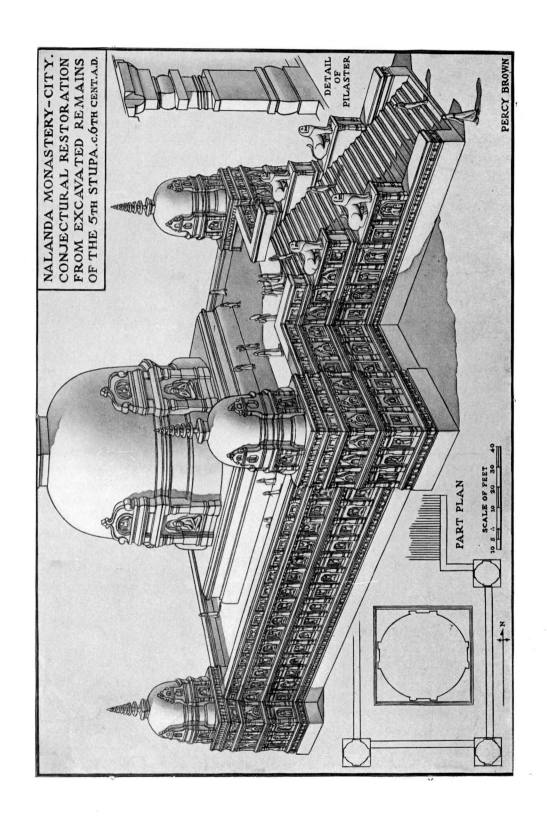

NALANDA MONASTERY-CITY.
CONJECTURAL RESTORATION
FROM EXCAVATED REMAINS
OF THE 5TH STUPA. c.6TH CENT.A.D.

DETAIL OF PILASTER.

PERCY BROWN

PART PLAN

SCALE OF FEET
10 5 ∴ 10 20 30 40

N

Fig. 1

Fig. 2.   Jor-Bangla, Vishnupur: Bengal; c. 18th century.

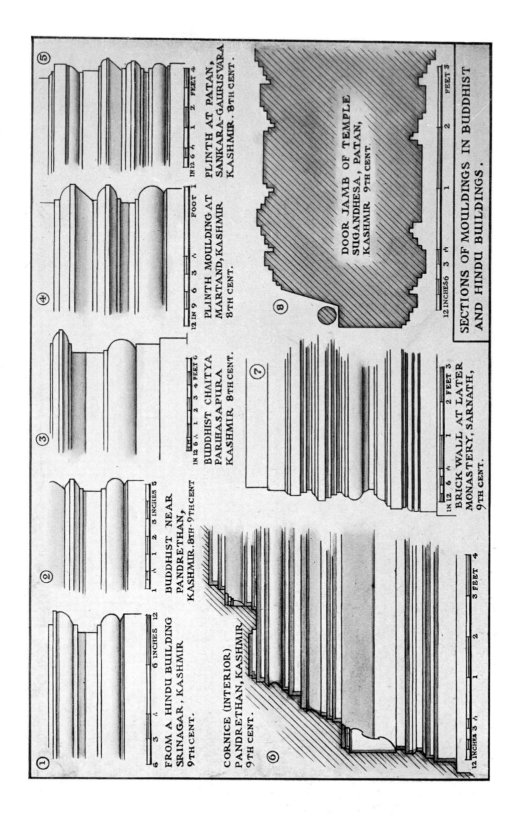

SECTIONS OF MOULDINGS IN BUDDHIST
AND HINDU BUILDINGS.

⑤ PLINTH AT PATAN,
SANKARA-GAURISVARA.
KASHMIR. 8TH CENT.

④ PLINTH MOULDING AT
MARTAND, KASHMIR.
8TH CENT.

③ BUDDHIST CHAITYA
PARIHASAPURA
KASHMIR. 8TH CENT.

② BUDDHIST NEAR
PANDRETHAN,
KASHMIR. 8TH-9TH CENT

① FROM A HINDU BUILDING
SRINAGAR, KASHMIR.
9TH CENT.

⑧ DOOR JAMB OF TEMPLE
SUGANDHESA, PATAN,
KASHMIR. 9TH CENT.

⑦ BRICK WALL AT LATER
MONASTERY, SARNATH,
9TH CENT.

⑥ CORNICE (INTERIOR)
PANDRETHAN, KASHMIR.
9TH CENT.

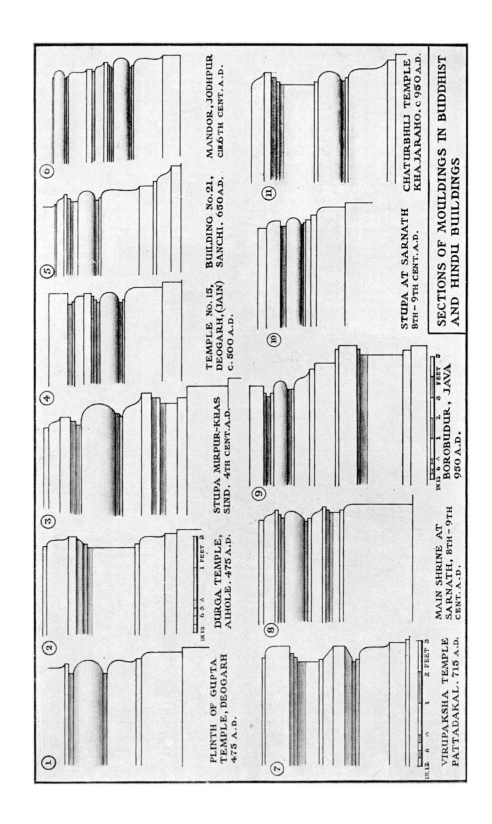

SECTIONS OF MOULDINGS IN BUDDHIST AND HINDU BUILDINGS

Turning to the pyramidal tower which surmounts the temples, the design of this outstanding feature is a compromise between on the one hand the sikhara of the Early Chalukyan type with its plainly defined stories, and on the other the closely moulded tiers of the Hoysala examples in Mysore. And the same remarks apply to the superstructure forming the apex of the tower, which is neither the bold upstanding cupola of the Pattadakal variety, nor the flat overlying parasol favoured by the builders of Mysore, but a faceted, double-flexured bell-shape, suggestive of a combination of the two conceptions. As a whole the sikharas of this phase display a not unpleasing mass contained within moderately strong contours, and sustained by a series of well-marked horizontal mouldings sufficient to preserve an appearance of some structural vigour.

In connection with the pillars of this mode, although they are richly moulded productions, there is little originality in their design, as they resemble the lathe-turned examples of the Hoysala style. But in one respect there is a slight departure, as in the majority of these pillars the principal moulding below the actual capital is very considerably projected, with a pronounced knife-edge section, a striking and distinguishing detail of the " order".

A notable feature of the later Chalukyan temple is the artistic emphasis given to the doorways, both in the case of those at the entrance to the building, and also those leading to the inner shrine. The practice of making the opening into the shrine-chamber the focal point of the temple embellishment has been previously noticed, but no other style has equalled the wealth of decoration and remarkable manipulative skill expended on some of the temple doorways of this region. Unlike those of the Hoysala type which, in keeping with their character are purely ornamental, there is an architectural framework as a basis to the design of these examples, consisting of a pilaster on either side with a moulded lintel and cornice above. Using this as his structural support, the craftsman has thrown over the whole a superb sculptured pattern of figures, foliage, and decorative effects, replete with mythical imagery, and carved with incredible detail and finish.

Within the country occupied by this phase of architecture there are upwards of fifty temples, and by means of selecting certain examples the development of the style may be readily followed.[1] Between the limits of the period, the dates of such examples and the sequence of their production, can only be largely conjectured, although these have been obtained by the sifting of several forms of evidence, as for instance inscriptions on or near the building, the local history, details of style, and the inference of certain elements in the construction. What are probably the earliest buildings are at Kukkanur, a village near the railway junction of Gadag, two of which depict not only the initial character of the movement, but provide a stepping-stone midway between the ancient type as at Pattadakal, and the later development now being described. For in these two buildings at Kukkanur we see the only examples of this phase executed in the somewhat coarse sandstone of the earlier period, all the subsequent temples of the group being built of the more refined and tractable chloritic schist. The older of the two structures, the Navalinga, or " Nine Lingas," can scarcely be termed a temple as it comprises a cluster of nine cells around three pillared compartments, with a

sikhara over each cell. These sikharas are in shape very similar to the type at Pattadakal, but the domical apex is already beginning to show signs of change. In the plastic decoration on the exterior there is that bold, almost coarse, modelling of their archetype above mentioned, and the pillars of the interior are substantial monoliths, with parts of their shafts turned into mouldings on a lathe.

The other example at Kukkanur is the temple of Kallesvara which, although of much the same architectural character as the Navalinga shrine, in its more refined treatment marks a slight advance on that structure, and is therefore, no doubt, a little later in date. Complete in all its parts, with an outer *nandi* porch, a four pillared hall, vestibule and cella, all in axial alignment, it measures 67 feet long by 37 feet wide, while its sikhara is 37 feet high, so that it is a compact and well-proportioned composition. Its exterior walls are simply but effectively decorated with pilasters at fairly close intervals, and an occasional mural shrine or similar structural motif is interposed between. The most instructive feature is the tower, which depicts the beginning of the departure from the earlier Pattadakal model. An increased definition in the separate stories, and a pronounced double-flexured curve in the outlines of the cupola at its apex, show that progress towards the flattened and more florid Hoysala type was already taking place. An unusual addition to the pillared hall are four windows tunnelled nearly seven feet through the thickness of the walls. In view of their style and that they are built of the same material, these two structures at Kukkanur appear to be closely allied to the temples of the Early Chalukyan group, as at Aihole and Pattadakal, and should be but little removed from them in date, although on historical grounds, one would place them as late as the last half of the tenth century.

Some little time after the production of the foregoing, a Jain temple was built at Lakkundi, a village seven miles from Gadag, which may be taken as the next step in the formation of the style. For not only does it denote progress in architectural experience, but it marks that change in material already referred to, when instead of the rougher grained sandstone hitherto used, it is built of the finer textured schist. The introduction of the latter reacted on the character of the workmanship as from now onwards the masonry courses are reduced in size, and the carving is more delicate and highly finished. The Jain temple is one of several buildings at Lakkundi, but it has every appearance of being the oldest, besides being the most imposing, as its dimensions are not inconsiderable, its length measuring 93 feet, its breadth 35 feet, and the sikhara is 42 feet in height. A distinguishing feature of its elevation is a high middle story in the tower, due, as in several Jain temples, to the imposition of an upper interior shrine-chamber, this supplementary sanctuary repeating, in several respects, the arrangements of the compartments underneath. On the eastern front is a large open-pillared hall, through which one passes to the sole entrance to the temple proper. Except for the more finished masonry and the finer character of the mural sculpture, there is nothing specially notable in the design of this building, save that the upper part of the tower indicates by the more flowing curve of its contours a still further trend towards the Hoysala model. As to the date of this temple it is recorded that Ballal II, one of the earliest of the Hoysala dynasty, made Lakkundi his capital in A.D. 1191, but even before that event it must have been

---

[1] *Chalukyan Architecture* by Cousens, H., Arch. Sur. of Ind., Vol. XLII, Calcutta, 1926.

an important city, so it is not unlikely from its appearance that this Jain temple was built in the last half of the eleventh century.

A new architectural feature now becomes evident in the style. Up to this point the temples of the Chalukyan mode were provided with a cornice of no particular prominence, but nevertheless its peculiar section denoted a special origin. This section takes the form of a simple quarter-round curve, added to which its bulky nature is obviously a heritage of the rock-cut type, which again derived from the overhanging thatched roof of the still older timber period. As a means of protecting the structural temple from the sun and the rain, it was ineffective, and a more suitable device now appears. This takes the shape of a wide projecting eave rather than a cornice, often with a double curved section, forming not only an artistic but a most useful addition to the building, serviceable as a protection against the strong light and also as a method of warding off the heavy monsoon rains. On most of the subsequent buildings this prominent eave, sometimes greatly expanded, although occasionally not curved but straight, and of exaggerated width, becomes a characteristic of this phase of the Chalukyan style. An early example of its introduction may be seen in the temple of Muktesvara at Chaudadampur, a hamlet on the banks of the Tungabhadra river towards the eastern boundary of the Dharwar district. This temple measures 80 feet in length and has a tower some 55 feet in height, but it is not exactly symmetrical in plan, as there are two entrance porches on the adjoining sides, with a kind of open portico confronting the eastern doorway. In addition to the emergence of the new form of eave, this temple signifies another stage in the evolution of the style, for it illustrates the fact that the formation of the tower has now matured. It shows in the design of this feature, that the well-defined stories distinguishing the early type, and also that of the Dravidian model, were being considerably reduced and their outlines obscured, by the wealth of plastic ornamentation which makes up the pattern of its sikhara. The Muktesvara, which was probably produced towards the end of the eleventh century, is an elegant little structure, its innovations denoting that the building art was living and moving, but even with the marks of progress and improvement recorded above, the zenith of the style was yet to come.

This consummation is exemplified in several temples of which the three finest are the Kasivisvesvara at Lakkundi, the Mahadeva at Ittagi, and the Mallikarjuna at Kuruvatti, all of which may date from the twelfth century. There are others, which in certain aspects, may be equally good, but as a whole this small series is representative of the phase in its most finished form. The Lakkundi temple indicates that some of the plainer parts of its structure may be of earlier date, but it is surmised that it was rebuilt at the time the city became a Hoysala capital in 1193. (Plate CXXXI, Fig. 1). It is one of several temples which adorned a once populous region, and is a double-shrined structure of conventional plan save for the unusual introduction of an open court towards the middle of its lay-out, from which various compartments extend axially on either side. What strikes one most in the elevational aspect of the building is the strength and vigour of its conformation, and the outstanding relief and richness of its architectural embellishment, the whole resulting in a powerful and effective composition. Provided with two shrines, one at each extremity, it has two separate towers, the larger one being at the western end, but both have lost their superstructures. The scheme consists of an alignment of four different sized squares, or elaborations of this figure, and its total length is 100 feet, with a width of 37 feet, while its main tower, when complete, would have been about 35 feet high. The principal entrance is on the south side, and leads into the *navaranga*, a chamber some 20 feet square with four pillars in the centre, and eight semi-detached pilasters around the sides, each pillar with a lathe-turned foundation of mouldings, but parts of these embossed with an intricate pattern as fine as chased metal. Where the temple excels however is in the bold character of the architectural ornamentation distributed over its vimanas, and the refined enrichment of its doorways, the one acting as a contrast to the other, evidently the productions of two different groups of workmen. In the decoration of the western vimana the customary system of mural design has been followed, but several motifs have been emphasised, including a large and prominent niche and canopy in the centre of each side above which rises a kind of foliated trefoil repeated up the centre of the sikhara, each repeat diminishing as it ascends. There is a voluptuousness and exuberance in the ornamentation, in temper not unlike that of the Baroque in Europe with its fantasy of grandiose excrescences, but, although impassioned, it is well-controlled and expressive of the style at the extreme height of its power.

The doorways of the Kasivisvesvara temple are its chief feature, one on the south, another on the east with a third leading to the cella, each of which is so treated as to possess all the qualities and essentials of a masterpiece. Each of these openings is designed on much the same principle, with a series of mouldings framing the rectangular aperture, but the sides are made structurally, as well as artistically firm by means of a prominent decorative pilaster. Above, is a moulded lintel surmounted by a carved cornice and overdoor, while a massive keystone, finely modelled into a scene of elephants anointing the goddess Lakshmi (*Gaja Lakshmi*) is a central motif. The south doorway is perhaps even more elaborate, much thought and imagination having been expended on its design, the effect being increased by the crisp texture of the relief. The remaining example, the doorway leading to the inner shrine, in its plastic handling is equally effective, a spirited battle between elephant-riders and horsemen sculptured almost in the round on the ogee curves of the cornice, assumes the quality of an ivory carving, in the microscopic nature of its technique. There are other temples at Lakkundi, including that of Nanesvara, which is a reproduction to a smaller scale of the foregoing, and is probably of the same date but none of these approaches in size or rich appearance that of the Kasivisvesvara.

At the town of Ittagi, the temple of Mahadev is another illustration of this phase of the builders' art at its meridian and is situated some twenty-two miles east of Gadag. This temple was the centre of an important group of religious structures arranged on a terrace specially built for the purpose and containing an ornamental tank the whole a very fine conception, evidently the focus of much spiritual activity early in the twelfth century A.D. Now the only building which is intact is the Mahadev, and this has lost the upper part of its sikhara, while the roof of its pillared hall has also been damaged. Even with these defects it is a beautifully harmonised structure, orthodox and symmetrical in its arrangements as it consists of a hypostyle hall, chamber of assembly (*navaranga*), with a pillared porch on either side, a vestibule and a cella, all grouped together in a simple and appropriate manner. It is of a fair size, as it measures, 120 feet long by 60 feet wide, and its tower would have been over 40 feet high, the general appearance of the whole proving that these proportions produce a very pleasing result. According to some standards its decorative treatment may be considered excessive, but nonetheless it is all balanced and orderly, and, although rich, its elements are well thought out and carefully distributed. In style it is much nearer to the Mysore phase previously discussed, particularly in the suave curves of its tower, in which there are no stories but only horizontal tiers, and a sculptured pattern is repeated over its entire surface. The hypostyle hall confronting the eastern aspect of the temple, and which measures some 55 feet across, is a striking part of the composition, as it originally contained as many as sixty-eight pillars, each of no mean size. Of these the twenty-six interior ones are massive lathe-turned columns with highly decorated pedestals, while the four forming the central group support a coffered ceiling, wrought into a most intricate design of figure-subjects and spirited foliage scrolls. In the interior of the *navaranga*, on each of the four walls, are two rectangular recesses, each one provided with a kind of altar table and a pedestal for the reception of sacred symbols, vessels, etc., a system strangely suggestive of the Easter Altar in some Christian churches. In the same way the circular niche on the front face of the tower, now empty, was utilized for a change of image whenever this was desired. (Plate CXXX).

The remaining example of this class, and of approximately the same date as the foregoing, is the temple of Mallikarjuna at Kuruvatti, a village on the Tungabhadra river, about seventeen miles west of the taluk headquarters of Harpanahalli. With a perfectly symmetrical plan, its sikhara quite complete, and its roof in tolerable condition, in many respects it may be regarded as a standard example of its kind. The length of the temple building itself is 38 feet, and its width, with the two entrance porches one on each side, is 36 feet, while its sikhara is 44 feet in height. If, however, the large *nandi* pavilion on its eastern front is included the whole composition is some 130 feet in length. The architectural treatment of the entire structure is of the same order as that of the buildings previously described, although, as a whole the decoration on its surfaces is less congested, and there is more restraint in the distribution of the motifs which enrich its walls both inside and out. Across the entrance to the vestibule of the inner shrine there is a *toran* or archway consisting of a massive lintel on two free-standing pillars, each portion elaborately carved, while the bracket figures at the upper part of the pillars are more delicately sculptured than in any other example.

One other group of temples belonging to this phase should be referred to on account of an unusual feature which finds a place on one of them. This is a cluster of three temples at Gadag, dedicated to Trikutesvara, Sarasvati, and Somesvara, all representative of the style at its culmination, but one of these, that of Somesvara is distinctive because it displays a form of mural treatment which carries it entirely away from the Dravidian tradition, and draws it very close to that of Mysore. In the profusion of plastic elements decorating the exterior of this temple, towards the centre of its vertical wall surface, there appears an attempt to reproduce that type of niched figure sculpture which is so characteristic of the Hoysala temples at Halabid and Belur, each niche shaped like a " stele " and each containing a statue of a divinity carved in high relief. A little uncertain in form, this significant element emerges in the Somesvara

temple, and is repeated around the building, supplanting the framework of pilasters, which in the Mysore type has almost completely disappeared. (Plate CXXVIII). By the introduction of such a motif in the Gadag example the two phases of the Chalukyan style, the Hoysala and the Kanarese, make definite contact. A further interest in this temple lies in the fact that its decoration is such that it appears to have reached the limit of its powers, it is inclined to be confused and its forms are lacking in vitality, conditions which may prefigure the beginning of the decline.

Before finally leaving this development of the later Chalukyan style some account of the remarkable exception already referred to, is indicated, and which relates to the temple of Dodda Basappa at Dambal. (Plate CXXIX, Fig. 2). Dating probably from late in the twelfth century, this temple is the only one of its kind, as all the others of the phase are rectangular in their lay-out, so that this star-planned structure is conspicuous as a work of notable originality. For although many of the temples of the Hoysala phase in Mysore, as previously shown, had stellate sanctuaries, at Dambal not only the sanctuary, but also the pillared hall, or *navaranga*, is star-shaped in plan. In the case of the sanctuary of the Dodda Basappa temple, this is worked out on a system of twenty-four points to the star, while the pillared hall would have as many as thirty-four, but owing to the amount of wall surface taken up by the junction of these two compartments and the introduction of two doorways, the former has in reality only ninteeen points and the latter twenty-one. (Plate XI, Fig. 12). As the stellate plan is carried up right through the elevation of the building, the effect of such a close array of vertical offsets on the appearance of the structure as a whole is singular and arresting. Whereas in the upright portions of the *vimana* walls, and also of the *navaranga*, these angular projections present vivid passages of chiaroscuro, their vertical tendency adding to the strength of the building, when they pass into the tower to intersect the horizontal string-courses of that feature, the pattern thus produced is too exiguous to be architecturally convincing. It is noticeable that the pillars of the porch to the main entrance of the building, which is on the south side, are fluted from base to capital, the idea being to maintain throughout the entire scheme its angular character, a commendable effort at architectural consistency. Such an innovation, however, raises the question as to whether the angularity in this instance has not exceeded its legitimate limits and so made to dominate the composition until it has become almost incongruous. One part of the conception stands out as a first-rate piece of work, showing that the builders had a highly developed sense of values, but at the same time not quite sufficient competence to apply it to all parts of the structure. This refers to the architectural treatment of the offsets of the vimana, a design consisting of forms alternating with motifs and motifs with forms, all gracefully attenuated so that the whole is not unlike the traceried walls of some fifteenth century northern Italian cathedral, or the panelled buttresses of sixteenth century Perpendicular Gothic.

In addition to the selected buildings of the style described above, there are many places within the area referred to where temples of the same type may be found, such as Haveri, Hangal, Bankapur, Niralgi, Harahalli, Galganatha, Harihara, Rattihalli, Belagamve, Unkal, Degamve, Belgaum, Bagai, Magala, Hirahadagalli, Nilagunda, Huvinahadgalli, and Halavagalu. Finally, for the phase in its decadence, there is the temple of Koppesvara at Khedrapur, a village thirty miles east of the town of Kolhapur. This is a large building, planned in the usual manner with a spacious pillared hall in front, but its construction seems to have been interrupted, being eventually completed at a much later date in brick and plaster. Most probably, it was being built, therefore, just at the moment when the forces of the Moslem invader Malik Kafur overran the Dekkan early in the fourteenth century, and on that account was left unfinished. From the design of the pillars particularly, the decline of the style can be understood, as these, although copying generally the shape of the fine moulded examples of the previous structures, are wrought in a dry and lifeless manner indicating plainly that by this time much of the fine spirit of the movements had gone out of it.

REFERENCE

Cousens, H., *Chalukyan Architecture* (Arch. Sur. of Ind.), Cal. 1926.

CHAPTER XXXI

THE BRAHMANICAL BUILDINGS OF BENGAL

(8th to 17th Centuries)

IN view of the large extent of country represented by Bengal and the territory adjacent to it, the extreme eastern position of India is not rich in buildings of an architectural character. There are the records of more than one great civilization, which flourished within this region, but the structural remains of these are extremely scanty. For this the nature of the soil and the climate are mainly responsible : both conditions encourage the rapid growth of jungle vegetation, and once a building ceases to be cared for, the creeping shrubs and trees speedily take charge, soon to tear it to pieces so that before long it becomes merely an unrecognizable mound of ruin. At the same time the destruction brought about by the hand of man cannot be omitted from any account of the architecture of this portion of the country, as the remains of some of the finest buildings amply testify. In no part of India are the two great cultural movements, the Hindu and the Muhammedan and the manner in which the one superseded the other more vividly illustrated than in some of the ancient remains of Bengal, as for instance in the ruined Adina Masjid, built by Sekander Shah (1358-89) at his new capital of Pandua, as this great congregational mosque was constructed almost entirely of materials taken from the demolished city of Lukhnauti, the capital of the Hindu dynasty of the Senas.

It is however the character of the country itself, and the nature of the building material most readily available, which have mainly conditioned the architecture of these parts. In those rare places where there is an outcrop of stone, this material has been employed, as in the case of a few laterite temples towards the south-west, and in the basalt buildings of the Malda district, situated more in the middle of the State. On the other hand as the country is deltaic and composed mostly of alluvium, everywhere there are deposits of clay suitable for the manufacture of bricks. Therefore much of the construction is produced in this manner. In addition a good supply of timber was procurable in many parts, as well as heavy growths of bamboo, the plaint nature of the latter giving that curvature of cornice characteristic of the building art of Bengal.

In spite of the destruction brought about by the various forces mentioned above, it is possible to identify from the remains of these productions, three separate movements illustrating the course of architectural development in this region. The first of these assuming more or less an end in itself, was confined mainly to the Southern area, and resolved itself into two distinct phases. What may have been the older of these phases was an offshoot of that very virile movement, already described, which flourished in Orissa in the early mediaeval period, as shown at Bhuba-

neswar. The other, of ancient origin, but represented by examples of a more recent date, was an indigenous style of building, appertaining to a form of folk architecture, notable on account of its sectarian and sociological aspects. The second of these movements, but one destined to have important implications, was part of that powerful Hindu-Buddhist development responsible for those immense monastic settlements, previously referred to, which flourished in Bihar and the Gangetic plain towards the end of the first millennium. The third was the outcome of that " Eastern School " of art and architecture, which under the patronage of the Pal and Sena rulers of Bengal, influenced greatly the arts of the surrounding countries until it ended with the Muhammedan invasion in the thirteenth century. It will be shown that the two latter movements coalesced in the course of time to form the chief inspiration of that powerful current of Hindu-Buddhism which, carried eastward, stimulated the creation of the magnificent monuments of Greater India.

Taking the first of these movements, that which found favour in the southernmost portion of the Bengal area, and was in some respects a provincial phase of the Orissa School, this may be studied at various places but principally in Mayurbhanj State, and in the Bengal districts of Bankura and Burdwan. In Mayurbhanj is the ancient site of Khiching, now a small village near the western portion of the State, but at one time comprising the capital of a principality, its ruined shrines and sikharas indicating that in the eleventh and twelfth centuries the Bhanja rules maintained a school of architecture and sculpture of no mean order.[1] Obviously a derivative of that great group of monuments at Bhubaneswar, although there are remains of an earlier date, the most significant example is the unfinished temple of Khandiya Deul, the fine doorway of which is still preserved. A feature of the Khiching shrine is that none of them possesses a *mukhamandapa* or portico, and most of those of the same class built in Bengal follow a similar plan, which has led a Hindu authority to observe that " a richly ornamented temple without a portico appears a more pious structure than one with a portico ; for in the former the lamp of sacrifice burns with greater brilliance."[2] Apart from the style of this small group as well as in other respects Khiching forms a connecting link between the development in Southern Bengal and that of Orissa.

As already mentioned the Southern Bengal development, chiefly illustrated by temples in the districts of Bankura and Burdwan, resolves itself into two distinctive types, one of which is allied to the Orissan movement, and the other is a self-originated mode, expressive of the people and their environment. The former are built mainly of stone masonry

---

[1] *Journal of the Bihar and Orissa Research Society, June* 1927.

[2] Dr. Ramprasad Chandra in " *Note on the Ancient Monuments of Mayurbhanj* " (*Journal of the Bihar and Orissa Research Society, June* 1927.)

and, as in the Khiching pattern are isolated towers or sikharas enclosing a cella for the image or symbol. Designed on the same principle as those of Bhubaneswar, but usually smaller in size, their height is approximately three and a half times the diameter of their square plan, while their elevation is in two stories, divided by a decisive double cornice, the relation between the lower and upper portions being in pleasing proportion. On three sides of the lower story are openings in the shape of elegant niches, while the front has a projecting doorway, but no outstanding portico. In one or two instances however a *mukhamandapa* may have been provided but which in the course of time has disappeared. As the scheme of these sikharas is one of verticality, mouldings of a lateral order provide the principal decoration, the skilful combination of the two contrasting elements presenting an attractive appearance to the entire composition. These shrines are sometimes found in groups as at Barakar in the Burdwan district, one of which, enumerated IV, owing to its outline and proportions bearing a resemblance to the sikhara of the Parasrameswar temple at Bhubaneswar is presumed to be of somewhat the same date, namely the eighth century, but is more likely much later. Locally known as the Begunia group owing to a fancied resemblance to the fruit of the egg plant, (*begun*), they are probably of the Pala period and therefore of the ninth and tenth centuries.[1] Among other examples of this class is the temple of Telkupi in the Manbhum district of Bihar, but undoubtedly the most ornate, is the Siddheswara Temple at Behulara in the Bankura district of the tenth century. Built of brick enriched with terracotta reliefs carried over its entire surface, yet this profusion of pattern does not offend, it serves to emphasize its graceful lines. Numerous other temples of this order are to be found distributed throughout South-Western Bengal and in the Manbhum district of Bihar, all apparently built while the Pala Dynasty was in power and therefore dating between the eighth and eleventh centuries.

The other phase of architectural development in the Southern region of Bengal has been defined above as an indigenous form of the building art peculiarly expressive of the inhabitants of these parts. Constructed sometimes of laterite, but generally of brick, and so actually moulded out of the very composition of the earth from which these agriculturists wrested their living, it speaks of the soil itself, and few things can be more fundamentally influential than the nature of one's native soil. Obviously originating from a somewhat primitive and cabin-like structure it gradually evolved into a system derived from the wooden houses and bamboo thatched huts of the ancestral forest dwellers. This is shown specifically in the sloping roof, curved eave, and other similar features, which could only be the result of long years of building in timber and bamboo. Such expedients are the logical outcome of a mind ingenuous yet practical, a consciousness which concerned itself mainly in dealing with the elements or powers of nature as these affected the course of daily life by the profound reality of their existence.

This mode of building, although superior to what may be termed folk-architecture, never rose to classical heights, but it possesses a freshness and spontaneity, and makes an appeal as it is a reflection of certain racial characteristics. The population being largely rural there are no outstanding monuments in this mode, but there are a number of temples of moderate proportions most of which display formations common to all. These temples are designed on the principle of a main structure, square in plan, its walls vertical, but the lines and planes which in most buildings are ordinarily horizontal, in this type are carried across its front in a series of parallel curves, bent in the form of a bow. Such a distinctive application of curves specially affects the form of the roof and its cornice or eave, which, in contour, are parabolic, and clearly inherited from a bamboo framework given this shape in order to throw off heavy monsoon rain. Huts with thatched roofs built on similar lines are common in most parts of Bengal, and the somewhat indeterminate curved effect of the upper portions conveys the impression of a people bending before the elements, of yielding to them rather than defying them in view of their relentless power. As an instance of the persistence of this tradition in the building art of Bengal, the principle of the curve is reproduced in modern roofs of corrugated iron, a material which, in spite of its intractable nature, is forced to follow the shape of the bent bamboo.

Such is one of the characteristics of the later temples of Bengal, but there are further features, individual in their treatment, which differentiate this style of architecture from that of other parts. Over the curved roof a tower is erected, and according to the number of these the temples were classified, for instance that with a cluster of five towers or turrets, was referred to as a *puncha-ratna*, literally five gems, meaning towers, or *nava-ratna*, nine towered and so forth. Wherever there is a cornice to these towers or turrets, it is also curved in keeping with the regional practice, while the upper portion of the tower forms itself into a kind of sikhara, with horizontal courses of moulding. The facade usually consists of three arched openings comprising the entrance, each opening separated by a substantial pillar, the arches themselves being of the pointed variety often engrailed with numerous prominent cusps. The pillars are remarkable, as they are not only exceptional in their proportions, but these massive supports found favour in most of the different phases of architecture as developed in other places in Bengal. In no part of India have such ponderous piers been employed, so that this abnormally wide and often short type of pillar is specially characteristic of the building art in this eastern region.

As to the interior of these temples a single hall or *thakurbari* is the main feature, on one side of which is the *vedi* or altar for the image, while above is an upper story in the shape of a continuous gallery around the circuit of this compartment. One of the attractions of these temples, particularly those constructed of brick, is the external decoration, which is in terracotta relief, and resolves itself into a diaper of square panels repeated over the entire surface of the facade, each panel containing a picture in relief, and to a relatively small scale, of some subject of peculiar interest. Many of these represent episodes taken from the ancient epics, while others are incidents in the daily life of the people, some of which are of no little sociological significance. (Plate CXXXIII).

There are many examples of this class of structure distributed throughout the townships and villages of Bengal, but a typical group may be seen at Vishnupur in the Bankura district due to the encouragement given to temple building

---

[1] *The Begunia Group of Temples*, S. K. Saraswati, *Journal of the Indian Society*, Dec. 1933.

by the Malla Rajas, a dynasty which held sway in these parts for several centuries. Of this group the principal temples date from the seventeenth and eighteenth centuries and include the Laljui which is a single towered structure in laterite and dated 1658, and the Madan Mohan, built of brick also with one sikhara, erected in 1694. Temples of the pancha-ratna type, or those with five towers are the Shyam Rai constructed of brick in 1643, and the laterite example of Madan Gopal dated 1665.

A variation in design is a form of double temple, and thus known as a *jor-bangla*, which differs but little in its interior plan, although it has a distinctive exterior. As its name implies, it is a " twin " (*jor*) shape, resembling two thatch and bamboo huts joined together but constructed of brick and surmounted by a single tower. A good example is the Kestaraya built at Vishnupur in 1726, a temple of fair size as it is a square of forty feet side, and the roof is thirty-three feet high, with its tower rising to nearly fifty feet from the ground. The sanctuary, or *thakur bari*, is a square cell of eight feet side occupying the centre of the structure, and there are surrounding side-chambers, one of which leads by a staircase to an upper gallery carried, rather like a clerestory, around the building. Another temple of this type is that of Chaitanya at Guptapara in the Hughli district.

Of the other movements in this region, that referred to as the Hindu-Buddhist development which produced the great monastic settlements in the Buddhist holy land towards the end of the first millennium, this also extended its influence into Bengal. For at Paharpur in the Rajshahi District excavations have revealed the remains of a monumental edifice of such stupendous proportions, that although now a mound of ruins, it appears to have been the largest and most important of its kind. Founded by the Pala ruler Dharmapala towards the end of the eighth century, it was known as the Great Vihara or Monastery of Dharmapala. Constructed very largely of brick, some idea of the plan and arrangements may be gained from the inset on Plate CLIII, where it will be seen that on the ground it took the form of a cross measuring 361 ft. by 318 ft., and it is calculated that it attained a height of well over one hundred feet. Its elevation shows that it rose up into terraces with the central core of the building resolving itself into a square cell enshrining an image or symbol of exceptional sanctity. The approach was by a stairway on the northern side leading to a corridor carried round the entire structure and communicating with four supplementary cells, one in each arm of the cross. Each of these cells presumably contained a large statue of metal, one of which may have been that fine figure, a product of the famous Varendra foundry, discovered at Sultanganj and now deposited in the Birmingham Art Gallery. For the instruction and edification of the multitudes of devotees who paid homage to this shrine, as it is recorded that it was venerated by the followers of all creeds, Buddhist, Hindu, and Jain, the exterior faces of the terraces were embellished with a continuous series of terracotta plaques illustrating in bas-relief the mythology and folklore of the country. Among the subjects depicted incidents have been identified relating to the life of the god Krishna, said to antedate the emergence of this cult by several centuries. In addition to this great central structure it was enclosed by an extensive range of monastic dwellings sufficient to accommodate a large establishment of priests. That such a grand monument, a landmark in the religious and architectural history of the country should have been almost entirely effaced is regrettable, but it is a matter of satisfaction to know that recent research and modern scientific methods have rescued what remains, and brought to light a building, which it is recorded formed at one time the cultural centre of eastern India.

There now remains the last of the great movements enumerated above, which brought into Bengal a phase of the building art of considerable beauty and consequence. This may be described as an extension of the " Eastern School " of architecture and art, which, due to the incentive of the Pala and Sena dynasties appears to have flourished with great effect at Lakhnauti, the capital of the Senas, now almost a lost site near Malda, but originally comprising a large complex of basalt buildings of a particularly substantial and ornate description. It was, however, completely despoiled by the Muhammedans after its capture in 1197, in order to provide materials for their own capital at Gaur. From the remains incorporated in the mosques and tombs of the conquerors, it is possible to obtain sufficient evidence for the character of the style of the Sena architecture to be conjectured. Situated as Lakhanauti was on the banks of the Ganges, yet within easy reach of the Rajmahal hills, it was not difficult to obtain from this rocky range a fine textured grade of black basalt, of which stone the principal buildings were constructed. Records of two kinds of buildings are recognizable, one religious, consisting of temples and shrines, and the other secular, apparently a royal palace and fortress.

That there was a certain class of religious structure produced in these parts and which has been referred to as the " lost temple type of pre-Islamic Bengal," seems more than probable, yet concrete evidences of such a development are rare and fragmentary. No complete example has survived, as all the ancient Hindu sites became convenient quarries from which the Moslems extracted the ready-made masonry required for their own purposes. As in the mosques at Ajmir and the Qutb at Delhi, so from the great congregational mosque of Adina at Pandua, and other Islamic buildings in this area, some idea of the regional type of temple architecture, as it existed in the twelfth century, may be abstracted. Out of the masses of sculptured stones incorporated in these Islamic structures, it is not difficult to envisage the manner in which the Hindu buildings were decorated, but their architectural appearance can only be a matter of inference. Two structural factors however emerge from this miscellaneous collection of material, and these supported by other circumstances, indicate that there was a sikhara over the temple shrine, a tall structure in tiers of a very ornate, almost florid character, and that a distinguishing feature of the style as a whole was the invariable use of a trefoil arch. Even with such slender data thus provided, it is possible to conceive that in general shape and treatment the Brahmanical temples of Varendra (Nothern Bengal) were not dissimilar from the Buddhist temple at Budh Gaya, a monumental building of more than ordinary significance, and which lay in the course of the art current as it was carried eastward into Bengal.

As to the manner in which the temples of Bengal were architecturally decorated, there is ample evidence provided in the mosques of Gaur and Pandua, for these Islamic buildings are rich repositories of sculptured remains. From the carved stones indiscriminately built into the later masonry, it is unmistakably apparent that under the Sena kings there flourished a school of plastic art, which for variety of design and skilled execution, could have had few equals in India. There is little doubt that this was the grand and final flowering of that art movement which three centuries before had taken form under the previous regime of the Pala dynasty. For on the authority of Taranath,[1] the Buddhist historian, it is known that at Varenda under these rulers in the ninth century, there lived the famous and versatile artists, Dhiman and Bitpalo, father and son, the Lorenzo Ghibertis of India, as, like the celebrated Florentine they were accomplished, not only in the arts of sculpture and metal work, but also in mural design and colouring. And so powerful was the influence of their productions that from them emerged that eastern school of sculpture with its ultimate development under the Senas at Lakhnauti, and now visible, embedded in the subsequent structural schemes of the Moslems.

Among the many carved fragments within these buildings, there is one example more complete than any of the others, and from which a fair conception of the style may be obtained. This is a small subsidiary doorway on the west and back wall of the Adina mosque at Gaur, evidently torn from a Vishnu temple of the eleventh-twelfth centuries and inserted into its present position. Originally forming the entrance to the cella, it shows clearly the architectural character of this feature, and from it the quality of the whole may be estimated. It represents a square-headed opening, with pilasters on either side and a cornice above, showing that its designers favoured a structural framework for their doorway design. A moulding formed of the rope-like convolutions of Sesha, the " endless serpent," surrounds the jambs, with a close and realistic cluster of the same coils comprising the " keystone." Outside this is a series of trefoil niches, and, wherever required, are scrolls of foliage, enclosing various symbolic forms, among which an interpretation of the " vase-and-foliage " of the Guptas may be identified.

In addition to the rich beauty of the design and workmanship of this doorway, it exhibits a singularly interesting expedient employed by the Hindu masons for bonding their stone construction. Within the lintel, exposed by fracture, it revealed a system of channels, vents, and plug-holes, for the purposes of enabling molten metal to be poured in, and for the courses of stone to be joined in this manner. Bonding by means of metal such as bronze dowels and copper cramps, is part of the builder's equipment, but the process shown in this example, and probably freely employed in their architecture, is unusual, and appertains more to the workshop practice of the foundry than to that of the stoneyard. Can it be that the influence of that forceful school of metal-casting brought to such perfection by Dhiman penetrated into the technique of the building art, so that the Pala builder was a metal-worker first and a mason afterwards ? In the hard metallic manipulation of the carving, in the bronze-like texture of the basalt itself there is implied the sharp incisive touch of the chiseller and chaser of cold metal.

As with the temples of old Bengal so with the secular architecture, the style of this is also mainly speculative. But a large rectangular space on the site of the ancient Hindu capital is still called Ballalbari, no doubt referring to the

palace of Ballal Sena, the last but one of his line, and who reigned in the twelfth century. *In situ* nothing remains, but in the mosques there are scores of huge black basalt piers and pillars, certainly not wrought for their present purpose, and hardly likely to be part of any temple-scheme. The inference, therefore, is that they are spoils from Ballal's grand palace and fortress, removed bodily from the columned halls, and accordingly representative of the temporal architecture of that ruler's time. Whatever their original function was, these pillars are remarkable productions, not monolithic, as were nearly all the pillars of this period, but built up of stone masonry in the most expert manner. Some of the shafts are round, but the majority are executed on a square or octagonal basis, strong, solid constructions averaging nine feet in height and three feet in width, such unusually thickset proportions being evidently so devised in order to support a heavy load, presumably a building in several stories. The style of the capitals is in keeping with the shafts, which are also massive but simple and severe in their design consisting of plain mouldings and chamfers with brackets of leaf scrolls. If the remainder of the architecture of which these pillars formed a part was of the same substantial and dignified character, then the building art of the Hindu kings of Bengal must have been of a standard equal to that of any other part of India. Except in the rock-cut temples there are no other pillars with such strength and stability combined with a stolid purposeful grace, as the black basalt piers from Lakhnauti ; those who produced them built them to last, little thinking that in a few short years an unexpected force would sweep through the land, to destroy and afterwards readjust them under entirely different conditions.

Much of the foregoing is confirmed by the remains on another site, that of Tribeni. Now merely a straggling village, Tribeni, originally Saptagrama or Satgawn in the Hooghly district, has a long history, but considerably obscured by the passage of time and events. Owing to its position at the junction of three streams—hence its name—it acquired great sanctity, and many religious buildings grew up in its neighbourhood. Among them there appear to have been some in the same style as those at Lakhnauti, and therefore of the Pala-Sena period, chief of which are two buildings now converted into a tomb and its adjacent mosque, known as the Mazar of Zafar Khan Ghazi. In the aisles of the mosque are the same square solid masonry pillars as at Gaur, evidently dismantled from a similar palace or fortress, although one of the columns, different from the others, seems to have formed part of a chaitya or shrine, as it was carved with Buddhist images. The tomb-structure itself, however, tells its own story. It is a rectangular enclosure formed of two roofless compartments built of black basalt, and in spite of the whole having been materially damaged in adapting it to its present purpose, its two compartments have been identified as the vestibule or *antarala*, and the assembly hall or *mandapa*, of a Vaishnavite temple. Most of the sculpture has been defaced, and portions of the structure are a mere jumble of stones, but it is quite clear that this temple was a finished example of the building art, its ashlar masonry is precise and orderly, and the architectural treatment of the parts still in position show knowledge and experience. There are four doorways to the compartments, one facing each of the cardinal points, and from these, and the design of the wall surface between,

[1] *Indian Antiquary*, Vol. IV, p. 101.

Fig. 1. Kashmir: Temple of the Sun, Martand; 8th century A.D.

Fig. 2. Temple at Barakar, Bengal; c. 18th century.

Fig. 3. Java, Dyeing Plateau; Arjuna Temple (c. 750)

Fig. 1
Kashmir: Temple of Wangath; c. 8th century.

Fig. 2
Avantipur, Kashmir: Temple of Avantisvami; 9th century A.D.

CONJECTURAL
RESTORATION OF
AVANTISVAMI TEMPLE
KASHMIR, 9TH CENT. A.D.

SCALE OF FEET
0 10 30 50 70 90 110 140

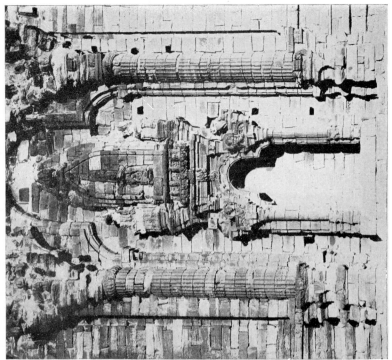

Fig. 2
Temple at Malot, Salt Range (Singhapura), Punjab; c. 9th century.

Fig. 1
Sankaracharya Temple (Takht-i-Sulaiman); 8th century.

Fig. 1.   Pandrethan Temple; c. 12th century.

Fig. 2. Detail from ruined temple in Srinagar; 9th cent.   Fig. 3.   Detail from cella of the Temple at Martand.

Kashmir Temples

Nepal: Stupa at Swambhunath.

Nepal: The Bodhnath.

Nepal: Mammath Temple, Patan.

the style may be judged. The doorways are square-headed openings, contained within mouldings, among which that of Sesha, or the snake emblem, may be recognized, and above the centre of the lintel is the customary dedicatory block. Where the builders of the structure have shown notable restraint is in their treatment of the wall-spaces between these openings, which have been conceived and carried out in a simple refined manner. At intervals plain flat buttresses having little projection, were imposed, intersecting both the mouldings of the cornice above, and of the basement below. This procedure divided the surface into a series of shallow sunk panels, within each of which was placed an ornamental foliated arcade. Such an appreciation of plain spaces and their value in emphasising the structural proprieties of a building are rare in Indian architecture, and in this instance are further proof that the building art under the Pala-Sena patronage was produced with more than ordinary intelligence and good taste.

Apart from the intrinsic quality of the art and architecture of two of the movements described above, namely that which expressed itself in the great Hindu-Buddhist monastic monuments on the one hand, and that which produced the temples and palaces of the Palas and Senas on the other, in a word the Eastern School, these two movements together were destined to affect profoundly the advancing tide of Indo-Buddhist civilization which was already beginning to overflow into the wide range of countries comprising Greater India. While the medium by which this Indian religio-culture was conveyed eastward was fundamentally the dynamic power of Hindu-Buddhism, which carried all before it, towards the later centuries of the first millennium, the form it eventually assumed took its source from the movements which grew up and were so firmly founded in the holy land of Buddhism on the Gangetic plain. Changed in outward appearance by their change of environment and other influences the architectural achievements of such countries as Burma, Cambodia, Java and, to a certain extent Ceylon, in the mediaeval period, were basically of Indian extraction. So much so that the building art of the various civilizations which comprise Greater India may be regarded as belonging to one broad school, each of the races concerned working out its architectural conceptions according to its own individual ideals, but with the whole evolution created, developed, unified and to a certain extent standardised by an intellectual, religious and physical awakening which originally proceeded from India.

An analysis of some of the decorative effects found in these more distant architectural productions reveals similarities which cannot be coincidences but are actual facts. There are reproductions, both in design and in relief, of patterns which might be the identical handiwork of the stone carvers of Lakhnauti in Bengal. The same applies to some of the constructional features, as for instance in Java where the arch motifs and pilasters appear to be derived from the same source. But it was in the aims and intentions of these architectural achievements in Burma, Cambodia and Java, that the growth of the Indian conceptions is most significantly expressed. While the stupa still held its place as the premier Buddhist symbol, it was too abstract in its nature to appeal to the physical senses. Something was required endowed with more humanistic qualities, and such qualities were represented by the great monastic monuments of mediaeval India, of which the Dharmapala Vihara at Paharpur previously described was a notable example. In all the countries therefore which drew inspiration from this movement there evolved, in addition to the stupa, magnificent architectural creations in the form of temples, or similar religious edifices, enclosing chambers or cells in which were enshrined images, often colossal in size, invested with halos and aureoles, emblazoned with gold, glorifying the creed to which they gave concrete form. Through the spiritual power thus generated, man's imaginative faculties were so stimulated that he felt impelled to express himself in some substantial manner, worthy of himself and his belief. By some such means the grand monuments of Greater India were conceived, such as Angkor Vat and Borobudur. In these immense works of architecture we see the spirit of the monastic movements in India further materialized, taking its shape from the " Eastern School " of India, and not a little from the building art of Bengal.

REFERENCES

Mitra, J. N., *The Ruins of Vishnupur*, Calcutta 1940.
French, J. C., *The Art of the Pal Empire of Bengal*, Oxford 1928.

CHAPTER XXXII

KASHMIR

THE BUDDHIST AND BRAHMANICAL REMAINS (A.D. 200 to 1300)

THROUGHOUT its history Kashmir has experienced an art life very much its own. The natural position of the country encouraged this condition—a valley at a height of six thousand feet above sea level, enclosed within snow-clad ranges, and approached only by long and tortuous routes, imposes an isolation which would normally tend to make its inhabitants self-supporting and self-contained. On the other hand, although itself remote, Kashmir lay within that part of Central Asia which at one period was the clearing-house of several separate civilizations and the influences of these found their way into this natural retreat. Moreover, there was a time early in the first millennium when it came into contact with the wide-spread eastern conquests of the Sassanid empire with its neo-Persian culture, to be followed not long afterwards by a period in which its own territories extended far beyond their natural geographical limits. Yet with all these events and powerful cross-currents, with the ebb and flow of great external movements on its borders, Kashmir continued consistently to maintain a certain indigenous and independent type of culture, as reflected in several of its activities, not the least of which was its form of expression in the field of art. Much of the high quality of the latter was due to the inherent aesthetic sense and rare adaptability of its inhabitants.

These artistic instincts were certainly stimulated by—if not actually derived from—the reactions of a receptive people to the exquisite natural scenery by which they were surrounded, and in the beauties of which their lives have been for ever steeped. Those who have been fortunate enough to dwell for any length of time in the valley of Kashmir can appreciate these conditions, which are not only produced by the superb formation of the country, of lake and river, meadow and forest, mountain and snow-clad peak, but by the atmospheric and other phenomena acting on such an enchanting environment, by its cloud and sunshine, its light and shade, its dawns and sunsets, its changes of season, its pageantry of colour and all those moving effects which nature so artistically stages with never-failing harmony. It can only be these that have given the inhabitants of this country that acute aesthetic understanding that has enabled them to design and create works of art of such a distinctive character. And combined with this natural gift is that of assimilation, that power to select extraneous elements and to absorb them so skilfully that they become an integral part of their own conceptions.

Of all the arts practised by the people of the valley in the pre-Islamic period, the greater part of which corresponds to what is ordinarily termed the Middle Ages, the building art was one in which they were notably proficient, as the remains of their large monuments in stone are a standing proof. Three phases of this architectural movement are discernible. The first was an early or primitive form which developed about A.D. 200, the records of which are merely foundational remains. This was followed by an epoch of

building on such a grand scale that it may be defined as the classical period of their building art, and lasted from 700 A.D. to the beginning of the fourteenth century, after which date the country came under the influence of Islam. This long period of some seven centuries is itself resolved into two phases, during the earlier of which the buildings were mainly of Buddhist attribution, while later they were entirely Brahmanical.

The first phase, or early Buddhist period, is represented by bare foundations, but these are of the utmost significance, as they serve to explain the origins of the building art in Kashmir, with some of its influences and associations. These remains are the result of excavations, two sites having been thus explored, one at Harwan near Srinagar, and the other at Ushkar near Baramula. The former has yielded the more important material, from which the character of the building art at its beginning may be realized. Harwan occupies an ideal situation on the slopes of high ground overlooking the crystal waters of the Dal Lake, with a glorious range of mountains in the distance. Here, in the early centuries of the Christian era, on a series of terraces covering a large area, there grew up a prosperous Buddhist settlement, which included the usual group of buildings forming such a monastic establishment, as for instance a stupa within its courtyard, accommodation for the resident monks, several chapels, and a chaitya-hall, or temple. The stupa was square in plan, with its base in three tiers, and approached by a flight of steps on its western side, the whole being contained within an open quadrangle, an arrangement corresponding in every particular to the stupa courts of Gandhara, with which country Kashmir at this time was closely connected. As to the upper part of the stupa, this has entirely disintegrated, but fortunately by the aid of certain small terracotta plaques bearing miniature replicas in bas-relief, and found in the debris, its shape and character have been revealed. The stupa itself was the customary stilted ovoid surmounted in this instance by a disproportionately large finial in the form of an umbrella of thirteen tiers, the great size of the superstructure necessitating as supports a number of sloping struts, probably of wood, between the body of the stupa and its lowest rim ; there also appears to have been a free-standing pillar of the Asokan type erected on each side.

The other building of consequence on this site was the *chaitya* or temple, a large structure occupying a prominent position on the highest terrace with the remaining edifices grouped below. What is remarkable in this building is that it was a typical chaitya-hall with an apsidal end, a distinctive form of a Buddhist temple common in the rock-architecture of the more southerly parts of India, but rarely found elsewhere. Yet it should be noted that the remains of a chaitya-hall almost exactly similar in plan and dimensions to that at Harwan, with a circular apse separated from an oblong nave surrounded by a processional passage, and enclosed within a rectangular courtyard, were unearthed at the Indo-Greek city of Sirkap in Taxila (Chapter VII), dating presumably from about the first century B.C. There can be little doubt that the settlement in Kashmir was an outlying branch of that Buddhist movement which had its monastic establishments widely distributed over a great part of north-west India and beyond, at this period of its history.

However interesting the plans and general arrangements of such early buildings were, the manner of their construction, and, above all, the character of their embellishment, were even more so. Three methods of building have been disclosed ; the earliest, a curious and primitive process of walling consisted of embedding quantities of pebbles in masses of mud mortar. This was followed about A.D. 300 by a process of reinforcing the wall of pebbles by the insertion at intervals of irregular blocks of stone, a system not unlike the large diaper masonry at Texila of the second century A.D., so that it has been designed " diaper pebble." Finally, about 500 A.D., a third method appears resembling in some respects rubble masonry, the walls being composed of large untrimmed stones with the spaces between filled by smaller stones. This has been called " diaper rubble." Such rough and rudimentary methods of construction naturally cried out for some system of surface treatment, and this took the form of a facing of terracotta tiles or panels, which were not only used to cover up the diaper pebble core of the walls, but also laid on the pavements of the courtyards, and applied so freely everywhere that as a stage in the development of the architecture of Kashmir, it may not inappropriately be referred to as the terracotta phase.

These terracotta plaques at Harwan each of which was moulded with a design in bas-relief, are of a character which makes them unique in Indian art. Pressed out of moulds so that the same pattern is frequently repeated, although spirited and naive in some instances, they are not highly finished productions, but their value lies in the fact that they represent motifs suggestive of more than half a dozen alien civilizations of the ancient world, besides others which are indigenous and local. Such are the Barhut railing, the Greek " swag," the Sasanian foliated bird, the Persian vase, the Roman rosette, the Chinese fret, the Indian elephant, the Assyrian lion, with figures of dancers, musicians, cavaliers, ascetics and racial types from many sources, as may be seen by their costumes and accessories. Moreover, as their size is approximately 18 inches by 12 inches, these terracotta facings are not exactly tiles, but slabs or small panels, and, it may be noted, of the same dimensions, and attached to their background in much the same manner as the *typos* or terracotta mural reliefs of the Romans, found in their *opus doliare* of the first century B.C. The remains at Harwan indicate that the memorable impact of diverse historical cultures, which took place in this part of Asia in the early centuries of the first millennium, also had repercussions on the arts of Kashmir.

Sometime after the close of this early Buddhist phase, the mediaeval movement comes into view, the beginning of a grand classical development of architecture, of which the first records emerge in the eighth century. And the difference between the two phases is remarkable. These subsequent productions are so vastly superior to the earlier, that the two appear to have no relation to one another, and so advanced are the later classical achievements that it seems to

exemplify the phenomenon, which occasionally happens, of a movement born fully matured. Such a manifestation recalls the almost spontaneous bursting into brilliant florescence of Gothic architecture in Europe in the latter part of the twelfth century ; and in Asia that structural and sculptural perfection which presents itself so unexpectedly in the majestic stupas, temples and palaces of Java and Cambodia in the ninth to the twelfth centuries. Whether on such occasions finality was reached by practising with impermanent materials until exact results were obtained, or whether such aesthetic outpourings signify that all conditions conspired to create works of genius, can only be conjectured. But whatever were the circumstances which brought forth these great historical masterpieces of the building art without any evidence of gradual growth, few countries can show a more decisive leap forward in the materialization of its architectural ideals than Kashmir in the eighth century A.D. It was a change from the productions of children or pigmies, to that of experienced giants. For, as already shown, the building technique of the early period was of an almost elementary description, consisting of walls formed of pebbles held together with mud. Then, after a comparatively short interval, without any recorded transition, the face of the valley was transformed by the appearance of a number of monumental buildings on a grand scale, constructed of immense stones wrought with astonishing precision, their surfaces finely dressed, and bonded by exact and scientific means, all showing profound experience and patient skill. In spite of the fact that the productions representing this development in its initial aspect are now in complete ruin, the remains are sufficient to prove that at this time there flourished in Kashmir a style of stone architecture, which for massive strength, simplicity of statement and expert technical accomplishment can have had few equals.

Some of this sudden progress in the architectural evolution of the country was undoubtedly due to the inspiration and forceful personality of one of Kashmir's greatest rulers. Lalitaditya (724-760), who among other notable activities, encouraged with outstanding impartiality both Buddhism and Brahmanism by the foundation of imposing monuments dedicated to each creed. It is scarcely likely, however, even with the incentive of this powerful monarch, that buildings in such a form can have been entirely self-originated, nor do they appear to have been derived from a similar movement in India proper although, at a slightly earlier date, under the Guptas, buildings of massive ashlar masonry had been erected in many parts of the adjacent plains of Hindustan. And in spite of indications of influence from such a direction having been identified in the sculpture of Kashmir, there is apparently little or no affinity between the two architectural styles ; each is obviously the result of a different sequence of experiences. Moreover, Lalitaditya's masons showed a much more profound knowledge of the building art than that ever acquired by the Indian craftsmen of the Gupta regime.

From what source, then, did the master-builders of Kashmir obtain this extensive practical proficiency in the art of building, from whom did they learn how to quarry immense blocks of limestone, to dress them so evenly, to move them over broken country by river and road, to hoist them into position, to bind them into course, to dispose them coherently so that they form an architectural unity, and finally, to carve them into sculptured forms of such effective appearance and quality of breadth ? Operations of this nature usually require a long term of preparation and practice before the results attain the high standard displayed by the stone monuments of Kashmir. An investigation of the aesthetic and technical characteristics of these buildings may throw some light on the points thus raised.

The style of the architecture may be first examined. In its design the Kashmir temple is a conception which may be best described as of a classical order, one may go so far as to say that it recalls distant memories of the productions of the Graeco-Roman schools. Such a generalization is emphasised by the peripteral treatment of the composition, with its pillared porticos and peristylar arcades, thus by association of ideas bringing to mind the colonnades and columned perspective of the Parthenon, and other Hellenic buildings. The source of some of this classical character is fairly obvious, as it was most certainly derived from contact with the monastic buildings of Gandhara, for in a manner the Kashmir style was a continuation of that Graeco-Buddhist movement, which as already shown, penetrated into Kashmir in the early centuries of the first millennium. In addition to this attribution, however, there are distinct evidences of influences from a more distant origin, as is shown by the particular kind of capital, or order, employed almost exclusively in the temple architecture of the country.

This capital bears no little resemblance to that known as the Doric order of the Romans. Here it should be noted that in the Gandhara architecture another and equally distinctive type of Graeco-Roman capital called the Corinthian was invariably used, other examples of the classical orders being extremely rare. Therefore the quasi-Doric capital found in the Kashmir temples could not, on this account, have been a contribution from Gandhara. On the other hand there are records that Lalitaditya's conquests carried his influence far and wide—for a period his power was absolute over a very extensive region in High Asia. Is it not possible, therefore, that some distant descendants of the Graeco-Roman schools, Asiatics no doubt, but still maintaining in their building practice reminiscences of the Hellenic-Latin traditions, brought to Kashmir certain architectural principles and precedents drawn from what remained at the fountain-head ? In their evident feeling for size, combined with breadth of treatment, and perfection of execution, the early mediaeval monuments of this country bring to mind, although indistinctly, recollections of some older architectural experiences, suggesting the final infiltration, towards the east, of the Graeco-Roman ideal.

Support to this view is provided by the technical details of the construction, of which the method of bonding is an instance. This has been effected in two ways, by the use of cement, and by the introduction of dowels, neither of which methods has been found except on rare occasions, in the masonry of India proper. Yet mortar, perfected by the Roman was now in universal use in all the countries of the west. Similarly the other system, that of jointing by dowels had been in vogue with the Ptolemaic Egyptians (323 to 30 B.C.), the Achaemenid Persians (B.C. 550-350), and by the Greeks (B.C. 500-300), but had been largely superseded at this time by lime mortar, the advantages of which were obvious. It is more than probable, therefore, that failing to find an acceptable process of bonding within their own experience, the architects and builders had gone much further afield, to the more advanced countries of the west, for a solution of this particular problem of structural technique.

The earliest monuments produced in this classical mode were Buddhist, the two principal sites being at Parihaspura, fourteen miles north-west of Srinagar, and at Puranadhish-thana, now the modern village of Pandrethan. Both these were the centres of important monastic communities, as their extensive remains plainly testify, but of the great buildings in which the priestly orders lived and worshipped, only the bases and foundations, exposed by excavation, have been preserved. The largest amount of material is provided by the ruins of Parihasapura, for on this site, in close proximity to one another, are substantial evidences of what at one time were three large and imposing monuments —a stupa, a monastery, and a temple or chaitya hall, with enough of their architectural construction and sculptured embellishment left to show the character of their style.

The central structure of this group of buildings was the stupa, attributed to Chankuna, a minister of Lalitaditya, and occupying a square of 128 feet side with projecting stairways on each face directed towards the cardinal points. Though we know it rose in two terraces, forming platforms for ambulation, yet the actual shape of the stupa cannot be determined, as it has entirely disappeared, but if in ordinary proportion to its base it must have been over 100 feet high. A monastery adjoined the stupa, planned in the manner of similar buildings elsewhere in India, and consisting of an enclosure of 175 feet side with an open courtyard in the centre surrounded by twenty-six cells averaging 16 feet side. This enclosure was entered from the east by a flight of steps, and on the far side was a larger chamber for the residence of the abbot. Although it may not have accommodated many monks, from its dimensions this monastery was obviously a large and sumptuous establishment, comparing favourably with the somewhat cramped quarters generally provided for the priestly brotherhood in the plains. The remaining building, the chaitya, was contained within a large quadrangle of 235 feet side surrounded by a wall and entered by a gateway on the east. Exactly in the centre of this open courtyard was the chaitya or temple, which took the form of a shrine or sanctuary for the reception of an image or its symbol rather than a hall of worship. This central structure was also square in plan, and stood on a double platform, the lower of which measures 95 feet across with a stairway on its eastern side ; within this building was the cella, a square chamber of 40 feet diameter. Judging from these dimensions it is not improbable that the building rose to a height of over 100 feet. It will be seen from this account that the chaitya in no way resembled the traditional Buddhist chaitya-hall ; there was no attempt at a pillared nave and aisles with an apsidal end, or any of those features characteristic of this type of temple in the plains. On the contrary it is an original conception, signifying the beginning of an indigenous style of religious architecture evolved by the people of the country in which it first appeared.

The architectural treatment of these Buddhist buildings is on the same scale as their size. This is particularly noticeable in the immense bulk forming the plinth of the stupa which is divided into simple broad contours by bold string-courses, the structural principle employed being that of two heavy torus mouldings appearing like great girdles and holding the whole firmly in position. Scattered about are ponderous fragments of architectural features, mouldings, capitals, and cornices, all of the same massive proportions. Among these is a portion of a pillar nearly 4½ feet in diameter with sixteen shallow flutes, and also the remains of a Doric capital having an ovolo of 12 inches in depth, in its measurements not very different from that of the same order brought to such perfection in the Parthenon at Athens. Another torus moulding, probably from the drum of the stupa and nearly 2 feet in diameter, has a simple spiral band raised on its surface which when in position must have been a very effective form of architectural enrichment. It is however from the nature of the masonry itself that the largeness of these buildings becomes most apparent. This is composed of well-made ashlar with most of the stones of stupendous size, particularly those used in the stairways, while there is one colossal block forming the base of the chaitya sanctum measuring 16 feet by 14 feet by 5½ feet, and weighing approximately sixty-four tons. Although this great stone is only one-seventh the size of one of the famous trilithons at Baalbek in Syria (second and third centuries A.D.), it implies that those who wrought and wielded such materials were both physically and intellectually of more than ordinary capacity.

The stones forming the triad of structures at Parihasa-pura were evenly dressed and united by means of lime mortar, or in some instances with metal dowels. The use of mortar in the building construction of India proper was practically unknown until the thirteenth century when it was introduced by the Muhammadans, all masonry previous to that date being of the dry order. The appearance of this adherent, freely and skilfully applied in the buildings of Kashmir as early as the eighth century A.D., as already remarked, is a matter of no little significance. As to the dowels none of these has been preserved, but they were almost certainly of metal, and from the appearance of the sockets, were of the usual flat section with expanded ends of hour-glass profile, in this respect not unlike the ebony cramps found occasionally in Egyptian masonry of the Ptolemaic era. But, in accordance with the scale of the Buddhist construction, they were of large size some of the sockets being as much as 18 inches in length. That there was a certain greatness, if not an appearance of supreme grandeur in these monuments there is every evidence, and no loss is more regrettable in the field of Indian architecture than their almost complete destruction.

Appearing not much later than the first examples of the Buddhist structures, the other form of architectural development, consisting of the temples and shrines of the Brahmans, continued to be produced over a longer period, for at least five centuries. All these Brahmanical buildings are considerably ruined, but not to the extent of those of the Buddhists, so that their appearance, when intact, can be readily conjectured. From the design of these mediaeval temples of Kashmir, it is clear that the creed of that country differed in its ceremonial from that in most parts of India. The temple of the valley included in its scheme no assembly hall but consisted of a main central shrine, or sanctuary, and to this, with the divinity in its cella, the devout paid their homage. This central building was isolated within a rectangular courtyard surrounded by a cellular peristyle, with a large gateway giving admission to the sacred enclosure on its front side. It will be seen therefore that the composition, as a whole, appertains more to a central tabernacle, or sanctuary for the accommodation of the deity, than a place for congregational worship. In this respect and also in others, the conception of the Brahmanical temple in Kashmir seems to have taken some of its character and arrangements from the stupa-courts of the Buddhists monasteries of Gandhara. Moreover, in its architectural treatment, it appears to have derived little from that important development of temple building which at this time was taking place in Hindustan. There is no sign of the Indo-Aryan mode in its structure, nothing of the sikhara nor of the columned hall ; the Kashmir temple, to all intents and purposes, is a manifestation of an independent ideal.

In the conception of this architectural style, there are three structural formations of such a prominent nature that they go a long way towards shaping its character. These are, (a) a recess or niche composed of a trefoil arch within a high-pitched triangular pediment, (b) the pyramidal roof, and (c) the employment throughout of a variety of fluted pillar, with capital and entablature complete, resembling in some respects the Doric order of the classical mode. The most distinctive of these is the trefoil arch and pediment, introduced into the scheme in the manner of a leit-motif, or a theme which can be disposed or manipulated at will, and around which others can be added as required. The origins of both arch and pediment are fairly clear. The former was derived from the trefoiled cell of the Gandhara stupa court, as used for instance in the monastery of Takht-i-Bhai (Plate XXXIII), while the pediment had its prototype in buildings of the same school, an illustration of which may be seen in a niche on the Shrine of the Double Eagle at Sirkap, Taxila, (Chapter VII). Such are the immediate sources, but both go still further back into the past, as for example the real origin of the trefoil motif is to be found in the conventional shape produced by the chaitya arch with its side aisles, a combination forming the facade of the early rock-cut temples of Buddhist India.

Turning to the second characteristic formation in the design of the Kashmir temple, the pyramidal roof, this feature was obviously derived from a wooden expedient, such a structure composed of over-lapping planks of wood being most suitable to the climate, where a heavy fall of snow in the winter months is not unusual. The connexion of this class of superstructure with the gabled and pyramidal roofs of India has been already dealt with (Chapter XXVII). Although these stone roofs of the larger temples of Kashmir have fallen, their general character may be assumed from some of the smaller shrines, which are exact copies, and are intact.

The third and remaining architectural element is the pillar, to the capital of which reference has been already made. It is not so much the application of this feature to every part of the composition, which is of consequence, although it is undoubtedly the keynote of the style, but it is the character of the pillars and specifically of its capital, and the supposed resemblance to a classical model, that is significant. On comparing the Kashmir example with, for instance, the Doric order of the Romans, there is a certain similarity of form, but this will be found to be more apparent than real. Where the orders of the two styles do correspond is in the ovolo member, a conspicuous element in both types of capital, decorated in each instance with a typical motif, in the Roman example with an "egg and dart" design, and with a series of full-blown lotus petals in that of Kashmir. Above the capitals of both styles is an abacus having somewhat the same appearance in each, but here the similarity ends, for the range of mouldings over this in the Kashmir example does not compare with the Roman entablature. There are moulded bases to each type of pillar, and the shafts of both are fluted, although as in all Indian building construction, these shafts are monolithic with their ends socketed into the capital and base the Indian stone-mason never learning to build these up in drums as did the Greeks and Romans.

Certain other factors are also noticeable in the mediaeval temples of Kashmir, which affect their architectural style. Among these was the practice of placing some of them in the centre of a shallow tank of water as may be seen at Ludov, Pandrethan and elsewhere, thus denoting the prevalence of a form of Naga or serpent-worship, water being a symbol of the cult. Another striking feature, already referred to in connexion with the earlier phase of building in Kashmir, is the character of the masonry. Most of the temples are constructed of abnormally large blocks of stone almost megalithic in appearance. But these huge blocks are by no means crudely or incompetently worked, on the contrary although of immense size they are highly finished productions laboriously hammer-dressed into level faces and fitted together in horizontal courses of remarkable regularity. Many examples may be studied of this fine stone-mason's work, notably in a retaining wall at Wangath, while the manipulative skill shown in the masonry as a whole recalls that in the Herodian buildings of the Roman Age. The labour involved in such construction must have been considerable, and although now the preparation of stonework in this manner is almost a lost art, the tradition may still be traced in the large stone mortars for pounding grain, which are to the present day hammered out of natural boulders by the same arduous process.

A further interesting feature in the Kashmir temples is the constructional principle applied in the production of the ceiling. In one of the earliest examples, that of the Rudresa in the village of Ludov, there are the remains of a semicircular dome of no mean dimensions formed of over-sailing courses of stone, while there are other instances in which a similar system of roofing is discernible. Any attempt at doming at such an early date is a matter of note, and that at Ludov, although not of the true variety in its technique, displays evidence of no little experience in dome construction. On the other hand most of the shrines are roofed by means of stone beams and slabs, seemingly the outcome of a wooden prototype. But the appearance of the two systems of covering a space, that of the dome and of the cross-beam, the former evidently being relinquished in order to make way for the latter, introduces another minor problem into the origins of the building art of Kashmir.

This mediaeval development of Brahmanical architecture in Kashmir is represented by two golden periods, or, to be more precise, rose to its greatest heights under two prominent building rulers, Lalitaditya, who as already shown, brought the style into being in the middle of the eighth century, and Avantivarman, under whom it attained its most refined form in the latter half of the ninth century. From certain buildings presumed to belong to the earlier stages of the movement, the growth of the style may be outlined. What is probably one of the oldest examples is the Rudresa temple at Ludov, situated sixteen miles south-east of Srinagar, a plain and simple square walled structure having every appearance of a primitive type. Its early character receives confirmation from the fact that it resembles in several respects one of the buildings of Gandhara, the vihara of Guniyar in the Swat Valley of the Frontier Province, which is hardly likely to be later than the fifth century A.D., although the Ludov temple may have been built at least two centuries after that date. The next stage may be studied in the Sankaracharya temple on the Takht-i-Sulaiman, a building occupying a unique position on a hill overlooking the city of Srinagar and with the great loop of the Jhelum river at its foot. Although of unusual shape,

as its plan is square with recessed chases and its interior is circular, the triangular headed offsets which project from each side of this structure suggest an embryo form of the high-pitched pediment and trefoil arch which characterize the following stage. This pediment and arch motif, in a further process of development, appears next in the temple at Narastan, situated some thirty miles south-west of Srinagar, where the flat offsets have been elaborated into moulded niches with triangular canopies and the sunk trefoil arch introduced. Around the shrine is also thrown an enclosure wall forming a courtyard entered by a prominent gateway. Here the style is seen to be approaching its final form.

This completed form was attained with magnificent effect in the great Temple of the Sun at Martand which became the model for all subsequent Brahmanical temples in Kashmir. (Plate CXXXVI, Fig. 1). Occupying a superb site five miles from the ancient town of Anantnag, although now a crumbling ruin, it is still possible to understand readily its original appearance. Its design in the main followed that previously outlined, of a comprehensive central structure including the sanctuary standing within a rectangular courtyard surrounded by a cellular peristyle which is entered by an imposing gateway. In one particular however this temple is not exactly according to type, as in front of the central building is a detached portico with two chambers in each of its wings, additional compartments evidently especially provided for the accommodation and performance of some ceremonial connected with sun-worship. Even with this supplementary formation the whole scheme is comparatively simple and it is the skilful manner in which all its parts are adjusted and treated that gives this temple its supreme aesthetic and architectural character. In the central building itself the outstanding features are the great trefoil arched recesses under their angular pediments, one of these occupying each face, and separated by a massive pilaster at each angle. The entire composition is raised on a high plinth and is terminated above by a pyramidal roof. Where emphasis was required, this was provided by suitably devised and boldly-shaped mouldings, and richness was obtained by a considerable amount of carving in high relief, chiefly of figures in niches, such plastic decoration being applied in strict accordance with the ceremonial of the sun-worship, as well as with the aesthetic needs of the architecture. The great trefoils are not true arches, but are constructed by means of oversailing courses of masonry, the undersides of the stones being shaped to produce the necessary semicircular curves.

Of the same character, although smaller yet similar in its proportions, was the entrance gateway to the temple, a substantial portal sufficiently large in size to balance the main shrine of which in appearance it was a modified replica. It contained an inner and outer compartment with the doorway in between, the whole surmounted by a pyramidal roof, and its surfaces were moulded and carved. As a contrast to the massive volume of both the central building and the gateway, the pillared arcade of the enclosure wall supplies the lighter values of the scheme, and quickened tempo with its fluent alternations of light and shade. The outward semblance therefore of the temple in its entirety is that of a well-balanced composition, the structural principles employed providing for an upward tendency in the lines and masses of the central building, areas of lateral space in its surrounding courtyard, equilibrium by the introduction of the gateway, and rhythm in the regular inter-columnation of the encircling peristyle. In spite of its appearance of largeness the dimensions of the whole are quite moderate. On plan the central structure occupies a rectangle 62 feet long and 35 feet wide, the projecting wings of the portico extending the width at the front to 56 feet. Although the main shrine is a square, the cella in its interior is an oblong of 18½ feet by 14 feet placed trans-versely, while the entire height of this central building was in the vicinity of 70 feet. The quadrangle measures 220 feet long by 142 feet broad, the pillars facing this enclosure being 84 in number, each 9½ feet in height with a space between of 6¼ feet at the base. As an indication of its proportions it may be noted that the total area of the en-closure corresponds to that of the cloisters at Wells Cathe-dral, while the central structure itself approximates in its ground plan to the dimensions of its Chapter House.

It will be seen therefore that the temple of Martand is a building of average size, but throughout a feeling of a large scale is consistently maintained, as there is nothing small or sparing in its composition. In its appearance of simple dignity, and in the solid nature of its masonry it has some-thing of that power expressed in the amphitheatres and aqueducts of the Romans when these seem to form part of the landscape itself. In its prime in the eighth century, few spectacles can have been more enchanting than Lalita-ditya's grey stone masterpiece, with its bold trefoil arches, stupendous walls, and elegant arcades, symmetrically elevat-ed against its mountain background, and looking out on the solitary splendour of the everlasting snows.

This sense of aesthetic agreement between the works of man and those of nature, as illustrated by such archi-tectural achievements, introduces the subject of the relation of a building to its environment. Different surroundings ordinarily call for different methods of architectural treat-ment, and, as at Martand, a site encircled by majestic ranges of mountains demands a composition having features of a special order for it to be in harmony with conditions of such exceptional grandeur. In these circumstances a structural conception formed of a powerful central pile, and supported by lines of mass so devised as to emphasize the quality of horizontality, appears to be the motive principle on which to proceed. The built-up forceful formation in the centre suggests by its volume the immense bulk of the adjacent mountains, while the implied parallelism with the ground conveys the impression of security and peace. The Kashmiri builders, sub-consciously perhaps, appear to have conformed to these principles for some such ideal seems to underlie their temple compositions. That those concerned had the genius, and the requisite imagination and capacity to attain this ideal, is proved by the superb manner in which these monuments accord with the surrounding landscape.

The temple at Martand was the supreme effort of Lalitaditya's builders, but there are other temples, not so large although in the same grand style, which belong to this period. Among them is a collection of buildings at Wan-gath, some thirty miles north-west of Srinagar, their size and position indicating that here was an important halting place on the pilgrims' way to the sacred waters of Gangabal, a solitary tarn cradled among the mountain peaks. (Plate CXXXVII, Fig. 1). The remains at Wangath are magni-ficently situated in the midst of a steep pine-clad gorge, with the white foaming river as its base. Three groups of build-ings are discernible within a short distance of one another,

the production of the whole probably extending over a consi-derable period and to have been begun at a relatively early date, one structure having been identified as the Jyesh-thesa temple of the ruler Lalitaditya (eighth century). Two of the groups consist of temples and shrines of the typical Kashmir order, while the third was a large and substantial building of which only the plinth remains, but was probably a refectory. All are now ruined and deserted, their worn and rugged shapelessness giving them the appearance of being part of their wild and rocky environment rather than the work of human hands.

The southern group comprises a central temple around which cluster several shrines, all poised on a terrace of partly a natural and partly a structural formation. Each edifice follows the conventional temple plan, the general propor-tions being good and the masonry well finished, but the surfaces are simpler and less ornate than those in the valley itself, probably owing to their more remote position. The other range of temples towards the north of the site is con-tained within a walled enclosure with a fine revetment wall on the mountain side specially provided to protect the entire group from being overwhelmed by rock-falls or similar contingencies. Among the confused and shattered struc-tures which now encumber the enclosure, the main temple is least ruined and consists of a building in the characteristic style but with several supplementary shrines attached to its front and sides. Such additional compartments were evidently required for a particular form of ritual, and that water was an essential accessory is shown by the presence in a prominent position of an immense cistern, eighteen feet long with its other dimensions in proportion, hammered out of one huge boulder, a work of astonishingly patient skill and stupendous labour.

But the most original achievement at Wangath is the solid masonry plinth standing separate from the temples and evidently the remains of a building of a special type. Measuring about one hundred and twenty feet long by seventy-five feet wide with a height of ten feet and appro-ached by a stairway on its southern face, along its sides are over thirty massive monolithic bases or piers at regular intervals of some twelve feet. Enough therefore remains of this structure to indicate that it was a pillared pavilion of imposing dimensions and appearance, although it is not unlikely that its immense span or roof could only have been composed of some system of wooden construction. The pier bases each over three feet in width are boldly moulded in a characteristic style, and each contains a socket for the insertion of a large monolithic shaft. As with much of the architecture of the country its chief features are the size of the structural units and the resultant largeness of its parts, inspired possibly by the great scale of the natural surroundings.

The second golden age of the mediaeval architecture of Kashmir was brought into being more than a century later by the patronage of king Avantivarman (855-883), and his immediate successors. As was not an uncommon proce-dure in India this ruler began to build a capital city according to his own ideas and requirements and selected a comman-ding site overlooking a bend in the river Jhelum, eighteen miles south-east of Srinagar, calling it Avantipur. All that now remains of this city are the ruins of two temples some little distance apart, one being the Siva temple of Avantesvara, and the other the Vishnu temple of Avante-svami. The former is much the larger, and may have been intended for public worship, while the latter, which although smaller is lavishly planned, was probably for the use of the royal family and the court only. Of the great Siva temple little more than the foundations remain, but it must have been an imposing structure, as the exterior dimensions of its courtyard measure 218 feet by 200 feet, and the base of the shrine building in the centre of this was over 57 feet square, so that in size at least it was second only to that at Martand. An elaboration in the composition of the central structure took the form of four supplementary shrines, one projecting from each corner of the main platform, thus aggregating five shrines in all, and making it therefore into an example of the *panchayatana* or five-shrined type.

Much better preserved is the other temple, that of Avantesvami, which appears to have been a very complete conception, and embellished with many additional features. (Plate CXXXVII, Fig. 2). In its general scheme it reproduces to a reduced scale the arrangements of its predecessor or Martand, with a rectangular courtyard of 174 feet by 148 feet, and a central building 33 feet square, the latter approached by a double flight of steps on its front or western side. It is a temple also of the *panchayatana* class, but in this instance the four subsidiary shrines are not attached to the large central erection of which they were small-scale copies, as each is an independent structure standing by itself and occupying a space in one of the angles of the courtyard. In front of the flight of steps leading to the main shrine there was a square shallow tank for ablutions, and again, in front of this, a *kirti-stambha* or free-standing pillar so that with all these additions, this courtyard contained its full complement of structures connected with the ceremonial. Forming the enclosure wall were sixty-nine cells and these were fronted by a colonnade of seventy pillars, each shaft having sixteen sides, surmounted by a quasi-Doric capital and standing on a plain cubical base. On the western side of the enclosure was the entrance gateway, a large building having a square plan equal in size to that of the main structure within. Pillars, both detached and engaged, add to the architectural effect of this gateway, while a colonnade of these was continued along the entire external length of the front enclosure wall, thus providing the main approach with a handsome facade. Decorating the wall surfaces was a considerable amount of sculpture, not however applied with that profusion which characterises the architecture of other parts of India, but judiciously distributed, and contained within panels or other prepared spaces.[1]

In endeavouring to appreciate the scope, appearance, and character of the temple of Avantesvami, it will be useful to compare these with the same qualities as they are shown in the temple of Martand for, the two buildings are the touchstones of the style. An interval of over a century separates the two examples, and the advance made during this period, although not great, is instructive. Avantivarman's fine architectural effort repeats much the same technical procedure as the older building; it illustrates no fresh experiences. During the hundred years that ensued, the art seems to have pursued its evolutionary course, without any notable innovations. But in a close study of the two buildings one does see in the later example an increased refinement of form, a more polished effect generally, evidently a reflection of that riper cultural atmosphere which prevailed

during this ruler's reign, and of which there are definite records. The main lineaments of this building are pronounced and clear cut, and the essential parts are more finely adjusted, a fact specially noticeable in the disposition of the central structure and its relation to the subsidiary shrines, and in the insistent consonance of tonality provided by the surrounding colonnade, while the whole appearance of the building is one of sensitive grace. As a contrast to the embodiment of massive bulk expressed in the temple of Martand in which we see the working of first principles, the temple of Avantesvami displays an intellectual and reasoned application of these principles, with a finished architectural unity as the result. (Plate CXXXVIII).

Yet in spite of the fact that there is much in both buildings that is rightly intentioned and thoroughly conscientious, there are certain features, not only noticeable in these two examples, but common to the style as a whole, which it is difficult to reconcile with what is ordinarily regarded as wholly good architectural design. One instance may be noted in the arched and pedimented recess, a motif repeated so frequently as to dominate the style. There is a lack of suavity in the rather inadequate curves of the trefoil, as they contrast abruptly with the acute angles of the pediment, neither of these elements flowing evenly by themselves, or with one another. But the least appropriate feature is the pyramidal roof, which the Kashmiri masons never succeeded in making really convincing. Steeped in the tradition of the lap-jointed gable of their wooden structures, they copied this expedient ingenuously in stone, disregarding the fundamental principle that what is asked of stone construction is that it should look like stone, and so with regard to all the materials used in the building art. In addition to these particular inconsistencies in the Kashmiri style, there are other subsidiary architectural elements, not entirely satisfying. These include a certain immaturity in some of the forms, which give the impression of a combination of artlessness and experience, a paradox probably not unconnected with the isolated position of the country itself.

After Martand and Avantesvami not very much remains of this style; nonetheless what there is reveals several interesting facts. There were other temples which may belong to Avantivarman's period, but as these are outside the actual limits of the valley, being on the route leading into it, they are inclined to be provincial in character, as distinct from the imperial quality of those in the capital. Such is a temple at Buniar, and another near Uri known as the Dhathamandir, both on the Jhelum Valley road. The former is by far the best preserved of the larger examples, and although the workmanship is slightly crude, its value lies in the fact that owing to its good condition it throws useful light on certain aspects of the style. This specially refers to the entrance gateway, always an important part of the composition, and the Buniar portal explains how the detached pillars were utilized in connection with the doorways and its trefoil arch.

A late and final flowering of the style may be seen in a group of buildings erected by Sankaravarman (A.D. 883-902), who succeeded Avantivarman, and adopted the town of Patan, seventeen miles north-west of Srinagar, as the site of his architectural activities. Here are the remains of two

---

[1] In the course of constructing the main road through the Valley, on a site between the two temples here described, some huge stones have become exposed, moulded and sculptured, which appear to have belonged to another and third temple at Avantipur. A large mound nearby may contain the remains of this building, and further exploration might bring its foundations to light.

Nepal: Bhatgaon Durbar Square.

CXLV

Nepal: Wood and Metal Window.

Nepal: Durbar Square, Patan.

Nepal: Facade at Patan.

Nepal: Temple of Changu-Narayan.

Wata Dage Temple, Polonnaruwa, Ceylon.

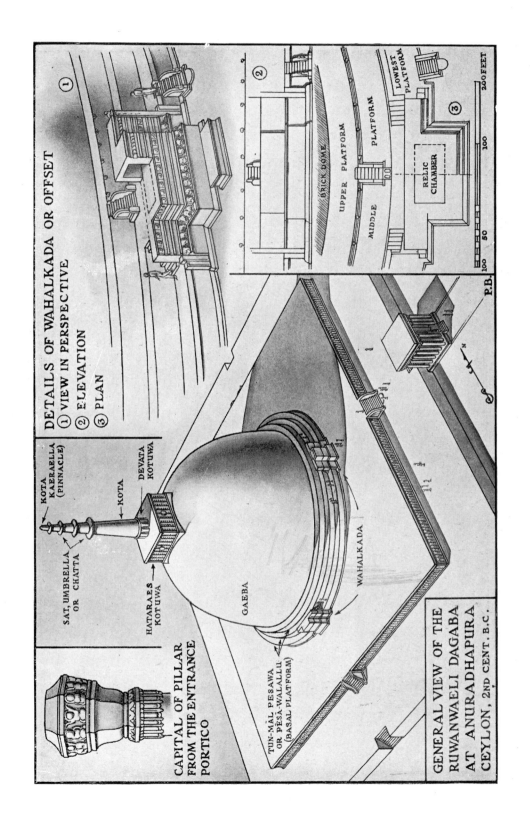

CAPITAL OF PILLAR
FROM THE ENTRANCE
PORTICO

DETAILS OF WAHALKADA OR OFFSET
① VIEW IN PERSPECTIVE
② ELEVATION
③ PLAN

KOTA KAERAELLA (PINNACLE)

SAT, UMBRELLA OR CHATTA

KOTA

DEVATA KOTUWA

HATARAES KOTUWA

GAEBA

TUN-MAL PESAWA OR PESA-WALALLU (BASAL PLATFORM)

WAHALKADA

BRICK DOME

UPPER PLATFORM

MIDDLE PLATFORM

LOWEST PLATFORM

RELIC CHAMBER

50   100   200 FEET

100   50   100

P.B.

N

GENERAL VIEW OF THE
RUWANWAELI DAGABA
AT ANURADHAPURA.
CEYLON, 2ND CENT. B.C.

LANKATILAKA (JETAWANARAMA)
TEMPLE AT POLONNARUWA,
CEYLON. 12TH CENTURY A.D.

P.B.

CONJECTURAL SUPERSTRUCTURE
OF WOOD, BRICK AND PLASTER
OVER STONE PILLARS IN CEYLON

PILASTER FROM
NORTHERN
TEMPLE

FROM
POLONNARUWA

Fig. 1.

Fig. 2. Burma: Pagan, Ananda Temple (c. 11th century).

Fig. 3. Lankatilaka (Jetawanarama): Temple at Polonnaruwa, Ceylon; 12th century A.D.

important Siva temples, Sankaragaurisvara built by the ruler himself, and the other Sugandhesa, named after his queen, but both are woefully ruined. Neither of these differs in shape from the other temples in Kashmir. They are each designed on much the same plan, and their elevations are similar in general appearance to those already described. But a close investigation of these structures reveals a refinement of workmanship, both in the handling of the materials and in the treatment of the ornamentation. The individual stones are large, in size recalling those of Lalitaditya's masons, particularly in the length of the blocks forming the lintels, one of these being eighteen feet long. Then their shaping is so precise and their angles so exact that they might have been produced by some mechanical process, instead of by hand. In one instance, in the formation of a complicated combination of roof and cornice in several planes meeting at different angles, where, ordinarily, a number of stones would have been fitted together, the whole is monolithic, being skilfully but laboriously cut out of one entire block. Some of the large beams were fixed into position by means of neatly shaped joggle-joints, and the courses of masonry generally are exceptionally well fitted. The details of these two buildings are of the same highly finished order, no mouldings could be cut with greater mechanical accuracy, and the carving, specially of the repeating patterns and borders, has an incisive quality rarely equalled. Few buildings can show such facile directness and dexterity of manipulation as the remains of these two temples at Patan.

By the beginning of the tenth century the growth of the style had come to an end, as, owing largely to political circumstances, temple building received little encouragement after that date. Small shrines continued to be produced but no notable architectural enterprises were undertaken. If the miniature Siva temple at Puranadhisthana (Pandrethan), three miles from Srinagar has been correctly identified as one built in the middle of the twelfth century, then this example carries the progress of the style another stage. (Plate CXL, Fig. 1). The building which is only 17½ feet square externally and 24 feet in height is a perfect type of the later development, and displays several interesting features. In this example it will be noticed that the horizontal moulding cutting across the upper angle of the high pitched pediment is omitted, and this member rarely appears again. The ceiling is also unusually attractive, as it consists of diagonally placed beams, with brackets, like dentils, supporting its outer framework, all very wooden in treatment, but on the other hand the general principles applied in this design are much the same as those in the coffered ceilings of many Hindu temples. There are mainly several other shrines, some much smaller even than this example, so that they are not constructed, but mainly are monolithic, such as those at Payar, Mamal, Kother, and Bumazu, which illustrate the declining period of the style.

A concluding manifestation of this type of architecture is illustrated by a series of temples outside the present borders of Kashmir and occupying various sites in the Northern Punjab and the North West Frontier ; they may accordingly be referred to as a provincial offshoot of the Kashmir style. These buildings are contained in several small groups distributed over a tract of country between and in the vicinity of, the upper reaches of the Jhelum and Indus rivers, following approximately the line of low hills known as the Salt Range

(Singhapura). This region, in the early centuries of the Christian era, appears to have been more or less an independent country until the seventh century, when it was absorbed into the territory of Kashmir. Its architecture links up the style of Gandhara with that of Kashmir, and exhibits some of the affinities of each. Yet these temples differ in character sufficiently to form themselves into three sub-groups, such as (a) those at Amb, Katas, Malot and Nandna in the Jhelum district, Punjab, (b) several at Bilot and (c) others at Kafir Kot, both the last named being on the river Indus in the North West Frontier Province. All these temples are square in plan, rising up into a sikhara or tower, and containing a square cella, but the architectural treatment of this structural foundation, which is common to all, shows numerous variations. Those of the first group are more nearly related to the Kashmir style, of which the example at Malot is the most typical. (Plate CXXXIX, Fig. 2). This temple which is built of sandstone, appears to have consisted of a central square shrine with its entrance on the east, and a separate gateway also on the east, so it may be assumed that the whole was surrounded by an enclosed courtyard in the manner of those in Kashmir. Both the shrine and the gateway were surmounted by pyramidal roofs, while the sides of the former were composed of recessed bays having trefoil arches above. The whole of the recess formed by each of these trefoiled bays is occupied by a carved motif, in high relief, a copy to a reduced scale of the actual temple it decorates, with a trefoiled arched niche like an altar at its base, the entire conception being an illustration of form and ornament developing out of the construction. The entrance to the shrine projects so as to include a vestibule, and the portal is a very elegant composition, formed of a trefoil arch supported on a fluted column engaged on each side. The size of this temple is 30 feet square while the addition of the portico makes its length 37 feet, the cella being 18 feet in diameter, and its height when complete about 50 feet. Although its style is obviously influenced by that of Kashmir, there is an originality in the architectural treatment of this temple which betokens the presence in the locality, at the time, of a group of workmen of a superior order.

The shrines at Bilot (b), while recalling some of the features of the previous group are more ample in their proportions, with decidedly more graceful plastic embellishment. A high vaulted porch projects on the entrance side of the square plan, and the whole is surmounted, not by a pyramidal roof, but by a sikhara or tower. The Kashmir attribution may appear in the cusped or cinquefoil arches of the entrance porch, which are repeated in the niches on the exterior sides, but the direct influence, if any, of the parent style in these examples is remote. Exteriorly they are richly decorated with tiers of carved plasters, dentil cornices, foliated medallions, and " horse-shoe " and *amalaka* motifs, all of which denote a closer association with the Gupta style than with that of Kashmir. The use of a remarkably hard grade of mortar to bind the stone masonry has been brought forward as evidence in favour of a late date. Slightly more classical in their appearance are the shrines of Kafir Kot (c), owing mainly to the presence of a range of tall low-relief pilaster around their outer walls. In general character and intention, however, they are little more than a variation of those at Bilot, as their square sanctuary, projecting porch, and tapering sikhara, suggest a similar source.

REFERENCES

Cole, H. H., *Illustrations of Ancient Buildings in Kashmir*, 1869.
Kak, R. C., *Ancient Monuments of Kashmir*, Ind. Soc., London, 1933.

CHAPTER XXXIII

THE BUILDING ART OF NEPAL

THE buildings in the independent kingdom of Nepal, together with the arts associated with these structures, display many original features, and at the same time provide a number of provocative factors relating to the evolution of the building art in Asia as a whole. In the sphere of architecture Nepal illustrates, with marked significance, the impact of two of the most forceful civilizations in the East, that of India on the one hand, and of China on the other, the two meeting within the region of Nepal's mountainous borders. For geographically, historically, and politically, the country occupies a position between these two great empires, and during its course has drunk deeply from the cultural springs issuing from each, drawing its inspiration first from one and then from the other, alternatively, as the political currents ebbed or flowed. The influence of these powerful streams of racial ideals is envisaged clearly in the building art of Nepal, while in addition there is the effect, religious and graphic, of that great tide of Buddhism which swept through the continent of Asia before and after the beginning of the Christian era, inspiring every people and every activity in its porgress.

Although the country of Nepal extends in the shape of an irregular parallelogram along the ranges of the Himalayas, occupying a region some 450 miles in length and averaging 150 miles in breadth, the main tenor of its life is almost entirely concentrated within a relatively localised area towards the centre, spoken of as the "Valley of Nepal." The remainder of the State is composed of a rugged mountainous terrain, sparsely inhabited, and containing few features of note. Within the valley, however, prehistorically a shallow lake but anciently drained so that it now presents an undulating landscape of considerable beauty, the vital pulse of the country beats. Here in this depression measuring twenty miles long by fifteen miles wide are distributed towns and villages, but more important still, in a middle position, are closely grouped the three capitals of the kingdom, Katmandu, Patan, and Bhatgaon, the remarkable architectural character of each representing the building art of the country in all its aspects.

This triad of capitals accounted for by the division of the kingdom in the fifteenth century into several different and separate states, each of which had its own royal residence or Durbar. And the groups of buildings which grew up around these Durbar palaces, each eventually to form a moderately sized and picturesquely planned township, were the work of the people who at that time, and up to the eighteenth century comprised the original inhabitants of the country. These were a race known as the Newars who occupied the country from a very early date, and although of indeterminate origin, appear to have entered the country from the north, probably from the direction of Tibet. But whatever their derivation, their productions in the field of architecture are proof, as the capitals of Nepal amply testify, that they possessed an artistic sensibility of a particularly exuberant nature. That this indigenous aesthetic tendency was stimulated and influenced at intervals by currents from sources exterior to the country is clearly shown in the charac-

ter of their creations during the course of their history. And that at certain periods they received ardent patronage from their own rulers is also obvious from the number and style of their buildings and monuments. But the fundamental fact remains that the consistent standard of art maintained throughout the whole of the mediaeval era was due to the natural aspirations of the Newars for an artistic environment, which found expression not only in their architecture, but in all the accompaniments of their daily lives.

The undercurrent of Buddhism which runs throughout the religious system of the country during its entire history originated at an early date. It is recorded that in the third century B.C. the Mauryan emperor of India, Asoka, made a pilgrimage into the valley of Nepal, and commemorated this event by the foundation of innumerable stupas as a token of his success in bringing the inhabitants into the Buddhist fold. After the passage of considerably over two thousand years it is believed that two of these monuments may be identified, one forming the central feature of the temple of Shwayambhu Nath, and the other known as the Bodhnath, both situated in the neighbourhood of the existing capital of Katmandu. The main shape of these stupas is of the orthodox semiglobal form, but in each instance this spherical body is surmounted by a large finial of unusual design and imaginative treatment, no other Buddhist superstructure bearing any resemblance to it. Primarily derived from the conventional three-fold umbrella, which in a somewhat fantastic but identifiable form still crowns the entire scheme, the steeple-shaped structure below this is in thirteen diminishing tiers, symbolizing the thirteen Buddhist heavens. But it is the design of the cubical base supporting this "steeple," corresponding to the *harmika* in the Indian examples, that presents the most striking appearance. For on each of its four gilded sides is embossed a face in metal and ivory with a large pair of human eyes. Such an innovation produces as startling and almost mesmeric effect, the eyes following the course of the pilgrim in a mysterious manner as he circumambulates the base of the sacred memorial. Some have attributed this evice on the harmika to a certain aspect of sunworship, recalling the motif known as the *suraj-mukh* or "sun-face," of Indian temples, but more probably the eyes looking so searchingly into space are an outward sign of the "All Seeing One." (Plate CXLII & CXLI).

Except however for their elaborate finials, the two examples of this class of stupa, are two very different conceptions. The Bodhnath for instance, has every appearance of having been, within modern times, thoroughly restored, but none the less, such conservation is of a convincing nature, suggesting that the old forms have been retained, and that the building as a whole is not far removed from its original design. Its chief character lies in the substructure which comprises a number of concentric terraces, with turrets at the angles, the whole approached by a simple and dignified flight of steps. The Bodhnath is an impressive monument by virtue of its plain and almost austere combination of planes and surfaces, contrasting emphatically with the intricate and elaborate nature of the subsequent mediaeval structures shortly to be described.

The other stupa, that at Shwayambhu Nath, must also when originated, have been little more than a tumulus of consolidated earth erected on a prominent site, a hill arising abruptly out of the low lying valley around it. This rough mound is now crowned by an immense finial of the type previously described, and stands amidst a confused complex of temples, shrines, alcoves and symbolic accessories crowding the flagged terrace of which it forms the central feature. In marked comparison with the profusion of fretted forms which have accumulated in its vicinity during many centuries, the stupa itself appears as an unadorned pile of earthwork, creating the impression that the bulk of this elemental monument may indeed be all that is left of one of Asoka's original tumuli erected to the order of that zealous and royal Buddhist some twenty-three centuries ago. (Plate CXLI). Primitive Buddhism, as in India, has almost passed out of Nepal, but these two stupas are a record of that period when this religion occupied a premier place in the life of its people.

Of the subsequent progress of this Buddhist development the material data is scanty, and much the same applies to such productions as took form during the centuries comprising the greater part of the first millennium. There are remains which indicate that the building art was maintained in a fairly substantial manner during this long interval, but no important or entire structures have survived to which reference can be made in order to throw light on the actual shape that these assumed at this stage of their history. Gradually, however, it becomes apparent from the nature of their handiwork that the Newar artisans were coming within the compass of that powerful movement eventually to be known as the " Eastern School," which flourished in the adjacent country of Bihar under the Pala and Sena dynasties in Bengal from the eighth to the twelfth centuries. The influence of the experienced Indian craftsmen during this period, supported by the traditions of the historical schools of Magadha and Varendra had a profound and far-reaching effect on the arts of Asia in the early middle ages, and there is certain evidence that the handicrafts of Nepal became one of the provincial or regional developments of this great religious and artistic movement having its head-quarters in the Gangetic plain. But it was not until a dynasty of royal patrons known as the Mulla Rajas who reigned over Nepal from the thirteenth to the eighteenth centuries and up to the conquest of the country by the Gurkhas in 1768, that the arts flourished in their most exuberant form. The Mulla regime attained its prime, as shown by its architectural achievements, under the seventh ruler of the line, Jayastithi (1386-1429) and also during the reign of his successor the eighth raja Yaksha, although much good building and numerous artistic productions were executed under Raja Bhupatindra as late as the first half of the eighteenth century.

It was during the Mulla ascendency that the three capitals previously mentioned came into being, and it is possible to visualize the manner in which these gradually evolved. First the residential palace for the ruler was located, with an adjacent Durbar Square, consisting of a paved open space for ceremonial occasions. Around this were arranged the administrative buildings the whole forming an enclave reserved for governmental purposes. From this focal point

streets radiated irregularly to supplementary squares each marking a quarter, or ward, known as *tols*, wherein a certain class of citizens resided and carried on their business. There is however little evidence of town-planning in this system, the fortuitous manner in which these lesser squares were placed in relation to the Durbar Square, and their unmethodical approaches, form one of the picturesque characteristics of these royal townships. In the course of time even this apparent attempt at orderliness has been lost, but the foregoing was obviously the general principle on which they were first laid out. Such is the present aspect of these architectural complexes, and it has been observed that " Nepal is still an authentic replica of an India that has disappeared."[1] Up to a certain point this is a correct appreciation of the concentrations of building art in the valley, but Nepal's geographical position is such that certain factors exist in its architecture, which are not found in India. The influence from India has already been explained, but on the opposite borders of the country are the immense and powerful civilizations of China and Tibet, which at certain periods, owing to political and other circumstances, affected not a little the outlook of its people. In its broad aspect this contact, especially that of Tibet, brought into the art of the Newars a certain Lamaistic quality, a mysticism and symbolism due to the elemental nature of thought in that country, conceptions inspired and stimulated by its great heights and empty spaciousness. But on its architecture the pylonic buildings of Tibet had little influence, the Newars were not impressed by the plain surfaces and sloping lines and planes of the monasteries or temples of the Lamas as their productions amply testify, their natures cried out for elaboration and detail. On the other hand there are definite indications that what may be termed the " pagoda " motif, that dominating feature in the building art of the Far East, was readily accepted by the Nepalese builders, and much of the architecture of the valley takes after this pattern. To sum up, regarded as a whole the structures of Nepal notably those of a sectarian ascription fall into two categories, those of the " sikhara " variety clearly derived from the style of temple favoured in India, and those of the multiple roof design associated with the pagodas of China, the former being mainly constructed of masonry, while the latter are largely composed of wood.

The first impression conveyed by the buildings forming this group of royal towns of Nepal is that not only do they represent architecture, but they also display picturesque and profuse accretions of applied art. For it was the practice of the Newars to embellish the exteriors of their temples, and also many of their other structures, with such a confused array of supplementary religious and decorative features, in metal, stone, and wood, as almost to obscure the original design of the building. This particularly refers to the pagoda type of structure as the surfaces of these buildings specially lent themselves to such additional treatment. But by no means were all these superimposed elements supplied by the actual designers of the building as part of their architectural scheme, many being subsequently donated as acts of devotion and fixed in position by those who wished to show reverence to the temple wherein they worshipped. In this manner most of the better known religious edifices provide positive museums of Newar art, in which the imaginative designs of the artificers and the facile manipulation of their materials may be readily studied. While the prodigality of the Newar's handiwork was applied without stint

---

[1] Le Nepal, par Sylvain Levi, Paris 1905-08.

to all classes of building, both religious and secular, the temples were the chief object of these artistic contributions. (Plate CXLIII). These buildings, whether of the " sikhara " or " pagoda " kind, were not designed for congregational worship, but were really shrines enclosing a cella or chamber for the divinity, or a symbol, and were therefore objects of devotion in themselves. Around them would sometimes be a courtyard for assembly or processions, but the abode of the deity was the sacred substance of their prayers. This will explain why these buildings supplied a foundation on which to attach such artistic treasure as the ardent devotee could spare, either physically to support his entreaties or in view of the hereafter. Certain prominent features on the pagoda type of temple are however not only accessories to the building but also are invariably applied as an essential part of the structural and artistic effect. Among these are the elaborately carved wooden struts which support the overhanging roofs, the great metal griffins which guard the entrance, and the massive tympanums which project over the doorways and not infrequently the windows, this last artistic convention being a characteristic and arresting architectural component universally used throughout the entire course of the architecture of Nepal. Carved in wood or embossed in gilt metal this ponderous semi-ovoid pedimental attachment is rarely omitted, inclining forward over all the openings of the facade, and standing out not only on account of its prominent sculptured relief, but also because of the involved allegory which it so emphatically pictures. A disquisition on this feature and its origin and interpretation, with other accompaniments which are so lavishly distributed over the surfaces of the Nepalese buildings, besides being beyond the scope of the present subject would require a volume in itself. One motif is however of exceptional historical and structural interest. It was the custom of the Newar builders to follow the ancient procedure of projecting the wooden lintels of their doorways and other openings beyond the uprights forming the jambs. To act as a support to this projection they introduced a curved bracket which they decorated with a figure, and it is not difficult to recognize in this a later edition of that dryad support holding up the other ends of the cross-bars of the toranas in the Sanchi stupa dating some two thousand years previously. Through all these centuries this artistic and structural motif has preserved its identity, modified during its long period and altered by circumstances but performing its original purposes as in the days of primitive Buddhism in India.

Of the " sikhara " form of Napalese temple, this structure, although obviously derived from the Indo-Aryan type of India, has been adapted to conform to different ideals. The sikhara surmounts a single cell, to which no mandapa is attached, but the whole is surrounded by a columned verandah, and is elevated on a series of diminishing plinths. All the main elements of the sikhara of India are visible such as the *urusringas* (attached turrets) the *amalasila* (fluted finial) and the characterisitc offsets (*paga*), but each treated in a manner different from its prototype, and therefore peculiarly expressive of the Newar idiom. A typical example of this class of building is the Krishna temple in the Durbar Square at Patan, which rises up in three arcaded stories, and is notable for the carved stone frieze of considerable length minutely chiselled depicting in full detail the romantic episodes of the divinity to whom it is consecrated. The arcading of this temple may be studied as in some respects it illustrates the " order " that was adopted not only in Nepal, but in the building art of the Himalayas generally. Tra-

beate in principle, the lintels are carried on brackets, a system which has led to this device being described as the " crutch " type of support, almost invariably employed in the wooden construction of these mountainous regions. Consisting of monolithic pillars, their shafts octagonal in section, these columns are provided with very rudimentary bases, but have capitals of a distinctive design. There is a square moulded abacus, but beneath this, part capital and part necking, is a circular chaplet of ovoid petals, an element which seems to be essential in all the fully matured capitals in Nepalese architecture. Whether this feature is associated with the lotus flower, or is a derivative of the Indo-Aryan *kalas* or fluted vase is not clear, but it is a prominent motif not only in the building art of the Newars, but also in the earlier architecture of another Himalayan country, that of Kashmir.

The secular or civic architecture of Nepal is of the same general character as the religious, except that it is constructed almost entirely of wood, supplemented by brick masonry with occasional accessories of metal added for adornment. While most of the buildings are planned on the principle of a square interior open court around which are disposed the main compartments looking inwards, it is on the facade abutting on the public thoroughfare, or bazaar, that the chief architectural effect is concentrated. This facade is often a most elaborate conception, the artistic treatment of the frontages in a continuous arrangement along the streets being the architectural key-note of the towns as a whole. It was usually the practice to design these facades in three stories, the lowest or ground floor being let off as a shop recessed within the building, with " crutch " pillars to support the superstructure. Above this ground story in most instances the first floor was composed of brick in which were interposed windows of a highly ornate and often intricate pattern. Over this the uppermost story consisting of a substantial wooden construction was projected on brackets and struts, all most decoratively carved, often painted in variegated colours and the openings filled with wooden screens. The roof of red curved tiles with metal gutters and cornerings overhung the whole by means of a prominent cornice, shading the upper story and keeping out rain. Such a composition in itself forms a highly picturesque production, but when it is realized that each feature is carved, embossed, overlaid and wrought with the most ingenious and fanciful patterns including tinkling metal bells and hanging lamps, some idea of the general effect may be imagined. For instance the wooden and painted struts protruding from the dark background of the heavy eaves were most fantastically carved and coloured in the form of figures in spirited action and holding symbols, an effective method of breaking up the deep shadow of this portion of the conception. It was, however, on the wooden windows of the intermediate story that the artisans lavished their infallible artistic skill, the variety and inventiveness shown in these being limitless. The system employed was derived from a very ancient and traditional type already referred to in which the upper and lower supports were horizontal lintels extending beyond the square window frame placed between. Both lintels, especially the upper, were freely carved and decorated, while the lower, or sill, was ornamented with metal. But it was on the actual opening, in lieu of glass, that the woodworker exercised his ingenuity by filling this space with complex geometrical lattices of jointed wood, corresponding to the *pinjra* of the Punjab and the *mashrabiya* of the Arabs. (Plate CXLV). The Newars were remarkably adept in the manipulation of their materials, both metal, and wood, treating these in a manner which suggests something of a much more tensile nature, twisting and turning the former, and taking advantage of the texture, grain, and even colour of the latter in obtaining their artistic effects. They were also fully aware of the fact of " beauty in utility." so that every object in their daily lives, however humble, was aesthetically treated, an outstanding example, among many, being the metal spouts of their conduits converted by means of a spirited and appropriate *makara* motif into works of art, on which the craftsmen must have spent laborious days in sheer enthusiasm for their subject.

One architectural feature in the civic aspect of the royal towns of Nepal, which is of striking originality, is the monumental pillar, as these exist in considerable numbers in the durbar squares. But these were something more than an isolated column, as they supported on their wide capitals a large metal group of statuary of elaborate design, recalling in a manner the Asokan columns of a previous and very distant era. The free-standing pillar of the Newars is a monolithic erection, moulded and ornamented with patterns of historical derivation and crowned with a capital of lotus petals, expanded so as to form a circular basis for the metal superstructure. Apart from groups of divinities, mystic symbols, and other emblems, the most ideal use of these pillars was for the display of portrait statuary, so that several of the most illustrious rulers of the Mulla dynasty are commemorated in this elevated and dignified manner. Of these one of the finest is that of Bhupatindra (cir. 1750) therefore a relatively recent production. Raised some thirty feet above the flagged pavement of the Durbar Square of Bhatgaon, kneeling in a devotional attitude on his Lion Throne under a ceremonial parasol, this statue in gilt metal and of heroic size is not only a crowning effort on the part of the craftsmen, who set effective achievement for above idealism, but a sculpturesque representation, conventionally treated, of a ruler whose record is one of marked personality. Moreover this fine bronze portrait of a kingly figure faces and looks down on the main portal of the Durbar Hall, the ruler's own conception and one of the most gorgeous works of art in the entire State. This doorway stands within a red brick pylon surmounted by an elegant metal roof, the combination of colours forming a pleasing setting to the actual opening in the centre. Of the characteristic design of such entrances, square-headed and with an immense gilt tympanum above, the composition as a whole is charged with symbolic elements embossed in the highest relief of which the metal and its skilled manipulators were capable. This " Door of Gold " represents the consummation of the Nepalese artificers handicraft, a work of art of the most splendid order. Other stone columns also examples of this method of displaying portrait statuary grace the squares of the royal towns, some supporting several figures or family groups all of exceptional interest and artistic merit but none attain the simple dignity of the one described above.

As a whole the complex of buildings forming the royal boroughs of Nepal presents a picture of sheer mediaevalism which can have few equals ; but it symbolises more than such a material view implies. The art thus gathered together in rich profusion is a record of a time when beauty and humanity were the birthright of the people, to be enjoyed as an essential part of their lives. It embodies an architecture which may not possess the qualities of supreme greatness, but it expresses to the full the soul not only of those who produced it, but of those for whom it was wrought.

REFERENCES

Levi, Sylvain, *Le Nepal, 3 Vols.* Paris 1905-08.
Wright, D., *History of Nepal.*
Brown, Percy, *Picturesque Nepal*, A. & C. Black, London, 1912.

CHAPTER XXXIV

THE CAPITAL CITIES OF CEYLON

THE general impression first conveyed on viewing the remains of the deserted and partially buried cities of Ceylon is that of an area of desolation containing groups of square granite pillar shafts, each group marking the site of some building long since destroyed. These monolithic pillars, owing to the ravages of time and to the want of support often inclined at diverse angles, are attached by sockets to substantial and elegantly moulded stylobates of dressed stone, approached by a massive stairway in the middle of one side. Such are the remains of the ground stories which these ruins represent, but what kind of upper structure these pillars supported is a matter very largely of conjecture. It is clear however that what survives is a record of two contrasting constructional systems almost invariably employed in the same building. On the one hand the foundations and ground stories prove the use of permanent materials effectively jointed and solidly united and therefore capable of supporting an equally strong and stable superstructure. On the other hand, the builders, after this notable exposition of an enduring fundamental storey seem to have given up any further ideas of stone construction and rather inconsistently carried out the remainder of their conceptions in the lighter but less durable materials of wood, brick and terracotta. The results of this combination of two dissimilar methods of structural procedure are plainly visible in the existing remains, for while the granite pillars and basements are still standing, every vestige of the upper portions has disappeared. The foregoing relates mainly to the larger architectural productions of the cities, but there was another important development of a somewhat different order. Prominent among the ruins of the earlier period are the remains of numerous stupas or dagobas, some of immense size, in certain instances of colossal proportions, all constructed of solid brickwork, but with approaches and appurtenances of granite in which pillars predominate. It will be seen therefore that the historical architecture of the country resolves itself a style of building composed partly of indestructible granite which, although damaged, still remains in situ, and partly of a variety of materials of a perishable nature which under the influences of the climate and from other causes has entirely disappeared.

But before the historical productions of the Sinhalese are studied, some mention may be made of the aboriginal people of the island, and the effect, if any, of their cultural activities on the origins and subsequent evolution of the building arts. This especially applies to one aspect of architecture, that of the rock carved method, which it may be noted was the beginning of the development in the adjacent country of India. The indigenous inhabitants, a primitive race, the Veddahs, with notable enthnological characteristics, worshipped among their deities the " god of the rock " (*Gale Debiya*), and considerable ceremonial was performed in his honour, but it does not appear to have found expression in architectural form. At Anuradhapura there is a Galge, or rock-chamber, prepared with some care for the accommodation of hermit priests, parts of which are however of brick construction. It is entered by a moulded doorway of simple but elegant design and leading to three cells, the date probably being of the first century A.D. Later in the fifth century the parricide king Kyaspa planned his eyrie at Sigiriya on a rocky mountain forming a natural fortress and palace combined with a remarkable walled gallery as a means of access, the whole of a romantic and fantastic order, but of no particular architectural significance. That the early Sinhalese were however adepts at rock sculpture is proved by the high quality of a colossal statue of king Parakrama Babu at Weligama, carved out of the living rock and equal to any work of a like nature in India itself. From these productions two facts emerge, firstly that the aboriginal inhabitants of the island exercised little influence on the architecture of the historical period, and secondly, although capable of manipulating hard rock for constructional and also plastic purposes, rock architecture which flourished with such vigour in India at this correspondingly early period made little appeal as a form of expression to the creative instincts of the Sinhalese.

Yet although the people of Ceylon appear to have received no stimulation from the great rock-cut temples that were being actively produced with the propagation of the Buddhist religion throughout India, it was by means of the transmission of that faith into the island, even before the Christian era, that its architectural procedure was initiated and developed. For as early as the middle of the third century B.C. the son and emissary of the Indian Emperor Asoka brought the word of the Buddha to Ceylon, an episode commemorated at the time by the erection of a colossal stupa at Mihintale where the gospel was first preached. During the succeeding years other stupas, also of immense size, arose on different sites, but with certain accessories and elaborations which give them a distinctive appearance and character. Founded in such a substantial and realistic manner it is only natural that the architecture of the country continued, with certain exceptions due to inroads by Hindu conquests from India, to be entirely Buddhist in its ideals, a condition which has been steadfastly maintained throughout the whole course of its history.

The principal remains of Ceylon's architectural development are distributed over two extensive sites, the ruined and deserted capital cities which represent the two great periods of the country's history. The earlier of these, at Anuradhapura, illustrates all that survives of an important civilization which flourished for several hundred years from the third century B.C. to the eighth century A.D. The later is that at Polonnaruwa to which place the seat of government was removed in the eighth century, and where it remained until the thirteenth century, both are situated in the North-Central Province. Other ruins of some consequence have been revealed in various widely-spread localities, but those of most significance and which depict the building art in all its aspects are contained within the area of these two ruined and abandoned capitals. From the mounds and scattered fragments which mark these sites, not only the architecture of the past may be studied and, in some instances, partially reconstructed, but it is possible to visualize even in their ruin the greatness of Ceylon's culture and civilization during these two notable historical periods. Finally there ensued a third phase, when, after the end of the thirteenth century the seat of Sinhalese authority was transferred to the heights of Kandy and where in its later aspect it was maintained until as late as 1815. Consistently Buddhistic throughout its course of two millenniums, yet as already mentioned there were short interludes when the continuity was interrupted by incursions from the Indian mainland, and during which certain buildings in the Tamilian styles of the Pallavas (600-900) and the Cholas (900-1150) intrude themselves on the indigenous mode, influencing it however only to a modified degree.

The earliest Buddhist structures in Ceylon are stupas, and these are found mainly within the region of Anuradhapura. Composed almost entirely of brick these tumuli display features which differentiate them from monuments of a similar order in other Buddhist countries. For instance the Sinhalese divide their stupas as a class, into six varieties according to their appearance, such as the " bell," the " bubble," the " lotus " etc., each signifying the general shape of the domical portion known in India as the *anda* or egg, but in Ceylon by the name of *gaeba*. Here it should be mentioned that the common name for the stupa is *dagaba* from *dhatu-garbha* or relic-chamber, the nomenclature of its component parts being shown in Plate CLXXVII. The stupa itself is ordinarily semi-globular in form and stands on a range of concentric circular platforms almost invariably three in number, the whole based on a square terrace approached by a flight of steps in the middle of each side. Over the summit of the dome arose the finial consisting of a box-like member in which valuable offerings were placed, previous to the *chhatravali* or conventional parasol being erected, as a spire, crowning the whole. The tumulus structure is composed entirely of solid brickwork, the bricks of the earliest examples, such as those erected before the first millennium, being similar to those used in India which were of a large size being as much as seventeen inches in length, but decreasing in the course of time until in those of the twelfth century they were only about twelve inches long.

The actual construction of some of these immense mounds of brickwork, several of which date from before the Christian era, implies considerable skill and experience. After over twenty-two centuries of the effects of the climate and the destructive action of vegetable growth, not to mention spoliation by the hand of man as instanced by driving tunnels into the structure in a vain search for hidden treasure, the fact that these monuments are still in existence, and also identifiable, speaks highly both of the quality of the materials employed and the manner of their application. To support a solid mass of brick and rubble some 270 feet in height and nearly a thousand feet in circumference, as in the case of the Ruwanwaeli Dagaba at Anuradhapura, of which the foundations were laid by king Duthagamini in the 2nd century B.C. would need special preparations and these are fully described in an ancient chronicle known as the Mahawansa. This royal founder ordered " round stones to be brought by means of his soldiers, had them well beaten down with pounders, and to ensure greater durability he caused that layer of stones to be trampled by enormous

elephants whose feet were protected by leathern shoes. He had clay spread upon the layer of stones : over them a network of iron : over that a layer of *phalika* stone, and over that he laid a course of common stones." On the top of this prepared basis, which in its technique is singularly suggestive of reinforced concrete, the monarch, making the occasion into a picturesque and formal ceremony, " guarded by his officers of state decked in all the insignia of their gala dress, himself captivating all by the splendour of his royal equipment, surrounded by a throng of dancing and singing women—rivalling in beauty the celestial virgins—decorated in their various embellishments, attended by forty thousand men, accompanied by a full band of musicians, repaired to the site for the royal hand itself to lay the first and festival brick of the edifice." The foundational rites having been performed with all the requisite regal and priestly observances, the actual construction was then put in hand. Firstly the groundwork of the raised terrace was prepared, with the stone revetment next fitted with great care backed by rubble (no mortar being used), and the interior packed to the level of the coping with earth and brick debris. Upon this, when it had settled, was laid the pavement, and on the centre of the platform the extreme circumference of the tholobate was marked out, and its lower course or courses built. At this stage it was usual to sink in the platform the brick foundations and walls of the chambers to enshrine the relics.[1] When these had been deposited within the receptacle it would be closed by stone slabs, and the dagaba finished by the completion of the tholobate, the dome, finial and spire. The surface of the whole would be thickly coated with white plaster, adornments of various kinds added, parts painted and gilt, so that the monument would present a chaste and at the same time brilliant appearance.

Such was the system by which these great sacred piles were inaugurated and created, some of which were of phenomenal size, while there were many others not by any means of insignificant dimensions. Of those erected in the vicinity of Anuradhapura shortly before and after the Christian era the following are the largest and most notable ; Ruwanwaeli, second century B.C., diameter 254 feet ; Thuparama, third century B.C., diameter 165 feet ; Abhayagiriya, 300 A.D., diameter 327 feet, and the Jetawanarama, 4th century, diameter 325 feet. As only one of the Indian stupas is more than 150 feet in diameter, namely the Amaravati, which is 162 feet, it will be realized that immense solid content was one of the aims of the Sinhalese dagaba builders. Various efforts have been made in an attempt to calculate the cubic volume of the largest of these Ceylon monuments, as for instance the Abhyagiriya, which, when perfect, must have been 270 feet in height. One authority has[2] stated that the quantity of bricks used in this structure would be sufficient to build a moderately large-sized town, while another[3] has estimated that the mass is equal in general dimensions to the Menkaura or Third Pyramid at Gizeh. Computations of this order do not lay claim to any degree of exactitude but they may give some idea of the stupendous size of the Ceylon dagabas, which in their later and dismantled condition, overgrown with vegetation, have more the appearance of a natural feature in the forest landscape than the handiwork of man. And it is not improbable that some such instinctive ideal party inspired the creation of these immense tumuli,

---

[1] Here the account is obviously referring to subsidiary relics immured in the relic chambers of the four *wahalkadas*, or offsets, projecting from the base of the dagaba. See Plate CLXXVII.

[2] Sir Emerson Tennent, *History and Topography of Ceylon*. Longmans 1860.

[3] H. Parker, *Ancient Ceylon*, Luzac & Co., London, 1909.

for mountains and peaks appealed to the Buddhist mind as sacred elements reaching upwards and charged with mystic power. To imitate these and to deposit at their summit some emblem of the Buddha may explain the urge to produce such mountainous masses of masonry. For unlike the Indian stupas, as for instance Amaravati or Sanchi, the Sinhalese dagabas were not highly decorated works of architecture, nor did they contain sculpture galleries narrating incidents of the Buddha cult, a certain amount of painting may have been added and some statuary was included in the scheme, but the general impression conveyed was the vastness and solidity of the conception, within the womb of which, unseen and inviolate, reposed some physical attribute of the Great Teacher.

Of these monumental dagabas raised during the early period, that known as the Ruwanwaeli at Anuradhapura is a characteristic example. It was built in the second century B.C., by king Duthagamini, a devout Buddhist who was also responsible for the Mirisavetiya, another but smaller dagaba about a mile distant and equally typical of the style. With a diameter of over 250 feet, this immense tumulus stands in the centre of two spacious square platforms, one above the other, their sides facing the cardinal points, with a pillared portico in the middle of the eastern side marking the entrance. Mounting the outer terrace through this columned approach, the pilgrim was confronted by a stepway leading to the inner terrace, the sides of which were supported by a frieze of innumerable elephants facing outwards. Occupying the middle of this terrace were the three orthodox concentric basal platforms, above which rose the great dome, or *gaeba* semi-spherical in shape. Interrupting these three platforms, facing the points of the compass, were four structures imposed on its circular outline which give some of the character to the Ceylon dabaga. These are " offsets " or projecting shrines known as *wahalkadas*, a special feature attached to the Sinhalese type. Somewhat similar offsets supporting *aryaka* or " worshipful columns " project from the Amaravati stupa of Southern India, but the wahalkadas displayed no such row of free-standing pillars, they were small chapel-like additions enshrining cells or diminutive relic chambers reached by a short flight of steps from the lowest circular platform. That both however had the same ascription is clear, yet the Sinhalese example being the earlier it is not improbable that the Indian development was derived from that source. (Plate CXXVII). But while the latter was merely one of the many elaborate embellishments of the Amaravati type of stupa, the wahalkada was the only ornate feature, except the finial at the summit, which adorned the otherwise relatively severe scheme of the Sinhalese dagaba. On the wahalkada therefore the Sinhalese sculptors lavished their skill, decorating its surface with mouldings and carved borders of elephants' heads at close intervals. In front of the offset was a pedestal for a statue, and at the side an elegant *et hondaval*, or " elephant's trunk " stairway for mounting the platform. There is something almost " precious " in the shape and rich treatment of this notable accessory to the dagaba design.

The remaining feature of note ornamenting the dagaba was the finial, a crowning emblem consisting of several superimposed elements, the whole comprising many mythical properties. Here was the heart and nerve centre of this immaculate monument. Briefly, this *kota* or *kotuwa* was composed of two main parts, the cubical casket or *hataraes kotuwa* at the base, supporting the ceremonial umbrella, or *chatta*, but in the course of years the ritual connected with

these went through forms of change. In the first place the *chatta*, although associated with the honorific parasol, bears little resemblance to this essential symbol of the Buddha, and, furled in the shape of a staff, is more reminiscent of the totem post of the Veddahs, and may therefore be of aboriginal extraction. This *chatta* post (*yasti* or staff of the *chhatravali*) was originally embedded in the cubical *hataraes*, a receptacle intended for the principal relics of the dagaba, but it was eventually found that this system of socketing left little space in its interior for the accommodation of the sacred deposit. Therefore a small compartment was made below, and actually within the brickwork summit of the gaeba itself, and into this was lowered the *yantragala* or Mystic Stone, a granite block the surface hollowed into nine small recesses to contain the relics and votive offerings, the finial or *kota* sealing up and surmounting the whole.

As with the stupa in India, so with its counterpart the dagaba in Ceylon, this Buddhist tumulous was by no means an isolated monument, but formed the central feature of a complete monastic settlement. Besides this great sacred pile a typical monastery or *sangharama* would consist of a temple, or image-house (*pilima-ge*), a preaching hall (*bana salawa*), the temple close (*simana*), a processional path (*vidiya*), with an enclosure (*prakaraya*) bordering this path, a priory (*prasada*), a tank (*pokana*) for ablutions, all of which were enclosed within a perimeter wall (*sima*) entered by a guard-house or lodge (*mura-ge*). To the main building of the monastery there was also a portico (*doratuva*) as well as various other supplementary structures for different purposes disposed within the enclosure walls. Remains of most of these buildings are to be found in conjunction with the Ruwanwaeli dagaba which in its prime must have been a very large and well-established institution. But in addition to these monastic premises, around the immediate precincts of the lowest platform of the dagaba were three or four concentric colonnades of free-standing monolithic pillars, presumed to have been so placed in order to carry lighted lamps on ceremonial occasions. The building art of this period was distinctly of the peristyle order, and it is the frequency of these pillars that form the most striking feature of the remains.

There are the shattered portions of many such monastic establishments in and around Anuradhapura and elsewhere, mainly represented by the massive stones of their foundations. And from one of the largest and most sumptuous of these priory halls, now incorrectly known as the Brazen Mansion or Peacock Palace, some idea of the architectural style of this period may be gained. Since identified as the famous Lohaprasada monastery built by king Duthagamini early in the first century B.C., partly from descriptive records and partly from intensive study of the remains the original shape of this historical structure can be conjectured. When first built it rose up as a great pyramidal pile in nine stories crowned by a domical roof of bronze, evidently an imposing conception, spacious in plan and striking in its appearance. For from what survives of its ground story, consisting of portions of its moulded stylobate with voluted balustraded stairways the quality of the workmanship may be determined, while from the forest of granite pillars which are still grouped upon its site the extent of its ground plan can be readily estimated. When it is realized that these monoliths have been calculated to be as many as sixteen hundred in number, each twelve feet high, and covering an area of 250 feet side, the dimensions of this priory hall and its great size generally may be imagined.

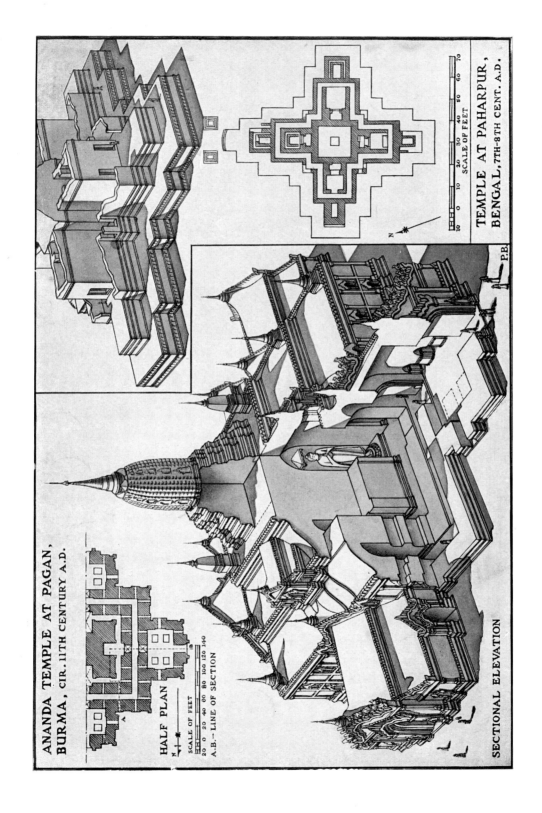

ANANDA TEMPLE AT PAGAN, BURMA, CIR. 11TH CENTURY A.D.

HALF PLAN

SCALE OF FEET
20 0 20 40 60 80 100 120 140
A.B.—LINE OF SECTION

SECTIONAL ELEVATION

TEMPLE AT PAHARPUR, BENGAL, 7TH-8TH CENT. A.D.

SCALE OF FEET
10 0 10 20 30 40 50 60 70

Burma: Buddhist Monastery.

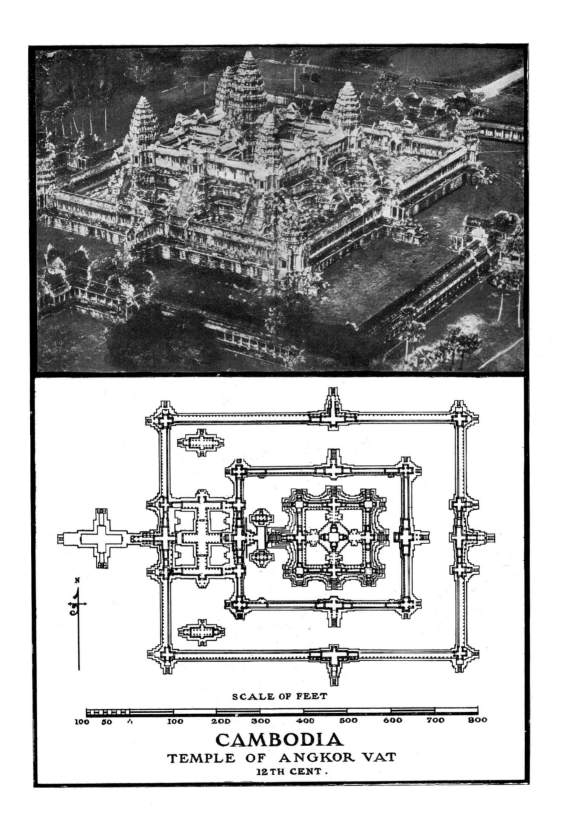

SCALE OF FEET

100   50   0   100   200   300   400   500   600   700   800

CAMBODIA
TEMPLE OF ANGKOR VAT
12TH CENT.

THE TEMPLE OF ANGKOR-VAT, CAMBODIA, FROM THE N.W. 12TH CENT. A.D.

LONGITUDINAL ELEVATION

P.B.

CAMBODIA
SECTION IN PERSPECTIVE OF
THE TEMPLE OF ANGKOR VAT
12 TH CENT. A.D.

PERCY BROWN

CAMBODIA.
ANGKOR THOM.
TOWERS OF THE
TEMPLE OF
BAYON
END OF 12 TH CENT. A.D.

PLAN OF
BAYON

SCALE OF   FEET
50   50   100 150 200 250 300 350 400 450 500 550 600

CAMBODIA.
ANGKOR

SOUTH SANCTUARY
OF THE TEMPLE OF
BANTEAY-SREI
A.D. 969.

OCTAGONAL
PAGODA AT SUNG
SHAN, HONAN (BRICK)
523 A.D.

P.B.

THE WAT MAHADHATU (RESTORED) LOPBURI CIR. 9TH CENT. A.D.

SIAM

PLAN OF THE WAT MAHADHATU

DETAIL FROM A TEMPLE AT PITSANULOK

DETAIL FROM A TEMPLE AT PITSANULOK

P.B.

TYPES OF TEMPLE PORCHES
BANGKOK

VAT RAJABOPHIT   VAT CHETUPHON   VAT ANONG   VAT PRAKEO

As to the elevational aspect of the Lohaprasada it may be assumed with a fair amount of certainty that it followed the pattern of a type of monastery building which was evolved in southern India, including Ceylon, during this early period of Buddhist monachism. This pattern may be studied, translated into a monolithic stone monument in the Dharmaraja ratha at Mamallapuram (Seven Pagodas) near Madras. Although this rock-cut model is several centuries later than the Lohaprasada, it preserves a tradition, of which the Anuradhapura building is an early example. The pillars of the ground story are the remains of the spacious hypostyle hall where the priests would assemble for congregational worship. Above this were the eight remaining floors each containing a row of cells for the accommodation of the resident brotherhood, these floors diminishing as they ascended, each with a courtyard or narrow passage to give access to the cells, the backs of which formed the exterior elevation. A reference to the Mamallapuram ratha (Plate LXI, Fig. 2) will explain the principle of this system, while a study of the sectional elevation of the Vaikuntha-Perumal temple (Plate LXIV) at Conjeeveram, in Madras State, will give some idea of the interior arrangements, although in this instance they have been modified in order to adopt them to the Hindu ritual. It has been already remarked that from the combination of cells in the Buddhist monastery the sikhara of the Indian Dravidian temple was developed, and in some of these sikharas the domical shape surmounting the entire structure of the Hindu example was of the same type as that which, bronzed and gilt, crowned the Lohaprasada, thus accounting for its name the Brazen Mansion. But, alas, the value of its bronze cupola no doubt attracted the cupidity of a later generation of invaders, while the considerable amount of wood in its construction would account for its ready destruction by fire. Some of the lintels of the lower stories were of stone but timber beams were mainly used, and these supported roofs of terracotta tiles shaped like wooden shingles. It is true the data for an attempted reconstruction of this building is scanty, but there are records that enable its great size, towering height, probably in the vicinity of 120 feet, and the crowning glory of its gilt metal cupola, to be dimly visualised.

If, however, the general architectural appearance of these early monastic buildings is denied us, on the other hand there are vast quantities of dressed stone elements in their composition which have survived and serve to give an excellent idea of the manner in which some of the essential features of these structures were treated. Chief among these, owing to their substance and position, were the stylobates of which there are innumerable examples among the ruins of Anuradhapura, together with their stepped approaches, which were made singularly ornamental. Nor should the ablution tanks (pokana) or bathing places be omitted in a survey of the style, as these were usually of distinctive design. But of the utmost significance in a development of the building art which is emphatically peristylar in character, are the capitals of the pillars, in other words, the " order " of the Sinhalese style of architecture. As these capitals are so original and expressive they may be described first. The shafts of the columns were invariably monolithic, without bases, generally square or octagonal in section and carved out of gneiss. Socketed into the upper surface was the puhul, or capital, of a design which has no counterpart outside Ceylon. The central portion of this feature is a double flexured vase-shaped element hexagonal in section and usually left plain. Contrasting with the simplicity of this unadorned member is the richly carved and substantial

abacus which it supports, and the deep necking below with ornamental mouldings between. (Plate CXXVII). There is no mistaking this " order ", as it is expressive of the style, and although in some instances it varies in detail, the principle of its design in this early period is as indicated above. In a later phase of the art occasionally a more exuberant type was devised in the form of lotus pillars, as in the Nissanka Malla Mandapaya, but this was a development of the twelfth century, when the style was becoming more florid. (Plate CXXVIII).

Turning to the massive stone blocks forming the plinths on which most of the main buildings were erected, these are appropriately moulded, dressed, and jointed in a highly finished manner. The same good workmanship is observable in all the stone remains of this period, amply proving that in the preparation and handling of stone construction the Sinhalese mason had little to learn. Specially noticeable in this connection are the tanks for drinking purposes and also for ablutions found in the vicinity of most monasteries, which, owing to the fact that they are below ground level have escaped destruction. Some of these are elaborately planned and laid out in cruciform and other geometrical patterns, while all are executed with a precision and technical ability which is admirable. It was however in the stairway approaches to the principal monastic buildings that the stone-mason showed the most originality and ingenuity, as these entrances breaking into the side of the plinths amply testify. Instances of somewhat similar flights of steps may be seen occasionally introduced in designs in India, as for example at Ajanta of a relatively early date, and later, in the fourteenth century in the Alankara Mandapa at Darasuram, Tanjore (Plate LXVI, Fig. 2) ; but the Sinhalese developed this feature into its most striking form. The component parts of these stairways are four in number : (1) the steps (2) the balustrade on each side (3) the guardstone and (4) the moonstone fronting the whole. Except for an occasional pattern carved on the " rise," the steps themselves were kept severely plain, but the balustrades alongside are heavily voluted in such a manner that they are referred to as et-hondaval or elephant trunk, although there is something more than a suggestion of the known makara or river gryphon of the Ganges in their flowing forms. As a finish to the balustrade are the guardstones or stele-shaped panels containing a bas-relief of the conventional door-attendant corresponding to the dwarpalas at the Indian temple entrance. But perhaps the most interesting portion of the whole conception is the moonstone or chand a large semi-circular stone forming the threshold to the steps. These are carved in a series of concentric borders with a beauty of pattern and mysticism of symbols that present an appropriate introduction to the building they confront.

Although the influence of India by means of the Buddhist contact is observable in the art of Ceylon during this early period, such influence is not great and only reveals itself in relatively minor evidences. For instance that characteristic feature, the conventional Buddhist " railing ", does not seem to have commended itself to the Sinhalese builders as it figures in only one example at Anuradhapura near the Abhayagur Dagoba, but it is most distinctively treated. Carried around a platform square in plan, the uprights, with their cross-bars, copy almost exactly to a smaller scale the more famous stupa railing at Sanchi in India. Where this differs from its prototype is in its more ornamental manipulation as it is elevated on a massive moulded pediment nearly half its own height, with its coping stone also moulded, the whole rising to a height of 7½ feet. Moreover it is entered not by the usual torana gateway, but by means of a stepway having its ends finished with tall guard stones of the stele form, the entire scheme presenting an almost reluctant concession to the traditional Indian origin. Yet that in the style of all this early work there are traces of a definite Indian affinity is obvious, and in some of the patterns there are the same liner and plastic qualities which give character to the arts of Mysore, a circumstance which in view of its geographical proximity, is in no sense remarkable. The remains at Anuradhapura illustrating this first phase of the building art in Ceylon, are sufficient to prove that the inhabitants of the island at that time were naturally of an aesthetic disposition, and only required the stimulus of the Buddhist religion to express this in architectural form. This characteristic shows itself not only in the large monuments of which unfortunately only fragments survive, but it is particularly noticeable in all the accessories of these great compositions, thus conveying the impression that whatever the craftsmen of this period handled, however humble or material, they converted it into a pleasing work of art. But at the beginning of the eleventh century the great and ancient kingdom of Anuradhapura was destroyed by an invasion from Southern India, and the northern portion of the island thus became included in the mighty empire of the Cholas, under a ruling dynasty which extended its influence from the tenth to the twelfth centuries over a very wide expanse of southern Asia. While this encroachment from the Indian mainland signified the end of an important era in the history of Ceylon, owing to the devastation which accompanied this event, at the same time it brought into the building art of the island the architectural style of the Tamil country, or Dravidadesha, thus affecting to some extent the subsequent character of Sinhalese art as a whole.

Although geographically Ceylon is so closely allied with its powerful neighbour India, and associated with it by the bonds of religion, the independence of the island has remained practically intact throughout its history. With the advent of Buddhism certain influences in the sphere of the building art may have been derived from the productions of the Andhras, a Buddhist people of pronounced architectural ideals whose chief structures occupied a region towards the south of India before and after the beginning of the Christian era. Later, the art of the Pallavas, as already indicated, may have affected the style of the Sinhalese monastery buildings when these began to be erected at Anuradhapura. These however were peaceful penetrations brought about by the demand on the part of the people for a constructional procedure to aid them in their building projects. But when the Cholas came in the eleventh century as ruthless invaders to force their Hinduism and its form of building art on the inhabitants of the island different circumstances prevailed. Whereas previously the features from India were incorporated in the indigenous style to give strength and character to the Buddhist architectural productions of the Sinhalese, on the other hand the Cholas destroyed the historical monuments which had been so laboriously evolved, and raised Siva temples in their place. And so there was imposed on the people during their period of occupation, extending over the eleventh and twelfth centuries, a style of building alien both in its structure and in its expressiveness, in a word a provincial development of the Tamilian type of Hindu temple architecture as this existed in Southern India at such places as Tanjore and Pudukottai. Examples of this architectural importation from the mainland may be seen at Polonnaruwa in the two temples of Siva

Devale of the eleventh century, related clearly to a somewhat earlier Chola temple at Srinivasanalur in the Trichinopoly District. (Plate LVI, Fig. 1). Constructed of stone masonry in the characteristic Tamilian manner, these Siva temples, among other buildings of the same period, mark plainly the effect of the south Indian invasion at this stage of Sinhalese history. With their prominent pilasters crowned by the Tamilian order of capital distinguished by its wide scalloped abacus, its walls divided by the " split " openings and sunken alcoves, its foundational string-course displaying the typical motif of immured gryphons, the entire composition manifests all the architectural attributions of the Dravidian mode under the Chola regime.

Such a forceful style as that which flourished with so much vigour in southern India naturally influenced the building productions of the country even after the Chola invaders had been driven out of the island, and the Sinhalese sovereignty restored by Vijayabahu (1070-1114) towards the end of the eleventh century. One aspect of this may be seen in the Thuparama temple at Polonnaruwa of the twelfth century, built by the greatest of all the kings of this line, Parakrama Bahu I, and to whom much of the architectural glory of the capital was due. In the main obviously of Dravidian extraction inspired no doubt by the style of those Siva temples of the Cholas which preceded it, yet it differs from its archtypes in one important constructional particular, it is not built of stone, but of the Sinhalese masons' favourite material, brick. Apart however from the changes brought about by this difference of technique, the Thuparama is obviously a provincialized conception, an attempt to reproduce a classical type of building without the finished knowledge and experience necessary for such an effort. Of considerable size but with much of its substance taken up by the abnormal thickness of its walls, although hardly decadent, it shows how the robust ideals of the Pallavas, developed more fully by the Cholas, could in less practised hands result in this somewhat uninspiring composition. In its mass there is a certain dignity and a sense of proportion, with an imposing tower-like structure surmounting the whole, but the surface treatment is inclined to be crude and unconvincing. The Thuparama is significant because it marks a stage in the course of the building art of Ceylon, not exactly a transition but the finale of an architectural intrusion which both directly and indirectly affected to a degree the arts of the island generally.

With the return of the rule in Ceylon to an indigenous dynasty in the twelfth century, the second era of the greatness of the country began. And as the first era centred round the capital of Anuradhapura, so it came about that the succeeding historical period had as its focus the royal city of Polonnaruwa, situated some fifty odd miles towards the south-east of the older metropolis. It was however under Parakrama the Great (1153-86) that this city assumed premier rank, as this ruler devoted all his resources to the production of monumental buildings, with the result that Sinhalese architecture had a second and brilliant flowering under his enthusiastic patronage. But this monarch's reign, in spite of its length, proved but a short, although illustrious episode in the chronicles of the country, recalling in some respects the Moghul Emperor Akbar's magnificent civic scheme at Fatehpur Sikri in India some centuries later, for both these imperial cities after a transitory but dynamic existence were abandoned and fell into decay after experiencing little more than a generation of sumptuous ceremony and regal splendour. At Polonnaruwa spoliation began as early as the thirteenth century, and although an attempt was made to revive some of its ancient glory in the fourteenth century, it availed little, since when it has remained a ruined record of the past, its temples and palaces fighting a steadily losing battle against the merciless inroads of the surrounding vegetation.

In reviewing the remains of Polonnaruwa one feels that something of the contemporary feudal system in Europe, which expressed itself in impregnable fortresses, may have in some manner communicated itself to king Parakrama the Great as well as to his nephew and successor Nissanka Malla (1187-1196), and so moved the former to construct his capital as a great walled city. But there was an oriental spaciousness, luxury and splendour in the Sinhalese conception rarely found in the strongholds of the West. What is further remarkable is that in such a relatively limited time so much should have been accomplished, and all of the most superb quality. Moreover in the broad lay-out of this city the ramparts of which cover a circuit of nearly four miles, there are definite evidences of that traditional form of planning observable throughout the ages in many capitals of the orient. With its trace in the shape of a parallelogram, one of its long sides is built on a " bund " or rampart overlooking the expansive stretch of water known as the Topa Vewa, and against this in the form of a smaller parallelogram also enclosed by a wall and within the city area, was the citadel. Apart from the fact that the lake acted as a protection, it also brought cool air and an open view to the palace buildings on its verge, the entire scheme being worked out on a general principle which underlies most imperial city plans. Within this enclosure an aggregation of buildings was erected which in number and variety few cities can excel. These comprised palaces, temples, monasteries, audience and council chambers, stupas and bathing places, together with all the miscellaneous structures, large and small, which go to make up an eastern capital of the first class. Polonnaruwa thus in the twelfth century became not only a city of marked architectural grandeur, but it was significant of a movement of great importance in the history of the building art in Ceylon. From its remains, now emerging throughout a large area of tangled undergrowth, certain important examples may be here selected which will explain the trends of the art at this period. One of these buildings, although perhaps not specially attractive in its composition, is notable as its conformation is fully expressive of the ideals which motivated Buddhism at this stage of its development. For it represents a change in the structure of the creed which reacted in a marked manner on the religious architecture of the time, as may be seen in such distant places as in the building art of Bihar in India, Burma, Cambodia, and even extending into Java. Briefly, in place of the abstract tumulous in the form of the stupa or dagoba, a desire arose for an anthropomorphic conception of the founder of the religion for the purposes of worship, and so in the course of time temples were erected enshrining colossal figures of the Buddha within halls specially adapted for this purpose. This movement naturally affected to no inconsiderable degree the formation of the building as a whole, and the Lankatilaka or Jetawanarama Temple is a typical example of the procedure adopted to attain this end. (Plate CXXVIII). Constructed entirely of brick covered with stucco, even the statue of the Buddha which is nearly sixty feet high in the interior being built up by the same process, the external appearance of this building shows how the Tamilian sytle of Southern India maintained its hold. Clearly designed as a shrine rather than a temple, the interior consists of two compartments longitudinally aligned measuring 170 feet in length by 70

feet wide, the outer one forming a kind of portico leading to the great cella containing the standing statue, obviously the main intention of the scheme. Except for the fluted buttresslike pilasters which flank the main entrance, no special originality is shown in the architectural treatment of the building, but when in its prime it must have been a stately and dignified structure, worthy of the city which it adorned.

That the Sinhalese builders of this period could however rise to great heights in their architectural productions is plainly shown in another of the many monumental buildings which constituted the glories of Polonnaruwa in the twelfth century. This is the Wata-dage, or " Hall of the Relic," a building constructed mainly of stone masonry and designed on an elegant plan of concentric circular platforms and passages, enclosing a round central shrine, within which is a memorial in the form of a small dagoba. Such an exquisite example of the building art was evidently intended to contain some very precious and sacred emblem, and it is accordingly presumed to have been the edifice known as the Dalada Maligawa built by Parakrama the Great to enshrine the immortal tooth-relic. This relic reposed in the votive stupa within the building, and it may have been the rounded shape of this dagaba which suggested the circular treatment of the structure as a whole. Not only is the Wata-dage an architectural conception of a notably graceful kind, but its accessories and plastic embellishment are equally, well executed, while originally the interior wall surfaces were decorated with paintings. The main elements of its composition are three in number, in the first place the circular configuration is the basis of the scheme and is maintained throughout, secondly the designer has made skilful use of pillars to accentuate the essential lines of his circular elevation, and thirdly at the appropriate places he has interrupted these lines by means of an entrance at each of the cardinal points, the main one on the east being a work of great beauty. One of the most attractive monuments throughout the entire range of Sinhalese building art, although of no great size, it was not only the conception of a genius, but it was evidently carried out in its mass as well as in its detail by the leading master craftsmen of the time. The same high standard of handwork may be seen in other and lesser structures at Polonnaruwa, such as some of the " pokanas," including the famous " Lotus Bath," and the architectural gem known as the " Floral Altar," all of which serve to prove that in the twelfth century under enthusiastic patronage, the arts of Ceylon attained their consummation.

Political conditions however brought this short-lived period of high maturity to a speedy end, Polonnaruwa was abandoned at the close of the thirteenth century, and the arts consequently suffered a considerable interval of decline, only to be revived when Kandy became the seat of the Sinhalese monarchy from 1592 to 1815. On this romantic site, some sixteen hundred feet above sea level, the last phase of the building art of the island is recorded. Picturesque and colourful but merely a pale reflection of the grand classical movement which died with the line of the Parakrama Bahu, its combination of timber and masonry has a certain attraction, but it is no longer a great art. It is represented by such buildings as the Audience Hall of the Kandyan kings, and now used as a Supreme Court House. There is also the Dalada Maligawa, or " Temple of the Tooth Relic " in a style of architecture which accords with modern taste its projecting caves with supporting corbels and massive pillars, all painted in schemes of primary colours displaying a sense of vivacity which is not unpleasing. Added to this there are patterns of figures and grotesques with floral accessories and other familar motifs which tend to associate it with the folk-art manner. But the great ideals of the early mediaeval period have deteriorated, under more modern conditions, the spirit of that remarkable movement has ceased to exist, and wood and painted pavilions are now sufficient to satisfy the public eye.

REFERENCES

Milton, G. E., *The Lost Cities of Ceylon*, Murray, 1928.

Parker, H., *Ancient Ceylon*, Luzac, 1910.

Cave, H. W., *Ruined Cities of Ceylon*, 1900.

Burrow, S. M., *Buried Cities of Ceylon*. 1906.

Smither, J. G., *Architectural Remains, Anuradhapura*, Ceylon, 1894.

Still, J., *Ancient Capitals of Ceylon*, 1907.

Coomaraswamy, A. K., *Mediaevel Sinhalese Art* (1908).

Paranavitana, S.,   *The Stupa in Ceylon*, Vol. V. Memoir of the Archaeological Society of Ceylon.

Annual Reports on the Archaeological Survey of Ceylon.

CHAPTER XXXV

THE "PAGODAS" OF BURMA

THE historical development of the building art in Burma falls into three periods, the first of which may be referred to as the "Early Phase," beginning from approximately the 2nd century A.D. and continuing until the 8th or 9th century. This was followed by a period when the architecture of the country assumed such a character and impressiveness that it becomes entitled to the designation of the "Classical Phase," and which flourished from the 9th to the 13th centuries. From the ending of this phase to the present day the country has reverted to a more intimate form of architectural expression, akin to a folk art, executed chiefly in wood in a very distinctive style, and which may be suitably defined as the "Pagoda" period.

Of the first of these developments, namely the "Early Phase," although it is known that a form of the building art existed at the historical centres of Thaton is Pegu the capital of a Mongolian tribe known as the Mons or Talaings, and at Prome the capital of another tribe, the Pyu, definite traces of the mode that then prevailed have disappeared. Partly on account of the destructive nature of the climate especially in the deltaic region, and partly owing to the continuance of devastating wars, the actual architectural remains of this period, which covered the earlier centuries of the first millennium, are so scanty as to be negligible. From the geographical position of these remains, however, and other evidences, it appears that a religio-cultural approach from Buddhist India, probably early in the Christian era, was made by sea. The land barriers between India and Burma at this period were of such a nature as to prevent ready intercourse, and accordingly the earliest historical material has been located in Lower Burma. Here, in the kingdom of the Pyus, with its seaport in the Gulf of Martaban, access to the country was obtained by means of the lower reaches of the Sitang river. The Pyu capital was at Srikshatra, near Prome, on the Irrawady, and was a city of considerable size and importance. It is described as being twenty-seven miles in circumference, with its walls and moat faced with glazed bricks, and that it contained over a hundred Buddhist monasteries richly furnished and endowed. There were twelve gates with pagodas at each corner, and mention is made of a great white image, one hundred feet high opposite the gate of the place.[1] Few traces, if any, of this city remain, yet, on the other hand several buildings have survived of a rather later date which may be regarded as a connecting link between the two periods, the Early and the Mediaeval, or, more precisely, a stage of transition leading up to the grand Classical Phase which followed.

These earlier structures consist of three examples at Hmawza (Old Prome) dating from about the 10th century A.D., and two others of the 11th century at Pagan. The former group comprises a stupa, the Bawbawgyi, and the two temples of Bebe and Leymethna. The stupa is a massive pile composed of a conical superstructure based on five diminishing terraces, the appearance of the whole recalling similar Buddhist monuments in India, and thus supporting the assumption that this architectural movement was derived from that country. But it is on the two temples mentioned above that interest chiefly centres, as although relatively small in size, they appear to have been the models for the much larger structures evolved slightly later at Pagan. The Leymethna is a type of temple gradually becoming characteristic of the religious architecture of the Buddhists at about this period in which the predominant features are a substantial central core of masonry surrounded by corridors with a portico projected from each of the four cardinal faces. Over the whole is carried the superstructure of the central block rising above the vaulted ceilings of the encircling corridors, so that the roofs of these form elevated terraces around the upper portion of the building.

The two temples at Pagan, are those of Patothamya and of Nanpaya in the village of Myinpagan both comparatively early examples of temple building in Burma, as they appear to date from the 11th century, thus illustrating an intermediate phase of some significance. The Nanpaya temple, attributed to Manuha, the last king of Thaton when a prisoner of war, may therefore be a survival of the style of architecture favoured by the Mons or Talaings as this mode existed just previous to the great classical movement which subsequently developed on the same site. Constructed of stone masonry over a brick foundation it is decorated both inside and out with carving, that on the exterior being of a bold simple order confined to the pediments over the stone lattice windows, while in the interior the pillars are ornamented in low relief with figures of Brahma.

With these two temples might be included a stupa, also at Pagan, that of Shivesandaw, as it is believed to date from the middle of the 11th century. Raised on five receding terraces, each designated by a legendary name, the stupa itself in its main outlines assumes a conical shape, its campaniform superstructure being divided into zones with the whole edifice crowned by a tapering finial ending in a stone *amalaka*.[2]

All these comparatively early examples of Burmese architecture show Indo-Buddhist influences, but none more so than the general scheme of the Nanpaya temple, referred to above, which recalls at once, both in its plan and elevation, the lay-out of similar buildings of an earlier or corresponding period in parts of India. There is the rectangular body of the temple surmounted by a sikhara, with a portico in front, all according to the arrangements found in the early examples at Aihole in Dharwar, or Bhubaneshwar in Orissa, and yet with a difference. It is an Indo-Aryan temple conceived according to Burmese ideals, but that it is based on an Indian model there can be little doubt. The other temple at Pagan, the Patothamya, although designed on much the same plan, with rectangular body and projecting portico, differs, in its architectural treatment, yet all these structures, whether

---

[1] Majumdar, R. C., *Hindu Colonies in the Far East*, p. 200.

[2] Archaeological Survey of India, Report 1926-27.

stupas or temples, while appearing to be fundamentally derived from Indian sources, disclose an attempt to effect in their design something original and indigenous, and in them are implied the racial sentiments of their creators.

With the production of these earlier structures the stage began to be set for that remarkable display of religious building in Middle Burma which has been referred to as representing the Classical Period of the architecture of the country. The sacred structure comprising this great group are Buddhist of the Hinayana order, and are all found on one site, at Pagan, the capital of Burma from 819 A.D., at which date it was founded, until 1286 when it fell, owing to invasion, and ceased to be the leading city of the state. Here, in this expansive but arid locality, the excessively dry climatic conditions being the main reason for their preservation, there grew up within a period of four centuries such an immense concourse of religious buildings that in number and size it can have few equals. This vast temple city, deserted in the thirteenth century, and ever since remaining a mere empty embodiment of its one time glory, must have consisted, when in its prime, of nearly a thousand " pagodas " of note, and which even now boasts of some eight hundred of these edifices, more than a few being monuments of exceptional proportions. Glistening brilliantly white in the searing sunlight, distributed over an area eight miles by five of bare and uninteresting landscape, these stupas and temples, bereft now largely of their spiritual content and priestly establishment, are a record of a time when Buddhism was foremost in the minds of the people, a condition which found expression in architecture of a grand order.

The style of the monuments at Pagan is such as to give support to a credible theory. History has revealed that in the evolution of the building art throughout the ages, and viewed in its broadcast aspect, some mysterious law of compensation has manifested itself so that architecture has developed in alternating cycles the result of two major elemental forces. These are Repose on the one hand and Energy on the other. In Europe the outstanding instance of this evolution by balanced movement is the underlying ideal of Classical architecture signifying Repose, being succeeded by Gothic architecture implying Energy. In India and beyond, to a somewhat lesser degree, a similar sequence is observable, beginning with the Buddhist stupa, a monument static in principle and even earthbound in structure, followed by the Hindu temple, with its qualities of animation and aspiration as shown in the sikhara and other features expressive of beauty in energy. In the vast expanse of stupas and temples spread out over the plain at Pagan, these appear to illustrate that stage in the process of architectural development when the two forces were silently contending for supremacy, to culminate finally in the emergence of energy in the form of the more modern soaring pagoda.

Such a prodigality of building production as that maintained at Pagan over so long a period during the early mediaeval era was largely the outcome of a flood of religious fervour, but not entirely so. The political circumstances were also favourable. Stimulated as the people were by the absorbing power of Buddhism, a state of being discernible in all the countries of Asia wherever the teachings of the Buddha penetrated, the religious movement in Burma was accompanied by another force. This was the realization in the country of a national consciousness, which eventually

brought about a unification of the people, a consummation achieved by the administrative genius of king Anoratha (1044-1077), who succeeded in welding his subjects into a homogeneous whole. To the combination of the two factors, religious and political, initiated and put into effect by this ruler in the middle of the eleventh century, these architectural records of Burma's mediaeval greatness are mainly due.

A study of this phase of Burmese architecture is simplified by the fact that all the examples are confined within a circumscribed area, and also that they resolve themselves almost entirely into two classes of structure consisting of (a) Stupas and (b) Temples. There are however two exceptions to this classification as a prominent building there, the Mahabodhi, is in imitation of the original Budh Gaya in Bihar, India, and another edifice, erected for the particular occasion by which it is designated and known as the Ordination Hall, both of which date from the thirteenth century. Of all the other buildings at Pagan, whatever their function, these are as completely expressive of the building art in Burma during the early mediaeval period as the Gothic cathedrals are typical of the same age in England. And, in much the same manner as the architectural ideals of the cathedrals were partially derived from external source, so there is little doubt that the basic design of the stupas and temples of Middle Burma originally came from Buddhist India. So much so that it has been authoritatively affirmed that the workmen who constructed these buildings were artisans actually brought from Bihar and Bengal for this specific purpose.[1] On the other hand such a view leaves out two important modifying factors, namely in the first instance the un-Indian appearance of these buildings as a whole and their definitely Burmese treatment, while, secondly, it does not take into account the marked aesthetic temperament of the Burmese people themselves which, if anything, is even more pronounced than that possessed by those from whom they are presumed to have drawn their inspiration. In short the buildings at Pagan may be most nearly defined as fundamentally of Indian extraction but designed and adapted to conform to Burmese conceptions.

Although the monuments in this ancient temple-city are mainly of two kinds, the stupa and the temple, the architectural treatment of both is of much the same order, as the difference lies largely in that of intention. The stupa is the shrine or reliquary, and is therefore in itself an object of worship, while the temple is planned with its interior arrangements consisting of galleries and corridors devised for religious ceremonial. Such were the primary attributions of these two types of structure, but in the course of time the Buddhist temple began to combine the two purposes, where the central block took the form of a great shrine with interior corridors carried around it for circumambulation and processions. The colossal Buddhist monumental shrine and temple at Paharpur in Bengal, at the height of its glory in the eighth century, but now a mound of ruins, is believed to have been the model for this form of structure, although only in its underlying essentials, and not in its architectural scheme. For in the buildings of Pagan, as in much of the structural art of Further India, is illustrated the contact of two diverse trends, that from India implying in its exterior mass the quality of convexity shared by the stupa and the sikhara, and that from the Far East revealing the characteristic concavity or inward sweep of the pagoda. In the whole of the architecture of this great region lying between India

---

[1] Memoirs of the Archaeological Survey of India, No. 56. *The Ananda Temple of Pagan* by Chas. Duroiselle, M.A. (p. 9).

and China, exemplified particularly in the buildings of Burma, there appears to have been a continual struggle for supremacy between the bulbous mass of the orthodox stupa combined with the outward curve of the Indo-Aryan sikhara on the one hand, and the ascending attenuated outlines of what is ordinarily known as the Chinese pagoda on the other. In an effort to bring about an agreement between these two somewhat conflicting architectural formations, the Burmese master masons were helped very considerably by adopting a form of elongated finial as a summit to their pagoda "spires," instead of the lateral *harmika* of the Indian stupa, or the short thick-set *amalaka* of the Hindu temple. This finial or *hti*, as it is called, is an adaptation of the multiform umbrella, and makes an appropriate finish to the tenuous shape of the Burmese superstructure. In spite therefore of the fact that although " Burma is surrounded by India, Tibet, China, Siam and the Malay States " and " the culture of its people, their art and monuments are almost exclusively derived from India "[1] a glance at the elevational effect of the architecture of the country will show that it owes not a little of its character, or at least its external appearance, to Far Eastern sources.

Referring more specifically to the two kinds of structure that make up the majority of the buildings in Pagan, among the stupas one of the most typical examples is that known as the Mangalazedi, erected in 1274. The system of receding terraces, usually three of five in number, square in plan, and approached by stairways in the middle of each face, is the principle adopted in the generality of buildings of this order, and in the Mangalazedi stupa the five platforms comprising the high basement are excellently proportioned. Having circumambulated these processional paths, the pilgrim, on attaining the uppermost terrace, sees mounting up above him the circular stupa, concentrically moulded as its base, then rising in the form of a massive bell-shape to terminate in another ringed feature crowned by the slender pointed *hti*. To produce a rhythmic quality into the structure as a whole miniature replicas of the main stupa, in the form of ornamental turrets, break the outline of the angles, while bas-reliefs, are introduced at the various stages to enrich the entire composition and at the same time to attract the attention of the devout in the course of their progression around the shrine.

Although in its architectural treatment far removed from the tumulous mound of the Indian stupa, the terraced substructure is, in a more simplified form, observable in some of the examples in the Punjab, while the bell-shaped feature surmounting the whole, recalls, in certain of its aspects, the *anda*, or globular body of the historical original form which it was traditionally derived. Following in its main outlines those of a pyramid, giving the idea of a great mass in repose there is in the Mangalazedi stupa at Pagan a dignity, grace, and effect of permanence, reflecting no little credit on those responsible for its composition and construction.

Of the other class at structure at Pagan, the temple, there are numerous excellent examples, such as the Gawdaw-palin ("Throne of the Ancestral Hall," built in 1200), the Thatpyinnyu, the Shwegugyi, and the Sulamani, but the largest and by far the most imposing of all, besides being the noblest monument in the whole of Burma, is the Ananda Pagoda, founded by king Kyanzittha (1084-1112) in 1090 A.D. A description of this typical temple will give some idea, not only of the character of the group as a whole, but also of the architectural perceptions of the Burmese builders during this, their finest period.[2] In size alone this grand building is of no mean proportions as across its width including its porticos it measures 300 ft. each way, while the four-entranced enclosure within which it is centrally placed is a square of 570 ft. side. Its height too is impressive as from the ground level to the finial of its main spire it is over 160 ft. But its architectural effect lies not so much in its dimensions as in the disposition of its parts, in the fine projecting porticos, the graduated terraces of its roofs, and its ascending tapering volume as a whole. The underling intention of the building has also been carefully considered, while the relation of the exterior features to the arrangements within, leaves nothing to be desired. That some of the treatment of the external facades verge on the extravagant, if not inclined to be fantastic, may of course strike the eye of the occidental spectator, but it should be remembered that the entire appearance of the building was designed to please the taste of a people with whom form and colour have few limits, a people who revel in brilliant hues, and where curves and foliations, spirals and volutes are favourite elements in their ornamental patterns. On plan the Ananda temple is cruciform in shape, its extended porticos reaching out to produce its four expansive arms, thus converting the whole into the semblance of a Greek cross. For the central portion of the structure is an immense solid square block of masonry above which rises the main sikhara or spire. On each face of this middle core is a tall arched alcove, each enshrining a large standing figure of a Buddha, 31 ft. high, with hands raised to the breast in the pose of the *dharmachakra mudra*, while around the entire interior are carried two concentric corridors, their vaulted ceilings partly supporting the terraced ogee roofs above. (Plate CXXX).

In addition to the main spire which rises above the centre of the building, there are other supplementary pinnacles over the angles of the receding roofs and above the porticos, of significant design. For they represent two traditions, as some of these, imitating the central spire are derived from the Indo-Aryan sikhara, while others, particularly the lower and subsidiary turrets, and what may be termed, a pagoda variation of the stupa. The former are rectangular in section but have recessed chases and are patterned with horizontal ribbed mouldings as seen in the *deuls* or towers of the Orissan temples, India. On the other hand the latter has a bell-shaped body, an attenuated development of the stupa. It is however in the exterior enrichments of the architectural scheme of the Ananda as a whole with which one is inclined to deal critically, as much of it is of an excessively flamboyant order and, although not decadent, is somewhat reminiscent of that later period of the building art in India, when the Nawabs of Oudh threw across the openings of their palaces foliated arches, and broke their skylines with florid merlons in an effort to attain a super-richness of effect. But the Burmese architectural decoration was by no means debased, it was a form

---

[1] "Revealing India's Past," India Society, London, 1939, Chapter VIII, Burma, by Chas. Duroiselle, p. 325.

[2] Over 40 years ago, the author was permitted to reside for a week in the Ananda temple, as in those days other accommodation in Pagan was either unsatisfactory or unavailable. There, in the benign presence of the colossal statue of the Buddha in the northern alcove, towering on its pedestal some 30 feet high, he was allowed to pass the nights, occasionally in wakeful moments to notice by the reflected light of the moon the ivory and nielloed eyes under their heavy overhanging lids ever watching over him with protective smile.

of genuine artistic exuberance which expressed itself plastically in cusped overdoors, wave-line pediments, and flowing, undulating shapes generally. That this method of decoration breaks up effectively the solid mass of the entire composition is conceded, but taken as a whole, it borders on the ultra-florescent, a reflection probably of the luxurious natural growth with which much of the country abounds.

In the execution of these buildings brick masonry was almost employed, having the surface finished off with a coating of plaster painted dead white. An inferential feature in the style of achitecture adopted, and also of the construction, is the introduction of that scientific method of bridging a space by means of the arch and vault. As already explained Hindu India made little use of the arch, the builders in that country preferring for their purpose the lintel, or horizontal beam. The appearance of such a constructional principle as the arch indicates that not all the building technicalities of the Burmese were derived from India, but none the less in other directions considerable borrowings are discernible. Although in the earlier examples of the arch those of a semi-circular order are not uncommon, in many of the Pagan buildings an arch of the pointed type is noticeable. In shape these arches are not dissimilar in outline from those associated with the " Decorated " period of Gothic architecture in England, and with which it is a coincidence they are more or less contemporary. These arches in Burma are, in a sense, of the " true " variety, as they are built up of radiating voussoirs, although the bricks forming these members are not laid face to face in the accepted manner, but edge to edge, other instances of which may be seen in India at Budh Gaya in the 7th century,[1] and also earlier still at Ctesiphon in Iraq (Plate XXXII). It is probable that the size and shape of the bricks used in all these buildings may have conditioned the method by which they were constructionally applied. Some of the archways in the Ananda temple are of spacious proportions, those in the porticos having a span of over 28½ feet and a height of 54 ft., while the fact that they have stood intact for more than eight and a half centuries is evidence of their strength and stability.

With the fall of Pagan in 1286, owing to the invasion of the country by the forces of the Asiatic conqueror Kublai Khan, Burma politically disintegrated and the architectural movement as this flourished in the mediaeval temple city suffered accordingly. The end of the 13th century therefore marks the end also of the grand classical style of the building art of the Burmese, a style which was never revived. Decadent forms of it appear in some of the subsequent capital cities, such as at Mekkhaya, Ava, Sagaing, and Amarapura, but on account of inferior construction most of these structures are crumbling to ruin. A considerable interval of separative rule then ensued, to be followed by a period of some four centuries when Burma appears to have turned away from India and to have been directed more towards the Far East for inspiration, its builders thus coming gradually under the influence of Chinese ideals, with the resultant change in their orientation, as exemplified by the recent architecture of the country. From the eighteenth century therefore there developed in the more important centres of Burma a style of architecture in which that distinctive feature commonly referred to as the " pagoda " element is predominant. The principal examples of the phase are the famous Shwe Dagon Pagoda at Rangoon, the Monasteries at Mandalay, as for instance the Queen's Golden Monastery, and more particularly, as it represents the secular architecture of the country at this period, the imperial city and palace at Mandalay.

Of the various forms of architectural expression which were evolved during the final period of the building art in Burma, as illustrated by the stupa, the monastery, and the palace, although the intentions of these three conceptions are widely different, and their functions are as dissimilar as their structural appearance, the architectural pattern underlying each class of building represents the same derivative sources, the same constructional experiences, and displays much the same aesthetic standards. None of these buildings can be described as great architecture when compared with the productions of the previous period, but nevertheless they are characteristic of the people, reflecting that light artistic temperament which shows itself in many aspects of their lives, from their instincts and aspirations to their customs and costumes.

That the Far Eastern influence in the buildings of this period is readily discernible will no doubt be admitted, but at the same time the racial reactions of the people have translated the forms communicated to them from the profoundly ancient civilization of China, into their own idiom. Perhaps the monument that is least effected by this change of direction in the minds of the Burmese from westward to eastward, and one that indicates in the most marked manner the connecting link between India on the one hand and China on the other, is the great Shwe Dagon Pagoda at Rangoon. This stupa-pagoda is not only a national monument, but is also fully representative of the spirit of Burma in its more modern phase. It enshrines within its reliquary eight sacred hairs of Gautama, and is recorded to be of very ancient foundation, although the present structure dates principally from the middle of the sixteenth century. From the ground level of the platform on which the stupa stands it rises to a height of about 370 feet, or a little higher than St. Paul's Cathedral, London. Its imposing appearance is however increased by the fact that it is poised on a mound, partly natural and partly artificial, shaped into two rectangular terraces, one above the other, each side, according to the customary orientation of this type of building, facing one of the cardinal points. In its architectural aspect, the Shwe Dagon Pagoda shows how far the Buddhist stupa, in the course of time and when removed from the country of its origin, has departed from the traditional mound-shaped pile to become a tall tenuous structure with only a suggestion of the tumulus body traceable in its composition. Summarized it consists of a wide terraced base of 1355 feet circumference supporting a tapering spire of slender proportions, divided into zones by transverse concentric string-courses, and surmounted by a richly decorated finial or *hti*.

Such is the Shwe Dagon Pagoda concisely described as an example of the building art, but no account however brief

---

[1] Early in the fourteenth century, the Buddhists of Burma, hearing that the sacred shrine at Budh Gaya in Bihar was in a state of ruin, undertook the restoration of this monument, and accordingly despatched to India a party of Burmese masons for this purpose. It is possible therefore that the remains of a form of the true arch afterwards exposed in the interior of the building were introduced into the structure at the time of this restoration. These arches are of the same type as those described above, and such as are used in the Ananda structure.

MI SON B6.

MI SON B3.

DONG DUONG 11.

MI SON B14.

PO KLAUN GARAI.

MI SON B3.

BINH LAM.

BUILDINGS OF THE CHAMS
(ANNAM, INDO-CHINA) C. 9TH CENT.

SCALE OF FEET

P.B.

Bhima Temple (c. 700)

Punta Deva Temple (c. 750)

Djeng Plateau, Mid-Java.

Prambanam (c. 900), Mid-Java

Panataram (c. 1370), East-Java

JAVA

CONJECTURAL RESTORATION OF
SARI VIHARA
AT PRAMBANAM
MID-JAVA
C. 800 A.D.

DETAIL OF AN ANTEFIX
(FOLIATED ARCH OVER
OPENINGS)

MOULDINGS
OF PLINTH

PILASTER

GROUND PLAN

N

SCALE OF   FEET
10 5   0   10   20   30   40   50   60   70

P.B.

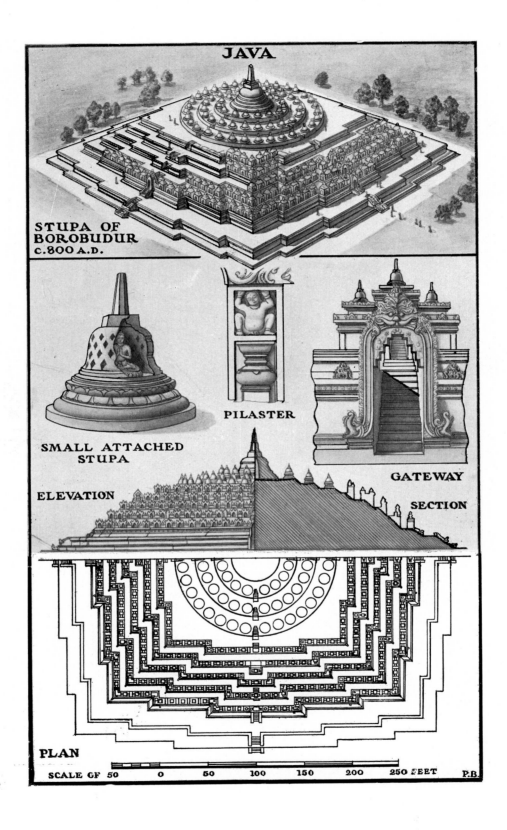

JAVA

STUPA OF
BOROBUDUR
c. 800 A.D.

SMALL ATTACHED
STUPA

PILASTER

GATEWAY

ELEVATION

SECTION

PLAN

SCALE OF 50   0   50   100   150   200   250 FEET

P.B.

of this monument would be complete without a reference to the complex array of structures which cluster around its base, the entire scene presenting a picture of sheer orientalism unequalled in any other Asiatic structural creation. Crowding each side of the processional circuit are groups of tall pointed shrines, their superstructures imitating in miniature the central pile, and each treated as a pattern of tawdry glitter and fretted ornament. A close study, however, reveals among this confusion of enrichment, here and there specimens of lovely handiwork in wood and metal, often painted and gilt, but the appearance as a whole is one of over-wrought exuberance, nevertheless not unattractive on account of its barbaric effectiveness. Surrounded by this medley of glass-mosaic, intricate carving, and gilded metal, the spectator can only stand amazed at the fervency of the people whose one aim is to show their devotion by embellishing in such a manner this supreme material manifestation of their religious belief.

In much the same style as the shrines and chapels around the Shwe Dagon Pagoda are the monasteries especially those in the vicinity of Mandalay, which not infrequently are buildings of some magnitude. As with most structural edifices in Burma they are raised on a substantial ground story to preserve them from damp exudations and destructive pests. Solid round pillars of teak (a wood impervious to insects) and supports of masonry form this foundational stage, above which in strange contrast rise the light and fantastic wooden gables and decorative halls of the monastic building itself. Ornamenting the angular roofs are prominently projecting eaves and barge-boards overhanging commodious balconies which encompass most of the structure, all covered with intricate carving but at the same time acting as useful protective screens against the elements, either sun or rain. To enter the higher halls of the monastery a stairway with an immense voluted balustrade is provided, and this approach, together with other ground constructions such as parapets formed of massive masonry merlons attached to the foundation story, differs in a marked degree from the light wooden architecture above. Here it becomes evident that these solid masonry appendages are a survival of the grand classical style which characterised the mediaeval monuments of Pagan. They represent an almost forgotten memory of that supreme effort, and their substantial forms are in forced contrast with the elegant, animated but fanciful woodwork they support.

One other notable example of the later phase of Burmese architecture, and of a very comprehensive order, is the city and palace of Mandalay.[1] This modern capital of the country, although not so important in its architectural aspect, is of considerable significance on account of its plan and general layout, as it represents the traditional conception of a royal residence, citadel, fortress, and city combined according to Far Eastern ideals. That Mandalay is a survival of the historical principles applied in planning a capital city in the orient is fairly clear, and receives confirmation from an interesting source. For Marco Polo's description of Khan Baliq, the Pekin capital built by the great Mongol Kublai

Khan in the thirteenth century, shows that Mandalay embodies the same essential features laid out on the same general plan, although founded some six hundred years later. This seat of the Alaungpra rulers of Burma was received and put into effect by King Mindon in 1857, and a striking view of its shape and the disposition of its parts may be readily obtained from Mandalay Hill, an eminence immediately overlooking the city on the north-west. Taken as a whole the layout is a system of concentric square enclosures the perimeter walls of which act as a series of protective barriers to the palace buildings occupying the centre. Surrounding the precincts of the palace itself was a high stockade of teak posts (since removed), while below the outer bastioned wall thus isolating the entire fortress is a deep and formidable moat seventy-five yards wide. Bridges over this moat, and doorways in the sides of each enclosure complete the general outline of the scheme.

The principal architectural features of this palace-fortress are to be found in the elaboration of the outer wall, and in the elevation aspect of the royal residence in the centre of the composition. The outer wall, a square of $1\frac{1}{4}$ mile side, is built of red brick 26 feet high, battlemented above, and fortified with 48 bastions each surmounted by a graceful wooden pagoda. Five bridges span the moat and there are twelve gates, the whole forming an attractive picture mirrored in the waters which surround it. Right in the heart of these encircling walls the palace stands, a large group of single-storied wooden buildings occupying a platform, more than a thousand feet at its greatest length and over 6 feet high, and presenting a spacious cluster of roofs, gables and parapets, with spire-like pagodas indicating the more important halls. Highest and most prominent of these pagodas is one in seven diminishing tiers, a slim and graceful structure some 256 feet in height, well-proportioned and profusely decorated with carving, gilding and colour. This pagoda marks not only the central and principal hall of the palace in which is situated the Lion Throne, but is also traditionally regarded as the axis of the universe around which all systems revolved. In addition to these pagodas, from each pointed roof and every angular gable rise small ornamental spires enriching the skylines of all parts in a manner typical of the style. The interiors of this palace are designed and decorated on the same general lines as the exterior, the walls and ceilings being covered with intricate wood carving, emphasized with gilding and striking schemes in colour. Appertaining more to a fine handicraft than to serious architecture, with portions sometimes trivial and added only for showiness of effect, in the entire range of structures forming this palace there are few outstanding features, nor is there any definite attempt at a unified whole. It is a composition of picturesque, colourful, grouping, an expression of that pulsatile quality that permeates every aspect of Burmese life. To the scenes of imperial pageantry staged from time to time by the Burmese Court, the palace at Mandalay provided an ideal background, but it can hardly be regarded as an example of the building art in its realistic and substantial form.

---

[1] Since very severely damaged in World War II.

REFERENCES

Memoirs of the Archaeological Survey of India, No. 56. The Ananda Temple at Pagan by Chas. Duroiselle, Delhi 1937.

Guide of the Mandalay Palace by Chas. Duroiselle, Calcutta 1931.

Revealing India's Past. The India Society, London 1939.

CHAPTER XXXVI

THE ARCHITECTURE OF GREATER INDIA

(1) CAMBODIA

THE previous chapters of this work have confined themselves entirely to the architectural productions contained within the strict geographical limits of the peninsula of India itself. But it has been truly observed that "to know Indian art in India alone, is to know but half its story."[1] For with the impulse mainly provided by the indigenous religions of the Indian people, Hinduism and Buddhism, the civilization and culture of India, together with the arts that these inspired, were carried eastwards into several of the great countries of Asia, there to flourish in some respects, with a more sustained vigour, than in the country of their origin. In the field of architecture, specifically, this movement led to the creation of large groups of buildings of marked significance, several of which, basically in the Indian tradition, are of such remarkable character and stupendous proportions as to equal any in the Western world. This eastern development of the religious, social and even material life of India spread over a large region in the south-central portions of the continent corresponding to what are now the countries of Siam, French Indo-China, Java and Bali, Malaya and Sumatra, all of which for the present purpose have been grouped under the designation of "Greater India."

The approach from India to these lands beyond the seas, was made from more than one direction, but was mainly maritime, from an early date ships sailing due east from ports on the Coromandel Coast crossed the Bay of Bengal to arrive at the nearest landfall in the Malay peninsula. This point was what is now known as the Isthmus of Kra, where, disembarking at Takuapa, the immigrants traversed the narrow neck of the peninsula to the Bay of Bandon in lower Siam. Again taking to the sea—the Gulf of Siam—they fanned out north-easterly to Champa, now Annam, believed to be one of the earliest of these settlements, and south-easterly to Java, and Banka (Sumatra).[2] Others, of a more adventurous disposition, may have taken the longer sea route through the Straits of Malacca, and so in this manner eventually reached the island of Java. In addition to this approach by sea there are evidences of a penetration by land from the direction of Bengal, and Assam through Burma, down the great rivers into northern Siam, and so into the regions beyond.

Such is the generally accepted view, based largely on legendary evidence and supported in a lesser degree by inscriptional testimony, that the Indianization of these lands was brought about by immigration, whereby colonial organizations were founded and developed, with the result that the light of India's culture was communicated wherever these were established. On the other hand another aspect of this expansion may be considered. Religion, and that was the basis of the movement, has no frontiers, and so probably owing to the power and impulse of Buddhism, in the first instance, a racial and cultural drift ensued, gradually penetrating into the whole of this portion of Asia, together with the civilization that accompanied it. This may have taken the form of a slow but persistent infiltration eastwards, often along the valleys of the great waterways on account of easier progress. At times this peaceful penetration came into contact with races having definite art instincts, either a folk art, or, on occasion, an indigenous aesthetic sense of some character, but being recorded in impermanent materials no actual remains have survived. The traditions however of this aboriginal art show their traces in that which the intruding movement superimposed on them, and which was subsequently so highly developed. That the inhabitants of these parts were receptively inclined and so prepared for such influences is clear from the primitive conditions under which many of them lived, all that was needed was some incentive of this kind to stimulate their progress in the natural course of evolution.

Here may be mentioned the historical fact that at this period intercourse between different peoples, was not only regionally but universally very prevalent. For in the first millennium, and particularly during the earlier centuries, there appears to have arisen a world-wide movement on the part of individuals and groups, who journeyed from one country to another, a condition largely due to a state of spiritual unrest. There was a marked coming and going of pilgrims, of missionaries, of searchers in quest of ideals, impelled by some mysterious urge which carried them over immense distances and sustained them over long intervals of time. In the West, these were the means by which Christianity, and all that it implied was conveyed from Asia to the northern countries of Europe, while in much the same manner in the Middle East, inspired by Buddhism, the religio-culture of India was communicated to the distant regions of Asia. The famous Chinese pilgrims who spent years travelling to the holy lands of Buddhism are a case in point, and there are doubtless many others of whom no records remain. Some of these were intellectual men who brought with them ideas on art and architecture and kindred subjects which left a permanent impress on the countries in which they often sojourned for a considerable time.

But whatever the process which brought about the extension of the Indian religions and much of the social structure of its people eastwards, its force was great and its results even greater. So much so that it was sufficient to inspire at least two races, the Khmers of Cambodia, and the inhabitants of Java, to produce monuments consecrated to the Indian religions and in the Indian tradition, which exceed in size and magnificence anything of a similar order in the land of India itself.

---

[1] Sir John Marshall in the Foreword to Dr. le May's "*Buddhist Art in Siam,*" Cambridge, 1938.

[2] Prof. G. Coedes in *Indian Art and Letters*, Vol. II, 1928, and Vol. IV 1930.

Of these two countries, Java being an island, the building art for which it became famed, was limited by its geographical boundaries, so that its effect on the architecture of this region as a whole was restricted. But the country of Cambodia, lying on the mainland, the influence of the Khmer style of architecture extended over the entire peninsula of Indo-China and even beyond. The historical progress of the building art of the Khmers, having wider implications, will accordingly be dealt with first.

The rise, development, architectural accomplishments, and final dissolution of the Khmers of Cambodia is one of the most remarkable and dramatic episodes in the history of Asia. And the record of their greatness is proved by the size and number of their structural productions. These cannot by any means be described as the result of an Indian colonial settlement, nor the expression of a talented few, but that of a large cultured, organised, and technically qualified race of people. From a relatively insignificant tribe of aborigines, settled on the lower reaches of the Mekong early in the Christian era, in the country of a few hundred years, the Khmers emerged as a nation of mighty warriors, who founded a powerful empire, evolved a civilization of marked intellectuality and refinement, and above all, created a style of architecture having outstanding character and expressed by monuments of such magnitude that in the words of the renowned authority Fergusson, they figure as " one of the greatest building races of the world." Such is a brief outline of the development of the Cambodians up to the twelfth century. Then, equally dramatically, in the thirteenth century came their dissolution, followed by their complete disappearance from the country they had so magnificently ruled. For after consolidating over a large region their imperial power with its enlightened administrative and social system, they were over-run by the Siamese (Thais) and dispersed, forced to abandon their possessions, to desert their cities, palaces and temples, and to leave their architectural monuments to be swallowed up and obliterated by the tropical vegetation and other devastating forces of nature. So completely was this effacement effected that for some four hundred years this once influential empire and its vast structural undertakings were lost to sight as if they had never existed, they passed beyond human ken unknown and forgotten even by the people of the continent in which they had so magnificently flourished. During this long period, unchecked, silently, slowly, but with deadly persistence, the sinuous roots of the jungle trees laboured to disintegrate the material proofs of its one time proud glories, built up after centuries of patient endeavour. In one instance, the temple of Angkor Vat, referred to by an authority as " one of the greatest, if not *the* greatest work of man standing " it seems as if nature, jealous of such an incomparable example of human handiwork, finding it left unguarded, threw a dense screen of vegetation around it and under its cover proceeded remorselessly to tear it to pieces. Fortunately complete destruction has been stayed, as by little more than mere chance what remained of these monuments was brought to light. For, as late as the year 1858, a French naturalist[1] while exploring the impenetrable forests surrounding the Mekong and Menam rivers, stumbled on the vast complex of ruins comprising the city of Angkor, the Khmer capital, and from this accidental discovery, the significance of the Cambodian empire, and the grandeur of its building creations became revealed. But so recently has this disclosure been made, that in spite of an intensive study of these remains by eminent scholars, a number of problems relating to the sequence of events in the history of the Khmers, and especially those regarding the founders and dates of their buildings, still await accurate solution.

Racially the Khmers were the result of a fusion of the "aborigines of Indo-China with Aryan and Mongolian invaders " and derived their name from the Hindu Kambu, the mythical founder of their race, hence Kambuja, with its European form Cambodia. The actual beginnings of the Khmer empire date from the second half of the sixth century A.D. but there are records of the Khmers much earlier than this time, when they occupied the town of Angkor Borai, or Vyadhapura, on the lower reaches of the Mekong river in Southern Cambodia. During the primitive period Brahmanism and the Sanskrit language were introduced, and probably due to this civilizing influence, under a rule of the name of Srutavarman about the fifth century the Khmers assumed some prominence as a growing power. Apart, however, from the inspiration caused by the spread of this culture, such a contact was bound to have an effect on their spiritual, intellectual, and physical activities, conditions which expressed themselves notably in the art of building so that a brief reference to the life of the people, together with their aspirations, appears to be a necessary preliminary to a study of their architectural ideals, and, subsequently, to their interpretation of these in structural form.

From an account by one of those ubiquitous Chinese travellers who spent much of their lives in visiting the countries of Asia during the early and middle ages some idea of the conditions that prevailed at Angkor when the Cambodian kingdom was at the height of its power becomes possible. It may be inferred from a description by Tcheou Ta-kouan[2] who sojourned there towards the end of the thirteenth century, that the Khmers were resolved into two social strata, ethnologically widely separated, consisting of a high caste ruling class on the one hand, and the aborigines of the country on the other. Such a state recalls that which existed in India when that country was becoming populated by the Indo-Aryans. In Cambodia the ruling class was evidently composed of people of refinement and marked intellectual ability with notable cultural aspirations, while the indigenous inhabitants were merely " hewers of wood and drawers of water." The former, with their vision and perceptive minds, conceived the architectural schemes which are the surviving records of their rule, and being endowed with supreme power these were materialized by exploiting the original race in a manner not far removed from slavery. But between these two extremes of human strata there must have been a large and very vital community corresponding to a middle class, in all respects superior to the unskilled labour mentioned above, from whom were recruited, among others, the artists, craftsmen, designers, the master masons and the numerous skilled personnel who would be an essential factor in the production of such superb examples of architecture and the plastic art.

Here a study of the monuments themselves may throw light on this aspect of the subject. For the walls of these

---

[1] Henri Mouhot. He died shortly afterwards, but his name should be remembered. See *Introduction a la Connaissanse d' Angkor* by the late Victor Goloubew.

[2] *Record of the Customs of Cambodia*, translated by Pelliot. B. E. F. E. O. 1902.

buildings are engraved with a long series of pictures in bas-relief illustrating scenes from the rich mythology of India, and from the Hindu religion, in detail and in technique equal to if not excelling anything the Indian sculptors ever produced. But although conceived in the Indian tradition, they are staged in a Cambodian setting, much as if, a western parallel, episodes from the Old Testament were depicted in an environment similar to that of the "Field of the Cloth of Gold," the famous historical pageant which took place in France in 1520. The result is that we are not only presented with Khmer interpretations Indian themes, but, incorporated with these, there runs throughout the entire series the physical and spiritual pattern of Cambodian life during its most dynamic period. And from the evidence so graphically provided it seems implicit that to the Khmers a sensitiveness to art was even something more than a matter of common interest, it was the essence of life itself, the breath of their existence. With such aesthetic perceptions it is not therefore surprising that this element in their racial consciousness manifested itself in all forms of art, specially the building art, and in the raising of grand architectural monuments, as the Cambodian remains are abundant proof.

And in the same manner that an appreciation of art and beauty entered so fully into the rhythm of their lives so did their religious belief, for not only are the majority of their buildings dedicated to the prevailing divinity, Buddhist or Brahmanical, as they worshipped at the shrines of both, but they embodied in these structures the same thought, piety, spirituality, and workmanship that moved the builders of the Gothic cathedrals in Europe at a slightly later date. For the meridian of the architecture of the Khmers was attained towards the 12th century, so that at this point such a significant movement appears to merit reference to outstanding building accomplishments in other lands, in order that the architecture of Cambodia may be compared to, or related historically with, correspondingly great phases of the building art.

In India the important art of rock architecture which is one of the main features of the country's technique, had produced its finest achievement in the Kailasa at Ellora in the eighth century, much earlier than the Cambodian apogee, which at this time was only at the beginning of its classical development. Slightly previous also to the culminating century of the Khmers, were the two large temples of the Cholas in Southern India, at Tanjore and Gangai-kondacholapuram, both erected in the first quarter of the eleventh century. Much further west, in Asia Minor, contemporaneously with the Cambodian movement but inspired by very different ideals, the rulers of the Seljuks were raising Islamic palaces, fortresses and mosques of a specialized character of which the Qutub Minar at Delhi dated A.D. 1200 is a distant Indianized interpretation. Turning to Europe the eventful era of cathedral building was being initiated, with the Gothic style in England assuming the form known as Early English (12th-13th centuries). And here one cannot fail to be struck by the manner in which destiny affected the two movements, the Gothic and the Cambodian, as the subsequent history of both conclusively reveals. Whereas the Gothic cathedrals gradually evolved eventually to become outstanding records of the spiritual life and to exist as permanent possessions of mankind, while these majestic monuments were rising in their rich beauty in all the important cities of the West, the immense

temples and proud cities of the Khmers, deserted and forsaken were crumbling to ruin under the devastating encroachment of the tropical forest. Where the Gothic movement signifies a great and momentous episode, not only in the history of architecture but in the building of character, the vast structural schemes of the Cambodians remains only to display the ruined and empty splendour of their prime.

In viewing the wide range of building undertakings attributed to the Khmers during the period of their domination the magnitude of the labour involved, and the amount of material required are astonishing. The layout, excavation, preparation of the foundations, the quarrying of the stone, the transport, the shaping of the blocks, and the mason-craft all these imply, must have been prodigious. Moreover these operations were evidently maintained at full strength for several hundred years, necessitating a large and efficient organization and the regular employment of an immense amount of skilled and unskilled labour. For such purposes a very considerable proportion of the population must have been directly or indirectly engaged on these stupendous building enterprises, so that the development of the building art in Cambodia postulates a mass concentration of constructional sensibility almost without precedent. When in addition to this preliminary process the architectural and plastic manipulation of the building material so laboriously won from the distant quarries is studied, some idea of the high standards achieved by the Khmer craftsmen may be realized. It should be noted however that in their constructional practice the masons displayed no special mechanical aptitude, for instance the system of the true arch was not employed, the bridging of spaces being effected by means of the beam or lintel, although in certain parts of the buildings, as for example in the curved roofs of the corridors, an arcuate treatment may be detected, but this effect was obtained by oversailing course, and not by the scientific method of voussoirs. Further, the masonry, was of the " dry " order, no adhesive such as mortar or cement being introduced, so that in their building technique, the structural principles put into effect by the Khmers corresponded in several essential particulars to those prevailing at this time in India. But if the constructional procedure was not according to that being developed in Western countries, on the other hand the artistic character of the architecture of Cambodia has been accorded high praise. In the words of one writer the Khmers possessed " the imagination of the Gothic worker, the gift for harmonious charm of the Greek, the power of the Renaissance craftsman, and the prodigality and wealth of ideas that can exist only in the East."[1]

It has been remarked however that although this aesthetic sense was distinctly pronounced, the Khmers never seem to have been aware of the fact that their constructional ability was not of an equal order. Yet in spite of many technical failings, the buildings, after being subjected to such adverse climatic conditions and other stresses, have on the whole preserved much of their original appearance in a most remarkable manner. That they are seriously ruined is obvious, but following centuries of neglect accompanied by year after year of uncontrolled devastation from jungle growth, they show by their condition, deplorable though this may be, that the Khmers built better than they knew. The materials employed consisted mainly of stone supplemented by a certain amount of brickwork. Two varieties of stone were favoured, laterite mainly for the foundations, and

---

[1] *Angkor Ruins in Cambodia* by Jeanneret de Burski.

sandstone for the walls. Both these were obtained from quarries located some 35 miles southeast of the capital, and conveyed to their destination in blocks, partly by waterway and partly by road. The bricks were well made and kiln fired, the average measurements in inches being $10 \times 5 \times 2$, a size which corresponds very nearly to those being used in Southern Europe at about the same date.

Throughout the course of their history extending over some nine centuries, the first three hundred years from A.D., 500 to 800, during which the Cambodian Empire was in process of formation, may be referred to as the Early Period. Then ensued some four and a half centuries, from A.D., 800 to 1250, leading up to and including what may be termed the Classical Period. After the thirteenth century, as far as the building art is concerned, there is little to record, and this therefore signifies the finale. Such long periods as those designated above may be simplified for the purposes of study by being sub-divided into a succession of phases, according to the following table which gives the stages of development from the time when the Khmers dwelt in huts on piles, through the period of their greatness to that final effort when fantastic giant forms heralded the end.

(1) Up to A.D. 500 Prehistoric Phase	Early Period.
(2) A.D. 500 to 800 Primitive Phase	
(3) A.D. 800 to 1000 Formative Phase	Classical Period.
(4) A.D. 1000 to 1100 Foundations of Classical Phase	
(5) A.D. 1100 to 1200 Culmination of Classical Phase	
(6) A.D. 1200 to 1250 Flamboyant or Baroque Phase	
(7) A.D. 1350 Decline	Finale.
(8) A.D. 1431, End, conquered by Thais (Siamese)	

The table indicates that the art of Cambodia reached its meridian in the twelfth century, a century of marked architectural activity, distinguished by numerous notable building undertakings, but particularly by the erection of the temple of Angkor Vat, the grandest achievement of the Khmer builders. But before this architectural culmination was attained, the building art progressed logically through its various stages of development beginning with what has been referred to as the Prehistoric Phase. Of this initial period few material records have survived, but from the subsequent character of their buildings, it is surmised that the early Khmers, living on low ground raised their huts above the swamp of the delta by means of horizontal layers of logs readily obtained from the exuberant forest growth in their vicinity. This primitive system was so indelibly impressed on their consciousness that it survives in the distinctive parallel course of torus mouldings forming the excessively high plinths characteristic of the stone structures at a much later date. Moreover that these original habitations were roofed with terracotta tiles arranged on a flexured slope with transverse runnels to carry off heavy rain, is also evident from the same method, but copied in stone, being employed to roof the corridors of the more sophisticated buildings which followed. Then the abnormally steep staircases leading from terrace to terrace in these later edifices seem to

be reminiscent of the ladder-like flights of steps peculiar to wooden houses elevated on piles. Other rudimentary elements may be identified, subsequently converted into elegant stone features, but these are some of the main evidences associating the Khmers, in their prehistoric existence, with timber-built dwellings raised above the low-lying deltaic region of the Mekong.

From this elementary beginning an advance may be recorded, for about the fifth or sixth centuries A.D. what may be termed the Indianization of the Khmers seems to have taken place, when the Primitive Phase (A.D. 500 to 800) of the Early Period comes into view. Of this stage of development also actual remains are rare, but it is possible that under the influence of Indian culture, buildings of a more substantial nature were erected, and were distributed over a wider area, as the power of the Khmers became more extended. In place of the wooden abodes of the previous period, brick construction was favoured, of which several examples believed to be of this period have been identified. Among these the temple of Tat Panom on the Mekong, although rather distant from the original settlement, may be a clue to the progress of the building art at this stage. Presumed to date from " the sixth or seventh century A.D., at the latest," it is a Buddhist structure, built " of large rectangular red bricks " with the lower story containing a series of carvings in bas-relief of a pronounced Indian character, " a link with the Amaravati school."[1] Here it is worthy of note that about the same time, in India, there was a brick building, Hindu and Buddhist, the technical features of which, such as carving and modelling in brick and terracotta, were not dissimilar from those found at Tat Panom. Among the Indian examples, a temple at Bhitagaon of the fifth century and, more important still, the great Buddhist shrine at Budh Gaya, while, at a later date, the brick temples at Raipur, are all illustrations of this structural method, which may have some bearing on the contemporary development of the brick technique in Cambodia. Such evidences, it is admitted, are however slight, but firmer ground is encountered when the next phase, that referred to as the " Formative " comes to be studied.

Marking the first stage of the Classical Period, the Formative Phase comprising the two centuries from A.D. 800 to 1000, this opens with a decisive event in the history of the Khmers. For when the king Jayavarman II (802-854) transferred the centre of his rapidly expanding dominions to Angkor, a site on the Mekong near the lake of Tonle-Sap, he not only planned the creation of a capital city, but also began the process of consolidating the empire. This ruler has left behind him the reputation of an ardent builder— a royal palace and important temples being his architectural contributions to the rising metropolis of the Khmers, but particulars of these await exploration. On the other hand, rather later, towards the end of the ninth century, a successor, Yesovarman I (889-910), either re-constituted the original capital or established another on its site which he named Yasodharapura, now only defined by mounds and other extensive remains hitherto unidentified. But some idea of its extent and arrangements have been obtained by an aerial survey, which shows that the quality of spaciousness, afterwards a notable characteristic of the subsequent architectural creations, was in process of germination. For the hill of Phnom Bakheng marking the original temple of the city, indicates the geometric centre of a rectangle about ten square

[1] Dr. le May in *Buddhist Art in Siam*, pp. 59, 60. Cambridge 1938.

miles in area, with the remains of a wide moat on the west and south sides, while on the east it was aligned parallel to the main city gate. The city temple, the focus of the scheme, raised on an eminence was contained with a walled rectangle having a cruciform terrace in front of the ramp and a stairway leading to its entrance on the east. From a square space which probably corresponded to a forum, or ceremonial parade ground, main roads radiated symmetrically in four directions connecting with the city gates, thus dividing the whole city into four wards each reserved for and inhabited by a certain class of citizen. In addition therefore to the grand dimensions of the layout of this city, it shows a system of town planning in symmetrical lines and rectangles on a broad scale, which seems to have been the ideal underlying most of the Khmers' architectural compositions.

Yet all that is visible of Yasovarman's capital of Cambodia of the ninth century at the present day is an immense area of mounds and plantations, under the surface of which lie the remains of this once great city. Such complete obliteration leaves no material record of the architectural style that comprised this civic scheme, but fortunately several detached buildings, away from the site of the capital, provide sufficient evidence to enable this to be visualized. Among these are the temples of Mébon, Pré Rup, and Banteay Srei, the last named, although small, is in many respects a typical example of its kind. Known to have been erected in A.D. 969, during the reign of Jayavarman V (965-1002), when the empire was beginning to become conscious of its power and domination, the temple of Banteay Srei, situated fifteen miles from Angkor, represents in every one of its sculptural stones that effort to obtain supreme richness in architectural design which is not infrequently indulged in by handicraftsmen and encouraged by their patrons in the orient. As elaborate in its plan as in its plastic decoration, this temple suggests a stage in the evolution of the building art when this calling was largely in the hands of sculptors rather than in those of masons, although even if this should be the case, as a miniature replica of a larger original built in the grand manner it implies definite architectural knowledge and structural experience. If the buildings buried under the mounds and swamps marking the destroyed capital were of the same order, then this phase of the architectural development in Cambodia must have been rich in the extreme. The temple of Banteay Srei formerly named Isvarapura, consists of an assembly of several buildings comprising three shrines or sanctuaries with two other structures presumed to have been libraries or rooms for vestments, the principal external feature of the scheme as a whole being the grouping of its three towers and their architectural treatment. These towers or sikharas, show an originality in their design and a marked play of imagination in the shape of the curved arches over the doors and alcoves, elements repeated on the face of each story, the entire conception being so freshly ingenious as to bear but little relation to the sikharas of temples in any part of India. (Plate CLIX).

With the long reign of Jayavarman's successor Suryavarman I, who ruled the empire for nearly the whole of the first half of the eleventh century, the foundations of the building art of the Khmers were well and truly laid, so that this century may be said to denote the Foundational Phase of the Classical Period. During this king's reign the city of Angkor Thom, the existing capital, was planned and built, an undertaking of great significance in the history of architecture in Cambodia. The establishment of this

imperial seat of the Khmers on such a permanent basis, with its walls 22 ft. high having a perimeter of 7½ miles, containing magnificent buildings grouped around the pyramidal temple of Baphuon, was in itself a notable achievement, and not unlike other royal enterprises it had the effect of stimulating the architectural ambitions of the people to a remarkable degree. For the remains of buildings of note dating from this period within the vicinity of Angkor are in themselves sufficient to establish the artistic reputation of any people and any age. These are however only a portion of the whole, for distributed with a lavish hand over a large part of the peninsula of Indo-China, a number approaching a thousand structures of note has been listed, either examples of the building art of the Khmers or of a character associating them with that style. Such a wide extent of low-lying country over which these buildings were dispersed naturally led to a system of built-up causeways with ornamental bridges and other means of direct communication, paved throughout not unlike those of the Romans, which with canals, waterways and other irrigational projects indicate that the Khmers were possessed of no little engineering knowledge and experience, while they also postulate that Cambodia teemed with active life and had attained a civilization of a standard unknown at the present time. It is not however certain that all this building construction and these technical and mechanical enterprises of works of public utility relate to the eleventh century only, but it is not improbable that they were largely inspired by Suryavarman with his conception of an imperial capital worthy of the empire and the aspirations of the people he ruled. The grand scale of the city is a proof that this monarch was gifted with preception, great ideas, and resources sufficient to enable his plans to be materialized. Apart from the dimensions mentioned above, the Cambodian capital was surrounded by a moat 300 feet wide over which were thrown five bridges connecting with the five entrance gates, the most imposing of which, the Gate of Victory, cruciform in plan, led to the Palace a large building confronted with an extensive enclosure, the terraced walls sculptured with figures of elephants. Another great structure was the pyramidal temple of Phimeanakas its elevational effect being produced by a series of ascending terraces which together with other structures all in the impressive architectural styles of the time, each made a notable contribution to this vast imperial undertaking.

But fully to appreciate the building art of the Khmers at its apogee, the architecture of the succeeding century, that of the twelfth, and here referred to as the " Culmination of the Classical Phase " should be studied. This century in Cambodia was one of marked constructional activity, and several important buildings were erected, but one edifice, of such a monumental character as to stand out above all others, is the temple of Angkor Vat, considered to be the largest and most impressive stone temple in existence. This magnificent architectural composition was the conception of King Suryavarman II (1112-1151) during whose reign the main part of it was constructed, the final completion, however, for it was a huge building project, being due to his successor King Dharanindravarman II (1152-1181). The name Angkor is a corruption of the Sanskrit " Nagara," meaning city, or capital, while " Vat " is a relatively modern Siamese name for any Buddhist building, so that the Angkor Vat is the " City Temple " or " Grand Cathedral " of the Khmers. Originally consecrated to the Hindu deity Vishnu, whose image was installed in the adytum, at a later date, believed to have been under King Jaiyavarman VII (1181-1201), the last of the great Cambodian rulers, it was adapted to Buddhism.

Situated about one mile towards the south of the walled capital of Angkor Thom, too spacious even to be located within its ample perimeter, the principal approach, instead of being as was the custom from the east, is from the west, to bring it into alignment with the royal city. No doubt partly for the sentimental reason of isolating the great sacred pile from the material world, as well as with the object of propitiating the Naga spirits, the entire scheme was laid out within an environment of water in the form of an immense moat 650 ft. broad, square in plan, and having a total length of 2½ miles. It is recorded that the vast quantity of earth excavated for this purpose was piled up in the centre of the site to create the massive mound on which the actual temple structure was erected. But this system may also explain the presence of a wide moat surrounding other architectural undertakings of the Khmers, as the soul thus removed provided a substantial foundation to carry the load of a heavy building. In the design of Angkor Vat the only communication across the water barrier of the moat was by means of a bridge supported on piers on the western side and approached by a raised causeway consisting of a broad paved avenue 36 feet across and 1500 feet long elevated seven feet above the ground and bordered on each side by a massive balustrade. As this causeway nears the main building it is expanded into a cruciform terrace raised above the surface of the foundational platform on which the whole temple stands. This immense stone platform is square in plan and considerably over three thousand feet side, in the centre of which the temple gathers itself up into a towering turretted mass. In terminating the approach in such a manner the cruciform terrace thus forms an appropriate prelude to the imposing entrance gateway which immediately confronts it. From here the actual structure begins.

The entrance portico leading to the temple proper is a finished architectural conception in itself, but none the less it composes with and forms an appropriate contribution to the scheme as a whole. The facade consists of an elaborate storied structure breaking effectively the long lines of the arcaded enclosure, which, with its corridors and corner towers forms the outer perimeter of the entire composition. Interiorly the portico resolves itself into a square plan of pillared halls with two diametrical corridors crossing the rectangle of the central space leaving four open courtyards, one in each angle. These entrance halls are symmetrically grouped on the wide raised terrace, the first of three such courts which, superimposed serve the important purpose of elevating the monumental pile of the main structure above its surroundings. In the open parts of this terrace on each side of the entrance halls small detached shrines have been placed, recalling the *panchayatana*, or five shrine planning of some of the temples of India.

A stairway, continuing the axial line of the portico ascends to the second terrace, which consists of a platform raised approximately double the height of the first, and contained within another enclosure of pillared corridors having towers (sikharas) at each corner, the whole forming a rectangle of 185 feet by 200 feet side. Above this a third terrace rises, approached by a long and steep flight of steps, for the height of this uppermost story is again twice that of the one below and which supports it. At each angle of this terrace, the inner space of which is a square of 130 feet side, is a sikhara, while in the centre is a cella for the accommodation of the deity, above which soars the tall central spire, bringing the total height of the whole structure from the ground to the golden lotus pinnacle to 210 feet.

From even this brief outline of the temple of Angkor Vat, it may be inferred that the scheme revolves itself into a somewhat complicated composition, but such is not actually the case. On analysis it will be found that, in spite of certain elaborations, it is a comparatively uninvolved arrangement, the plan consisting of a series of rectangles concentrically disposed, while the elevation is a system of superimposed diminishing terraces with the angles emphasized by towers and a larger and higher one in the centre. Orderly and balanced, and logically symmetrical it is readily comprehensible, and from this view alone the Angkor Vat stands out as an architectural masterpiece. But there are other and more subtle qualities in this building which raise it above the material plane of mere stone and its physical manipulation by means of immense labour and skill. Its grouping of terraces and halls, colonnades and towers enunciates a profound sense of rhythm which is characteristic of the Khmers as a people and a very real factor in their being. From their art, which is intensely expressive of their life, it is clear that rhythm in all things was their ideal, in the dance, music, their figure drawing, dress and ornament ; but in no aspect of their aesthetic and social environment is this quality more pronounced than in their architecture, as exemplified in the design and composition of the Angkor Vat. In some of its details this building has certain faults of structure, but as a correlation of parts to the whole, in the measured movement of the entire conception, in a word in the cadency of its articulation it has few equals.

And towards this architectural consummation the artistic and structural treatment of some of the more important elements, so skilfully united, may be individually studied. In such an immense undertaking, and where every constituent part is so experientially worked out and applied, it is not possible to refer to many of these, but some of the more salient may be selected. On account of their singular character as well as for their significance in the scheme as a whole, the towers or sikharas of the Cambodian temples merit special reference, those on the Angkor Vat being fully representative of the style. The obvious cognate relationship of this form of spire to the sikhara in the Indian temple cannot be overlooked, but there are differences between the two types which in many aspects are fundamental. Except for its main outlines and volume conforming to the same structural principles as those employed in the better-known Indo-Aryan examples, the surface manipulation of the Khmer sikhara manifests definitely original attributes. The shape of the Cambodian tower has been likened to a gigantic fir cone and the simile is not an inapt one. Apart from its intentionally aspiring quality the most pronounced feature is its texture, produced by a horizontal system of zoning, and herein lies its resemblance not so much to the Indian style but more to the conventional design of the pagoda as seen in buildings in the Far East, an example of which is a brick structure at Sung Shan (Honan) dated A.D. 523. Here the horizontal courses are emphasized in the same manner as those in the Angkor sikharas, the designers of the latter apparently at some formative stage of their development having looked more to the East than the West for inspiration on this point of detail. On the other hand the fact that the Khmer Sikhara is stellate in section allies it to some of the Dravidian examples in Southern India which assume this distinctive shape. In view of its architectural significance the scheme of the Khmer sikhara may be described more fully. On plan, and in its lower portions, the sikhara is rectangular, although this square shape is interrupted by re-entrant angles, and also on the free sides there are shallow recesses. Rather less than half way up the height, the rectangular base changes in section to become star-shaped and this continues in diminishing zones, usually nine in number, to terminate in a metal crowned finial, the height of the whole being 2½ times the diameter of the square base. The diminishing zones are sharply defined by prominent string courses, also stellate in plan, with wide cavetto intervals between each course. These intervals of dark shadow are relieved by a series of semi-detached motifs, not unlike Greek acroteria, known to Indian craftsmen as a *khudu*, an element in miniature derived from the chaitya-arch form of the Buddhists. Each zonal cornice is supported on small decorative arches, simulating in some respects the technique of Islamic honeycomb vaulting. The appearance of the whole is rich and animated, an appropriately vibrant treatment to this outstanding feature of the style.

Another architectural constituent remarkable on account of its originality, is the great depth of the range of torus mouldings, particularly those forming the high stylobate of the middle storey of the building. As already mentioned, presumably a memory of the logs supporting their primitive dwellings, although the repetition of these string courses has reached its reasonable limit as shown in certain parts of the Angkor Vat, at the same time they do not fatigue the eye and fit into the scheme in a rational manner. Some of this effect is due to the introduction at correct intervals of massive cornice-like elements, suggesting equilibrium, stability, and strength just where such qualities are most needed. It is instructive to compare these with the bold torus mouldings at the base of the Chola temples of Southern India proving how virtually the same results may be obtained but in a somewhat different manner. Similarly, also derived from a usage found in the earliest phase of Khmer history, are the double flexured fluted roofs over the corridors, originally executed in terracotta now appearing as slabs of sandstone, their rippling texture not only affording a pleasing contrast to their more conventional lithic surroundings, but serving the practical purpose of speedily throwing off the heavy rain. In the formation of these corridors, pillars and piers are extensively used, having shafts generally square or octagonal in section, and monolithic in structure as was also the practice in the temples of India. No special treatment was accorded to the capitals of the pillars, they were commonly moulded or patterned, but not sufficiently distinctive in the design to constitute an "order." The application of these pillars to produce light in the corridors and also to form by their long colonnades and arcades effective passages of alternating solids and voids in the elevational aspect of the composition indicate that the builders realized the increased vitality that such a procedure brought into their scheme. In connection with the method of lighting, rectangular window openings were devised and also, on occasion, a continuous screen of apertures was inserted, but broken up in an effective fashion. For in these openings moulded mullions, evidently turned on a lathe and resembling slender balustrades, were set at close intervals, thus providing most effectually and also artistically the admission of light and air. It is tolerably clear that these uprights were copied in the first instance from either wooden slats or sections of bamboo originally used as windows in their primitive wooden huts. Such mullioned openings are found in many of the temple buildings of Cambodia, as in that of Prah Khan and of Banteay Srei, in their pattern and intention recalling similarly balustrated apertures in some of the temples of India, particularly at Bhubaneswar in Orissa of about the same date.

There are other architectural elements forming essential and artistic portions of Angkor Vat and the buildings of this period, all well worthy of study, of which the elaborately sculptured tympanums over the openings, niches, and gable ends, hold an important place. These "overdoors" take a variety of shapes, often being composed of arches with emphatically involuted curves and invariably enriched with figures and foliage, the figures in high relief occupying alcoves, thus by their structure contributing to the stability of this feature as a whole. Although the carved figures are mainly drawn from the religious and mythological records of the country some of the subjects appertain more to the secular in which *apsaras*, or nymphs, and others of semi-divine attribution display their voluptuousness elegantly posed on the sides of pillar, pilaster and pier. Of the carved patterns the foliage convention, the modelling and technical manipulation of these arabesques are of a very distinctive character, so much so that they might actually be the handiwork of the sculptors who decorated the temples and palaces of Oakhnauti, the ancient capital of the Pal empire in Bengal of the tenth and eleventh centuries, so exactly do they resemble in design and relief the productions of the famous Varendra School.

Where, however, the Khmer sculptors excelled was in the high standard and lavish display of their plastic art as represented in the long series of bas-reliefs on the walls of their buildings particularly those in the corridors of Angkor Vat, in which temple alone they form a continuous frieze of over two thousand feet, resolved into eight compartments, six feet in height, the figures of all kinds thus portrayed aggregating upwards of eighteen thousand in number. Episodes of war and peace, pomp and pageantry, ceremony and cavalcade, the forest and the field, every picturesque event of a picturesque age, allegory and legend sacred and profane, all are imaged in this absorbing national art gallery. Moreover these reliefs hold a mirror to the Cambodian people themselves, from which it is possible to sense their reactions to art and life, and to realize something of their emotional nature generally. And all are drawn, composed, and in a form of relief that has rarely been equalled. Delicately but firmly modelled, a comparison of this method of plastic art with that practised in other countries may be useful. Nothing could be more emphatic than their contrast with the reliefs in the adjacent country of Java, especially on the famous stupa of Borobudur, the sculptured galleries of which are almost as extensive and continuous as those at Angkor. But whereas the former are moulded in high, bold, rounded forms almost aggressively robust, the Cambodian school has obtained its results by means of a more subtle treatment of gradations and planes, less impressive at first sight, but with a more sensitive feeling for artistic quality, recalling in a manner that of tapestry. Turning to the schools in India, the Khmer reliefs bear the nearest resemblance in technique to those on the stupa of Amaravati in Madras, executed several centuries previously, but here also there is a difference in modelling and in the actual height of the projection, besides other variations which seem to rule out any definite relationship. On the other hand although the Angkor art displays an originality in every aspect of its treatment, it is worthy of note that the same textural attributes may be discerned in the bas-reliefs of some of the contemporary schools in China.

A substantial change in the architectural effect of the building art of Cambodia has now to be recorded. Towards the end of the twelfth century certain major elements began to appear in the art of the Khmers of sufficient significance to alter or at least to modify its nature. These impositions are of such a character as to entitle the development at this stage to be referred to as the Flamboyant Phase, and were brought about mainly through the personality and ardent zeal of a ruler who has been described as the " Grand Monarch " of the Khmer dynasties, Jayavarman VII (1181-1201), in certain respects the Louis the Fourteenth of his line. Standing forth as the last great king of the Cambodian empire and possessed with overpowering ambitions together with unlimited resources, these conditions found expression in architectural undertakings of a grandiose order. Not only were his building schemes on an unprecedented scale but they imply a definite change in artistic values, so that the building art under this ruler's patronage assumed a different orientation, its manner being not far removed from what may be termed the mood of the Baroque. And in the fantastic exuberance of its architecture this phase presages the final stage of the Cambodian epoch. Much of the building activity of this period was concerned with elaborate additions to the capital city of Angkor Thom, among which may be mentioned an imposing causeway including a Gate of Victory, and above all, the monumental temple of Bayon rising in the centre of the city itself. Other buildings, chiefly temples belonging to this phase are Prah Khan, Ta Prohm, Banteay Kedai and Banteay Chhumar, none of which however attempts to attain the magnitude or phenomenal character of those in the Khmer capital. This character is chiefly notable for the introduction in the architecture of a form of imagery of titanic proportions and cryptic intention, so that superhuman figures and giant statuary dominate the style. Although displaying certain spectacular qualities, the effect on the architectural propriety of the building art may be imagined. For instance the massive parapet on each side of the causeway leading to the Gate of Victory instead of being supported by a conventional balustrade, takes the shape of a monstrous serpent, its coils wreathed in the muscular arms of a team of Paladins, represented by fifty-four figures of heroic proportions, on both sides amounting to the mystic number of one hundred and eight, while the enlarged expanded hydra head of the reptile is raised menacingly at the entrance. But the keynote of the style may be seen in the treatment of the gate to which this extravagant conception leads, for the towers or sikharas of this building have imposed on each of their four sides a gigantic human mask, smiling, inscrutable, enigmatical, expressing some thought beyond all understanding. The Gateway of Victory is however only an introductory to the temple of Bayon, within the city, which has fifty such towers grouped above its ranges of terraces, halls, and corridors, aggregating some two hundred of these faces, each gazing with sphinx-like smile on the slow irresistible sapping by the forces of nature of its own stability. (Plate CLVIII.)

As the Bayon temple is typical of the style at this particular phase, it may be described more fully, although covering in its widest dimensions an area hardly so large as that of Angkor Vat, none the less the extreme outside walls form a rectangle 700 feet by 500 feet while the plan of the building itself fills a square of 500 feet side. This plan consists exteriorly of a system of double galleries enclosing a courtyard, in the centre of which stands the main structure rising up into two stories to a height of 130 feet. It is not therefore the dimensions of the building, although these are not inconsiderable, which give the Bayon its character, but the intricate yet logical disposition of the component parts in its plan, and the strikingly unique appearance of its elevation. Taking the plan first, this resolves itself into a central cruciform layout, with the external angles of the cross thus formed filled in with courtyards contained within pillared galleries, by these means converting the ground plan as a whole into a square. This square and the transepts within, are then divided up into a system of arcaded courts, vestibules, chambers, galleries and corridors, all interrelated and each having its specific shape and place according to its purpose. Then, in the centre, occupying the intersecting space of the cross, is the circular basement of the main tower, which rising high over the entire conception enshrines the sanctuary of the deity. It will be realized that although in parts apparently involved, the planning of this temple was worked out with a full and complete knowledge of the various objects for which it was intended, and in its entirety was obviously devised by the master-craftsman of his time possessing marked experience and a thorough grasp of essentials.

As to the elevational aspect of the Bayon this approximates a pyramid in mass, an effect produced by the whole being raised on two tall platforms supporting the great central structure. One of the ideals of the Cambodian architect was a composition of this nature, a substantial pile of masonry to provide a basis on which he could construct processional galleries one above the other and concentrically disposed, while over all he raised a tower to contain the sacred image. The Bayon, as well as the Angkor Vat, are designed on this principle, which, in a manner, was also followed in Java, as the stupa at Borobudur is a colossal stone mound furnished with concentric corridors and terminating in a finial shrine. Long pillared halls are prominent in the Dravidian temples of Southern India but there is no counterpart to the system of concentric ascending galleries as found in the monuments of Greater India. As at Angkor Vat and also in the Bayon there are several entrances, but in this instance the main approach is by means of a pillared portico on the east, having on each side a small detached shrine within the angles of the first enclosure. But undoubtedly as was intended, the outstanding characteristic of the exterior is the orderly and balanced distribution of the towers over the entire scheme, each one of its fifty sikharas distinguishing externally some conspicuous feature of the interior, those of the inner group being fifty feet in height, while the main central tower is more than double this size. As already remarked it is in the surface treatment of these sikharas that the imagination has been allowed to exceed the bounds of accepted architectural procedure, and in straining after originality the designer has purposely ventured into the realms of phantasy. A certain rigidity of surface and stability of outline is a recognized convention in structures having exceptional height, and the observance of this principle has been universally approved. Yet although this convention in the Bayon towers has been disregarded, thus reducing their static quality, the great human masks on each side of these have in a manner compensated for the loss by adding to the entire conception that spectacular effect combined with an atmosphere of profound mystery which was obviously the intention of its creators. The smile on the face of each, exactly reproduced in every example, recalling that on the Sphinx of the Pharoahs, propounds a riddle which may for ever remain unsolved.[1]

---

[1] More recent research has now identified these gigantic masks as representations of the Boddhistva Lokesvara "Lord of the world."

With this *tour de force* as exemplified by the Bayon temple, the course of architectural development under the Khmers draws to a close. The mystic titanic imagery introduced into the building art under Jayavarman was a reflection of the sensuous conditions that were beginning to appear in Cambodia at this time, thus implying the pride that goes before a fall. It is recorded that there was no appreciable decline of imperial power, the Khmers had become masters of most of Indo-China at this date, as their buildings freely distributed over the entire region are sufficient testimony, while the actual influence of their architectural style extended even further. But the soaring ambitions of the ruler and his people overmastered them, they undertook more than they could accomplish, and eventually the Thais of Siam, who for a considerable period had been gradually increasing in strength, triumphantly swept through the country, finally in 1431, capturing and dispoiling the capital at Angkor ; from this catastrophe the Khmers never recovered. The civilization which they had evolved during several centuries with such labour and application disappeared and with it, for a time, the superb monuments recording the material evidence of their greatness were also submerged. Just as the rich Cambodian soil stimulated the Khmers in their architectural productions, so the same favourable conditions, acting on the natural forces by which they were encompassed, when uncontrolled, brought about their ruin. Yet it is pleasing to relate that through the efforts of the Ecole Francaise d'Extreme Orient, not only has the disintegration been stayed but much has been done to remove the veil obscuring this lost empire, and to rescue its achievements from oblivion. It has now become possible to realize, through its architecture, the significance of this culture as developed in Cambodia, to study its relations with the civilization of India, and to observe its position in the pattern-content of the art of Asia as a whole. As a people with a genius for monumental architecture, at once splendid, magnanimous, and devotional, the Khmers of Cambodia hold a high place. With this natural gift they also maintained throughout their history a supreme and instinctive ideal in that they invariably aspired to do great things and to do them in a great way.

REFERENCES

Aymonier, E., *Le Cambodge*, 3 Vols., Leroux, Paris, 1900-4.

Beylie, L. de, *L'Architecture Hindoue en Extreme Orient*, Paris, 1907.

Coedes, G., *New Archaeological Discoveries in Siam*, Indian Art and Letters, Vol. IV, London, 1930.

Le May, R., *Buddhist Art in Siam*, Cambridge, 1938.

Wales, H. G. Quaritch, *A Newly Explored Route of Ancient Indian Cultural Expansion*. Indian Art and Letters, Vol. IX, London, 1935.

Journal of the Greater India Society, Calcutta.

Nag, Kalidas., *India and the Pacific World*, Calcutta, 1941.

The Influences of Indian Art, The India Society, London, 1924.

Majumdar, R. C., *Hindu Colonies in the Far East*, Calcutta, 1944.

De Coral-Remusat, G., *L'art Khmer, les grandes etages de son evolution*, Paris, 1940.

Parmentier, H., *L'art Khmer classique*, 2 vols., Paris, 1940.

Glaize, M., *Les Monuments du Groupe d'Angkor*, Saigon, 1944.

Finot, L., Goloubew, V., Coedes, G., Parmentier, H., *Memoirs Archaeologique de l'Ecole Francaise d'Extreme Orient*, Paris, 1926-1932.

CHAPTER XXXVII

GREATER INDIA

(2) THE BUILDING ART OF SIAM

FROM a general view of the historical building remains of Siam there is a tendency to assume that its people were not specially distinguished for the character of their architecture, they aspired to erect temples and shrines often of a sumptuous nature, fully emblematic of their faith, but although in all these there are invariably evidences of a notable spiritual content, the genius which produces outstanding examples of the building art was never sufficiently pronounced. This is the more significant because on each side of them, towards the north-west in Burma, and, nearer still, on the east in Cambodia, as at Pagan in the former country, and at Angkor in the latter, the art of building was developed in a very magnificent manner. It is worthy of mention however that whereas these two adjacent and powerful schools of architecture came to a definite end towards the thirteenth century, the less forceful art of Siam, although nominally supposed to have completed its course in the seventeenth century, is still a living form of expression to the present day.

Essentially Buddhistic, the architecture of Siam, owing to the geographical accessibility of the country, shows perceptibly in its characteristics the influences of the Buddhist countries with which in the course of its history it came into contact. A few references may suffice to explain the extent and diversity of these external currents on the Siamese style of building at different periods. For instance in the temple of Maha-Tat, presumably of the twelfth century, at Sawank'alok, the tower, or sikhara, shows an affinity to those erected in the tenth and eleventh centuries by the Palas of Bengal, and in its detailed treatment to those of Angkor in Cambodia, or the Bhubaneswar temples of Orissa in Eastern India. The temple of Na Pra Tat (c. eleventh century ?) " is akin to the Javanese style of the seventh or eighth century", while in the temple of Chat Yot near Chiengmai there is a distinct resemblance to the shrine of Budh Gaya in Behar ; it should be explained however that this great Indian monument, owing to its special sanctity on account of its personal associations with the Buddha, has been the original model for a number of buildings in Buddhist Asia. At Lamp'un the temple of P'ra Yun is reminiscent of the That-Byin-Nyu at Pagan, and, from a more distant source, the shrine of the temple at Shri-Sarap'et in Ayudhya there is an approach to that of the Lankatilaka (Jetawanarama) of the twelfth century at Polonnaruwa in Ceylon. The list might be extended, the resemblance of some of these examples being more convincing than others, but they provide evidences that the master-builders of Siam not only received the impact of these external currents but were also sufficiently impressionable, as well as skilful, as to be able to make use of them in giving variety to the style of their own architectural conceptions.

From these references to examples of the building art in various parts of the country in which influences from a foreign origin are plainly discernible, it will be realized that any attempt at a classification of the several styles of architecture presents difficulties. In support of this it may be mentioned that it has been found expedient to resolve the plastic arts of Siam into as many as nine separate schools or periods each of which exhibits definite characteristics differentiating it from the others.[1] Moreover, although the country measures only a little more than one thousand miles long, and at its greatest part is only half that in width, owing largely to racial movements, and the diverse nature of the people who at certain periods have inhabited its territory, it has been considered useful to divide the entire region into four parts (1) Northern (2) Central (3) North-Eastern and (4) Southern or Malay Peninsula Section. It is not to be inferred however that the various architectural developments coincide with this geographical distribution, but it may help to simplify the subject. As a preliminary the architecture of Siam may be made to fall into three broad periods (1) the Mon-Indian or Dvaravati period up to the tenth century (2) the Khmer period, from the tenth to the thirteenth century when much of the country came under the domination and influence of the adjacent empire of Cambodia, and (3) the Tai or national period from the thirteenth to the seventeenth century, and afterwards to the present day.

Before referring specifically to the buildings illustrating these periods, the various types of structure peculiar to the architecture of Siam may be defined. As with most Buddhist sites, these consist of a group of buildings including the temple (*Vat* or *Wat*), a stupa (*P'ra*), a monastery (*vihara*), a consecration hall (*bot*), and the usual additional edifices for service purposes. Occasionally, and only connected with the imperial places of worship or chapels royal (*prakeo*), there is a *chattamukh* (chaumukh, or shrine of four images), and a *mandob* (*mandapa*) a large open hall. Of these different buildings, the stupa, in its Siamese form, is the most distinctive, and is of two kinds (a) the *p'ra-jedi* and (b) the *p'ra-prang*. These are apparently derived from two separate traditions, the p'ra-jedi being circular in plan, and the p'ra-prang being rectangular, and accordingly the former has its origin attributed to the Indian stupa, while the latter has been traced to the spire or sikhara of the Indian temple in the Indo-Aryan style. That the p'ra-jedi is a Siamese development of the stupa is quite clear, as the circular plan, and the bell-shaped element in its superstructure are ample proof, but its tapering elongation and finial have removed it far from the original tumulus or mound. Yet as with the stupa, the p'ra-jedi is a solid structure with no interior compartments, and is venerated, like the Crucifix in Christendom, as the most sacred symbol of the Buddhist faith. The derivation of the p'ra-prang is not so certain, but it has much the same significance and sanctity as the p'ra-jedi, although it differs structurally inasmuch as it may include an alcove or cella within its interior. Of the same

---

[1] Dr. le May, *Buddhist Art in Siam*, p. 15.

tall aspiring shape, yet instead of the tapering finial it terminates at its apex in a rounded or domical form, thus recalling in this respect the amala-sila crowning the sikharas of the Brahmanical temple type.

Turning to the three historical periods into which it is proposed the architectural development of Siam might be resolved, the first of these, the Dvaravati, is so designated as it was the name of an ancient kingdom situated between the countries corresponding at the present time to Burma on the one hand and Cambodia on the other. Of this kingdom the principal inhabitants were of the Mon race from lower Burma, who having accepted Buddhism from India, brought this and the culture which accompanied it to Dvaravati. Except the few sculptures that have survived of this period and described as "based on Gupta models"[1] the remains of this civilization, particularly in the sphere of the building art, are rare. Those discovered consist of fragmentary remains of buildings, chiefly foundations, which although they may give some idea of the plans of these structures, their architectural style is unknown. Composed of laterite or moulded brick, these plinths evidently supported superstructures of timber, while for the reception of the wooden pillars, granite bases were provided with mortice holes in which they were socketed. A small model found at Kedah recalls the system of roofs reproduced in the group of monolithic temples at Mamallapuram (Madras, 7th cent.), for example those of the rathas of Bhima and of Ganesha. Such evidence implies a southern approach by sea through Malaya, which may have brought with it contributions from Southern India, as for instance from Amravati (Andhra, second to seventh centuries), Pallava (seventh century) and also by means of currents of Sinhalese art from Ceylon. Further traces of an early Indian penetration have been found at P'ong Tuk, a site about one hundred miles northwest of Bangkok. Here also only the foundations remain of a rectangular and a circular building, identified as a temple and a stupa respectively, the former having an entrance at one end with projections and recessed chases at the sides, very similar to the plans of ancient shrines in India. Also of interest are the profiles of the laterite stylobates which have mouldings of much the same characteristic section as those in many Buddhist buildings from Ceylon to Kashmir of the first millennium.[2] There are other remains of the Dvaravati period, as may be seen in a bell-shaped structure or stupa at P'rapatom, presumed to date from the fifth century, as well as in the foundations of the Maha Tat temple at the ancient and historical town of Lavo (Lopburi), possibly of the seventh century. All these records of this early kingdom in Siam serve to confirm either a direct or indirect association with India, chiefly through Buddhist influences.

But the real development of the building art in Siam began when the second, or Khmer period was initiated in the tenth century, and the central portion of the country came under the domination of the adjacent Khmer empire of Cambodia. This supremacy lasted for three hundred years, until the thirteenth century, when the Cambodian empire itself began to crumble. In some respects implying a provincial phase of the Khmer style as this flourished at Angkor, none the less the buildings, of this period in Siam display in their character a certain independence of treatment significant of their historical background and earlier traditions. On the other hand some of this variation from the classical type of the Khmers has been traced to the notable infusion into the country of the Mons or Talaings from southern Burma, who brought into Siam the ideals of the Burmese as expressed in the great architectural movement at Pagan which flourished there with such vigour from the ninth to the thirteenth centuries. So much so that in the field of the plastic arts this has been referred to as the Mon-Khmer School. Most of the buildings of the Khmer ascription are much ruined, and although examples survive in such old regions as Sawank'alok, Suk'-ot'-ai, and Pitsanulok, two typical temples are to be found in the historical town of Lopburi, the ancient Lavo, eighty miles due north of Bangkok. That Lopburi was of importance even in the pre-Khmer times is evident from its records, but as the centre of Khmer sovereignty in Siam from A.D. 1000 it reached its highest state. Of the two principal buildings here having Cambodian affinities that of the temple of Wat Mahadhatu, and attributed to the twelfth century, is the most distinctive. Within a walled enclosure, and consisting of a sanctuary tower with its attached portico or mandapa, its general appearance conforms to that of certain mediaeval temples in India. And although the architectural treatment combines elements recalling both the Indo-Aryan and Khmer styles, it is no slavish copy of either of these modes, but a definitely original effort. It is true the tower or sikhara, in the main, follows the outlines and also the substance of the Angkor type, and to a lesser degree those of the temples of India, but there any similarity to either of these styles ends. Certainly the massive arch-shaped tympanums rising above the openings have their counterpart in the Cambodian buildings, and the excessively high moulded plinth may have been derived from the same source, but a similarly tall stepped basement was characteristic of the contemporary temples at Khajuraho in Central India. It is, however, when the plastic surface forms, especially those on the tower, are studied, that the self-originated nature of the conception becomes apparent. For instance in the design of the sikhara there is no attempt at the ringed zoning which gives its principal effect to the Angkor examples, nor is there the grouping of turrets (urusringas), that produces the vertical quality in the Indo-Aryan type. On the contrary the upper part of the tower, although in horizontal stages, these are obtained mainly by the imposition on the central core of a series of alcoves or niches diminishing as they rise, and as the tower tappers to its apex. This apex, although ruined, appears to have ended in some form of amalasila, thus pre-figuring the domical terminal of the Tai p'ra-prang of the succeeding period. There are other variations in this tower, some of them refinements, such as the concave sections of the moulded corbel tables, which, in the Angkor type, are plainly angular, and, again, the diminishing effect of the Mahadhatu sikhara is obtained by sloping stages, whereas the Cambodian are vertical. One important improvement in constructional technique the Khmers introduced which has a marked effect on the building art of Siam at this period ; this was the use of làterite stone to replace the brick or rubble previously employed. Such a change in the nature of the building material may be an aid in solving the problem of the classification of Khmer architecture within Siamese territory. (Plate CLX).

---

[1] *Buddhist Art in Siam*, p. 25.
[2] Prof. G. Coedes in *Indian Art and Letters*, Vol. II, 1928 and Vol. IV, 1930.

The other temple of Khmer attribution at Lopburi is that of P'ra Prang Sam Yot, so different in character from the preceding example that it is difficult to connect it with the same phase of development. This difference may however be due to two factors, on the one hand it is presumed to be considerably later in date, possibly built during the end of the Khmer supremacy in Siam, and on the other it displays certain elements, which associate it not with the prevailing Buddhism but with the Brahmanical faith. A triple temple the Sam Yot consists of three detached shrines each surmounted by its tower, and these super-structures which are the most distinctive features appear to be more closely affiliated in style to the later Cambodian type. Broader and even more suggestive of the fir-cone simile, the sikharas, although basically in zones are so overlaid with decorative details, in which the "acroteria" or *kudu* form predominates, that they recall the embellishment so profusely encrusted in strata on the gopurams of Southern India. Yet, unlike the Khmer examples, these too terminate in the "amalasila" as in the blunted finial of the p'ra-prang. Another temple not in Lopburi, but in old Suk'ot'ai an ancient site considerably further north on the Yom river, is that of Wat Sisawai, also composed of triple towers and presumably of Khmer extraction. Built of laterite below and brick above, with ornamentation in stucco liberally applied between the massive string-courses of its upper diminishing portion the entire treatment implies no little originality of pattern. The diversity of style in these provincialized Khmer buildings is remarkable, being traceable either to strong indigenous local influences, or to the importation of artisans from a Cambodian source working in a specialized regional mode. Several other significant examples of the effect of the Khmer domination may be referred to, such as a temple at Pimai, built towards the end of the tenth century, another at Panom Wan possibly dating from the eleventh century, and that at Panom Rung of the twelfth, which, if these dates are con-firmed, will give a series of examples showing the progressive development of the style. The temple at Pimai, the earliest, is richly decorated with carving in bas-relief, some of the border patterns, both in design and modelling, being almost exact replicas of similar ornamentation on the remains of the Pala structures at Gaur in Bengal of the ninth century. At Panom Rung the ruins include a range of buildings which may be identified as a palace, with corrugated roofs over the corridors of that distinctive type seen at Angkor. The list might be extended with references to the temple of Culamani at Pitsanulok of the twelfth century, built of laterite having additions in stucco, the temple of Wat P'ra Pai Laung at Suk'ot'ai, and "a truly magnificent temple at P'ra Vihara on the summit of the Dangrek range"[1], to mention only a few. Finally there is the temple of Maha-Tat at old Suk'ot'ai comprising a complex of structures, some of which are of Khmer ascription, while others belong to the succeeding phase of Siamese architecture, that referred to as Tai, the third division of the style.

The Tai period of the building art in Siam began to make its appearance during the thirteenth century, when a Mongoloid race of that name, whose original habitat is believed to have been southern China, gradually overran the country eventually becoming the paramount power throughout almost the entire peninsula of Indo-China. Of the varied influences which had been finding their way into the country during the course of centuries, that from the Far East was now strengthened, and the subsequent art of

Siam shows evidences of an attenuated but persistent current from this source. Further, owing to intermittent intercourse with the islands of Java and Ceylon, the buildings of the Tai period display to an extent the effects of both of these contacts. Out of this diverse amalgamation of architectural styles there is however one development of the building art which although on the one hand may have been indirectly inspired by Sinhalese conceptions, and on the other by those of Pagan, has a distinctive national character. All the examples of this phase of the Tai movement are in a ruined condition, being marked by colonnades of dismantled pillars, for they appear to have been not only inspiring structures when entire but to imply an original approach in the ritual of Buddha worship. Skilled in the fashioning of statues of the Great Teacher, notably in bronze and some of great size, the central feature of these temple complexes, for they resembled a group of connected structures rather than a co-ordinated scheme, was a colossal statue of the Buddha, screened by a high and massively built wall, not unlike a roodscreen, through which the sacred image could be viewed, and therefore worshipped, by means of a tall narrow lancet-shaped aperture. Leading up to this shrine, altar, and divinity combined, was a pillared hall, corresponding in its intentions to the Indian temple mandapa, while in the rear rose a tapering sanctuary tower or *pra-prang*. Other edifices utilized in the ritual are grouped around, but the foregoing are the main and central elements of the composition. Such are the temples of Maha-Tat at Sawank'alok, and another having the same dedication at old Suk'-ot'-ai, where also is situated that of Cri Chum of a similar type, all found in the more northerly region of the country, while at Ayudhya towards the south, nearer Bangkok, is the temple of Cri Sarap'et (cir. 1490). This class of temple appears to have emerged during the earlier centuries of the Tai period, and in their architectural character as well as in their ritualistic aspect, they recall in some respects the planning and perceptions of the Sinhalese in their temple of Lankatilaka at Polonnaruwa. In the con-struction of most of these temples, brick, with a surfacing of stucco took the place of the more substantial laterite masonry introduced during the previous period by the Khmers, thus no doubt partly accounting for their dilapidation, to which also the climate has contributed its share.

Although the Tai kingdom was founded in the thirteenth century, and has continued until recent times during this long period of some six hundred years, it has naturally experienced several decisive political and other changes, which have reacted on the course of the building art. The earlier examples of the movement are to be found in the northern region, where the first advancing tide of the Tai race swept into the country soon to become prominent in North-Central Siam in the areas of Suk'-ot'-ai, Sawank'alok and Pitsanulok, as the remains of the buildings already referred to bear witness. Progressing still further southwards in 1350 the city of Ayudhya became the capital, situated, some forty-five miles north of Bangkok, thus bringing the Tai ascendency into the southern region and so completing the domination of the entire country. Ayudhya was des-troyed by the Burmese in 1767, and is now a scene of desol-ation and ruin, but in the seventeenth century according to writers of the date, it was a city of great size and import-ance. The principal record of its one time greatness are the extensive remains, now a vast array of disintegrated buildings holding the imagination, but implying the decay of a

---

[1] Indian Art and Letters, Vol. VIII, 1935.

significant yet all too transient phase. Among these are the ruins of the temple of Cri Sarap'et of which sufficient is still standing to show that in the fifteenth century, in spite of indications of an approaching decadence, it was a notable work of architecture. In the mode of the more northerly group of temples, as at Suk'-ot'-ai, to which class it obviously belongs, the columns of its pillared hall, the stupas, including two of considerable size fully representative of the style at this period, and above all the colossal seated Buddha, fifty feet high, from these remains some idea of the magnitude, if not the sumptuousness of this temple composition may be surmised.

With the establishment of the capital at Bangkok in 1782, shortly after the destruction of Ayudhya, Siam entered on its modern phase of the Tai period, when the arts of all kinds received encouragement from the throne. Many important buildings have been erected in Bangkok within the last century, comprising palaces, temples, stupas and shrines, which although they maintain the general character of the historical examples, such as the p'ra-jedi and the p'ra-prang, it has become the custom to overlay these traditional forms with so much ornamentation that the simple dignity of the originals is obscured by a superfluity of mouldings and stringcourses, rich in themselves, but made more so by each being embellished with lesser patterns until the whole presents an appearance of meretriciousness significant of a decline in taste. Steps are being taken to correct this departure from true expressive architecture, so as to bring back the art more into proper relation with the simpler understanding of the people.

To sum up, it will appear from the foregoing that although there are buildings in Siam, and also groups of buildings, which display considerable architectural qualities, yet there is little evidence of any combined effort on the part of the people to materialize their ideals in structural form on anything like an adequate scale or in an inspired manner. When they were moved to create large buildings they found themselves with only limited perceptions and capacities for such undertakings and accordingly they were compelled to borrow extensively from the self-activities of others with whom they were brought into contact. The result is that there emerges at no period a definite national style, their buildings are largely the effect of "influences," and their architecture is therefore not exactly a logical development or a natural growth. Diverse elements from external sources enter freely into its character, often indeed to its improvement, but it appears to be rarely a genuine expression of the people themselves, probably because they were never sufficiently coalesced to formulate a unified ideal. On the other hand the sculpture of Siam shows marked indigenous ability, as may be seen in the metal and stone statuary which attained a very high standard during most of the country's historical periods. Architecture, therefore, may have been largely regarded as subordinate to the plastic art, and more as a background on which to display their great skill as sculptors and workers in bronze.

REFERENCES

Le May, Reginald, *A Concise History of Buddhist Art in Siam*, Cambridge, 1938 (The standard work on this subject, and to which the author is greatly indebted).

Majumdar, R. C., *Hindu Colonies in the Far East*, Calcutta 1944.

Nag, Kalidas, *India and the Pacific World*, Calcutta 1941.

Beylie, L. de, *L'Architecture Hindoue en Extreme-Orient*, Paris 1907.

CHAPTER XXXVIII

GREATER INDIA

(3) THE BUILDINGS OF THE CHAMS

(Annam, French Indo-China)

A portion of the Indo-China Peninsula, where the inhabitants appear to have made at an early date contact with India, is that now known as Annam. Originally, however, this eastern seaboard of the peninsula was occupied by the Chams, a race of Austronesian extraction, who derived their name from Champa, by which the country was known to India. First coming into notice towards the beginning of the Christian era the kingdom of the Chams remained in power until it was overrun by the Chinese Annamites in the 14th century, who thus shared with the Indo-Khmer dynasties of Cambodia the domination of the entire region now known as Siam and French Indo-China. In the architectural remains of the Chams there are definite evidences that their civilization was fundamentally Brahmanical, although in the tenth century there was a short interval when Buddhism was favoured. The principal groups of buildings are at Mi-Son, a Hindu "temple-city," and at Dong-Duong, a Buddhist site, both seventy-five miles south of Hue, the present capital of Annam. Much further south is a large collection of remains at Po Nagar, near the seaport of Nha Trang, and there is also a group near Kwi Nhon known historically as the "Towers of Gold, Silver, and Copper." All these structures indicate by their architectural treatment that the building art of the Chams was an independent regional movement, but obviously of Indian ancestry.

In working out their temple scheme it was the custom of the Cham builders to plan these in groups of three, the principal shrine being in the centre with its subsidiary shrines placed on either side. These were arranged on a square terrace, and each of the buildings was square in plan with a square cella forming the interior. Above this ground plan in each instance arose a tall tower, and the design of this triad of towers, called *kalan*, is the chief feature of the style. The kalan is usually an isolated structure corresponding to the sikhara, vimana, or deul, of the Indian examples, and is constructed of brick with elaborate ornamentations. Access to the cells within is obtained by a doorway projected from the east or west sides, but some have porticos connected with the cella by a vaulted passage. The interiors are all vaulted structures, with plain walls, and the arches and vaults are formed, not by the "true" method, but by means of oversailing courses of bricks gradually reducing the space until these meet at the apex.

Contrasting with the severe simplicity of the interior, the exterior of these towers, and also any supplementary buildings, are loaded with elegant relief decoration or architectural motifs of a special order. The proportions of these towers are approximately the same as those of the Indian sikhara, the width at the base being about one-third of the height, although this may vary according to the period in which they were built. Moreover they are not crowned by a flat member, such as the Indian *amalasila*, but finish with a pointed finial or small spire. In their architectural design these towers display two methods of treatment, the lower half being emphasized by means of a scheme of vertical lines, while the upper portion consists of an arrangement of horizontal mouldings and other lateral features, the two systems in juxtaposition presenting as a whole a very harmonious contrast. It will be observed that the vertical appearance of the lower portion is obtained by means of a series of tall shallow pilasters grouped on each side of the central space, and also forming the quoins. These are continued up to the cornice, above which the lateral treatment predominates by means of a composition of diminishing stories, generally three or four in number, each defined by a plain coping.

Such are the broad outlines of these Cham towers, but over and above this structural basis, additional features have been superimposed of a sufficiently distinctive nature as to add very considerably to their character. Below, on the vertical portion, in the centre and between the ranges of pilasters on each side, an ornamental offset is projected, rising from pediment to cornice and completely filling this otherwise vacant space. In its design it resembles a tabernacle and alter combined, having a foliated and arched canopy supported on pillars, very often with the apex of the lower arched feature penetrating into the base of the same motif above. Over all are carried low relief arabesque patterns enriching the entire edifice like a finely woven fabric. On the portion above, the same elaborate treatment is followed, but in this instance in the centre of each story the ornamental offset breaks the lateral lines by being in more pronounced relief, the line of vertical projections continuing until they join the pinnacle rising spire-like over all. (Plate CLXI).

It is not uncommon to find in certain styles of art a motif used so persistently that it identifies that art at once. Such is the rampant steed in the mediaeval sculpture of Southern India, the chaitya element, "kudu" in Buddhist rock architecture, and the trefoil with the angular pediment in the temples of Kashmir, to mention only a few instances. But probably in no country has this system of reiteration of a particular form been carried to such an excess as a certain flame-like form, used both architecturally as well as decoratively in the art of Indo-China, and specially in that of the Chams. Introduced, as referred to above, in the manner of an offset, or repeated in miniature in countless numbers on the towers, it is so invariably employed that the eye is wearied by its unrestricted frequency. A distant derivative of the chaitya arch, through the "kudu", it has now become a kind of "acroteria" on the shrines of the Chams. But although this motif is so universal in the design of these kalans, it does not conceal the fact that in appearance, shape, proportions, and technical treatment, these shrines bear a textural resemblance to that almost isolated example at Bhitagaon, in the United Provinces of India, a brick temple of the sixth century. Not that there is any noticeable structural likeness, for as previously stated, the building art of the Chams shows considerable evidence of being an independent phase of Hindu architecture, approximating only to the parent art of India in some of its details, implications and general trends, but at the same time an affinity is apparent.

At Mi-Son there is the most representative series of these towers, where some eight groups of temples remain, as here was a "temple-city", and from these examples, together with those at other sites, some idea of the progress of the building art from the seventh to the tenth century may be gained. It is tolerably clear that previous to this period, in the third and fourth centuries A.D., a wooden style of architecture existed, very similar to that which was afterwards copied in brick, but no examples of this have survived. Then ensued the phase as illustrated at Mi-Son, which shows the art of the Chams at its most mature period. Later, the design of the towers became more stylized, detached turrets became a feature of the upper portions, corresponding in some respect to the *urusringa* of the Indian sikhara, and the buildings lose some of their original ingenuousness. Although the tall shrine is the outstanding characteristic of the style, occasionally long rectangular halls were introduced in front of the main tower, but detached from it. Sometimes these contained columns, and usually there were doorways at both the short sides, evidently for the entrance and exit of ceremonial processions. Window openings of a graceful design find a place in the Mi-Son structures, square apertures sunk between pilasters, and with elaborate entablatures having carved friezes of figures. The openings themselves have baluster-shaped mullions, not unlike a similar device seen in the Rajarani temple (cir. 1000) at Bhubaneswar in Orissa. On the other hand contact with the architecture of China is shown in several features of the Cham buildings, as illustrated by the treatment of some of the "kalan" roofs. These are of the keel-shaped kind with an arched chaitya gable, but curving upwards at each end after the pagoda style of the Far East, examples of which may be seen in the shrines at Po Nagar.

In the tenth century a departure took place, when the king Indra-Varman, an ardent Buddhist, built a temple to that faith at Dong-Duong, which although following the same general principles of the prevailing style, was designed to accommodate, in its much enlarged interior, figures and symbols of the Buddha. These consist of a stupa in the centre on a high and decorative plinth and approached by elegantly designed steps, with an enthroned figure of the Buddha on a tall pediment attended by his disciples. The pedestals and thrones, platforms and steps within this interior hall are all profusely embellished with high relief figure-subjects relating to the Buddha cult, and it is evident that the people rejoiced in richly ornamented shrines. Part of the exterior scheme consists of tall fluted pilar-like structures grouped on each side, the Cham interpretation of a stupa, but very far removed in appearance from the original tumulus mound.

REFERENCE

Parmentier, H., Inventaire descriptif des monuments Cams de l'Annam (1909-1918).

CHAPTER XXXIX

GREATER INDIA

(4) JAVA AND BALI

THE island of Java in the Malay Archipelago received the same form of religio-culture as that which developed in India, conveyed to it in the same manner as the other countries of Greater India, by means of progressive movements which infiltrated into it during the course of the first millennium. Specific indication of this contact are first seen in certain Sanskrit inscription of the fourth century discovered in the western portion of the island, but of any structures connected with these, there are no traces. It is in the region east of this, towards the centre of the country that the earliest and principal architectural remains are to be found. Here it may be explained that owing to the longitudinal shape and orientation of the island as a whole, it has been found expedient to resolve the country politically into three regions, referred to as West, Middle, and East, and accordingly in this order the building art of Java will be described.

The western region possessing no architectural records, a study of the subject begins with the central division, termed Mid-Java, where on a site known as the Djeng Plateau, a group of Vaishnavite temples was erected about the eighth century A.D. These Hindu temples represent the earliest phase of the building art in Java. About a century later, the teachings of Mahayana Buddhism began to make their appeal to the people, and for some considerable time, as shown by their monuments, the two religions flourished side by side. This combined movement led to the consummation of the architectural effort in the island, referred to as the Golden Age, where in Mid-Java, in an area not far removed from the more recent capital of Jokyakarta, the finest examples were created, culminating in the grandest of all Buddhist buildings the stupa of Borobudur (c. 850 A.D.). Then,

early in the tenth century, for some reason hitherto unexplained, the erection of buildings of all forms abruptly ceased, authority in the centre was relinquished, and no further constructional activity in this part of the country is recorded. The Golden Age of Javanese architecture was ended.

An interval then appears to have ensued, a break in the continuity of the style occurred, and when the pendulum came into action again it swung over to the eastern division of the country, where a new regime rose to political power, and a fresh development of the building art resulted. From East-Java, therefore, from the eleventh to the fifteenth centuries, the island was administered, and in the course of time a considerable number of buildings were erected, which although possessing certain architectural qualities, were not equal to those of the previous era, so that this eastern movement has been designated the Silver Age. (Plate CLXII). In the fifteenth century this period also came to an end owing to the acceptance by the people of Islamism, a condition which has prevailed to the present day. But merged with this new orientation, or more correctly parallel or co-existent with it, arose another movement on the part of the Indonesians, a reversion to a form of folk-art, with the *Wyang* or puppet shadow-play as its basic structure. Finally the occupation of the island by the Dutch in the eighteenth century, brought in European forms and these are becoming the main features in the modern style.

Such in outline is the course the building art in Java pursued during the main periods of its history ; this outline will now be amplified according to the chart set out below.

ANTIQUITIES AND MONUMENTS OF JAVA, (HINDU AND BUDDHIST)

WEST-JAVA	MID-JAVA (Golden Age)			EAST-JAVA (Silver Age)		
to 625 A.D.	A.D. 625 to 928			A.D. 928 to 1478		
Hindu	Indo-Javanese			Indonesian		
	Hindu	Buddhist	Hindu	Hindu-Buddhist		
	625-750	750-860	860-950	11th & 12th cents.	1250-1292	1294-1478
Kingdom of Taruma	Djeng Plateau	Sailendra-Sumatra	"Restoration"	Kadiri	Singasari	Majapahit
Inscriptions of 4th and 5th centuries	Temples of Bhima, Arjuna Punta Deva Srikandi Bagelen Pekalongam Parikesit	Temples of Kalasan (778) Mendut Sari (800) Sewa (825) Sewu (859) Pawon Plaosan Stupa of BOROBUDUR (c. 850)	Temples of Asu PRAMBANAM (Loro-Jonggrang, c. 900).	Lalatunda (tomb & bath) Belahan (bath built by Erlinga 1010-42).	Temples of Singasari (1250) Kidal (1250) Jago (1268)	Simping (1295) Papoh (1300) Jaboeng (1354) PANATARAM (Palah) (1370) Sawentar Surawana. Tigawangi Djedong Sukuh (1450)

Beginning in Mid-Java with the emergence of the group of stone temples on the Djeng Plateau, these represent the first phase of three developments which form the Golden Era as this flourished from the seventh to the tenth centuries. The initial movement in the architectural history of Java, as this originated on Djeng in the seventh century, is exemplified by some eight relatively small temples, recorded however to be the sole existing remains of a temple-city of considerable proportions of much the same character as similar concentrations of religious buildings exist in India, for instance at Sonagarh near Datia in Central India, and elsewhere. Some of these temples that have survived on the Djeng Plateau have been designated colloquially in more recent times by the names of the heroes of the Ramayana, such as Bhima and Arjuna, but they were all originally dedicated to Vishnu. Comparatively limited in size, averaging in plan not more than fifty feet side, they consist of a single cell contained within an architectural exterior based on a cubical system of design and construction. This is emphasised by marked horizontal and vertical projections, a massive portico with stairway, the whole rising up into a solidly built double storied building of agreeable proportions. What makes these Djeng examples of special significance is that in their character they prefigure the architectural style of the Javanese development as a whole. It is possible to see for instance in the temples of Arjuna and Srikandi of this group a certain structural procedure which marks the beginning of the movement, a feeling for simplicity and mass, a broad and robust treatment comparable with the first efforts of the Gupta builders in India (A.D. 350). Not that there are any signs of a definite relationship with this Indian mode but the same textural temper is observable in both forms of structure. Yet there is one example of the Djeng series, which differs from the generalization outlined above, and may be the earliest of its kind. This is the Bhima, which has a resemblance in some respects to that "key" temple of brick at Bhitagaon near Cawnpore although it must be admitted that the likeness to the Indian type is more in intention than in substance. There is however the tall tower or sikhara in receding chases, tapering as it rises, while the cella is entered by a projecting portico. Then the surfaces are freely decorated with reproductions of the chaitya-arch motif, alternating with panels and string-courses, all of which features, both architectural and ornamental, are combined with much the same effect in each instance. Moreover on the quoins are *amalakas*, those ribbed elements so distinctively of Indian origin that the conception of the Bhima as a whole has evoked the opinion that "in all probability Indian architects were at work here."[1] (Plate CLXII). No account of the temples on the Djeng Plateau would be complete without a reference to one of these known as the Punta Deva, built presumably about A.D. 750. This is a lovely little building exquisitely designed and wrought, a gem of its kind, and presenting an architectural scheme in miniature treated in a notably classical manner. From such a beginning, and denoting a keen sense of refinement allied with a certain quality of vigour the style was launched upon its course. (Plate CLXII).

After this initial Brahmanical phase as illustrated by the shrines at Djeng, a period of Buddhism intervened, when a number of large and important buildings were erected on a separate site in Mid-Java some distance to the south-east of the earlier group. It is recorded that these were inspired by the advent in the island of the Sailandras of Sumatra

(760-850), a powerful Buddhist dynasty whose influence extended over a very large portion of south-east Asia towards the 8th century A.D. Their domination over a great part of Java stimulated the architectural aspirations of the people to a remarkable degree, so much so that the productions, of the Sailendra-Sumatra period in Mid-Java were of such a high order as to entitle this movement to be designated as already mentioned the Golden Age in Java's architectural history.

Of these temples dedicated to the Buddha, the most notable are the Kalasan (c. 778), the Sari, the Mendut (c. 800), and the Pawon, and although none of these is of any great size—the largest, the Sari, (Plate CLXIII) being only eighty feet in its extreme width—they represent a phase in the building art of Java of great significance. But contrasting with the relatively moderate dimensions of the above, and included with this group, as it was built about the same time, is the stupa of Borobudur, the largest and most remarkable monument erected to the Buddhist faith, and therefore in every way standing in a class by itself. Taking the lesser buildings of this period first, the earliest is the Kalasan, its date being verified by an inscription, and it is accordingly the first Buddhist temple to have been raised in Java. Dedicated to the goddess Tara it is planned in the shape of a Greek cross, its projecting wings forming side chapels each approached by a stairway through a prominent portico. Standing on an elegantly moulded base, it appears to have been of one story only, but above is a substantial cornice, supporting a cluster of ornamental stupa-finials, the whole crowned by a graceful central tower. On the broad middle wall-space of the exterior, sculpture has been freely applied in a scheme of niches, alcoves, and openings, each embellished with a foliated pediment in the form of a *kirti mukha* of intricate design. In spite of being considerably ruined, it is clear that the Kalasan temple presents a complete and finished example of a style of architecture, not self-originated, but the logical result of a long tradition of structural experience in the art of building. The question naturally arises from whence was this experience obtained, thus enabling this fully matured structure to emerge towards the end of the eighth century in the heart of Mid-Java ? An analysis of the mode illustrated in this building may partly solve the problem. In some of its aspects the Kalasan recalls the manipulation of the Khmer productions in Cambodia of the same date, and also in a similar manner with the earlier monuments at Pagan in Central Burma. But the general character of much of the work on the Kalasan temple and other examples of this group seems most nearly allied to the art of Bengal at the beginning of the Pala period (8th century A.D.). As almost all the productions of this Indian School have perished, mainly owing to the Muhammedan invasion of the thirteenth century, a comparison is difficult, but what has been referred to as the "lost temple type of pre-Islamic Bengal" may provide some data. Fragments of this type of structure recovered from various sites in Bengal and Bihar, bear a peculiar resemblance to some of the plastic art on the buildings in Java, while the same patterns and relief treatment are observable in the architecture of Burma and Cambodia of approximately the same date. It appears therefore that during the latter half of the first millennium an art movement encompassing a very large region extending from the lower Gangetic plain to the islands of the China Sea was in operation, carried to distant places mainly through the medium of the Indo-Buddhist faith.

---

[1] Coomaraswamy.

Such may be an explanation of the form and finished structural appearance of the Kalasan temple in Mid-Java in the year 778.

But while the Kalasan temple acts as a pointer in the movement, other examples of this group, built rather later, show the trend of the style at a more advanced stage. Of these the temple of Mandut is the most expressive, as it represents this particular phase in the development of the building art in its most refined mood. As with all the buildings of this group it is raised on an expansive and ornate base, approached by a graceful and prominent stairway. The central structure resolves itself into a scheme of rectangular elements, the combination of which, mounting up by diminishing stories each defined by a bold cornice, forms an elegant and well proportioned whole. Contrasting with the simple vigour of the upper and lower portions is the broad middle area of the exterior surface which is left free for an arrangement of fiat wall spaces, but all richly carved in patterns of relatively low relief. The interior is a single cell, plain in its treatment but enshrining three statues of great sculptural merit, illustrating the high standard the plastic art had attained in Java at this early period. Decorating the throne of the central figure are certain symbolic motifs, not only exquisitely carved, but displaying features closely associated with the contemporary art of Southern India. It should be noted here, that throughout its course, although pilasters and similar attachments figure in the building art of Java, the style itself is distinctly astylar, as no use of pillars is made in its structure.

Yet although this group of shrines contains some admirable architecture, these buildings may be regarded as merely the satellites of the stupendous structure of the Borobudur, which rose in their vicinity, and is of virtually the same period. This immense stupa, undoubtedly the largest monument dedicated to Buddhism, and one of the most remarkable architectural productions achieved by the hand of man, not only on account of its vast dimensions, but also by reason of its endless galleries of bas-reliefs and statuary, must have taken many years to complete. No definite date of its construction is recorded, but it probably occupied the large army of skilled workmen engaged in its creation part of the eight and probably the whole of the first half of the ninth century, a total of at least seventy-five years. It is the only stupa of note on the island, but the entire Buddhist community at the time appears to have concentrated its efforts on this one grand symbol of their faith. As with most Buddhist monuments the site of the Borobudur was selected with great care, and is a singularly appropriate one, as it crowns a high commanding position which adds not a little to its impressive appearance. The elevated plateau on which it stands overlooks the undulating wooded country-side, interrupted by areas of vivid green rice fields, while the distance is encircled by ranges of mountains, some of them still active volcanoes, from which pillars of smoke erupt to disperse themselves into the upper atmosphere. Wrapped in that supreme spirit of peace emblematic of the creed with which it is identified, yet the Borobudur has gazed for over a thousand years on a landscape where the forces of nature are ever restless and frequently display their most turbulent mood. And over

all is bathed a golden light, characteristic of this tropical island, an iridescent refulgence probably occasioned by the volcanic vapour with which the whole air is surcharged.[1]

It is however a strange irony that from the harvest, so to speak, of these volcanic ranges the materials for the construction of this stupa were obtained, as the blocks of which it is built are what is known as trachyte or volcanic rock, in a word solidified lava. This is a roughly textured substance (hence its name), and the surfaces of the blocks, sometimes even worked from the boulders erupted from the craters, were ground down by hand to level beds and joined together without any cement, following the dry masonry technique of the builders of India. Afterwards the sponge-grained surfaces were made smooth by the application of thick lime-wash, or a form of plaster, remains of which treatment are still discernible on the sculptures, where it was specially necessary to produce a finished appearance to the carved figures or ornaments. It is also understood that a considerable amount of colour was applied to the sculptured forms, in which case a general view of the entire monument may have been very different from the monotone appearance it now presents. The above system of construction applies not only to this stupa, but it was also the method by which most of the buildings in Mid-Java were produced.

The stupa of Borobudur, or "Many Buddhas," so called on account of the innumerable images distributed over its various surfaces, stands on the summit of a low hill-top, the upper portion of which was levelled for its reception. Square in plan, but its right lines interrupted by projecting faces, it measures some five hundred feet side, and mounts up by a series of terraces to a total height of one hundred and sixteen feet. It assumes therefore the appearance of a huge mound of masonry with its paraboloid skyline fretted by a range of turrets, replicas in miniature of the stupa-shape, thus giving it a serrated contour. As a whole, and seen from a distance, the Borobudur presents no inspiring architectural composition as it lies tortoise-wise basking on the wide rocky bed prepared for it, yet one cannot fail to be moved by its immense size and massive bulk, and also on closer approach by its overwhelming spiritual significance emphasized by the long galleries of sculptured friezes carried around the corridors of its elevated terraces. These terraces, three in number, make up the square formation of the building, and each is approached by a steep flight of steps through an elaborately carved arched doorway. It is by means of these doorways that access is obtained to the galleries of sculpture, probably the most remarkable feature of the monument. Up to this height the stupa has followed the shape of a low pyramid in its general configuration but above the third terrace this pyramid becomes truncated to produce a wide flat surface, and from this stage what may be referred to as a change of key in its structural scheme takes place. Here the square system ceases, and a circular formation is introduced. For over the square platform three circular terraces arise, one above the other, diminishing in size, on each of which is disposed a regular series of smaller stupas amounting to seventy-two in all, and it is from these that the crenellated outline of the composition is derived. Then to crown the summit of the entire conception is a larger stupa

---

[1] In the year 1910 the author had the fortunate experience of seeing this vast structure under the most unique circumstances. It was the last appearance of Hallys comet then at its zenith, and the spectacle of this monumental pile with its "Many Buddhas" gradually emerging from the darkness lit by its great luminous beam mysteriously rising from behind the heavy smoke emitted at regular intervals from a distant volcano, is unforgettable.

raised in the centre forming the finial or pinnacle of the whole. (Plate CLXI).

In somewhat the same manner as all colossal monuments make their appeal, as for instance the pyramids of the Pharoahs, the stupa of Borobudur stirs the emotions not so much on account of its architectural character, but more through its phenomenal proportions, for what to the spectator seems to form part of the natural landscape, dwarfing its immediate surroundings, he realizes is a structure laboriously built up stone upon stone by means of the puny hands of his own kind. And it is also within the nature of things that such a unique creation should evoke feelings of a mystic quality with which in the course of time it has become associated. For example an attempt has been made to interpret its plan as a structural form of a " mandala," a subject pictured not unfrequently in the imaginative designs painted on Tibetan " tangkas " or temple banners. The mandala is a visionary conception reproduced in one dimension, of an assembly of celestial " mansions in the skies," as viewed by the Buddhist artist priests working in the Lamaseries on the heights of the Himalayas, and in some of the concentric passages and geometrical shapes of the Borobudur there is a certain resemblance to these magic buildings. The fact that this great pile takes the form of a tumulus, but in plan is square has moved one writer to state that the architect's conception was " to erect a stupa on at pyramid."[1] Another has described it as " in its mass a cupola half rising from the earth, and holding within its bosom a stepped pyramid, loaded with images."[2] While a third remarks that its designer " instead of putting the stupa above the pyramid, really put the pyramid inside the stupa,"[3] adding that it is a " symbolic microcosm, of which the superimposed stories symbolize the different stages of the ecstasies of dhyana." The actual facts no doubt were that under a powerful Buddhist hegemony and an inspired hierarchy it was resolved to raise a monument which while conforming in its general scheme to the traditional stupa ideal, should in the first place exceed all previous productions of a like nature in its dimensions, and secondly excel them in the prodigality of its sculptured themes. That both these objects were attained in the Borobudur is clearly demonstrated, on the one hand its immense size cannot fail to fill the spectator with awe, while on the other, the vast amount of statuary and the continuous friezes of plastic forms all of the highest quality are excelled in no other building. These friezes consist of a double series of panels numbering some thirteen hundred in all, and which if placed end to end it is estimated would extend in length for over three miles. In these reliefs the projection is bold, what may be described as almost in the half round, and the vigour, perceptivity, and emotion expressed in the compositions entitle this Javanese school of plastic art to take a prominent place in the field of sculpture as a whole.

Regarded in all its aspects therefore the Borobudur represents not only the high water mark of Javanese creative genius, but stands forth as one of the world's greatest constructional and artistic masterpieces. Here it may be noted that this immense stupa corresponds in its vast bulk and sculptured magnificence to that other stupendous building undertaking rising somewhat later also in Greater India, the temple of Angkor Vat in Cambodia. Both these grand architectural productions were an expression in material form of Hindu-Buddhist ideals emanating from an Indian source. It is also significant that both were the conception and creation of people living outside the accepted geographical limits of the country in which these ideals originated. No Hindu or Buddhist monument in India can compare with either of these achievements, not in size, architectural character, plastic embellishment, or in the vision that incited them. It yet remains to be explained how these supreme accomplishments came to be planned and brought to such perfect consummation in both countries so far removed from the origin of their inspiration.

Despite however the *tour de force* as exemplified in the Borobudur, a monument intended no doubt to act as a stimulant to the declining faith of pure Buddhism, almost before it was completed there appears to have been a reversion to the creed of Hinduism in the form that this had previously found favour in the island. Referred to as the " Restoration," as the country seems to have been restored to its original belief, this movement, which began about A.D. 860 and continued until the middle of the succeeding century, produced several important temples dedicated to the Hindu deity Shiva. But as a proof that the two cults flourished contemporaneously in this area, a Buddhist temple, the Plaosan, was also erected about the same time. Yet an outstanding work of architecture, representing this Restoration phase, is a complex of shrines known as the Prambanam, or the Loro-Jonggrang[4] group, which, in view of its size and importance, was probably conceived and constructed as a Hindu rival to the Buddhistic Borobudur. This great Brahmanical temple-scheme in Mid-Java was completed about A.D. 900, and was clearly designed with the object of reviving the practice of Hinduism throughout the country. And just as the Borobudur made its appeal mainly on account of its colossal size, so the Hindu hierarchy realizing that in this respect it could not be surpassed, proceeded in an attempt to rival it by a numerical effort. For the Prambanam consists of an expansive composition aggregating over one hundred and fifty individual shrines arranged in rows on a commodious terrace, and, so that its influence should be as wide as possible, the main buildings were consecrated respectively to the deities Vishnu, Shiva and Brahma, thus providing an all-embracing dispensation. Further, in order to be abreast with the sculptured reliefs proving so effective at Borobudur, a long frieze was carved on the walls illustrating the mythology of these age-old Indian divinities. In its architectural appearance the Prambanam temple could not have been very imposing, the main effort being concentrated on the range of temples on the upper platform, that dedicated to Shiva being most important and representative of the style at this juncture. The structure is square in plan with re-entrant angles, having flights of steps in the middle of each side, thus producing a cruciform shape on the ground. Only one of the stairways leads to the central square cella, the remainder ending in small independent chapels. The elevation, unfortunately much ruined, shows a symmetrical tower-like edifice, ascending in diminishing tiers, its projecting faces merging by stages to form a broad sikhara. In the design of this temple there is evidence of a refinement and elegance expressive of an advance on the more robust examples of the previous phase. The figure subjects with which it is embellished are

---

[1] M. Stutterheim, [2] G. Coedes, [3] M. Mus (Indian Art and Letters, Vol. VIII, London 1934).

[4] This is a comparatively modern name and relates to a local legend having no real connection with the temple.

a confirmation of this progressiveness, and these are usually regarded as the consummation of the plastic art in the hands of the Javanese sculptors. While there is admirable breadth and restraint in the bolder forms of the Borobudur reliefs, the Prambanam carvers have improved on these by means of a more delicate and suave method of modelling, in the subtle grading of one passage into another, and in the play of surface as a whole. Architecturally this temple illustrates a movement towards a riper and more polished type of structure, a natural stage in the course of evolution in the building art.

It is significant that some of the sculptures at Prambanam are left unfinished, and it is not improbable that the period of Brahmanical supremacy, with the architectural movement that this temple exemplifies, ended at this date. It represents therefore the passing of the " Golden Age," the conclusion of an era, an event which took place in the first half of the tenth century. For not only was this Hindu Buddhist site, with all its varied types of religious structure abandoned, but the region of Mid-Java, as the main administrative centre of the island, for the time being in its history ceased to function. When next the ruling power comes into view, a transfer has taken place, for the seat of the government has been moved to a position in East-Java, and from here the third and last period of the building art was developed. This period began about A.D. 950, and continued until the latter half of the fifteenth century, when it was gradually submerged by the approach of Islamism, finally coming to a prolonged and attenuated end. During this eastern phase, extending over nearly five centuries, the art still maintained evidences of being a living force, yet compared with the grand monuments of the Golden Age, it falls short of the same high standard, and has rightly been designated the " Silver Age." Apart from the fact that no buildings of outstanding importance were produced in East-Java, there is a noticeable decline in the quality of the designs, although on occasion some of the old spirit was revived, as for instance in the Kidal temple (1250), and even as late as the Jaboeng temple (1354), it is obvious that in spite of these transient efforts the style was drawing towards its close.

During this last period, a marked change gradually came over the arts, they took on a certain character, not of an extraneous nature, on the contrary they absorbed some of the indigenous qualities of the people, in other words they ceased to draw inspiration from any Indian source, so that there finally evolved a style having national attributions which has been defined as Indonesian. And as it progressed its indigenous character became more pronounced. Throughout its course the movement in the Eastern region resolved itself into three historical periods, according to the dominant rule at the time. These are (1) the Kadiri, in the eleventh and twelfth centuries, (2) the Singasari, from 1250 to 1292, and (3) the Majapahit, 1294 to 1478. Although during the first of the phases, a ruler of some note, Erlanger (1010-1042), occupied an important place in the historical archives of the country, few remains of consequence have survived. But from these it is surmised that the decisive change of location referred to above affected very considerably the outlook of the people. Two facts emerge, one of these being that the rulers were arrogating to themselves divine power, which found expression in canonization after death, as the sculptured statuary shows, and the other is that a form of royal tomb associated with a sacred bath was taking the place of the temple which had been almost the only structure erected hitherto. An example of this may be seen at Djalatunda, dated 977, while there are several others of a like nature to be found in East-Java. It should be remarked that although the building art was not prominent during this phase, which may be referred to as a stage of transition, some fine sculpture was produced under this and the succeeding regime, although perhaps of a somewhat florid order. Briefly the plastic art maintained its original supremacy while the structural art declined.

With the advent of the Singasari rule and the second phase in East-Java which began towards the end of the thirteenth century, temple building appears to have been revived, as the leading example, dedicated to Shiva amply proves. This Singasari temple consists of a central shrine surmounted by a tall tower and having a supplementary shrine to a smaller scale projecting from each of its four sides. Another temple is the Kidal, erected in 1250, and from the style of these, together with a third example, the Jago (1268), some of the trends of the art may be surmised. The general tendency of these structures shows a definite departure from type, so that in no manner do they resemble the parent art in India. Neither is there any likeness to the stupa or the Buddhist temple of Jago, nor to the Indo-Aryan style in the Hindu temples of Singasari or Kidal. All of them are more or less of a self-originated order, having only a remote connection with the style of the previous period in Mid-Java. It is true there is the pronounced and expanded base on which rises the cubical body of the cella, and above this a massive and heavily projected cornice supporting a tall pyramidal tower. But a striking and invariable feature is a boldly executed makara-head above each opening, while large circular medallions, a favourite decorative device with the Indonesians, were frequently distributed over the wall surfaces.

Following the ascendancy of the Majapahit dynasty (1294-1478), the third and final phase of the East-Java development comes into view ; it also signifies the close of the Hindu-Javanese architectural productions on the island. More prolific builders than their immediate predecessors, and dominating most of the country, the important capital city of Majapahit was one of the undertakings of this regime, near what is now Majakista. Completely ruined, mainly from volcanic eruptions, what remains indicates that the style of the previous phase was continued, but carried even further away from its original derivative. Still maintaining much of its solid square and cubical character, with finely moulded members both on its spreading platform and overhanging cornice, the general outlines of the structure tend to become more pronounced, as may be seen in the temples of Panataram (1370), and of Sawentar (c. 1400). Although there is an appearance of strained elegance in the shape of these buildings of this last effort, the high standard of the masonry is remarkable, and in the manipulation of the stonework combined with the precision of the finely chiselled mouldings the craftsmen of this period were unequalled. That a sense of originality still survived is shown in the Buddhist shrine of Jaboeng (1354) near Kraksaan, executed when the Majapahit rule was at the height of its power. Less formal in its composition than most of the Javanese buildings, as, although the typical terraced basement is retained, somewhat higher than usual in this instance, the superstructure, instead of being cubical in its treatment takes the form of a circular tower as its basis with its entrance and side alcoves imposed on its curved surfaces in a strikingly able manner. Above is the richly moulded expanded cornice, with probably a tapering pyramidal sikhara, all however, in such a ruined condition that this part is unrecognizable. But the " phase of transition " from the square basement to the circular plan of the body of the shrine, and the attachment of the openings, both difficult problems, have been most artistically solved, and the whole structure shows that even at this late stage the art was still a living movement. An example of the final development may be studied in the small shrine of Papoh, a diminutive monument of a somewhat " precious " order, in a manner recalling the small scale productions signifying the last stage of the classical period in the Indo-Buddhist architecture of a slightly earlier date in the distant country of Kashmir.

One of the symptoms of the indigenous trend in the building art of Java is noticeable in the plastic designs which decorate these later structures, where a grotesque treatment of the human figure gradually began to insinuate itself. This represents the influence of the *Wyang* or " Shadow Show" movement, a phase of Hinduism-cum-entertainment of a theatrical nature. The Wyang phenomenon appears to have captured the imagination of the Javanese in a most remarkable manner, so much so that not only their art became intensely stylised but their figure compositions in a sense are replicas of the people themselves, who seem to have cultivated deliberately a stiff and emphatic form of pose and progression, as if the Wyang figures had come to life. At this stage therefore the sculptures on the buildings show that the art as a whole was losing its pronounced classical ideal, which gave such a distinguished and dignified quality to the productions of the Mid-Java development, and on the other hand was assuming a character, which although it may have a certain attraction, tends towards a formalized method of expression, and particularly a somewhat distorted, if not fantastic interpretation of the human form.

Throughout the whole course of the building art in Java it is noticeable that the same method of technique in the process of carving the reliefs seems to have been maintained. The stone to be decorated was first "boasted" into a plain projected surface, and on this the figure subject was inscribed, afterwards being blocked out in the form of a " silhouette." Where unfinished it has been found there is every indication that the composition was first traced out on the prepared surface by means of a drawing, then the background was chiselled away by an apprentice, who merely followed the outlines of the tracing. Then came the hand of the master craftsman to put the modelling into the " silhouette," and carve it into the subtle planes of the relief and so form the finished picture.

What has enabled many of the historical buildings in Java to be studied most advantageously is that within recent years their restoration has been perfected in a singularly scholarly and scientific manner by experienced officials employed for this particular work by the Netherlands Government. This operation may not have been so difficult as in other countries owing to the circumstances by which their ruin was brought about, but this is no reflection on the skilled and conscientious methods by which these reconstructions have been made. For while no doubt considerable dislodgment of the stones may have been due to the insidious growth of vegetation within the joints of masonry, in all probability the main demolition has been caused by earthquakes,

to which the island is frequently and often violently subjected. Such disturbances, while sometimes throwing down large portions of the building and damaging in the process some of the materials of which it is composed, do not usually entirely destroy these stones, as has often been the case in other countries, as for instance when iconoclastic man is bent on utilizing these for his own base purposes. In Java the masonry though displaced, lies about where it has been thrown in a more or less uninjured condition and in the vicinity of the structure it previously adorned, so that with care and judgment it can be returned to fulfil the specific purpose for which it was originally prepared. In this operation the Netherlands officials have definitely shown the way in which such responsible work may be undertaken, with the result that a considerable number of the historical buildings on the island present now much the same appearance as when first erected over a thousand years ago. Specially does this apply to the vast structure of the Borobudur, which from a tumbled mass of scattered blocks strewn over the entire site, as was its condition at the beginning of this century, the whole monument is now in the most perfect order, having been rescued from impending disintegration, thus enabling its remarkable character to be studied under ideal circumstances.[1]

Resuming the account of the course of the Hindu-Javanese mode in the island, the end of this movement approached with the close of the Majapahit power in the fifteenth century, which coincided with the introduction of Islamism, and with it the great classical school of Javanese art terminated. From this time the people took on a new orientation, and although buildings of an Islamic order, such as mosques, are to be found in several of the towns, showing occasionally some slight evidence of a revival of the ancient and mediaeval forms, the minarets and mihrabs with which these are provided proclaim the dominance of other ideals. Such are a mosque at Kudus, and another at Sendang-duwar. Later, towards the end of the sixteenth century, the Dutch occupation brought with it the influence of the European style of building. As an example of the transition from the indigenous to the alien and more modern is a palace or water-castle, the Taman Sari at Jokjakarta, described as an oriental Trianon, and erected in the middle for the eighteenth century for the Sultan Mangku Buwono. Designed by a Portuguese, it is a synthesis of eastern and western elements, but is now a picturesque ruin so that its parts are almost unidentifiable. A further Portuguese connection with the country is shown by a church at Batavia, containing a handsome pulpit typical of the style. Buildings of a Dutch character however predominate, of which the Government Record Office in Batavia is a copy of the old type found in the Low Countries ; others such as the Amsterdam Gate and the Palace of the Governor-General, also in Batavia, are of the more recent order.

In the small island of Bali, detached by a narrow passage of sea from the mainland of Java, it is recorded that when the latter was submerged by Islamism what remained of the Hindu belief found a retreat in this little dependency. Although Bali retains the old culture of the Javanese as seen in the character of its minor handicrafts, its structural productions are but a pale reflection of the works of the great classical period as this flourished in the larger island. The Balinese appear to have been by nature too care-free

---

[1] In 1910, the author for over a month, was a witness of the scientific and scholarly manner in which Col. Van Erp, who was entrusted with the work, carried out his exacting duties extending over a period of several years.

to rise to any great heights in the creation of examples of serious architecture, their buildings, chiefly local shrines, although valuable ethnologically, have no special significance except as objects of worship and in their decorative aspect. A few instances of rock-architecture are to be found in Bali including an ancient monastery known as the Goenoeng Kawi near Tampak-sering, and another in the vicinity of the pilgrim shrines of Poera Wato Kaoe in the Tabanan section. At the former a series of cells have been excavated in the rock containing rudely shaped altars hewn out of rock slabs, and there are also niches in the walls believed to have a royal funerary origin, the whole presumed to date as late as the eleventh century. Also in the Tabanan area at Bedhulu there is an "Elephant Cave", the Goa Gadjah, consisting of a rock carved in the semblance of a giant elephant's head with an opening under its trunk leading to a dark cell, in some respects recalling the "Tiger Cave" (c. 150 B.C.) at Udaigiri, Orissa, India. Mention should be made of a hunting scene of some spirit carved in rock relief, and known as Tojo Poela also near Bedhulu. Such attempts in the rock technique are however relatively unimportant except that they may support the theory of an early and direct contact with India.

Of the buildings composed of masonry these are comparatively rare and show a connection with the mediaeval School of Majapahit, which, in view of the proximity of Bali to East Java is not surprising, as proved by the temple of Pura ye Ganga dating from the fourteenth or fifteenth centuries. The more modern type of Balinese temple, although usually of a simple and primitive order displays in its arrangements certain features of interest. Dedicated to Hindu divinities, there are often images of these, such as Shiva, Vishnu and Brahma, carved in a black stone and enshrined within the interior courts. It is the disposition of these courts, with a large and highly decorated entrance gateway, which, although in a very rudimentary form, are reminiscent of the Hindu temple system in Southern India. Rectangular in plan the three courts are concentrically arranged, in the outer of which the *gamelan*, temple bells and musical instruments, are kept, while feasts are also held in this portion. In the second court, or *vale-agoeng*, the council meetings take place, while in the innermost court, or *djeron dewa*, the holy of holies, are the shrines and altars, generally carved in limestone, elaborately moulded and decorated in fantastic patterns in high relief similar to the later and Eastern Javenese School of sculpture. Architecturally the temple building is distinguished by pagoda-like structures, called *meroes* (probably referring to Mount Meru, the Olympus of the Hindus) which rise up into tiers of diminishing thatched roofs, seven or nine in number, sometimes even as many as thirteen, similar to those in the Buddhist umbrella finial. The main entrance to the enclosures is of brick with columns in pairs, or imposing stone gates, the whole elaborated with a confusion of ornamental attachments. Such are the temples of Poonkulang near Sangsit, the Taman Sari, Bengali, Sockawati, Den Pasur, Gelgel, and many others.

REFERENCES

Java :

Krom N. J. and Erp, T. Van, *Barabudur, Archaeological Description* (The Hague, 1927).

Erp. T. Van, *Hindu Monumental Art in Central Java.* (Twentieth Century Impressions of Netherlands India 1909).

Coomeraswamy, A. K., *History of Indian and Indonesian Art*, Leipzig (1927).

With, Karl. *Buddhistische und Brahmanische Architektur und Plastik Auf Java*, Hagen 1922.

Bali :

Krom N. J., *L'Art ancien de Bali* (Revue des Arts Asiatiques, 1924).

Stutterheim, W., *Archaeological Research in Java and Bali* (Indian Art and Letters, London 1927).

Stutterheim, W., *Indian Influences on Old Balinese Art*, India Sec. London 1935.

APPENDIX

The following are extracts from a note on the presumed chronology of the Ajanta and Ellora rock-architecture prepared recently by the Hon'ble Mr. Justice Edgley who has devoted some time to an investigation of the sequence in which these excavations were made. Appended is a table showing the dates of the chaityas and viharas according to Mr. Justice Edgley's researches and deductions.

*   *   *

Ellora was probably regarded as a holy place from the earliest times by the principal religious communities of ancient India. Moreover its most important temples date from a period when complete toleration was observed by Hindus, Buddhists and Jains. At Ellora, side by side with Buddhist monasteries, which were constructed between the sixth and eighth centuries A.D., magnificent groups of early Brahmanical and Jain temples have been cut out of the rock. Most of the Hindu temples were probably constructed in the seventh and eighth centuries A.D. They culminate in the Kailasa Temple, which belongs to the middle of the eighth century and is the finest monument of its kind in India. The earliest of the Jain Temples, the Indra Sabha, is probably contemporaneous with the Kailasa Temple while the latest of the Jain group appears to have been constructed in the thirteenth century.

Ajanta shows Buddhism at the zenith of its power. At Ellora, on the other hand, we see Buddhism being gradually overshadowed by a vigorous Hindu reaction. Ellora in fact represents a period when Buddhism began rapidly to decline in influence and authority ultimately to disappear almost completely from India. In the light of available information, the cases of this decline are difficult to explain with any degree of accuracy and this remarkable phase in religious history opens out a wide field for speculation.

*   *   *

It is sometimes suggested that Ajanta and Ellora were abandoned by the Buddhists in 642 A.D., as a result of the defeat in that year of the Chalukyan, Pulakesin II, by the Pallava King, Narasimhavarman I, and consequent disturbances in the Deccan. Although Narasimha succeeded in capturing Badami he does not appear to have been able to establish himself for any length of time in any considerable portion of the Chalukyan territories. The dynasty of his rivals was certainly not extinguished as is shown by the fact that, some thirty years later, Pulakesin's son, Vikramaditya I, waged a victorious war against the Pallavas and captured their capital, Kanchi. Even if Narasimha had reached Ajanta and Ellora it is hardly likely that he would have been instrumental in suppressing Buddhism in Western India. From the observations of Hiuen Tsiang, who visited Kanchi in 640, it would appear that the Pallavas actually protected the Buddhists in South India. As part of the spoils of war Narasimha may possibly have removed to his country the sculptors and stone-masons who were actually employed at Ajanta and Ellora in order that they might work for him at Kanchi and Mahabalipuram. It is, however, highly probable that the unskilled members of the monastic communities would have been allowed to remain in their settlements and to continue their religious activities unhampered, except possibly by the withdrawal of financial support from the Chalukyan kings whose treasury must have been sadly deplected by the Pallava invasion.

*   *   *

It is difficult to say whether the first excavations at Ellora were made by Buddhists or Hindus, but, from the general appearance of the older temples, I incline to the view that the earliest work here must have been undertaken almost simultaneously by the followers of both these religions. The influence of the Badami style of cave-architecture is very apparent in the early temples at Ellora, particularly in the use of the elaborate pillars with "cushion" capitals, which from so characteristic a future of the Badami work. In fact, it is not unlikely that, after the completion of the work at Badami, many of the artizans at that place were sent to work at Ellora.

An inscription in Cave III at Badami fixes the date of the construction of that cave approximately 578 A.D. We may, therefore, infer that those Ellora temples which show a close connection with the Badami style were constructed during the period from about 580 to 642 A.D. In the latter year work was probably suspended for a time owing to the Pallava invasion of the Deccan.

The Badami influence may be detected in the capitals of the pillars in Buddhist Caves II and V and in the Dumar Lena (XXIX) which is a Hindu temple. From its position Cave I is likely to have been constructed at approximately the same time as Cave II. Probably the Buddhist Caves, I, II, and V (Maharwada) and the Dumar Lena (XXIX) are the only caves at Ellora which were completed before 642 A.D.

*   *   *

The most interesting of the early group of Buddhist caves mentioned above is the Maharwada (V). It contains a long central hall flanked by pillars of the Elephanta type and, along the whole of its length, run two parallel stone platforms. Whether these served as refectory tables or were provided for use in connection with some religious ceremonial is not altogether clear.

The next group of temples and *viharas* in chronological sequence would probably include those in which the "vase and foliage" capital begins to be adopted as one of the main architectural features for decorative and structural purposes. This particular form of capital seems to have been borrowed from Ajanta towards the middle of the seventh century. I shall deal with this matter more in detail in connection with Ajanta where something happened which interrupted further work just at the identical time that the "vase and foliage" capital was in the process of being adopted on an extensive scale as an architectural order. It is not unreasonable to suppose that the same sort of thing happened at Ellora. I therefore think that it is probable that some of the early caves in which this form of capital appears at Ellora were in an unfinished condition in 642, and that the work there was interrupted for some years ultimately to be completed during the last quarter of the seventh century.

Within this group I would place Buddhist Caves III and IV and Hindu Caves XXI (Ramesvara), XXV (Kumbharwada) and XXVII (The Milkmaid's Cave). The most remarkable of these is the Ramesvara (XXI) with its verandah supported by four massive and richly carved pillars to which elaborate struts with female figures have been added. The pillars of the interior are of the Elephanta type. The temple contains some interesting sculptures one of the best of which is a representation of the Dancing Siva.

The next group appears to me to be still later in style than those last mentioned, and to have been constructed probably between 700 and 750 A.D. It includes Buddhist Caves VI to XII and Hindu Caves XIII to XV. The sculpture to the right and left of the shrine in *vihara* VI shows signs of Hindu influence and, in this respect, it may be compared with the sculpture to be found in Cave VII at Aurangabad. In my view, the Hindu influence which is sometimes noticeable in the later Buddhist sculptures at Ellora and Aurangabad does not indicate that Buddhism at that time was merging into Hinduism but merely shows that the sculptors engaged in the work had spent more time working for the Hindus than for the Buddhists. Indeed some of them might have spent many years working at Mahabalipuram as captives of the Pallava king.

The most interesting cave of this group is the Visvakarma (X). It is the only *chaitya* hall at Ellora. There is some realistic sculpture of the late Mahayana period in the triforium and in the galleries. The style of the interior decoration of this chapel—particularly that of its facade—is later than and not so satisfying as that of the last Ajanta *chaitya* hall (XXVI) and, on a comparison with work of a similar character at Bhubaneswar, it is difficult to avoid the conclusion that the Visvakarma must have been constructed nearly a hundred years after the completion of the last Ajanta chapel (XXVI).

*   *   *

The Do Thal (XI) and the Tin Thal (XII) are three storied *viharas*. They belong approximately to the same period as the Visvakarma, although they may have been cut a little later than the other *viharas* compared with which they seem to be better constructed and to represent a more advanced stage of architectural development. Further, they contain many more sculptured figures of the Buddha, the Bodhisattvas and other divine or semi-divine beings connected with Buddhist mythology than are usually found in Mahayana *viharas*.

The most interesting of the Hindu temples of this group of the first half of the eighth century is the Das Avatar the walls of which have been elaborately sculptured. This temple contains an inscription which suggests that it was probably completed during the reign of Dautidurga Rashtrakuta who conquered the Chalukyans about the middle of the eight century.

*   *   *

By far the finest of the Ellora temples is the Kailasa (XVI) which was probably begun about the year 760 A.D., in the reign of Krishna I of the Rashtrakuta dynasty. To cut out of the rock a temple of this size would be in itself a remarkable achievement. The further work connected with its detailed elaborate decoration and the construction of the subsidiary shrines and the sculptured corridors must have been phenomenal.

*   *   *

AJANTA

The question as to the chronological sequence according to which the caves were constructed is one which presents considerable difficulties. Historical records throw very little light on the subject and relevant contemporary inscriptions are few.

*   *   *

The earliest caves are those which have been cut towards the centre of the crescent (VII to XIII). Caves IX and X are *chaitya* halls or chapels and the others are *viharas* or monasteries. Their style indicates that these caves (with the possible exception of XI) were excavated during the first and second centuries B.C. by Buddhists of the Hinayana community. Cave XI may have been cut during a slightly later period than the other caves of this group. The shrine at the back of this cave and the sculptures in the verandah are much later additions and clearly belong to a period when the Mahayana form of worship had been established.

*   *   *

The next cave to be cut was probably XV. The shrine contains an image of the Buddha of the early Mahayana type and the cave appears to have been constructed between 400 and 440 A.D.

Cave XIV has been cut above XIII. It is not easy to attribute a date to it but, as it has been left unfinished, it probably belongs to the middle of the seventh century when all constructional work then in progress seem to have been abandoned. From the beginning to the fifth century, however, for a period of at least two hundred and fifty years, the work at Ajanta continued almost without interruption.

*   *   *

Cave VII probably belongs to the same period of construction as Cave XV, but it may be a few years later. Cave VI was probably begun after VII had been completed. Cave VI is double-storied and both VI and VII are remarkable for the number of small sculptured figures of the Buddha which they contain. These caves are of an earlier type than XVI and XVII which are among the finest of the entire series, and, as the last two caves can be attributed with tolerable accuracy to the concluding years of the fifth century (possibly 470 to 480), I would assign Cave VII to 400 to 440 and VI to 440 to 480 A.D.

Caves XVI and XVII are magnificent *viharas*. From an architectural and artistic point of view, they are perhaps the best specimens of Gupta art in India. Fortunately both these caves contain inscriptions which connect them with Harishena. He was the last king of the Vakataka dynasty of whom we have any definite record, and reigned from about 465 to 500 A.D. From these inscriptions it appears that Cave XVI was dedicated by Varahadeva, Harishena's minister, while Cave XVII was cut during the same reign by the minister of a ruler who seems to have been subordinate to Harishena. It would, therefore, be safe to estimate that these caves were constructed about 470 or 480 A.D.

*   *   *

The next group consists of Caves XVIII to XX. As regards style they show a development from that of Caves XVI and XVII, especially as regards the ornamentation of the pillars in the fine *chaitya* hall (XIX). The probable date of their construction would be from about 500 to 550 A.D. The interior of the *chaitya* cave (XIX) is a magnificent piece of work. The pillars of the nave are particularly pleasing and the sculptured decoration is in the best Gupta style. In the *chaitya* caves of the earlier period considerable use had been made of wood for the purpose of completing the facade and for internal decoration. Here wood has been discarded and all the work is of stone. There is a large representation of the Buddha in bas-relief in the stupa, which indicates a complete break with Hinayana traditions as regards the ritual of worship.

A further demand for accommodation led to the construction of *viharas* XXI to XXIII, which were probably cut between 550 and 600 A.D. Of this group Cave XXI is extremely interesting. At each end of the verandah and also to the right and left of the shrine some beautiful little chapels have been constructed, separated respectively from the verandah and the side aisles of the main hall by two pillars and two pilasters. The pillars support delicately sculptured friezes of the ' jewel pattern,' depicting various scenes from Buddhistic mythology.

A further notable feature of these chapels is the use, probably for the first time, of the "vase and foliage" capital, which subsequently came to be very widely adopted as an architectural order in the principal mediaeval buildings of Northern India.

There is some difference of opinion among archaeologists with regard to the period when *viharas* I and II were completed. Most of the authorities seem to agree that they may be assigned to the first half of the seventh century A.D., but it has also been suggested that Cave I may have been constructed towards the end of the fifth century and that Cave II belongs to a slightly later period, possibly the first half of the sixth century. The latter theory, if correct, would place the four caves (XVI, XVII, I and II) which contain the best of the Ajanta paintings within a period which is generally held to have produced the finest specimens of Gupta art. On the other hand, it would be equally interesting if the theory could be reaffirmed, that Caves I and II belong to the first half of the seventh century A.D. as this would indicate that the Gupta tradition at Ajanta was sufficiently strong to ensure its survival there long after the disruption of the Gupta Empire in North India under the impact of the Hun invasions. I must confess that I find the latter theory the more attractive one and I would be loath to discard it except in the face of very convincing evidence.

On page 320 of the "Cave Temples of India" there is a discussion regarding the age of the first five westernmost caves of Ajanta and the last seven at the other extremity in which the following observation occurs :—"There are no inscriptions from which their age can be ascertained with precision, but their architectural details and other indications

are sufficient to enable us to feel confident that nearly the whole of them belong to the seventh century, as those of the central group certainly belong to the sixth." The joint authors had assigned the inscriptions in Caves XVI and XVII to about 500 A.D. and it was on this account that they attributed the central group to the sixth century. They are, however, quite definite that Caves I and II cannot belong to the same period. They seem to base their opinion principally on architectural style which is often the safest and clearest indication with regard to the period of construction of ancient monuments.

It seems to me that Caves I and II are nearer in style to the unfinished *viharas* at Ajanta than they are to Caves XVI and XVII. I incline to the view that the last excavations to be completed at Ajanta were *viharas* I and II and *chaitya* hall XXVI and that they may be attributed to the period between 600 and 642 A.D. They are all splendidly decorated and must rank among the best examples of Buddhist architecture in India.

*   *   *

This brings us to the caves at Ajanta, which were never completed, *viz.*, Caves III, IV, V, XIV, XXIV, XXV, XXVII, XXVIII and XXIX. They were probably under construction in 642 A.D., when further work was interrupted by the Pallava invasion of the Deccan. Two of these caves, (*viharas* IV and XXIV) if they had been finished and decorated, would have been the most magnificent of the entire series. The hall of Cave IV is considerably larger than that of I and is supported by twenty-eight pillars. There is an interesting Buddhist Litany near the main door. Sculptures of this kind are characteristic of the late Mahayana period.

Cave XXIV would have been the largest *vihara* in the series after IV, the hall being about 75 feet square with twenty columns. The sculptures which still exist in the verandah show that it was intended in this *vihara* to use the "vase and foliage" capital as one of its main architectural motifs. In Cave XXI this form of capital seems to have been introduced experimentally into the decorative scheme of the *vihara*. Now for the first time we find it being adopted on a larger scale.

Architectural details of this nature may possibly throw some light on the general history of the time. It is, I think, reasonable to suppose that, once the use of the "vase and foliage" capital had emerged from its experimental stage at Ajanta, the place of its origin, its general adoption on a larger scale as a prominent architectural feature would take place almost simultaneously at Ajanta and the other Buddhist centres in the immediate neighbourhood of that place. As might have been expected, we find this form of capital in use in a number of the caves at Ellora and Aurangabad. These caves are certainly later in style than any of the completed caves at Ajanta. In fact, they seem to continue the development of Buddhist cave-architecture from the point it had reached when the excavation of Cave XXIV at Ajanta ceased.

Cave I at Aurangabad, in which the "vase and foliage" capital has been used with great effect in the verandah, was intended to be a large *vihara*, but further work therein was abandoned at almost the same stage of construction as Cave XXIV at Ajanta. I cannot help thinking that the cause of the cessation of work must have been the same at Ajanta and Aurangabad, and it is highly probable that the same cause must also have brought work to a standstill at Ellora. As already stated, this cause was probably the invasion of the Deccan in 642 A.D., by Narashimhavarman I and the overthrow of the Chalukyan king. At the same time, there seem to be every reason to suppose that a good deal of constructional work must have been done in the Buddhists caves at Aurangabad and Ellora long after it had ceased at Ajanta.

It is sometimes assumed that work in connection with the Buddhist caves in this part of the Deccan was discontinued permanently about the middle of the seventh century. I think that can only be correct as regards Ajanta. I therefore venture to put forward another theory.

I suggest that what really happened was that after defeating the Chalukyans in 642 A.D., the Pallava king removed the artisans and sculptors from Badami, Ajanta, Ellora and Aurangabad to Mahabalipuram and other places in his own country and that they or their successors were taken back to the Deccan about 647 A.D., when the Chalukyan king, Vikramaditya I, defeated the Pallavas and captured Kanchi (Conjeeveram).

This theory finds some support from the fact that the style of the work at Mahabalipuram seems to show a close connection with the Deccan. The cave-sculptures at Mahabalipuram both in the subject represented and in the manner of their execution bear a certain resemblance to those at Badami. Further, there is a remarkable similarity between the Pallava sculpture known as "Arjuna's Penance" and some of the work at Ajanta. On this point, the authors of the "Cave Temples of India" observe (p. 157) that "Even if this great bas-relief does not afford us much information regarding the rock-cut architecture of Eastern India, it has at least the merit of fixing almost beyond cavil the age of the various objects of interest at Mahavallipur. The sculptures, for instance, of Cave XXIV at Ajanta, are so nearly identical that their age cannot be far apart. We have in these the same flying figures, male and female, the same Kinnaras (harpies) the same style of sculpture in every respect, and such as is not found either before or afterwards. As this Ajanta cave is only blocked out, and only finished in parts, it is probably the latest excavation there and may therefore with certainty be assumed to belong to the seventh century of our era, and most probably the later half of it."

As regards architecture, the Badami tradition seems to have been continued in the Pallava country. One of the most characteristic features of the Badami cave temples is the use of very effective pillars with "cushion" capitals, a motif which had probably developed from the bell shaped capital found at such places as Karle and Bedsa and in some of the earlier Buddhist monuments. Further developments of the "cushion" capital are to be found at Ajanta and Ellora, for example in the *chaitya* Caves XIX and XXVI at the former place and in the Maharwada at the latter. In Pallava territory we notice its introduction in the later cave temples of the Bhairavakonda groups, which were probably constructed during the reign of Narasimhavarman I and also in that king's temples at Mahabalipuram where good examples are to be found in the Mahishasura and Ramanuja Mandapas.

It is also not without significance that some use is made of sculptured tracery of the later Ajanta variety in some of the Mahabalipuram caves (*e.g.*, the Mahishasura).

It must be remembered that apparently during the latter half of the seventh century the work at Mahabalipuram was brought suddenly to a standstill and many ambitious projects which had been begun there were abandoned. At approximately the same time there seems to have been a resumption of constructional operations at Ellora and Aurangabad where the old traditions are followed and to some extent developed. This was probably due to the restoration of the Deccan stone-masons and sculptors (or their descendents) to their former country. The non-resumption of work at Ajanta may possibly be explained by the fact that there was already sufficient accommodation there for ordinary monastic requirements and that the Chalukya-Pallava war may have prevented the further development of Ajanta as a seat of learning. The Buddhist settlements at Aurangabad and Ellora, on the other hand, seem to have been purely monastic institutions but very little progress could have been made in constructional work at either of these places before 642. At Ellora only Caves I, II, and V appear to have been completed by that date. If it be assumed that the use of the "vase and foliage" capital was adopted simultaneously on a large scale at Ajanta, Aurangabad and Ellora, it is probable that Cave III at Ellora, in which this form of capital first appears at that place, had reached about the same stage as Cave XXIV at Ajanta. Similarly at Aurangabad the completed work in 642 A.D., could only have consisted of the existing *chaitya* hall and a small remodelled *vihara*. The work on the other later *viharas* must have been in a very incomplete stage. If monastic communities of any size existed at Ellora and Aurangabad, as seems to have been the case, further accommodation was clearly necessary and I am inclined to think that, from the time of the return of the stone-workers from the South about 674 A.D., the work in the Buddhist caves temples at those places was continued from the point it had reached in 642. In some of the caves, however, the work was not resumed. This may have been due to want of funds or to be the reduction in the numbers of the monks since 642. For instance, no further work seems to have been done in Cave VII at Ellora and Cave I at Aurangabad. But, as regards the other caves which were unfinished in 642, (*e.g.* Caves III and IV at Ellora and most of the Caves at Aurangabad) the work seems to have been continued until about 750 A.D., when it may have been interrupted by the demand for large numbers of stone-workers in connection with the construction of the Kailasa Temple at Ellora.

CHRONOLOGY OF THE PRINCIPAL ELLORA CAVE TEMPLES

No.	Description			Local Name		Date		Remarks
1	Vihara	(Buddhist)	..	Dherawara	..	580-642 A.D.		
2	Hall	,,	..		..	580-642 ,,		
3	Vihara	,,	..			Begun c. 640 A.D.	}	Work probably interrupted and completed after 675 A.D.
4	,,	,,	..			,, c. 640 A.D.	}	
5	,,	,,	..	Maharwada	..	580-642 A.D.		
6	,,	,,	..		..	700-750 ,,		
7	,,	,,	..		..	700-750 ,,		
8	,,	,,	..		..	700-750 ,,		
9	Annexe to 6	,,	..		..	700-750 ,,		
10	Chaitya Hall			Visvakarma	..	700-750 ,,		
11	Vihara	,,	..	Do Thal	..	700-750 ,,		
12	,,	,,	..	Tin Thal	..	700-750 ,,		
13	Small Hall	(Hindu)	..		..	700-750 ,,		
14	Temple	,,	..	Ravana-ka-kai	..	700-750 ,,		
15	,,	,,	..	Das Avatara	..	700-750 ,,		
16	,,	,,	..	Kailasa	..	750-850 ,,		
21	,,	,,	..	Ramesvara	..	Begun c. 640 A.D.	}	Work probably interrupted and completed after 675 A.D.
25	,,	,,	..	Khumbharwada	..	Begun ,, ,,	}	
27	,,	,,	..	The Milkmaid's Cave	..	,, ,, ,,		
29	,,	,,	..	Dumar Lena (Sita's Nahani)	..	580-64 A.D.		
33	,,	(Jain)	..	Indra Sabha	..	750-850 ,,		
33	,,	,,	..	Jugannath Sabha	..	750-850 ,,		

CHRONOLOGY OF THE AJANTA CAVES

No.	Description			Date		Remarks
1	Vihara		..	600-642 A.D.	..	Paintings
2	,,		..	600-642 ,,	..	,,
3	,,	(unfinished)	..	Begun c. 640 ,,	..	
4	,,	,,	..	,, c. 640 ,,	..	Buddhist Litany
5	,,	,,	..	,, c. 640 ,,	..	
6	,,		..	440-480 ,,	..	Traces of paintings
7	,,		..	400-440 ,,	..	
8	,,		..	c. 100 B.C.	..	
9	Chaitya Hall		..	c. 100 ,,	..	Traces of paintings
10	,,		..	c. 150 ,,	..	Paintings Facade has fallen
11	Vihara		..	c. 100 A.D.	..	Shrine later
12	,,		..	c. 150 B.C.	..	
13	,,		..	c. 100 ,,	..	
14	,,	(unfinished)	..	Begun c. 640 A.D.	..	
15	,,		..	400-440 ,,	..	
16	,,		..	470-480 ,,	..	Paintings
17	,,		..	470-480 ,,	..	Paintings
18	Porch		..	500-550 ,,	..	
19	Chaitya Hall		..	500-550 ,,	..	
20	Vihara		..	500-550 ,,	..	
21	,,		..	550-600 ,,	..	First appearance of vase and foliage capitals
22	,,		..	550-600 ,,	..	
23	,,		..	550-600 ,,	..	
24	,,	(unfinished)	..	Begun c. 635 ,,	..	Vase and foliage capitals
25	,,	,,	..	c. 640 ,,	..	
26	Chaitya Hall		..	600-642 ,,	..	
27	Vihara	(unfinished)	..	Begun c. 640 ,,	..	
28	Chaitya Hall	,,	..	,, c. 640 ,,	..	
29	Vihara	,,	..	,, c. 640 ,,	..	

GLOSSARY OF TERMS

A

Abacus, *phalaka* or *palagai*, a square or rectangular table forming the crowning member of a capital.

Acanthus, a genus of plants, used conventionally in Greek art.

Achchaday, lit. envelope, the outer stone facing of a stupa.

Acroteria, a figure or ornament placed on the apex or at the lower angles of a pediment.

Addorsed, back to back.

Adytum, inner and most sacred chamber.

Aisle, lateral divisions running at the sides of the nave.

Alcove, vaulted recess in wall.

Alinda, verandah.

Amalaka, amalasila or *amalasari*, flat fluted melon-shaped member usually at the summit of the Indo-Aryan type of *sikhara* or spire.

Ambulatory, *pradakshina patha* or processional path.

Amman, shrine or pavilion attached to temples of southern India for ceremonial reception of the *amman* or goddess.

Amphitheatre, oval or circular building, with seats rising above and behind one another round a central open space.

Anardha-paga, projected surface adjacent to the surface at the angle of a building.

Anda, literally " egg," spherical portion of the stupa.

Anghri, dwarf-pillar.

Antae, pilasters terminating the side walls of a classic building.

Antarala, vestibule, chamber in front of shrine or cella.

Antechamber, chamber or small hall in front of a larger hall, vestibule.

Apse, Apsidal, the circular termination of a building ; first applied to a Roman basilica.

Arabesque, decoration with fanciful intertwining of ornamental elements.

Arbour, a structural retreat, often of lattice-work in a garden.

Arcade, range of arches supported on piers or columns.

Architrave, the beam or lowest division of the entablature which extends from column to column.

Arcuate, arched.

Ardha-Chandra, semicircular doorstep before a shrine door.

Ardha Mandapam, compartment in front of main hall of temple.

Aruna-Stambha, a pillar dedicated to Aruna who personifies the dawn, or the Sun.

Arris, corner or angle ; sharp edge formed by the meeting of two surfaces.

Aryaka, worshipful columns ; row of five pillars symbolizing the Five Dhiyana Buddhas.

Asana, a seat or throne.

Ashlar, squared stonework in regular courses, in contradistinction to rubble work.

Ashta-bhadra, eight faced or sided ; star-shaped.

Ashta-dikpala, the eight regents or guardians of the four cardinal and four intermediate points of the compass ; ceiling, divided into nine panels, in the central one is Brahma, while surrounding eight contain images of the eight regents of the compass Favourate ceiling design in later Chalukyan temples.

Astragal *kumuda*, small moulding round top or bottom of columns; torus.

Astylar, without columns.

Asvathara, the "horse moulding" in the basement of a temple.

Athisthana, base.

Atlantes, *kichaka* bracket, sculptured human figures used in place of columns or pilasters.

Atrium, court open to the sky in the centre (Roman).

Attic, the upper story of a building above the main cornice : of Athens or Attica.

B

Bada, cubical portion of a temple up to the roof or spire.

Balcony, outside balustraded platform.

Bali-mandapa, front hall (Chalukyan).

Baluster, balustrade, a small pillar or column supporting a handrail.

Bamli, court or courtyard.

Bandhana, a division or group of mouldings in the wall surface.

Baoli or *Wav*, step-well of Gujarat and western India.

Baradari, lit. "twelve pillared," a pillared portico or pavilion, columned building.

Barajhanji, carving on the doorway of a temple (Orissa).

Barandi, a division within the *bada* or cubical portion of the temple.

Barge-board, projecting roof to a gable.

Baroque, fantastic, grotesque, a style common in Europe in the first half of the 18th cent.

Barrel-vault, cylindrical form of roof or ceiling.

Basalt, dark green or brown igneous rock.

Basana, a division or element in the wall surface.

Base, *kumbli, athisthana*, lower portion of any structure or feature.

Basilica, applied to a large hall for the administration of justice.

Bas-relief, carving of low projection.

Basti, temple, (Kanarese districts.)

Bastion, projecting part of a fortification.

Batter, slope, rake.

Battlements, indented parapet, *kanjur*.

Bay, a division or compartment ; between pillars, a *chauki*.

Bazaar, market.

Bead and Fillet, small cylindrical moulding resembling a string of beads.

Beam, lintel, long piece of stone or wood supported at both ends.

Bedi, hall for reading the *beds* or *vedas*.

Begun, egg plant, hence the Begunia group of temples in Bengal as they are presumed to resemble this fruit.

Beki, the cylindrical stone below the *amla* in the finial of a building.

Berm, ledge, or narrow open passage.

Bhadra, flat face or facet of the sikhara (tower).

Bhamli, cells in the inner face of the containing wall of a temple.

Bhoga-mandapa, the refectory hall of a temple (Orissa).

Bhrama (Guj.) circumambulatory passage (*pradakshina patha*).

Bhumika, story, stage.

Boast, boasting, stone projection left for purpose of carving.

Bodhika, capital of a column.

Bodigai, pushpabodhica, projecting bracket or corbel of a Dravidian capital.

Boss, ornament projecting in form of a large knob.

Bracket, projecting ornament or support.

Brahma-kanda, column, rectangular in section, in the Northern style.

Bulbous, shaped like a bulb, nearly spherical.

Bund, dam or embankment.

Burj, tower.

Buttress, support built against a wall.

C

"Cable" moulding, resembling a rope.

Campa, fillet.

Campaniform, bell-shaped.

Campanile, Italian for a bell-tower, usually detached.

Canopy, covering over a niche.

Capital, *siras ;* upper portion of a column or pilaster.

Carralls, small study rooms.

Caryatid, sculptured human female figures used as columns or supports.

Casemate, vaulted chamber in thickness of wall.

Casement, a form of window.

Cathedral, principal church of a Bishop's district (diocese).

Causeway, raised road.

Cavetto, simple concave moulding.

Ceiling, covering surface under roof.

C—(contd.)

Cell, *kulika*.

Cella, small chamber, compartment for the image of symbol.

Chaitya, originally a tumulus (*chita*), but subsequently a sanctuary of any kind ; the Buddhist temple.

Chakra, Sacred Wheel of the Law (Buddhist) : also discus of Vishnu.

Chamfer, bevel or oblique surface, produced by cutting away a corner.

Chandrasila, moon-stone, the semi-circular doorstep before a shrine.

Chankrama, place of the promenade of the Buddha at Budh Gaya.

Chapel Royal, church in connection with a royal palace.

Chaplet, wreath or necklace.

Char rasta, junction of four roads : central place of a town.

Chauki, bay between pillars : also entrance to a porch.

Chaultri, pillared hall attached to outside of Dravidian temple.

Chaumukh, four images placed back to back, with the four faces looking towards the four cardinal points.

Chauri, fly-whisk, symbol of royalty.

Chavada, pavilion (western India).

Chhatra, honorific umbrella ; a pavilion (Buddhist).

Chhatravali, triple umbrella (Buddhist).

Chhatrayashti, the staff or rod of the honorific umbrella.

Chunam, lime, also plaster or stucco.

Citadel, fortress, especially guarding or dominating a city.

Classical, of the first class : of the standard of the ancient Greeks and Romans : style of antiquity.

Clerestory, upper division of the walls of a building from which light was obtained.

Cloister, covered corridors, or passages usually surrounding an open square.

Coffer, sunk panel in a ceiling.

Colonnade, series of columns.

Column, vertical support, pillar.

Coping, *ushnisha*, capping or covering to a wall.

Corbel, blocks of stone projecting from a wall or pier : brackets.

Core, inner construction of a wall, or other architectural feature.

Corinthian order, the most ornate of the Greek orders of architecture.

Cornice, any crowning portion or projection.

Corridor, passage in a building.

Cramp, metal bar for holding masonry.

Cruciform, in the form of a cross.

Crutch, pillar or support surmounted by crosspiece.

Cupola, *sringa ;* spherical roof.

Cushion-member, a form of capital in the shape of a cushion, generally found in the rock architecture.

Cyma, moulding in an outline of two curves : cyma recta, the concave curve surmounts the convex : cyma reversa, the convex surmounts the concave.

D

Dado, portion of a pedestal between its base and cornice ; also applied to the lower portions of walls.

Dagoba, stupa, (Sinhalese).

Dais, raised platform.

Dali, scroll work.

Daric, wood, woodwork.

Darwaza, door.

Decorated, the second of the three divisions of English Gothic architecture, evolved during the fourteenth century.

Devagosta, niche.

Devayatana, house of gods.

Dewl, deul, in Bengal and Orissa generic name for a temple as a whole, but it is also used to signify the sanctuary only, such as the cella and its tower, the *vimana*.

Dharmachakra, Wheel of the Law (Buddhist).

Dharmsala, hostel, Hindu caravansarai.

Dhvajastambham, lofty pillar in front of temple.

Diaper, small floral pattern repeated continuously over a wall surface.

Dikpala, guardian of one of the cardinal points.

Dipdan, lamp pillar.

Dipmala, high tower or pillar for festival light.

Distyle in antis, term for a facade having two columns between pilasters or antes.

Dola, swing.

Doric Order, first and simplest order of Grecian architecture.

Dormer, window in a sloping roof.

Dormitory, sleeping room with several beds or cubicles.

Dry masonry, stones laid without mortar or any adhesive.

Durbar, Indian court or levee.

Dvarpala, doorkeeper.

Dwarf pillars, *anghri*.

E

Early English, first of the three divisions of Gothic architecture in England, evolved during the thirteenth century.

Eaves, *chajja*, lower portion of a roof projecting beyond the face of the wall.

Echinus, evolo member of the Greek Doric capital, also a somewhat similar feature in the Ionic capital.

Enceinte, enclosure.

Entablature, upper portion of a structure supported by a colonnade.

Entasis, slight convex curvature of the shaft of a column thus preventing a concave appearance.

F

Facade, front view or elevation.

Faience, earthenware, porcelain.

Fan-light, fan-shaped window over door.

Fenestration, with windows or openings.

Filigree, fine ornamental work : delicate tracery.

"Filling," the repeating pattern on the largest or central space of a wall.

Finial, finishing portion of a pinnacle.

Flamboyant, florid, showy style.

Flange, projecting flat, rim, collar or rib.

Fleche, slender spire.

Flexured, curved or bent.

Fluting vertical channelling on the shaft of a column.

Forum, public place, place of assembly, especially at Rome.

Fret, fretwork, ornamental pattern usually carved and perforated.

Frieze, upper border : middle division of entablature.

G

Gable, gable-end, triangular portion of roof.

Gallery, passage common to rooms in an upper story.

Galli, small street or lane.

Gambhara, (Jain) sanctuary cell.

Gana, child figures in ornament, urchins.

Gandharvas, celestial musicians of Indra.

Garasmukha, same as *kirtimukha*, a grotesque mask used in ornamentation.

Garaspatti, a particular string-course or moulding in the basement of temples decorated with the *garasmukha*.

Garbha-griha, adytum, shrine, the most sacred part of a temple.

Garbha-mudra, carved lotus on the topmost course of corbels of the *rakha* (curvilinear portion).

Gargoyle, projecting water-spout in Gothic architecture.

Garth, small garden within cloisters.

Garuda, *vahana* or vehicle (riding bird) of Vishnu.

Govaksha, small ornamental niches on lowest turrets.

Gajaprishthakriti, shaped like an elephant's back, whale-backed.

Gelbai, carving around a doorway.

Ghadi, upper part of the *kalasa*, or vase member of the capital.

Ghanta, bell.

Ghat, platform or steps at edge of water.

Ghatapallava, "vase and foliage" pillar.

Girder, beam for support.

Gokhala (Jain) niche.

Gopuram, monumental gateway.

Gothic, pointed arched style prevalent in Western Europe during the 12th to the 16th centuries.

Grille, grating, latticed screen.

Guda mandapa, closed hall in front of a door, vestibule.

Guldasta, pinnacle.

Gumpha, monastery.

H

Half-timbered construction, building formed of a wooden framework with the interstices filled with brick or plaster.

Hammer-beam roof, late Gothic form of wooden roof without a direct tie.

Hamsa, goose.

Harmika, the finial of a stupa in the form of a pedestal in which the shaft of the honorific umbrella was set.

Headers and stretchers, bricks bounded with their short or long faces placed alternately.

Hellenic, ancient Greek.

Hemadpanti, name given to a type of Deccani temple supposed to have been introduced or designed by Hemadpant, minister of the Yadava king of Devagiri in the 13th century.

Hinayana, primitive Buddhism, an earlier form of this great religious movement, as distinct from the later, or Mahayana.

Hippogryph, fabulous griffin-like creature with body of horse.

Hira, bead moulding.

Hira, *grihas*, corbels.

Honeysuckle and palmette, border in Grecian art consisting of these decorative elements.

Hti, finial (Burmese).

Hypostyle, pillared hall.

I

Icon, image, statue.

Iconography, illustration of subject by drawings or figures.

Idaie, flower-shaped member in a Dravidian capital.

In antis, within or between antae or side walls.

Ionic, second order of Grecian architecture.

Ishtaka, brick, brickwork.

J

Jaga mohan, audience hall or ante-room, compartment of an Orissan temple fronting the sanctuary.

Jagati, railed parapet.

Jakanacharya, mythical architect or builder of temples in Southern India.

Jali, literally "net," any lattice or perforated pattern.

Jamb, sides of the openings of doors and windows.

Jangha, applies to the broad band of sculpture towards the middle of the temple wall (exterior) ; sometimes called *panchakama*.

Jatakas, stories of the Buddha's former births.

Jaya Stambha, Tower of Victory.

Jhappa-sinha, rampant lion motif.

Jina, Jaina, Tirthankara, or religious reformer of the Jains.

K

Kailasa, Shiva's Heaven.

Kakshasana, sloping seat-back of stone.

Kalan, temple tower (Cham).

Kalasa, vase, an ornamental pot found in finials and capitals.

Kalasa and *amla*, "vase and melon" capital.

Kalyana mandapa, "hall of marriage" in temples of Southern India: pavillion where the marriage of the deity is celebrated annually.

Kanti, in Orissan temples the recess between a bracket or cornice.

Keel, like the keel of a ship.

Khunta-ra-mandir, (Jain) small subsidiary shrine.

Kirtimukha, "face of fame," an ornamental mask of great antiquity in Indian art.

Kirti-stambha, "pillar of fame," free standing pillar in front of temple.

Konakapaga, the pilaster or projection on the angle of a temple.

Kottara, temple granary.

Kudu, antefix, foliated arch on Dravidian temples, ornamental motif derived from the Buddhist chaitya arch.

Kumbha, a motif resembling a vase.

Kumbha pancharam, recessed pilasters.

Kumuda, astragal or torus moulding.

L

Labyrinth, complicated irregular structure of many intricate passages : maze.

Laminated arch, formed by layers as of thin wood.

Lat or *stambha*, pillar.

Laterite, ferruginous rock.

Latin Cross, cross with upright longer than arms.

Lattice, screen of cross laths : perforated structure.

Leogryph, *vyali*, lion-griffin.

Lintel, beam, the timber or stone covering an opening.

Loggia, a gallery open to the air ; verandah.

Lunette, crescent shape ; semicircular space or opening.

M

Machicolation, parapet of fortress with opening for dropping missiles.

Madapalli, cooking room, kitchen.

Madar (Jain) large subsidiary shrine.

Mahabharata, great Sanskrit Epic of India.

Mahadvara, outer gate surmounted by a lofty superstructure, (Chalukyan).

Maha Govinda, in Buddhist writings the name of an architect who built several important cities and fortresses.

Mahall, palace.

Maha-mandapam, large enclosed hall in front of main shrine : also transepts.

Mahayana, later development of Buddhism.

Makara, crocodile-shaped creature presumed to symbolize the river Ganges.

Malleable, adaptable, pliable, can be hammered or pressed into shape.

Manasara, ancient Indian architectural treatise.

Manastambha, free-standing pillar in front of temple.

Mandapa, *mandapam*, large open hall.

Mandir, temple.

Mandovara, central and principal space in the outer wall of a Gujarati temple.

Mashrabiya, lattice-work formed of small pieces of wood jointed together.

Matha, monastery or convent.

Mausoleum, large tomb building.

Medhi, terrace.

Megalithic, structure in which there is a marked use of large stones.

Merlon, part of embattled parapet between two embrasures.

Meroes, pagoda (Bali).

Moat, deep wide ditch surrounding a fort.

Modillions, projecting brackets in the classical orders.

Monobloc, single piece of concrete composition.

Monolith, single block of stone shaped into a pillar or monument.

Monoptoral, circular type of temple.

Mortar, mixture of lime, sand, and water for joining stone or bricks.

Mortice, hole cut to receive a projection especially a tenon.

Moulding, the contour given to projecting members.

Mudra, language of the hands and fingers.

Mukka-mandapam, front hall or colonnade in front of main shrine.

Mullion, upright members used to divide openings into smaller spaces.

Mural, wall, wall decoration.

N

Nagara, city or capital (*Sanskrit*).

Nal, staircase, flight of steps.

Nal mandapa, porch over a staircase.

Nandi Mandapa, portico or pavilion erected over the sacred bull (*nandi*).

Naos, sanctuary cell or principal chamber.

Nat-mandir, dancing hall, usually the middle structure in an Orissan temple.

Navagraha, nine planets, represented usually on the lintel or architrave of the front door of a temple.

Navaranga, middle or central hall of temple.

Navaratha deul, a structure showing nine pilasters on its facade.

Nave, the central or main compartment of a building.

Neck-moulding, *padma-bhandam*.

Niche, recess in wall for the reception of a statue or ornament.

Nook-shaft, detached pillar in a recess of a doorway, opening, or pier.

Nritya sala, dancing hall of temple.

O

Obelisk, tapering and usually monolithic shaft of stone with pyramidal apex.

Ogee, a form of moulding or arch, the curves of which resemble the cyma reversa (q. v.)

Opisthodomos, in Greek architecture an open vestibule within the portico.

Order, in architecture signifies a column with its base, shaft and capital, and the entablature which it supports.

Oriel, projecting window.

Oversailing, system of construction in domes or arches where the course of bricks or stones projects over the course below.

Avoid, oval with one end more pointed.

Ovolo, convex moulding.

P

Pada, foot or base.

Pada-vinyasa, ground plan.

Padma, lotus, moulding having the curves of the lotus petal, cyma reversa or recta.

Padmabhandam, neck moulding.

Padmam, pedestal.

Padmasana, lotus throne.

Paga, projecting pilaster-like surface of an Orissan temple (exterior).

Pagoda, tall structure in several stories.

Paksala, kitchen.

Palagai, square member forming upper portion of Dravidian capital ; abacus

Palimpsest, an inscription or manuscript over which another has been subsequently written.

Pancharam, attic or superstructure ; also pavilion.

Pancharatha deul, structure having five pilasters on its facade.

Panchayatana, temple consisting of five shrines in a group.

Panel, recessed compartment in a wall, etc.

Pansala, cell.

Parapet, upper portion of a wall above the roof.

Parastara, entablature.

Parichakra, half medallions on the uprights of a Buddhist railing.

Parterre, level space in a garden occupied by flower-beds.

Parthenon, Greek temple at Athens, ideal of classic architecture.

Parvis, priests' chamber.

Pata, lintel or beam.

Patina, green film that covers materials exposed to the air.

Patio, open court of a Spanish dwelling.

Pavilion, chavada, chabutri.

Pediment, triangular termination of the roof in a classic temple.

Peripetral, surrounded by a range of columns.

Peristyle, range of columns surrounding a court or temple.

Picture-gallery, chitragara.

Pida, pitha, basement.

Pier, supporting mass other than a column.

Pilaster, square pillar projecting from a wall.

Pillar, khumbhi.

Pinjra, lattice work.

Pinnacle, guldasta, small turret-like termination.

Pitha, base, pedestal.

Piu-lu, torana, or gateway of the Chinese.

Plan, representation of a building showing the general distribution of its parts in horizontal section.

Plastic, modelled or moulded.

Plateresque, plateresco, over-florid ornamentation in the Spanish Renaissance style, resembling intricate silver-work.

Plinth, (pitha) lower portion, or base, of a building or column.

Podium, stone bench ; low pedestal wall.

Pokana, bathing tank (Ceylon).

Polychromatic, many-coloured.

Porch, structure in front of doorway.

Portal, doorway.

Portico, space enclosed within columns.

Pra, stupa (Siam).

Pradakshina patha, vedika, processional passage or ambulatory.

Prakaram, open courtyard.

Prasada, palace, also shrine.

Prastara, entablature.

Pronaos, porch, part of a classic temple in front of the naos : sometimes portico.

Propylaeum, entrance gate or vestibule.

Pteroma, space between the wall and columns of a temple.

Purna kalasa, vase of plenty, "pot and foliage" capital in style of northern India.

Pushkarani, sacred pool or tank.

Pushpabandha, pushpa bodhica, projecting bracket or corbel of a Dravidian capital.

Pylon, propylon, tall monumental gateway.

Pyramidal, including to an apex a pyramid.

Q

Quadrangle, four-sided figure or court.

Quattro-cento, fifteenth century as period in Italian art.

Quoin, corner stones at the angles : angle of a building.

R

Raha paga, central projection or pilaster.

Rakshasas, earth spirits.

Ramayana, Sanskrit epic poem of great antiquity.

Rampart, broad-topped defensive mound or structure.

Random rubble, masonry formed of stones of irregular size and shape.

Ranga mandapa, painted hall or theatre.

Ratha, lit. a car ; car used in the temple ceremonies of southern India ; also applied incorrectly to the monolithic shrines of the Seven Pagodas, Mamallapuram.

Refectory, dining hall in a monastery or college.

Rekha, curvilinear portion of a spire or sikhara.

Rekha deul, a towered sanctuary (Orissan).

Reliquary, receptacle for relics.

Renaissance, revival of art and letters in Europe under the influence of classical models in 14th and 16th centuries.

Rib, projecting band on a ceiling or vault.

Ridge, highest point of a roof, running from end to end.

Rococo, style with debased Renaissance features.

Roll moulding, also called scroll moulding from its resemblance to a scroll of paper.

Rood-loft, raised gallery in front of the chancel of a church or cathedral.

Rood-screen, framing separating the chancel from the rest of the building.

Rosette, rose-shaped ornament.

Rose window or wheel window, circular window with millions converging like the spokes of a wheel.

Rotunda, building of circular ground plan, circular hall or room.

Rudra Kanda, sixteen-sided pillar.

Runnel, small hollow.

Rustication, method of forming stonework with recessed joints.

S

Sabha mandapa or chavadi, assembly hall.

Sal, hall.

Salunkha, alter.

Sanctum, holiest portion of a temple ; inner sanctuary ; garbha griha.

Sangarama, monastery.

Sankha, a shell, emblem of the god Vishnu.

Santhagara, mote, moot or meeting hall.

Saptaratha deul, structure with seven pilasters on its facade.

Sarai, caravansarai, halting place.

Sarsen, large sandstone block as at Stonehenge.

Schist, type of rock, metamorphic, and fissile (split) in character ; dark slate coloured.

Seni, guilds.

Seljuks, Turkish Islamic dynasty of western Asia, in the 11th, 12th & 13th cents.

Sesha, serpent deity.

Shaft, portion of a column between base and capital.

Sikhara, spire or tower.

Shrine, sanctuary, most sacred portion of a temple.

Sill, shelf or slab in front of window.

Silpa sastra, ancient Indian treatise on building construction and allied arts.

S—(Contd.)

Silpi laksmana, architect.
Sinha, lion.
Sinhasana, lion throne ; throne for a statue of the Buddha, usually supported on figures of lions.
Sinha stambha, lion pillar.
Siras, capital of a pillar.
Siva kanda, pentagonal pillar.
Skanda kanda, hexagonal pillar.
Soffit, underside of any architectural member.
Soma sutra, spout to carry away oblations in the shrine of a temple.
Sopana, flight of steps, stairs.
Sridhara, pillar with octagonal shaft and square base.
Sringa, quarter sikhara like a turret attached to the main sikhara.
Staggered, not opposite, not in line.
Stambha, column, pillar (in Gujarati, *tekana*).
Steeple, spire, *sikhara*, lofty structure above a church.
Stele, upright slab or pillar sometimes inscribed as a gravestone.
Stellate, arranged like a star, radiating.
Stencil, pattern inscribed or painted by means of a cut plate.
Stereobate, solid platform.
Sthapti, master craftsman.
Stockade, line of posts as a fence or barrier.
Story, *bhumikha*, space between two adjacent floors.
String-course, a horizontal moulding often under a parapet.
Strut, wood, stone or iron set up to bear weight or pressure ; a brace.
Stucco, kind of plaster or cement for coating surfaces.
Stupa, originally a funeral mound or tumulus, but erected by the Buddhists either to enshrine a relic or to commemorate some sacred site.
Stylobate, the base or sub-structure on which a colonnade is placed.
Suchi, cross bars in a Buddhist railing.
Sukhanasi (Chalukyan) temple vestibule.
Sun window, chaitya window, large arched opening in the facade of a chaitya hall or Buddhist temple.
Supercolumniation, one row of pilasters or pillars in a story above another.
Suraj-mukh, "sun-face", a symbolic decorative element.
Surya, the sun god.

T

Tabernacle, small movable sanctuary ; also canopied stall.
Tadi, a kind of necking in a Dravidian capital.
Tala, story.
Talapattana, pavement.
Tala prishtha, lower of the two tiers of a plinth.
Tandava, dance of Siva.
Temenos, sacred precincts of a temple or sanctuary.
Tempera, distemper ; method of mural painting by means of a "body," such as white pigment.
Thakur bari, sanctuary (Bengal).
Tirthankara, Jain religious reformer.
Titanic, gigantic, superhuman.
Tol. quarter or ward of a town (Nepal).
Topiary, art of clipping shrubs into ornamental shapes.
Torana, gateway of Indian design.
Torri, gateway of a Japanese temple.
Torus, convex moulding chiefly used in pillar bases.
Tower, *sikhara*.
Trabeate, use of beams in construction as distinct from arches.
Tracery, ornamental perforated pattern.
Transept, cross or transverse compartments of a building.
Transom, horizontal divisions or cross-bars to windows.
Trefoil, arranged in three lobes.
Triforium, gallery or arcade above the arches of the nave.
Trikutachala (Chalukyan) triple shrine or three-celled temple.
Trimurti, Hindu Triad.
Triptadhara, short cylindrical member over the *amla*.

Triple Umbrella, *chhatravali* (Buddhist).
Triratha deul, a structure having three pilasters on the facade.
Trisula, trident, emblem of Siva.
Truncated, cut off at top.
Truss, support for a roof, bridge, etc.
Tudor Gothic, late perpendicular style which flourished in England from the reign of Henry VII to that of Elizabeth ; 16th century.
Tumulus, a mound, often funerary, presumed origin of the stupa.
Turrets, small towers.
Tympanum, triangular space within the cornices of a pediment.

U

Ubapitam, pedestal.
Uda sinha, flying lion.
Ugrana, store house (Chalukyan).
Umbrella stick, *chhatrayashti*.
Upana, pedestal of a pillar.
Upapitha, pedestal.
Urusringa, half-*sikhara* like a turret attached to the main *sikhara*, or spire.
Ushnisha, coping.
Uttira, entablature.
Uyyala, *Unyal mandapam*, (hindola) hall for swinging the deity (Tamil).

V

Vahana mandapa, (Chalukyan) hall in which the *vahanas* or temple vehicles are stored.
Vastu Sastra, " Rules of Architecture."
Vat, Buddhist monument (Siamese).
Vault, arched covering over any space.
Vedas, ancient sacred books, the foundation of Hinduism ; they give their name to the Vedic Age.
Vedi, alter, also a wall or screen.
Vedica, Buddhist railing.
Vestibule, ante-room.
Vihara, Buddhist or Jain monastery.
Vimana, towered sanctuary containing the cell in which the deity is enshrined.
Vira ghanta, sacred bell, a common decorative motif.
Vishana, horns.
Visvakarma, Lord of the Arts, patron saint of the craftsman.
Vitruvius, Roman architect, military engineer and writer, in the days of Cæsar and Augustus.
Volute, scroll or spiral.
Vyali, leogryph.

W

Wagon-vault, semi-cylindrical roof like a wagon tilt or cover.
Wahalkadas, decorative projecting shrines on Sinhalese stupas or dagabas.
Wattle and daub, primitive walling of twigs plastered with mud or clay.
Wav or *Baoli*, step-well in Gujarat and western India.
Wheel, *chakr*, also discus of Vishnu.
Wing, sides, the lateral extremities of a building.
Wyang, Javanese theatrical performance.

Y

Yagasala, hall where the sacred fire is maintained and worshipped ; place of sacrifice.
Yaksha, semi-divine being.
Yali, hippopotamus-like creature in the ornamentation of Chalukyan temples.
Yamuna, Jumna river.
Yashti, stick, pole or shaft, (Buddhist).

BIBLIOGRAPHY

GENERAL

Barman, Christian. Architecture. London, 1928.
Blomfield, R. Touchstone of Architecture. Oxford, 1925.
Fergusson, J. History of Architecture in All Countries. 5 vols. 1893.
Fletcher, Banister. A History of Architecture on the Comparative Method. London, 1938.
Lethaby, W. R. Architecture, An introduction to the History and Theory of the Art of Building. London, 1929.
Scott, G. The Architecture of Humanism. London, 1924.
Simpson, F. M. A History of Architectural Development. London, 1905.

INDIAN GENERAL

Archæological Survey of H.E.H. the Nizam's Dominions : Annual Progress Reports from 1914-15. Hyderabad, Deccan.
Archæological Survey of Mysore : Annual Progress Reports from 1886. Mysore.
Batley, C. Indian Architecture (Plates). London, 1934.
Benoit, F. L'architecture L'orient Medieval et Moderne. Paris, 1912.
Beylie, L. de, L'architecture Hindoue en Extreme Orient. Paris, 1907.
Burgess. J. The Ancient Monuments, Temples, and Sculptures of India. London, 1911.
Chatterji, S. C. Magadha. Calcutta 1945.
Cole, H.H. Buildings in the Punjab. Simla, 1884.
  ,,   ,,   Preservation of National Monuments in India. Simla, 1882-85.
Coomaraswamy, A. K. History of Indian and Indonesian Art. Leipzig, 1927.
Cumming, Sir John. Revealing India's Past, The India Society. London, 1939.
Cunningham, A. Archæological Survey of India. Vols. I-XXIII. Simla, Calcutta, 1865-77.
De Forest, L. Indian Domestic Architecture. Boston, U.S.A., 1885.
Fergusson, J. History of Indian and Eastern Architecture. London, 1910.
  ,,   Picturesque Illustrations of the Ancient Architecture of Hindostan, 1848.
Griggs, W. Photographs and Drawings of Historical Buildings. London, 1896.
Havell, E. B. The Ancient and Mediæval Architecture of India. London, 1915.
  ,,   ,,   A Handbook of Indian Art. London, 1920.
  ,,   ,,   The Ideals of Indian Art. London, 1920.
  ,,   ,,   Indian Architecture. London, 1913.
Indian Art and Letters. India Society, London.
India Society, Revealing India's Past. India Soc. London, 1939.
Jacob S. S. Jeypore Portfolio of Architectural Details. London, 1891-94.
Journal of the Indian Society of Oriental Art, Calcutta.
Kramrisch, Prof. Stella, The Hindu Temple, Calcutta, 1946.
Latif, S. M. Agra, Historical and Descriptive. Calcutta, 1896.
  ,,   Lahore. Lahore, 1893.
La Roche, E. Indische Baukunst. Munich, 1921.
Le Bon, G. Les Monuments de I'Inde. Paris, 1893.
Maindron, U. L'Art Indien. Paris, 1898.
Marshall, Sir John. Annual Reports of the Archæological Survey of India, 1902-3 to 1930. Calcutta.
  ,,   ,,   Sanchi, the Monuments of. Government of India Press 1938.
  ,,   ,,   Mohenjo-Daro and the Indus Civilization. London 1931.
Memoirs of the Archæological Survey of India, Vols. 1 to 40. Simla and Calcutta.
Reuther, Oscar. Indische Palaste und Wohnhauser. Leonhard Preiss, Berlin.
Rowland, Benjamin. The Art and Architecture of India : Buddhist-Hindu-Jain. Penguin Books.
Rupam, Magazine of the India Society of Oriental Art, Calcutta.
Smith, E. W. Portfolio of Indian Architectural Drawings. London, 1897.
Smith, V. A. A History of Fine Art in India and Ceylon. Oxford, 1911.

i